Saving the Twentieth Century: The Conservation of Modern Materials

Proceedings of a Conference
Symposium '91 - Saving the Twentieth Century
Ottawa, Canada
15 to 20 September 1991

Organized by the Canadian Conservation Institute, Communications Canada

Edited by

David W. Grattan

Canadian Conservation Institute
Ottawa, Canada

1993

Sauvegarder le XXe siècle : la conservation des matériaux modernes

Les actes de la conférence
Symposium 91 - Sauvegarder le XXe siècle
Ottawa, Canada
du 15 au 20 septembre 1991

Organisé par l'Institut canadien de conservation, Communications Canada

Sous la direction de

David W. Grattan

Institut canadien de conservation
Ottawa, Canada

1993

Canadian Cataloguing in Publication Data

Symposium '91 - Saving the Twentieth Century
(1991 : Ottawa, Ont.)

Saving the twentieth century : the conservation
of modern materials : proceedings of a conference, Ottawa, Canada, 15 to 20 September
1991 = Sauvegarder le XXe siècle : la conservation des matériaux modernes : les actes de
la conférence, Ottawa (Canada) du 15 au
20 septembre 1991

Prefatory material and abstracts in English
and French.
Includes bibliographical references.
ISBN 0-660-57854-9
DSS cat. no. NM95-58/2-1992

1. Museum conservation methods — Canada —
Congresses. 2. Museum techniques — Canada
— Congresses. 3. Materials — Conservation
and restoration — Congresses. I. Grattan,
David W. II. Canadian Conservation Institute.
III. Title. IV. Title: Sauvegarder le XXe siècle.

AM141.S28 1992   069'.53'0971
C92-099400-0E

**Données de catalogage avant publication
(Canada)**

Symposium 91 - Sauvegarder le XXe siècle
(1991 : Ottawa, Ont.)

Saving the twentieth century : the conservation
of modern materials : proceedings of a conference, Ottawa, Canada, 15 to 20 September
1991 = Sauvegarder le XXe siècle : la conservation des matériaux modernes : les actes de
la conférence, Ottawa (Canada) du 15 au
20 septembre 1991

Texte préliminaire et résumés en anglais et
en français.
Comprend des références bibliographiques.
ISBN 0-660-57854-9
N^o de cat. MAS NM95-58/2-1992

1. Musées — Méthodes de conservation —
Canada — Congrès. 2. Muséologie — Canada
— Congrès. 3. Matériaux — Conservation et
restauration — Congrès. I. Grattan, David W.
II. Institut canadien de conservation. III. Titre.
IV. Titre : Sauvegarder le XXe siècle.

AM141.S28 1992   069'.53'0971
C93-099400-0F

Proceedings published subsequent to Symposium '91 - Saving the Twentieth Century, organized by the Canadian Conservation Institute, Communications Canada, and held at the Skyline Hotel, Ottawa, 15 to 20 September 1991.

© Communications Canada, Ottawa, 1993.

All rights reserved. No part of this publication may be reproduced or transmitted, in any form or by any means, electronic or mechanical, including photocopying, recording, entering in an information storage and retrieval system, or otherwise, without prior written permission of the publisher.

Cover Design: Sophie Georgiev, Canadian Conservation Institute

Printing: Groupe Harpell Inc.

PRINTED IN CANADA

Available from:
Extension Services
Canadian Conservation Institute
Communications Canada
Ottawa, Ontario
K1A 0C8

Ce document a été publié à la suite du Symposium 91 - Sauvegarder le XXe siècle, organisé par l'Institut canadien de conservation, Communications Canada, et présenté à l'hôtel Skyline, Ottawa, du 15 au 20 septembre 1991.

© Communications Canada, Ottawa, 1993.

Tous droits réservés. La reproduction d'un extrait quelconque de ce livre, par quelque procédé que ce soit, tant électronique que mécanique, ou par photocopie, microfilm, bande magnétique, disque ou autre, sans l'autorisation écrite de l'éditeur est interdite.

Graphisme de la couverture : Sophie Georgiev, Institut canadien de conservation

Impression : Groupe Harpell Inc.

IMPRIMÉ AU CANADA

Vendu par :
Services de diffusion externe
Institut canadien de conservation
Communications Canada
Ottawa (Ontario)
K1A 0C8

Acknowledgements

Organizing Committee

J. Cliff McCawley (chair)

Henri Benoît
Malcolm Bilz
Marie-Claude Corbeil
Valerie Dorge
David Grattan
Maureen MacDonald
Janet Mason
Wanda McWilliams
Charlotte Newton
Jean Tétreault
David Tremain
Season Tse

The Organizing Committee thanks the speakers, session chairs, presenters of posters, and participants in the panel discussion for their contribution to the Symposium.

Editorial Committee

David Grattan (chair)

Valerie Dorge
Charlotte Newton
Jean Tétreault

Production Committee

Deborah Robichaud (chair)

A.P. Dorning
Sophie Georgiev
David Grattan
Sandra LaFortune
Linda Leclerc

Remerciements

Comité organisateur

J. Cliff McCawley (président)

Henri Benoît
Malcolm Bilz
Marie-Claude Corbeil
Valerie Dorge
David Grattan
Maureen MacDonald
Janet Mason
Wanda McWilliams
Charlotte Newton
Jean Tétreault
David Tremain
Season Tse

Le comité organisateur tient à remercier les conférenciers, les présidents de session et tous les participants à la table ronde pour leur contribution au symposium.

Comité de rédaction

David Grattan (président)

Valerie Dorge
Charlotte Newton
Jean Tétreault

Comité de production

Deborah Robichaud (présidente)

A.P. Dorning
Sophie Georgiev
David Grattan
Sandra LaFortune
Linda Leclerc

Publication

The editor thanks the authors for their manuscripts and for their kind cooperation during the editorial process. The editor also acknowledges the help of the following people in the preparation of this publication:

Caroline Shaughnessy:
    English editing
André La Rose:
    French editing and translation
Sophie Georgiev:
    Design and layout
Sandra LaFortune and Linda Leclerc:
    Editorial assistance and proofreading
Valerie Dorge, Charlotte Newton, and
Jean Tétreault:
    Technical review
Translation Bureau, Department of the
Secretary of State:
    Translation of abstracts

Consultation

We acknowledge the advice and assistance of the following people in planning the Symposium:

Dr. David J. Carlsson:
    National Research Council Canada,
    Ottawa
Karen Graham:
    Canadian War Museum, Ottawa
Robson Senior:
    National Museum of Science and
    Technology, Ottawa
Dr. David M. Wiles:
    Plastichem Consulting, Victoria, B.C.

Publication

Le rédacteur en chef tient à remercier les auteurs de leur contribution au projet ainsi que de leur coopération. Il désire également exprimer sa gratitude à toutes les personnes qui lui ont prêté main-forte :

Caroline Shaughnessy :
    Révision des textes anglais
André La Rose :
    Révision des textes français et traduction
Sophie Georgiev :
    Graphisme et production
Sandra LaFortune et Linda Leclerc :
    Aide à la rédaction et correction d'épreuves
Valerie Dorge, Charlotte Newton et
Jean Tétreault :
    Révision des textes techniques
Bureau des traductions du
Secrétariat d'État :
    Traduction des résumés

Consultation

Nous tenons à remercier certaines personnes qui, par leurs conseils et leur aide, ont contribué à la planification du symposium :

David J. Carlsson, Ph.D. :
    Conseil national de recherches Canada,
    Ottawa
Karen Graham :
    Musée canadien de la guerre, Ottawa
Robson Senior :
    Musée national des sciences et de la
    technologie, Ottawa
David M. Wiles, Ph.D. :
    Plastichem Consulting, Victoria (C.-B.)

Introduction

The conference "Symposium '91 - Saving the Twentieth Century" took place in Ottawa in the autumn of 1991. Organized and hosted by the Canadian Conservation Institute (Communications Canada), Symposium '91 formed one of a series of international meetings devoted to specific conservation problems.

Each Symposium addresses topics of major importance to museums — particularly to museums in Canada. Topics are selected that have been generally overlooked and that pose new and demanding challenges. In this way, we hope to create a better awareness of problems, to stimulate thought, and to encourage research. The theme for Symposium '91, modern materials, meets all these criteria.

Museums and galleries reflect society, and are influenced by opinion and fashion. As material culture becomes more sophisticated, museums collect a much wider range of objects. Museum curators are, therefore, assembling collections that include new synthetic materials, complex electronic circuitry, sophisticated alloys, and many new types of coatings. Consider the following list: compact disc, radio, computer, spacesuit, aircraft, plywood, and plastic doll. All are among the rapidly degrading artifacts that were discussed at Symposium '91.

"Complex" is perhaps the word that best describes modern objects. They are becoming increasingly complex in structure, in materials used, and especially in function. Conservators are expected to stabilize and conserve artifacts from all periods in history. However, perhaps by inclination and certainly by training, they have concentrated on studying past technologies rather than current ones. Although modern materials are generally perceived as being more stable than traditional substances, nothing could be further from the truth. Many twentieth-century artifacts are very unstable, and some have problems that are new to conservators, such as radioactivity, polymer degradation, and aluminum corrosion.

Introduction

La conférence « Symposium 91 - Sauvegarder le XXe siècle : la conservation des matériaux modernes » a eu lieu à Ottawa au cours de l'automne de 1991. Symposium 91, mis sur pied par l'Institut canadien de conservation (Communications Canada) qui en était également l'hôte, s'inscrivait dans le cadre d'une série de rencontres internationales consacrées à l'étude de problèmes de conservation particuliers.

Chacune de ces rencontres porte sur un sujet d'importance pour tous les musées — surtout pour les musées du Canada. Et chacun de ces sujets correspond à un domaine qui, bien que généralement négligé, n'en constitue pas moins un nouveau défi de taille. Les conférences visent donc à sensibiliser davantage les gens à certains problèmes, tout en favorisant la réflexion et en stimulant la recherche. Symposium 91, qui portait sur les matériaux modernes, respectait tous ces critères.

Les musées et les galeries d'art sont le reflet de la société, et ils ne sont dès lors pas à l'abri de l'opinion et des modes. Au fur et à mesure qu'évolue la culture matérielle, les conservateurs de ces établissements en viennent à collectionner une gamme toujours plus variée d'objets, faits à partir de nouvelles matières synthétiques, de circuits électroniques complexes et d'alliages de haute technicité, et dont le recouvrement comporte lui aussi de nouveaux matériaux. Les disques compacts, les radios, les ordinateurs, les combinaisons spatiales, les aéronefs, les contreplaqués et les poupées en plastique ne sont que quelques-uns des objets qui, se dégradant rapidement, figuraient au programme de Symposium 91.

Le mot « complexe » est sans doute celui qui permet le mieux de décrire les objets modernes, qui deviennent en effet toujours plus complexes quant à leur structure, aux matériaux qui les composent et, surtout, à leur fonction. On s'attend donc à ce que les restaurateurs arrivent à stabiliser et à conserver des objets de toutes les époques de l'histoire. Or, peut-être par

Conservators are having to cope with these objects using their limited training in materials science and an ethical code conceived with more traditional artifacts in mind.

The degradation of recently acquired artifacts is forcing curators to review collecting policies. Should museums acquire examples of modern artifacts after extensive use has accelerated the degradation process? Should more emphasis be placed on documentation in order to preserve information about the artifact if the artifact itself cannot be preserved? How are we to preserve and maintain this rapidly developing material culture?

The aim of Symposium '91 was to approach these issues over a broad front. It involved experts in science and technology, both from within the museum field and outside, and included many museum professionals. We hoped to outline the current state of knowledge and to set future directions for research. As the following pages show, these goals were accomplished. As for the conservation of modern materials, we have only just begun....

Editorial Committee

penchant naturel et sans doute en raison de leur formation, les restaurateurs se sont consacrés davantage à l'étude des techniques du passé plutôt que celles du monde contemporain. Et même si l'on a généralement tendance à croire que les matériaux modernes sont plus stables que les anciens, rien n'est moins sûr. Nombre d'objets du XXe siècle sont en effet fort instables, et posent aux restaurateurs des problèmes inédits, qui tiennent entre autres à la radioactivité, à la dégradation des polymères et à la corrosion de l'aluminium. Lorsqu'il ont à résoudre de tels problèmes, les restaurateurs ne disposent donc que d'une formation rudimentaire dans le domaine de la science des matériaux, et se voient contraints d'appliquer des règles d'éthique qui ont été conçues pour des objets beaucoup plus anciens.

La dégradation des objets récemment acquis force les conservateurs de musées à revoir les politiques qui président à l'établissement des collections. Les musées devraient-ils acquérir des modèles d'objets contemporains qui ont été grandement utilisés et dont le processus de dégradation est d'autant plus avancé? Vaut-il mieux privilégier la documentation, la conservation de renseignements sur les objets, si ces derniers ne peuvent pas être conservés? Comment réussira-t-on à conserver les modèles de cette culture matérielle qui évolue si rapidement, et à maintenir ces collections d'objets?

Ces questions devaient être envisagées, lors du Symposium 91, dans le cadre d'une perspective plus large. Aussi a-t-on fait appel tant à des spécialistes des sciences et de la technique œuvrant à l'intérieur ou à l'extérieur des musées qu'aux professionnels de ces établissements. La conférence visait à fournir un aperçu des connaissances actuelles dans ce domaine, et à décider des orientations que prendra la recherche dans le secteur. Les pages suivantes montrent, de façon éloquente, que ces objectifs ont été atteints. Et, pour ce qui est de la conservation des matériaux modernes proprement dite, force est de constater qu'elle n'en est qu'à ses débuts...

Comité de rédaction

Table of Contents / Table des matières

1. Modern Materials in Collections / Utilisation des matériaux modernes au sein des collections

2. Conservation Policies and Plans / Politiques et projets en matière de conservation

3. History of Technology / Histoire de la technologie

4. Processes of Deterioration / Processus de dégradation

5. Case Studies and Specific Problems with Materials/
Études de cas et problèmes particuliers posés par les matériaux

6. Testing and Development of Conservation Processes / Élaboration et mise à l'essai des méthodes de conservation

7. Methods of Analysis and Identification / Méthodes d'analyse et d'identification

Modern Materials in Collections
Utilisation des matériaux modernes au sein des collections

Les matériaux modernes au Musée de la civilisation à Québec : un défi passé, présent et futur

Sylvie Marcil

Musée de la civilisation
Québec (Québec)
Canada

Résumé

Les matériaux modernes prennent de plus en plus d'importance dans les collections du Musée de la civilisation à Québec, qui présente, sous différents thèmes, un patrimoine souvent assez récent. La variété de ces matériaux ne cesse de croître — caoutchoucs, plastiques de tous genres, laques et vernis, métaux —, et leur composition nous est souvent inconnue. Ils se retrouvent dans presque toutes les collections — alimentation, accessoires de mode et de beauté, ameublement, jeux et jouets, outils et équipement, transports et communications — dans des proportions variées.

Qu'ils entrent dans la composition d'objets exposés ou mis en réserve, ces matériaux complexes posent de nouveaux défis à l'équipe de conservation-restauration, compte tenu du mandat qui a été confié au Musée par le ministère des Affaires culturelles du Québec. La présente communication fait précisément état de ces défis.

Dans le cas d'expositions, ces défis tiennent surtout à des questions de responsabilité — qui est partagée entre deux services — et d'attitude, de même qu'au statut des objets eux-mêmes et aux conditions ambiantes particulières qu'ils exigent. Dans le cas des collections, ils se posent, pour ainsi dire, à toutes les étapes : depuis l'identification et la numérotation des objets ou l'évaluation de leur état, jusqu'à leur nettoyage, leur traitement et leur entreposage, et en passant par les divers contrôles — des objets eux-mêmes tout autant que des conditions ambiantes des réserves — qui doivent s'effectuer.

Le Musée ne dispose que de ressources limitées, si l'on prend en compte son calendrier d'expositions chargé. Aussi son équipe de conservation-restauration doit-elle s'en tenir à la mise en application de mesures préventives et à des interventions minimales. Et il lui tarde de mettre sur pied un programme préventif global pour ces matériaux.

Introduction

En reprenant, au terme du présent symposium, le sujet de la communication d'introduction, à savoir « Les matériaux modernes dans le musée », nous voulons en quelque sorte boucler la boucle. Nous n'aurons pas nécessairement fait le tour de la question mais, en effectuant ainsi un retour au point de départ, nous serons mieux en mesure de déterminer si cette rencontre nous a effectivement permis d'avancer un peu.

Sans offrir de solutions ni tirer de conclusions des communications précédentes, le texte qui suit présente tout simplement une réalité, celle, très commune, d'une conservatrice-restauratrice d'un musée qui collectionne l'histoire en devenir, dans divers secteurs, et qui utilise différentes thématiques pour l'illustrer. Le contenu témoigne des défis que présente la conservation des matériaux modernes, présents dans un nombre croissant d'objets de la collection.

Au fil du texte sont insérées plusieurs photographies : les figures 1 à 5 offrent quelques exemples de matériaux modernes en exposition; les figures 6 à 10 sont des exemples de la détérioration de matériaux modernes et les figures 11 à 13 offrent quelques exemples d'interventions. Il est à noter que si certains objets ont le statut d'objets fabriqués ou proviennent de collections privées, il s'en trouve aussi d'autres qui ne constituent encore que des accessoires, mais qui pourraient bien éventuellement devenir des objets de collection. Tous ces matériaux se côtoient dans les expositions.

Le Musée de la civilisation

Le Musée de la civilisation est situé à Québec même, au bord du majestueux fleuve Saint-Laurent. Il loge dans un immeuble très récent, qui a ouvert ses portes en 1988. L'équipe du Musée est jeune, dynamique et ambitieuse. Elle réussit à attirer quelque 800 000 visiteurs par année, en faisant en sorte que le Musée soit ouvert et accessible à tous.

La réserve du Musée, où sont entreposées les collections, est située dans la ville de Vanier, à environ 10 km du Musée. Une importante partie du Service des collections y travaille, dont les équipes chargées du registrariat, du catalogage, de la recherche et des prêts d'objets, ainsi que celle de la conservation-restauration.

La conservation-restauration

L'équipe de conservation-restauration se compose d'une technicienne en conservation préventive, Élisabeth Forest, et, depuis mai 1989, d'une conservatrice-restauratrice. Des techniciens en restauration viennent, au besoin, se greffer à cette équipe. Le mandat que le ministère des Affaires culturelles a confié au Musée n'est pas un mandat de recherche. Le Musée est plutôt chargé des fonctions préventives, tandis que le Centre de conservation du Québec (CCQ) continue d'assumer en grande partie la fonction curative.

Compte tenu de ce mandat et du roulement des expositions au Musée, le travail de conservation-restauration s'effectue plutôt à un niveau de consultation, de prévention ou d'intervention minimale. L'équipe dessert tous les services du Musée — et plus particulièrement celui des expositions —, ainsi que quelques agences extérieures et, à l'occasion, le grand public. Les interventions se font surtout à la réserve, dans un atelier équipé à cette fin.

Les matériaux modernes au Musée de la civilisation

Déchet hier, trésor aujourd'hui, déchet aujourd'hui, trésor demain. Il ne fait aucun doute que les objets modernes, faits de matériaux modernes, se retrouvent déjà dans nos expositions, et qu'ils entrent en grand nombre dans nos collections. Leur variété ne cesse de croître : caoutchoucs et plastiques de tous genres, laques, peintures et vernis, métaux, cartons, contreplaqués, textiles, etc. Ils se retrouvent dans presque tous les secteurs — l'alimentation, les accessoires de mode et de beauté, l'ameublement, l'art populaire, les jeux et les jouets, les outils et l'équipement, les transports et les communications, etc.

Ces matériaux sont très complexes, hétérogènes et en constante évolution, et nous devons donc désormais apprendre à les conserver et à les restaurer, au même titre que les autres. Il s'agit là d'un défi de taille pour tous les conservateurs-restaurateurs, mais plus particulièrement pour ceux qui sont isolés dans des musées où les collections sont assez diverses et nombreuses.

I. Les expositions

Outre les expositions itinérantes, le Musée présente une vingtaine d'expositions par année dans les 10 salles du bâtiment principal, qui occupent approximativement 5 700 m^2, et dans deux autres bâtiments, à savoir la maison Chevalier et l'entrepôt Thibodeau*. Une proportion marquée des objets exposés se compose de matériaux modernes. Les deux tiers environ des objets de chaque exposition sont empruntés ou acquis à cette fin.

Les expositions ont une influence considérable sur le travail de conservation-restauration et sur le développement des collections, qui comportent de plus en plus d'objets créés à partir de matériaux modernes. Ces matériaux sont en effet très présents, car les thèmes qui sont

Figure 1 : *Autopsie d'un sac vert (Photo : Pierre Soulard, Archives du Musée de la civilisation, 348-PH-6).*

Figure 2 : *Éphémère (Photo : Pierre Soulard, Archives du Musée de la civilisation, 330-PH-21).*

Figure 3 : *Jeux (Photo : Pierre Soulard, Archives du Musée de la civilisation, 341-PH-3).*

Figure 4 : *Québec sur glace (Photo : Pierre Soulard, Archives du Musée de la civilisation, 319-PH-20).*

abordés lors de telles expositions — l'alimentation, la beauté et l'environnement, pour n'en nommer que quelques-uns — établissent une comparaison entre le passé et le présent, tout en explorant les tendances futures.

Cela met donc en valeur un patrimoine souvent très récent : depuis les ensembles de cosmétique ou un canot de fibre de verre d'une des dernières courses sur glace jusqu'aux systèmes audiovisuels qui ne sont pas encore sur le marché chez nous.

Tous ces objets n'aboutissent pas nécessairement dans nos collections, mais il faut quand même assurer leur conservation pendant leur séjour au Musée. Et c'est de là que proviennent les difficultés, qui tiennent surtout à des questions de responsabilité et d'attitude, ou au statut des objets eux-mêmes. Le Service des expositions est, avec celui des collections, responsable des objets. Vu la nature consultative de sa fonction, la conservation-restauration n'intervient qu'au besoin, à différents moments de la planification. Un objet récent — quel qu'en soit le propriétaire ou la personne responsable — ne

Figure 5 : Souffrir pour être belle (Photo : Pierre Soulard, Archives du Musée de la civilisation, 303-PH-21).

commande pas autant de respect qu'un bronze de l'Antiquité, par exemple. De plus, certaines pièces de même genre ont tantôt le statut d'objets de musée, ou d'artefacts, tantôt celui d'accessoires, et ne reçoivent donc pas toujours la même attention, ce qui porte parfois à confusion.

En ce qui concerne les conditions d'exposition (la lumière, la température et l'humidité relative), on opte plutôt pour la prudence. Le Musée possède d'ailleurs un système évolué de contrôle, mais pour les salles d'exposition du bâtiment principal seulement. Les facteurs qui posent la plus grande difficulté sont les polluants atmosphériques et la compatibilité entre les matériaux — entre ceux qui composent l'objet lui-même, de même qu'entre ces derniers et les matériaux de construction environnants. De plus, il arrive souvent que l'on ne connaisse ni la composition des objets ni celle des objets environnants, et on ne peut donc prévoir les réactions qu'ils auront dans un montage où ils se côtoient.

Il est par ailleurs possible que, au terme d'une exposition, l'objet passe du statut d'accessoire à celui d'artefact. On essaie toutefois de déterminer son statut futur avant le montage, pour s'assurer qu'il sera, au besoin, adéquatement restauré et pour éviter qu'il ne soit inutilement

abîmé pendant l'installation — s'il était collé, épinglé ou peinturé, par exemple. La démarcation entre l'artefact et l'accessoire n'est d'ailleurs pas toujours évidente. Il est difficile pour les conservateurs d'établir la valeur d'une acquisition en comparant les coûts de gestion et d'entreposage de l'artefact à ceux de l'objet neuf et en prenant en compte les axes de développement de la collection. Mais le défi ne s'arrête pas là. Lorsque les objets ont intégré les collections, ce sont d'autres préoccupations qui entrent en jeu.

II. Les collections

Actuellement, près de 65 000 objets sont entreposés à la réserve du Musée, dans un espace d'un peu plus de 3 000 m^2. Il est difficile d'établir le nombre d'objets qui comportent des matériaux modernes, car leurs fiches ne font pas toujours état des matériaux qui les composent, mais ils constituent, de toute évidence, un pourcentage non négligeable de cet ensemble. On sait déjà que les plastiques et les caoutchoucs font partie, à eux seuls, de plus de 2 000 de ces objets. Ce nombre augmente rapidement au fur et à mesure que progresse la validation des fiches d'objets aux fins d'intégration à la base de données sur vidéodisque, un système dont l'efficacité dépend de la précision et de l'exhaustivité de l'information qui y est versée.

Quel que soit le matériau, il faut donc l'identifier, numéroter l'objet, en déterminer l'état, le nettoyer, le traiter au besoin, l'entreposer dans les meilleures conditions possibles et, finalement, le contrôler. Beaucoup plus facile à dire qu'à faire, surtout lorsqu'il s'agit de matériaux modernes. Pour y arriver, il faut avoir une connaissance approfondie de la nature des matériaux et disposer de bons outils de travail. La tâche est énorme et les priorités, difficiles à établir.

1. L'identification
Dans un tel contexte, l'identification est le premier problème qui se pose. L'absence d'identification des matériaux rend difficile le catalogage et les autres étapes de la mise en réserve, de même que la rédaction des vignettes accompagnant les objets.

L'identification exige une formation en science des matériaux et un bon sens de l'observation. Même si on reconnaît la présence d'un matériau moderne, il faudra faire appel à un conservateur-restaurateur, qui est souvent le seul à posséder la formation qui permettra de l'identifier. Ce spécialiste ne dispose néanmoins pas toujours de tous les outils dont il a besoin pour trouver les réponses, et il devra donc trouver des moyens simples et rapides pour y arriver : tests, équipements, ouvrages de référence, etc. Si on veut que le catalogage suive le rythme des acquisitions, on ne peut, en effet, se permettre d'effectuer une recherche poussée pour chaque objet. Aussi une formation plus approfondie et continue facilite-t-elle le travail.

2. La numérotation

Lorsque le matériau a été identifié, il se peut que l'on ne puisse pas numéroter l'objet en employant la méthode traditionnelle de l'encre et du vernis — qui risquerait de faire fondre le matériau. C'est le cas de certains plastiques — les nitrates cellulosiques, par exemple —, caoutchoucs, surfaces vernies et métaux laqués. Il est donc bon de faire part de cette mise en garde aux personnes qui sont chargées de cette étape, s'ils n'ont pas déjà reçu la formation pertinente.

Dans ces cas, nous utilisons parfois des étiquettes de polyester dactylographiées, qui servent habituellement à la numérotation des textiles. Nous les fixons à l'objet avec un adhésif soluble à l'eau — en l'occurrence, du Cellofas —, mais il adhère plutôt mal à certaines surfaces. Nous n'avons pas encore, de toute évidence, trouvé la méthode idéale.

3. L'état de l'objet

Contrairement à ce qu'on aurait pu imaginer, la plupart des matériaux modernes mis en réserve au Musée paraissent stables et ne montrent pas de signes de détérioration avancée. Une évaluation très sommaire a permis d'établir que la majorité des matériaux serait en très bon état. Ceci résulte probablement du fait que plusieurs acquisitions d'objets modernes sont récentes, et qu'on a choisi, dans la mesure du possible, des objets en bon état.

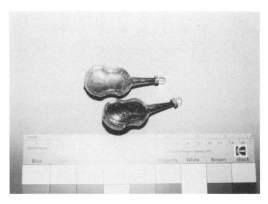

Figure 6 : Ornement de Noël en forme de violon (Musée de la civilisation, 89-1679). La laque présente de grandes fissures, qui laissent paraître le verre soufflé sous-jacent. (Photo : Élisabeth Forest)

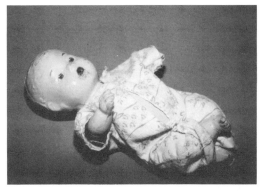

Figure 7 : Poupée (Musée de la civilisation, 79-138) constituée d'un matériau composite, possiblement une pâte de bois et recouverte d'une couche de plastique non identifié. Ce recouvrement craque et se soulève. (Photo : Élisabeth Forest)

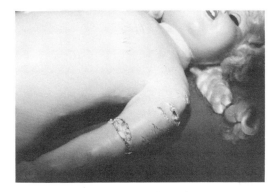

Figure 8 : Poupée (Musée de la civilisation, 88-6495) de caoutchouc rembourrée. Le caoutchouc sous tension se fissure et laisse paraître la bourrure, probablement de laine. (Photo : Élisabeth Forest)

Figure 9 : Jeu de parchési (Musée de la civilisation, 89-1655). Le papier verni est déchiré, ainsi que les bandes de tissu du centre et des côtés. (Photo : Élisabeth Forest)

Figure 10 : Parapluie (Collection privée). Les couleurs du tissu ont pâli et le bouton de plastique est complètement fissuré. (Photo : Élisabeth Forest)

Les manifestations de détérioration, lorsqu'il s'en trouve, sont caractéristiques : les plastiques et les caoutchoucs craquent, durcissent, jaunissent, suintent; les laques, les peintures et les vernis craquent, se soulèvent, s'effritent; les métaux se cassent, se corrodent, et leurs placages tombent; les cartons se déchirent, plient, se déforment et jaunisssent; les textiles se tachent et se déchirent; les contreplaqués fendent et se délaminent, etc. Certains matériaux sont plus touchés — les caoutchoucs et les plastiques mous, certaines laques et les cartons notamment. L'utilisation qui a été faite de l'objet à l'origine, combinée à la nature du matériau, est responsable en grande partie de cette détérioration.

4. Le nettoyage

Le nettoyage demeure l'opération la plus courante à laquelle sera soumise l'objet. Le temps, les ressources financières et les données sont souvent trop limités pour pousser plus loin l'intervention. On s'en tient donc à de simples tests, à l'aide de méthodes et produits usuels. Il est certain que cette étape est plus facile si le matériau a été identifié. En cas d'effet négatif, on se limite au dépoussiérage.

Lorsque la méthode de nettoyage a été définie différentes questions se posent. Jusqu'où doit-on aller? Faut-il conserver tous les éléments? Doit-on disposer systématiquement des contenus à caractère pharmaceutique ou alimentaire, par exemple? Et comment doit-on s'y prendre?

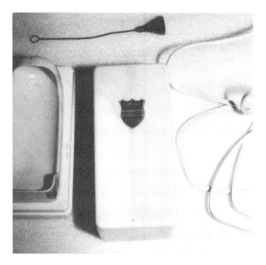

Figure 11 : Rasoir (Collection privée). La plupart des interventions se limitent à un nettoyage de surface lorsque le matériau réagit bien.

5. Le traitement

Un simple nettoyage n'est parfois pas suffisant pour assurer la stabilité d'un objet. Si on connaît la cause de la détérioration, on peut parfois intervenir. Il est toutefois difficile de formuler un traitement et d'en évaluer les conséquences sans avoir de solides connaissances du matériau. Les ouvrages de référence, rares, épars et souvent trop théoriques, ne sont pas d'un grand secours. On se réfère plutôt à des collègues plus expérimentés. On doit aussi affronter des questions d'éthique, car il est difficile d'établir un principe directeur d'intervention qui tienne compte de l'intention du fabricant et des autres considérations pour la conservation.

Comme pour le nettoyage, les quelques interventions curatives qui s'effectuent au Musée sont limitées, compte tenu du manque de temps et de connaissances approfondies. Les résultats sont de ce fait inégaux. La diversité des matériaux ne nous permet pas de passer en revue tous les genres de traitements qui ont été mis à l'essai, mais nous en retiendrons tout de même quelques-uns.

Figure 12 : Carrosse (Musée de la civilisation, 89-1655). La capote était fendue et trois des cerceaux de caoutchouc manquaient aux jantes.

Les meubles, les valises ou les jouets, par exemple, ont souvent un recouvrement qui est fait de textile enduit, de plastique (du vinyle, notamment) ou de carton laminé et parfois verni. On réussira à refermer les fentes dans les textiles à l'aide d'une doublure de soie de polyester collée avec du BEVA, à faire adhérer le vinyle au bois avec du Rhoplex AC-33 et à consolider des cartons délaminés avec du Cellofas.

Figure 13 : Le traitement, fait au Centre de conservation du Québec (CCQ), a permis de stabiliser la capote de cuirette « American Leather » avec un entoilage de mousseline de soie collé avec du BEVA et de rééquilibrer les roues en adaptant des tubes de néoprène. (Photo : Michel Élie, CCQ)

Les caoutchoucs — vulcanisés, mousse ou latex — demeurent non traités pour l'instant. On les protège avec du Armor-All, quand ils sont en bon état, mais on remplace aussi certaines parties manquantes avec des matériaux équivalents modernes, ce qui est parfois plus rapide et plus économique, et qui permet mieux de respecter l'original et son utilisation. Il faudra voir comment de telles interventions résisteront aux années.

6. L'entreposage
Déterminer les meilleures conditions d'entreposage possibles n'est pas toujours facile lorsqu'il s'agit de matériaux modernes. Bien que les règles générales d'entreposage s'appliquent, il faut déterminer les besoins particuliers des matériaux en ce qui a trait à l'humidité, à la température et à la lumière, et à leur protection contre les polluants atmosphériques. L'identification des matériaux est également primordiale pour établir leur compatibilité avec les autres matériaux environnants.

On a déjà beaucoup amélioré l'entreposage général au Musée, et on continue de le faire, mais on n'a toujours pas de système de contrôle environnemental adapté aux collections, et on ne s'est pas encore penché sur les besoins particuliers des matériaux. Le fait que les objets soient souvent composés de plusieurs matériaux vient compliquer les choses. L'espace diminue déjà à vue d'œil avec les acquisitions, surtout quand on doit entreposer séparément chacun des éléments de l'objet (un jeu en boîte, par exemple, où l'on retrouverait des pions en métal et en plastique dans un contenant de papier et de carton). Devrait-on entreposer ces éléments par matériau, si les matériaux constituants sont incompatibles? La question demeure sans réponse pour l'instant. Il y a beaucoup d'arguments contre cette option, d'ordre logistique notamment.

7. Le contrôle

Puisque la plupart des matériaux modernes de la collection du Musée semblent, pour l'instant, en bon état, il importe de nous concentrer sur l'aspect préventif. Dans un avenir rapproché, il faudra définir un plan d'évaluation global pour ces matériaux et en assurer un certain contrôle. Cette étape sera facilitée par le vidéodisque, mais compliquée par le fait que ces matériaux sont dispersés dans l'ensemble de la collection. L'œil averti des conservateurs responsables de secteurs sera d'une grande utilité pour les repérer et pour établir les priorités de traitement. Encore faudra-t-il trouver des traitements qui soient efficaces!

Conclusion

Il est évident qu'on ne peut ignorer l'arrivée continuelle de nouveaux matériaux au Musée. Pour un établissement possédant une telle quantité et une telle diversité d'objets, la conservation-restauration constitue un défi énorme, et les besoins sont proportionnels. Pour bien s'acquitter de cette tâche, il faut s'attaquer globalement au problème, même si cela ne semble pas évident de prime abord.

Le conservateur-restaurateur ne peut être un spécialiste de chaque matériau qu'il rencontre. Il faut qu'il puisse compléter sa formation par des ateliers ou des séminaires spécialisés. Il faut aussi qu'il ait facilement accès à une information regroupée à l'intérieur de bibliographies choisies, etc. Le bulletin du groupe de travail de l'ICOM sur les matériaux modernes est une excellente initiative et un grand pas dans la bonne direction. Il regroupe une foule de renseignements pertinents. Je suis certaine que le symposium aura également été profitable. Il s'agit « simplement » de continuer dans cette direction. Maintenant que les problèmes et leurs causes sont mieux connus, les conservateurs-restaurateurs isolés misent davantage sur leurs collègues pour pousser plus loin leur recherche, et pour publier les résultats de leurs travaux, autant les bons que les mauvais.

Remerciements

J'adresse mes très sincères remerciements à Élisabeth Forest, qui participe activement au travail dont j'ai fait état dans la présente communication, et qui a exécuté bon nombre des photographies qui ont été présentées. Les autres diapositives ont été tirées des archives du Musée. Je tiens également à remercier les manutentionnaires Gaétan Giguère et Lise Dionne, responsables de la numérotation et de la mise en réserve, qui ont emballé les objets qui n'ont malheureusement pas pu être présentés en démonstration.

Note

*Pour obtenir de plus amples renseignements techniques, prière de communiquer avec :

Sylvie Marcil
334, rue de la Tourelle
Québec (Québec) G1R 1C8
Téléphone : (418) 648-1590
Télécopieur : (418) 529-4195

Abstract

Modern Materials in the Collection of the Musée de la civilisation

Modern materials have become increasingly important in the collections of the Musée de la civilisation, which presents a thematic view of recent history. The composition of these artifacts is often unknown, is becoming increasingly diverse, and includes such materials as rubber, plastics, lacquers and varnishes, and metals. These materials can be found in varying proportions in almost every area of the collection: food, fashion and beauty accessories, furniture, games and toys, tools and equipment, transportation, and communications.

Whether one considers the composition of displayed or of stored artifacts, these complex materials present new challenges to the conservation team. This is particularly true in light of the mandate given to the Museum by the Quebec Ministry of Cultural Affairs. This presentation outlines these challenges.

In the case of exhibitions, these challenges mainly relate to issues of responsibility, which is shared by two departments within the museum, and of

attitude as much as to the status of the artifacts themselves and to the particular ambient conditions they require. In the case of collections, these challenges exist at all stages, for example, identifying and numbering the objects; evaluating their state; cleaning, treating, and storing them; and monitoring — of the objects themselves as much as of the ambient storage conditions.

The Musée de la civilisation has limited resources, considering its heavy exhibition schedule. Hence, its team of conservators must adhere to preventive measures and use minimal intervention. A global program of prevention for these materials has yet to be established.

The Condition Survey of Sound Recordings at the National Library of Canada: Implications for Conservation

Jan Michaels

The National Library of Canada
Ottawa, Ontario
Canada

Abstract

The National Library of Canada is the deposit library for, among other things, published sound recordings in Canada. In the summer of 1990, as part of a three-year program, a condition survey of sound recordings was conducted of National Library collections. Separate surveys of reel-to-reel tapes, cylinders, LPs, 45s and 78s were done.

Information was obtained, which will assist in collection management as well as in preservation and conservation planning. Shelving methods and containers were examined for suitability and condition. Lignin and pH tests were conducted on containers made of paper-based materials. As for the sound recordings themselves, base materials and oxide layers were identified. For open reel tape, rub and smell tests were carried out, as well as physical examination for over 20 categories of damage, including creasing, stretching, flaking, blocking and plasticizer migration. Similar tests for the other media were conducted as appropriate. For discs, groove wear also was examined.

This paper discusses the survey's results and implications. In the short term, our new-found information will help in planning preservation activities including re-housing and copying. The survey also directs attention to unresolved conservation issues, both technical and ethical. An unresolved ethical issue remains: is the aim to repair in order to play an item one more time, or to conserve for posterity? The paper concludes with a discussion of the National Library's attempts to come to grips with the problem of establishing a discipline of sound recording conservation.

Introduction

The phonograph was invented in 1877 by Thomas Edison. Like many inventors of genius, he claimed that it was by "the merest accident":

> I was singing to the mouthpiece of a telephone, when the vibrations of the wire sent the fine steel point into my finger. That set me to thinking. If I could record the actions of the point, and then send the point over the same surface afterwards, I saw no reason why the thing would not talk.

> I tried the experiment, first on a strip of telegraph paper and found that the point made an alphabet. I shouted the word 'Halloo! Halloo!' into the mouthpiece, ran the paper back over the steel point, and heard a faint 'Halloo! Halloo!' in return. I determined to make a machine that would work accurately, and gave my assistants instructions, telling them what I had discovered.

> They laughed at me. I bet fifteen cigars with one of my assistants, Mr. Adams, that the thing would work the first time without a break, and won them. That's the whole story. The discovery came through the pricking of a finger.[1]

From that "merest accident" was born a technology that has transformed cultural life.

This transformation is described by an anonymous Canadian in Moogk[2]:

> Records have done more to spread music and culture to the far-flung corners of Canada, and indeed the world, in the first fifty years of its [sic] invention, than personal performances did in all the centuries that passed before. Until the advent of radio, and even for many years after that, the gramophone was the main source of entertainment for the settler, the hunter and trapper, the isolated farmer, and the little hamlets and communities in the Canadian north and far west.

The National Library, as keeper of the Canadian published heritage, has been receiving published sound recordings through legal deposit since 1969. In order to fulfill its mandate, it has purchased or received as gifts or donations tens of thousands more recordings that were made prior to legal deposit. The National Library also has thousands of tapes recorded by or for Canadian composers and performers. As well, there are talking recordings, children's tapes, Canadian National Institute for the Blind cassettes and educational kit recordings. The Library has piano rolls, cylinder recordings, 78 rpm records (78s), 45 rpm records (45s), 33⅓ rpm records (also known as long-playing records or LPs), reel-to-reel magnetic tapes, cassettes, 8-track cassette tapes, compact discs (CDs), and music videos. All told, the National Library of Canada's Recorded Sound Collection now holds over 120,000 recordings of Canadiana.

In the summer of 1989, as the first step of a new initiative in preservation planning, the National Library undertook the examination of the nature and condition of all its collections. Starting with eight categories of printed items, the surveys continued, evaluating microforms and sound recordings. In 1992 the last of the surveys, manuscripts, will be completed. Once all surveys are concluded and the analyses finished, the National Library will have a comprehensive picture of the state of its holdings and the areas of greatest threat. This will greatly facilitate preservation management.

In some senses, our sound recording survey was the least successful of the surveys carried out. Ambitious plans were made to survey all major media in the collections and to do some sound tests, too. In the end, within the allotted time, only the cylinders, 78s, 45s, LPs and reel-to-reel tapes were surveyed. No sound tests were conducted. A decision on whether or not to complete the survey as originally planned has not been made. Costs will have to be weighed against the potential value of any additional information.

The surveys of the discs and magnetic tapes were conducted using a stratified random sample with approximately 400 items per stratum. This provides a 95% confidence level. (Further information on the sampling method can be found in Bullock.[3])

In the questionnaire we recorded the physical condition of the sound recordings and their containers. Base materials and oxide layers were identified. Over 20 categories of damage to the recording media were surveyed. pH of the containers was assessed using Phydrion Instacheck surface pH pencils and lignin content using the phloroglucinol test.

Results and Implications

This paper briefly discusses some results of the disc and reel-to-reel tape surveys. The cylinder survey is not discussed. Detailed analysis of all the sound surveys will be available at a later date.

Discs

78s: The phonograph was invented in 1877. Twenty years later, in 1897, shellac was introduced as the major component in the disc. The 78 rpm disc was the principal commercial recording medium of the 1930s and 1940s.[4] McWilliams describes these shellac recordings in the following way:

> The term shellac, as used in record manufacture, did not mean — at that time or subsequently — a disc made entirely of shellac. It was, rather, a convenient way of referring to a compound material. Shellac contained fillers, such as limestone or slate, pigment (usually carbon black), lubricants, such as zinc stearate, and binders and modifiers, such as Congo gum and vinsol.[5]

Fortunately, most shellac discs are really very stable. McWilliams goes on to say, "Properly formulated shellac cures as it ages — a cross-polymerization occurs, which guarantees good long-term life."[6]

However, McWilliams has reported that the composition of shellac compounds deteriorated during the World Wars when shellac supplies were interrupted. As a result war-year discs may be less stable.

Despite their long-term stability, shellac discs are nonetheless quite brittle and relatively easy to damage. Results indicate that all of the National Library's collection of 78 rpm recordings are damaged because of dust and dirt. Figure 1 depicts the major forms of damage to these 78s.

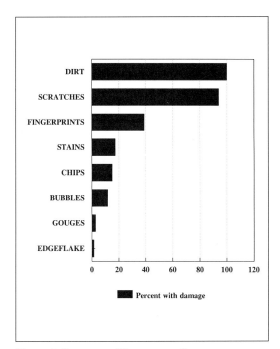

Figure 1 Damage to 78 rpm recordings.

LPs: The long-playing disc or LP was first manufactured in the early 1950s and by the 1960s was ubiquitous. The National Library collection is not stored on proper shelving or with adequate support. Results indicate that 99% are still stored in their original outer jackets. Of these outer jackets, 98% are composed of acid paper, and 81% are of ligneous paper.

Of the inner sleeves, 92% are originals. Sleeves composed of paper constitute 55% while those of paper with plastic liners make up 26%. Of the paper sleeves, 97% are acid paper and 93% have a surface pH of 3 or 4.

Unfortunately data indicates that all of these recordings also are damaged: 74% are scratched and 99% are dirty. Figure 2 depicts the major forms of damage to these $33\frac{1}{3}$ rpm recordings.

45s: The 45 rpm record with its large-diameter spindle was first introduced by RCA in the 1950s. Currently, these 45s are stored in their original outer jackets. Results indicate that 98% of the National Library's outer jackets are acid paper. All of the 45s show some kind of damage. Figure 3 depicts the major forms of damage to these 45s.

Overall Comments

Records are published with jackets on the outside and sleeves as inner protectors. Data indicates that 99% of all types of discs in the collection, as a group, are in acidic record jackets. Of the inner liners, 92% are originals. Of

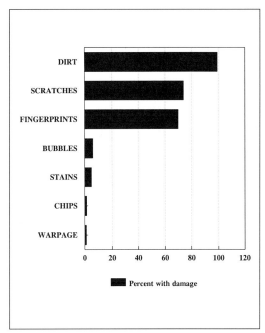

Figure 2 Damage to $33\frac{1}{3}$ rpm recordings.

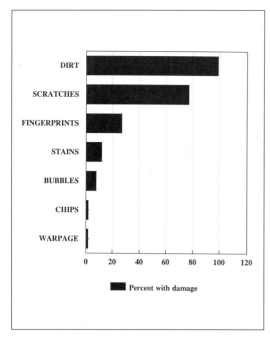

Figure 3 Damage to 45 rpm recordings.

the inner sleeves, 58% are paper, 97% of which are acidic. In general, paper inner sleeves should be avoided because paper breaks down over time, contaminating the surface and grooves of the recording with dust-like paper debris. Obviously acidity in the paper accelerates this breakdown. As well, there is a possibility that ligneous paper can damage recordings.[7]

Clearly, we are facing a massive re-sleeving program. As well, the original jackets will require de-acidification and storage space.

Results indicate that 99% of the discs are dirty. As dust easily can be imbedded permanently into the plastic, it is considered damage for purposes of the survey. This high level of dust must be related to the inadequate air filtering system in the Library as well as the large number of acidic sleeves and jackets. According to St.-Laurent, when a record is played:

... only a small point of the stylus is actually making contact with the groove walls. One and a half grams of stylus pressure on such a minute surface translates to several tons of pressure per square inch. The resulting

drag generates enough heat that the plastic partially melts (though not enough to deform), causing a microscopic flow around the stylus into which dust can be embedded permanently.[8]

Record player needles cause additional damage to recordings because of the friction between the record grooves and the stylus. The friction contact is needed to reproduce the signal, but it is also harmful because it causes gradual deformation or bending of the grooves. The result is a progressive distortion that builds up from one playback to the next.[9] This is why it is recommended that a record only be played once in any 24-hour period.

The single greatest problem in the preservation of disc recordings is groove wear.[10] This damage is not visible except under a microscope. Another major form of damage to discs, and the second most common found in the survey, is scratching. Most scratches occur as a result of use. As playing is one of the major causes of damage to recordings, a priority must be the minimizing of damage to originals. Clearly the best solution to the potential damage caused by dust is not to play the recordings. A second-best solution is not to use a stylus to play the recordings. This is no longer impossible. Within the last year a record player has become available commercially that uses a laser beam rather than a stylus to play the disc. This revolutionary piece of equipment has taken almost a decade to develop. The National Library recently acquired the first such laser turntable outside Japan.

The ELP laser turntable uses five laser beams to track the record. It can compensate for warpage, discs of various sizes and speeds, certain types of groove damage or variable groove widths. Even discs that are flaking can be played successfully with this system.[11] Use of this turntable will assist in minimizing damage to the collection.

Fortunately the long-term prognosis for discs is quite good. Their predicted life expectancy is more than a century when stored in ordinary library environments. The Pickett and Lemcoe report states:

The actual potential storage life with respect to chemical degradation of an individual disc is dependent on its exact formulation (including both kinds and amount of stabilizer and extender used) and its thermal history prior to acquisition (including processing and molding). Apparently, small changes in these parameters can change the potential storage life with respect to chemical degradation by several decades.[12]

Unfortunately evidence does exist that 45s may not be so permanent. Very early 45s seem to be quite stable, but later, polystyrene was commonly used for 45s due to greater economies in manufacture over vinyl. These polystyrene discs are inherently unstable. They fracture relatively easily.[13] The outer layer of the record surface can peel off at the area of contact — like old house paint.[14] Though the National Library's collection of 45s does not appear to be in worse condition than the other discs, this may be a result of benign environmental conditions and relatively short life rather than any inherent longevity in their makeup. Clearly it is important to conduct further research before the 45s begin to self-destruct.

Reel-to-Reel Tapes

Magnetic recordings have existed since the end of the 19th century. However, the first successful tape recordings were not demonstrated until 1935 at the Berlin Radio Exhibition. Harold Lindsay built the first Ampex machine in 1947, successfully introducing the medium to the United States.[15] Low-priced units became available in the mid-1950s.[16]

There are usually three layers in a magnetic tape: the base or substrate onto which the binder and recording material is coated; the binder, which bonds the recording material to the base; and the recording material, which is capable of being magnetized and contains the information recorded.

The survey indicated that in the National Library's collection 78% of the tape bases are polyester, 20% are cellulose acetate and only 1% is paper. McWilliams states:

Many tape recordings from the 1950s will be found on acetate-base tape. Cellulose acetate is unstable. It will eventually crumble, destroying the sound recording, or cause patches of the magnetic coating to fall off, destroying areas of the recording. Acetate-base tapes may hold up well for years but eventually they will self-destruct.[17]

Polyester or pre-stretched poly(ethylene terephthalate) (PET) was reserved initially for products exposed to severe conditions, such as those used in the military. Its use spread very gradually over a period of 10 years beginning around 1960. Until about 1970, both cellulose triacetate and polyester tapes were produced.[18]

Experts project a life expectancy (i.e., the acceptable maintenance of mechanical properties) for cellulose triacetate at approximately 300 years, and for PET at several millennia. Under adverse storage conditions, the polyester base appears to be much more stable than the acetate base. Degradation of cellulose acetate at very high humidity (RH 80%) is extremely rapid. Cellulose acetate tapes stretch with dampness to produce waviness and contract with drying.[19] This is corroborated in our results: the cellulose acetate tapes were reported to be curled much more frequently than the polyester. Conversely, as the production of acetate tape requires the use of plasticizers, overly dry storage conditions contribute to the loss of these agents and the film becomes extremely brittle.[20] As well, cellulose acetate is decomposed by acids and alkalis.[21] This is of great concern as results indicated that 93% of the tape storage boxes are acidic. The thin base layer has a front coating, namely the binder, which contains a magnetic recording material, which is commonly ferric oxide. Brown et al. decribe these binders:

> The magnetic material is embedded in a polymeric binder. Common binders are based on polyester polyurethanes. Sometimes there is a carbon coating on the back, which is also embedded in a polymeric binder. The carbon coating dissipates electrostatic charge.
>
> The polyester polyurethane binders used on tapes are highly cross-linked materials with complex structures. They can be expected

to have 5-10 times as many ester groups as urethane groups. Aliphatic esters are used; these are more susceptible to hydrolytic degradation than the PET substrate.[22]

And in a later paper Smith et al. state:

Other materials such as lubricants, adhesives, or stabilizers are frequently added to this layer. Polyester polyurethane is subject to auto catalytic hydrolysis, which was expected to limit the lifetime of the tape. Some types of magnetic tapes contain chromium oxide particles, which do affect the chemical degradation mechanisms. This has recently been reported by researchers at IBM.[23]

In order for the magnetic tape to work properly, the binder must adhere so firmly to the base material and to the iron oxide that it will resist the stresses of playback and storage without crazing, flaking, or peeling. It must maintain these properties despite chemical degradation and loss of residual solvent or plasticizer.[24] Brown et al. indicate:

Thus the degradation of interest in magnetic tapes is primarily that of the binder. On degradation this softens; adjacent layers of tape may stick together or the binder may stick to the recording heads. Ultimately the tape becomes unreadable.[25]

The binder is more sensitive to hydrolysis than PET.[26] The short estimated useful tape lifetime of 20 years[27] is directly related to the failure of the binder layer. In some cases, binder breakdown has been discovered in items only five years old.[28]

The results of the reel-to-reel tape survey were very worrisome: for 30% of the tapes, the oxide rubs off; 23% cannot be played. Figure 4 indicates damage to the tape recordings.

The reels onto which tapes are wound can be another source of damage. Results indicate that 69% of the National Library tape reels are plastic and 31% are metal. Waites indicates that the reel's "...basic function is to protect the tape from damage and contamination. It is often the reel itself, damaged through mistreatment, that in turn damages the tape."[29]

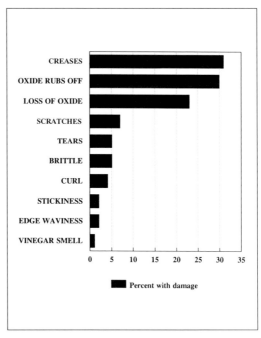

Figure 4 Damage to reel-to-reel tape recordings.

Sound recording experts have recommended that tape should not be stored on plastic reels. Metal, unslotted reels are recommended.[30] These solid, unslotted reels prevent uneven exposure to the environment. Waites explains:

Because the hub is the strongest and most stable part of the reel, it is the best means of reel support during storage. When the reel is supported by the hub, there is little if any weight resting upon its flanges. This protects the flanges from problems such as bending and nicks.

Under no circumstances should a reel be stored resting on its flanges. Paper notes about stored data or other sources of contamination should not be put in the storage container.[31]

The Association for Recorded Sound Collections (ARSC) report also recommends that liner notes be stored separately from the sound recordings.[32] The effect of acid migration on tapes is reflected in the condition survey results. The pH of paper notes for all items where the oxide rubbed off was reported to be 5 or less.

Clearly the potential loss of information that is indicated by the results is distressing. Information is quickly disappearing in large amounts. Unfortunately very little research is being carried out to allay this worldwide problem. Gerry Gibson of the Library of Congress said in 1989:

> With the exception of work now being carried out on magnetic tape for the National Archives [in the United States] by the National Bureau of Standards (United States et al. 1986), reported evaluation of Sony's optical Century Media data by the NBS, and of the effects of fire upon sound and audiovisual recording supports by the French Ministère de la culture et de la communication for the Bibliothèque nationale (Paris) (Fontaine 1987), virtually no independent work is going on at this time on topics directly related to audio preservation. Further, relatively little is known about the preservation, conservation, or aging problems or properties of sound recordings from directly related scientific study.[33]

In fact, the 1959 Pickett and Lemcoe study *Preservation and Storage of Sound Recordings*, long out of print, remains the basis of most of the conservation knowledge in the field.[33]

Conservation Issues

Pickett and Lemcoe point out that shellac and poly(vinyl chloride) (PVC) discs deteriorate in opposite ways. Whereas shellac discs will slowly, progressively become embrittled even in a good storage environment, PVC discs suffer from an increasingly rapid embrittlement at the end of their storage life. They recommend skilled judgment to determine when a disc has become so embrittled that it should be re-recorded. They indicate that:

> Such embrittlement is often noticed by the decrease in flexibility of a disc or by playback (with good equipment) resulting in disc wear so serious that the powder will dirty a soft white cloth wiped across the surface.[34]

This is reminiscent of a short poem I used to know, written by the Danish poet and inventor Piet Hein, about making perfect toast: one was supposed to put it in the toaster until it began to smoke and then toast it for two minutes less.

Pickett and Lemcoe recommend a surveillance procedure of inspection and test based on stabilizer exhaustion as the most feasible means of determining the need for re-recording these discs. They say:

> ...there is evidence that detectable changes in the chemical composition of the record can be used to indicate incipient failure due to chemical deterioration, although more information is needed to develop analytical techniques and surveillance procedures. This aspect of the problem might be made the subject of additional study.[35]

Thirty years later, analysis of residual products is being pursued in France by Fontaine with the intention that these can be used as indicators of degradation.[36]

A remedy for another area of concern for tape recordings, binder breakdown, is feasible. Commercial firms can, through a carefully controlled time-temperature cycling process, reverse the binder breakdown. Kent describes the technique:

> Heat allows the binder system to rebond temporarily. The treatment is not permanent, but gives at least a 30-day time window in which to work with the tape. Provided the time-temperature cycling is done correctly, there is no measurable high-frequency loss, noise increase or increase in print-through. Treated tapes appear to play with no difficulty and no apparent damage. It also appears that the tape could be re-treated later for another use period.[37]

Similar environmentally based binder rejuvenation programs that reverse tape hydrolysis are discussed in papers by Sidney Geller[38] and Edward Cuddihy.[39]

There is a critical need for basic research into both the conservation science and treatment of sound recordings. The problem is that the profession of sound recording conservator does not exist. Even the question of proper cleaning of recordings has not been examined by a conservator or scientist. Gerry Gibson laments, "What is known is based upon trial and error, not upon controlled, objective, scientific study."[40]

The National Library is in the initial stages of plans for a conservation program for its sound recordings. The intention is to create two positions for sound recording conservators: one to concentrate on disc technologies and the other, magnetic tape technologies. Such positions will be challenging. Clearly a strong background in chemistry will be needed to ensure that non-destructive, reversible, ethical conservation techniques are developed. Much scientific research will be required before treatment decisions can be made. How exactly can we repair a broken 78 so that it can be played again? How can we simulate grooves so the needle can track the record at least one more time? Are we talking about repair for only one more play or a more permanent repair? If a one-play repair is adopted do we immediately reverse the repair once completed in order to preserve the original?

As we have seen, tapes are even more problematic. Can anything be done when there is catastrophic failure, that is, when the binder has separated from the backing? Can something be done when the lubricant or plasticizer has dried, making the tape very brittle?

Perhaps the most stimulating and challenging debate of this Symposium is that of retention: can we, should we, at what price? There are many analogies that can be drawn between sound recordings and books: both are mechanical, they function, they move, they are used. Both can be damaged through use. Both carry information and are usually mass produced. Both are relatively easily copied: microfilm, photocopy, dubbing. And both speak of a culture and its time. That trapper and his cylinder player, the isolated homesteader listening to gramophone recordings in retreat from the surrounding wilderness, a teenager pouring over his or her favourite 45s. Just as bibliographic integrity and artifactual value are important considerations when deciding on whether to retain a book after microfilming, similar considerations are important for sound recordings.

Unquestionably at least a proportion of original published sound recordings should be kept. Criteria based on rarity, value, examples of different media, major changes to carrier or sound recording technologies could be used to help select items for retention and the remainder could be dubbed onto an archival medium.

At this time, however, there are two major problems with this solution of selective retention and global copying. There is no proven archival medium for sound carriers.[41] In the case of discs, records may well last longer than any medium onto which they are dubbed. Copies themselves must, over a period of years, be copied. Though tape is most often used for dubbing, Smith et al. report:

> It has been found that in many cases old tapes can be read only once. Therefore a tape testing program involving random sampling might eventually destroy a substantial portion of a tape library without finding bad tapes.[42]

The second problem is related to the increased sophistication of sound systems. A copy made today is usually dubbed using a computerized system that easily filters out the original's clicks and pops, adjusts the pitch and removes background noise. But this adjustment in sound is not reversible on a copy. We still need to have the original to get as close to the performer's or composer's original intent.

A major study of preservation needs for sound recordings was undertaken in 1987 by the international Association for Recorded Sound Collections. The results and recommendations, compiling more than 400 pages, call for action:

> There is a clear and urgent need to preserve our surviving heritage of sound recordings. Sound recordings have been created and disseminated for nearly a century, for the most part with little thought for their lasting significance to society. For the most part, recognition of their scholarly value has come about only recently along with the creation of archival facilities, collections, and preservation projects. ... In the meantime, very large numbers of sound recordings — including unique material — are rapidly deteriorating.

> Preservation of archival collections of sound recordings, both in theory and practice, has only recently begun to receive widespread, serious attention. As with any field of study which is only now moving through the early stages of development, the field of audio

archiving is characterized by widely divergent practice, doubt, confusion and a myriad of questions.[43]

Nearly all of the conclusions reached by the planning study group reflected the lack of co-ordinated, carefully planned research into audio preservation and conservation problems.[44] Gerry Gibson has expressed it best:

> Clearly, the solution can not be to endlessly rerecord holdings. We must search to find a more permanent storage media [sic] and to accept an archival format good for 50 or more years. Further, we must actively and aggressively work together, since the job is far too large for any one or two collections to undertake. We must carry out coordinated research into the various factors that affect the long term storage and retrieval of the data and materials in our collections. We must work together to build the shared pool of knowledge which is necessary to prevent premature failure of the items in our care, and, thus, loss of the knowledge of our civilization. Only in that manner can we assure that the information that they carry will be transmitted to future generations.[45]

It is time that the conservation community took up the challenge!

Résumé

Les enregistrements sonores à la Bibliothèque nationale du Canada : une étude d'état et son incidence sur la conservation

C'est à la Bibliothèque nationale du Canada que sont archivés, entre autres, les enregistrements sonores produits au Canada. Au cours de l'été de 1990, les enregistrements sonores conservés à cet établissement ont fait l'objet d'une étude d'état, menée dans le cadre d'un programme de trois ans. Les rubans de magnétophone à bobines, les cylindres, les disques longue durée, les 45 tours et les 78 tours ont tous été soumis à une évaluation distincte.

L'information ainsi recueillie facilitera la gestion des collections, de même que la planification des mesures à prendre pour assurer leur préservation et leur conservation. On a ainsi cherché à savoir si le rangement sur étagères et les contenants convenaient, et à évaluer l'état des objets ainsi conservés. Des tests portant sur la lignine et le pH des contenants à base de papier ont été menés, et l'on a identifié les matériaux qui entrent dans la composition du support des enregistrements sonores eux-mêmes, de même que ses couches d'oxyde. Dans le cas des rubans de magnétophone à bobines, on a effectué des essais de frottement et d'odeur, et l'on a tenté d'identifier plus de 20 genres de dommages, dont le plissement, l'étirement, l'effritement, le blocage et la migration du plastifiant. Les autres supports d'enregistrement ont été soumis, dans la mesure du possible, à des essais analogues. Dans le cas des disques, l'usure des sillons a en outre été évaluée.

Au cours de la présente communication, nous traiterons des résultats et de l'incidence de cette étude. À court terme, les renseignements nouveaux que nous fournissons faciliteront la planification des mesures qui seront prises pour assurer la préservation de ces enregistrements — leur relogement et leur copie notamment. L'étude fait par ailleurs ressortir certains problèmes de conservation qui demeurent non résolus, et qui sont aussi bien d'ordre technique qu'éthique. Ainsi, sur le plan de l'éthique, la questions demeure de savoir si la réparation du médium doit d'abord viser à obtenir une audition supplémentaire de l'enregistrement ou à assurer sa conservation pour la postérité. Nous terminerons en traitant des efforts que déploie la Bibliothèque nationale en vue de résoudre la difficulté que pose la création d'une discipline distincte pour la conservation des enregistrements sonores.

References

1. Quoted in Moogk, Edward B., *Roll Back the Years: History of Canadian Recorded Sound and its Legacy. Genesis to 1930* (Ottawa: National Library of Canada, 1975) p. 5. Original source, J.B. McClure, ed., *Edison and His Inventions*, (Chicago: Rhodes and McClure Publishing Co., 1895).

2. Moogk, *Roll Back the Years*, p. 8.

3. Bullock, Allison, *National Library of Canada 1989 Survey of the Non-rare Printed Collections* (Ottawa: National Library of Canada, 1989, in press).

4. McWilliams, Jerry, "Sound Recordings in Swartzburg," in: *Conservation in the Library: A Handbook of Use and Care of Traditional and Non-traditional Materials*, ed. Susan Garretson, (Westport: Greenwood Press, 1983) p. 164.

5. McWilliams, Jerry, *The Preservation and Restoration of Sound Recordings* (Nashville: American Association for State and Local History, 1979) p. 6.

6. McWilliams, "Sound Recordings in Swartzburg," p. 165.

7. David Grattan and Helen Burgess, personal communication, Canadian Conservation Institute, 1991.

8. St.-Laurent, Gilles, "The Care and Handling of Recorded Sound Materials," *Commission on Preservation and Access Report*, (Washington, D.C.: Commission on Preservation and Access, 1991) p. 8.

9. Heckmann, Harold, "Storage and Handling of Audio and Magnetic Materials," in: *Preservation of Library Materials*, ed. Merrily A. Smith (Paris: Saur, 1987) p. 68.

10. Gibson, Gerald, "Preservation of Non-paper Materials," in: *Conserving and Preserving Library Materials*, Kathryn Luther Henderson and William T. Henderson, eds. (Urbana-Champaign: University of Illinois, 1983) p. 103.

11. Gilles St.-Laurent, personal communication, 1991.

12. Pickett, A.G. and M.M. Lemcoe, *Preservation and Storage of Sound Recordings* (Washington: Library of Congress, 1959) p. 30.

13. McWilliams, *Preservation and Restoration*, p. 42.

14. Alexandrovich, George, "Phono Cartridges and Communications," *Broadcast Engineering*, August 1982, p. 26.

15. Gibson, Gerald D., "Preservation and Conservation of Sound Recordings." Paper presented to the [U.S.] National Archives, February 28, 1989, p. 4.

16. McWilliams, "Sound Recordings in Swartzburg," p. 164.

17. McWilliams, "Sound Recordings in Swartzburg," p. 169.

18. Fontaine, Jean-Marc, *Dégradation de l'enregistrement magnétique audio* (Paris: Ministère de la culture et de la communication, 1987) p. 10.

19. Fontaine, *Dégradation de l'enregistrement*, p. 11.

20. Fontaine, *Dégradation de l'enregistrement*, p. 13.

21. Blank, Sharon, "An Introduction to Plastics and Rubbers in Collections," *Studies in Conservation*, 35, 1990, p. 53.

22. Brown, D.W., R.E. Lowry and L.E. Smith, *Prediction of the Long-term Stability of Polyester-Based Recording Media*, NBSIR 82-2530 (Washington, D.C.: National Bureau of Standards, June 1982) p. 9.

23. Smith, L.E., D.W. Brown and R.E. Lowry, *Prediction of the Long-term Stability of Polyester-Based Recording Media*, (Washington, D.C.: National Bureau of Standards, June 1986) pp. 2-3.

24. Pickett and Lemcoe, *Preservation and Storage*, p. 56.

25. Brown, Lowry and Smith, *Prediction of Long-term Stability*, 1982, p. 9.

26. Brown, Lowry and Smith, *Prediction of Long-term Stability*, 1982, p. 2.

27. Smith, Brown and Lowry, *Prediction of Long-term Stability*, 1986, p. 1.

28. Kent, Scott, "Binder Breakdown in Back-Coated Tapes," *Recording Engineer/ Producer*, July 1988, p. 80.

29. Waites, J.B., "Care, Handling, and Management of Magnetic Tape," in: *Magnetic Tape Recording for the Eighties*, ed. Ford Kalil, NASA Reference Publication 1075 (NASA, April 1982) p. 50.

30. Ad Hoc Subcommittee on the Preservation of Sound Recordings of the National Archives and Records Administration (NARA) Advisory Committee on Preservation. Minutes of meeting July 29-30, 1987, Washington, D.C., p. 13.

31. Waites, "Care, Handling, and Management," p. 54.

32. Association for Recorded Sound Collections (ARSC), Associated Audio Archives Committee, *Final Performance Report. Audio Preservation: A Planning Study* (Washington, D.C.: ARSC, December 31, 1987) p. 54.

33. Gibson, "Preservation and Conservation," p. 1.

34. Pickett and Lemcoe, *Preservation and Storage*, p. 26.

35. Pickett and Lemcoe, *Preservation and Storage*, p. 49.

36. Fontaine, *Dégradation de l'enregistrement*, p. 18.

37. Kent, "Binder Breakdown in Back-Coated Tapes," p. 81.

38. Geller, Sidney B., *Care and Handling of Computer Magnetic Storage Media*, NBS Special Publication 500-101 (Washington, D.C.: U.S. Dept. of Commerce, June 1983) pp. 94 and 115.

39. Cuddihy, Edward F., "Stability and Preservation of Magnetic Tape," in: *Proceedings of Conservation in Archives: International Symposium*, Ottawa, Canada, May 10-12, 1988, (Paris: International Council on Archives, 1989) p. 204.

40. Gibson, "Preservation and Conservation," p. 7.

41. Association for Recorded Sound Collections (ARSC), *Final Performance Report*, p. 5.

42. Smith, Brown, and Lowry, *Prediction of Long-term Stability*, 1986, p. 20.

43. Association for Recorded Sound Collections (ARSC), *Final Performance Report*, p. 11.

44. Association for Recorded Sound Collections (ARSC), *Final Performance Report*, p. 4.

45. Gibson, "Preservation and Conservation," p. 17.

Plastics in the Science Museum, London:
A Curator's View

Susan Mossman

Collections Division
Science Museum
London, U.K.

Abstract

It is only in the fairly recent past that plastics have become a feature of many museum collections. During the last five years, curators have begun to notice that objects made of plastics degrade with time, and sometimes very rapidly, indeed. These provide problems for the curator, particularly in a technological museum such as the Science Museum, where we collect artefacts that may be wholly or partly made of plastics. As time goes on, our plastics artefacts, with their attendant problems of degradation, will only increase in number.

The Science Museum's collection of plastics contains about 1,500 objects, and is of great importance because it contains a rich selection of historic plastics, ranging from Parkesine, the first semi-synthetic plastic, to a sample of the earliest polyethylene. We continue to collect actively in the field of modern plastics materials, in particular composites and biodegradable plastics. In addition, plastics appear in many of our other collections where they play an increasingly important role, especially in telecommunications, electrical engineering, medicine and transport.

Particular problems we have noted occur in the earliest semi-synthetic plastics, that is, those containing cellulose nitrate.

We are in the process of improving the storage of our plastics, giving due attention to the effects of photodegradation and high temperatures as well as ensuring that the various types of plastics are stored separately, and, in cases of severe degradation, are isolated from those which, so far, appear to be "healthy."

Current research into the degradation of the earliest cellulosic plastics appears to suggest that in 50 years' time few of these will remain. The curator has to consider very carefully whether to display the most vulnerable types of plastics, which will then be subjected to quickened rates of photodegradation. Should the curator acquire two of every plastics object: one for display and hence disposable and another to keep in optimum storage conditions to give it the longest life possible?

Introduction

How long will our plastics collections survive? This is the question that curators are now having to ask themselves. It has become evident over the last few years that collections of plastics might not last forever. They degrade, and some faster than others. Sadly, it also appears that the most historic and earliest plastics are the ones that are most vulnerable.

John Morgan explains elsewhere in this publication what a polymer is and briefly introduces some of the historic plastics. This paper refers to many of the same plastics, but from the point of view of a curator of plastics of varying kinds, from the oldest to the most modern, referring in particular to objects in the Science Museum's collections. The paper's first part maintains a roughly chronological framework.

The Science Museum's collection of plastics (about 1,500 in number) is rich in the highlights of plastics' history, and many pieces are (as far as we can tell) in quite good condition. We have obtained specimens from a variety of sources, ranging from industry to relatives of the inventors of certain plastics. We are also fortunate in owning two large groups of plastics (together numbering over 500 objects) that are not only useful because they cover the full range of plastics materials from the late 19th century until ca. 1970, but also because they contain objects of aesthetic importance. Some of the more important items are addressed in the following discussion.

The collection includes the rubber-based products that predate what is regarded as the first plastic, Parkesine. Some of the rubber-based compounds were used in their unmodified state, such as gutta-percha. These fall into the category defined as natural plastics.

Gutta-percha is a dark brown substance obtained from the palaquium tree, which is found in Malaysia. It became a very popular material in the early Victorian period and was used for a multiplicity of purposes. The Science Museum possesses a number of examples of this material, including an inkstand dated to about 1851 (moulded to commemorate the use of gutta-percha to insulate the first submarine telegraph cable from England to France in 1850). Gutta-percha possesses excellent insulating properties, and so was ideal for this purpose. The main problem we have with gutta-percha is that with age the surface cracks, and the object becomes brittle and fragile.

Other natural plastics in the collection are horn, tortoiseshell and shellac, as well as a very rare material called Bois Durci (literally translated as "hardened wood") blended from sawdust and albumen.[1]

Certain other rubber-based substances, such as vulcanite, are themselves sometimes regarded as semi-synthetic plastics, since they are modifications of a natural substance. In the case of vulcanite, sulphur is added to natural rubber to produce a harder material.

Vulcanite is well represented in the collection that includes many pieces made by Thomas Hancock, including a plaque of himself, dated ca. 1843, and made of vulcanized rubber. Remarkable are some ornate vulcanite plaques made by Hancock and sealed up in glass-fronted passe-partout frames, which were displayed in the Rubber Exhibition at the Science Museum in 1929. These have survived in excellent condition; possibly linked with the fact that their sealed environment has set up a stable micro-climate, with no access to oxygen to encourage the degradation process (Figure 1). Only one plaque has begun to fade slightly.

Figure 1 Vulcanite plaques, ca. 1843, are elaborately decorated and in excellent condition. This is probably linked to the lack of oxygen available in their sealed environment.

Perhaps the greatest treasures in the plastics collection are the 87 examples of Parkesine dated from 1855 to 1881. Parkesine, invented by Alexander Parkes, is generally accepted to be the first plastic, although at this early date, of course, it was a modified natural product rather than a fully synthetic material. Parkesine is made of cellulose nitrate, which is made from nitric acid, sulphuric acid and cellulose (obtained from such sources as cotton flock). It is then mixed with vegetable oils and small amounts of organic solvents. This mixture forms a pliable dough that can be moulded into a variety of shapes. A collection of Parkesine objects presented to the Science Museum in the 1930s by the family of the inventor contains a wide range of items, from crude samples to ornate hair-slides inlaid with silver, brass and mother-of-pearl (Figure 2). Other pieces of Parkesine also convey religious themes. A remarkable piece is a tiny carved head of Christ, measuring 2.7 cm in height. A significant number of these pieces show Alexander Parkes' skills as a carver.

Figure 2 Parkesine hair-slides with brass, silver and mother-of-pearl inlay, ca. 1862. Metal inlay is lifting due to shrinkage of Parkesine.

Parkes set up the Parkesine Company Ltd. to manufacture Parkesine. After the company failed in 1868, his one-time Works Manager, Daniel Spill, tried to make money out of Parkes' invention, which Spill renamed Xylonite. The Xylonite Company (set up by Spill in 1869) also produced material made of imitation ivory (called Ivoride) and coral. The Science Museum possesses objects made of Ivoride and imitation coral, which were manufactured by Spill's company in the 1870s. Of particular interest is the Ivoride *Death's Head* walking-stick handle, which was Spill's own.

Neither Parkesine, Xylonite nor Ivoride were very satisfactory products due to problems with flammability. John Wesley Hyatt, an American, experimented to develop a more stable product. Hyatt made the breakthrough in 1870 when he found that camphor made an excellent solvent and plasticizer for cellulose nitrate. Hyatt patented his invention on 12 July 1870[2] and called his product Celluloid, the name by which most products based on cellulose nitrate are known today.

Spill then entered painful years of litigation with Hyatt, who by 1872 had set up the Celluloid Manufacturing Company. Spill finally lost the battle, and Hyatt made a great success of

celluloid, combining innovation with sharp marketing skills. He realized there would be a keen market for celluloid combs and wipe-clean collars and cuffs.

A fibre based on cellulose nitrate, and described as artificial silk, was patented by Count Hilaire de Chardonnet in 1884, and samples were shown at the Paris Exhibition in 1889. We have an advertisement for Chardonnet silk showing dyed and undyed samples that date to 1896 (Figure 3).

Figure 3 Chardonnet silk, 1896. Yellowing; liquidizing; based on cellulose nitrate (artificial silk patented by Count Hilaire de Chardonnet in 1884, of which samples were shown at the Paris Exhibition in 1889).

Our collection includes samples of other semi-synthetic plastics, such as the milk-based plastic, casein, and the less flammable cellulosic plastic, cellulose acetate.

In 1909 came the next important development in the history of plastics, when a brilliant Belgian chemist, Leo Baekeland, patented the first phenolic polymer. When combined with a filler, such as wood flour or cotton flock, phenol-formaldehyde forms an excellent material that can be moulded into a durable plastic with excellent electrical insulating properties. Baekeland's invention was quickly adapted to many uses, primarily electrical fittings, but was also commonly used for telephones and radio casings. A point to note is that phenolic plastics are dark in colour, due to their fillers. A remarkable object in our collection is a coffin, invented by James Doleman and made in 1938 by the Ultralite Casket Co. Ltd. The coffin is claimed to be the largest phenolic moulding ever made. It was manufactured from imitation walnut phenolic with a wood flour filler (a special type of moulding material produced by Bakelite Ltd. of London). Various stories are told as to why the coffin did not go into large scale production. According to the inventor's son (personal communication) it was due to his father's death in 1944, during World War II.

By 1928, a method had been perfected of casting phenol-formaldehyde without a filler. The result was the ability to produce cast phenolics in bright colours. Cast phenolic was used to imitate natural materials, such as amber and jade. The Science Museum collection includes a FADA Radio, dated to the 1940s. This is a collector's item and made of imitation amber catalin (cast phenolic).

The mid to late 1920s saw the advent of the colourful as well as durable and waterproof plastics made of thiourea-formaldehyde and urea-formaldehyde. Identified by such trade names as *Beetleware* and *Bandalasta Ware*, these plastics were popular for domestic ware and picnic sets. They are well represented in our collection.

With the 1930s, came polyethylene, polystyrene, acrylics, and polyamides. We have a sample of the first polyamide knitted tubing, made by du Pont in July 1935. Nylon was to be its successor and would become a runaway success as an excellent thread for stockings, and later in solid form as a material for gears and bearings.

As well as very practical objects, the plastics collection includes items important for their artistic merit. Among the finest is the Fornells

Material. This consists of a number of cosmetic boxes of cellulose acetate and later, urea-formaldehyde, made in Paris by the workshops of *Editions Paris E. Fornells* between the years 1913 to 1940 (Figures 4 and 5). Eduard Fornells Marco, an Andorran by birth, was a master carver recognized for his skills and taken on as a craftsman by René Lalique. Fornells was responsible for the famous cherry box design marked Lalique, made between 1911 and 1913, of which the Museum also has an example in its collection (Figures 6 and 7).

In addition to a wide range of products illustrating the applications and particular advantages of individual plastics materials, the Science Museum collects machinery used for the

Figure 4 Fornells Material: cosmetic boxes of cellulose acetate and later, urea-formaldehyde, made in Paris by the workshops of Editions Paris E. Fornells, ca. 1913 to 1940.

Figure 5 Close-up of Fornells' trade mark.

Figure 6 Cherry box made by Eduard Fornells Marco (between 1911 and 1913) shows Lalique trade mark.

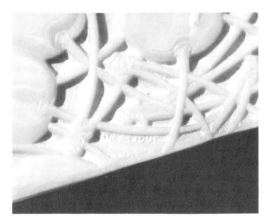

Figure 7 Close-up of trade mark on Lalique cherry box.

production of plastics. The machinery has separate conservation problems (i.e., metal, wood and rubber), which are dealt with elsewhere in this publication.

An important example of such machinery is a pilot-plant, nine-litre reaction vessel for polyethylene, which was used at Imperial Chemical Industries (ICI), Winnington, in 1938 to produce the first ton of polyethylene (of which we are fortunate to have a sample). ICI had begun the chemical work that led to polyethylene as early as 1932[3] and were finally successful in repeating the discovery somewhat fortuitously in 1935. Due to the very high pressures required to produce polyethylene, ICI regarded producing larger amounts as an engineering problem,

not one of chemistry.[4] There was a need to develop a reactor that could produce greater quantities without a runaway reaction leading to an explosion in the reaction vessel. By 1939, ICI had developed the first full-scale polyethylene plant, which was capable of producing 100 tons (based on a 50-litre reactor). ICI continued to expand their production capacity, which was necessary, as polyethylene played a vital role during the Second World War, for example, in radar. The nine-litre reaction vessel was an important step in this development.

The Science Museum is also active in collecting archive material, for example, trade catalogues, associated technical literature and sample books. Particularly significant is a gutta-percha catalogue from the Gutta-Percha Company, ca. 1851, which shows a range of objects from cherubs to coats of arms moulded in this material. In addition, the Museum holds a number of casein button sample cards (part archive and part object) dated to the first half of the 20th century.

Such archive material is useful because it helps us assess the range of objects that were available at the time the catalogue was produced and it also helps us identify objects. Work diaries and private papers often give us insight into the development of the plastic, working practices, and problems encountered.

It is essential when acquiring an object, particularly a modern one such as a composite ski boot, to acquire the relevant technical literature at the same time. A modern Salomon ski boot (1985) in the collection is made of four injection-moulded parts in nylon with polycarbonate clips; the boot is lined with a polyurethane foam sock.

In the absence of technical literature, it would be almost impossible to find out what plastics a complicated object is made of, without much time and expense. However, sometimes manufacturers are reluctant to reveal the secrets of their latest invention. Occasionally, we have to wait for over 50 years before the full story behind a particular plastic is released.

Another area to explore and collect is oral history. Although we have no formal programme in this area at the Science Museum, it is often invaluable to record interviews with pioneers of plastics and later have the text transcribed.

On a broader level, plastics materials are not only confined to the plastics collection; many other Science Museum collections contain objects of plastics in combination with other materials. Some that deserve mention are collections of electronics, telecommunications, medicine and aeronautics.

Are plastics worth preserving? We of course are biased and hope that the brief resumé of some of the treasures in our collections are convincing proof of their value and importance. Many, in particular the Parkesine and polyethylene objects, hold great significance for the history of the science and technology of plastics.

The curator has to make decisions as to what to collect, both on the grounds of the object's significance and longevity. This does not mean that the more vulnerable plastics should not be collected; however, it is important to be aware of their probable lifetime as well as ensure that all important information is recorded about them upon acquisition. Other ways of recording the shape of a plastics object should be considered. Various suggestions of doing this are explored later.

Which Plastics Are Most at Risk?

Cellulose Nitrate-Based Plastics
Our immediate concern is with those plastics based on cellulose nitrate: Parkesine, Ivoride, Xylonite and Celluloid, of which we have examples in our collections. Certain examples have shown characteristic signs of degradation, as also discussed in detail by John Morgan. These include sweating, crazing, discolouration (yellowing in the case of imitation ivory cellulose nitrate objects) and the giving off of acidic fumes.

Curiously enough, the majority of our Parkesine objects are in good, and sometimes excellent, condition. The items that have suffered most are the thin films and smaller pieces, such as a pen nib and a tiny carved head that are both now in fragments (Figure 8). The main

problem we have with other Parkesine objects is shrinkage. This is particularly evident with decorative combs that have metal inlays. In some cases, the object has shrunk so much that the inlay has popped out.

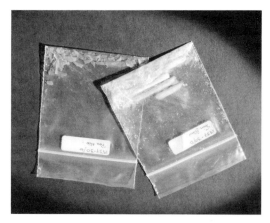

Figure 8 Samples of deteriorated Parkesine (thin films and pen nib), ca. 1862.

In the case of a Parkesine denture, degradation was rapid. The denture had been on display for two years. We noticed that yellowish powder was deposited around it; when we examined the denture, it was so brittle, it immediately fell into pieces.

Other pieces on display appear to be fairly stable, but these are monitored regularly.

When a material has been stressed, for example a cellulose nitrate comb made of imitation tortoiseshell, it crazes where it has been bent into shape.

When metal is in contact with cellulose nitrate objects, in the form of inlays or hinges for example, it appears to speed up the degradation of the cellulose nitrate, providing a focus around which degradation begins and then spreads throughout the object.

Other Plastics
At present our cellulose acetate objects do not appear to be exhibiting signs of degradation. However, the Tate Gallery in London has experienced problems with sculptures made from cellulose acetate by Naum Gabo.[5] In addition, the problems of deteriorating cellulose

triacetate film are well known.[6] So we can foresee problems with our cellulose acetate objects.

Currently our casein (also known by such trade names as Erinoid and Galalith) objects appear to be in remarkably good condition; however, we are well aware of their moisture-retaining qualities as well as the danger of warping and cracking if the humidity levels change too radically.

Phenolic plastics (generally referred to as Bakelite) appear to be fairly stable unless broken (when they become susceptible to biological attack due to their fillers made of wood flour and cotton flock). The main problem appears to be with fading (green to brown).

Cast phenolic plastics (often known as catalin) are also susceptible to colour change, having a tendency to turn yellow.

Solutions: What Are We Doing at the Science Museum?

Thorough Records
The first priority is to record the object fully, both in writing and visually. We are doing this for the Science Museum's plastics objects. We write a detailed description of the object on a record card, including date and manufacturer's name. Other space on the card is available for dimensions, material, and most important of all, condition. We date the card so that we have a report of the item's condition at the time it is recorded. This information will be important as more plastics begin to deteriorate, either by discolouring, shrinking or by showing various other symptoms, such as crazing and cracking.

It is important to photograph the object with a scale, preferably using colour. We are undertaking a programme that incorporates this practice.

Stores
We have improved the storage conditions for our plastics, thus:

- The plastics are separated by type of material.

- They are stored in stable conditions that are kept as cool as possible.

- The objects in store are kept in the dark. This is essential as plastics are very susceptible to photodegradation, particularly when exposed to ultraviolet light.

- Deteriorating plastics, especially cellulosics, are separated from "healthy" objects.

- Gloves are always worn when handling plastics, as fingerprints can indelibly mark certain types.

- Sticky labels are not applied to objects as we have found that the glue can "eat into" the surface.

We have to deal with the practicalities of storing a large number of different plastics as well as our other collections (which are themselves made of many and varied materials).

If we keep cellulose nitrate-based plastics, such as Parkesine and Celluloid, on open shelving for ventilation, as is recommended practice, any gases released may attack other plastics. Currently most plastics, apart from the largest pieces, are wrapped in acid-free tissue and packed in acid-free boxes. We are well aware this may not be ideal for the cellulosics in particular.

A few pieces have been laid out on open shelves on plastazote, which appears to be a relatively stable base. We are monitoring this arrangement.

Of course, a separate, well-ventilated room for each type of plastic, with a separate room for those that have begun to degrade, would be ideal. However, every museum has constraints on space, and we are no different. Cost is another limiting factor.

We might consider using another room at our store in which we might install a ventilated case for those cellulose nitrate objects that are deteriorating. Even the air for ventilation is not without attendant problems: the store is at Olympia, Kensington, in a busy part of London and so suffers from air pollution due to heavy traffic. We cannot allow air to come into the case without filtering it or cleansing it in some way.

Display Material

Whilst we try to protect our plastics in store from many of the dangers that could initiate or accelerate their degradation, what about those plastics on display? We have to accept that, at present, displaying plastics will shorten their lives.

Light levels can be reduced and ultraviolet light can be excluded by the use of optical filters. We have excluded natural light from our plastics gallery at South Kensington.

We also look forward to the results of the work being carried out by Julia Fenn at the Royal Ontario Museum, in setting up a sealed case for plastics, and using a system of cleansing the atmosphere using scavengers and absorbents as well as a method of ensuring the circulation of air within the case.[7]

Using traditional display methods will mean that in some cases, for example with the cellulosics, complete breakdown may come very rapidly. Indeed, it is vital for the curator and conservator who are mounting the display of plastics, to be fully aware of the implications of their actions.

It would be most sensible to display only those plastics objects that are duplicates or easily replaceable. This revision in curatorial attitudes would have a direct influence on collecting policies. The most satisfactory solution would be to collect two of everything: one to be kept in ideal collections in store, and the other to be kept for display purposes.

Solutions to the Problem of Display: Pros and Cons

Replicas

A mould could be taken of the object, in order to make a replica. This might be suitable where original machinery has survived. However, the use of the original machinery provides an ethical dilemma for the curator of technology, as well as practical difficulties. Should the machinery be maintained in working order and

parts replaced as they wear out? Or should the machinery be preserved in a suspended state, but in good condition?

Moreover, many of the early plastics were produced using somewhat rough and ready methods, which could on occasion be quite dangerous. For example, producing cellulose nitrate-based plastics, such as celluloid, is potentially a fire hazard. Within the plastics manufacturing centre at Oyonnax (in La Val Plastiques, Jura Mountains, France) is located La Grande Vapeur, a factory that was used to produce objects, mainly combs and spectacle frames, initially of cellulose nitrate, and later of cellulose acetate from ca. 1908. The factory had an in-built sprinkler system as well as a system of cells with steel doors for each workshop, so that if fire broke out in one workshop it could be contained.

To be realistic, the factory inspector and the Science Museum's safety officer would not be happy if we tried to reproduce these types of fireproof "cabines" in the Science Museum. In fact, we were not allowed to display a block of celluloid together with its pilot machinery in the 1970s due to fears about the flammability of the plastic.

The recipes used to make early plastics were not standard. Rather like cooking, they varied according to the person making the plastic. We have recipe books for casein in the Science Museum. Other recipe books exist for celluloid.* However, records show that the plastics pioneers spent a fair amount of time unjamming the machinery when it became clogged due to variations in the mixture. Of course today, things are very different. Mixtures and temperatures are precisely measured, and provided one has access to the amounts used, it would be possible to replicate these. However, modern machinery is usually on an enormous scale, and this might well prove impractical.

---

* Ipswich Public Records Office holds recipe books for the manufacture of Cellulloid, from BXL Plastics, Wardles Story, Brantham in Essex, the site of the old Xylonite Factory.

Three-Dimensional Recording

The object could be copied in a more technological fashion. Three-dimensional photography is an option; the object could be photographed stereoscopically, so that the picture could be viewed in three dimensions through special spectacles. This would give a clear idea of shape. Three-dimensional photographs could be taken from all important angles. If the object degraded, a three-dimensional record of its form would at least exist. Such a system is already in use in the archaeological world, and in the Victoria and Albert Museum department of sculpture conservation.[8]

A more advanced technique would be to record the three-dimensional image electronically. Such a system is available, for example, the company Tektronix produces a suitable package. However, all such systems cost money. The Science Museum is currently undertaking a programme of photographing objects with the long-term view of transferring the images to computer; our outstation, the National Museum of Film, Photography and Television at Bradford, is considering doing the same for its photographic archives. Another outstation, the National Railway Museum at York, is exploring digital storage for its photographic material. Three-dimensional computer imaging is some way down the line (on current judgement, about five years).[9] However, if the objects are already photographed in this format, the images could be transferred to computer when sufficient funding is available. Currently such a proposal is in preparation for the Science Museum's collection of plastics.

In the long term, the computerized three-dimensional recording of the object would have many benefits. The image would be readily available at the touch of a button. It would no longer be always necessary to unpack the object from store, which would reduce both unnecessary handling as well as superfluous exposure to light. Equally, computer terminals could be put in the plastics gallery and at information banks throughout the museum. The museum visitor would then be able to look at objects not on display. This would also satisfy the visitor who wants to look at items made of a particular plastic, without having to put the objects on display and thus contribute to their degradation. Moreover, it would be beneficial to those visitors with a particular interest. They could select only the objects they wished to view for study purposes. Again, this practice would cut down the unnecessary handling of objects in store.

However, such a system would have to be used with caution. Visitors will always want to see objects. Though this system will allow visitors to see objects not on display due to lack of space or fragility of the objects, it will never totally replace the display of real objects.

Conclusion

Today the Science Museum is active in collecting new plastics materials, specifically those engineered for a precise purpose, or those that have found a new use. For example, recycled and biodegradable plastics are an increasingly important area in which to collect. We have even collected a flowerpot made of recycled plastic. Another recent acquisition is a Biopol bottle, a degradable plastic produced by ICI.

As for the rich collections that we have inherited, we are now becoming increasingly aware that we have to put into practice what we learn about their stability. We have had to assess them for condition and probable lifetime. We have improved our storage; in particular cutting out exposure to light wherever possible, and maintaining stable storage conditions, specifically of temperature and humidity. We are keeping a careful eye on the more vulnerable plastics, in particular those based on cellulose nitrate and cellulose acetate. As yet, we have no ideal solution to the problems of their degradation but we are exploring new ways of prolonging their lives and watching with interest work being done at other institutions in Britain and abroad, notably in Ontario, Canada.

Acknowledgement

The author thanks Sue Cackett and Dr. Derek Robinson for their helpful comments on this paper, and Ben Booth for the information he supplied.

All photographs are provided courtesy of the Trustees of the Science Museum, London.

Résumé

Les plastiques au National Museum of Science and Industry — le point de vue d'une conservatrice

Ce n'est qu'assez récemment que les plastiques ont fait leur entrée dans les collections de musée. Au cours des cinq dernières années, les spécialistes de la restauration ont par ailleurs commencé à constater que les objets en plastique se dégradaient avec le temps, et parfois même très rapidement. Une telle dégradation n'est pas sans poser des problèmes à ces spécialistes, surtout dans un musée technologique comme le National Museum of Science and Industry, où les collections comportent des objets qui sont partiellement ou entièrement constitués de plastique. Le nombre des objets de musée en plastique continuera par ailleurs de s'accroître, multipliant d'autant les problèmes de dégradation de ce matériau.

La collection de plastiques du musée regroupe quelque 1 500 objets. Elle est très importante car elle renferme une riche sélection de plastiques qui ont une valeur historique — depuis le Parkesine, le premier plastique semi-synthétique, jusqu'à un échantillon du premier polyéthylène. Et des matières plastiques modernes continuent de s'y ajouter — des plastiques mixtes et biodégradables notamment. Les plastiques sont en outre présents dans nombre d'objets des autres collections, puisqu'ils jouent un rôle de plus en plus grand dans des domaines comme les télécommunications, le génie électrique, la médecine et le transport, pour n'en citer que quelques-uns.

Les problèmes particuliers que nous avons relevés se posent dans le cas des premiers plastiques semi-synthétiques, c'est-à-dire ceux qui renferment du nitrate de cellulose.

Nous cherchons actuellement à améliorer la mise en réserve de nos plastiques. Nous accordons ainsi aux effets de la photodégradation et des hautes températures toute l'attention qu'ils méritent, et nous veillons à ce que les divers genres de plastiques soient mis en réserve séparément et à ce que les plastiques qui se sont gravement dégradés soient isolés de ceux qui semblent toujours « intacts ».

S'il faut en croire les résultats de la recherche actuelle sur la dégradation des premiers plastiques cellulosiques, il semble qu'il n'en restera que fort peu dans 50 ans. Aussi les spécialistes de la restauration doivent-ils ne décider d'exposer les plastiques les plus vulnérables qu'après avoir soigneusement analysé la question, puisque ces matières seront alors sujettes à une photodégradation accélérée. Et il convient sans doute de se demander s'il ne faudrait pas toujours acquérir deux exemplaires du même objet en plastique : un premier qui serait exposé — et dont on pourrait éventuellement disposer — et un second qui serait mis en réserve — et qui serait conservé dans des conditions optimales pour durer le plus longtemps possible.

References

1. Williamson, C., "Bois Durci," *Plastiquarian*, vol. 1, Winter, 1988, p. 8.

2. Hyatt, J.W., "Improvement in Treating and Moulding Pyroxyline," U.S. Patent no. 105338.

3. Kennedy, C., *ICI: The Company That Changed Our Lives* (London: Hutchinson, 1986) p. 64.

4. Wilson, Gordon, personal communication, ICI Petrochemicals and Plastics Division Licensing Manager, U.K., 9 August 1991.

5. Pullen, D. and J. Heumann, "Cellulose Acetate Deterioration in the Sculptures of Naum Gabo," *Modern Organic Materials*, The Scottish Society for Conservation and Restoration, Edinburgh, 1988, pp. 57-66.

6. Edge, M. et al., "Cellulose Acetate: An Archival Polymer Falls Apart," *Modern Organic Materials*, The Scottish Society for Conservation and Restoration, Edinburgh, 1988, pp. 67-79.

7. Fenn, J., "Scavengers for Controlling Combinations of Emissions from Exhibitions of Mixed Polymers," *Polymers in Conservation*, Congress, Manchester Polytechnic and Manchester Museum, July 17-19, 1991.

8. Larson, John, "The Three Dimensional Recording of Sculpture," Lecture in the series *The State of the Art*, Royal College of Art/ Victoria and Albert Museum, London, March 15, 1990.

9. Booth, B., personal communication, July 1991.

Suppliers

Plastazote:

U.K.
  Polyformes Ltd., Cherrycourt Way, Stanbridge Road, Leighton Buzzard, LU7 8UH.

EUROPE
  Wilhelm Koepp Zellkautschuk GmbH & Co., D5100 Aachen, Postfach 848, Hegelsbendenstrasse 20, Germany.

  Companie Internationale de Plastique Biodégradable, 24 Boulevard Princesse Charlotte, Immeuble Est-Ouest, MC98000 Monte Carlo, Monaco.

EASTERN EUROPE
  BP Chemicals GmbH, Zaunergasse 4, A-1030 Vienna, Austria.

NORTH AMERICA
  United Foam Plastics Corporation, 172 East Main Street, Georgetown, Massachusetts 01833-2107, U.S.

AUSTRALIA
  Dunlop Foam Products Group, P.O. Box 1, Mordialloc, Victoria 3195, Australia.

Membership and Aims of the Plastics Historical Society

John Morgan

Plastics Historical Society
Plastics & Rubber Institute
London, U.K.

Abstract

The centenary of plastics was celebrated in 1962, yet it is only in comparatively recent years that an interest in collecting plastic materials has emerged. In 1968, a History Discussion Circle was formed in Britain by the Plastics Institute. The idea of recording the reminiscences of some of the plastics pioneers, first mooted at the time of the centenary celebrations, was re-affirmed. However, the Circle was short lived, and it was not until 1986 that sufficient general interest in plastics had developed for the Plastics Historical Society (PHS) to become a reality.

The PHS is an independent society, affiliated to the Plastics & Rubber Institute with which it shares headquarters. Its aims are "to promote the study, preservation and sharing of information on all historical aspects of plastics, and to encourage the recording of any current development adjudged to be of value to future generations." A long-term aim is the establishment of a National Plastics Museum, but in the meantime effort is being devoted to saving historically important records and objects from being consigned to the rubbish tip. This is especially important when old, established firms are taken over by someone who has little sympathy for the historical significance of the company.

The PHS forms links with other organizations having associated interests, for example, the Kunststoffe-Museums-Verein (KMV), a German plastics museum society. In addition, the PHS and The Conservation Unit (of the Museums & Galleries Commission) have started a cooperative program of work into the degradation problems of plastics materials. The international membership of the PHS encompasses a variety of people, including some from industry, education and research as well as designers, collectors and staff from museums and auction houses. Many members have their own plastics collections, covering a diversity of themes. The society is thus able to call upon a wide range of expertise and experience, and its journal, Plastiquarian, *contains news and articles of interest to collectors and plastics historians.*

What Is Plastic?

In general terms we all know what plastics are, but a simple definition that includes only plastics materials and excludes everything else is not easy to find. One definition that has previously been suggested[1] includes the following characteristics:

- Solid materials

- Organic, or organic/inorganic polymers

- Natural, chemically modified natural or wholly synthetic polymers (or mixtures of these)

- Capable of being compounded with colourants, plasticizers, etc.

- Capable of being moulded at some stage in production

There are some arbitrary exclusions, such as adhesives, fabrics, paints and rubbers, but opinions on this differ and the Plastics Historical Society (PHS) takes a fairly broad view in its definition of plastics.

How Old Are Plastics?

It is generally considered that plastics materials were first exhibited in England at the International Exhibition of 1862 by Alexander Parkes. The material was called Parkesine and was made from cellulose nitrate, a chemically modified natural polymer.

The roots of the industry, however, lie in the earlier manipulation of naturally occurring plastics. Detailed mouldings were being made from horn as long ago as the 17th century; the vulcanization of rubber was discovered in 1839 and in 1850 gutta-percha was used to protect and insulate the first submarine telegraph cables. Also in the 1850s, shellac was compounded with wood flour to mould Union cases to protect and display early photographic images. Albumen, principally from blood, was also compounded with wood flour to make Bois Durci, which was widely used to make decorative inkwells, plaques and other items.

At first, the new plastics were mainly regarded as substitutes for naturally occurring materials, such as shellac, tortoiseshell and ivory. Such material was in short supply and was becoming technically inadequate for the demands of industry. At the turn of the 20th century, casein, a plastics material based on the protein from milk, was introduced in Germany, and for many years it was known as artificial horn. At about the same time the search for a synthetic substitute for shellac produced the material that many consider the real starting point of the plastics industry — Bakelite. This material was produced by compounding phenol-formaldehyde, a new and entirely synthetic resin, with wood flour, the same type of filler that was compounded 60 years earlier with natural shellac to mould such items as Union cases and mirror and brush backs.

It was not until the 1920s that the word plastics was first used as a generic name for the new materials. During this same period the polymeric nature of plastics was elucidated and this scientific understanding enabled new polymers to be researched and to be established in new ways. Even so, new polymers were still discovered by accident during other investigations, but their polymeric nature was immediately recognized — unlike generations earlier when polymers were sometimes produced by experiment, but the sticky residues were discarded as failures. Injection moulding, one of the key processes in plastics fabrication, was also developed during the 1920s. This and the various factors already mentioned are reflected in the sharp rise in the output of plastics, starting in about 1930 and continuing to the present day, the progression being hindered only slightly by the oil crisis in the 1970s. Figures 1 and 2 respectively show the growth in world plastics production during 1900 to 1940 and 1940 to 1990, from 20 thousand to 100 million tons per year, a five-thousand-fold increase.

The fact that plastics were initially regarded as substitutes no doubt contributed to their poor popular image — an image that was reinforced in those and later years by the inferior quality of their design and application — a criticism that is sometimes levied even today.

The Formation of the Plastics Historical Society

A History Discussion Circle was formed in Britain in 1968, but it was short lived and it

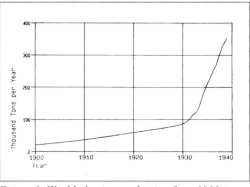

Figure 1 World plastics production from 1900 to 1940.

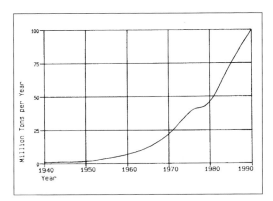

Figure 2 World plastics production from 1940 to 1990.

was not until almost 20 years later that sufficient general interest in the historical aspects of plastics had developed for the Plastics Historical Society to become a reality.

The PHS, founded in 1986, has established the following aims:

- To promote the study, preservation and sharing of information on all historical aspects of plastics

- To encourage the recording of any current developments adjudged to be of value to future generations

- To establish a National Plastics Museum

- To co-operate with other organizations interested in the historical aspects of plastics

The international membership of the PHS encompasses a variety of people, including some from all sectors of the plastics industry, staff from museums and educators, as well as designers, historians and many others.

Approximately half of the members are collectors of plastics whose themes range from "anything so long as it's plastic" to specialized collections of one particular era, one particular material or a particular type of object. Reasons for collecting are as varied as the objects collected. Those from the industry itself are often influenced by materials and processes with

which they have been involved, whereas many others are motivated by the design possibilities of plastics compared to other materials. The warm touch and handling qualities of plastics are also important to some collectors.

How to best care for a plastics collection is one question that remains largely unresolved, but an equally important consideration is the extent to which plastics should be cleaned, polished or restored. An example is the brown discolouration that occurs to cast phenolic resins, such as Catalin and Bakelite, the effect being particularly apparent with blue or white colours. Their ready discolouration in natural or artificial light is one reason why warm colours, especially amber, were more popular. Many, if not most, cast phenolic objects now appear much darker in colour, and in many cases are of an entirely different hue to what they were at the time of manufacture. The colour and polish may be restored by an abrasive cleaning process, but at the expense of the removal of surface material. The same is true of the more familiar moulded Bakelite, but because of discolouration during moulding, original colours were usually drab. Nevertheless, colour change does occur — the original colour can usually be seen by inspecting an unexposed part of the moulding, and one may be tempted to remove the discolouration. Opinions on the advisability of such treatment differ widely and debates on these and related topics are lively and sometimes a little controversial.

With the aim of addressing these concerns, and the more urgent questions about conservation, the PHS and The Conservation Unit (of the Museums & Galleries Commission) have started a co-operative program of work into the degradation problems of plastics materials in museum and private collections. (This is discussed in more detail in a second paper by Morgan in this publication).

Activities of the Plastics Historical Society

The PHS is an enthusiastic body of individuals engaged in widely differing aspects of plastics history. Some of the topics listed below are covered in their discussions.

- Recording reminiscences of the "old-timers" who worked on many of the processes and materials that have been developed this century

- Rescuing records from factories that are closing

- Researching particular manufacturers, items or materials

- Arranging exhibitions of plastics

- Organizing meetings or visits of interest to plastics historians

These topics, and many more, are reported in the PHS magazine *Plastiquarian* together with news items and articles of general interest.

Résumé

La composition de la Plastics Historical Society et ses objectifs

Si 1962 a marqué le centenaire du plastique, on n'a pourtant commencé qu'assez récemment à collectionner des objets faits à partir de ce matériau. En 1968, le Plastics Institute a créé un cercle de discussion historique en Grande-Bretagne, et on a alors repris l'idée, lancée pour la première fois lors des célébrations du centenaire, de noter les réminiscences de certains pionniers du domaine des plastiques. Ce cercle n'a toutefois pas fait long feu, et il faudra attendre jusqu'en 1986 pour que l'intérêt général pour les plastiques devienne assez grand pour amener la création de la Plastics Historical Society (PHS).

La PHS est une société indépendante, affiliée au Plastics & Rubber Institute, dont elle partage les quartiers généraux. Ses objectifs sont de promouvoir l'étude et la conservation des plastiques, ainsi que le partage d'informations sur l'histoire de ces matières, et de favoriser la consignation de toute nouvelle découverte qui pourrait être jugée importante pour les générations futures. À long terme, elle envisage de créer un musée national des plastiques. Dans l'entre-temps toutefois, elle met tout en œuvre pour éviter que des dossiers ou des objets d'importance du point de vue historique ne soient détruits. Et ce genre d'action prend tout son sens lorsque, par exemple, une entreprise établie de longue date passe aux mains de gens qui se préoccupent peu de ce qu'elle représente sur le plan historique.

La PHS entretient des relations avec d'autres organismes qui partagent les mêmes intérêts, dont le Kunststoffe-Museums-Verein, une société muséale allemande qui s'intéresse aussi aux plastiques. Elle s'est de plus unie au Service de conservation de la Museums & Galleries Commission pour créer un programme qui permettra d'approfondir les problèmes de dégradation des matières plastiques.

Parmi les membres diversifiés de la PHS qui proviennent de la communauté internationale, certains représentent les secteurs de l'industrie, de l'éducation et de la recherche, tandis que d'autres se recrutent parmi les concepteurs, les collectionneurs ou le personnel des musées ou des entreprises de vente aux enchères. Par ailleurs, nombre des membres de la PHS possèdent leurs propres collections de plastiques, qui couvrent toute une gamme de thèmes. C'est donc dire que la PHS peut faire appel à des compétences et à des expériences variées. Son bulletin Plastiquarian *contient enfin des nouvelles et des articles qui sauront intéresser toute personne qui se spécialise dans la collection des plastiques ou dans l'histoire de ce matériau.*

Reference

1. Redfarn, C.A., "What is Plastic?" *Plastics and Rubber International*, vol. 2, no. 3, 1977, p. 134.

Conservation Policies and Plans
Politiques et projets en matière de conservation

A Joint Project on the Conservation of Plastics by The Conservation Unit and the Plastics Historical Society

John Morgan

Plastics Historical Society
Plastics & Rubber Institute
London, U.K.

Abstract

Mounting concern about the deterioration of early plastics artefacts has led to co-operation between The Conservation Unit of the Museums & Galleries Commission and the Plastics Historical Society of London to devise a program of work aimed at combating the problem.

A step-by-step approach has been adopted, the first part of which is the publishing of preliminary guidelines for the storage and display of plastics objects. These guidelines are based upon our current understanding of the ageing of these materials.

The second part of the program is the determination of the nature and extent of present degradation problems so that appropriate priorities for research can be established. A survey encompassing a wide range of historical collections has been started, the aims being to: provide details on the type of material collected; ascertain the present condition of objects; determine the atmospheric conditions under which artefacts are stored and displayed; and give information about preventive and curative measures already being followed by conservators and collectors.

It is already clear from the work to date that if plastics are to survive they will require more in the way of preventive conservation than has hitherto been given to most other materials. Procedures for arresting deterioration of plastics already affected need to be established so that curative techniques may be researched and applied, whilst anticipation of future degradation problems may enable the development of appropriate preventive measures.

Different plastics degrade in different ways, and it is therefore necessary to classify objects according to material. It is particularly important that plastics susceptible to auto-catalytic degradation mechanisms—the most damaging form of deterioration—be identified and kept under observation.

The progress and preliminary results of this work will be presented and discussed.

Introduction

Museums and private individuals collect increasing amounts of plastic, both as artefacts in their own right and as component parts of a wide range of items. This is an inevitable consequence of the increasing importance of these materials in our daily lives, starting with the exhibition of the first semi-synthetic plastics in 1862 and culminating with the arrival of "The Plastics Age" in 1979, when the volume of plastics produced world-wide exceeded that of steel.

Polymer degradation was observed in the 16th century by explorers who were returning with samples of a newly discovered material. Later known as rubber, the material was said to have "perished" during the long sea voyage. Thomas Hancock studied the degradation of rubber by measuring the water loss from a sealed rubber bag over 30 years, from 1820 to 1850. The result, shown in Figure 1, illustrates a typical course of degradation for many polymers; a relatively long induction period showing little change followed by a period of accelerating degradation. In the 1850s problems due to degradation of gutta-percha were encountered when this material was first used as insulation on telegraph cables.

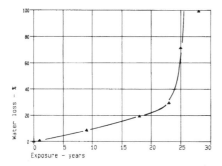

Figure 1 These data are from an experiment to determine water loss from a sealed rubber bag. The experiment was conducted by Thomas Hancock over a period of 30 years, from 1820 to 1850. The data illustrate a typical course of degradation for many polymers: a relatively long induction period showing little change followed by a period of accelerating degradation.

Degradation has serious economic implications to plastics manufacturers who have devoted much effort to limiting the extent of degradation during the service life of their products. Improved quality control and the use of stabilizing additives has enabled plastics to be used in applications from which they would otherwise be excluded. However, little attention has so far been paid to limiting the slow deterioration of historical plastics, some of which were manufactured before their true nature had been elucidated and when the science of additives was little more than a "black art."

In recognition of mounting concern about the deterioration of plastics in historical collections, The Conservation Unit (of the Museums & Galleries Commission of Great Britain) and the Plastics Historical Society have started a co-operative program of work, the aims of which are to:

- publish preliminary guidelines for the storage and display of plastics

- carry out a survey of plastics held in U.K. collections

- collate information relevant to the degradation of plastics in collections

- provide training workshops for conservators and collectors

- research stabilizing treatments and curative techniques

The project is still in the early stages, but the preliminary guidelines have been published[1] and the first of the training seminars took place in May of 1992. The first stage of the survey is in the form of a questionnaire, which has been sent to a wide range of British museums, and also to several private collectors of plastics.

Preliminary Findings from the Survey

First, many private collections are devoted almost exclusively to plastics while others, for example, button or toy collections, contain a significant proportion of these materials. Quite often the objects are made entirely of plastic. In museum collections, plastics are widely distributed but often in comparatively small numbers and usually form only a part of the objects. Very few museums have displays devoted to these modern materials. Figure 2 shows the distribution of plastics in collections by period of manufacture.

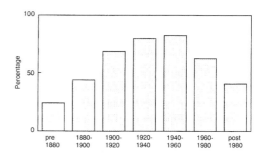

Figure 2 Popularity of various periods in plastics collections.

The survey reveals that approximately half of the museums replying to the questionnaire possess more than 100 objects wholly or partly made from plastics. A slightly smaller proportion report between 10 and 100, with only a few (less than 10%) recording less than 10 or more than 1,000 such objects in their care.

The most popular kinds of objects are those for the home, followed closely by personal items and toys. Mostly, they date from 1920 to 1960, but surprisingly, more than one-third of the museums report holding items manufactured since 1980.

Approximately two-thirds of the museums report some deterioration of plastics, the most common being crazing, discolouration or fading. Figure 3 shows the extent and kinds of deterioration in plastics collections.

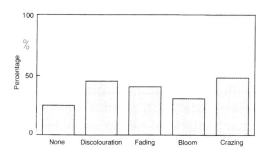

Figure 3 Proportion of collections reporting various forms of degradation in plastics objects.

The next stage of the survey will be to visit a wide range of collections in order to obtain more detailed information about the composition of objects and materials, particularly those giving cause for concern. The results will be used to determine priorities in the final part of the program, which is the setting of standards for the care of collections, and the development of stabilizing treatments and curative techniques for plastics materials.

Degradation of Plastics

Plastics are made from long-chain molecules, or polymers. The polymer chains can be essentially linear or they can form a three-dimensional, crosslinked network of relatively short chains. The former group comprise the thermoplastic materials, that is, they soften and flow when heated; the crosslinked polymers are thermosetting, and once formed do not soften when heated and will normally char before melting. Rubbers are a special class of thermosetting polymer having long, flexible polymer chains with few crosslinks.

Some linear polymers, such as polyethylene and nylon are partially crystalline, the degree of crystallinity varying with purity, processing conditions and grade of polymer. Crystalline regions are less permeable (e.g., to oxygen) than amorphous regions and as a consequence, degradation may be less pronounced in the more crystalline material.

Polymers are also divided into two types, addition polymers that are formed by "chain growth" reactions, and condensation polymers that are formed by "step growth" mechanisms. Thermoplastics may be of either type whereas thermosetting plastics are almost always formed from condensation polymers. Examples of addition polymers are polyethylene, polypropylene, polystyrene, vinyl polymers and acrylic polymers. Examples of condensation polymers are polyesters, polycarbonate, nylon and phenol formaldehyde. The two types differ structurally in that addition polymers contain only carbon atoms along the backbone of the polymer chain whereas condensation polymers also contain atoms other than carbon (e.g., oxygen) at regular intervals along the chain. The two types are generally susceptible to different degradation processes. The hetero-chain polymers, for example, may be susceptible to hydrolysis — chemical reaction with water resulting in decomposition, or scission of chemical bonds.

Physical Effects
These effects are associated with loss or migration of additives, absorption of liquids or vapours, crazing due to stress or fatigue, mechanical damage, or excessive heat or cold.

Physical causes may be responsible for the following changes:

- distortion or dimensional change
- crazing or cracking
- surface deposit (often tacky)
- changes in flexibility

(Figure 4 shows typical degradation for cellulose nitrate.) Cellulosic materials, casein and nylon are among the plastics that contain significant quantities of moisture, and their moisture content can vary with changes in humidity. Moisture absorption results in dimensional changes and consequently the formation of stress. Varying humidity levels therefore present a low frequency fatigue stress and this is partly responsible for the crazing of casein plastics.

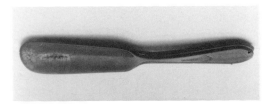

Figure 4 Cellulose nitrate shoehorn showing degradation typical of this polymer.

The combination of stress and certain liquids or vapours, which would otherwise have little or no effect, can produce environmental stress-cracking. The stress may be an applied stress or it may be residual from moulding or machining operations, or it may have developed with age. This phenomenon became widely known from the premature failure of early polyethylene bottles containing detergents. Rigid thermoplastics, such as polystyrene and poly(methyl methacrylate), are subject to stress-cracking in the presence of lower alcohols, paraffins, white spirit or oils. Acrylic materials intended for outdoor exposure need to be annealed at a temperature of 80°C in order to minimize risk from this effect.

Many physical effects can be controlled by the maintenance of stable conditions of temperature and humidity and by avoiding mechanical stress or contact with liquids and vapours that might be absorbed. Migration of plasticizers in such materials as cellulose acetate and poly(vinyl chloride) result in these plastics becoming more rigid. This rigidity may cause distortion,

which may eventually lead to cracking, but the maintenance of stable conditions will limit the rate and, possibly, the extent of such changes.

Plasticizer migration and loss may also occur due to changes in miscibility of the polymer/plasticizer system brought about by chemical degradation. In such cases, attempts to reverse the process and replace lost plasticizer by re-absorption would be ineffective.

Chemical Effects

As with all materials, polymers can react chemically by coming into contact with other substances. This includes those substances carried in the atmosphere, such as oxygen, ozone, moisture and pollutants. Chemical reactions that involve scission of the polymer chain are potentially the most serious. Because of their network structure, thermosetting polymers can withstand more chain scission than thermoplastics and are generally found to be more stable.

Chemical effects are nearly always progressive and irreversible, leading eventually to complete disintegration. They are, therefore, usually more serious than physical effects.

Evidence for chemical effects may be:

- colour change
- chalkiness or surface bloom
- crazing
- embrittlement with loss of strength
- evolution of degradation products (often acidic)
- softening or tackiness

Major factors involved in bringing about chemical changes are:

- light, especially ultraviolet
- heat
- stress
- oxygen
- moisture, including humidity
- ozone and other atmospheric contaminants (including those from nearby degrading objects)
- contact with other materials (intentionally or by accident)
- some forms of biological attack

Not all of the above are damaging to any particular material, but combinations of two or more may be synergistic (i.e., the combined effect is much greater than the sum of the effects considered individually). Antagonistic effects, more simply known as "bad neighbours," can occur between two materials. In this case, the close proximity of one material adversely affects the stability of another. For example, the copper core of electrical cables can accelerate the degradation of plastics insulation. A similar effect was observed in the early 19th century by Thomas Hancock — the rubber coatings of his waterproof textiles were prematurely decomposed by colouring matter present on some dyed cotton fabrics.

Hydrolysis by atmospheric moisture is the main degradation mechanism for the cellulose esters, such as cellulose nitrate and cellulose acetate. Hydrolysis plays a significant part in the degradation of polyesters (thermoplastic and thermosetting) and nylon, and can also contribute to the degradation of polymer additives, such as plasticizers. The process usually results in the formation of acidic by-products, which accelerate hydrolysis so that decomposition proceeds at an accelerating rate and the build-up of acidity itself can initiate other degradation processes. Depending on the polymer, the site of hydrolysis may be in the polymer backbone (as is the case with many condensation polymers) or in side groups. The former is more serious because it causes chain scission.

Hydrolysis is accelerated by acids or alkalies and it is therefore important to ensure that traces of such materials are not present in the vicinity of plastics prone to hydrolysis.

Chemical bonds are also broken by other forms of energy, such as heat, light and mechanical forces. The broken bonds generally form highly reactive species, namely free radicals, and the fate of the polymer is controlled largely by chemical reactions associated with these. Light, especially from the more energetic ultraviolet region, causes bond scission in many polymers. In particular, it may initiate an auto-catalytic form of degradation, known as autoxidation, to which hydrocarbon polymers are especially vulnerable. Polyethylene, polypropylene, nylon, gutta-percha and plastics based on natural or synthetic rubbers are susceptible to this type of degradation, which is potentially very damaging as it can propagate at an accelerating rate throughout the material.

Light fades many colourants and discolours many materials. Colour change can therefore be a useful and responsive indicator of excessive exposure to light. However, colouring matter may also mask early signs of deterioration.

Sometimes, degradation is confined to the surface, as may be the case with some reactions initiated by light on opaque materials. This type of deterioration should be distinguished from that where the whole of the material is affected, as the consequences are much less serious.

Conditions to which a material has been exposed in the past often play a part in determining the nature and extent of future deterioration. Removal of the object from adverse conditions does not necessarily halt the degradation processes. Conditions during polymer manufacture, compounding or moulding may also influence future degradation. For example, during the manufacture of cellulose nitrate and cellulose acetate polymers, acidic treatments are used and acidity that is not completely removed by subsequent processing is known to affect the stability of these polymers. Degradation may also be initiated by overheating the material during moulding.

Control of Degradation

Early detection of degradation and its likely cause is most important — this can only be achieved if objects are examined regularly and their condition noted. Sometimes it may be necessary to conduct physical or chemical tests in an attempt to monitor the extent of any change.

Plastics respond in different ways to the various environmental factors, and identification will be necessary in order to appreciate how the material might degrade. The minimum requirement will be the recognition of those materials that need to be kept under special environmental conditions. The following tests and observations may be sufficient for this purpose: colour and appearance; handling qualities; hardness; density; end use; method of manufacture;

trademark; chronology; smell; signs of typical degradation; and specific tests.

Confirmatory tests using various analytical procedures may still be necessary, especially with objects giving cause for concern. The large range of plastics now in production makes the task of identification more difficult for recent material.

Illumination
Light has long been recognized as a major factor in the deterioration of polymers. It is damaging to all plastics and its exclusion is the single most effective step that can be taken to minimize degradation. Since ultraviolet (UV) is the most damaging part of the spectrum of light, it is important not to expose objects to it. Even with ultraviolet removed, the light levels should be maintained as low as circumstances permit.

Temperature Control
Temperature influences the rate at which physico-chemical reactions proceed — the higher the temperature the faster the rate. It affects the rate at which reactants, such as oxygen and moisture, permeate into a material as well as the rate at which reaction products permeate out of the material. The optimum storage temperatures for longevity of the various materials have yet to be determined. Long-term maintenance of temperatures much below ambient would be expensive and may prove to be of little benefit.

For all plastics, the provision of a stable temperature is advised especially with objects containing other materials that may have different thermal expansion coefficients.

Humidity Control
The required level of humidity will depend upon the particular plastics material. For the cellulosic plastics, relative humidity should, ideally, be maintained below about 40%. Casein and nylon become brittle and subject to stress if their moisture content is allowed to become too low, and for these materials a relative humidity of 60% is better. The moisture level is less important with most other plastics but for all groups it is important that it remains

constant. Most plastics absorb moisture to some degree and stress may develop as a result of changing moisture content — stress is a contributory factor in many kinds of degradation.

Ventilation
Ventilation is important for those materials that emit gaseous degradation products. For example, the cellulosic materials and poly(vinyl chloride) emit acidic products, which as well as accelerating degradation may affect other parts of the object or other materials and artefacts in the vicinity. Metals may be corroded by the acidic vapours.

Cleaning
Plastics materials often become soiled during storage, handling and use. Many are electrostatic in nature and attract dust whilst others slowly bleed plasticizer to the surface and become tacky. They do not seem to benefit from the polishing action of repeated handling as do some other materials (e.g., horn and bronze). Perhaps they lack the right combination of hardness and wear characteristics. Only occasionally does a plastics object develop an attractive appearance or patina from the combined effects of ageing, wear and polishing. The most likely plastics to do so are those for which colour plays only a subtle part of their attraction, for example, vulcanite and moulded Bakelite. In such cases cleaning with a soft, dry brush or cloth is probably all that is necessary.

It is recommended that plastics (with certain exceptions) should be cleaned periodically to remove surface contamination that may have built up over a period of time and, particularly, to remove any degradation products that might accelerate deterioration. The frequency at which this should be carried out will depend upon circumstances, but with cellulosic materials and casein it is recommended that this should be done not less than once every five years.

Objects should be washed with tepid water containing a small quantity of liquid detergent; the use of a soft brush may be necessary for textured surfaces. Afterwards, the material should be rinsed with clean water and immediately dried using an absorbent material. Do not soak for long periods of time — it is much better to rewash if soiling remains. Only in rare circumstances and after careful consideration should solvents be used. Even if the material is not directly attacked by the solvent, stress-crazing may result and this might not appear until later.

Care should be exercised with objects containing metals that might corrode, or with hollow objects that may be difficult to dry on the inner surfaces. Disassembly, if possible, is advised in such circumstances.

There may be occasions when objects, perhaps soiled with tar or the residue from self-adhesive labels, are difficult to clean with aqueous solutions and in such cases one of the following solvents should be considered: white spirit, petroleum spirit fuel for cigarette lighters and isopropyl alcohol (propan-2-ol). These solvents possess optimum combinations of cleaning power and inertness towards most plastics. Use a cloth moistened with the minimum amount of solvent. Do not immerse, rub too harshly or subject to stress, and do not use on rigid thermoplastics, such as "untoughened" polystyrene or acrylic because of the risk of stress-crazing. Even for other materials, a wise precaution is to test a small area on a hidden part of the moulding. Remember that these solvents are highly inflammable and toxic.

Degrading cellulose nitrate and cellulose acetate that show crazing or porous areas should not be washed. Stabilizing treatments are being sought and the work on ESBO by Williamson[2] described below shows promising results.

ESBO and Cellulose Nitrate
Cellulose nitrate is susceptible to hydrolysis by atmospheric moisture. Nitric acid is released and this promotes further hydrolysis so that, once started, degradation proceeds at an accelerating rate. It is possible that the application of an acid acceptor, in a form that could migrate into the material, might prove effective in retarding degradation by neutralizing the acidic by-products. Epoxidized soya bean oil (ESBO) has been tried. A mirror back, probably from the 1920s, exhibited typical degradation in the thick rim section in four distinct areas. It was

half immersed in ESBO and left at room temperature for about two years. As shown in Figure 5, the increase in size of the crazed area exposed to the atmosphere indicates continuing degradation. The areas immersed in the ESBO have not increased in size. Other objects showing initial signs of degradation have been smeared with ESBO and the initial results are also encouraging.

Conclusion

Some plastics objects have already undergone serious changes to their properties and appearance. These changes are unlikely to be reversible and all that can be done is to attempt to retain those objects in a stable condition for the future.

5a   5b

Figure 5 Cellulose nitrate mirror back showing pronounced degradation in four areas of the perimeter at one-quarter and three-quarters of the height. (Photo: courtesy of C.J. & M.L. Williamson, The Mansion House, Ford, Shrewsbury, U.K. 0743 850267.) Fig. 5a shows the mirror at an early stage of the degradation. Fig. 5b shows the mirror at a later stage. The degraded areas in the top half of the mirror that were not treated with ESBO continued to grow. The degraded areas in the lower half, which had been immersed in ESBO, appeared to remain stable.

Plastics do slowly degrade in the atmosphere and their life will be considerably shortened if kept under the wrong conditions. Since it is not generally possible to eliminate completely the various environmental factors responsible for the deterioration of plastics, it becomes necessary to control the degree of exposure to them.

This will require classification of objects into groups of materials, an assessment of the various risks followed by the provision of appropriate storage and display conditions. Light, humidity, temperature, ventilation and cleaning procedures all need to be controlled and monitored.

It is probably not feasible to provide the best environmental conditions for storing everything collected and so it will be necessary to optimize the use of those facilities that can be made available. This will require an assessment of which materials and objects are at most risk from deterioration. Such considerations should not be excluded when determining the collection policy (i.e., what artefacts are collected).

Résumé

La conservation des plastiques : un projet mixte du Service de conservation de la Museums & Galleries Commission et de la Plastics Historical Society

Source grandissante d'inquiétudes, la détérioration des premiers objets de musée en plastique a amené le Service de conservation de la Museums & Galleries Commission et la Plastics Historical Society de Londres à unir leurs efforts pour mettre sur pied un programme qui vise à enrayer ce problème.

Pour y arriver, on a adopté une approche comportant diverses étapes.

Ainsi, dans un premier temps, des directives préliminaires sur la mise en réserve des objets en plastique et sur leur exposition seront publiées. Elles seront établies en fonction des connaissances que l'on a déjà sur le vieillissement de ce matériau.

Dans un autre temps, on cherchera à déterminer la nature et l'ampleur des problèmes actuels de dégradation, afin de définir les secteurs de la recherche qui devront être considérés de façon prioritaire. Une étude, couvrant un grand nombre de collections historiques, a ainsi été amorcée dans le but de : fournir des détails quant aux genres de matériaux qui se retrouvent dans les collections; évaluer l'état actuel des objets; déterminer les conditions ambiantes dans lesquelles les objets sont mis en réserve et exposés; offrir de l'information sur les mesures préventives et curatives qu'utilisent déjà les spécialistes de la restauration et les responsables de collections.

Les travaux effectués révèlent clairement que, pour durer, les plastiques doivent, comparativement à la plupart des autres matériaux, faire l'objet de plus de mesures de conservation préventive. Aussi faut-il élaborer des méthodes qui permettront d'arrêter la détérioration des plastiques qui sont déjà touchés — et donc effectuer de la recherche dans le domaine des techniques curatives et les mettre en application —, et tenter de prévoir les problèmes de dégradation que risquent éventuellement de poser ces matériaux — et donc définir les mesures préventives les plus appropriées pour les combattre.

Des plastiques différents se dégradent de manière différente, et il devient dès lors nécessaire de classifier au préalable les objets en plastique suivant leur composition. Il importe tout particulièrement de reconnaître les plastiques qui sont sujets à l'action des mécanismes de dégradation autocatalytique — soit la forme de détérioration la plus destructrice — et de les garder sous observation.

Nous décrirons, dans la présente communication, l'évolution des travaux, tout en fournissant un aperçu de leurs résultats préliminaires.

References

1. Morgan, J., *Conservation of Plastics, An Introduction* (London: Museums & Galleries Commission, 1991).

2. Williamson, C.J., *Polymers in Conservation*, International Conference, Manchester, U.K., July 1991. (Proceedings to be published).

Conserving the Science Museum Collections

Roger Price and Anne Moncrieff

Science Museum
The National Museum of Science and Industry
London, U.K.

Abstract

During 1989 to 1990 a new conservation section was established at the Science Museum in London. Because its facilities are, at present, relatively modest compared with some other national museums, the conservation section aims to protect the Museum's collections by rigorous management of its resources.

In recognition of some damage that might have occurred because of the lack of clear guidelines, a new Code of Conservation Practice is being drawn up. This will include standards for storage and display (drawing on the Storer Report, sponsored jointly by the Science Museum and the Museums & Galleries Commission), observations on available treatments for various materials, and an explanation of the new conservation recording system. This document will serve as the basis for actions that might affect the preservation of the Museum's collections.

In most technical museums, conservation is undertaken by skilled craft technicians. However, few of them operate in the mainstream of conservation practice as it is understood, for example, in fine arts or archaeology. Largely for that reason, some objects have been over restored, which effectively destroys evidence of historical significance. To remedy the situation, the Science Museum runs a three-year Conservation of Industrial Collections Training Course specifically designed to meet the needs of technicians. Similarly, object-cleaning practices have been reviewed. Object cleaners are now included as members of conservation staff and are given basic training.

Like other museums that collect modern artefacts, one of the greatest challenges facing the Science Museum is how to deal with the problem of the degradation of modern materials. Although improved quality of storage and display might help, research into new methods for treatment is urgently required. In the absence of its own research facilities, the Museum has begun sponsoring research at properly equipped institutions. By such collaboration, which need not be prohibitively expensive, some progress can be made in this difficult field.

In view of the diversity of materials collected, all of which have their own special problems, it would be sensible to broaden the research. Ideally, this should be organized on a world-wide basis, with like-minded museums agreeing upon some way of avoiding duplication of work so that resources can be more effectively directed towards solving the problems that beset us.

Introduction

Many museums specialize in aspects of industrial and technological history and numerous non-specialist museums now acquire such artefacts as part of their wider collecting activities. Among long-established museums of industrial history, the size and scope of the collection is greater than ever. New materials are replacing traditional metals and wood, making the conservation of industrial artefacts a complex and demanding task.

The National Museum of Science and Industry, which includes the Science Museum in London, the National Railway Museum and the National Museum of Photography Film and Television, is widely acknowledged as the world's pre-eminent museum devoted to the history of science, technology, industry and medicine. Its collections are the largest, the most comprehensive and the most significant anywhere. To ensure that the preservation of these outstanding collections fully meets the requirements of modern museum practice, a new conservation section was established during 1989 to 1990.

Maximizing Our Resources

The conservation section's most urgent task was to identify and quantify the major problems that threatened the well-being of the Museum's objects so that, by rigorous management, the available resources could be deployed most effectively. Quickly realizing that clear guidelines or procedures were needed, work commenced on the compilation of a detailed Code of Conservation Practice.

The Code contains instructions to all staff on how to use the conservation facility. This includes everyone who is in any way involved in taking actions that might affect the preservation of the collections, including curators, designers, stores officers and building managers. It also contains an explanation of the new conservation recording system, environmental standards for storage and display, and guidelines for conservation staff on materials and techniques.

Central to this initiative is the work of the Conservation of Industrial Collections Forum. Founded in 1987, this group consists of conservators, curators and engineers from national and local authority museums and related institutions, as well as restorers in private practice. For industrial collections in general, the approach to conservation is not as developed as it is in, for example, fine arts or archaeology; rather, the care of industrial objects is based upon traditional engineering craft skills, often of a very high order, but all too frequently

lacking the rigour and discipline of modern conservation practice. The Forum meets twice yearly with the Director of the National Museum of Science and Industry to discuss ways in which the conservation of industrial material can be raised to a standard more appropriate for the needs of today and tomorrow.

An early achievement of the Forum is the 1989 publication by J.D. Storer, *The Conservation of Industrial Collections: a Survey*, sponsored jointly by the Science Museum and the Museums & Galleries Commission. In this important work, Storer surveys the facilities for conservation and storage in 43 museums throughout the country holding industrial and related material, and makes a number of recommendations on standards that should be met.

Another direct result of the Forum's work is the 1989 inauguration of the Conservation of Industrial Collections Training Course, run by the Science Museum. As its most urgent priority, the Forum advocates staff training in two distinct areas: first, the need to recover traditional engineering craft skills (a need that must be and to some extent is being met by apprenticeship to experienced craftspersons in museums and private workshops); and second, the need for a conservation approach based on the methodical study of an object, its history, deterioration and treatment, of which a written record must be made.

This new training course is specially designed to meet the needs of engineering technicians in the full-time employ of a museum. Over three years they receive 70 days of theoretical instruction during which they gain experience in the wider issues of conservation. They must also compile a written portfolio based on work they have undertaken to meet the requirements of a practical syllabus. Their progress is assessed regularly and there are examinations at the end of each year. Successful graduates are awarded a Certificate in the Conservation of Industrial Collections.

The Science Museum has always employed staff to clean the objects displayed in the galleries. Staff cleaners have considerable practical experience but, until now, have had no formal training. In recognition of the continued need for this work, 12 cleaners were assigned to the conservation section in 1990. Three of them have since been promoted to act as supervisors for each of three cleaning teams. In the last year, they have all had some training, which was based on standards used by the National Trust. The large number of objects on display means that these cleaners will be busy dusting for most of the time, however, they will be integrated more fully into the section and given more training so that they can work with conservators on more specialized cleaning tasks.

Through this endeavor the Science Museum ensures that the objects on display are presented attractively and are also treated with appropriate care. Another important gain from such a regular cleaning programme is that the objects displayed are subject to frequent detailed observation and any change in their condition can be recorded and treated where necessary.

Our Approach to Degrading Modern Materials

Like other museums that collect modern artefacts, one of the greatest challenges facing the Science Museum is how to deal with the problem of the degradation of modern materials. Although improved quality of storage and display might help, research into new methods for treatment is needed. With no research facilities of its own, the Museum has begun to sponsor research at institutions that have the staff and equipment for such work.

The Science Museum has some aluminium alloys, especially castings, that are corroding. In collaboration with the Corrosion and Protection Centre at the University of Manchester Institute of Science and Technology (UMIST), the Museum has obtained a Science and Engineering Research Council Award for a Ph.D. student to carry out research into this problem. The aim is to develop a technique that will reduce the rate of decay to a minimum. The first two years of this three-year project have brought some success on simulated objects, but the methods have yet to be tested in a real situation.

Objects made from cellulose nitrate are also showing signs of deterioration. Because the Centre for Archival Polymeric Materials at Manchester Polytechnic was already working on the degradation of cellulosic film materials, the Science Museum provided funding for additional work. The project seeks to characterize the polymer in both original and artificially aged samples, with the aim of finding methods to assess the state of deterioration and to slow down the rate of decay.

The Museum has a few 19th-century cars whose original upholstery is in poor condition. To conserve the upholstery rather than restore it with new materials, a joint project was set up with the Leather Conservation Centre in Northampton. New materials and methods were investigated to effect the repair and reinforcement of the old leather. So far, certain experimental methods have been successful and have been used on two of the cars.

Condition surveys on objects in the stores have confirmed early impressions that some commercial protective coatings are effective in retarding metal corrosion. The Museum will continue to use these, drawing on the experience of other users. The Museum is also discussing the choice of oils for lubrication and hopes to sponsor research into the degradation of oils and metal surfaces in collaboration with a university research department outside London.

While working with existing research groups has the advantage of having access to expertise, it also has the slight disadvantage of not having complete control over the project and the direction that it might take. It is not easy to find research groups to work on the materials that interest the Science Museum; nor are most students prepared to work on old materials. Furthermore, the problems do not always fit neatly into the time available to Ph.D. students. Nevertheless, this is an effective way to use limited resources and with the right partner such cooperation can be successful and rewarding.

There is a very real problem with complex objects, such as older computers. An example of one approach used by the Science Museum is the formation of the Computer Conservation

Society. Collaborating with the British Computer Society, the Museum has allocated a curator post and provided facilities for the enthusiastic and expert volunteers; the technicians, engineers and computer operators who once actually worked with these same early computers.

The Society first focused on restoring to working order a *Ferranti Pegasus* vacuum-tube computer dating from 1958 and an *Elliott 803* germanium-transistor machine dating from the early 1960s. This work has been fully documented and is regarded as a continuation of the working life of these objects. In the process of this work young engineers and technicians are trained to care for these machines. Though the computers will only work for a few more years, the experience enables the Museum to capture and record the expertise of the designers, builders, maintainers, programmers and users of early computers.

The partnership between the Museum and these computer professionals has also created a programme of emulation whereby software is designed to make a modern computer behave just like the old machines, including their idiosyncrasies. This enables anyone who is interested to experience something of the work of the early pioneers. A publication on the work of the Computer Conservation Society is planned for 1992.

Conclusion

Conservation staff at our Museum keep in touch with work going on in other museums by attending conferences and through many informal contacts, for example, the ICOM Modern Materials Working Group and The Conservation Unit of the Museums & Galleries Commission (whose Conservation Research Policy Group is keeping a record of conservation research in the United Kingdom).

In view of the diversity of materials now collected by museums, all of which have their own special problems, it would be sensible to broaden research into their deterioration and remedial measures. Ideally, this should be organized on a world-wide basis, with like-minded museums agreeing upon some way of avoiding duplication of work so that resources can be more effectively directed towards solving the problems that beset us.

Résumé

La conservation des collections du National Museum of Science and Industry

En 1989-1990, une nouvelle section de conservation a été créée au National Museum of Science and Industry de Londres. Comme ses installations sont, pour le moment, relativement modestes comparativement à celles de certains autres musées nationaux, cette section a pour mandat de préserver les collections du musée en assurant une gestion rigoureuse des ressources.

Il a été reconnu que l'absence de lignes directrices claires explique certains des dommages qui se seraient produits, et l'on travaille donc actuellement à la rédaction d'un nouveau répertoire des règles et usages en matière de conservation. Ce document renfermera des normes pour la mise en réserve et l'exposition des objets — qui s'inspireront du rapport qu'a préparé, sous le patronage mixte du musée et de la Museums & Galleries Commission, la personne responsable des réserves —, des observations sur les traitements qui peuvent être appliqués aux divers matériaux et des explications au sujet du nouveau système d'enregistrement aux fins de conservation. Et il servira de document d'orientation lorsque viendra le moment de prendre des mesures qui pourraient influer sur la conservation des collections du National Museum of Science and Industry.

Dans la plupart des musées de la technique, les travaux de conservation sont confiés à des techniciens et techniciennes qualifiés et expérimentés. Il s'en trouve néanmoins peu parmi eux qui travaillent suivant les règles de conservation qui ont cours, par exemple, dans un musée des beaux-arts ou de l'archéologie. Et c'est sans doute ce facteur qui explique le mieux que l'on retrouve parfois, dans ces musées, des objets qui ont été beaucoup trop restaurés, jusqu'à en perdre pratiquement toute signification historique. Soucieux de faire sa part pour remédier à cette situation, le musée a mis sur pied un cours de formation de trois ans qui, portant sur la conservation des collections industrielles, est spécialement conçu pour répondre aux besoins de ces techniciens et techniciennes. Les usages entourant le nettoyage des objets ont également été passés en revue, si bien que des personnes spécialement affectées à cette tâche ont été intégrées au personnel de conservation, et qu'un cours de formation de base a été mis sur pied à leur intention.

Le problème de la dégradation des matériaux modernes constitue sans doute l'un des plus grands défis auxquels le musée ait à faire face à l'instar des autres musées qui collectionnent des objets modernes. Et s'il est sans doute utile de chercher à améliorer la qualité des méthodes de mise en réserve et d'exposition, il n'en demeure pas moins urgent de poursuivre la recherche de nouvelles méthodes de traitement. Ne disposant pas d'installations de recherche qui lui permettraient de poursuivre lui-même de tels travaux, le musée a commencé à parrainer des recherches qu'effectuent, dans ce domaine, des organismes adéquatement équipés. Il devient dès lors possible, grâce à une telle forme de collaboration, de réaliser des progrès dans ce secteur plutôt difficile, et ce, sans que le musée ait à effectuer de gros déboursés.

Compte tenu de la diversité des matières qui se retrouvent dans les collections, et qui présentent toutes des problèmes particuliers, il serait raisonnable d'élargir l'horizon des recherches. Une telle entreprise devrait idéalement être intégrée à un projet de portée mondiale, dans le cadre duquel les musées ayant les mêmes intérêts se seraient mis d'accord sur une façon d'éviter les dédoublements, et feraient ainsi en sorte que les ressources servent effectivement à la résolution des problèmes.

History of Technology
Histoire de la technologie

Rubber: Its History, Composition and Prospects for Conservation

M.J.R. Loadman

Malaysian Rubber Producers' Research Association
Tun Abdul Razak Laboratory
Brickendonbury, Hertford
United Kingdom

Abstract

Everyone living in the "modern" world is familiar with rubber and its properties. Perhaps it is that very familiarity that has bred, if not contempt, at least an unthinking acceptance of the material and its position in our civilization. The term "rubber" is used to describe any polymer that has or appears to have elastic properties, and there are many such polymers of both natural and synthetic origin on the market today. In a "rubber" product, the elastomer may well be less than 50% of its total mass since many additional chemicals may have been added to produce a serviceable article, and these in turn may have been selected from hundreds of possibilities.

It is not intended, in this paper, to delve deeply into the scientific details of rubber product formulation, but it is essential that, before starting any conservation process, the conservator is aware of the material with which he or she is dealing and how inappropriate treatment can do more harm than good. The history of elastomeric materials will be reviewed, with particular attention to developments in the 20th century, which might assist the conservator in classifying and possibly dating any elastomeric product. To further these aims, a brief description of some simple methods of analysing these materials will be included.

Visually displeasing changes to the surface of an elastomeric product are a common event and can sometimes presage surface degradation, although this is not always the case; some surface changes are intended and are beneficial to the life of the material. Possible causes and effects of surface changes will be discussed and ways of distinguishing between them presented.

Knowing what the material is, and from the state of its surface what has happened to it so far in its life, consider now what can be done to optimize its display life. Whilst there is no one answer for all elastomers and their products, many suffer degradation through a series of common phenomena: oxygen, ozone, heat, light, mechanical work, pro-oxidant metals, bacteria and even that dreaded word "chemistry"; combinations of these phenomena often have a synergistic effect. An attempt will be made to weave a path through this minefield so that the best conservation procedure is chosen for each of the various types of elastomeric products on display.

Introduction

There can be no-one living in the "modern" world who is not familiar with rubber and its properties, but perhaps it is that very familiarity that has bred, if not contempt, at least an unthinking acceptance of the material and its position in our civilization.

The natural material has been used for at least 2,000 years. It may, even today, be used "raw" for crêpe soles of high quality shoes, or mixed with chemicals in the latex state, prior to having formers dipped into it to produce such articles as baby bottle teats, condoms or surgeons' gloves. The mixed (or compounded) latex may also be treated to produce latex thread suitable for the finest underwear whilst, at the other extreme, the dried rubber can be mixed with more chemicals, often including carbon black, to manufacture the strongest of engineering products, such as base isolation units for buildings in earthquake zones, conveyor belts and, accounting for by far the greatest area of usage of elastomers, aircraft and car tyres. If you doubt the remarkable properties of this material, remember the faith you put in the four 'handprints' of the tyres on the road beneath your car.

In the last 150 years or so, hundreds of chemicals have been added to rubber to modify the polymer itself, or its properties. And numerous synthetic elastomers have been invented and manufactured, put through the same process of mixing with all the chemicals used with natural rubber, and more. Yet still, for general purpose applications, and, indeed, many specialized ones, the sap from the weeping tree, which originated in Brazil, gives rubber, a material unequalled in its many useful properties.

With such a wide variety of end products and constituent chemicals it is impossible to do other than generalize, but there are some useful observations that can be made.

Materials on display must look good, be they in a shop window to encourage sales, or on display in a museum. Surface deterioration is a common event in both environments and can sometimes presage surface degradation, although this is not always the case; some surface changes are intended and beneficial to the life of the material. The possible causes and effects of surface changes will be discussed, and ways of distinguishing between them presented.

Knowing what the material is, and from the state of its surface what has happened to it so far in its life, consider now what can be done to optimize its display life. Many ideas have been put forward, some possible and some definitely counter-productive. Whilst there is no one answer for all elastomers and their products, many suffer degradation through a series of common phenomena: heat, light, mechanical work, pro-oxidant metals, bacteria, oxygen,

ozone and even that dreaded word "chemistry"; combinations of these phenomena often have a synergistic effect. An attempt will be made to weave a path through this minefield so that the best conservation procedures may be selected for the various elastomeric products on display.

The history of natural rubber, or NR as it is usually known, from a plaything over 2,000 years ago to the founding member of one of the most important classes of materials of modern day is a fascinating story, unequalled, I believe, for any material. The more recent development of synthetic elastomers is equally interesting, arising as it did from a mixture of the chemist's basic desire to mimic and improve on nature and the absolute need for a synthetic replacement for NR by both Germany and the United States during the Second World War.

Highlighted in an appendix are those events in the history of rubber that seem to me to be important, or interesting, in the development of the rubber industry of today. The list, although extensive, is still superficial and very personal, but even more brief is the summary included here.

Although the oldest rubber known is fossilized and some 60 million years old, the detailed modern history began some 2,000 years ago with the New World involvement in "rubber" produced from a "weeping tree." It is probable, however, that the earliest rubber came from *Castilloa elastica* and not the *Hevea braziliensis*, which produces essentially all the world's natural rubber today.

Skipping past references from Columbus and Torquemada, the first real European involvement was by the French during the middle of the 18th century, when de la Condamine and Fresneau attempted, without success, to start the first manufacturing plants for rubber goods in Europe. Their main interest was in latex dipping but they could not ship the latex to Europe without it coagulating — a visual and olfactory effect similar to milk curdling!

For 50 years little happened, except that Priestly coined the name "rubber" for the material that rubbed out pencil marks. Then, within a very short period from 1820 to 1839, there was a tremendous growth of interest, when in the United Kingdom, Hancock invented his machine to convert lumps of solid rubber into a useable homogeneous gum (a process he called "pickling" to confuse his competitors), and Macintosh developed his three-layer waterproof fabric. In North America, at the same time, a substantial market developed for dipped rubber shoes, whilst Chaffee invented his mill and calender, the designs of which are basically the same as those in use today. Chaffee also founded the first American rubber company.

By 1839 the American rubber bubble had burst, mainly due to the stink of crude unstabilized rubber as it decomposed in the heat of summer, but also accelerated by the economic collapse of the country. In the U.K. Hancock and Macintosh survived due to their company's "Macintosh's Waterproof Double Textures." However, the product, although better than anything else, was still liable to putrefy and, whilst "state of the art," it could not be considered perfect.

In that same year of 1839, Goodyear discovered, by accident, that heating a mix of rubber, white lead and sulphur resulted in a highly elastic material that was rubber "cured" of its problems. It no longer went brittle in the cold and soft in the heat, nor did it seem to putrefy so easily. Thus the process of heating rubber with sulphur became known as the "curing" process as well as vulcanization, a name probably coined somewhat later by an otherwise unremembered friend of Hancock's, Mr. Brockedon.

In 1857 Thomas Hancock published his classic guide to the U.K. rubber industry and his illustrations give some idea of the breadth of uses to which rubber was being put. Not many are missing from a list of today, since these include air-proof products, hoses and tyres, nautical, domestic and travel equipment as well as a range of seals and washers.

In the second half of the 19th century explorers around the world were searching for plants that could produce "rubber." These were being shipped to politically and climatically acceptable locations in the hope of discovering one that could be "harvested" profitably. In fact,

none succeeded in the long term except *Hevea braziliensis* and this has not been bettered, although the American government research continued into Guyaule right up until last year, and during the 1930s the Russians used dandelions as a source material, having access to nothing else.

In 1873 Henry Wickham appeared, and the story of his shipping 70,000 seeds of *Hevea braziliensis* to Kew Gardens in London has entered rubber folklore, mostly due to Wickham's and others' fireside embellishments of the diaries and notes that Wickham kept on his trip. What *is* known is that 2,397 seeds germinated at Kew, and 1,919 of these were sent to Sri Lanka, 18 to Java and "a few" to Singapore. Yet little is made of the fact that the British government forgot to pay freight charges and most of the seedlings died! Here precise details become cloudy, but a month later another 100 seedlings were sent to Sri Lanka from Kew and yet another 100 were sent in the following year (1877).

In 1878, 22 seedlings were sent from Sri Lanka to Singapore. Ridley, the Director of the Botanic Gardens of Singapore and the man who could fairly claim to be the father of the rubber plantations in Malaysia, believed that these were seedlings from a batch of Brazilian seeds sent to Kew by another collector, Robert Cross. These were the seedlings from which most of the world's rubber trees have developed. Thus it is possible that Cross, not Wickham, should be thought of as the true father of the natural rubber industry. In 1899 the first "plantation rubber" was shipped from Sri Lanka and the rubber production industry was born. For another 50 years "wild rubber" from trees, not necessarily *Hevea braziliensis*, continued to come out of Brazil. This was often called "Para rubber," after the port of Para from whence it was shipped.

To the following people, therefore, lies the credit for founding the rubber industry of today: Goodyear, the idealist and fanatic who sacrificed his family, income and health in his attempts to do anything and everything with rubber; Hancock, the pragmatic businessman first, and engineer second, who came to grips with the mastication of rubber; Chaffee, unknown to most today, but the inventor of the still standard two-speed, two-roll mill and its extension, the calender. On the rubber production side is the famous Wickham (or perhaps less known, Cross), Hooker and Markham at Kew Gardens and Ridley at the Botanic Gardens of Singapore. Perhaps, finally, the motor car should be mentioned, hardly conceived during the period covered by those listed above, but the undoubted catalyst to launch the rubber industry into the 20th century on an increasingly large scale.

In this century a few critical dates can still be picked out from the great mass of scientific advancement:

- 1921 to 1923 - The development of most of the chemicals used to "accelerate" and clean up the chemistry of sulphur vulcanization

- 1925 - Can be considered the start of the synthetic rubber industry

- 1930s - The introduction of amine derivatives as antioxidants

- 1933 to 1945 - The development of familiar synthetics, such as polybutadiene, styrene-butadiene, nitrile, chloroprene (neoprene), polyurethane and silicone

- 1950s - The introduction of non-staining phenolic antioxidants

- 1958 - The introduction of fluoroelastomers

- 1962 - World production of natural and synthetic rubbers each reaches two million tons per annum

- 1990 - World output of rubber around 15 million tons; 2:1 synthetic:natural

It is worth noting that, whilst many special elastomers have been developed that can operate in environments where NR would not function satisfactorily, none of the general-purpose elastomers can offer any improvement over NR for run-of-the-mill applications. These

general-purpose elastomers, including NR, account for some 80% of the current elastomer market.

To my mind, the most important features of this summary in the area of conservation are the following:

- Any artefact manufactured before 1840 is not vulcanized.

- Identification of curatives/additives will help in dating products manufactured between 1840 and 1920.

- Identification of the polymer is essential after 1930.

- Non-black filled products were not protected with antidegradents before the mid 1950s.

Obviously, more detailed datings may be possible by considering all ingredients found, and thus it is worth considering what can be done in this field. I have not gone into scientific detail here, as knowing what can be done, not how to do it, is the important thing and analytical details are not needed to ask the experts to look for something.

Aspects of Analysis

Excluding surface effects, which are considered later, useful information can be obtained through these three questions:

- What is the polymeric system?

- What can be said about the cure and protective systems?

- What inorganic materials are present?

The first is most easily answered by pyrolysis followed by either infra-red spectroscopy (P-IR) or gas chromatography (P-GC). Characteristic traces that are obtained for each polymer using both techniques and polymer blends can be quantified if the analytical conditions are right. Typical patterns for NR are illustrated in Figures 1 and 2. These techniques suffer from one disadvantage in that they cannot be considered non-destructive. Nevertheless, P-IR can use only l0 mg whilst P-GC requires, say, 100 µg and this can usually be spared from any material. Figure 3 shows a sample ready for P-GC analysis; the baby feeder teat gives an idea of the scale. The equipment need not be highly sophisticated and costs would be 10,000 to 15,000 dollars.

Examination of the cure and protective systems is potentially the cheapest of all analytical techniques, if a gram or two of material can be spared, since thin layer chromatography (TLC) can be used to separate and visualize virtually all of the candidate chemicals. The sample is extracted with a suitable solvent, and this solution is then concentrated and spotted onto the bottom of a TLC plate. This is then placed in a special tank containing a low volume of a liquid, which elutes the various components up the plate at differing rates. Treatment of the "developed" plate with particular chemicals produces variously coloured spots from the components present, which enables identification of the materials with a high degree of specificity, provided reference materials or data are available. Thus, for a few cents, much useful information can be obtained. It may also be of interest to note that one spray is relatively

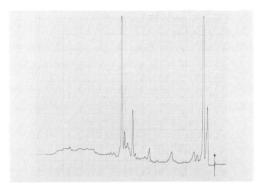

Figure 2 Pyrolysis — gas chromatogram of natural rubber.

specific for oxidative degradation of NR, giving an orange spot and streak, whilst another enables a distinction to be made between NR and the material that is its nominal synthetic equivalent, generically called "PI" for polyisoprene.

If the sample size is limited to milligrams, high performance liquid chromatography (HPLC) is the analytical method of choice. This method can give as much data, and quantify it, but costs more — 30,000 dollars upwards!

It should be noted here that I have talked only of sulphur vulcanization and not of any other types. Since the discovery of modern accelerators in 1920, sulphur vulcanization has dominated the methods of crosslinking polyolefins and probably accounts for over 95% of the market. Peroxide, urethane, and radiation

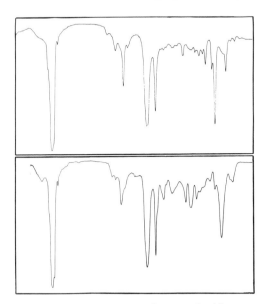

Figure 1 Infra-red spectra of a natural rubber pyrolysate (top) and thin film (bottom).

Figure 3 Sample being inserted into a pyrolyser coil for P-GC identification.

crosslinking of polyolefins must be considered "niche" areas for very specific properties. Considering the whole elastomer field and pseudo-elastomer field, there are two significant exceptions to sulphur vulcanization, the polyurethane and silicone rubbers. These have multi-functional groups in a few molecules of low molar mass that enable three dimensional networks to build up during polymerization. Here the word "vulcanization" is not appropriate whereas "curing" might be. In fact, this latter word is used by the resins and plastics industry quite happily, and reasonably, since their crosslinking processes also cure the sticky and flow problems of the starting materials.

Finally, any inorganic elements present must be considered and this includes any added sulphur that would indicate a cured product. For simplicity, and even the chance of true non-destructive analysis, the scanning electron microscopy (SEM) with a built-in electron microprobe X-ray analyser must be considered. The X-ray spectrum will immediately identify the elements present and allow a "guesstimate" of their levels. Figure 4 shows the spectrum of a vulcanizate with zinc and sulphur together with aluminium and silicon, the last two indicating a clay filler. The characteristic peaks of barium suggest barium sulphate, used to increase the density of certain materials, and there is also a trace of iron. In Figure 5 an impurity is identified as rust; it must be emphasized that this is a surface technique with a sample penetration of about 10 microns. This feature is obviously relevant to the next section; in the context of bulk element composition care must

be taken to examine a piece free of surface contamination or, more safely, a section through the bulk of the material. These instruments are not cheap but my experience in the U.K. is that most museums know of their potential and are able to persuade either a local university or industrial organization, such as my own, to have samples examined.

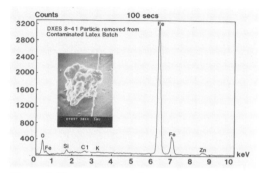

Figure 5 X-ray spectrum of contaminant with, inset, a micrograph of the particle.

Such a technique was of instant importance a few years ago when I was asked to identify the "elastic" material found inside a sealed amphora during a Middle-Eastern excavation (Figure 6). It was assumed to be a seal of some sort and, whilst having a brittle skin, was obviously "elastic" or rubbery underneath. A minute sliver was taken from within a whorl and identified by P-GC as NR. This was exciting as there was no record of rubber being used outside the New World prior to 1500, although with dandelions and the many hundreds of other rubber-bearing plants around, it was not impossible. SEM X-ray analysis threw the "cat amongst the pigeons" as this showed both zinc and sulphur at "modern" levels of addition. HPLC examination of a further sliver showed mercaptobenzothiazole (MBT). This placed the artefact after 1920 and thus raised doubts about the other artefacts found in the vicinity of the amphora. It certainly caused local red faces, but at least prevented a much larger scale of embarrassment. There are many different sources of analytical techniques that can be used to examine elastomers, and one of which I am co-author, listed in the bibliography, discusses these in some detail. Many useful tricks are documented there and perhaps there is one that deserves mention here, as it is cheap! All that is required is a press with platens that can be

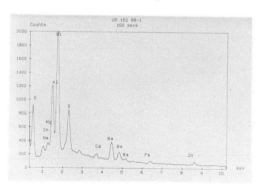

Figure 4 Scanning electron microscope — energy dispersive X-ray spectrum of a filled rubber vulcanizate.

Figure 6 Artefact discovered in "sealed" amphora.

heated to about 175°C. Hot pressing non-vulcanized rubber will result in a smooth film, but if the rubber is vulcanized it will stretch and tear before shrinking to something like its original size. One important application is in distinguishing between vulcanizates and such materials as plasticized PVC (arguably called "rubber") and the thermoplastic elastomers, which are taking an increasing share of the current elastomer market.

Surface Effects

Examination of the surface of a rubber product or artefact immediately reveals whether the surface looks good and "respectable" or whether there is something wrong with it. If the latter is true, there could be several reasons and these need to be identified before carrying out any treatment. The following categories of surface effects can be defined. But before discussing each in turn, I must emphasize that it is possible for more than one of these effects to be present at the same time.

A **true bloom** is a thin layer on the surface of a rubber article of one of the chemicals added before, or produced during, vulcanization. This chemical actually migrates from the bulk to the surface by a mechanism that will not be discussed here beyond saying that the chemical has to be soluble to a certain extent in the rubber and be present at a level above that solubility. Chemicals that can bloom are sulphur, zinc dialkyldithiocarbamates, mercaptobenzthiazole and zinc mercaptobenzimidazole. With the possible exception of the last, they are not intended to bloom in a properly formulated product. One

chemical that is intended to bloom is wax, the sole reason for its adding being to bloom and produce an ozone-impervious film on the surface of the rubber product.

Modified blooms result from protective agents on or near the surface of the rubber reacting with the environment and undergoing a chemical change. The non-reacted chemical in the bulk of the rubber then migrates to the surface to decrease the concentration gradient, where it is then further consumed, eventually building up a protective skin. At this stage the migration stops until the skin is removed or broken and "repairs" are needed. Classic examples of this are the paraphenylenediamine antidegradents.

Pseudo blooms are what I call dull surfaces, which appear to be suffering from a bloom but which on closer examination, often under an electron microscope, are actually suffering from surface degradation of the rubber. In very extreme cases, sometimes called "chalking" or "frosting", the rubber is completely eaten away leaving a powdery surface of the inorganic filler. This has led some people to claim that fillers can bloom, but this is not possible as they are insoluble in rubber. They only "come to the surface" because the surface is eaten away. Also included in this category is surface crazing, to which I will refer later.

Surface contamination, staining and discolouration are always problems, particularly with the sort of materials conservators might be examining. These have to be identified, possibly by SEM, before taking action to restore the material, remembering that any "clean-up" procedure must take into account surface effects or defects if further damage is to be avoided.

The final category, **hazing**, only applies to transparent or translucent products and is caused by either insoluble crystals, particles or immiscible liquid droplets suspended in bulk rubber. These may or may not migrate as well, but little can be done about them. Although not a surface effect, it is not always possible to distinguish between the two with a cursory examination. Tables I and II illustrate some simple tests that can be used to provide information on possible surface effects. It is usually possible to find some part of an article that can be experimented on, but as I mentioned earlier, more than one effect may be present at any one time and therefore a degree of care is required in drawing any conclusions. The tests themselves are perfectly straightforward and do not require any further elaboration.

A more sophisticated examination should be carried out if possible and it is obvious that the SEM with X-ray analytical microprobe must be the technique of choice, although some information is available from chemical spot tests and multiple internal reflection infra-red spectroscopy as well as IR microscopy. Once again, there are many tricks that can be used to facilitate examination, but these are beyond the scope of this paper. For more details in this

area, once again I recommend the book *The Analysis of Rubber and Rubber-like Materials*, as listed in the bibliography.

Ageing

In any discussion about ageing it is enlightening to begin by quoting from Hancock's classic book *The Origin and Progress of the CAOUTCHOUC, or India-rubber Manufacture in England*, which was published in 1857. The following observation seems to have been made sometime during 1825 to 1826:

The injurious effects of the sun's rays upon thin films of rubber we discovered and provided against before much damage accrued. All these things are now cheaply known to those who have followed us by men leaving our employ and the specifications of our patents; but they had all to be undergone in

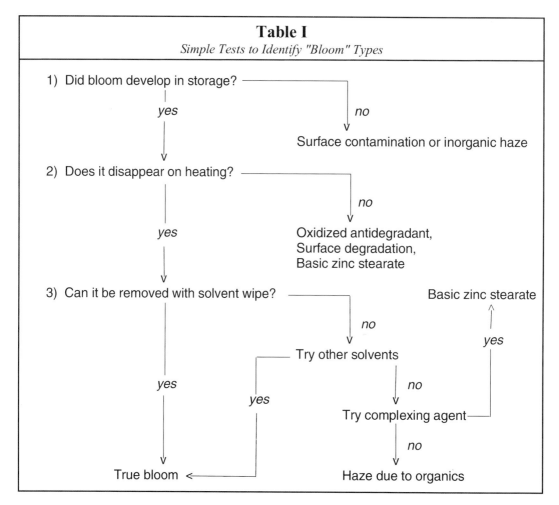

Table I

Simple Tests to Identify "Bloom" Types

1) Did bloom develop in storage?
   yes / no
   no → Surface contamination or inorganic haze

2) Does it disappear on heating?
   yes / no
   no → Oxidized antidegradant, Surface degradation, Basic zinc stearate

3) Can it be removed with solvent wipe?
   yes → Basic zinc stearate (yes)
   no → Try other solvents
      yes
      no → Try complexing agent
         no → Haze due to organics

True bloom

our early progress at an enormous cost, as well as trouble and vexation: and none but those who have passed through the ordeal can conceive the mortification experienced during those years.

It would appear that there really is nothing new under the sun! Unfortunately there is a great difference between knowing about something and circumventing it — particularly for the time scale that interests museums. The factors that can influence the life of an elastomeric product fall into two categories, which I will call "product characteristics," about which nothing can be done, and "ageing processes," about which something can be done.

Product characteristics describe the product as it was made and include such variables as: which elastomer was used; whether the product is filled or not and if so, whether it is black, coloured or white; the vulcanizing system; the protective system; whether it is properly designed and manufactured or has built-in stresses; and the size and shape.

All of these have an effect on the product's service and storage lives but unfortunately there is a conflict in that the manufacturer is concerned with optimizing the product's performance during an acceptable service life with some pre-use storage, but the manufacturer is

not prepared (quite reasonably) to compromise this performance so that the product might be displayed for a few hundred years in a museum. These effects may also interact so, with the exception of the protective agents themselves, none will be discussed in any detail. Their significance will become apparent as the discussion continues.

Ageing processes involve three distinct mechanistic routes that can be identified as follows:

- continuing sulphur vulcanization chemistry

- shelf ageing

- atmospheric ageing

Sulphur chemistry is particularly important in vulcanized products that are resisting a distorting force. Chemistry does not stop when the vulcanizing temperature is reduced from some 150°C to ambient — it just proceeds more slowly. One of the features of a vulcanizate is known as its "set" and this is due to the fact that the C-Sx-C bonds, which form the chemical crosslinks between polymer chains, can break between sulphur atoms and then the loose ends re-attach to either their original partner or another loose end. If the vulcanizate is under a distorting force, then, as the bond breaks, the elasticity of the polymer chain causes it to relax against the force so that the bond will re-form further down the chain. The result is a slow "slippage" of the vulcanizate, which cannot be reversed. This can be minimized by the appropriate choice of crosslinking agents, since the so-called "efficient" vulcanizing systems, which are low in sulphur and high in accelerator, have a much higher proportion of monosulphidic crosslinks than "conventional" cure systems. As the C-S bond is stronger than the S-S one, it will not break so easily, but, once there is a vulcanizate, its propensity to set cannot be changed. It is essential, therefore, that vulcanized (and of course non-vulcanized) artefacts are stored and displayed with as little distorting forces as possible. Vehicles, for instance, should not be left on inflated tyres, but should be blocked up and the tyres deflated to a few pounds per square inch (psi). Although the chemical changes will continue in an unstressed object and are significant in terms of

Table II

Colour Changes and Their Significance in "Bloom" Analysis

1) Is the colour change light-induced? (Mask some of sample for reference)

Grey/Brown	amine a/o
Pink	phenolic a/o

2) Is the colour change heat-induced?
   If yes, with

stickiness/embrittlement	oxidative degradation

   If yes, without

stickiness/embrittlement	amine a/o

3) Is the colour change patchy?
   Reaction of external contamination with rubber chemicals

4) Does colour change appear after laundering or contact with metals?
   Copper/Iron reaction with dithocarbamates

5) Does colour change accompany poor ageing?
   Further evidence for Copper/Iron contamination

product usage, they will not significantly affect the appearance of a display object.

Shelf ageing is basically oxidative ageing and, apart from the obvious influence of oxygen, the catalytic effects of heat, light and pro-oxidant metals have to be considered. If the chemistry of oxidative degradation was considered in detail it would fill in a lifetime or two and still leave unanswered questions, but in a simplistic form, it is fair to say that oxidation of a sulphur vulcanizate proceeds via at least one chain reaction sequence. This, fundamentally, introduces C-C and C-O-O-C crosslinks between polymer chains as well as C-O-O-C rings within the same polymer chain, whilst another set of reactions between the sulphur atoms of the crosslinks and oxygen breaks the crosslinks. The mechanism of chain scission is still not completely understood but theories have been proposed that involve both the "in-chain" C-O-O-C groups and the C-O-O-C crosslinks. The reactions between sulphur and oxygen are those that eventually lead to sulphuric acid formation, which is a particular problem with ebonites.

Therefore, there is a large range of both sequential (or chain) reactions and competing reactions, and the ones that predominate depend on factors such as the formulation or composition of the vulcanizate as well as the influences of heat, light and metal catalysis. Heat ageing balances the rate of reaction of oxygen with the elastomer and the rate of diffusion of the oxygen into it. If the temperature is relatively low, it has been postulated, for an unprotected elastomer, that diffusion through the elastomer predominates and therefore there is slow oxidation throughout the product, but at higher temperatures (e.g., >80°C) the rate of oxidation becomes much more important than the rate of diffusion, so substantial oxidation occurs on the surface and an oxidized (hard) surface skin forms. As oxidation continues, the chain breakdown may become more significant and the hard surface can then soften and turn sticky. To complicate matters further, under certain conditions this order can be reversed and an initially sticky degraded surface can harden with further oxidation.

In real life vulcanizates, particularly when black-filled, it seems that the ingress of oxygen is limited and, apart from the surface 0.5 mm or so, the bulk rubber remains in excellent condition. It is this experimental fact that enables conservation scientists to predict with confidence service lives well in excess of 100 years for engineering products, such as base isolation units for buildings, or bridge bearings that take up the expansion and contraction of most modern bridges.

Light-catalysed oxidation is particularly noticed in unfilled or light-coloured objects and can result in an inelastic skin which, as it thickens, cracks in random directions and produces a pattern known as "crazing" and this is illustrated in Figure 7. In thin sheets the effect has been called "light stiffening", whilst in highly filled articles the degradation can result in complete loss of the resinified elastomer, ending up with the "chalking" effect that I mentioned earlier. Because of the light-absorbing properties of black-filled materials, this effect is not normally seen, although a "bronzing" effect has been claimed to result from light-induced ageing of some very smooth-surfaced, black-filled products. I must emphasize that light itself does not cause degradation of rubbers; oxygen must be present and the effect is light-catalysed oxidation. The effect varies with wavelength, UV being the most dangerous and red/orange the least so.

Figure 7 Crazing pattern induced on a thin white disc of rubber.

The effects of trace levels of pro-oxidant metals, such as copper and manganese, have been known for years and were used by Goodyear in 1837 to *improve* his sticky raw rubber by painting the mouldings with a concentrated solution of copper nitrate. The "improvement" was actually a hard oxidized skin! These metals accelerate the oxidative degradation, again forming brittle skins on both raw and vulcanized rubbers as well as eventually degrading the elastomer to a sticky mess, as illustrated in the baby feeder teats in Figure 8. There has been much dispute as to how much copper an unfilled vulcanizate can reasonably tolerate without specific protection. There is no doubt that it depends upon the "state" of the copper and "state" probably relates to its chemical form and degree of solubility. Certainly 10 parts per million copper is sufficient to destroy a product, as Figure 8 shows.

Figure 8 Baby feeder teats, one degraded through high copper contamination.

Atmospheric ageing is different from shelf ageing in that it is characterized by the attack of ozone on the rubber. It is often called flex cracking or ozone cracking as detailed examinations of the types of cracking have shown the same pattern. It is interesting to note that this type of cracking occurs more readily at night than in the day as light-catalysed oxidation tends to obscure the ozone cracking. Following from this, ozone cracking will occur in black-filled materials, where light-catalysed oxidation is minimal. A classic picture in Figure 9 illustrates an aircraft tyre where the top (black) area shows the typical ozone-induced

cracks perpendicular to the stress in the side wall, whilst the white strip in the side wall, which must have had an identical life, shows the random crazing of oxidative degradation.

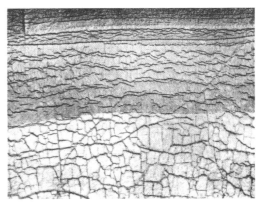

Figure 9 An aircraft white wall tyre showing crazing in the white region and ozone/flex cracking in the black region.

I have not discussed ageing by work, other than flex cracking, as in most exhibits this will not be valid. However, once movement is introduced into an elastomeric product, complications can occur — none of which is beneficial to the life of the product. The two dangers for any dynamic exhibit are first that any protective layer of oxidized rubber, antidegradent or wax is cracked, in which case oxidation will proceed very rapidly from the location of the crack, and second that a cycle of work on a thick piece of rubber can result in heat build-up within the rubber, which is eventually dissipated by catastrophic failure from within the bulk, as shown in Figure 10. Obviously this should be considered and investigated prior to initiating any "dynamic" exhibit. Indeed, in any such exhibit it may well be appropriate to replace the moving elastomeric components with

Figure 10 Heat build-up test pieces showing catastrophic internal failure.

modern replicas. For a much more exhaustive account of the ageing of rubber, please refer to the Malaysian Rubber Producers' Research Association publication *Natural Rubber, Science and Technology*, as detailed in the bibliography.

Conservation Options

After that brief glimpse of what is going on during the life or storage of an elastomeric product, consider now what can be done to prolong its display life. In truth, options are restricted to adding protective agents, coating the product with an impermeable membrane or removing the cause of the trouble — oxygen and ozone. Assuming that the light is adjusted as indicated, the temperature kept low, and all unnecessary sources of stress removed, these actions still will not stop some of the sulphur chemistry from continuing. But, as pointed out earlier, the sulphur chemistry will not, by itself, harm the exhibit for several centuries.

There have been well over 1,000 patents issued concerning protective agents for rubber vulcanizates — antioxidants and antiozonants — but there are relatively few on the market. The situation is complicated by the many trade names used, but for chemically different materials, the number is probably no more than 100. Because of the cost of introducing new chemicals and testing against various consumer regulations, it is not likely that any new wonder material will be produced. Current efforts are aimed at meeting market requirements through blends of chemicals, but remember, "market" requirements are not the same as a museum's!

Essentially the antidegradents in use today can be divided into two types, those derived from aromatic amines and those from hindered phenols. There are a few others such as phosphites, used with phenols in the plastics area as there is a synergistic effect, and mercaptobenzimidazole (MBI), which is effective against metal catalysis. Again, this is used in conjunction with a conventional antidegradent.

For simplicity, trade names will be used in this section. These are easier than many of the chemical names that take a line or two of print, but have the disadvantage that one chemical

can have half-a-dozen trade names. The ones I shall use are those familiar to me in the U.K., but in books, such as the BRMA toxicity guide to rubber chemicals listed in the bibliography, they can be related to their equivalents from other manufacturing sources.

The main difference between the amines and phenols is that the former stain to a lesser or greater extent and the latter do not — again within limits (see Table III).

Table III
Amine and Pherol Antidegradents for Rubber

The amines consist of four basic categories:

keto-amine condensates	good antioxidants	BLE25
quinolines	good antioxidants poor ozone resistance	Flectol H
substituted diphenylamines	good antioxidants some ozone resistance	DDA Octamine
substituted p-phenylenediamines	good antioxidants good antiozonants	IPPD Wingstay 100

The phenols can be divided into four categories:

mono-phenols	moderate antioxidants least staining	Ionol/BHT
polyhydroxyphenols	moderate antioxidants relatively non-staining	Wingstay L
bis phenols	good antioxidants possible staining	2246
thiobis phenols	good antioxidants weak antiozonants slight staining	Santowhite crystals

---

If the intention is to add one of these materials to a vulcanizate then there is little option other than to dissolve the chemical in a suitable solvent, immerse the vulcanizate and wait for diffusion to take place. As long ago as 1931 this was proposed as a method of giving protection to objects made without added antidegradents, but it never found commercial favour and, although I have seen no experimental ageing results based on this method, I am not surprised. The usual idea is to use a solvent for the antidegradent that will swell the rubber surface and allow diffusion of the antidegradent into the bulk of the rubber. This may be acceptable for a new vulcanizate, but if the object is not vulcanized, or is degraded so that the surface is structurally weak, it will either dissolve or swell to such an extent that the surface will be severely damaged. The rates of diffusion of antidegradents are quite slow — this is essential to their operation — so they will also take a long time to diffuse into the rubber and, on this time scale, much damage could be done to the network, particularly since the solvent will be extracting whatever it can from the vulcanizate whilst the antidegradent is diffusing in. If this method is used for long-term protection, then a non-solvent for the rubber should be used, methanol perhaps, as the antidegradent will still diffuse into the rubber, but there will be less extraction from the bulk of existing chemicals. There will, of course, still be dissolution of any soluble layer and, if there is a stable surface skin already, either of oxidized rubber or insoluble oxidized antidegradent residues, this may be impervious to the antidegradent being added!

If the choice is not to diffuse protective chemicals into the unprotected rubber, there is still the option of adding a protective surface coating, but before considering the various treatments that are available, one point must be made. Antidegradents can be considered to operate by physical (barrier) means, chemical reactions, or both. It is crucially important to understand that the different types of antidegradents work in different ways and thus give visually different surface finishes.

The p-phenylenediamines (PPDs) function as both antiozonants and antioxidants and at least one of their modes of operation is to migrate or bloom to the surface of a product where they react with the oxygen and/or ozone to form a brittle skin, which increases in thickness until it presents an impermeable barrier to the gas. Any damage to the skin, such as by cracking, is repaired by further blooming. There are many different PPDs and one of the main reasons for selecting a particular one is its solubility in the polymer system being protected. This affects the rate of blooming, which is crucial to long-term protection. PPDs oxidize to blue/purple/black materials and readily stain; this causes no problems with a black-filled material that is not in contact with a light coloured one, but obviously would be catastrophic for, say, a white thread in underwear. A surface skin can

be built up by topical application, provided the limitations of cracking, repair and surface finish are appreciated.

The phenolic antidegradents are *not* considered antiozonants, only antioxidants. When oxygen attacks a rubber molecule various chain reactions occur, which result in, among other things, polymer chain breakage as well as the insertion of further crosslinks. The phenols offer an alternate path in the chain reaction sequence, which stops the chain breakage from progressing. They do not stop chain reactions from starting, so their effect is, at best, to slow down the oxidative breakdown by perhaps five times. They do not form a protective skin if oxidized on the rubber surface and they need to be intimately dispersed/dissolved in the rubber to function.

Any physical barrier will stop or reduce oxygen/ozone diffusion into the rubber and might or might not crack depending on its brittleness. Again, its capability to self-heal will depend on whether it can migrate from the bulk or whether it is an added surface layer.

There is also the problem of light coloured articles and UV catalysed oxidation. As with plastics, UV stabilizers can be added to the bulk product or in a surface finish. As mentioned, light by itself does not degrade rubber, it catalyses oxidative degradation.

Finally, there is the "tart-up" factor. Treatment with a wax, polish or silicone oil can make a rough degraded surface look beautiful just by reducing the light scattering. The coating material will also have some barrier effect and so might prolong the life a little, but there will be no great long-lasting effect.

There is one word of warning about any topical application; as mentioned earlier, any surface disruption by solvent swelling/drying will potentially be disruptive and could do more harm than good. If the product is black and protected with PPDs (i.e., post early 1930s) or non-black and made after the mid 1950s, thus probably containing phenolic antioxidants, any protective layer could be washed away by a solvent and this would not be a good idea. If the intention is to apply any such application, it should be the mildest water-based emulsion or a relatively dry spray of a solvent-based system.

Another well-established barrier technique is the coating of the product with an oil lacquer that is then vulcanized. The procedure is described in detail by Gottlob, and Figure 11 shows rubber shoes over 70 years old that were given this finish and that are immaculate today; they were stored underwater, which may be relevant. The electron micrograph illustrated in Figure 12 clearly shows the layer of lacquer on the surface (running vertically slightly left of centre) and, as this layer is over 70 years old

Figure 11 Rubber overshoes recovered from a ship sunk some 70 years ago.

90211 30KV 50U

Figure 12 Scanning electron micrograph of cross-section through the rubber layer of the overshoe showing the lacquer as a smooth film about 15 μm thick running vertically just left of centre.

and still perfect, its projected life in the same environment must run to many hundreds of years.

It is obvious that none of these methods meets the conservator's ideal of doing nothing irrecoverable to the samples, but in the chemistry area at least, there are few options. Indeed, if the sample is light-coloured and thin, the additional strengthening supplied by a vulcanized coating might be a considerable advantage. After all, old Master works are revarnished, why not old elastomers?

Since the degradation to be prevented is caused by oxygen, and to a lesser extent by ozone, the obvious answer must be to prevent these gases from reaching the elastomer. In the absence of a barrier layer the exhibit must be in an enclosed vessel that can either be evacuated or filled with an inert gas. Evacuation is not to be encouraged because of both the potential danger should the case implode and the possibility of chemicals being volatilized from the rubber and condensing on the glass. Nitrogen is cheap and easy to acquire, and a low pressure gauge, showing that the pressure is one or two psi above atmospheric pressure, will give an easy check on leaks.

The shoes discussed earlier are by no means the only case of rubber being recovered from underwater. The tyre and inner tube of a Wellington bomber lost during the Second World War in a Scottish loch were recovered and the tube inflated with no problems. Similarly, a seal from a hatch of the first British submarine *Holland 1*, lost during trials in 1901, was found to be in perfect condition under a layer of surface oxidation. The oldest industrial sample I have ever examined was a sewer seal, installed in 1861 and removed during the replacement of rusted iron pipework in 1963. The sewer is illustrated in Figure 13, with the seal just visible under the rubble as a gentle arc in the foreground. In spite of the distinctly hostile environment it had been in, and the surface loss through abrasion, it was still a good seal and would have lasted many more years if only the pipework had lasted. Storage under cold water might be a viable preservation option although I have never seen it suggested as a deliberate ploy.

The one essential point is that whatever mode of preservation is attempted, the object should be mounted as it is intended to be displayed, as soon as possible after the treatment or even before, and then not touched, flexed or otherwise distorted. Obviously any mounting should be as stress-free as possible.

Conclusion

In summary, therefore, the only real danger to elastomeric artefacts displayed in museums is oxygen, although light, heat and ozone might have a part to play in some environments.

Figure 13 An 1861 sewer with functional rubber seal arcing across the foreground.

There is no wonder chemical that will prevent oxidation — nor is there even one that could be universally recommended for all elastomers —nor is there ever likely to be.

The best that phenolic antioxidants can do is slow down oxidative damage by a factor of about five. What this means depends on the individual article and its initial life expectancy.

Black products of a reasonable thickness (i.e., >5 mm) should cause no problems over many decades and probably centuries, although the surface may appear to deteriorate marginally. There might be a benefit from coating these products with a mix of wax and an amine antioxidant.

Light-coloured or non-vulcanized articles are at great risk and should be barrier protected. This must be the best option for long-term protection, and the best barrier is a sealed case and an inert atmosphere. If the storage temperature can be reduced to 2°C to 5°C, this could be an added advantage.

Acknowledgement

The author thanks the Board of the Malaysian Rubber Producers' Research Association for permission to attend *Symposium '91* and to publish this paper.

Figure 7 first appeared in *Revue Générale du Caoutchouc*, 31, 1954: 479 and is reproduced with permission of that journal.

Figure 9 first appeared in *Transactions Institution of the Rubber Industry*, 21, 1945: 49 and is reproduced with permission of the Plastics and Rubber Institute.

Résumé

Le caoutchouc : son histoire, sa composition et ses perspectives de conservation

Quiconque vit dans ce monde dit « moderne » connaît fort bien le caoutchouc et ses propriétés. Et c'est sans doute justement parce que cette matière nous est si familière que nous l'abordons, sinon avec un certain mépris, du moins avec une certaine indifférence, malgré la place qu'elle occupe désormais dans notre civilisation. Le terme « caoutchouc » désigne tout polymère qui possède ou semble posséder de l'élasticité, et il existe aujourd'hui nombre de polymères d'origine naturelle ou synthétique qui répondent à cette définition. Or, l'élastomère peut très bien constituer moins de 50 % de la masse totale d'un produit dit « de caoutchouc », puisque plusieurs substances chimiques, choisies parmi des centaines, peuvent avoir été ajoutées pour lui donner une forme utilisable.

La présente communication ne vise nullement à fournir une analyse scientifique détaillée de la préparation des produits de caoutchouc. Il n'en demeure toutefois pas moins que, avant d'amorcer tout travail de restauration d'un objet de musée, les spécialistes de ce domaine devront absolument connaître les matériaux qui le composent et être bien conscients du fait qu'ils risquent, s'ils n'appliquent pas le traitement approprié, de lui faire plus de mal que de bien. Aussi tenterons-nous de présenter un historique des élastomères qui met tout particulièrement l'accent sur certaines découvertes du XXe siècle qui permettront aux spécialistes de la conservation de mieux classifier, voire de dater, les produits élastomères. Au-delà de cet objectif, nous décrirons brièvement certaines des méthodes simples qui peuvent être utilisées pour analyser ces produits.

Il arrive souvent que la surface d'un produit élastomère en vienne à présenter des changements qui, quoique déplaisants sur le plan visuel, ne sont pas toujours le présage d'une dégradation de la surface; certains de ces changements sont même voulus, pour permettre au produit de durer plus longtemps. Nous passerons en revue les causes et les effets éventuels de tels changements de surface, tout en fournissant des techniques qui serviront à les distinguer entre eux.

Si l'on connaît bien les matériaux qui composent un objet de musée et que l'on peut, d'après l'état de sa surface, déterminer ce qui lui est arrivé, il sera d'autant plus facile de définir les mesures à prendre pour optimaliser sa vie utile d'exposition. Il n'est pas de solution qui puisse s'appliquer à tous les élastomères et à leurs produits, mais on retiendra qu'ils se dégradent le plus souvent sous l'action de toute une série de facteurs courants (l'oxygène, l'ozone, la chaleur, la lumière , le travail mécanique, les métaux oxydants, les bactéries et même, la « chimie », ce mot redoutable), qui ont souvent un effet synergique. Aussi tenterons-nous, dans le cadre de la présente communication, de nous frayer un chemin à travers ce véritable « champ de mines », et d'élaborer une méthode qui permettra de choisir, pour chacun des divers genres d'élastomères exposés, la technique de restauration qui convient le mieux.

Bibliography

History of the Rubber Industry, eds. P. Schidrowitz and T.R. Dawson (Cambridge, U.K.: W. Heffer and sons, 1952).

Hancock, T., *The Origin and Progress of the CAOUTCHOUC, or India-rubber Manufacture in England*, eds. Longman, Brown, Green (London: Longmans and Roberts, 1857).

Gottlob's Technology of Rubber 1925, Eng. Trans., J.L. Rosenbaum (London: Maclaren and sons, 1927).

Wolf, H. and R. Wolf, *Rubber, a Story of Glory and Greed* (New York: Covici and Friede, 1936).

Chemistry and Technology of Rubber, ed. C.C. Davis (New York: Reinhold Publishing Corp., 1937).

Buist, J.M., *Ageing and Weathering of Rubber* (Cambridge, U.K.: W. Heffer and sons, 1956).

Cook, J.G., *Rubber* (London: Frederick Muller, 1963).

Wake, W.C., B.K. Tidd and M.J.R. Loadman, *Analysis of Rubber and Rubber-like Materials* (London: Applied Science, 1983).

Natural Rubber Science and Technology, ed. A.D. Roberts (Oxford: Oxford University Press, 1988).

Toxicity and Safe Handling of Rubber Chemicals (Birmingham: British Rubber Manufacturers Association, 1990).

Appendix

Natural Rubber: History of Its Industrial Development to the 20th Century

	1st Millenium B.C.	Mexico	Ball courts/figurines holding balls.
Aztecs Mayas	6th Cent. & possibly earlier.	South America	Balls, dipped feet -> shoes, coated fabrics. Pictures copied in National Museum, Mexico.
	—> 10th Cent.	SW US	Ball courts and ball games. Objects in Peabody Museum, Harvard University.
Columbus	1493	Haiti	First European recorded to have seen rubber balls and returned some to Europe.
Torquemada	1615	Mexico	Taught Indians how to waterproof cloth and make dipped goods.
Charles de la Condamine	1735 to 1740	South America	In the Andes, described how Indians "milked" trees for liquid to waterproof fabrics. The Indians called the tree "HEVA" and the gum from the liquid "CAHUTSCHU." de la Condamine christened the "milk" "LATEX."
Fresneau	1743 to 1746	French Guiana	Realized the potential of the material and infected France with enthusiasm for rubber research. The problem was that latex could not be shipped to Europe without 'going bad' and solidifying. Tree was *Hevea braziliensis*.
Herrisant/ Macquer	1761	France	Found dry rubber would dissolve in turpentine but the resulting dried film was sticky and soft.
Macquer	1768	France	Replaced turps with ether and cast strong films that were not sticky.
	1769	France	Made riding boots for Frederick the Great by multiple dipping process.
Priestly (of oxygen fame)	1770	UK	Noted that an artist's shop in London sold a half inch cube of material for erasing pencil marks for three shillings. He called it "INDIA RUBBER" having found from whence it came.
Roberts/ Dight	1790	UK	First patent referring to rubber — rubber solution for treating canvas before oil painting.
Hummel	1813	US	Gum elastic varnish — first US patent that mentions rubber.

Thomas Hancock	1819	UK	First saw rubber.
	1820	UK	First patent for dry rubber; cut strips for elasticating clothes, braces, etc.
	1820	UK	Invented his "pickling" machine, which enabled dry rubber to be worked into a "dough."
	1820	US	Dipped shoes appeared in the US, made in South America, exported to Paris — gilded, "fashioned" and exported back to America.
	by 1823	US	Direct imports from Brazil.
Charles Goodyear	1820	US	Born.
Macintosh	1823	UK	Realized that if fabric coated with rubber solution then had another layer of fabric applied to rubber, the three-layer sandwich was waterproof and not sticky —"MACINTOSH."
	1825	UK	Pitch/rubber solution —> sheets for coating ship bottoms, etc.
Faraday	1826	UK	Established empirical formula as C_5H_8.
	1825 to 1830	UK	Dozens of uses.
	by 1830	US	Over 500,000 pairs of rubber overshoes had been imported.
Chaffee	1831	US	Rubber/turps/lampblack paint to waterproof leather.
	1832	US	Roxbury India Rubber Co. founded (first US rubber company).
	1834 to 1836	US	Invented the two-roll, two-speed mill and then enabled it to be heated. Still the standard mill of today.
Hancock/ Macintosh	1834	UK	Formed Chas. Macintosh and Co.
Chaffee	1835	US	Invented the three-roll mill for "calendering," which is still the basic procedure today.
Goodyear	1834 to 1835	US	Became intrigued by rubber — some say obsessed.

Hancock	1837	UK	Invented the spreader, the standard coating machine of today.
	by 1837	US	Economic crisis. Rubber "bubble" burst.
	1839	US	Existing rubber industry in the US finished but 500,000 non-vulcanized shoes per annum still coming from Brazil.

But in the same year:

Goodyear	1839	US	Left a mix of rubber, sulphur and white lead on a hot stove and the resulting material was "CURED" of all its defects. No longer softened on heating/hardened on cooling and lost its stickiness.
	1840	US	First commercial vulcanized material — rubber thread for "shirred" cloth.
Goodyear	1843	US	First application for US vulcanization patent.
Hancock	1842 to 1843	UK	Identified sulphur in a piece of Goodyear's cured rubber. Could not duplicate "CURE" as did not know about white lead, but effectuated cure with rubber/molten sulphur.
	1843	UK	Produced "Hard rubber" (Ebonite) with long treatment of rubber with molten sulphur.
	1843	UK	In November Hancock obtained UK prov. patent.
Goodyear	1844	UK	In February UK patent application refused.
Parkes	1846	UK	"Cold cure" process discovered (sulphur chloride).
Thompson	1845	UK	Patented the pneumatic tyre but no vehicles suitable to make it a commercial success!
	1851	US	Vulcanized rubber shoes being manufactured at a rate of over 5 million pairs per annum.

But in the UK there was more interest in vulcanized "Macintosh" material:

Hancock	1857	UK	Published his "Personal Narrative."
Williams	1860	UK	Decomposed natural rubber and isolated isoprene (C_5H_8).

Thompson	1861	UK	First commercial solid vulcanized tyres.
	1861	?	"Hard rubber" first called Ebonite.
Murphy	1870	US	Recognized "oxidation" as cause of deterioration in rubber.
Collins	1872	UK	Commissioned to report on Rubber in Brazil.
Wickham	1873	Brazil	Commissioned by Kew to collect seeds of *Hevea braziliensis*.
	1875	Brazil	Dispatched 70,000 seeds to Kew; 2,397 germinated.
	1876	Singapore	50 seedlings arrived. Died due to neglect.
Cross?	1877	Singapore	22 seedlings arrived and survived. Basis of virtually all Asian trees today.
Bouchardat	1879	France	Re-polymerized isoprene to "rubber."
Daimler/ Benz	1885	Germany	Invented the motor car.
Ridley	1888	Singapore	Took over Botanic Gardens. Began a one-man crusade to develop plantations.
Dunlop	1888	UK	"Reinvented" the first pneumatic tyre but now bicycles and vehicles available to use it.
Bartlett/ Welch	1890	UK	Developed tyre rim designs essentially similar to those in use today.
	1899		First plantation rubber shipped from Sri Lanka.
	1900		World production of NR approaches 50,000 tons.
Kronstein	1902	Germany	Polymerized styrene.
Oenslager	1906	US	First chemical to "accelerate" vulcanization (Aniline) then diphenylthiourea (DPU).
Lebedev	1910	USSR	Polymerized 1,3-butadiene to give a rubbery material.
	1910		Wild rubber peaks at about 90,000 tons per annum. Plantation rubber (Malaysia/Sri Lanka) reaches 10,000 tons.

Ostromislenski	1915	USSR	First organic vulcanization systems without sulphur: nitrobenzene and peroxides.
			About this time the importance of zinc oxide in accelerated cures was appreciated.
Kratz	1920		Diphenylguanidine (DPG).
	1920		World production of NR 350,000 tons.
Bruni	1921	Italy	Mercaptobenzothiazole (MBT)
Bedford	1921	US	independently.
Lorentz	1922	US	Thiurams.
Caldwell	1922	US	Xanthates.
Bruni	1923	Italy	Zinc dithiocarbamates.
Russell	1923	US	Patented organic fatty acid/zinc oxide use in vulcanization.
	1924	Germany	Fossilized rubber 60 million years old found.
	1925	Germany	Serious work began on the synthesis of Synthetic polybutadiene (Buna).
	1925		First commercial antioxidants (amines) introduced. They were staining.
Rosenbaum	1926	US	"Synthetic rubber is dead."
Patrick	1930	US	"Thiokol" — first commercial synthetic rubber. Note that this is not a sulphur cure — just metal oxides and possibly quinones.
Semon	1930	US	Suggested diffusion after vulcanization of protective agents into rubbers.
	1930		World production of NR 850,000 tons.
Tschunker	1930	Germany	Buna N and Buna NN discovered (nitrile rubbers of 25% ACN and 35% ACN).
	1930s		Introduction of amine derivative antioxidants (staining).
du Pont	1931	US	Duprene. Became polychloroprene (Neoprene).
IG Farben	1932	Germany	Sulphenamides — adducts of MBT with amines.
	1932	USSR	Russia manufactured SKA — followed by SKB (polybutadiene rubbers).

Tschunker	1933 to 1934	Germany	Buna S patented and produced (Styrene butadiene copolymer).
	1935	USSR	Sovprene; equivalent to Neoprene.
Thomas	1937	US	Butyl rubber.
Union Carbide/ Goodrich	1939	US	First use of plasticized PVC as cable sheath.
	1939 to 1941	US	Nitrile rubber produced.
	1940		World production of NR 1.5 million tons. World production of Synthetic Rubber (SR) 100,000 tons.
	1940	USSR	SKI — polymerized isoprene (synthetic "NR").
	1943	US	GR-S production started (now known as SBR) Government rubber-styrene —> styrene butadiene rubber (similar to Buna S).
Pintin	1943	Germany	First patent relating to urethane rubbers.
Dow Corning/ General Electric	1945	US	Silicone rubber. Again not normally a sulphur cure, peroxides used.
	1950s		Introduction of Phenolic antioxidants (non staining).
			Last wild rubber exported from Brazil.
Goodrich	1954	US	Announced high cis synthetic "NR."
	1954	US	Introduction of substituted para-phenylenediamine antiozonants.
Firestone	1955	US	Low cis synthetic "NR."
du Pont	1958	US	Fluoroelastomers.
	1960		World production crossover point. Both NR & SR about 2 million tons.
MRPRA	1970	UK	Urethane crosslinking of NR.
	1990		World production of NR 5 million tons. World production of SR 10 million tons.
	1990		Perhaps 5 billion *Hevea braziliensis* trees worldwide.

Ardil: The Disappearing Fibre?

Mary M. Brooks

York Castle Museum
York, Yorkshire
United Kingdom

Abstract

Ardil is a regenerated protein fibre produced commercially for clothing and domestic furnishings by Imperial Chemical Industries between 1951 and 1957. This paper examines the development, characteristics, manufacturing methods and marketing of Ardil. Few examples of Ardil are known, so this paper represents current work toward identifying textiles containing Ardil and makes recommendations for their conservation. Ardil represents a particular challenge to both the conservator and the curator and highlights the importance of researching, identifying and recording manufactured fibres.

Introduction

Ardil is a relatively little-known regenerated protein fibre, which had a short but intriguing life as a "wonder fabric," manufactured by Imperial Chemical Industries (ICI) after the Second World War. So far, few named examples have been identified in British collections. This may indicate the nature of the long-term stability of the fibre or problems in distinguishing Ardil from other fibres and blends unless it is trade-marked.

Development of Ardil

The development and eventual failure of Ardil as a technologically and economically viable fibre involved a complex mix of interacting factors. There was great interest in developing new regenerated and synthetic fibres in the early 20th century. The acetates using cellulose pulps were well established by the late 1920s. Truly synthetic fibres came a little later. Du Pont developed nylon in the U.S. and in 1939 granted ICI a production licence. There was a real need for suitable fibres and textiles to satisfy both a growing world market and specific military requirements.*

However, the cellulose-based fibres did not yield fabrics that felt warm to wear and there was much competition to create an artificial wool-like fibre using a protein source. In order to form a fibre, a polymer must have large molecules that are capable of crystallizing, achieving a reasonable degree of orientation and having a high degree of polarity to give intermolecular cohesion. Possible alternative fibre sources included casein, a milk-rerived product, waste leather and fish protein. Casein-based fibres were developed under trade names, such as Lanitol (Italy), Fibrolane (Britain) and

---

* In 1942, the Ministry of Economic Warfare in London was urgently questioning British legations in Berne and Stockholm regarding the Axis powers textile supplies: "What is the output by Solanum GmbH of cellulose pulp from potato tops and other new forms of cellulose? ... What is the extent of fibre production by Germany and Italy respectively from Broom plant (Ginstra)?... Your answers to all the above may have an important bearing in enemy supply position."[1]

Aralac (U.S.) and companies in both Europe and America were experimenting with vegetable protein sources. Interest and development was such that in 1946 the American Society for Testing Materials proposed that all regenerated protein-based fibres derived from sources, such as casein, peanuts, soya beans or other vegetable proteins, should be described using the generic term "azlon."

It was against this background that W.S. Astbury of Leeds University and A.C. Chibnall and K. Bailey of Imperial College, London, approached ICI with the results of their experiments in producing fibres from vegetable protein. Their initial research used protein extracted from hemp,[2] but by 1936 they had switched to peanuts, the nut of a sub-tropical plant *Arachis hypogae L.*, as the protein source. Peanuts contain the proteins arachin and conarachin. Hydrolysis of the amino acids in these proteins has shown them to be very similar to those in wool. Peanuts or groundnuts were grown widely throughout the British Empire as well as in America, China and Borneo. However, ICI was careful to stress that Ardil had no connection with the great groundnut scheme in Africa, which collapsed in scandal in the early 1950s. Nevertheless, peanuts were an important crop, with a yield of around eight million tons per annum during the 1930s.

Astbury, Bailey and Chibnall refined their research and proposed a process for producing a fibre from denatured vegetable protein dissolved in urea.[3] Their patent described it as "the production of artificial filaments, threads, films, and the like from solutions of denatured or degenerate or coagulated protein material by extruding such solutions into a diluent or other regenerating medium."[4] They approached ICI and reached an agreement whereby the company took over development.[5] The project was based at the ICI research plant in Ardeer, Scotland — hence the name Ardil was registered as the trade mark. Of the ICI divisions, the Scottish plant had the most experience of fibre spinning and weaving. ICI researchers developed practical processes for production that moved away from the original theoretical propositions and filed their own patents.[6]

It is worth noting here that Courtaulds were also working on regenerated protein fibres. They developed Fibrolane A, BC and BX, made from casein, and Fibrolane C, made from peanut protein.[7] The relationship between the two industrial giants was a complex mix of competition and integration. Courtaulds had vast experience in spinning and weaving silk and regenerated viscose mourning crepes, but relied on chemicals produced by ICI. Conversely, ICI had little knowledge of fabric manufacture or consumer-led marketing, but dominated the chemicals field. This relationship was formalized in a 1928 agreement by which Courtaulds agreed to abstain from chemical manufacture, taking all their supplies from ICI, whilst ICI promised to refrain from artificial "silk" fibre production. The respective textile technology skills of these two companies was to be crucial in deciding the fortunes of Ardil.

Under wartime production pressure, ICI and Courtaulds joined together in 1940 to form a company named British Nylon Spinners specifically set up to produce nylon for parachutes. Despite this, Courtaulds persisted in regarding nylon as a competitor to its traditional interests in artificial "silks," the viscose rayons based on cellulose. In fact, they campaigned to have nylon classified as a new type of rayon. In keeping with this conservative attitude, Courtaulds refused to join ICI in a proposed post-war joint venture to develop Ardil.[8] In 1943, the earlier agreement between ICI and Courtaulds lapsed. ICI felt free to move into the field of fibre production, but, significantly, they lacked Courtaulds's expertise in fibre technology and consumer marketing.

ICI felt sufficiently confident to announce the creation of Ardil just before the war. An Ardil production plan was launched in 1938, but suspended due to the outbreak of hostilities. Sufficient fibre was produced to make a few Ardil/wool blend suits; some of these were apparently still being worn in 1951 when full-scale production commenced.[9] Post-war, ICI urgently needed to diversify. In particular, they needed to find an alternative production activity for their Scottish Explosives Division. Ardil was selected as an ideal new product. The pilot plant was established in 1946 although production was initially limited to half a ton a week. In July 1947, ICI proposed a capital expenditure of 2.1 million pounds for Ardil with an expected return of 7% when the main plant was operating at half capacity.[10] Building of the manufacturing plant at Dumfries, Scotland, commenced in 1948 with an initial capacity of 22 million pounds per year although production was well below this amount.

Simultaneously with this development, Unilever, a company with various interests including margarines, was building a plant at Bromborough, Merseyside, to handle the raw peanut meal. Unfortunately, disputes with Unilever over processing charges caused delays. The major problem however was an unexpected shortfall in world peanut production associated with the failure of the East African groundnut scheme. Ardil manufacture commenced in 1951 — again, most unfortunately, coinciding with a depression in the textile trade. Of the 316 firms who had indicated interest in 1947, only 76 placed small trial orders in 1951. The auguries were not good.

Technical difficulties, which will be discussed more fully later, meant that Ardil was best used as a blend with wool, cotton or other manufactured fibres. This resulted in marketing problems as such blends could not be marketed as 100% pure single fibre products and therefore required special promotion to consumers. Despite the support of the Bradford Dyer's Association and other wool and cotton manufacturers who were prepared to invest in Ardil, some Divisions of ICI were always skeptical. The Dyestuffs Division, which had the most experience of the textile market, was never prepared to declare confidence in the fibre. In the end, internal dissension and technical problems meant that economic realities conquered.

If Ardil was to be attractive as a bulking agent for the more expensive natural fibres, it had to be cheap. Such cheapness could only be achieved when production levels were high enough to realize economies of scale and while costs were high it was hard to build up sales volume. Over the five years of production,

sales never rose above 2.6 million pounds. In 1955, producing Ardil cost 47 old pence a pound (approx. 20 new pence, or 40¢ Can.) as opposed to 24 old pence a pound (approx. 10 new pence, or 20¢ Can.) for viscose staple fibre despite the fact that the raw material was a comparable price.[11] A drop in wool prices further reduced the competitive advantage of Ardil as a bulking fibre.

Caught in this vicious circle, Ardil never gained a firm foothold in the market. However, synthetic fibres overall had made a significant impact. ICI set up Group F to develop their manufactured fibres including Terylene and Ardil in 1956 and were still expressing cautious optimism regarding the future of Ardil: "Sales of Ardil were disappointing ... but work is in hand to evaluate an Ardil fibre with improved properties."[12] This improvement never materialized, and in 1957 ICI took the decision to cut their losses, which had been running at 3.7 million pounds and Ardil production ceased. It had an effective commercial life of only six years.

Manufacturing Methods: Successes and Problems

The basic principle of manufacturing was to extract the proteins, arachin and conarachin, from the peanut and treat them so that they formed a solution from which a fibre could be spun.

The peanuts, whose fruits grow underground, were hand pulled, shelled and the reddish skin removed to prevent discolouration. For maximum protein yield, the nuts needed to be mature but ungerminated. The decorticated nut consists of 43% to 48% oil, 24% to 26% protein and 26% to 29% carbohydrate. After blanching, the nuts were ground to a meal and solvents used to extract the oil, which was a useful by-product used for salad oil or margarine.

Care was needed to select suitable solvents and to control temperature during this process. The oil-free meal contained about 40% to 49% protein. It was dissolved in dilute alkali and acidified with sulphur di-oxide to pH 4.5 to extract the protein. This process was carefully controlled to keep the colour as light as possible.*

The solid residue, mainly carbohydrate, was used as a base for cattle fodder. The precipitated protein was then washed and dried, giving a creamy powder known as "Ardein," which was almost pure arachin and conarachin. This was then dissolved in dilute caustic soda giving a viscose solution that was allowed to mature for 24 hours. This denaturation process allowed the folded long-chain molecules present in the soluble protein to open out into an extended form so giving better mechanical properties.

Once this process was completed, the solution was pumped through spinnerets into a coagulating bath of 2% sulphuric acid and 15% sodium sulphate to form the fibre. Urea or caustic soda solutions had been used in the earlier development stages. The tow fibre was then hardened by a formaldehyde treatment under acid conditions to improve insolubility. The chemistry of this process of forming molecular crosslinks was complex and not altogether understood.[14] Alternatively, improved wet strength could be achieved by acetylation or treatment with 0.3% glyoxal polymer. A natural crimp developed if the fibre was wetted, stretched and released. The fibre could be extruded in any diameter required. Although it could be produced as a continuous filament, it was often cut into staple lengths of between 1.3 cm to 20 cm depending on the application. It could then be spun using a woollen, worsted or cotton system.

Three types of Ardil were produced. Ardil B was pale cream and so could be easily dyed in

---

*Moncrieff details one example of this process as follows: "200 parts by weight of fat extracted peanut meal are stirred with 3500 parts water at 20°C for 10 minutes. Then 150 parts 1% to 2% caustic soda are added over a period of 20 minutes bringing the liquid to a pH of 8.0 to 8.5. Stirring is continued for one hour and the resulting solution is clarified. After clarification the solution is pH 8.3 and is claimed to have practically no colour. Next sulphur di-oxide gas is passed through the solution until the pH value is 4 to 5. This acidification results in a copious white precipitate, which allowed to settle, is centrifuged, washed and dried. The yield is 84 parts air-dry protein."[13]

light colours without bleaching. It was nearly neutral with not more than 0.3% acetic acid and a slightly higher moisture regain rating. Ardil F was a pale fawn colour and was used when dying darker colours. It contained 4% sulphuric acid and some formaldehyde. Ardil K was made in heavier deniers, but was otherwise similar to Ardil F. The range of deniers available corresponded with those of wool: ranging from fine grades to thicker deniers for carpeting.

Dyeing Ardil

Ardil dyed well both on its own and in blends. Mass-dyed Ardil was produced by introducing pigment into the fibre during manufacture, giving highly light and water fast colours. This was a cheaper dyeing process and 12 standard colours were available, chiefly for use in carpet yarns. Most wool dyes, such as acid and chrome dyes, as well as some direct and vat dyes, could be used successfully. Dyes sensitive to formaldehyde could not be used. The differential reactions of fibres to dyes meant that cross-dyeing of blends of Ardil with other fibres produced interesting ingrained speckled effects. Ardil could also be printed using traditional methods.

Fibre Properties

Physical Properties: Ardil had many of the characteristics associated with the natural protein fibres — warmth, softness, resilience and the ability to absorb moisture and generate heat when wet. It had a remarkable wool-like texture despite being less strong than wool. Although not thermoplastic, its good crease recovery and draping qualities were valuable in improving the performance of cellulose fabrics. Blended with synthetics, it improved wearing qualities through its ability to absorb moisture.

Key Characteristics

Colour: Probably as a result of some peanut skins remaining despite skinning and blanching, Ardil had a creamy yellow colour. Colour varied with Ardil F and Ardil K being darker than Ardil B. At one point, attempts were made to develop a peanut with a grey skin to reduce such colouration, but this was a long-term project and such peanuts were not used for production.

Elongation and Abrasion Resistance: Ardil had good elongation at 50% with good elastic recovery so it was hard to break the fibre. However, it had poor abrasion resistance unless blended with wool. A 50/50 Ardil/wool blend had improved resistance possibly due to lubrication of the wool by the Ardil fibre.

Behaviour with High Temperatures: Like wool, Ardil had low flammability and resisted high temperatures without softening or melting. It began to char at 250°C. Excessive dryness caused embrittlement, but if the fibre was returned to standard humidity and temperature, it regained flexibility. Contemporary technical information puts great stress on the low fire risk of Ardil, presumably reflecting problems encountered when working other highly flammable regenerated fibres. Extra fire cover was not required by insurance companies for factories processing Ardil.

Electric Properties: Ardil had a low dielectric rating and gave few static electric problems when processed at normal humidities.

Tensile Strength: This remained the great weakness of the fibre. The tensile strength of Ardil was calculated at about 8 kg/mm^2 to 10 kg/mm^2, which is lower than that of wool at 12 kg/mm^2 to 20 kg/mm^2. When wetted the fibre extends about 15% in length and about 5% in diameter, but on drying, returns to its original dimensions. Tensile strength was greatly reduced in the wet state, dropping from 1 g/denier when dry to 0.3 g/denier when wet. Proposals for chemical treatments to increase crosslinking and overcome this significant strength loss included stretching in a bath of mercuric acid and acetic acid, which had obvious safety problems.[14] Traill and Simpson showed that an increase of 50% in wet strength and 25% in dry strength was possible if the fibre was treated with basic chromium sulphate and formaldehyde after dyeing with acid or chrome dyes.[15]

Moisture Absorption: The moisture content was 14%. The moisture absorption and regain rates at standard conditions were similar to those of scoured wool. Comparative information is given in Table I.

Table I

Percentage Moisture Regain of Ardil in Comparison to Other Fibres at 65% RH and 20°C

Fibre	Moisture Regain (%)
Wool	15.0
Ardil B, neutralized/bleached	14.0 to 15.0
Casein fibre	13.0
Ardil F, Ardil K, mass-dyed, unneutralized	12.0 to 13.0
Viscose rayon	11.0
Vicara protein fibre	10.0
Cotton	7.5
Cellulose acetate	6.0
Nylon	4.5
Terylene polyester	0.4

Source: ICI Technical Bulletin GL. 1 "The Properties of Ardil Protein Fibre".

Felting and Shrinkage Behaviour Patterns: Due to the lack of any surface scales, Ardil did not felt, but felting could be induced. When blended with high grade wool, Ardil could accelerate felting shrinkage, possibly as a result of lubricating the wool fibres.

Behaviour under Ultraviolet Light: Ardil had high UV resistance. An Ardil/wool blended yarn exposed to UV light for 150 hours in a carbon arc fadeometer showed no significant strength reduction.[16]

Tolerance of Pests/Fungi: Unlike wool, Ardil was mothproof (a point that was made much of in advertisements) and was more resistant to mildew.

Comparison with Wool: Technical details, comparing the qualities of Ardil with wool, are given in Table II.

Chemical Properties

Ardil fibre is essentially made up of two proteins, arachin and conarachin. Chemical reaction with formaldehyde causes these to become insoluble in, and resistant to, the aqueous liquors used in textile processing. Ardil F and Ardil K and the mass-dyed fibres are acidic in

Table II
Technical Properties of Ardil

Properties	Ardil	Wool
Moisture regain at 65% RH & 20°C		
Types F & K	12%	16%
Type B	14%	16%
Tensile strength (kg/mm^2)	8 to 10	12 to 20
Tenacity (g/denier)		
conditioned	0.7 to 0.9	-
wet	0.4 to 0.6	-
Elongation at break (%)		
dry	40 to 60	30
wet	50 to 70	-
Heat of wetting (Cal./g.)	26.6	26.9
Torsional rigidity (dynes/cm^2)	1.2×10^{10}	1.3×10^{10}
Specific gravity	1.31	1.33
Young's modulus (g/denier % measured at 100 extension per minute)	0.14	0.20

Source: Anonymous untitled typescript, presumably ICI document, Whitworth Art Gallery, Manchester.

reaction and contain about 4% sulphuric acid. Ardil B differs in being nearly neutral with approximately 0.3% acetic acid.

Acid and Alkali Resistance: Ardil was highly resistant to acids and acid tendering. This enabled it to withstand many of the standard processes for textile production, which often involved acids. However, it had low resistance to alkalis. The fibre would swell making it sensitive to mechanical damage Unlike wool, however, Ardil does not require sulphur crosslinks for its structural stabilizing and therefore can resist chemical damage by alkalis. Normal vat dyeing could be carried out on Ardil/cellulose blends. This was an important factor as many of these fabrics were destined for use in women's and children's clothing and were often dyed.

Behaviour with Bleaches: Like wool, sodium hypochlorite and sodium chlorite could cause degradation in Ardil and hydrogen peroxide bleaching was preferred.

Behaviour with Solvents: Ardil is insoluble in the standard organic solvents. It may therefore be solvent cleaned, solvent selection depending on the behaviour of any blended fibre.

Ardil and Other Fibres

As a result of the poor tensile and wet strength, Ardil was almost always used in blends either as an economic bulking agent with such natural fibres as wool, or to improve the characteristics of cellulose and regenerated cellulose fibres. ICI recommended that it should not be used alone. The blended fabrics were designed to be suitable for a wide range of end uses from clothing to domestic furnishing fabrics. A ratio of 50% Ardil/50% merino wool was used for sweaters while 40% Ardil/60% viscose was used in carpeting. Ardil, viscose and nylon blends were used for hard-wearing, lightweight and cheaper suiting cloths. The Whitworth Art Gallery, Manchester holds a group of fabric samples from ICI in a wide range of blends and fabric types. These include mass-dyed grey Ardil/viscose/woolsuiting; Ardil/wool tweed; Ardil/viscose/nylon shirting; printed Ardil/Peruvian cotton dress fabric; Ardil/wool jersey knit; Ardil/viscose velour coating and Ardil/wool/viscose blanketing. Technical details of the yarns and weaves are given on the swatch cards.

An Ardil blended yarn may be used either as warp or weft. Amongst the Whitworth samples, shirting fabric Pattern 31 uses 30% Ardil B, 60% viscose and 10% nylon in both warp and weft. Other examples combine an Ardil blend with a pure fibre as the other yarn. Pattern 341, a lightweight printed fabric, combines a warp of 100% cotton with a weft composed of 33% Ardil and 67% Peru Tanguis cotton. A few swatches have differing blended yarns in the warp and weft. The velour coating sample, pattern No. 181, has a warp of 25% Ardil B with 75% viscose and a weft of 50% Ardil B with 50% viscose.

Due to the differential strengths of the various fibres, there were technical problems in preparing the fibres. It was important that a uniform blending was achieved to avoid problems and special techniques were required. In general,

Ardil and the complementary fibre(s) were blended together before carding. ICI published a range of technical information for the trade (see Appendix 1). Conventional processing machinery could be used avoiding the need to invest in an expensive new plant.

When blending with wool, Ardil needed particular care to prevent overstretching and breaking. Relaxation shrinkage was possible in Ardil/wool blends when wet. Altering the percentage of the blend allowed for the creation of fabrics with different qualities. Alone, Ardil would not permanent-pleat. However, when blended with a sufficiently high proportion of a natural fibre, the resulting fabric could be induced to carry a pleat. A 50/50 Ardil/wool blend gave a fabric that took a sharp crease but hung out well while 25% to 35%/65% to 75% Ardil/wool was softer and did not carry a crease well. Such blends were ideal in knits. Ardil was also used in hat felts. The British Hat and Allied Feltmakers Research Association recommended blends of Ardil and rabbit fur or Ardil and wool.

Lancashire cotton weavers were particularly interested in exploring blends to improve cotton's handle, crease resistance and drape. When working with cotton, it was recommended that Ardil, the weaker fibre, should be oiled.[14] Methods of dealing with Ardil/cotton mixes were extensively discussed by Dyke.[17] Ardil/cellulosic warps were sized either with sago or Cellofas B. In cotton blends, Ardil fibres showed a tendency to migrate to the surface during washing. This could be controlled by using a tightly spun yarn and problems were reduced with plain weaves.[18] These fabrics were used for nightwear, shirts, lightweight suits and dress fabrics.

Tertiary blends exploited the wool-like handle of Ardil whilst adding strength from the other fibres. Lightweight blends of Ardil/viscose and wool were used for velours, suitings and dress fabrics. Nylon was used to improve strength and abrasion resistance. Blankets were produced using a cotton or cotton/viscose warp with an Ardil/wool/viscose weft while carpeting could be produced using blends of Ardil, wool and viscose.

Fabric Care

ICI recommended that Ardil could be washed using normal domestic or commercial methods, the governing factor being the needs of the complementary fibre. They rather cautiously stated that, although Ardil/cotton blends could be washed as normal cotton, it was preferable that such blends should be "washed as for wool."[19] This presumably relates to possible increased loss of wet strength in a hotter washing process. Ironing temperatures were again governed by the requirements of the other fibres used in the blend.

As Ardil was stable in most organic solvents it could safely be commercially dry-cleaned.

Marketing Ardil

ICI launched Ardil with extensive marketing. The trade magazine *International Textiles, The British Export Journal of Textiles and Fashions* gave it wide coverage, reflecting the general sense of amazement at this new fibre: "Starting metaphorically with a bag of monkey nuts and an idea, British chemists of ICI have evolved a new synthetic fibre which, they claim, is wool-like, does not shrink and is not attacked by moths."[20]

In 1944, post-war shortages and technical problems were still holding up production and ICI was only able to promise that samples would shortly be ready for the trade. However, ICI held a major exhibition in London in 1946. As shown in Figure 1, the showcase factory in Dumfries was featured in an advertisement in the 1951 Scottish Festival of Britain publication.[21]

Manufacturers were courted. ICI staff lectured and published articles on the new fibre. For example, in 1952 F.M. Dyke from ICI addressed the Oldham branch of the Textile Institute and his lectures were subsequently published.[17] ICI went to considerable lengths to provide technical information to textile spinners and weavers. (Titles are listed in Appendix 1.) ICI proposed a wide range of end uses for Ardil, stressing the economic advantages of cheapness and price stability in comparison with pure natural fibres.

'ARDIL' PROTEIN FIBRE

This new ICI factory at Dumfries is now producing 'Ardil' protein fibre, and full production —at the rate of 22 million pounds per year—will be achieved by the end of 1951.

IMPERIAL CHEMICAL INDUSTRIES LIMITED
NOBEL DIVISION

Figure 1 ICI advertisement for Ardil featuring the showcase factory in Dumfries, Scotland.

Ardil was also promoted directly to the public. In the 1950s, advertisements appeared in women's magazines, such as *Good Housekeeping*. Ardil is described as "the man-made protein fibre — soft as cashmere, smooth as silk, warm and absorbent as wool. (It's moth resistant, too.) Blended with other fibres, it gives clothes the unmistakable touch of luxury at prices you can afford." A housewife of the 1950s is shown selecting clothes for her family — pyjamas for her son, dresses for her daughter and shirts for her husband. The copy encourages her purchases: "Happy families wear clothes that contain Ardil." Interestingly, she never seems to wear it herself.[22] A scarf made with Ardil, which is now in the Nottingham Museum of Costume and Textiles, may have been a promotional gift from ICI to troops in the Korean War.

There was considerable concern to make sure that consumers understood the new fibres and knew how to care for them. In 1956 the *News of the World, Household Guide and Almanac*

contained a useful section on the new synthetic fibres that aimed to do just this.[23] The new fibres are described as "Among the wonders of the post-war world." Ardil is included and praised as being wool-like whilst being cheaper and for improving the behaviour of cotton and viscose. The need for blending due to lack of strength is clearly stressed. Care advice includes a warning against shrinkage when washing wool/Ardil blends.

Examples of Ardil in U.K. Museum Collections

So far, few examples of Ardil have been located in U.K. museum collections.

The York Castle Museum Wallis archive consists of a donation of costume, spanning four generations of one family. It includes a nightdress belonging to Amy Wallis dating from the 1950s. Old-fashioned in style and similar to Viyella, a wool/cotton blend in handle and appearance, it was made by Potters (Museum number 431.78). As shown in Figure 2, the label indicates that the nightdress contains Ardil and that it is styled by Unique from Potter's Ardingle. The nightdress is in reasonable condition and has clearly undergone regular washing. Microscopic examination of the fibres showed cotton plus Ardil.

Figure 2 Label from nightdress of the 1950s, Wallis family archive, York Castle Museum (Museum number 431.78).

As previously mentioned, the Nottingham Museum of Costume and Textiles holds a scarf from the 1950s that is labelled "Nobel Division,

An Ardil Blend, ICI Ltd." (Museum number 1979, 609). The other fibre in the blend is not known. The scarf is woven with a crimson and green cross check and blue stripes with fringed ends. According to the donor, the scarf was supplied directly from ICI, but was not hard-wearing as it had an unfortunate tendency to dissolve in saliva.*

The largest collection of fibre samples, woven fabric swatches and technical literature from ICI, together with a bag of peanuts, is held by the Whitworth Art Gallery, Manchester. There are also tow samples, apparently of all three types of Ardil. With the exception of one swatch made by T. & J. Tinker Ltd. of Holmfirth, Huddersfield, all the fabrics are from ICI's Ardil Fibre Factory in Dumfries. The Science Museum, London, also holds some Ardil samples.

Identification of Ardil

Ardil is not easy to identify visually, particularly as it usually occurs as a blended yarn and may vary widely in appearance. This may help to explain why so few examples have been identified. It is important to sample both warp and weft in blends thought to contain Ardil as they may contain different fibres in different proportions. It is also necessary to identify the other fibres present.

Microscopic Analysis: On a microscopic level, the longitudinal appearance of Ardil is straight, uniform along the length and almost structureless although with some longitudinal striations. The edges are smooth. Liquid paraffin has been suggested as a suitable mounting medium. The cross-section is circular with some slight pitting, as shown in Figure 3.

---

* Scarf mid 1950s, 1105 mm x 216 mm. Label woven yellow on black, "Nobel Division, An Ardil Blend, ICI Ltd." A note from the donor, R.C.G. Williams, reads "Supplied direct from ICI Ltd. who developed the fibre type Ardil made from the protein part of peanuts. The fibre was made to augment the supply of wool and was of importance during the Korean War (1950 to 1953) when wool was in short supply. The fibre has a "wool-ile" (sic) handle but is not very hard wearing and so failed when wool became plentiful."

Figure 3 Ardil mounted in XAM, magnified 400 times.

Chemical and Physical Tests: When analysing blended fibres, it is necessary to use a scheme, such as that outlined by the Textile Institute to identify the various elements.[24] In this programme, the sample is tested using normal sodium hypochlorite and 0.5 normal sodium hydroxide to identify the presence of regenerated protein, wool or tussah silk. The presence of other fibres can also be established and suitable tests carried out. Other techniques are required to identify which protein fibre is presented.

Burn Test: This test will establish the presence of a protein fibre without specific identification. Ardil burns without forming a bead with a smell of burning feathers as do wool and other regenerated protein fibres.

Wet Strength: This test can be used to establish the presence of a regenerated protein fibre. A marked loss of strength when the fibre is wetted and then tested using a Strength Test machine indicates the presence of Ardil or another regenerated protein fibre.

Measurement of Fibre Density: This test will identify Ardil specifically. Moncrieff describes the method of establishing the specific gravity of textile fibres. A glass tube is filled with two liquids of contrasting density, which are allowed to diffuse into each other. The tube is then calibrated using fibres of known density before testing unknown fibres. Using this method, it is possible to distinguish Ardil with a specific gravity of 1.30 from wool (specific gravity 1.32) and casein (specific gravity

1.29).[24] An alternative method using a Tecam Density Gradient Column apparatus is set out by the Textile Institute.[24]

Infra-red Spectroscopy: Once a known standard has been established, Ardil can be recognized by the chemical constitution shown on the infra-red spectrum in comparison with the spectra of other known fibre samples. At present no such standard has been established. Infra-red spectroscopy showed a protein fibre, similar but not identical to silk.

Solubility Tests: Solubility tests can be used to distinguish Ardil from other protein fibres. In 80% sulphuric acid, Ardil is unchanged whereas wool and casein dissolve. Caustic soda 5% at boiling point can be used to distinguish between protein and regenerated protein fibres. Ardil will stay stable whereas wool dissolves and casein shrivels up. Ardil will dissolve when heated at 97°C in 18% solution of sodium hydroxide whereas other regenerated protein fibres remain stable.[25] The ability of Ardil to dissolve in a cold aqueous solution of sodium hypochlorite (3.5 g available chlorine/litre) is used to analyse percentages of component fibres present in blends.[26]

Stain Tests: Moncrieff reports that the regenerated protein fibres casein, Ardil, soybean and zein all give a yellow-orange colour with cold Shirlastain A stain.[7] Shirlastain A is used for the identification of non-thermoplastic fibres, such as cotton, wool and regenerated fibres. The presence of formaldehyde may affect the results of staining tests.

Tests for Formaldehyde: Ardil is strengthened with a crosslinking treatment using formaldehyde or glyoxal to modify the fibres so as to improve stability and to allow such standard textile processes as dyeing to be carried out. The presence of formaldehyde can be identified using the Chromotropic Acid Test.[24]

Implications for Conservation

Once the presence of Ardil has been established, the conservator should be able to make better informed decisions regarding the treatment of the textile.

Unfortunately, at the moment, there is insufficient evidence to establish a degradation pattern for Ardil. Once more textiles containing Ardil have been identified it will be possible to assess the behaviour of naturally aged examples. Tentative conservation recommendations can be developed based on documentary evidence. Experience in dealing with degraded wool fibres is also relevant. Full testing for fibre stability and dye fastness should precede any interventive treatment. The conservation requirements of other fibres and materials in the garment should also be considered.

Wet-cleaning should be approached with caution as Ardil never achieved good wet strength. It is possible that degradation could intensify this weakness. Relaxation shrinkage could occur, particularly in Ardil/wool blends. Little is known about the possible reaction of degraded Ardil with detergents or other wash bath additives. High alkalinity would be undesirable as the fibre becomes vulnerable to mechanical damage at a higher pH, and a non-ionic detergent with sodium carboxy methyl cellulose as an anti-soil redeposition agent would be preferable. The evidence from the donor of the Nottingham scarf that it dissolved in saliva would suggest that the fibre is not stable when exposed to certain enzymes.

Bleaching protein fibres is highly problematic and not recommended. Ardil was never stable in sodium hypochlorite or sodium chlorite.

When new, Ardil was stable in most organic solvents. Following testing, solvent cleaning may be acceptable. Suitable extraction facilities will be required to meet health and safety standards. It is not clear how the use of formaldehyde as an after-treatment will affect the long-term stability of Ardil. Neither is it clear whether textiles containing Ardil might be a potential risk to other vulnerable objects in a mixed media collection, particularly metals, pigments and paper, on account of organic acid vapours resulting from the formaldehyde treatment.[27] Isolating identified textiles and careful monitoring is recommended.

Conclusion

Until more textiles containing Ardil are discovered, it is difficult to assess the long-term stability and behaviour of the fibre. The author would appreciate receiving any information about such items. The speed with which both known examples and contemporary information about a recent commercially produced regenerated fibre have disappeared should alert both curators and conservators to the importance of acquiring suitable examples and recording information on modern fibres as fully as possible.

Acknowledgement

The author thanks The Conservation Unit, Museums & Galleries Commission for generous support and grant aid; Fiona Strodder, Castle Museum, Norwich; Michael Robertson, ICI Chemicals and Polymers Ltd.; Jeremy Farrell, Museum of Costume and Textiles, Nottingham; David Howell and Alain Colombini, Textile Conservation Studios, Hampton Court Palace for infra-red spectroscopy analysis; Jennifer Harris and Ann Tullo, Whitworth Art Gallery, Manchester; Sonia O'Connor, York Archaeological Trust; Helen Durrant and Josie Sheppard, York Castle Museum; and Mark Suggitt, Yorkshire and Humberside Museums Council. Photographs by Richard Stansfield, York Castle Museum, copyright City of York Leisure Services.

Source of Materials

Shirlastain A Stain is available from Shirley Developments Ltd., PO Box 61, 856 Wilmslow Road, Didsbury, Manchester M20 8SA England.

Appendix 1

Technical Bulletins

ICI published the following list of available and forthcoming Technical Bulletins on "Ardil — A New Staple Fibre for the Textile Industry," (ICI Fibres Division, Harrogate, no date, possibly 1949):

GL. 1 — The Properties of Ardil Protein Fibre
GL. 2 — The Construction and Finishing of Dimensionally Stable Ardil Fibre/Cellulosic Fabrics
WD. 1, 2, 3 & 4 — The Processing of $3\frac{1}{2}$ Denier and 5 Denier Ardil Protein Fibre on the Worsted System
WN. 1 — The Processing of Ardil Fibre on the Woolen System
CN. 1, 2, 3 & 4 — The Processing of 2, $3\frac{1}{2}$ and 5 Denier Ardil Protein Fibre on the Cotton Spinning System
WG. 1 — Sizing of Ardil Fibre/Cellulosic Warps
FF. — Ardil Fibre in Fur Felts
FW. 1 — Ardil Fibre in Wool Hat Felts
FG. 1 — The Scouring and Bleaching of Yarns and Fabrics Containing Ardil Protein Fibre
FG. 2 — The Application of Crease Resistant Resins to Blends Containing Ardil Fibre and Viscose
FG. 3 — The Finishing of Ardil/Cotton Blended Fabrics
AN. 1 — The Quantitative Analysis of Ardil Fibre/Nylon and Ardil Fibre/Cotton Blends
AN. 2 — The Quantitative Analysis of Ardil Fibre/Nylon and Ardil Fibre/Viscose/Nylon Blends
AN. 3 — The Quantitative Analysis of Ardil Fibre/Wool and Ardil Fibre/Viscose/Wool Blends
Forthcoming
    — The Dyeing of Ardil Protein Fibre "B", "F" and "K" and Ardil Fibre Unions
    — The Printing of Ardil Fibre Unions
    — The Application of Caledon Dyestuffs to Ardil Fibre "B"/Cellulosic Fibre Blends

Résumé

L'Ardil, la fibre qui disparaît?

Fibre obtenue par régénération de protéines, l'Ardil, qui a été produit commercialement par l'Imperial Chemical Industries (ICI) entre 1951 et 1957, a servi à confectionner des vêtements et à fabriquer des pièces d'ameublement. La présente communication traite du développement de l'Ardil et des caractéristiques de ce produit, de même que de ses techniques de fabrication et de sa commercialisation. Et puisqu'il n'existe que peu d'exemples connus de cette fibre, elle rend compte des travaux qui s'effectuent actuellement pour retracer les tissus contenant de l'Ardil, et fait un certain nombre de recommandations au sujet de la conservation de ce matériau. L'Ardil constitue donc un défi pour les spécialistes tant de la conservation que de la restauration, et il illustre toute l'importance que revêtent l'étude, l'identification et l'enregistrement des fibres synthétiques.

References

1. Ministry of Economic Warfare, London, Letter to NBM Legation in Berne and Stockholm, 21 October 1942. Public Record Office L40-9/1.

2. Chibnall, A.C., K. Bailey and W.T. Astbury, "Improvements Relating to the Production of Artificial Filaments, " British Patent 467,704, Provisional Specification No. 29161, 1935.

3. "A Perspective on the Preparation of Protein Fibres," Central Registry Papers (CR), 29 June 1939. ICI Head Offices Records Centre in: W.J. Reader, *Imperial Chemical Industries. A History* (Oxford: Oxford University Press, 1970).

4. Chibnall, A.C., K. Bailey and W.T. Astbury, "Improvements in or Relating to the Production of Artificial Filaments, Threads, Films, and the Like," British Patent 467,704, Provisional Specification No. 20927, 1936.

5. "Ardil Development," Notes of a Meeting on 14 February 1939. ICI Development Ex. Committee Papers in: Reader, *Imperial Chemical Industries*, 1970.

6. Various ICI Patents:
"Hardening of Protein Filaments," British Patent 492,677 (1932) and 492,895 (1938).
"Insolubilizing Protein Fibres," British Patent 766,360 (1954).
"Insolubilizing Protein Fibres," British Patent 787,588 (1955).
"Protein Filaments," British Patent 758,445 (1956) and 757,215 (1953).
"Method of Insolubilizing Protein Filaments," British Patent 763,501 (1954).
"Insolubilizing Protein Fibres," British Patent 758,560 (1954).

7. Moncrieff, R.W., *Man-made Fibres*, 6th edn. (London: Newnes-Butterworths, 1975).

8. Lutyens, W.F., "ICI/Courtauld's Relations," Central Registry 700/2/2 ICI, 2 February 1945, in: Reader, *Imperial Chemical Industries*, 1970.

9. "From Ground Nuts to Ardil," *ICI Magazine*, April 1951.

10. "Ardil Supporting Memo," Central Registry 3/1/1, 6/46, 8 July 1947, in: Reader, *Imperial Chemical Industries*, 1970.

11. "The Cost of Production of Ardil Fibre," Central Registry 3/15, 9 August 1955, in: Reader, *Imperial Chemical Industries*, 1970.

12. *ICI Review*, 1956, p. 21.

13. Moncrieff, R.W., *Man-made Fibres* (London: National Trade Press Ltd., 1957).

14. Traill, D., "Some Trials by Ingenious Inquisitive Persons: Regenerated Protein Fibres," *Journal Society of Dyers and Colorists*, July 1951, vol. 67, pp. 257-270.

15. Traill, D., G.K. Simpson and ICI, "Improvements in or Relating to a Method for Improving the Strength of Artificial Insolubilized Protein Filaments," British Patent 639,342 (1947).

16. Untitled, undated typescript, presumably from ICI, now held at the Whitworth Art Gallery, Manchester.

17. Dyke, F.M., "Ardil Protein Fibre Blends," *The Textile Weekly*, February 1952, p. 491.

18. "The Production of Shirting Cloths," *ICI Technical Bulletin* FG. 1, undated.

19. *Ardil Protein Fibre. A New Staple Fibre for the Textile Industry* (Harrogate, U.K.: ICI Fibre Division, undated).

20. "ICI Launch Monkey Nut Fibre," *International Textiles*, vol. 12, 1944.

21. Scott-Moncrieff, G., *Living Traditions of Scotland* (London: HMSO for The Council of Industrial Design Scottish Committee on the occasion of the Festival of Britain, 1951).

22. Advertisements: *Good Housekeeping*, August 1955, p. 16, November 1955, p. 7, December 1958, p. 5; *Woman's Journal*, April/May 1956, p. 4.

23. *News of the World, Household Guide and Almanac* (London: News of the World, 1956).

24. *The Textile Institute Identification of Textile Materials*, 7th edn. (Manchester: The Textile Institute, 1975).

25. Carroll-Porczynski, C.Z., *Manual of Man-made Fibres* (Guildford, U.K.: Astex, 1960).

26. "Qualitative Analysis of Ardil Fibre/Nylon and Ardil Fibre/Viscose/Nylon Blends," *ICI Technical Bulletin* AN. 2, ICI, 1956.

27. Hatchfield, P.R. and J. Carpenter, "Formaldehyde. How Great is the Danger to Museum Collections?" Centre for Conservation and Technical Studies, Harvard University Art Museums, 1987.

Plastics Found in Archives

Alan Calmes

National Archives and
Records Administration
Washington, D.C.
U.S.A.

Abstract

With the rise of plastics in the 1950s and 1960s, there emerged novel ways of recording information. Dictaphone belts, Thermofax copies, and all sorts of magnetic tapes joined vinyl discs and celluloid film as base materials for permanently holding valuable information, such as speeches, pictures, music, and data. Such materials typically reach an archive two or three decades after their creation, presenting a technically complicated preservation challenge. The cycle of development, usage, support, and obsolescence of polymers in recording media is examined. Aging characteristics, conservation measures, and conversion options are examined in the context of archival preservation administration.

Overview

Throughout the 19th century, paper was practically the only material used for record-keeping, except for some special applications of parchment. Often, papers were bound together and stored in leather volumes, or tri-folded together and pressed into wooden file boxes. Cellulose nitrate, as a filler for pyroxylin bindings and as a transparent substrate for photographic film, marked the advent of manufactured plastics in archives. During the first half of the 20th century, vinyl, in the form of phonograph records, replaced wax cylinders and joined film as a plastic material for holding information. Since 1950, more and more plastics have been used in record-keeping practices. Sound recordings, for example, have gone through a number of formats with different plastic materials, from physically embossed grooves on dictaphone belts, to magnetically charged particles on tape and, more recently, to laminated laser-produced, digitally encoded disc recordings. Each involves a complex combination of plastics.

The desire to have quick copies of paper documents led to the development of a variety of wet and dry and sometimes heat-processed coated papers during the 1940s and 1950s. Some of these processes involved plastics. Beginning in the early 1960s, the plain paper electrostatic photocopier produced an image using copolymers mixed with carbon black and fused to the paper surface. Early conservation methods used plastics for the lamination of fragile documents. The document, tissue paper, and sheets of cellulose acetate were heat-pressed into a melt. Plastic enclosures and boxes have been used in archives, and plastic parts are found in information recording equipment. Additionally, paints containing plastics have been used on surfaces of shelves and on containers, and plastic adhesives have been used to hold boxes and envelopes together.

Records are usually 20 to 30 years old by the time they reach the care of an archivist. Before records are transferred to an archive, they may have been stored in harsh environmental conditions and subjected to rough handling. Archival materials made of plastic often arrive in need of special attention. For example, cellulose nitrate film may arrive in an advanced state of deterioration and be highly flammable and in need of special handling, packaging and storage; dictaphone belts may arrive cracked and broken. An archivist needs to know the aging characteristics of plastics, conservation measures suitable for plastics, and copying techniques.

Especially vulnerable are non-paper records, such as motion pictures, video recordings, photographs, sound recordings, and computer data. Some of the most important information of the second half of the 20th century will require special conservation and duplication efforts to preserve the history of nations. A partial list of important events recorded on plastics would include: political debates, presidential addresses and news conferences on radio and television; satellite mapping and environmental observations; and motion pictures of historic events. An example of valuable information on a plastic medium is the sound recording of the Nuremberg Trials, which was recorded on a long loop of cellulose acetate film. The embossed grooves and bumps have nearly disappeared as the plastic material has gradually returned to its pre-embossed smooth state. A special machine had to be built with a special tracking stylus to play the loop.

The majority of plastics found in archives are thermoplastic materials, such as cellulose nitrate; cellulose acetate; polycarbonate; poly(methyl methacrylate) (PMMA or acrylic); nylon; poly(vinyl chloride) (PVC); polystyrene; poly(ethylene terephthalate) (PETP or polyester); polyurethane; and polyolefins, such as polypropylene. Some thermosetting resins are also found, such as polyurethane, epoxy resin, melamine formaldehyde resin, and phenolic resins, such as phenol-formaldehyde resin, and Bakelite.

The following are examples of plastics found in archives: cellulose nitrate film; various cellulose acetate films; vinyl (PVC) phonograph discs; polyester encapsulation; polyolefin shrink wrapping; polyethylene boxes and envelopes; polyurethane binders on magnetic tape; acrylic sheets and blocks used in exhibits; epoxy resin adhesives and coatings; and nylon gears.

Many product names are used by non-specialists as generic names of plastics, such as Du Pont's Mylar for poly(ethylene terephthalate), Rohm & Haas's Plexiglas for poly(methyl methacrylate), and General Electric's Lexan for polycarbonate.

Additives

Plastics are seldom used in a pure state. Polyester used for encapsulation is generally described as a simple polyester, but even it contains some by-products left over from the manufacturing process, such as lubricants and some silica compounds to prevent blocking. Polypropylene and polyethylene have antioxidants added so that they can be melted and formed into sheets or poured into molds without undergoing oxidation. Additives add to the complex nature of plastic materials. Lubricants in magnetic tape, for example, can ooze out of the tape onto its surface. The reading-head of a tape-drive will collect the oozed-out lubricants and this can cause the reading-head to either fail to read the data or gouge the surface of the magnetic tape, destroying the recorded information.

Since plastic products may melt, burn and spread a fire rapidly, flame retardants are often added. Some local fire codes require the addition of flame retardants in plastic materials found in household and office furniture, and, therefore, flame retardants should be included in plastics found in abundance inside any building. Some flame retardants, however, can evaporate in small quantities and affect materials in contact with them. Some halogens, for example, may produce oxidants that can react with the silver halides of photographic film.

Changes in the Composition of Plastics

Plastics have evolved rapidly since 1950. Chemical formulations have been replaced or modified to achieve desired results. New applications or improved materials brought about the obsolescence of one form of plastic in favor of another. As a result, it is difficult to identify old plastics found in archives without conducting laboratory tests.

Manufacturing processes have changed. Most plastics originally served more immediate needs and were not designed for long life. There was almost an assumption in our society that plastic products were disposable, and if continued use of the product was desired, it would have to be replaced by a new and better product. This philosophy is changing, as manufacturers are beginning to produce engineering plastics with substantial durability and environmental resistance. Paradoxically, there are now environmental concerns that plastics are here forever; this fear has led to the development of biodegradable plastics for throw-away products.

The need to carry out periodic duplication on plastic media extends to all types and formats: sound recordings, video recordings, motion picture film, and computer tapes. How often this is done depends on how the medium is stored and handled, and on the characteristics of the plastics used.

Physical Characteristics

Plastics can be rigid or flexible, soft or hard; they can be molded to almost any shape. During manufacturing processes, plastics are malleable and can be stretched as well as molded. These attributes, convenient for making any shaped item, can cause problems later. With sufficient heat, plastics can return to the malleable state and change shape. When stretched during a forming process, plastics can be made into thin films; however, the material will continue to have a memory of an earlier state, and try to revert back to a previous condition. Many plastic films will relax back to their pre-stretched dimensions if they are heated even briefly above a transition temperature that varies from one plastic to another.

Plastics can be made with such a smooth surface that when placed in contact with another smooth surface, such as a photograph, pressed, and then removed, the photograph will be left with a shiny surface. This process is sometimes called "ferrotyping" (a term borrowed from photography, referring to the process of transferring an image directly onto the smooth surface of a specially prepared iron plate). Such plastic sheets should not be used in albums. Another deleterious process, "offsetting," is when

plastics adhere to the ink and toner of paper documents or to the imaging layer of photographic prints. PVC plastic sheets have this quality because of the plasticizer, such as dioctyl phthalate, which acts like a solvent in dissolving and attracting the copolymer ingredients of toners and dyes used in electrostatic copies and photographic images. Furthermore, PVC should not be used for albums or filed with papers because it is an unstable plastic that decomposes to produce hydrogen chloride (HCl) and, with a little water, this forms hydrochloric acid.

Plasticizers are solutes placed in hard plastics to reduce the glass transition temperature, and consequently to improve the flexibility of the material. Poly(vinyl chloride) is an example of such a material that is normally glass-like. Plasticizers are not chemically bound to the polymer, and, over time, may come out of solution and be found on the surface of the plastic from which they may evaporate if heated, or rub off. Eventually, plastics that are plasticized will "dry out," shrink, and crack. Other additives, such as oils, lubricants, antioxidants, and cyanamides (also known as carbodiimides) may ooze out onto the surface of the plastic material as it ages. With the subsequent reduction in the solubility of the plasticizer in the plastic, a white powder is often found on the surfaces of old films and tapes consisting of a number of additives that have come out of solution in the plastic support and/or recording layer.

Aging Characteristics

Cellulose Nitrate
Originally, almost all black-and-white 35-mm motion picture film was on cellulose nitrate film. It was used exclusively for studio work from the 1920s to the 1950s. Cellulose nitrate was not used for color film, or for 16-mm and 8-mm home movie film.

When ignited, cellulose nitrate burns very rapidly. Nitrate film decomposes with the emission of oxides of nitrogen. The reactions are highly exothermic and are responsible for the spontaneous ignition of cellulose nitrate. Despite the hazards, commercial film makers preferred cellulose nitrate film over cellulose acetate safety film because it was easy to handle and produced a very clear, sharp image when projected. By 1950, however, after many theater fires, fire codes mandated the use of safety film. During the past 10 years, after several devastating and dangerous cellulose nitrate film vault explosions and fires, archives and libraries have copied most cellulose nitrate film images onto safety film (a cellulose acetate or polyester film) and disposed of the cellulose nitrate film. There remains, however, some spliced-in cellulose nitrate film within reels of safety film. Nitrate-based film stock can be identified by feel; it is softer and more supple than cellulose acetate or polyester film. When degrading, its appearance may be deceiving. It is therefore safer to have a laboratory test film to confirm its nitrate content.

The aging of cellulose nitrate is characterized by rapid change once the deterioration process begins. Prior to the onset of deterioration, there is no serious shrinkage of the material, image quality is good, and the images can be copied easily. The kinetics of the reaction are such that there appears to be virtually no intermediate stage between the time when the film is in good condition and the time when it is obviously deteriorated. Archivists have seen reels of cellulose nitrate film change from excellent to extremely poor condition in two months. When it deteriorates, cellulose nitrate film produces sticky-brownish, powdery-fibrous globs.

Gases emanating from deteriorating cellulose nitrate film can initiate the process of deterioration in neighboring films of all types. Chemically, cellulose nitrate, upon decomposition, produces its own oxidizer, and, therefore, once the chemical bonds begin to break down, a rapid autocatalytic reaction sets in. The reaction produces its own heat, which accelerates the initial breakdown. The process can be fast enough to produce fire and, if film is tightly compacted, an explosion can result. Once a degrading cellulose nitrate film has been identified, the archivist must move quickly to copy the images onto safety film and to dispose of the cellulose nitrate film. The continued usefulness of a reel of cellulose nitrate film depends upon good environmental conditions, such as clean, cool, and dry air.

Cellulose Acetate

The same general mechanism of deterioration of cellulose nitrate occurs in a similar way in other cellulose esters. The same acid hydrolysis occurs in all cellulose materials, but the other esters produce only an acid that catalyzes further acid hydrolysis, not an oxidizer like nitrogen dioxide in the case of cellulose nitrate. The degradation process of cellulose acetate film takes longer than that of cellulose nitrate film, but once started, the autocatalytic chemical reaction cannot be stopped. The result of the self-destruction of cellulose acetate film is somewhat different from cellulose nitrate film, in that an intermediate stage of deterioration between a good condition and a powdery condition can be seen. Acetic acid, a product of cellulose acetate degradation, can be detected by its vinegar odor. The presence of acidic gases and particles found in polluted air will initiate the degradation process of cellulose acetate film. Unlike nitrate film, however, the image layer is not chemically affected by the by-products of the decomposition of the acetate substrate.

The first safety-based films were cellulose mono-acetate and cellulose diacetate. The term "safety-base" was used because acetate films do not burn easily. By the 1970s, triacetate began to replace diacetate as the favored substrate for film.

Manufacturing experience found that the diacetate substrate took diazo salts more readily than the triacetate base and thus the diacetate base was used in diazo films until polyester began to be used in the 1980s.

Researchers at the Image Permanence Institute in Rochester, N.Y., are finding little difference between the degradation processes of cellulose diacetate film and cellulose triacetate film. One is not necessarily more stable than the other. The process, however, might take longer with a triacetate than with a diacetate. Within one category there are likely to be variations from one batch to another, depending on formulas and additives, and manufacturing processes.[1]

The long, intermediate stage of deterioration of cellulose acetate film is characterized by shrinkage. When the cellulose acetate film base shrinks, the emulsion layer on top, which does not shrink, is deformed into a mass of wrinkles. Since the image is within the emulsion layer, the image becomes illegible, unless there is a way to copy or transfer the emulsion layer before the wrinkling obscures the image. The choices are to copy the image before this occurs or to laboriously remove and reapply the image layer after it occurs. The greater the shrinkage, the more difficult it is to recover the information. When motion picture film shrinks, the sprocket holes are no longer in the right place, making the copying process, necessary to save the images, difficult and expensive. The shrinkage will be uneven; consequently, engineered sprockets with a different spacing may not provide a solution.

Until the late 1950s, cellulose acetate films were used as a very thin base material for sound recording tape and for some early video and computer tape. With age, and accelerated by elevated temperatures and high relative humidities, thin cellulose acetate tape becomes brittle and will break easily. Brittleness is an inevitable condition. Plasticizers used during the manufacturing process will ooze out onto the surface of the tape in the form of white droplets that look like powder. To complicate matters, a recording layer, such as one composed of iron oxides dispersed in polyurethane, will have characteristics of degradation different from that of the base material.

A break in cellulose acetate magnetic tape is usually clean. It can be spliced back together again with little loss of information for an analog sound or video recording. This is different from polyester-based magnetic tapes that stretch considerably before breaking.

Polyester
Poly(ethylene terephthalate) entered the scene in the late 1950s. Because of its strength it was used, even in a very thin film, as the substrate for all computer and video tapes. Soon thereafter, polyester replaced cellulose acetate as the base material for sound recording tape. The switch from cellulose acetate to polyester-based photographic film has been very slow. The demand for a strong, long lasting microfilm brought about the use of polyester for

microfilm in the 1980s, but it co-existed with cellulose triacetate-based microfilm.

With the right combination of conditions, acid hydrolysis can break the bonds between monomers of polyester. During this process acids are created that in turn break more bonds. Once started, degradation is autocatalytic. Hydrolysis can be initiated by acids present in polluted air or left over from the manufacturing process. Oxides of nitrogen from automobile exhaust form acids in the atmosphere that can accelerate the degradation process of plastics. Exclusion of water from the air, that is, maintaining a low relative humidity, is an effective strategy to prevent hydrolysis. Using scrubbing systems or treated charcoal filters to remove pollutant gases from the air are other strategies. The lower the temperature the slower the rate of chemical reactions. To slow down degradation, carbodiimides are added to react with acids and antioxidants are added to prevent reaction with oxygen; however, the additives will eventually be consumed, ooze out or evaporate from the plastic.[2,3]

Polyester film is bi-axially oriented or "balanced." Cellulose acetate is often uni-axially stretched. Due to its limberness, polyester tape is more difficult to handle than cellulose acetate tape. Polyester tends to respond to tension. For example, it will curl under tension. These characteristics vary with the thickness of the tape. The much thicker photographic film will demonstrate different properties, such as springiness rather than limberness. Polyester has what is called "plastic memory," and tries to go back to its pre-stretched state.

In order to reduce volume, polyester-based magnetic tape for computer use has become extremely thin, but there is, concomitantly, a higher risk of loss of information, as a small amount of stretching or some other dimensional change can cause the loss of data.

Engineering Plastics
Engineering plastics, such as nylon, polycarbonate, and phenolic resins, have replaced metal for machine parts in modern information recording and retrieving devices. For example, video players now have more plastic machine parts

than ever before. Plastic machine parts have the advantage of being lightweight, tough, and wear resistant, they do not need lubrication, and their gear trains operate quietly. Contrary to popular opinion that plastics are cheap substitutes for metal components, plastic machine parts are often more expensive than the metal parts they replace. Quality is a factor with plastic parts as well as with metal parts. Quality of the product depends upon quality of the manufacturing process for the plastic part and the quality of assembly into a machine.

There is a need for guidelines for the long-term maintenance of plastic machine parts. They should not be lubricated. There is a problem when part of a gear train is plastic and another part metal, because the lubricant needed for the metal part may cause the plastic part to deteriorate. Spare parts should be obtained before the machine becomes obsolete.

Acrylics, Polycarbonates and Epoxies

Acrylic resins, polycarbonates, epoxy resins, and various mixtures of these are used as shields, supports, adhesives, coatings, and toners for information recording systems. We have, however, very little experience on the use of these plastics in archives. Acrylics are better known by their product names, such as Plexiglas and Lucite, but acrylic products come in a variety of forms from solid materials to liquids. Some acrylic products turn yellow and become brittle upon exposure to ultraviolet light or unfiltered sunlight. Recent materials use ultraviolet blockers to reduce the damage caused by light.

Poly(methyl methacrylate) (PMMA) has been used for compact discs (CDs) and CD-ROM discs. Often, such discs were also coated with epoxy. Consumers began to note failures in these products in the late 1980s. Beginning in 1990, CDs and CD-ROMs were beginning to be made from polycarbonate, which is tougher and more resistant to change than PMMA.

Much work remains to be done on plastics used in adhesives. For example, pressure-sensitive labels may fall off archival boxes, tape splices on motion picture film or magnetic tape eventually may fail and need to be replaced. Plastic

adhesives can damage not only the surfaces where they are applied but also can initiate the degradation of nearby areas of papers, films, and tapes.

Polyolefins and Polystyrene

Plastic containers have significant advantages over metal cans and cardboard boxes. They do not corrode, are lightweight, and are unaffected by high humidity or water. Polypropylene motion picture containers are being used in some archives. There are no solvents or plasticizers in polyolefins. However, colorants may come to the surface and cause a problem and flame retardants required by fire codes may slowly, even at normal temperatures, emit small quantities of reactive materials, which might affect the contents of the container.

Plastic cartridges can warp and cause magnetic tape to mis-track when read and to mis-align when rewound. In the latter case the edges of the tape may rub against the sides of the container. Plastic pressure pads in magnetic tape cartridges have been known to crumble after a few years. The pieces of pad can damage the reading machine and get between the layers of tape, causing the tape to be wound unevenly.

Because magnetic tape is thin and will sag against the flange when stored horizontally, magnetic tape should be stored vertically, suspended on a hub; otherwise, an unevenly wound tape will result in having its outlying tape-edges folded under by the weight of the rest of the tape. Motion picture film is thicker and stiffer than magnetic tape and is stored horizontally without flanges with the film resting on the surface of the container. The film must be wound evenly and snugly. Instead of metal, hubs and flanges are sometimes made of polystyrene. In special cases glass has been used for flanges. Plastic is substantially cheaper and lighter than metal or glass; thus, we can expect to see more plastic.

Combinations of Plastic Materials

Combinations of materials abound in archives. Some of these are bound together into laminated "sandwiches." For example, bound volumes consist of many layers of materials glued together. An old phonograph record was constructed of a layer of shellac painted onto glass or metal. Magnetic tape base is made up of a layer of polyurethane laminated to a substrate of polyester. Each layer has a different coefficient of expansion. Changes in environmental conditions can cause the separation of layers. The chemical products of decomposition of one layer can affect the other layer. One layer may become brittle while the other remains flexible.

Static Electricity

Plastics can hold a static electric charge and can release sparks and electromagnetic radiation. Static electricity is a problem for the microelectronics of some machines. Some manufacturers try to mitigate the problem of static electricity by adding an anti-static layer to the back of tape or placing an anti-static additive directly into the plastic. Tapes coming out of long-term storage should be equilibrated at greater than 30% relative humidity to dissipate the electrical charge and metal reels should be grounded. Static electricity also attracts dust and grit that must be kept away from magnetic tape or disc surfaces to prevent a reading-head from bumping into them. Note that polystyrene, the plastic material used for tape flanges, can also collect a static charge. Dust and grit are also undesirable on film since they scatter light, cast shadows and scratch the emulsion. Also, it is undesirable to attract dust and grit at the time of polyester encapsulation of documents.

Obsolescence

Rapid changes in technology during the 20th century have compounded the problems concerning the maintenance of information in other than readable form. For example, from the 1930s through the 1950s, sound-recorded dictation was kept on a cellulose acetate belt, sometimes referred to as a dictabelt from a dictaphone. At first, the sound frequencies were embossed mechanically into the surface of the cellulose acetate belt; later, the sound was recorded magnetically onto the surface of the belt. A simple stylus can translate embossed vibrations into sounds, like that used for vinyl disc players. To play the magnetically recorded dictation on a belt, it will be necessary to obtain the same type of machine as that used to produce the recording, or research will be necessary to determine the appropriate size of stylus and use an appropriate transducer and amplifier and play the recording at the correct speed.

The pace of technological change has quickened during the 20th century. Vinyl records have been in use for over 50 years, analog sound recordings on magnetic tape for 50 years, digital recording for 30 years, and format changes are now occurring nearly every decade. Plastics have played a role in the quickening of change by providing an infinite variety of new materials for adaptation. For example, computer information systems are constantly being upgraded with increased information density and reading speed, such as dye-polymers used in some optical-magnetic recording systems to provide very high density storage and fast random access.

The preservation of machine-readable information depends on periodic copying. If copying is carried out properly and in a timely manner, there is little loss of information. However, there must be an assumption of continued cost to pay for periodic duplication and new hardware/software updates.

Conclusion

People in our society have ambivalent ideas about plastics. The memory of how plastic toys break and cannot be fixed gives the impression of plastics as cheap, ephemeral, and disposable. Certainly, most people would not give a plastic object for a keepsake. From another point of view, seeing plastics floating around in the mid-Atlantic Ocean stimulates environmental concerns that plastics pollute and will never go away. The replacement of metal parts with plastic parts is accepted by some as progress and is seen as an improvement; others would argue that the switch represents a cheapening of the product, even though it may look better.

Since plastics can be manufactured and molded into almost any shape at a fraction of the cost of other materials, there are economic forces driving the use of plastics. With an acceptable short life expectancy of most products today, perhaps attributable to rapid obsolescence, frequent changes in style, and the desire to reduce manufacturing costs, manufacturers are using the less expensive plastics in products that are virtually disposable after a few years. Some plastics, however, such as polyester and melamine are expected to remain durable and to last for centuries. The various plastics have their various environmental requirements, and as long as they are met, the plastic materials will serve their intended uses well. Maintaining a benign environmental storage condition is key to extending the life of any material. Constant low relative humidity between 30% and 50% should benefit all plastics. Temperatures should be kept as low as practical, between 5°C and 20°C.

Plastics are manufactured materials subject to endless changes in proprietary formulations. After a formula has been used and the plastic product is replaced by a new model, no one will know what formula was used or what additives were placed in the old plastic product; in which case, it is almost impossible to predict the life expectancy of the medium. Only when we know the history of the material and its chemical composition can we reasonably expect a certain performance and life expectancy of the plastic medium. We need the cooperation of manufacturers to reveal the complete formula of each plastic. With advance warning in hand, archivists, therefore, can program replacement costs to allow for a periodic migration of information from one plastic medium to the next.

Acknowledgement

The foregoing information on plastics found in archives was derived primarily from interviews with archivists and technical staff in the National Archives and Records Administration (NARA) and with polymer chemists and photographic film and magnetic tape standards experts at the National Institute for Standards and Technology (NIST). Susan Lee-Bechtold, Chief Chemist, and Charles W. Mayn, sound and video recording engineer, both of NARA, and Leslie E. Smith, polymer chemist, and Thomas Bagg, both at NIST, were particularly helpful.

Résumé

Les plastiques présents dans les archives

L'utilisation de plus en plus répandue des plastiques dans les années 50 et 60 a fait naître de nouvelles façons d'enregistrer l'information. Les bandes de Dictaphone, les copies Thermofax et toutes sortes de rubans magnétiques ont ainsi rejoint les disques en vinyle et les films de celluloïd au rang des matières de base qui servent de support permanent aux enregistrements de discours, de photographies, de pièces de musique, de données. Or, en général, ces documents ne sont placés dans les archives que deux ou trois décennies après leur création, de sorte que leur conservation n'est pas sans poser d'énormes difficultés techniques.

Nous examinerons, dans le cadre de la présente communication, le cycle de développement des polymères qui entrent dans la composition de tels supports et leur utilisation, tout en traitant des mesures de soutien qui peuvent leur être appliquées et de leur obsolescence. Nous aborderons également, du point de vue de l'administration d'un service d'archives, leurs caractéristiques de vieillissement, de même que les diverses mesures et options de conversion auxquelles on peut avoir recours pour assurer la conservation de ces supports et des informations qu'ils contiennent.

References

1. Adelstein, P.Z., J.M. Reilly, D.W. Nishimura, and C.J. Erbland, "Stability of Cellulose-Ester Based Photographic Film," *SMPTE Journal*, May 1992, pp. 336-353.

2. Smith, L.E. et al., "Prediction of the Long-Term Stability of Polyester-Based Recording Media," (Gaithersburg, Md.: National Bureau of Standards, 1986) Report No. NBSIR-86/3474.

3. Smith, L.E., "Factors Governing the Long-term Stability of Polyester-Based Recording Media," *Restaurator, The International Journal for the Preservation of Library and Archival Materials*, vol. 12, 1991, pp. 201-218.

Processes of Deterioration
Processus de dégradation

Changes in Polymeric Materials with Time

David M. Wiles

Plastichem Consulting
Victoria, B.C.
Canada

Abstract

Virtually all plastics, fibres, rubbers, paints and protective coatings, as well as paper, wood, skin and hides, owe their useful characteristics to the relatively high molecular weights of their molecules. Values in molecular weights range from a few thousand to several million. Unfortunately, fabrication, handling, use or misuse of these materials result in deleterious changes (usually decreases) in the molecular weights of the constituent molecules with concomitant reduction in the materials' useful properties. The detailed science of the changes at the molecular level is highly complex and, frequently, not well understood. Nevertheless, some features common to the degradation of many polymeric materials with time have been elucidated and can indicate the way to improved preservation practices.

Chemical aging includes oxidative deterioration as a result of exposure in air to light, heat or ionizing radiation, and also includes hydrolysis and attack by acids or bases. Biodegradation can be considered a special case of chemical breakdown caused by microbial enzymes. The reactions involved in chemical aging are numerous and somewhat material-specific, but the more important ones can frequently be related to the oxidation of liquid hydrocarbons. The discolouration, embrittlement and reduction in various physical properties that accompany oxidative deterioration can be minimized by the use of appropriate combinations of stabilizing additives. Microbial susceptibility is best dealt with by "good housekeeping" practices.

Less well known is the phenomenon of physical aging, whereby polymeric materials continue to alter for weeks, months or years after they have solidified or otherwise attained the physical form in which they are used. Originally observed in thermoplastics below their glass transition temperatures (Tg), physical aging arises because all temperature-dependent properties, which change abruptly at Tg, continue to change below that temperature, albeit very slowly. Physical aging is observed in amorphous, glassy polymers, in the amorphous phase of semi-crystalline polymers and in the rubbery matrix of filled rubbers. As a result, over time, many materials become stiffer and more brittle as "rates of relaxation" decrease. Because physical aging affects polymer segmental mobility, it should also affect chemical degradation, photo-oxidation, swelling and de-swelling, and crosslinking reactions in a wide variety of macromolecular systems.

Introduction

The degradation of materials is identified by the user/observer as an unacceptable change in characteristics, be they mechanical, chemical, optical, or electrical. In the case of polymeric materials, that is, those comprising very large molecules, it is usually an alteration in the molecular weight of these molecules that results in an undesirable change in properties leading, for example, to mechanical failure or discolouration. Occasionally, with some materials, crosslinking occurs (the formation of chemical bonds between molecules) with a resultant

105

increase in molecular weight, but more commonly chemical reactions cause a reduction in the molecular weight of the large molecules, which collectively are the origin of the useful properties of polymers. Not infrequently, however, unacceptable property changes can occur even though very little change in molecular weight can be measured. In short, polymer degradation is widespread, complex and sometimes difficult to evaluate; it can also be very difficult to prevent.

Much of the progress in elucidating the degradation of macromolecules is summarized in the articles and monographs listed in the references.[1-14] It is justifiable to look for simplifications and generalities that assist in understanding and dealing with polymer degradation. Turning first to chemical aging, there are numerous features common to the oxidative deterioration of many kinds of macromolecules as a result of exposure in air to light, heat, ionizing radiation or mechanical action. Some of these overall features are summarized in the figure below. It has proven useful to relate these kinds of chemistry to the oxidation of liquid hydrocarbons. Such model compound studies have identified mechanisms that apply (at least in part) to the degradation of solid polymers; kinetics, the rates of the critical reactions, are rather more composition- and state-specific. Nevertheless, considerable progress has been made in devising methods (largely chemical) of postponing for prolonged periods the inevitable degradation.

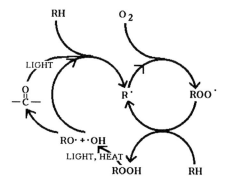

Hydrolysis, as well as deterioration from exposure to acids or bases, can be a problem in humid or "hostile" environments for polymers having specific structural features that are inherently susceptible. Ester linkages are hydrolyzable, for example, and molecules that can react with acids or bases will usually be degraded by them. Microbial attack may be a problem for natural polymers since, in warm, moist air, fungal enzymes can oxidatively degrade many such macromolecules. Biodegradation is fortunately not a factor in the deterioration of many synthetic polymers.

It is worth remembering that the molecular weights of polymeric materials are really very high and that their desirable properties will be lost when only a very small fraction of the bonds per molecule are broken. The molecular weight of the molecules in cotton averages over 2 million, in wood cellulose over 1.5 million, and in paper several hundred thousand. Among the synthetic polymers, nylons and polyesters having superior physical properties may have molecular weights of only 30 thousand or so, but polyolefins are characterized by values from a few hundred thousand to more than a million. The breaking of one bond in, say, 10 thousand in polymer chains will have a devastating effect on the properties of the material (unless the scission occurs near the ends of the molecules). Such sensitivity is rarely observed in small-molecule science.

Physical aging is an entirely different phenomenon in that it is thermodynamically driven and cannot be stopped although it is readily reversible. Moreover, it is by no means invariably undesirable. All temperature-dependent properties of materials that change abruptly at the glass-transition temperature continue to change below T_g. In effect, materials become stiffer and more brittle; rates of relaxation decrease so the response of a material to deformation or impact changes, usually for the worse. Physical aging in amorphous polymers and related materials persists for a very long time and affects a variety of properties so that repair and replacement is tricky and, of course, longevity may be compromised. Additional information can be found in the references.[15-20]

Oxidative Degradation

A very high proportion of the common polymers, both natural and synthetic, have molecules that consist of chains of carbon atoms bonded together or chains of carbon atoms interspersed with other atoms, such as oxygen (e.g., in polyesters, polycarbonates, polyethers) or nitrogen (e.g., in polyamides, polyurethanes). Invariably, hydrogen is bonded to most of the backbone carbon atoms but, occasionally, so is oxygen or chlorine, for example. Aromatic rings may be part of the polymer chains (e.g., PET, aramids) or pendant from them (e.g., polystyrene). Energy in one form or another is introduced into macromolecules either during fabrication (or other handling) or during use and, inevitably, chemical bonds of the types referred to above will be broken homolytically, that is, to produce highly reactive free radicals, in pairs. Sometimes, it is these primary reactions by which molecular weights are reduced below acceptable levels, but it is frequently the case that the damage is done in secondary or even tertiary reactions. The varied response of many common polymers to degradative environments is illustrated in Tables I and II, which are taken from Carlsson and Wiles.[1]

The identification of those processes that cause the loss of the essential properties of polymers has consumed a very great deal of research time during the past 40 years and it is by no means complete. One singularly useful approach has been to identify the more important products of polymer degradation and, using principles established with low molecular weight analogues for the polymers, "reconstruct" the chemistry that gave rise to the products. Thus, under thermal stress, the weakest bonds in the system are most likely to break; these could be tertiary carbon-hydrogen bonds, for instance, or peroxidic linkages. In the case of light-induced damage, it is the shortest wavelengths (highest energy) in the incident radiation that do most of the damage and there must be appropriate chromophores (light-absorbing groups) present for any damage to occur. For example, the more cotton or other cellulosic is purified, the whiter it becomes and the less susceptible it will be to actinic deterioration because the relevant chromophores are present in extractable impurities rather than in the polysaccharide chains themselves. Another example is that the purer a polyolefin, the less rapidly it will photodegrade, since it is the chromophoric impurities in these thermoplastic molecules that give rise to their photosusceptibility.

Table I
Susceptibility of Unstabilized Polymers to Degradation

Polymer	Thermal Oxidation	Photo-oxidation Weathering	Ozone	Hydrolysis	Oxidation
		Resistance to degradative process*			
polyethylene	p	p	e	e	f
polypropylene	vp	vp	e	e	p
polystyrene	f	p	e	e	g
poly(methyl methacrylate)	g	e	e	g	f
poly(tetrafluoroethylene)	e	e	e	e	vp
polyamide (Nylon-6 and -6,6)	f	f		f	f
polyacrylonitrile	p	g	e	g	f
poly(vinyl chloride)	vp	p	e	e	p
poly(ethylene terepthalate)	g	g	e	g	g
polyoxymethylene	p	p	f	f	vp
polycarbonate	f	p	g	g	g
poly(phenylene oxide)	vp	f	g	g	g
poly(ester urethane)	f	f	g	g	f
poly(ether urethane)	p	p	g	f	f
poly(*m*-phenylene isophthalamide)	e	vp	e	g	e
poly(*p*-phenylene terephthalamide)	e	vp	e	g	e
* Key: e = excellent, g = good, f = fair, p = poor, and vp = very poor					

Given that some carbon-carbon bonds are broken in due course, a general series of reactions may be written:

Polymer Molecules $RH \xrightarrow[\text{ionizing radiation}]{\text{heat, light}} 2R^\bullet$ Carbon-centred radicals, in pairs

$R^\bullet + O_2 \longrightarrow RO_2^\bullet \xrightarrow{RH} ROOH + R^\bullet$

$ROOH \xrightarrow[\text{light}]{\text{heat}} {}^\bullet OH + RO^\bullet \xrightarrow{RH} ROH + R^\bullet$

$H_2O + R^\bullet \qquad R^\bullet + \text{ketones}$

$2RO_2^\bullet \longrightarrow \text{stable products}$

Two features of this sequence should be obvious. Since each initial carbon-centred radical ($R^\bullet$) gives rise to several other radicals, this is a branching chain reaction overall and, if nothing interrupts the sequence, oxidative degradation of a polymer can proceed rapidly. A second feature is that there is likely to be some difficulty in sorting out all the degradation products and where they came from, especially since some are themselves heat- and light-sensitive. A third, less obvious feature of this reaction scheme is that it should apply (at least in part) to a wide variety of polymer types and it should apply whether bonds were cleaved initially by heat, light, ionizing radiation or mechanical stress. The behaviour of a reactive chemical species, such as a polymer radical, is determined by environment (both macro and micro) more than by origin; the radical has no memory (see Figure 1). This feature has been helpful in the elucidation of polymer degradation mechanisms as well as in the development of many highly effective stabilization systems.

There are many synthetic polymers that have chromophores as part of the repeat units, that is, they are built into the polymer chains. Carbonyl groups in polyesters, nylons (including aramids), polycarbonates and polyurethanes are examples of chemical structures that absorb specific wavelengths in terrestrial sunlight. Norrish-type photodegradation reactions ensue, leading to the formation of radicals that undergo the same kinds of chemistry illustrated in the scheme shown earlier. There are other kinds of photochemistry and other types of degradation reaction in the case of certain specific polymers, but the scheme is valid for a wide variety of macromolecules.

In addition to reducing the tensile or flexural performance of polymeric materials, oxidative degradation frequently results in surface

Table II
Thermal Deterioration of Polymers Maximum Use Temperature[a]

Polymer Generic Type	Film Thickness, mm	Maximum Use Temperature, °C
poly(vinyl chloride)	2.0	50
polyethylene	1.5	50
polyoxymethylene	0.7	50
poly(methyl methacrylate)	1.5	50
polystyrene	3.1	50
poly(phenylene oxide)	1.5	50
polyamide	0.7	65
polycarbonate[b]	0.7	65
epoxy resins	3.0	90
silicones	0.7	105
poly(ethylene terephthalate)	0.2	105
alkyd resin	1.5	130
polytetrafluoroethylene	0.9	150
phenolic resin	2.0	150
polyimide	0.1	200
aramid[c]	0.2	220

a Recommended use temperature at which 50% of the original dielectric strength, tensile, and impact properties are retained for 11,000 h under low continuous stress. In some cases, stabilizers may be present. Underwriters Laboratories data.
b Bisphenol A.
c Aromatic polyamide.

cracking, discolouration and enhanced surface wettability, for example. In all cases, the trick is to try to identify those chemical reactions that cause the loss of useful properties since these are the reactions that need to be prevented as much as possible. Commonly, materials are subjected to heat and light stress simultaneously. Conventional wisdom has it that photochemical reactions have no activation energy, that is, there is no significant effect on rate of increases or decreases in temperature. Even though this is true for most primary photoprocesses, a number of the subsequent reactions will, in fact, be governed by Arrhenius principles. No one has yet determined how to describe this situation quantitatively, for example, in terms of lifetime predictions, but it should be kept in mind that the effects of light and heat together on polymers are more severe, sometimes synergistically so, than either separately.

Moisture-Based Deterioration

It is self-evident that polymers that are highly hydrophobic are unlikely to be susceptible to hydrolysis; there are no hydrolyzable groups present. Using polyolefins as an example, these plastics cannot hydrolyze, are highly resistant to acids and bases, and are microbially inert. These characteristics give rise to applications in geotextiles, food packaging and automobile parts, for example. Some polyesters are more hydrolyzable than others. PET, being relatively resistant, is highly useful as textile fibres, soft drink bottles and prosthetic devices, whereas a simpler polyester, such as poly(glycolic acid), is an effective "biodegradable" suture material. Chemical structure at the molecular level is the critical factor and a very reasonable basis for material selection. It is not surprising, therefore, that many naturally occurring polymers are not soluble in water (or many other solvents) at ambient temperatures. Likewise, susceptibility to reaction with (and destruction by) acids and bases is predictable on the basis of polymer structure compared to that of analogous small molecules.

To simplify somewhat, biodegradation is commonly molecular fragmentation resulting from the chemical effects of microbial enzymes. A very common manifestation of this would involve one of the more than 80,000 kinds of

fungi that operate by excreting water-soluble enzymes onto a biosusceptible substrate. Subsequent breakdown of the molecules of the substrate material into water-soluble fragments, for example, two carbon-atom chunks, is followed by transfer back inside the mycelial cells. Fungi like to be warm and moist and they require oxygen because, like mammals, they derive energy from the oxidation of carbon to carbon dioxide. Over tens of millions of years, fungal systems have evolved that can degrade a wide variety of materials, some of them rather toxic. There is, however, as yet no fungus that has the enzymes to break down most synthetic polymers, which, by and large, do not occur in nature and have been invented within the past 60 years. Nevertheless, microbial growth can readily occur on surface dirt of bioinert materials like plastics, causing, at the very least, unacceptable aesthetic consequences.

Fungi proliferate by sporulation and fungal spores are literally everywhere, waiting for conditions favorable for germination. Commercial fungicides are available, but these are relatively toxic compounds unsuitable for many materials and situations. Whether there is a need to prevent growth on a susceptible substrate or on the contaminated surface of an inert material, the best way is to maintain "good housekeeping" practices. In other words, it is usually sufficient to keep things cool, clean and dry, in air conditioned premises if possible, in order to minimize the undesirable effects of fungi and other micro-organisms.

Physical Aging

As the temperature of a solid, amorphous polymer is raised, the kinetic energy of the molecules will increase, but the resultant vibrations and rotations will be significantly restricted as long as the material retains its glass-like structure. At a specific temperature, characteristic of each polymer type, there is a measurable change in the system where glass-like properties give way to rubber-like behaviour, owing to the onset of greater rotational freedom and more segmental motion (20 to 50 chain atoms) of the polymer chains. This temperature is called the glass transition temperature or Tg. Since the properties of a rigid glass and a rubbery plastic are very different, the Tg of a polymer is one of its most important characteristics. Values range from -102°C for cis-1,4-polybutadiene, -67°C for natural rubber, -20°C for polyethylene, 57°C for nylon 6,6, 69°C for PET, 81°C for PVC, 100°C for polystyrene, and up to 149°C for bisphenol-A polycarbonate. Thus, some common polymers are below their Tgs at room temperature. Moreover, this is the case also for the amorphous phase of semi-crystalline polymers and the rubbery matrix of filled rubbers and other composites. Amorphous glassy solids are not in thermodynamic equilibrium after solidification and thus, over a wide temperature range and for a very long time, will undergo characteristic property changes. This is called physical aging and is quite different than, and distinct from, chemical aging, such as thermal degradation and photo-oxidation.

The temperature range over which physical aging occurs can be quite broad and frequently includes the use-temperatures of common plastics. Physical aging can be explained qualitatively on the basis of the free-volume concept so that, for example, the time dependence of mechanical properties is found to be independent of chemical structure. Indeed, creep (stress relaxation) curves of numerous types of polymers measured at various temperatures and aging times can all be superimposed to form a single master curve.

The consequences of physical aging for the materials specialist are twofold. On the one hand it is a major phenomenon that determines the behaviour of a material to a large extent by changing its relaxation times. The ability of rigid plastics to withstand prolonged stresses, that is, the fact that they can be used as load-bearing materials for long periods, is not an inherent property but one that is developed by physical aging during the deformation period. On the other hand, because it persists for a very long time, physical aging affects segmental mobility of polymer molecules so it probably also affects chemical degradation, photo-oxidation, swelling and de-swelling, in addition to mechanical relaxation phenomena. A knowledge of the aging behaviour of a plastic is indispensable in the prediction of its long-term properties from short-term tests. Effects on crazing and environmental stress-cracking are important but almost impossible to quantify on the basis of any free-volume models that may be applied to the aging of plastics.

Polymer Stabilization

A very high proportion of the reactions that degrade polymers involve free radicals: reactive, neutral species that tend to be chemically self-perpetuating in a hydrocarbon matrix. Two ways of approaching the requirement to stabilize polymers are (a) reducing the rates of formation of these radicals, and (b) preventing their destructive reactions by deactivating them first. It is self-evident that in selecting a material, recognition of the need for longevity in the intended use environment will be factored in with mechanical, aesthetic, and cost criteria. In connection with approach (a), it is advisable to avoid the formation of relatively labile chemical groups or relatively weak bonds in a polymer during storage, handling, application or fabrication. If the material is heat sensitive, for example, the time that it is exposed to air at high temperatures should be minimized; likewise, light-sensitive materials should be protected from exposure to sunlight, light from arc lamps or from some fluorescent lamps. Longer wavelength light can be a problem for coloured materials. In the case of polymers that are to be exposed to near ultraviolet (UV) wavelengths (the erythemal, or sunburn region, 290 nm to 315 nm), UV-absorbing stabilizers are commonly incorporated as low-level additives. Some pigments are UV protective although the anatase form of TiO_2 can act as a photosensitizer.

Hydroperoxide groups fastened to polymer chains represent a particularly insidious type of thermal and photochemical instability. Present just at or below detection limits, hydroperoxides can initiate the degradation of polymers containing aliphatic and even aromatic carbon-hydrogen bonds. Sulphur- and phosphorus-containing compounds, as well as hindered amines and nickel chelates, are among the highly efficient stabilizers that are added to polymers to protect them by decomposing adventitious hydroperoxides to form more stable compounds, before those hydroperoxides can initiate polymer degradation.

It is inevitable that covalent bonds will be broken and radicals will be formed during the fabrication, application and use of macromolecular materials. With regard to approach (b) mentioned earlier, stabilization can be achieved by trapping radicals. The most common kinds of radicals that can be trapped (deactivated) are alkyl and alkylperoxide, with the former being much more reactive and, in the presence of air, converting in what is usually a very fast reaction into the latter. It is very common to use stabilizing additives that deactivate alkyl radicals; hindered phenols can protect thermoplastics during fabrication (in the melt) as well as during long-term exposure to warm temperatures. Hindered amines (HALS) react with alkyl and peroxide radicals catalytically, as well as decomposing hydroperoxides, and impart unusually good stability to many polymers, including paints.

A variety of other stabilizers is included in polymer formulations to cope with specific instability problems, for example, metal soaps to neutralize the HCl generated in the dehydrochlorination of poly(vinyl chloride); antiozonants to protect polymers containing carbon-carbon unsaturation, such as diene rubbers, from attack by ambient ozone. Indeed, it is noteworthy that synthetic polymers are never pure and may include additives of many kinds for the modification of mechanical, surface, aesthetic and chemical properties. Few of these will be significant in contributing to stability.

Conclusion

Energy, oxygen and time combine to change the characteristics of polymers. The rates of undesirable changes can be reduced by selecting the most durable materials initially, combining these where possible with stabilizing compounds, reducing the exposure to degradative influences, and ensuring the least harmful use conditions and service environments. The effectiveness of such approaches is maximized by developing a comprehensive understanding of macromolecules and the chemistry of them.

Résumé

La transformation des matériaux polymériques avec le temps

À l'instar du papier, du bois et des peaux, pratiquement tous les plastiques, toutes les fibres, tous les caoutchoucs, toutes les peintures et tous les revêtements protecteurs doivent leurs caractéristiques utiles à la masse, relativement élevée (variant de quelques milliers à plusieurs millions), de leurs molécules. Malheureusement, la fabrication, la manutention et la bonne ou mauvaise utilisation de ces matériaux peuvent modifier — voire habituellement abaisser — la masse de leurs molécules constituantes, et atténuer de façon concomitante leurs propriétés utiles. L'étude dans le détail des modifications qui se produisent à l'échelle moléculaire demeure un secteur scientifique très complexe, qui est souvent difficile à saisir. Il est toutefois certains aspects, communs au vieillissement de plusieurs matériaux polymériques, qui ont été élucidés, et qui peuvent ainsi ouvrir la voie à une amélioration des techniques utilisées pour leur conservation.

La dégradation chimique de ces matériaux s'explique notamment par la détérioration oxydative qui se produit lorsque, exposés à l'air, ils entrent en contact avec la lumière, la chaleur ou des rayonnements ionisants, mais aussi par leur décomposition sous l'effet de l'hydrolyse ou de l'action d'acides ou de bases. La biodégradation peut, par ailleurs, être considérée comme un cas particulier de décomposition chimique causée par des enzymes microbiens. Les réactions qui interviennent dans la dégradation chimique sont nombreuses et, dans une certaine mesure, particulières à chaque matière; néanmoins, les plus importantes peuvent fréquemment être rattachées à l'oxydation d'hydrocarbures liquides. Pour réduire au minimum les phénomènes de décoloration, de fragilisation et de perte de propriétés physiques qui accompagnent la détérioration oxydative de ces matériaux, il suffit d'utiliser un mélange approprié d'additifs stabilisateurs. Et la meilleure façon d'atténuer leur sensibilité aux microbes demeure la mise en pratique de bonnes méthodes d'entretien.

Le vieillissement de ces matériaux polymériques qui, solidifiés ou ayant atteint autrement leur forme définitive d'utilisation, continueront à se dégrader durant des semaines, des mois, voire des années, demeure néanmoins un phénomène beaucoup moins bien connu. D'abord observé dans les thermoplastiques, au-dessous de la température de transition vitreuse (T_v), le vieillissement de ces matériaux se produit parce que toutes les propriétés liées à la température, qui changent brusquement à T_v, continuent néanmoins à changer au-dessous de cette température, même si ce n'est que très lentement. Le vieillissement s'observe chez les polymères amorphes, vitreux, chez les polymères semi-cristallins en phase amorphe, de même que dans la matrice caoutchouteuse des caoutchoucs chargés. Avec le temps, nombre de matériaux deviennent ainsi plus rigides et plus fragiles, au fur et à mesure que diminue le « taux de relaxation ». Comme le vieillissement influe sur la mobilité segmentale des polymères, son action devrait aussi se faire sentir sur la dégradation chimique, la photo-oxydation, le gonflement et le dégonflement et les réactions de réticulation de toute une gamme de systèmes macromoléculaires.

References

1. Carlsson D.J. and D.M. Wiles, "Degradation," in: *Encyclopedia of Polymer Science and Engineering, Volume 4, 2nd edition* (New York: John Wiley & Sons Inc., 1986) pp. 630-696.

2. Grassie, N., ed. *Developments in Polymer Degradation*, volume series, nos. 1 to 5 (London: Applied Science Publishers Ltd., 1977, 1979, 1981, 1982, 1984).

3. Jellinek, H.H.G., ed. *Degradation and Stabilization of Polymers* (Amsterdam: Elsevier, 1983).

4. Allen, N.S., ed. *Degradation and Stabilization of Polyolefins* (London: Applied Science Publishers Ltd., 1983).

5. Davis, A. and D. Sims, *Weathering of Polymers* (London: Applied Science Publishers, Ltd., 1983).

6. Moiseev, V.V. and G.E. Zaikov, *Chemical Resistance of Polymers in Aggressive Media* (New York: Plenum Press, 1982).

7. Pappas, S.P. and F.H. Winslow, eds. *Photodegradation and Photostabilization of Coatings*, American Chemical Society Symposium Series No. 151, 1981.

8. *Durability of Macromolecular Materials*, American Chemical Society Symposium Series No. 95, 1979.

9. *Long-term Properties of Polymers and Polymeric Materials*, Applied Polymer Symposium No. 35, 1979.

10. McKellar, J.F. and N.S. Allen, *Photochemistry of Man-made Polymers* (London: Applied Science Publishers Ltd., 1979).

11. Allara, D.L. and W.L. Hawkins, eds. *Stabilization and Degradation of Polymers*, Advances in Chemistry Series No. 169, 1976.

12. *Ultraviolet Light-induced Reactions in Polymers*, American Chemical Society Symposium Series No. 25, 1976.

13. Wiles, D.M. "The Photodegradation of Fibre-Forming Polymers," in: *Degradation and Stabilization of Polymers*, Chapter 7, G. Geuskens, ed. (London: Applied Science Publishers, 1975).

14. Rånby, B. and J.P. Rabek, *Photodegradation, Photo-oxidation and Photostabilization of Polymers; Principles and Applications* (New York: Wiley-Interscience, 1975).

15. Road, B.E., P.E. Tomlins and G.D. Dean, "Physical Ageing and Short-term Creep in Amorphous and Semi-crystalline Polymers," *Polymer*, vol. 7, July 1990, pp. 1204-1215.

16. Bouda, V., "The Nature of Glassy State Instability," *Polymer Degradation and Stability*, vol. 24, 1989, p. 319.

17. Chai, C.X. and N.G. McCrum, "Mechanism of Physical Aging in Crystalline Polymers," *Polymer*, vol. 21, 1980, p. 706.

18. Aklonis, J.J. and W.J. MacKnight, *Introduction to Polymer Viscoelasticity* (New York: John Wiley and Sons, 1983).

19. Ferry, J.D., *Viscoelastic Properties of Polymers, 3rd edition* (New York: John Wiley and Sons, 1980).

20. Stuik, L.C.E. *Physical Aging in Amorphous Polymers and Other Materials* (New York: Elsevier, 1978).

The Physical Aging of Polymeric Materials

Christopher W. McGlinchey

Paintings Conservation
The Metropolitan Museum of Art
New York, N.Y.
U.S.A.

Abstract

Physical aging of polymers can be defined as the changes in spatial arrangement of macromolecules and side chains with respect to one another. This molecular reorganization can cause several observable changes. Thermal properties, such as melting point, glass transition and crystallization, can become modified, possibly transforming the solubility and optical characteristics in the process. More tactile qualities, such as flexibility, embrittlement and drape, are also changes brought on by the process of physical aging.

Polymer morphology, the study of polymer order, depends upon the chemistry of the polymer, its structure and the thermal history to which it has been exposed. Though the terms amorphous and crystalline are often applied to polymers, it is more accurate to think of these terms as extremes on a spectrum and to consider that polymers, depending upon their structure, have the potential of being crystallized (achieving a higher state of order) or quenched (achieving greater disorder or becoming more amorphous). Physical aging can have significant effects on the aforesaid properties, but unlike chemical degradation, physical aging would be completely reversible were it not for the complication that occurs when chemical degradation alters the relationship between temperatures of degradation and melting point.

In the early stages of commercial polymers, physical aging was poorly understood and not knowingly factored into formulations. More recent polymer scientists now carefully consider this phenomenon, and make superior products to the earlier ones comprised of identical materials. Distinguishing between differences in chemical and physical aging will enable conservators to think more clearly about their fundamental approach to the complex aging process of polymeric materials.

Introduction

The elusive property that made macromolecules a controversial subject from the time of their discovery until as recently as the 1920s is their "polymeric" nature. It was precisely this property that prevented macromolecules from being identified using existing methods of fractionation, purification and crystallization. Results from these methods appeared to be in direct conflict with results based on diffusion and viscosity measurements that gave inordinately high molecular weights. The methods that failed to properly detect polymers were the traditional methods that had been successfully applied for centuries in the characterization of inorganic and lower molecular weight organic materials. Early distillations of macromolecular materials resulted in the decomposition of the parent material into fractions of low molecular weight. Neglecting the possibility of degradation, one attempt to solve this paradigm was through the concept of colloidal forces. These colloidal forces, though undetectable, were thought to reside in the residue of the distillation process. Two of the prominent scientists that finally settled the "polymer" controversy were Staudinger[1] and Carothers.[2] They showed through synthesis that macromolecules consist of many (poly) smaller repeat groups (mers) joined by conventional covalent bonds.

These and other historic proofs that led to the acceptance of polymers soon gave way to their full scale development and specialization. Polymer materials rapidly began to be reliably processed into products and finishes with a wide variety of uses (e.g., automobile tires, plexiglass, traffic stripes and vinyl upholstery). This was largely due to the homogeneity of certain properties, which assure reproducible activation conditions, melting point and solubility for different batches of the same material. The most significant properties of the polymer include chemical composition, molecular weight, molecular weight distribution and branching. In addition, synthetic polymers are more likely to be free of unstable impurities common to many natural polymers, which can initiate degradative chemical reactions. However, while these new products were likely to have extended lifetimes, improperly selected processing conditions may have occasionally shortened their life spans. Polymers do not necessarily possess intrinsic properties whose qualities are immediately apparent. Selection of processing conditions can either bring out desired properties — transparency, strength and dimensional stability — or result in a product that exhibits hastened embrittlement, warpage or cloudiness.

In order to study the changes in synthetic polymers upon aging it is necessary to define the differences between chemical and physical properties. Chemical degradation processes are related to changes in the covalent bond structure. A covalent bond is defined as the strong attractive force derived from the sharing of two electrons between two atoms. They are graphically represented as the lines between monomeric units, as well as between the atoms within each monomer. Physical properties, in addition to being dependent on molecular weight, molecular weight distribution and branching of polymers, also depend upon secondary bond forces. Secondary forces are attractive and repulsive forces that arise from the local electron densities that surround the atoms in molecules, and are therefore in part

dependent upon the primary bond forces. Although secondary bonds are relatively weak compared to covalent bonds, they can have a significant cumulative effect on the macroscopic properties of molecules.

It is possible that changes brought on by the altered physical properties of the polymer can be reversed *in-situ*, while those derived from chemical degradation cannot. Therefore it can be advantageous to determine the source of observable changes. For example, the yellowing of organic materials is obviously due to the "irreversible" chemical production of chromophores. But graying, embrittlement and decreased solubility are due to alterations in a material's physical properties. Modified physical properties that result from chemical degradation cannot be erased; they merely become the new physical properties of the particular system. On the other hand, the components of physical changes not initiated by chemical degradation are theoretically reversible. It is evident that the glass transition temperature (T_g) increases as oxidative degradation proceeds due to an increase in polar secondary forces. However, it is also possible for a material to remain chemically unchanged while showing an increase in T_g through physical aging.

The purpose of this paper is to discuss and illustrate the reversible and non-reversible changes that occur for thermoplastic polymers after processing and the passage of time. It is hoped that this information will enlighten conservators' understanding of these materials, whether they are for their own use or as the medium of the artist or a previous conservator. This will enable conservators to not only choose their treatments more judiciously but also assess the aging mechanisms occurring within artwork containing such polymers.

Polymer Physical Properties

Thermoplastic polymers are by definition materials that can be cycled from the solid state to the fluid state a number of times without a change in their molecular composition; this trait is characteristic of their physical properties. The term thermoplastic is intended to distinguish these materials from those that require chemical reactivity or radiation to cure them into an irreversible polymerized state. Thermoplastic polymers, while stable, are not necessarily exempt from thermo- and photo-chemically induced degradation. Given this finite chemical stability, the physical changes derived from these chemical changes are therefore non-reversible.

Thermoplastic polymers have to somehow be transferred from their raw material form into a final shape or finish. This transformation requires energy that is supplied in the form of heat, pressure and/or solvent action. Whether polymers in this transient state are in the form of polymer solutions or are heated above their melting point (Tm) they are by definition amorphous. This is because polymers are not locked within an ordered matrix; neighboring molecules randomly exchange their position. Rheology, the study of the flow and deformation of matter, is frequently used to study the response of polymer melts and solutions to stresses imposed by processing forces. Instrumentation for these measurements include viscometers, dynamic mechanical analyzers, calorimeters, melt rheometers and melt indexers.

The crystallization of thermoplastics occurs only between Tg and Tm.[3] The conformation changes required for the transition to a crystalline state do not occur instantaneously. Time is required for polymer chains, side chains and functional groups to organize into a three-dimensional order. Annealing (heating a material between its Tg and Tm) combined with a slow rate of cooling will optimize the amount of organization for a given polymer. Conversely, quenching (rapidly cooling from above the Tm to below the Tg) of a polymer will minimize the crystallinity of its molecular structure. Thus, it is possible to achieve a range of conformations or morphologies for a polymer by controlling the duration of the cooling period. Annealing can also be governed by processing variables, such as pressure, temperature and solvent evaporation.

Below the Tg, molecular motion is drastically reduced. (Note: Tg is not as precise as melting point; the transition occurs over a temperature range.) This reduced molecular motion corresponds to a reduction in heat capacity; the intensity, or shift in baseline of the differential scanning calorimeter (DSC) measurement for the Tg, corresponds to the differences between heat capacity of the liquid and glass states.[4] Of crystalline polymers, those that are quenched will show a more intense Tg than those annealed because the phenomenon is derived from non-crystalline — conversely amorphous — domains.[5] Below the Tg the polymer matrix is sufficiently restricted in movement to prevent further crystallization. The physical processes that take place beneath the Tg in amorphous domains are termed physical aging. Physical aging occurs between the glass transition, Tg, and the next lower secondary transition defined as T_β.[6] Secondary transitions are denoted T_α, T_β, T_γ, etc.; T_α corresponds to the Tg, while lower transitions maintain their Greek symbols and are due to weaker molecular motions at lower temperatures.

Thermal Processing
It is important for thermally processed polymers to be stable at the necessary processing temperature. If thermo-oxidative degradation is expected to occur, antioxidants in small quantities can be introduced to extend the effective processing time. Common methods of processing include injection molding, film and fiber extrusion, calendaring and casting. These operations are discussed in greater detail elsewhere.[7] Solvents are sometimes added to aid processing. Afterwards, they are usually intended to evaporate out but sometimes small amounts remain as plasticizers (e.g., water in certain nylon processes). In processing, polymer choice depends upon both the intended use of the product and the actual processing method. There is no polymer that is ideally suited for all processing methods. Some polymers (e.g., polyethylene) can be easily adapted for different processing methods, but usually at some compromise, for example, mechanical properties at the expense of optical properties or vice versa.

In thermal processing, crystalline polymers tend to be turned into fibers and films while amorphous materials lend themselves well as molded objects that need good clarity and isotropic strength. Synthetic fibers are processed from crystalline polymers so that when they are drawn, their crystalline domains are oriented along the fiber axis (machine direction) resulting in their higher strength in that direction. For example, nylon fiber after drawing (extending its length by pulling at a rate faster than that at which it comes out of the die exit) has a greater strength in the machine direction. Additionally, polyethylene pellets are opaque, but after processing, films and fibers can become more transparent due to orientation of crystalline domains previously randomly distributed. Stress whitening is a result of orienting in one direction to such an extent that the polymer develops fine voids during processing that cause extensive scattering.[8]

Processing forces, in conjunction with the cooling effect of the mold, transfer significant stresses into the polymer. Stresses that are formed in patterns are observable by the technique of flow birefringence.[9] If these patterns are not allowed to relax sufficiently they will become frozen within the material. These frozen stress patterns may relieve themselves through the process of physical aging, or be coaxed along by heating. A significant effort has been spent in developing processing operations that ease these stresses prior to being frozen into materials.

Physical Considerations of Solvent-Borne Polymers

Those formulating coatings have developed a wide range of solvents and additives to accommodate the many specific end-use requirements in the coatings industry. A host of additives have been developed to prevent almost every defect known to coatings; some examples are additives to avert floating, flooding, flattening, fouling, skinning and settling. Rheological modifiers are also added to improve a coating's handling properties during application. While a solvent must have the appropriate solubility characteristics to make a proper paint, the rate at which it evaporates plays a significant role in how the surface sets up to dry. The evaporation rate of a solvent from a paint is different from the evaporation rate of the pure solvent and varies from polymer to polymer. The surface tension of the solution (which depends partially upon the solvent) controls film leveling.[10] Unsuitable surface tension is responsible for such flaws in appearance as "orange peel" and "cratering."[11] In order to help study the checking,

cracking and crazing within coatings' derived stresses imparted from drying processes, a laser interferometry technique has been developed to make these stress patterns observable.[12]

The preparation of polymer thermoplastic coatings can include a combination of heat, solvent and pressure. Usually, the less soluble these materials are, the greater their crystallinity. Solvent cast films high in crystalline content tend to be durable and impervious to attack by organic solvents when dry. (This is the benefit gained from materials that require additional energy to formulate.) Thermoplastic amorphous resins with a low Tg are often used as components to pressure-sensitive adhesive coatings because their soft, amorphous domains reduce the surface tension of adhesive formulations to improve their flow, or tackiness. Amorphous coatings of higher Tg are commonly found in over-the-counter applications because of their shelf stability, solubility in mild solvents and ease of application. Hard amorphous materials are also those most often used in conservation practices because they are most likely to remain soluble in solvents similar to the ones in which they were originally dissolved.

Amorphous polymers are easily dissolved because there is no three-dimensional order that must be broken up prior to entering the amorphous liquid state. The lack of order in amorphous substances permits more voids into which solvent molecules can penetrate, leading to the switching of polymer-polymer interactions to solvent-polymer interactions. These voids, or unoccupied spaces between atoms and molecules, are often referred to as the free volume of the system. Crystalline materials, on the other hand, require additional energy to break up the ordered structure that results from relatively strong polymer-polymer interactions and generally a *lower* free volume compared to amorphous substances.[13]

Free volume permits solvent molecules to penetrate and to replace polymer-polymer interactions with polymer-solvent interactions. Since free volume increases with temperature, solubility of both amorphous and crystalline materials is increased by heating.

While solvent evaporation cannot be strictly likened to the cooling of polymer melt, some parallels do exist; these depend upon the rate of solvent release and the ability of the polymer resin to crystallize. It has been shown that molecular relaxation processes have occurred for annealed organic glasses that are the result of solvent removal; furthermore, these relaxation processes are solvent dependent.[14] For coatings with crystalloid resins the rate of solvent loss may have a great bearing on the final properties of the surface coating. This is because the time required for crystallinity to develop will be based upon the free volume available per unit of time; a fast evaporator will cause the free volume to decrease at a fast rate, thereby restricting motions that would be allowable in a slow er evaporating solution. The quickly dried sample, with its lower crystallinity, will be subsequently more soluble. If the Tg of the amorphous component is low enough, physical aging processes mentioned above may also result. Latent crystallization can only occur for materials exposed to temperatures between their Tg and Tm for significant periods of time.

Results and Discussion

Degree of Crystallinity for Hydrocarbons

The range of crystallinity can be illustrated by comparing the DSC cooling curves of two aliphatic hydrocarbon solids, such as low density polyethylene (LDPE) and hydrogenated poly(dicyclo pentadiene) (h-PDCPD), as shown in Figure 1. LDPE is a long linear polymer with some branching and h-PDCPD is a cyclic bridged structure. LDPE crystallizes at 89°C while the h-PDCPD does not crystallize. This is to be expected because the highly branched structure of the h-PDCPD prevents crystallization. Secondly, DSC heating curves show that DCPD has a Tg at 49°C while LDPE has a Tm of 106°C (Figure 2). Notice that the progression for thermal transition for LDPE is Tg<Tc <Tm, where Tc is the crystallization temperature. It is clear that the morphology of LDPE may depend upon thermal history whereas h-PDCPD remains amorphous under the same conditions. The crystalline nature of LDPE makes it more difficult to dissolve compared to h-PDCPD, which is more soluble and hence appropriate as a solvent cast varnish.

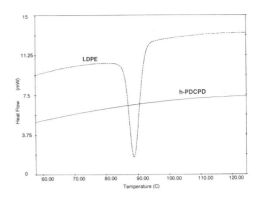

Figure 1 DSC cooling curves for LDPE and h-PDCPD.

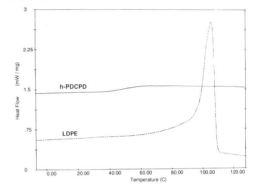

Figure 2 DSC heating curves for LDPE and h-PDCPD.

The effect of processing forces on the thermal properties of LDPE is determined by analyzing the DSC curve from the first heating cycle of the injection molded resin. In this instance, frozen stresses are derived from the imposed quench cooling of the high-pressure injecting of molten polymer into a mold much cooler than the plastic. As a result it does not have the opportunity to achieve the optimum degree of crystallinity. The DSC scan of the injection-molded sample shows a Tg of 41°C and a Tm of 105°C, which suggests the presence of both amorphous and crystalline components respectively (Figure 3). After the sample is annealed at 80°C, prior to the DSC heat, the diminished Tg is the result of enhanced crystallization.

Thin sections viewed in polarized light show a radial orientation orthogonal to the picture plane (Figure 4). Annealed radial and tangential samples cut from this circular cross-section show the stress-release mechanism:

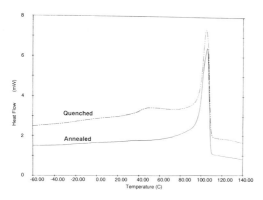

Figure 3 *DSC heating curves for injection-molded and annealed LDPE.*

Figure 4 *Thin section cut from injection-molded LDPE rod, viewed in crossed polars.*

unsymmetrical stress distributions in the tangential sample cause out-of-plane warpage while the radial cut sample does not (Figure 5). This warpage is similar to planks of wood cut with the same orientation, although the derivation of these stresses is radically different. For complex shapes of molded plastics frozen stresses can be equally complicated. For early plastics (whose color was a mixture of two different pigmented resins, such as red and white polystyrene) the incomplete mixing of these colors leads to a grain pattern in the product. It is possible that frozen stresses can follow this grain. This pattern, while visible, is not necessarily demonstrative of frozen stresses; the molding conditions may have eased these stresses by using a mild cooling temperature for the mold and/or a lower injection pressure.

Effect of Thermal History on Varnishes

The amorphicity of poly(vinyl acetate) (PVAC) is illustrated by DSC cooling curves. The DSC

cooling results (not shown) are similar to the h-PDCPD sample. However, first heat DSCs of a 34-year-old PVAC film, which was mechanically removed from a panel painting, indicate either the release of mechanical stresses in amorphous domains or the melting of crystalline domains both in the range of 37°C to 44°C (Figure 6). Normally the first heat is discarded because aging history makes it complicated and rarely reproducible. This is certainly true here because the peak in Figure 6 has taken as long as 34 years to develop. The fact that this is not reproducible does not make this result any less valuable. It is simply demonstrative of the aging history of this particular sample. This phenomenon must take a long time to form because, as can be seen from the annealed sample, it was not possible to regain this apparent Tm within the time frame of the DSC experiment.

After heating this sample to 45°C for five minutes and then reducing the temperature to 25°C, visible light transmittance, measured spectroscopically, increased permanently by 7%. It is therefore most likely that the opacification after

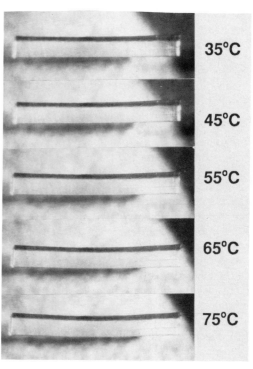

Figure 5 *Heat-treated sample tangentially cut from LDPE cross-section.*

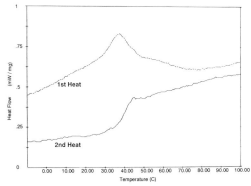

Figure 6 DSC traces 34-year-old PVAC film.

34 years is from the formation of crystalline domains that are large enough to scatter light and that the increase in transparency upon heating is due to the conversion of crystalline domains back into amorphous ones. PVACs, though not normally crystalloid, apparently are to a small degree when given enough time, in this case 34 years.

While long-term induced crystallization is certainly responsible for a portion of the increased opacification or grayness of these films it is likely not to be the only reason. The denser structure associated with the increase in crystallinity has (by definition) contracted during the aging process. If sufficient, this contraction may contribute to the lack of adhesion at the paint/varnish interface and furthermore may permit diffusing air to accumulate in this region, thereby increasing scattering even more. The fact that these films are so easily peeled off of paintings lends credence in some instances to this hypothesis. It is also possible that soft resins allow more airborne particles to stick to their surfaces.

Once the proportion of crystallinity has been reduced within the material through heating, solubility properties change. After a five minute exposure to xylene, the post treatment samples imbibe more solvent and coalesce more extensively. After measuring the solvent uptake for five pairs of heated and unheated samples, on average the preheated sample imbibed 0.51 µl and the untreated film took 0.11 µl in a five minute period. After two hours of exposure the results were less reproducible: in three cases the heated sample cleared away more

resin and in the remaining two pairs the appearance in effective solubility was about the same for both samples. These results suggest the main change in solubility is that the rate at which solvent is taken up varies significantly. Given enough time, however, eventual solubility is approximately the same.

This is not to suggest that all the changes in this film are derived from changes in purely physical properties. By comparing the IR spectra of this 34-year-old film to fresh PVAC, it is evident that some degree of chemical degradation has taken place (Figure 7). The increase in polarity from oxidation products chemically formed during aging is likely to require a solvent of enhanced polarity to re-dissolve the film. It is therefore apparent that these materials change as a result of both chemical and physical properties. Additionally, the change in physical properties, the result from the chemical changes illustrated in the IR spectra, impart their own effect on the physical properties that are not reversible. This is opposed to the portion of physical changes represented by the DSC results that are reversible.

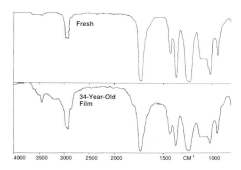

Figure 7 Infrared spectra of PVACs cast on salt plate.

Conclusion

The methods by which thermoplastic polymers are made into their final product is as varied as the class of thermoplastics themselves. While polymers have intrinsic properties that cannot be hidden, such observable properties as strength, clarity and solubility are contingent upon processing forces. It is understood that solvents, temperature and pressure can affect these observable properties. Stress-release mechanisms result from frozen stresses of improperly molded objects. The process under which these stresses are relieved depend upon polymer structure and ambient exposure conditions. After sufficient aging PVAC develops crystalline domains that are large enough to scatter light and modify solubility. Additionally, the risks involved in the removal of old synthetic restorations can possibly be induced by warming them to moderate temperatures (e.g., 40°C) in order to reduce the time required for their solubility.

Finally, with the ushering in of a class of chemically stable synthetic products, yellowing and other phenomena associated with oxidative degradation are no longer the only degradation processes that divert artistic works from their original meaning. Opacification, scattering and (when appropriate) warpage are changes that may or may not be easily reversible. It is our responsibility to learn more about these changes, if not for the conservator, for the sake of future generations so they don't romanticize about the "gorgeous grays" of the 20th century.

Experimental

The T_g, T_c and T_m of polymers were determined using a liquid nitrogen cooled differential scanning calorimeter, model DSC 7 (Perkin-Elmer). Temperatures and specific heats of transition were calibrated using indium and zinc standards.

Low density polyethylene (Rexene 143, Dupont) was injection molded (at 400°C under a pressure of 9.65 MPa using a water cooled Van Dorn injection molding machine) into the form of a rod with a diameter of 5 mm. Plates 1 mm thick were cut from the rod, tangential and radial samples were cut from this plate (Figure 1). These samples were placed on a heatable stage, Metratherm model 1200d (BBC), and observed through a stereoscope (Zeiss). Approximate temperatures were determined by correcting them against the observed boiling point of water. Stress-release mechanisms were photographed using a Polaroid camera attachment on the stereoscope.

Solubility tests were as follows. A pair of 2 microliter pipettes, mounted on a wooden

stick with wax, were suspended perpendicular to the microscope's stage. This assembly was attached to a plate of adjustable height on either side of the stage. The varnish films were placed beneath these pipettes and weighed down with small washers. Prior to filling with solvent, the pipettes were adjusted to ensure simultaneous contact with each surface. Samples were then rinsed with an aliphatic solvent and allowed to dry overnight and then photographed.

Visible light transmittance measurements were calculated at 550 nm using a Perkin-Elmer lambda array UV/VIS spectrophotometer.

Acknowledgement

The author thanks John M. Brealey and Hubert von Sonnenburg for creating and maintaining the interdisciplinary environment of the Sherman Fairchild Department of Paintings Conservation; Jeffrey Jennings and Marie L. O'Shea for providing valuable comments regarding the subject matter of this paper; and Marycolette Hruskocy for providing assistance during the investigative stages of this paper.

Résumé

Le vieillissement des matériaux polymériques

Le vieillissement d'un polymère peut se définir comme le réarrangement spatial des macromolécules et chaînes latérales qui le composent. Il s'accompagne parfois de plusieurs changements observables. Ses propriétés thermiques — son point de fusion, sa transition vitreuse et sa cristallinité, notamment — pourront ainsi se modifier, tandis que sa solubilité et ses caractéristiques optiques varieront d'autant. Le vieillissement suscite en outre une transformation des propriétés plus tactiles du polymère, telles sa flexibilité, sa friabilité et son drapé.

La morphologie du polymère — l'étude de la disposition des macromolécules les unes par rapport aux autres — est liée à sa chimie, à sa structure et aux températures auxquelles il a été exposé. Si l'on qualifie souvent les polymères de cristallins ou d'amorphes, il serait pourtant plus juste de considérer qu'il ne s'agit là que de deux extrêmes, que les polymères peuvent, selon leur structure, devenir plus cristallins — lorsque leurs macromolécules présentent, les unes par rapport aux autres, une disposition régulière — ou plus amorphes — lorsqu'elles offrent une disposition moins régulière. Le vieillissement peut avoir des effets importants sur les propriétés énumérées plus haut mais — contrairement à ce qui se produit dans le cas d'une dégradation chimique — ces effets demeureraient entièrement réversibles si ce n'était de cette complication qui survient quand une dégradation chimique altère le rapport entre les températures de dégradation et le point de fusion.

À l'époque des premiers polymères commerciaux, on comprenait mal le vieillissement, et on n'en tenait guère compte dans l'élaboration des préparations. Aujourd'hui, les spécialistes des polymères prennent soigneusement en compte ce facteur, si bien que l'on obtient, à partir des mêmes matières, des produits supérieurs aux premiers. Forts d'une telle distinction entre la dégradation chimique et le vieillissement, les spécialistes de la restauration seront en mesure de définir plus clairement leur approche fondamentale face à ce processus complexe que constitue le vieillissement des matériaux polymériques.

References

1. Staudinger, H., "The Constitution of Polyoxymethylenes and Other High Molecular Compounds," *Helvetia Chimica Acta,* 1925, pp. 67-70.

2. Carothers, W.H., "An Introduction to the General Theory of Condensation Polymers," *Journal of the American Chemical Society,* vol. 5, no. 1, 1929, pp. 2548-2559.

3. Hall, C., *Polymer Materials,* 2nd edn. (New York: Wiley Interscience, 1989) p. 47.

4. Turi, E., *Thermal Characterization of Polymeric Materials* (Orlando: Academic Press, 1981) p. 167.

5. Ferry, J.D., *Viscoelastic Properties of Polymers,* 3rd edn. (New York: Wiley, 1980) p. 280.

6. Struik, L.C.E., "Volume Relaxation in Polymers," *Rheologica Acta,* vol. 5, 1966, pp. 303-311.

7. Han, C.D., *Rheology in Polymer Processing* (New York: Academic Press, 1976).

8. Woodward, A.E., *Atlas of Polymer Morphology* (Munich: Hanser Pub., 1989) p. 363.

9. Meeten, G.H., ed., *Optical Properties of Polymers* (London: Elsevier, 1986) p. 101.

10. Keunigs, R. and D.W. Bousfield, "Analysis of Surface Tension Driven Leveling in Viscoelastic Films," *J. Non-Newtonian Fluid Mechanics,* vol. 22, 1987, pp. 219-233.

11. Quach, A., "Polymer Coatings: Physics and Mechanics of Leveling," *Industrial and Engineering Chemistry Product Research and Development*, vol. 12, no. 2, 1973, pp. 110-116.

12. O'Brien, R.N. and W. Michalik, "Laser Interferometry for Internal Stress Measurement in Coatings," *Journal of Coatings Technology,* vol. 58, no. 735, 1986, pp. 25-30.

13. Morawetz, H., *Macromolecules in Solutions,* 2nd edn. (New York: Wiley, 1974).

14. Petrie, S.E.B., "Thermal Behavior of Annealed Organic Glasses," *Journal of Polymer Science Part A-2,* vol. 10, 1972, pp. 1255-1272.

La prévision du comportement à long terme de matériaux polymères synthétiques d'après des expériences de vieillissement artificiel

Jacques Lemaire

Laboratoire de photochimie
Centre national d'évaluation de photoprotection
Université Blaise-Pascal
Clermont-Ferrand
France

Résumé

Nous décrirons le photovieillissement des polymères synthétiques se retrouvant couramment dans des sculptures modernes qui sont exposées dans les musées extérieurs. Les polyesters insaturés réticulés ainsi que divers polyacrylates et polyméthacrylates serviront d'exemples de matrices non stabilisées dont les propriétés peuvent être modifiées au cours de la polymérisation, par séchage à partir de la solution ou de l'émulsion et au moyen d'additifs. Nous décrirons également la photo-oxydation et l'oxydation thermique d'élastomères diéniques (butadiène, styrène-butadiène et caoutchouc de nitrile-butadiène), car on ne saurait élaborer une stratégie de stabilisation sans d'abord comprendre le mécanisme d'oxydation.

On peut avoir recours, pour tenter de prévoir la vitesse du vieillissement des polymères synthétiques qui ont été utilisés, à l'approche mécanistique. Aux termes d'une telle approche, les polymères solides sont considérés comme des « réacteurs » chimiques, c'est-à-dire comme des milieux qui sont le site de certaines réactions chimiques. Elle suppose l'identification des mécanismes qui se produisent, à l'échelle moléculaire, dans des conditions de vieillissement accéléré, artificielles, et d'utilisation normale, naturelles. Les effets les plus néfastes proviennent de l'oxydation causée par une trop forte exposition à la lumière, à la chaleur ou à d'autres contraintes statiques et dynamiques. Et une analyse chimique poussée permettra d'expliquer les modifications de propriétés physiques macroscopiques (propriétés mécaniques, opacité, aspect en surface, etc.). Le vieillissement accéléré se confond ainsi, en fait, avec une oxydation accélérée, et le facteur d'accélération peut être établi à partir de la vitesse de la formation, dans des conditions artificielles et naturelles, des produits d'oxydation critiques. C'est donc dire qu'il est possible de prévoir la durée de vie d'un polymère en se fondant sur les mesures de durée de vie obtenues dans des conditions artificielles et en prenant alors en compte le facteur d'accélération. Cette approche mécanistique se compare bien aux techniques empiriques fondées sur la simulation des conditions physiques et chimiques réelles et sur les variations de propriétés physiques macroscopiques qui en résultent.

Pour la plupart des polymères synthétiques, la dégradation oxydative, qui tient soit à la structure normale du monomère polymérisé, soit à des défauts chimiques, s'observe à un très faible degré d'oxydation. Il faut dès lors avoir recours à des techniques spectrophotométriques in situ très sensibles et informatives pour déterminer la nature des divers intermédiaires et produits finals.

Introduction

Les matériaux polymères, naturels ou synthétiques, que l'on utilise soit pour la conservation et la restauration des œuvres d'art, soit pour leur élaboration, présentent l'inconvénient majeur d'évoluer dans le temps, avec une perte progressive de leurs propriétés physiques et des modifications d'aspect. Les phénomènes de vieillissement, qui sont reconnus comme complexes depuis fort longtemps, ne font en fait l'objet d'analyses que depuis vingt ans, leur étude ayant été largement différée à la suite des premiers succès obtenus grâce à des méthodes très empiriques.

Les premiers problèmes de fiabilité des matériaux polymères en cours d'usage se sont en effet posés dès les années 1945-1950 aux mécaniciens qui utilisaient des pièces en plastique. Ces mécaniciens n'ont alors considéré que les aspects macroscopiques du vieillissement des systèmes, et ils n'ont étudié que les variations des propriétés physiques utiles en appliquant à ces systèmes, en laboratoire, des contraintes physiques et chimiques représentatives de celles auxquelles ils sont soumis en cours d'usage. Par exemple, le vieillissement en conditions climatiques était examiné dans des enceintes de « simulation » qui reproduisaient les contraintes naturelles de l'environnement (la lumière, la chaleur, l'O_2, l'H_2O, etc.). De telles méthodes ne permettaient de prévoir le comportement à long terme des polymères qu'en établissant une « corrélation » avec les situations réelles de vieillissement. Ces méthodes — de contrôle plutôt que de prévision — n'ont guère évolué depuis 1950; leur emploi s'est par contre beaucoup développé, et elles ont fourni de nombreux résultats que l'on n'arrive pas à « rationaliser ».

À partir des années 70, une approche plus cognitive du comportement à long terme des matériaux polymères s'est développée, qui se fondait sur des analyses, au niveau moléculaire, des modifications chimiques des chaînes macromoléculaires qui apparaissent en cours d'usage. Cette approche a surtout été utilisée pour les polymères synthétiques qui, contrairement aux matériaux organiques naturels, présentent un ordre au niveau moléculaire, avec une répétition plus ou moins régulière de l'unité monomère. Actuellement, on peut considérer comme acquis les principes suivants :

• Un matériau polymère évolue à la façon d'un **réacteur chimique ou photochimique**; sa dégradation suppose l'apparition de concentrations généralement faibles de groupements chimiques (oxydés, par exemple) et cette **évolution chimique** est responsable de la dégradation des propriétés physiques. Le **vieillissement physique** des polymères n'intervient que dans le cas des matériaux qui sont soumis à des contraintes physiques très importantes, et il n'a donc aucune importance dans le cas des œuvres d'art.

• L'**évolution chimique** ne dépend pas des contraintes mécaniques qui sont appliquées; ces contraintes ne modifient que les conséquences physiques de l'**évolution chimique**.

• L'**accélération de l'évolution chimique** ne dépend donc pas des contraintes mécaniques externes et internes. L'analyse de l'évolution chimique permet de **convertir** la durée d'expériences en laboratoire en durée d'usage dans des conditions naturelles (l'évolution chimique constituant dès lors la base de tout transfert de données).

• L'évolution chimique est une caractéristique de chaque mécanisme d'évolution d'un **matériau donné**. Une formulation précise (polymère + charges + pigments ou colorants + additifs) doit être caractérisée par un **facteur d'accélération** qui lui est **propre**. On ne peut transférer directement un classement de divers matériaux ou de diverses formulations obtenu en laboratoire aux conditions du terrain sans tenir compte de facteurs d'accélération **nécessairement différents**.

• L'accélération des évolutions chimiques est non seulement autorisée, mais elle est fondamentalement **indispensable** car :

a) **on ne sait pas** extrapoler les données recueillies dans les phases précoces d'évolution des matériaux (les méthodes de la cinétique homogène ne sont pas acceptables);

b) on doit amener le matériau à un niveau d'évolution chimique qui entraîne une dégradation mécanique.

• Il est, par contre, indispensable de provoquer une accélération des événements chimiques en maintenant **leur représentativité**. Cette représentativité doit d'abord être la conséquence des contraintes physiques et chimiques qui sont appliquées, lesquelles doivent elles-mêmes être représentatives des contraintes en cours d'usage. La représentativité doit être surtout vérifiée en comparant les **mécanismes réactionnels** en conditions accélérées, d'une part, et en conditions d'usage, d'autre part. Dans ce domaine, un mécanisme réactionnel peut être décrit à l'aide de séquences réactionnelles (et non de processus élémentaires), et chaque séquence réactionnelle doit être reconnue dans les évolutions artificielles et naturelles. Il s'agit là de la base de l'approche « mécanistique » qui, de 1975 à nos jours, a pu être développée dans notre laboratoire pour la plupart des polymères couramment utilisés.

• Tout vieillissement accéléré correspond en fait à une accélération de l'**évolution chimique**. Quand un mécanisme chimique suppose plusieurs chemins réactionnels d'importance équivalente, on ne peut espérer accélérer tous ces chemins réactionnels avec les mêmes facteurs d'accélération. L'expérience en laboratoire déforme alors la réalité des conditions d'usage. De même, si, à l'évolution chimique, se superposent des phénomènes de transfert physique (oxygène ou stabilisant, par exemple), la présence de plusieurs processus dynamiques interdit le transfert des conditions accélérées créées en laboratoire aux conditions d'usage. On ne peut opérer ce transfert que pour les systèmes dont l'évolution chimique est contrôlée par un **mécanisme chimique prépondérant**. Cette situation se présente assez souvent dans le cas du photovieillissement, où le mécanisme photo-oxydatif est alors contrôlant et les phénomènes de diffusion de l'oxygène, suffisamment rapides pour ne pas limiter l'oxydation.

• La description de l'**évolution chimique** doit, enfin, être associée au critère de dégradation choisi :

- La description basée sur les produits observables en **spectroscopie vibrationnelle** (infrarouge ou Raman) doit être associée aux variations de propriétés mécaniques. Ces produits correspondent en effet aux voies principales d'oxydation; ils sont en concentrations faibles mais leur apparition correspond à une vraie détérioration de la matrice.

- La description basée sur les produits observables en **spectroscopie électronique** (ultraviolet, lumière visible, colorimétrie ou émission de fluorescence) doit être associée aux variations d'aspect. Ces produits — les produits de jaunissement, par exemple — sont détectés à des concentrations très inférieures à celles des produits principaux d'oxydation observés en infrarouge ou en Raman, et ils ne correspondent généralement pas à une perte des propriétés mécaniques de la matrice.

Il est donc possible de prévoir la durée de vie d'un matériau polymère soumis à des contraintes lumineuses ou thermiques en présence d'O_2 et d'eau :

• en déterminant, en conditions accélérées de laboratoire, la cinétique de l'apparition d'un « produit critique », c'est-à-dire un produit qui s'accumule, selon une loi linéaire, avec la durée d'exposition et dont l'apparition traduit une coupure de chaîne macromoléculaire;

• en déterminant, toujours en conditions accélérées de laboratoire, la corrélation existant entre les variations de propriétés macroscopiques d'usage (propriétés mécaniques ou aspect) et les variations de la concentration de ce produit critique; on précise ainsi le seuil tolérable d'évolution chimique;

• en comparant la cinétique de l'apparition du produit critique en conditions accélérées, d'une part, et **dans une phase précoce** de vieillissement en cours d'usage, d'autre part, on obtient le facteur d'accélération qui permet de convertir la durée d'exposition en laboratoire en durée d'usage.

Dans le présent exposé, trois classes exemplaires de polymères seront évoquées, à savoir :

1. la classe des polyesters insaturés, comme exemples de matériaux polymères dont le comportement à long terme peut être modulé par la structure même du polymère et par l'introduction d'additifs stabilisants;

2. la classe des polyacrylates et des polyméthacrylates, comme exemples de polymères relativement stables dont le comportement à long terme dépend pourtant dans une large mesure du composé étranger qui a été introduit;

3. la classe des élastomères diéniques, comme exemples de polymères dont le comportement à long terme a été prévu, à tort, à partir d'essais non représentatifs.

La photolyse et la photo-oxydation des polyesters insaturés

Les polyesters insaturés sont des polymères de condensation résultant de l'action de diacides sur des dialcools (glycols). L'un au moins des diacides est insaturé, ce qui permet la réticulation par oligomérisation *in situ* d'un agent de réticulation. On obtient alors un réseau tridimensionnel donnant au produit final son caractère d'irréversibilité thermique le classant dans les thermodurcissables. Si l'on utilise le styrène comme agent de réticulation, on obtient des polyesters insaturés de structure :

où R peut être un noyau aromatique disubstitué en ortho ou en méta selon que le diacide utilisé est un acide orthophtalique ou isophtalique.

Ces polymères se retrouvent souvent dans des sculptures contemporaines (de T. Grand, de Niki de Saint Phale ou de J. P. Raynaud, par exemple). L'insolubilité de ces polymères réticulés rend l'analyse de l'évolution chimique particulièrement difficile. Il a été possible néanmoins de démontrer les faits suivants :

1. Les groupements responsables de l'absorption de la lumière naturelle extérieure ($\lambda \geq 300$ nm) ou intérieure ($\lambda \geq 340$ nm) sont les groupements de maléates-fumarates résiduels et les groupements de phtalates, les oligomères de styrène n'étant pas susceptibles d'absorber cette lumière. Ces groupements absorbants provoquent, par dissociation en radicaux, l'amorçage de la photo-oxydation.

2. Ces matériaux sont le siège de phénomènes de « jaunissement » photolytique (la photolyse désignant des événements photochimiques non modifiables par l'oxygène). Ces produits de la photolyse qui absorbent les rayons de la lumière visible ($\lambda \approx 400$ nm) peuvent être détruits par photo-oxydation.

3. Ces matériaux sont simultanément le siège de phénomènes photo-oxydatifs. Cette photo-oxydation — qui dépend de la nature des diacides et du glycol utilisés, du réticulant (styrène ou acrylates) et des modes de réticulation — provoque également des jaunissements, mais elle est surtout responsable de l'apparition de groupements oxydés (groupements hydroxylés et carbonylés), qui s'accumulent et qui sont associés aux variations de propriétés physiques (des microfissurations superficielles, par exemple).

4. Les jaunissements qui apparaissent de façon plus importante en l'absence ou en déficit d'oxygène qu'en présence d'oxygène sont dus soit aux seuls groupements de styrène (dans les polyesters insaturés élaborés uniquement à partir d'anhydride maléique), soit à l'action conjuguée de groupements de phtalates et de styrène (dans les polyesters élaborés à partir de mélanges d'anhydride maléique et d'acide phtalique).

5. L'oxydabilité des polyesters insaturés est surtout attribuable aux insaturations de maléates ou de fumarates qui n'ont pas réagi dans la réticulation. Une réticulation obtenue avec du styrène réduira ainsi l'oxydabilité, mais elle accentuera le pouvoir jaunissant. Une réticulation obtenue avec un acrylate et un méthacrylate diminuera le pouvoir jaunissant, mais le taux d'insaturation résiduel sera plus important et l'oxydabilité, plus grande. Dans ce dernier cas, les couches superficielles oxydées donneront lieu à des microfissurations, et il en résultera un blanchissement.

6. La nature du dialcool est également importante — l'usage de néopentylglycol permet de réduire l'oxydabilité, par exemple.

Les mécanismes d'évolution chimique des polyesters insaturés réticulés à l'aide de styrène sont schématisés dans les tableaux I et II, qui indiquent les groupes chromophores photo-amorceurs, les unités réactives et la nature des produits observés. Le tableau I porte sur les polyesters obtenus à partir d'un mélange d'acide phtalique et d'anhydride maléique et le tableau II, sur les polyesters obtenus à partir d'anhydride maléique.

Puisque la structure moléculaire d'un polyester insaturé réticulé peut varier très largement selon la nature des monomères, des réticulants et du mode de réticulation, la photoréactivité sera tout aussi variable. Elle pourra ainsi notamment être adaptée pour obtenir, par exemple, une microfissuration réduite, si l'on accepte qu'un jaunissement important puisse se produire. En fait, la durabilité de ce matériau peut être largement améliorée grâce à l'emploi de photostabilisants. Lorsqu'un polyester est simultanément le siège d'une photolyse et d'une photo-oxydation, ou d'un autre double processus photochimique du genre, il convient d'utiliser un mélange formé des substances suivantes :

• un « anti-U. V*. » qui inhibera partiellement la photolyse, ainsi que la photo-oxidation

Tableau I

Les mécanismes d'évolution chimique des polyesters obtenus à partir d'un mélange d'acide phtalique et d'anhydride maléique

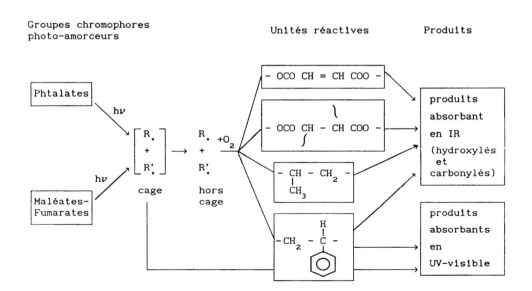

127

Tableau II

Les mécanismes d'évolution chimique des polyesters obtenus à partir d'anhydride maléique

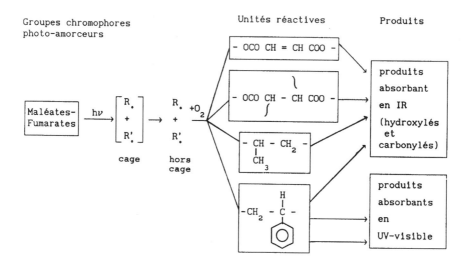

tant de la matrice que des produits de la photolyse (par compétition d'absorption);

• un « antioxydant redox » qui n'inhibera que la photo-oxydation de la matrice (sans inhibition de la photo-oxydation des produits de la photolyse).

L'emploi d'un seul anti-U. V. risque d'accentuer le photojaunissement. Il faut l'assister d'un antioxydant redox qui ne modifiera que les oxydations radicalaires sans perturber les photo-oxydations directes.

La photo-oxydation des dérivés acryliques

Les **polyacrylates** et les **polyméthacrylates** sont des polymères saturés qui ne présentent pas de sites intrinsèques de fragilité photolytique et photo-oxydative. Les processus de Norrish de type II qui interviennent dans les esters saturés ont une importance réduite. Par contre, ils peuvent être le siège d'une oxydation photo-induite par tout composé étranger susceptible d'absorber la lumière et de donner naissance à des radicaux. Ces polymères sont donc très sensibles à toute contamination (introduite, au moment de l'élaboration ou avec le temps, par migration dans les systèmes solides). Cette

circonstance se rencontre, en fait, de façon classique, dans tous les matériaux polymères qui n'absorbent pas la lumière lorsque $\lambda \geq 300$ nm; l'amorçage photochimique de leur oxydation est également dû à des composés étrangers chromophores et photo-inducteurs. Mais, dans la plupart des cas, cet amorçage ne correspond qu'à une phase initiale, les groupements oxydés formés sur la chaîne principale du polymère jouant très vite le rôle de chromophores photo-amorceurs. Les poly(méthacrylates de méthyle), ou PMMA, se caractérisent, au contraire, par le fait que leur durée de vie semble complètement tributaire des contaminants.

La photo-oxydation du PMMA se traduit par l'apparition de produits hydroxylés observables en spectroscopie infrarouge à transformée de Fourier (IRTF) à 3 580 et 3 320 cm^{-1}. Ces produits, qui atteignent une concentration constante au terme d'une phase précoce de formation, ont été identifiés à des groupements alcooliques associés, par liaisons « hydrogène », soit aux groupements esters (à 3 580 cm^{-1}) soit entre eux (à 3 320 cm^{-1}). Les produits hydroxylés sont les seuls photo-produits aisément observables; il se forme également des groupements responsables de l'élargissement de la bande d'absorption des groupements esters, mais il est impossible d'attribuer des caractères quantitatifs à cette observation.

À grandes longueurs d'onde (λ > 300 nm), la photo-oxydation est essentiellement le fait de composés extrinsèques chromophores et photo-inducteurs. Aucun photoproduit chromophore n'est formé au cours de la photo-oxydation du PMMA et n'assure le relais des photo-inducteurs initiaux. La photoréaction s'arrête donc quand le photo-inducteur est entièrement consommé; ceci intervient également à très faible taux d'oxydation de la matrice de PMMA exposée sous forme de film.

Quand, par contre, une plaque épaisse de PMMA est exposée en conditions accélérées ou en conditions naturelles, la photo-oxydation est localisée dans les quelque 1 000 μm de la couche superficielle; elle résulte tant de la diffusion d'oxygène dans la matrice que d'une diffusion qui se produit en direction opposée aux photo-inducteurs. Cette deuxième diffusion a été mise en évidence lors d'une expérience, au cours de laquelle deux photo-oxydations sont intervenues successivement, et où les 400 premiers μm les plus photo-oxydés ont été prélevés au terme de la première photo-oxydation. La deuxième photo-oxydation s'est produite à des vitesses nettement inférieures à celles qui avaient été observées lors de la première. Cette remarque justifie d'ailleurs les techniques de rénovation du PMMA qui se fondent sur une élimination des couches oxydées les plus superficielles.

Les insaturations résiduelles sont des sites réactifs qui disparaissent au cours de l'oxydation de la matrice de PMMA, bien que, n'absorbant pas les photons de λ >300 nm, elles ne soient pas responsables de l'amorçage de la photo-oxydation du PMMA.

La fonction d'un photo-inducteur — c'est-à-dire d'un composé susceptible d'absorber la lumière et de donner naissance à des radicaux libres réactifs, qui ne se recombineront donc pas entre eux — est peu spécifique. La nature des contaminants chromophores du PMMA peut être très variée et dépendre des conditions qui ont présidé à l'élaboration, à la mise en œuvre et à la formulation du PMMA qui fait l'objet de l'analyse, et il n'est pas utile de préciser la nature moléculaire du photo-inducteur, dont la présence se manifestera par une

absorption au-delà de 300 nm dans les spectres ultraviolets de plaques épaisses (de 3 à 6 mm).

Le mécanisme de l'oxydation photo-induite du PMMA peut être représenté ainsi :

```
            X  (photo-inducteur)

                  │ hν

            r.(ro₂.)

                  +
                 CH₃
                  │
        — CH₂ — C —
                  │
                 COOCH₃

                  │

               •   CH₃
                  │
        — CH — C —
                  │
                 COOCH₃

                  │  O₂ , PH

             H   CH₃
             │   │
        — C — C —
             │   │
            OOH COOCH₃

                  │ hν

             H   CH₃
             │   │
        — C — C —    + •OH
             │   │
            O•  COOCH₃

          /              \
         / réaction        \
        / en cage           \
                                        CH₃
      CH₃                   — CH ——— C —
       │                        │      │
   — C—C —  + H₂O               O      C
    ‖  │                        \     /‖ \
    O  COOCH₃                     H  O   OCH₃

                                    +
   (non observable)          groupements hydroxyles
                             associés entre eux
```

PH = Hydrogène du polymère

129

Les polyacrylates d'alkyle présentent des mécanismes de photo-oxydation analogues à ceux du PMMA. Un phénomène nouveau peut apparaître, par contre, quand on polymérise *in situ* des monomères ou des oligomères d'acrylates pour constituer des couches adhésives d'assez forte épaisseur. Cette polymérisation initiale est souvent inhibée par l'oxygène et elle ne s'effectue que très partiellement; les insaturations résiduelles restent donc en concentrations importantes au sein de la matrice au terme de la polymérisation. Ces insaturations résiduelles sont susceptibles de donner lieu à une polymérisation à long terme et il se crée alors un réseau polymérique dans la matrice initiale, avec une réduction du volume occupé. Il apparaît alors des zones d'hétérogénéité visibles à l'œil nu. Ce phénomène est courant dans le cas d'œuvres où de fortes épaisseurs d'adhésifs acryliques ont été utilisées.

La photo-oxydation d'élastomères diéniques

Jusqu'à ces dernières années, les élastomères diéniques n'ont pu, essentiellement à cause de facteurs d'ordre analytique, être examinés dans le cadre de l'approche « mécanistique ». Dans leur forme finie, ces matériaux sont fort complexes et profondément modifiés par la vulcanisation ou la réticulation, et ils contiennent généralement des pourcentages élevés de charges absorbantes en ultraviolet, en lumière visible et en infrarouge. Les méthodes spectroscopiques qui sont habituellement utilisées pour observer les quelques modifications chimiques des chaînes polymériques (à un degré d'avancement souvent inférieur à 1 %) ne peuvent plus être mises en œuvre aisément. La durabilité des élastomères synthétiques élaborés à partir de diènes n'avait donc été examinée que sur le plan macroscopique, le vieillissement de ces matériaux exposés en conditions naturelles ou simulées n'étant caractérisé que par des variations de propriétés mécaniques ou d'aspect (des microfissurations superficielles, par exemple). Une telle approche n'a pu fournir, à l'évidence, aucune indication sur la nature exacte de l'évolution chimique, les seules connaissances de cet ordre n'ayant pu être acquises que sur des composés modèles de faible poids moléculaire.

Depuis 1985, nous analysons le mécanisme de photo-oxydation de différents types de polybutadiènes (BR), de polyisoprènes (IR) et de copolymères styrène-butadiène (SBR) ou acrylonitrile-butadiène (NBR). Nous avons procédé à une étude détaillée des évolutions photochimiques en utilisant diverses techniques spectroscopiques (infrarouge, IRTF, micro-IRTF, ultraviolet ou Raman). En outre, les perturbations apportées par des noirs de carbone et des oxydes photo-actifs ont été analysées. L'emploi de nouvelles techniques analytiques bien adaptées aux milieux très opaques — la microspectrophotométrie IRTF et la spectrophotométrie IRTF avec détecteur opto-acoustique, par exemple — nous ont permis de reconnaître, lors de l'évolution de matériaux finis (vulcanisés et pigmentés), les mécanismes qui interviennent dans le cas d'élastomères non transformés.

Comme pour tout polymère « non absorbant », la lumière est en fait absorbée par des chromophores extérieurs aux élastomères examinés (probablement des impuretés ou des défauts que l'on ne peut contrôler). En outre, la vitesse initiale de photo-oxydation, généralement très faible, est une donnée qui dépend essentiellement des antioxydants résiduels, et la période d'induction ne peut être considérée que comme une caractéristique extrinsèque. Cette période d'induction n'excède pas une heure dans les conditions de photo-oxydation exploitées dans la cadre de la présente étude. Au terme de cette période, les contaminants inhibiteurs sont consommés et des chromophores intrinsèques se forment (hydroperoxydes, cétones $\alpha - \beta$ insaturées, cétones saturées). La photo-oxydation vraie de l'élastomère intervient alors, selon le schéma de la page suivante.

On sait que l'oxydation radicalaire des alcènes suppose généralement une extraction d'hydrogène sur le carbone situé en α de la double liaison. Ce mécanisme d'amorçage par extraction entre en compétition avec l'addition du radical avec la double liaison. Une réaction en chaîne d'hydroperoxydation permet d'expliquer la formation d'hydroperoxydes α-β insaturés. Aux hydroperoxydes associés qui apparaissent à des concentrations maximales de 60 mmol·kg^{-1} doit être attribuée la bande d'absorption à 3 400 cm^{-1} environ, qui n'est pas observée en oxydation thermique à 60°C et qui disparaît par photolyse sous vide à 35°C.

Il faut admettre que l'hydroperoxydation en α de la double liaison intervient avant toute saturation de cette double liaison pour expliquer la formation de cétones α-β insaturées par photolyse (ou thermolyse) de ces hydroperoxydes. Si les cétones α−β insaturées absorbant à 1 696 cm^{-1} se forment dans une réaction en cage, habituellement rencontrée dans les polymères, les groupements alcooliques résultent de radicaux alcénoxydes qui ne sont pas recombinés dans la cage.

La bande d'absorption à 1 726 cm^{-1} a été attribuée aux groupements cétoniques saturés que l'on peut observer aisément lors d'oxydations thermiques. En photo-oxydation, les cétones ne peuvent apparaître qu'en faibles concentrations stationnaires car les processus photochimiques de Norrish de types I et II provoquent leur conversion. En particulier, la formation d'acides saturés (absorbant à 1 717 cm^{-1} environ) intervient dans toute matrice polymérique où sont formées intermédiairement des cétones saturées; cette conversion de cétones saturées en acides suppose un processus de Norrish de type I.

La disparition des insaturations résiduelles est directement observée à partir des spectres infrarouges et elle est à l'origine de la formation de tous les produits d'oxydation. En outre, cette disparition permet d'interpréter la réticulation observée en R.M.N. Les données cinétiques

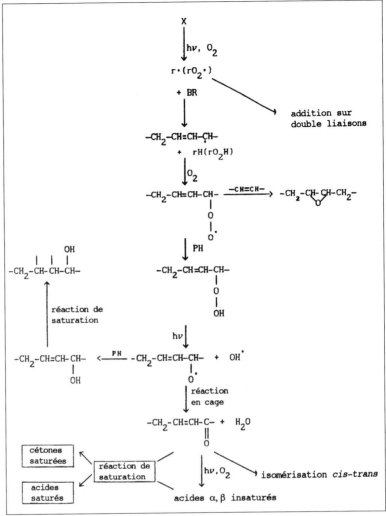

PH = Hydrogène du polymère

montrent que la photo-oxydation des polybutadiènes ne dépend guère du genre de microstructure, puisque toute insaturation, quelle qu'elle soit, entraîne une forte photo-oxydabilité de ces élastomères indépendamment de la structure.

La photo-oxydation d'un élastomère se traduit également par une modification importante du réseau. Aux scissions de chaînes intervenant lors de la formation des groupements oxydés, s'opposent des réticulations. Les photopassivations très remarquables, observées même en films minces (de 150 à 210 μm), s'interprètent par une augmentation de l'imperméabilité à

131

l'oxygène des couches superficielles oxydées et réticulées. Il convient de noter que, en photovieillissement artificiel d'élastomères non transformés, les films deviennent, sous exposition, des photoréacteurs très hétérogènes qui ne s'oxydent que superficiellement. Le cœur du film n'est alors pratiquement pas modifié.

Les copolymères SBR et NBR étudiés se sont comportés comme les homopolymères de poly-butadiène; les unités de styrène et d'acryloni-trile sont demeurées pratiquement inertes au cours de la photo-oxydation, ce qui signifie que tous les radicaux produits dans la matrice réagissent en fait sur les sites insaturés.

Les polyisoprènes présentent des photo-oxydations qui interviennent selon le même mécanisme général. Mais la structure même du polyisoprène entraîne les différences suivantes :

1. La dissymétrie de l'unité isoprénique laisse prévoir la formation de deux radicaux diffé-rents par réaction d'extraction d'hydrogène :

$$
\underset{(a)}{\overset{\displaystyle CH_3}{\sim CH\text{-}CH\text{=}C\text{-}CH_2\sim}} \quad ou \quad \underset{(b)}{\overset{\displaystyle CH_3}{\sim CH\text{=}C\text{-}CH\text{-}CH_2\sim}}
$$

Les hydroperoxydes apparaissent en plus fortes concentrations dans les polyisoprènes que dans les autres élastomères, ce qui est com-patible avec une structure tertiaire de ces hy-droperoxydes. Les radicaux **(a)** semblent donc être essentiellement formés et leurs formes mésomères :

$$
\overset{\displaystyle CH_3}{- CH\text{-}CH\text{=}C\text{-}CH_2 -} \quad <\!\!-\!\!> \quad \overset{\displaystyle CH_3}{- CH\text{=}CH\text{-}C\text{-}CH_2 -}
$$

permettent de rendre compte de cette structure tertiaire :

$$
\overset{\displaystyle CH_3}{\underset{\displaystyle OOH}{- CH\text{=}CH\text{-}C\text{-}CH_2 -}}
$$

2. Les radicaux alcénoxydes correspondants donnent naissance à des processus plus variés :

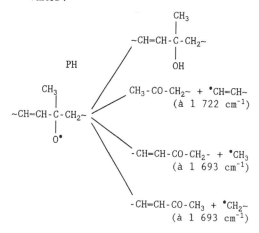

Dans le cas du polyisoprène, les processus de β-scission des radicaux alcénoxydes provo-quent donc des coupures de chaînes. Il s'agit là d'un facteur qui différencie nettement le poly-isoprène des autres élastomères pour lesquels les coupures de chaînes interviennent par d'au-tres mécanismes moins primaires et apparem-ment moins fréquents.

Il est maintenant possible de décrire l'évolu-tion chimique d'élastomères diéniques non transformés à l'aide des différents produits intermédiaires et finals qui se forment au cours d'oxydations photothermiques (à basse tem-pérature) ou thermiques. Il est donc possible de comparer cette évolution en photovieillisse-ment ou en thermovieillissement artificiel et celle qui se produira en vieillissement clima-tique. Il apparaît alors clairement que le vieillis-sement climatique d'élastomères diéniques non transformés se réduit essentiellement à une oxy-dation photochimique et qu'il ne correspond, en aucun cas, à une ozonisation (ce dernier genre d'oxydation présentant une stœchiométrie tout à fait différente de celle d'une oxydation photo-chimique ou thermique).

Par ailleurs, il convient de signaler que la présente étude a été prolongée pour permettre l'analyse de mélanges formés d'élastomères vulcanisés et contenant de forts pourcentages de noir de carbone et de pigments photo-actifs (ZnO et TiO$_2$). Les résultats obtenus jusqu'à maintenant montrent, à l'évidence — et malgré les difficultés d'ordre analytique rencontrées —, que le vieillissement climatique de ces polymères exposés à la lumière s'explique essentiellement par une oxydation photochimique, et non par une ozonisation.

Conclusions

La prévision du comportement à long terme des matériaux polymères synthétiques en conditions d'usage reste difficile. Mais l'avancement des connaissances sur les mécanismes d'évolution rend cette prévision de moins en moins aléatoire. En fait, les progrès réalisés récemment résultent de la conjonction de deux facteurs, à savoir :

• La mise au point de dispositifs expérimentaux d'étude en laboratoire qui permettent d'examiner les seuls phénomènes de photovieillissement en conditions anhydres (avec application de contraintes de lumière, de chaleur et d'O2) ou en conditions de concentration d'eau maintenue (avec application de contraintes de lumière, de chaleur, d'O2 et d'eau). Il devient alors possible de hiérarchiser l'importance des différents mécanismes de photovieillissement, de thermovieillissement et de vieillissement hydrolytique, et de n'accélérer en conditions artificielles que le mécanisme le plus important.

• Le développement de méthodes microanalytiques qui permettent de suivre *in situ* l'évolution chimique de microzones des systèmes polymériques. Ces techniques de microspectrophotométrie vibrationnelle — la microspectrophotométrie IRTF, par exemple — rendent possible l'analyse des couches élémentaires de 5 μm et l'élaboration des profils des produits d'oxydation et additifs qui se trouvent dans les parties les plus superficielles du matériau. Elles peuvent de plus être utilisées, grâce à des détecteurs opto-acoustiques, pour analyser des milieux très opaques. Enfin, ces reconnaissances analytiques des mécanismes d'évolution permettent, tout en garantissant la représentativité des essais de laboratoire, de

convertir les durées d'essai en temps réel d'usage dans des conditions moyennes d'utilisation.

Note

*Un anti-U. V. est un composé moléculaire qui absorbe fortement les rayons ultraviolets et dont les états excités sont susceptibles de se désactiver, de façon non radiative, avec une très grande efficacité.

Abstract

Prediction of the Long-Term Behaviour of Synthetic Polymeric Materials from Artificial Ageing Experiments

The photo-ageing of synthetic polymers commonly used in modern sculptures found in outdoor museums will be described. Cross-linked unsaturated polyesters and various polyacrylates and polymethacrylates will be presented as examples of unstabilized matrices whose properties can be modified during the polymerisation, on drying from solution or emulsion and by introduction of additives. Photo-oxidation and thermal oxidation of dienic elastomers (Butadiene, Styrene-butadiene and Nitrile-butadiene rubber) and oxidation of polyacetals will be described. A basic understanding of the oxidation mechanism is pre-requisite to any stabilisation strategy.

The prediction of the rate of ageing for synthetic polymers in use can be based on the "mechanistic" approach. This approach entails the recognition of solid polymers as chemical "reactors", that is, environments where certain chemical reactions are facilitated. The mechanistic approach involves the identification of mechanisms at the molecular scale, in artificial accelerated conditions and in use. The most detrimental effects on polymers are caused by oxidation which is induced by light, heat, static and dynamic stress. Variations in macroscopic physical properties (mechanical properties, opacity, surface aspect, etc.) can be explained by analyzing the chemistry fully. Thus, accelerated ageing is actually accelerated oxidation and the acceleration factor can be determined from the rates at which critical oxidation products form in artificial and natural conditions. Lifetimes of polymers can therefore be predicted from the measured lifetimes in artificial conditions, taking acceleration factors into account. This mechanistic approach compares favourably with empirical techniques based on simulation of actual physical and chemical conditions and the resulting variations in macroscopic physical properties.

In most synthetic polymers, the oxidative degradation, which is controlled either by the normal structure of the polymerized monomer or by chemical defects, is observed at a very low degree of oxidation. Very sensitive and informative in-situ spectrophotometric techniques are required to determine the nature of the various intermediate and final products.

Composition Implications of Plastic Artifacts:
A Survey of Additives and Their Effects on the Longevity of Plastics

R. Scott Williams

Canadian Conservation Institute
Communications Canada
Ottawa, Canada

Abstract

Plastic objects are usually described by reference to their main polymer component, i.e., polyethylene sheet, vinyl or poly(vinyl chloride) upholstery, acrylic sculpture, polystyrene or styrene box, etc. In fact, all manufactured plastic items are complex formulations of polymers with the additives that are required to give the base polymer suitable end-use properties. Additives such as plasticizers, stabilizers, colorants, processing aids, etc. are as important as the base polymer in determining how long an object serves its intended purpose, or how long it survives in a museum.

The main polymer groups that comprise plastics found in typical museum objects are briefly introduced, and the additives in the plastics made from these polymers are discussed in detail. Results of recent chemical analyses of deteriorated plastic objects are used to illustrate the effect of additives and base polymers on the longevity of the plastics. Deterioration and damage such as accretions, blooming, cracking, crazing, discoloration, embrittlement, oozing, softening, etc. are related to changes in, or loss of, the additives. These changes are influenced by the museum environment. General guidelines for storage of plastic objects, both to increase their longevity and to prevent damage to neighbouring objects, are given.

Introduction

A *plastic* is not a pure chemical product but rather a formulation or composition made by proper mixture of a *base polymer* with a combination of *additives*. Some common base polymers are listed in Table I. Polymers can be produced as pure materials but these are never adequate for serviceable products. To produce a useful plastic, the inherent chemical, physical, mechanical, optical, electrical, and other properties of the polymer must be modified by the incorporation of additives, such as those listed in Table II. Plastics also are subjected to a variety of physical treatments to modify such properties as appearance, printability, and shape. (Table III lists some of these.) The nature of the base polymer, additives, and fabrication all affect the service life and museum-longevity of objects. This paper discusses the mode of action of some additives and the deterioration of plastic objects due to their change or loss.

General Characteristics of Additives

Additives should be efficient, that is, effective at low concentration (most are used at concentrations of less than 1%, with the notable exceptions of plasticizers, pigments, fillers, and reinforcing fibres typically used at concentrations of 10% to 35%), low-cost, convenient, safe to use and handle, and should not impart undesirable characteristics such as colour, taste,

Table I
Common Base Polymers in Plastics

(Note: The abbreviations are those given in ASTM Standard D 1600-83: Standard Abbreviations of Terms Relating to Plastics by the American Society for Testing and Materials.)

Acrylonitrile-butadiene-styrene	ABS
Cellulose acetate	CA
Cellulose acetate butyrate	CAB
Cellulose acetate propionate	CAP
Cellulose plastics, general	CE
Cresol formaldehyde	CF
Cellulose nitrate	CN
Cellulose propionate	CP
Casein	CS
Cellulose triacetate	CTA
Epoxy, epoxide	EP
Ethyl cellulose	EC
Ethylene-vinyl acetate	EVA
Impact polystyrene	IPS
Melamine-formaldehyde	MF
Polyamide (nylon)	PA
Polycarbonate	PC
Polyethylene	PE
Poly(ethylene terephthalate)	PET
Phenol-formaldehyde	PF
Polyisobutylene	PIB
Poly(methyl methacrylate)	PMMA
Polypropylene	PP
Polystyrene	PS
Polytetrafluoroethylene	PTFE
Polyurethane	PUR
Poly(vinyl acetate)	PVAC
Poly(vinyl alcohol)	PVAL
Poly(vinyl butyral)	PVB
Poly(vinyl chloride)	PVC
Poly(vinylidene chloride)	PVDC
Styrene-acrylonitrile	SAN
Styrene-butadiene	SB
Silicone plastics	SI
Urea-formaldehyde	UF
Unsaturated polyester	UP

Compatibility and Permanence

Polymers and additives are compatible if they can be intimately blended with each other to form a homogeneous composition. Additives that are highly compatible with a given resin do not exude to form droplets or liquid surface films, nor do they bloom as a crystalline surface crust. Incompatibility is usually indicated by migration and exudation of substances on the plastic surface (also called spewing or blooming), or by poor physical properties. This is not always evident after short storage periods but may take months or years to appear. *Permanence* refers to the ability of an additive to remain unchanged within various environments so that the plastic retains its desired properties during use, as opposed to simple *incompatibility*, which becomes evident by time alone and is not related to the exposure environment. The permanence of an additive is usually determined by its volatility, migration, extractability, and stability to heat and light.

Compatibility can be thought of as mutual solubility, although phenomena other than solubility can create compatibility (e.g., molecular entanglement). Additives are often relatively small molecules that can diffuse through the polymer matrix. The larger the additive molecule, or the more crosslinked or crystalline the polymer, the slower is the diffusion. As a result

Table II
Additives in Plastics

Plasticizers (50% in some PVC)

Stabilizers
    Antioxidants
    Heat stabilizers
    UV absorbers

Processing Aids
    Internal lubricants
    Mould release agents
    Slip agents
    Blowing agents

End-use Modifiers
    Colourants
    - Organic dyes and pigments
    - Inorganic pigments
    Reinforcing fibres
    Fillers and extenders
    Antistatic agents
    Antiblock agents
    Barrier coatings
    Laminating process

or odour. They should also maintain their properties over time, be resistant to extraction during service, be thermally stable at processing temperatures, be stable to light, and be unaffected by pollutants. Additives should be compatible with the polymer and other additives, and be capable of blending mutually. They are intended to remain effective throughout the *service lifetime* of the plastic. Note that the designed service lifetime of a plastic object is always much shorter than the desired museum lifetime. It would be nice if additives remained effective throughout their museum lifetimes, but this is seldom the case.

of diffusion driven by concentration gradients, additives can migrate to surfaces where, if they are not volatile, they collect as a discrete exuded layer (this property is sometimes used intentionally as in the case of slip agents and antistats). This migration continues until the concentration gradient disappears, at which time the rate of diffusion from the interior to the surface equals the rate of reverse diffusion from the surface to the interior. If the exudate is removed, a new concentration gradient is set up and more additive migrates to the surface to replace the lost material. Volatile additives evaporate at the surface, to be replaced by more additive from the bulk of the plastic. In this situation there is a constant loss of additive to the atmosphere and a constant diffusion of additive from the interior to the surface. Eventually, all the additive will be lost (and possibly redeposited elsewhere to cause harm).

Although plasticizers will be discussed in detail later, additive/polymer compatibility using plasticizers as an example is discussed here to clarify discussions of all additives.

Compatibility and the Hildebrand Solubility Parameter

Plasticization is similar to dissolution of the polymer by the plasticizer compound. Thus the Hildebrand solubility parameter, which is a measure of solubility or solvent power, may be a predictor of compatibility (see Barton 1983,

Hedley 1980, or Horie 1987 for discussions of solubility parameters). Table IV lists the Hildebrand solubility parameters of some common polymers and compounds used as plasticizers. Compounds most commonly used as plasticizers for poly(vinyl chloride) (PVC) have Hildebrand solubility parameters between $17.2\ \mathrm{MPa}^{1/2}$ and $23.3\ \mathrm{MPa}^{1/2}$ bracketing $19.6\ \mathrm{MPa}^{1/2}$, the solubility parameter of PVC. The solubility parameters of other polymers (e.g., cellulose nitrate and polyethylene) are outside the compatibility range of plasticizers that are suitable for PVC. Thus different types of plasticizers are required for different polymers, as is verified by formulation practice.

Compatibility and Dielectric Constant

Solubility parameter is only one of many properties that can be evaluated to predict plasticizer/polymer compatibility. Dielectric constant is also an important property of a solvent. The dielectric constant of a compound is a measure of its polarity and its polarizability. Polarizability is a measure of the response of a molecule to an electric field and thus of the intermolecular forces between a solvent and a solute, that is, between a plasticizer and a polymer. The interaction of these forces affects compatibility. Observation of compatible plasticizers shows that those with dielectric constants between 4 and 8 are compatible with PVC, which has a dielectric constant of 3.2 (Table IV).

Exudation of Additives due to Incompatibility

Figure 1 shows the relationship between solubility parameter and dielectric constant for compounds commonly used as plasticizers (for all plastics, not just PVC). The zone of compatibility for PVC is indicated by the dotted lines. As can be seen there is a restricted group of compatible plasticizers for PVC. Similar zones of compatibility could be plotted for all other plastics and would include a different group of plasticizers.

This Figure helps to explain the occurrence of exudates and blooms. Some additives have solubility parameters and dielectric constants outside the zone of compatibility. We should expect these to exude because they are incompatible. Exudations may also occur if the

---

Table III

Plastic Fabrication Processes

Shaping Processes
    Molding, extrusion, casting
    Machining (cutting, grinding, drilling, stamping, etc.)
    Foaming

Surface Treatments
    Surface texturizing, embossing
    Surface activation (to permit printing)
    - Flame
    - Corona discharge
    Coating
    - Painting, printing
    - Metallizing, electroplating
    - Lamination
Joining
    Adhesive bonding
    Welding
    Mechanical fastening (screws, rivets, etc.)

Table IV

Plasticizers: Solubility Parameters
and Dielectric Constants

Plasticizers	Solubility Parameter (Mpa$^{1/2}$)	Dielectric Constant
Phthalate esters:		
Di(2-ethylhexyl phthalate), (dioctyl phthalate), DOP	14.9-18.0	5.2
Dibutyl phthalate, DBP	17.0-19.2	6.4
Butyl benzyl phthalate	15.5-18.2	6.4
Phosphate esters:		
Triphenyl phosphate, TPP	19.6 (20.7)	
Tricresyl phosphate, TCP	17.2-20.2	7.2
Diacid esters:		
Di(2-ethylhexyl) adipate, (dioctyl adipate), DOA	(17.4)	4.1
Di(2-ethylhexyl) azelate, (dioctyl azelate), DOZ	19.0	4.0
Diethylene glycol dibenzoate		7.1
Miscellaneous:		
Epoxidized soya oil, ESO	(18.2)	5.5
Adipic acid polyester	19.0	6.0
Tri(2-ethylhexyl) trimellitate, (trioctyl trimellitate), TOTM	18.4	4.7
Camphor	18.2	11.4
Castor oil		8.9
Polymers		
Polytetrafluoroethylene	12.7	2.0
Polyethylene	16.2-16.8	2.25-2.35
Polypropylene	18.8	2.2
Polystyrene	17.6-19.8	2.4-2.6
Poly(vinyl acetate)	18.0-22.5	3.5
Poly(methyl methacrylate)	18.4-19.4	3.3-3.6
Poly(vinyl chloride)	19.0-20.2	3.3-3.5
Polycarbonate	19.0-20.2	3.0-3.2
Poly(ethylene terephthalate)	21.9	3.0-3.6
Cellulose nitrate	21.5-23.5	7.0-7.5
Cellulose diacetate	22.3-23.3	
Cellulose acetate	27.2-27.8	3.5-7.5
Nylon 66	27.8	4.0

solubility parameters and dielectric constants of polymers and additives shift out of the compatibility zone as chemical reactions take place in the plastic as it ages. For instance, it is possible that dibutyl phthalate, a very compatible PVC plasticizer, may hydrolyze to form butyl alcohol and phthalic acid. The solubility parameter and dielectric constant of butyl alcohol are 23.3 MPa$^{1/2}$ and 36.4 MPa$^{1/2}$ respectively, values well outside the zone of compatibility. We would expect this hydrolytic degradation product (of an additive, not the polymer) to exude. This could happen for any additive that changes upon aging. Similarly, if the polymer changes enough to shift its solubility parameter and dielectric constant, then the changed polymer would have a new compatibility zone. Unchanged additives might now lie outside the new compatibility zone of the aged (changed) plastic. They might now be incompatible, and therefore exude.

Incompatibility due to Aging of Base Polymer and Additives

There is a particular relationship between the base polymer and its additives in an unaged plastic. Initially, everything is designed to be mutually compatible. Upon aging, compatibilities change. Light-, heat-, and oxygen-induced reactions of the various components occur. Stabilizers prevent reactions of the polymer macromolecules, but in doing so the stabilizers are changed into new products, with different compatibilities with the base polymers. And, in spite of the stabilizers, changes do occur in the polymer. Slow macromolecular rearrangements increase crystallinity. A few crosslinks pull polymer molecules together and decrease molecular free volume, squeezing out additives. Oxidation of macromolecules and additives tend to increase their polarities. All this leads to changes in

mutual solubilities and may lead to separation of components (incompatibility). As aging proceeds, these changes make the plastic composition more and more different from the initial design formulation. Since the initial formulation was designed by delicately balancing many properties of different polymers and additives, the likelihood of incompatibilities increases. The plastic should be designed so that these developing incompatibilities do not affect the properties of the plastic during its design lifetime. Unfortunately, over the extended duration in a museum, problems of incompatibility start to show up.

Deterioration of Plastics

Plastics deteriorate by 1) chemical degradation of the base polymer and/or the additives, 2) physical processes like bending and breaking or exudation of components (perhaps resulting from chemical changes), and 3) biological agents (molds, fungi, rodents, people, etc.), just as all other organic and biological museum objects deteriorate (Table V). Physical processes include diffusion and molecular redistribution where there is no change in the chemical bonds in the polymers or additives. These

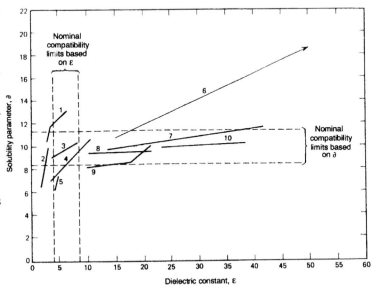

Figure 1 Compatibility zone defined by solubility parameter and dielectric constants of plasticizers. Curves: 1, carboxylic acids; 2, hydrocarbons; 3, chlorinated hydrocarbons; 4, esters; 5, ethers; 6, alcohols; 7, alkyl nitriles; 8, aldehydes; 9, ketones; 10, nitro compounds. (from Darby, Touchette and Sears 1967.)

Table V
Agents of Degradation

Heat	during processing and use
Light	during use
Atmosphere	oxygen and pollution
Moisture	hydrolysis
Solvents	dissolution and solvolysis
Biological Agents	bacteria, fungi, insects, rodents, people
Physical Changes	crystallization, migration
Mechanical Work	fatigue, creep

are usually slow and can be accommodated by compatibility considerations during design of the plastic (See also McGlinchey, this publication). This sort of degradation takes a long time to show. Often it is not detected, or not significant, during the service lifetime of a plastic, but becomes a problem after long periods in a museum. Chemical degradation alters the arrangement and type of chemical bonds present in the plastic. The primary chemical changes are due to oxidation, although hydrolysis is a factor in some polymers. Oxidation can be initiated or promoted by heat (thermal oxidation) and light (photo oxidation). Light in the absence of oxygen can also cause chemical degradation.

The inherent properties of plastics affect their degradation. For example, amorphous polymers allow easier diffusion of oxygen and water than do crystalline polymers, therefore oxidation and hydrolysis are likely to be more pronounced in the former. Plastics with glass transition temperatures below room temperature are in a rubbery state, which allows greater molecular mobility and greater opportunity for reactive degradative species or degradation products to move through the plastic thereby increasing the rate of degradation reactions. The presence or absence of certain functional groups in the polymer macromolecules affects the susceptibility to certain degradation reactions. For instance, esters and amides are susceptible to hydrolysis, aromatic rings and carbonyl groups absorb ultraviolet (UV) light and are sensitive to photodegradation, and pure hydrocarbons like polyethylene, polypropylene, and rubber contain no chemically bound oxygen and so will oxidize only if exposed to oxygen. Unfortunately these latter hydrocarbons contain tertiary hydrogens, which makes them very susceptible to degradation by free-radical processes.

Degradation Profile

To help visualize degradation processes, *degradation profiles* can be created by plotting changes in such properties as colour, brittleness, tack, surface gloss or crazing or chalking, release of volatile substances, and many other chemical, mechanical, and physical properties. Feller (1977) described four stages of degradation — inception, induction, increase to maximum rate or steady state, and decreasing rate stages — and introduced a generalized profile of oxidative degradation as measured by oxygen uptake. Examples of degradation profiles are shown in Figure 2 for yellowing, for weight gain due to oxygen uptake during oxidation, for solubility, and for oxidation (measured by IR absorbance due to hydroperoxide formation). These degradation profiles show the state of degradation of a plastic object at any stage in its lifetime and permit some prediction of the course of its degradation. This is valuable in the museum/conservation context. Chemical degradation follows the same general pattern for all plastics and organic materials although the breadth and height of the curve may change. It is worth examining degradation profiles in more detail to see how plastic objects degrade, to identify the stage of degradation achieved by a particular object, to predict what future can be expected for a particular object, and to determine how the course of degradation of objects can be altered so as to prolong their useful life.

Consider a plastic with a degradation profile shown in curve A in Figure 3. If the duration of the inception/induction stage can be increased, the amount of degradation that will have occurred at a future observation date will be decreased, even if the shape (slope) of the later portions of the curve is unaltered. This situation is shown on curve B. Note that the amount of degradation at the future observation date on curve B (labelled D_B) is less than that on the original curve (D_A). If the inception/induction period cannot be increased, but the *rate* of degradation can be reduced (i.e., reduced slope), then the total amount of degradation at the future observation date can be reduced. This is shown in curve C. Note that D_C is less than D_A. As another example of possible intervention, consider that the durations of the various stages cannot be changed but the magnitude of each can be decreased. This is shown in curve D.

140

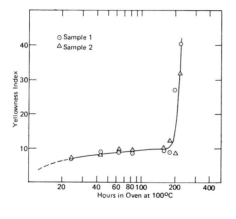

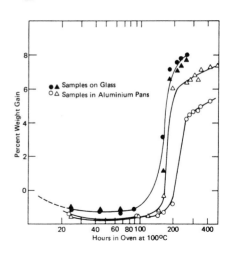

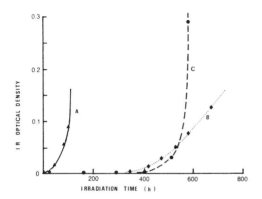

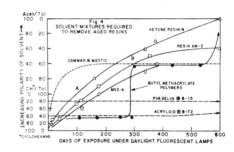

Figure 2 Degradation profiles produced by measuring different properties of plastics. Top left: Yellowing of rubber cement (from Feller and Encke 1982); Top right: Weight gain of rubber cement (from Feller and Encke 1982); Bottom left: Hydroperoxide concentration in photo-oxidized polypropylene as measured by IR absorbance at 3400 cm^{-1} with no inhibitor (A), with nickel chelate inhibitor (B) and with piperidine HALS inhibitor (C) (from Grattan 1978); Bottom right: Change in solubility of varnish resins (from Feller 1975).

Again, the total amount of degradation at the future observation date (D$_D$) is less than in the case without intervention.

In general, to decrease the degradation of a plastic at some future date the objectives should be to 1) increase the duration of each of the early stages of the deterioration profile (i.e., delay the onset of later stages), 2) decrease the rate of change from each earlier stage to the next, and 3) decrease the magnitude of degradation for each stage.

Stabilizers

Stabilizers (inhibitors) are additives that are used to make changes in the degradation

profile. They function either by preventing the initiation reactions caused by light and heat exposure, or by interfering with the free-radical chain reactions, thereby preventing propagation reactions. They also scavenge non-free-radical products of degradation that cause or catalyze further degradation. If stabilizers are effective they alter the degradation profile by lengthening the time scale and reducing the extent of degradation. When stabilizers fail (by loss or change) the degradation profile becomes much steeper and the plastic degrades more rapidly.

The stabilizers to be discussed here include antioxidants, heat stabilizers, and ultraviolet

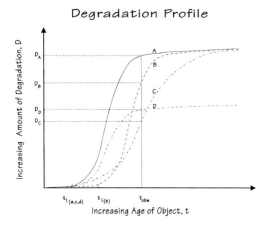

Degradation Profile

Figure 3 Altering the degradation profile of a plastic. Curves: A, unaltered profile; B, induction period increased but shape of profile unchanged (B is "parallel" to A); C, induction period unchanged but rate of degradation decreased (slope decreased); D, induction period and rate of degradation unchanged but magnitude of degradation decreased. D_A, D_B, D_C, and D_D are amounts of degradation at some arbitrary future observation time, t, for each scenario. The end of the induction period is indicated by time, t_i.

light stabilizers (including ultraviolet light absorbers).

Antioxidants

Oxidation Reactions

To understand how antioxidants work, the chemical reactions that take place in the base polymer during oxidation must first be considered. This subject is vast and has been discussed in the conservation context by Grattan (1978) and de la Rie (1988) and in much greater technical detail by Carlsson and Wiles (1986). For oxidation to occur, oxygen must be absorbed and dissolved in the polymer. It then diffuses to reactive sites on the polymer macromolecule where oxidation reactions can take place. Such reactive sites are usually free-radicals produced when energy in the form of heat, radiation (commonly UV and visible light but also gamma- and X-rays, or electron beams), and mechanical work, etc. is absorbed by the plastic and breaks chemical bonds in polymer macromolecules. These free-radicals react with oxygen to produce hydroperoxides. Hydroperoxides readily undergo thermal and photo

cleavage to produce two new oxygenated radicals (hydroxyl and alkoxyl). Thus the number of radicals multiplies and oxidative degradation of the polymer via free-radical reactions is accelerated.

In the initial stages of this chain reaction, radicals react with non-radical polymer macromolecules. Eventually, as the radicals multiply, their concentration becomes large enough that they react with each other as well as with the non-radical macromolecules. The reaction of one free-radical with another produces a non-radical. Thus radical-radical reactions terminate free-radical chain reactions. Eventually the rate of termination of radicals equals the rate of production of radicals and a steady state is reached. This corresponds to the steady state region of the degradation profile — degradation continues, but at a constant, non-accelerating rate.

Prevention of Oxidation

Key stages in the oxidation process are the initial formation of alkyl free-radicals by energetic processes and the subsequent production of hydroperoxides by reaction of the alkyl free-radicals with oxygen. Oxidation can be prevented if formation of either of these species is prevented or if these are converted to something innocuous before they have a chance to react with polymer macromolecules. Thus to prevent oxidation the aims should be the following:

- prevent access of oxygen to the plastic by removing oxygen from its surroundings (anaerobic conditions) or by using oxygen barrier layers on the plastic

- prevent initial formation of alkyl radicals, or scavenge those radicals formed before they have a chance to react with oxygen in the plastic (radical scavenger antioxidants)

- destroy peroxides that do form before they cleave to produce new radicals (peroxide decomposer antioxidants)

- prevent the development of, or remove, active sites from the polymer macromolecules

Anaerobic (oxygen-free) atmospheres can be produced using bell jars with inert gas purging or by enveloping objects in oxygen barrier membranes (including bell jars) with enclosed oxygen scavenger chemicals such as Ageless (Grattan 1991). This method may be suitable for a few special objects in a museum, but it is useless for plastics in normal use.

Oxygen-impermeable layers can be applied, or allowed to develop by controlled exudation from the body of the plastic. Some wax "antioxidants" function in this manner — during fabrication of the plastic a wax is incorporated that migrates to the plastic surface where it forms a thin oxygen-impermeable barrier layer that prevents oxygen dissolution in the plastic. This is an example of an intentional exudation of an additive. It is commonly used for rubber. Disruption of this barrier layer gives oxygen access to the plastic and oxidative degradation can occur. Thus conservation treatments and handling procedures should be designed so that this surface oxygen-barrier layer is not disrupted.

Protection by Antioxidants
Antioxidants are compounds that inhibit or retard oxidative degradation of polymers by atmospheric oxygen during fabrication, storage, and use. They are added during formulation and become intimately mixed with the polymer. They function at the molecular level by reacting with a particular functional group of a nearby polymer macromolecule that is reacting, or has just reacted, with oxygen dissolved in the polymer. There are two classes of antioxidants. *Free-radical scavengers* (radical or chain terminators) react with chain-propagating free-radicals before these free-radicals have a chance to react with oxygen or polymer macromolecules, thereby preventing the formation of more radicals and propagation of the chain reactions of oxidative degradation. *Peroxide decomposers* (sometimes referred to as secondary antioxidants or synergists) convert peroxides and hydroperoxides into non-radical and stable products before they become reactive free-radicals that propagate degradation reactions.

Many compounds are used as antioxidants and only the more common can be described (Table VI). A review by de la Rie (1988) describes polymer stabilizers and their reactions in

greater detail, with emphasis on conservation applications. Free-radical scavengers are typically hindered phenols (e.g., butylated hydroxy toluene, BHT) or secondary aryl amines (e.g., diphenylamine derivatives). These react with peroxy and alkoxy free-radicals to convert them to non-radicals. Organophosphites and various organic sulfur compounds, such as thiodipropionic acid, are effective peroxide decomposers. Organophosphites react with hydroperoxides to form alcohols and phosphates. Organic sulfides react with hydroperoxide to form alcohols and organic sulfoxides. These antioxidants are usually used in combinations with each other and with other stabilizers. A typical stabilizer package may consist of phenolic or amine antioxidant, a thiodipropionate ester, a phosphite, a metallic stearate (for lubrication), and a metal deactivator (for chelating any traces of detrimental metal ions, usually from polymerization catalyst residues).

Table VI
Antioxidants
Chain Propagation Radical Terminators

Alkylated phenols and polyphenols
    - Butylated hydroxy toluene (BHT)
    Secondary aryl amines

Hydroperoxide Decomposers
Organophosphites   Thioesters

Metal Deactivators
    Hydrazides
    Triazoles
    - Benzotriazole

Polymers with hydrogens on tertiary carbon atoms, such as polypropylene and its copolymers, are particularly susceptible to oxidation initiated by free-radicals produced by hydrogen abstraction. During manufacture and processing, unstabilized polypropylene yellows and changes in melt viscosity (a function of molecular weight). These polymers require antioxidant stabilizers. Since they are exposed to high processing temperatures, low volatility compounds should be used. Typical antioxidants for polypropylene are high molecular weight, low volatility alkylated phenols and polyphenols with esters of thiodipropionic acid (a sulfur-containing compound) and phosphites at total concentration of 0.25% to 1%.

Metal ions from catalyst residues, such as titanium and metal containing pigments (zinc, iron, chromium, cadmium, etc.), induce hydroperoxide decomposition and cause undesirable discolouration. Such metal deactivators as hydrazides and triazoles often are added in conjunction with antioxidants to protect against adverse effects of metals.

Most hydrocarbon polymers (e.g., natural and synthetic rubbers based on polyisoprene, polybutadiene and its copolymers or blends like acrylonitrile-butadiene-styrene, polyisobutylene, etc., and such synthetic plastics as high-impact polystyrene that have a rubber component) have unsaturated carbon-carbon double bonds that are subject to oxidation that is accelerated by heat and UV light. This oxidative aging is often characterized by yellowing and embrittlement. These are commonly protected by 0.1% to 2.5% of an antioxidant system generally consisting of organic phosphites and low-volatility hindered alkylidene bisphenols often in conjunction with UV stabilizers.

Heat Stabilizers

Heat stabilizers are added to polymers to retard their decomposition when exposed to heat energy and mechanical stress during mixing, processing, reworking of scrap, outdoor exposure, and/or other storage or use conditions throughout their service lives. Since they are most commonly used in PVC plastics, heat stabilizers for this plastic will be discussed in detail.

PVC degrades by a mechanism referred to as dehydrochlorination, in which hydrogen chloride is produced when hydrogen and chlorine atoms are eliminated from adjacent carbons on a PVC molecule. The acidic hydrogen chloride catalyzes further degradation of the PVC and corrodes production equipment. The hydrogen chloride elimination creates polyene sequences consisting of conjugated carbon-carbon double bonds. This causes yellowing, which deepens through red and brown to black as degradation increases. Oxidation reactions of non-reacted polymer molecules and of the polyene sequences of degraded polymer molecules result

in polymer chain breakage or *chain-scission* and the formation of various oxygen-containing species, such as peroxides, hydroperoxides, alcohols, aldehydes, and ketones. Physical changes accompany these chemical changes, leading to increased stiffness, insolubility, and exudation of plasticizers (in the case of plasticized products). The degradation and stabilization of PVC is described in great detail by Nass (1976).

The main degradation reactions involve certain labile chlorine atoms that are easily abstracted from PVC molecules. The aims of stabilization are to prevent the abstraction of chlorine atoms, and/or prevent the reaction between chlorine atoms and the polymer. This can be done by the following methods:

- exchanging chlorine atoms with stable substituents that become more firmly bonded to the PVC molecule

- preferentially reacting the abstracted chlorine with additives instead of PVC

- scavenging hydrogen chloride to prevent it from catalyzing further reactions

- using antioxidants to decrease oxidation reactions in the PVC or the polyene sequences to prevent chain-scission, crosslinking, and other free-radical reactions

Table VII lists some of the more common types of heat stabilizers for PVC. Predominant in use

Table VII
Heat Stabilizers for PVC

Primary Stabilizers

    Barium/cadmium soaps
    Calcium/zinc soaps
    Lead soaps
    Antimony compounds
    Organotins
    - Tin carboxylates
    - Tin mercaptides and mercaptoesters

Secondary (auxiliary) Stabilizers

    Epoxy
    - Epoxidized soya oil (ESO)
    Organophosphites

among these is the group with heavy metal salts (zinc, cadmium, stannous tin, etc.) paired with alkaline or alkaline earth metal salts (sodium, potassium, magnesium, calcium, barium, etc.). The synergism between the two types of salt make the combinations much more cost-effective than either single salt.

Primary stabilizers are a group of compounds that can be used as additives, by themselves, to impart significant heat stabilization to a PVC polymer. *Secondary* or auxiliary stabilizers cannot by themselves impart stability, but can dramatically increase the efficiency of other stabilizers by synergistic effects.

Primary Heat Stabilizers

Barium/cadmium carboxylate soap systems are the most widely used PVC heat stabilizers. Cadmium exchanges its carboxylate anion for labile chlorine atoms of PVC creating a carboxylate-containing PVC molecule that is stabilized against loss of other chlorine atoms in the form of hydrogen chloride. This exchange forms cadmium chloride, which, unfortunately, catalyzes PVC degradation. Degradation is prevented by reacting the cadmium chloride with the barium soap also present in the heat stabilizer to make barium chloride and regenerate the cadmium carboxylate soap. Barium chloride does not cause PVC to degrade. The regenerated cadmium soap is available for more stabilization by labile chlorine exchange. Eventually the barium soap is consumed by reaction with the cadmium chloride. Then, no barium soap remains to scavenge cadmium chloride, which then catalyzes PVC degradation resulting in catastrophic deterioration. Because these barium/cadmium stabilizers are toxic they are not likely to be found in objects that contact food and drug products.

Calcium/zinc soap stabilizers function in the same way as barium/cadmium soaps, but they are non-toxic and have been sanctioned for food-packaging film, blister packaging, blow-molded bottles, beverage tubing, blood bags, etc. Like the barium/cadmium system, the calcium/zinc system is effective as long as there is calcium soap available to scavenge zinc chlorides and regenerate zinc soaps. Eventually the calcium soap is exhausted and degradation proceeds.

Thus, PVC stabilized as above, has a period with no deterioration while the barium (or calcium) soap is present, followed by very rapid deterioration after the barium (or calcium) soap is consumed leaving the cadmium (or zinc) chloride to catalyze degradation. This sort of behaviour is exemplified by the deterioration of vinyl rooftops on cars, which takes place after about 5 to 10 years. On the degradation profile this manifests itself as a lengthened induction period followed by a very rapid rate of deterioration in the second stage (e.g., Figure 3, Curve B). It is the duration of the induction period that is of critical importance in the museum context.

Among the earliest effective heat stabilizers for PVC were inorganic lead compounds (e.g., basic lead sulfates, dibasic lead phosphite, basic lead carbonates, and complexes like basic lead silicosulfate). Now there is a larger variety of both inorganic and organic lead salts (mainly soaps like basic lead phthalates, basic lead maleates, and dibasic and normal lead stearates, which are also used for their lubricating properties). Lead functions in the same way as cadmium and zinc, stabilizing the PVC by exchange of labile chlorine atoms with other anions (e.g., stearates). Lead chloride is produced, but, unlike cadmium and zinc chlorides, this does not catalyze PVC degradation. Eventually these stabilizers are consumed and become ineffective. Lead stabilizers tended to be used in opaque, rigid, and flexible PVC extrusion and injection moldings such as phonograph records, conduit, pipe, and wire and cable. Lead stabilizers are common in wire and cable insulation because of their electrical properties (low volume resistivity) and because lead chloride is water-insoluble and non-conducting.

Antimony stabilizers have been used for about 25 years, especially in phonograph records. These have drawbacks because they are unstable in UV light and, like lead stabilizers, also suffer from sulfide staining (producing an orange stain) when in contact with any sulfides. They are cost-effective because they have a synergistic response with metal soaps and improve performance at lower concentrations.

Recently commercialized organotin stabilizers are most efficient for rigid PVC, because, although more expensive, they excel in the most demanding high temperature and high pressure (high shear) fabricating processes that must be used for non-plasticized PVC. These are based on tetravalent tin (they are usually dialkyl tin esters) and are true organometallic compounds where the metal is covalently bonded to carbon. Organotin carboxylates like dibutyltin dilaurate and dibutyltin maleate were among the earliest organotin stabilizers. These have low toxicity, low volatility, and good UV stability. Organotin maleate provides UV stability and sparkling clarity to flexible and rigid PVC. Some alkyl tins have low toxicity and are sanctioned by the U.S. Food and Drug Administration (FDA) (e.g., di-n-octyltinbis-(iso-octylthioglycolate) and di-n-octyltin maleate). Organotin mercaptides and mercaptoacid esters are liquids that are used in the most difficult-to-process rigid PVC applications, such as pipe and profile extrusion and injection and blow molding. These have poor UV stability relative to organotin maleates and strong characteristic skunky odours.

Secondary Heat Stabilizers

Epoxy compounds with oxirane and ester functional groups improve the performance of heavy metal carboxylate soaps. These are prepared by epoxidizing natural unsaturated vegetable oils like soya bean and linseed oil, or by epoxidation of synthetic esters of unsaturated animal or vegetable fatty acids (e.g., butyl-9,10-epoxy-stearate and octyl-epoxy-tallate). Their ability to accept chloride ions preferentially (thereby preventing the formation of heavy metal chlorides that catalyze degradation) is the source of their enhanced performance. Thus the more the oxirane content, the more effective is the epoxy. Epoxidized soya and linseed oils are also plasticizers that add low temperature flexibility. These are also FDA sanctioned.

Organophosphites (di- and trialkyl, di- and triaryl, and mixed alkyl aryl phosphites) are most often used in conjunction with barium/cadmium and calcium/zinc stabilizers or sometimes with organotin or antimony stabilizers. They provide heat and UV light stability and improve early colour and long-term UV light stability.

Advantages and Disadvantages of Different Stabilizers — Museum Consequences

Lead stabilizers are relatively inexpensive but they have several drawbacks. They are opaque salts and cannot be used in clear plastics. Lead compounds are toxic and do not have FDA approval. They are also susceptible to sulfur staining, which may be of some consequence in museums. Early "plastic" objects are often made of sulfur-vulcanized rubber. Storage of lead-stabilized PVC with sulfur-vulcanized rubber may lead to sulfur staining of the PVC, that is, the production of brown or black lead sulfide by reaction of lead from the stabilizer with volatile sulfur-vulcanizing agents from the rubber. Gaseous sulfur pollution may also cause lead staining. Additional sources of sulfur are other (more modern) PVC objects that contain organotin sulfide based heat stabilizers. Cadmium and antimony stabilizers undergo similar reactions with sulfur to produce yellow and orange stains. Thus heavy metal stabilizers and sulfur-containing stabilizers cannot be used in the same product because of the formation of lead sulfide stains. Similarly PVC with heavy metal stabilizers cannot be stored with sulfur-containing plastics and rubbers, direct contact especially should be avoided.

Ultraviolet Stabilizers

When exposed to light, especially UV, some plastics are degraded. To have an effect, the light must be absorbed by the plastic *and* must have sufficient energy to rupture chemical bonds. In general, UV light has sufficient energy and, for certain bonds, so does blue light. Certain functional groups, called chromophores, absorb light and transform into energetically excited and highly reactive states. Because the functional groups have absorbed UV light energy they contain more energy than in their unexcited normal or "ground" states. This excess energy must be dissipated and the extent to which the plastic will, or will not, be degraded depends on how this energy dissipation occurs.

Absorbed energy in the excited chromophore can be dissipated by 1) non-damaging conversion to heat (i.e., vibration of molecules), 2) non-damaging energy transfer to nearby molecules which in turn dissipate the energy as non-damaging heat, or 3) degradative rupture of weak chemical bonds in the chromophore molecule or in nearby molecules to which the energy is transferred.

Different plastics vary greatly in their resistance to light damage (Carlsson and Wiles 1986). Some plastics, such as polycarbonates, polyesters, and aromatic polyurethanes, have strongly absorbing chromophores as parts of their molecular structures. Other plastics, such as polyethylene and polypropylene, have no chromophores in the pure polymer, but unfortunately they usually contain small amounts of catalyst residues from polymerization, or ketones and hydroperoxides from oxidation, which are chromophores and absorb energy, leading indirectly to bond cleavage and formation of free-radicals in the plastic. In air, free-radicals trigger chain reactions leading to more bond cleavage and destruction. Once initiated by light, these oxidative chain reactions require no light to continue, so it is important to prevent or inhibit the initial photochemical events that produce these radicals. Since photochemical production of radicals leads to subsequent oxidation reactions, antioxidants (preferably UV-stable ones) are usually added to retard thermal oxidative degradation by scavenging free-radicals and chemically inactivating peroxides.

Thus there are two main mechanisms for UV degradation: 1) direct rupture of chemical bonds by absorbed UV energy followed by rapid oxidation of the radical fragments, and 2) rupture in nearby molecules caused by energy transferred from UV-excited impurities, such as catalyst residues or oxidation products in the plastic.

Choice of UV absorber stabilizers is governed by the spectral region in which light absorption leads to degradation. This spectral region, namely the "activation spectrum," is that portion of the UV (and/or visible) spectrum, primarily responsible for the degradation of a particular polymer. A UV stabilizer should thus do the following:

• absorb strongly at the wavelengths of maximum sensitivity of the polymer

• be compatible with the polymer

• be stable at processing temperatures

• have low volatility so that it is not lost during processing

• not contribute colour

Choice also is influenced by other additives present, such as antioxidants, heat stabilizers, fillers, and pigments.

Three types of UV stabilizers are used — *UV absorbers* (UV screens), *energy transfer agents* (quenchers), and *free-radical scavengers*. Each of these groups contains many compounds that are effective UV stabilizers, some of which are listed in Table VIII. Synergistic enhancement of stabilizing activity is often achieved by simultaneous use of stabilizers that act by different mechanisms. Some compounds act by several different mechanisms. In his review of polymer stabilizers de la Rie (1988) describes UV stabilizers and their reaction mechanisms in greater detail.

Table VIII

Ultraviolet Stabilizers

UV Absorbers

Carbon black
Zinc oxide
Substituted benzophenones
(yellow discolouration)
Substituted benzotriazoles
Substituted acrylonitriles
Aryl esters
- Salicylates and benzoates

Energy Transfer Agents (Quenchers)

Cobalt and nickel chelates
(green/blue discolouration)

Free-radical Scavengers

Hindered amines (HALS)

UV Absorbers

UV absorbers compete with the polymer for absorption of the incident UV light. The UV absorber absorbs the UV light before or more efficiently than the polymer molecule. The excess energy in the UV absorber is converted into harmless heat (vibrational energy of the molecule). By absorbing the UV light at the surface, less UV light reaches the interior of the plastic. It is important to note that this is essentially a surface phenomenon. Although the entire bulk of the plastic may contain UV absorber, only that absorber in a surface layer measuring a few tens of microns thick is the effective stabilizer.

Some inorganic pigments are efficient UV absorbers. Carbon black is most common and effective, but titanium dioxide and zinc oxide are also used. When high levels of inorganic pigments can be used, additional UV stabilizer is not required. The main disadvantage with these pigments is that they produce opaque plastics.

Colourless and transparent UV absorbers, such as benzophenone derivatives (e.g., ortho-hydroxybenzophenone) absorbing at 230 nm to 350 nm, and benzotriazole derivatives absorbing at 280 nm to 390 nm, can be used in clear plastics. Although these UV absorbers are not consumed during their interaction with the UV light, some are consumed by reaction with free-radicals (this is especially true for o-hydroxy-benzophenone, which is as commonly added for its free-radical scavenger antioxidant properties as for its UV absorber properties). An unfortunate property of benzophenones and benzotriazoles is that the products of their reactions with free-radicals are usually highly coloured, causing yellowing of the plastic. Aryl esters including aryl salicylate, resorcinol monobenzoate, and aryl esters of terephthalic and isophthalic acid undergo light-induced rearrangement to give photochemically stable products, which are derivatives of 2-hydroxy-benzophenone which absorb in the range of 230 nm to 350 nm and which are effective UV absorbers. Unfortunately these also cause discolouration by formation of quinoid by-products, like the benzophenone derivatives.

Quenchers (Energy Transfer Agents)
Quenchers interact with energetic excited-state chromophores. Excess energy is transferred from the excited chromophore to the quenching stabilizer, allowing the excited chromophore to return to its stable ground state. The excess energy in the excited quencher is dissipated by non-damaging conversion to heat (vibrational energy) in the quencher molecule.

Nickel chelate complexes are commonly used quenchers that function by absorbing UV light energy into their highly conjugated structures and dissipating the energy as harmless IR radiation by a resonance stabilization mechanism. They also have some hydroperoxide decomposing abilities. Unfortunately they are inherently greenish or tan coloured. Some benzophenone derivatives function both as direct UV absorbers and as energy-transfer agents, absorbing in the range of 230 nm to 350 nm. As noted, these have a tendency to yellow under processing or exposure to light.

Free-radical Scavengers
Free-radical scavengers do not absorb or block UV light. They scavenge the free-radicals produced by photolytic reactions. They prevent degradation by reacting so quickly that the free-radicals have no time to undergo subsequent photo-oxidative degradation reactions with the polymer.

Compounds typically used for this include substituted tetramethyl piperidines, a class of compounds referred to as hindered amine light stabilizers (HALS). These HALS have exceptional activity that is attributed to mechanisms in which the active species are regenerated and recycled. They are not consumed by their stabilizing reactions and therefore have long lifetimes in the plastic. HALS function as energy quenchers, peroxide decomposers, and/or alkyl radical terminators.

Plasticizers

A polymer is said to be plasticized when it is made more flexible by the addition of compounds to the base polymer. Typical plasticizers are high-boiling organic liquids or low-melting solids that are added to hard or tough resins to impart softness or flexibility, reduce stiffness, increase impact resistance, and ease processing by lowering melt viscosity and fabricating temperatures. Camphor, the first plasticizer, introduced about 1870, was used at concentrations of about 50% in cellulose nitrate to make celluloid. This formulation was the principal thermoplastic until camphor supplies from Japan were threatened during WW II. Increasing scarcity combined with camphor's objectionable odour led to its gradual replacement with phosphate esters, particularly triphenyl phosphate. Phthalates were developed in the 1920s. Di-2-ethylhexyl phthalate, commonly referred to as dioctyl phthalate or DOP, currently the predominant plasticizer for all plastics, was patented in 1933. Modern plasticizers are used at concentrations of 10% to 25% but sometimes as high as 50% (Figure 4). Eighty-five per cent of plasticizers are used in PVC and these are most commonly esters of carboxylic acids or phosphoric acid. Plasticization of PVC is reviewed in detail by Darby and Sears (1976).

Plasticizers are not chemically bound to the polymer but merely dissolved in it. Plasticizer

softening action (plasticization) usually is attributed to their ability to reduce the intermolecular attractive forces between the polymer macromolecule chains. The plasticizer molecules insinuate themselves between those of the polymer, thereby preventing the polymer-to-polymer interactions that create rigidity (i.e., increased tensile strength and decreased elongation). The plasticizer acts as a lubricant to facilitate movement of the polymer macromolecules over each other and provides internal lubricity. Plasticizers have varying degrees of solvating action on resins. A plasticizer is a solvent that is involatile.

Different plasticizers have different efficiencies — different concentrations are required to achieve the same level of plasticization. In general, monomeric plasticizers are the most efficient. Plasticizer efficiency may be measured by a number of physical properties, such as tensile strength, modulus of elasticity, elongation at break, and hardness. Figure 4 shows the variation of the mechanical properties of tensile strength and elongation at break with plasticizer concentration and plasticizer type. Horizontal lines indicate the onset of plasticization. At higher concentrations plasticization is evident, whereas at lower concentrations the plastic remains stiff and relatively unaffected by the plasticizer content. Figure 4 also shows that different plasticizers have different efficiencies, that is, at a particular concentration different compounds produce different levels of flexibility.

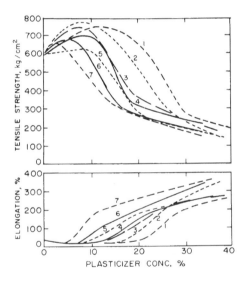

Figure 4 Effect of concentration of various plasticizers on tensile strength and elongation at break of PVC. Plasticizers: 1, dicyclohexyl phthalate; 2, phthalate polyester; 3, adipic polyester; 4, tricresyl phosphate; 5, liquid butadiene-acrylonitrile copolymer; 6, di-2-ethylhexyl phthalate; 7, di-2-ethylhexyl adipate (from Darby and Sears 1976). The concentration at which the curves cross the line marking the initial value of tensile strength or elongation indicates the onset of plasticization. At any plasticizer concentration greater than this, the plastic will be softer and more flexible than in the non-plasticized state. For these plasticizers the concentration at onset of plasticization ranges from about 6% to 22% plasticizer content. This is also a measure of the efficiency of the plasticizer—the lower the onset concentration, the more efficient the plasticizer.

Plasticizers that exhibit good compatibility are designated *primary* plasticizers. Those that exhibit partial compatibility or that exude or bloom on standing are usually called *secondary* plasticizers and cannot be used alone. The distinction between primary and secondary plasticizers is vague, depending partly on polymer, concentration desired, and environment and conditions of end use (see previous discussion of plasticizers in section on additive compatibility). These are *external* plasticizers, compounds added to the base polymer. *Internal* plasticization can be accomplished by copolymerization of a flexible polymer with a rigid polymer. Vinyl chloride-vinyl acetate copolymer is an example where the vinyl acetate imparts flexibility to the PVC. In this type of plasticization, no "external" compounds are added to the base polymer. Instead a new polymer with greater flexibility is chemically produced by modifying the polymer backbone with flexible units. Such "internally plasticized" plastics avoid plasticizer migration problems. Internally plasticized plastics will not be discussed further.

Pressure exerted on plastics can cause migration of plasticizers. This can lead to exudation and blooming of plasticizers or to loss of plasticizer from specific areas in compression (Figure 5). This might cause excessive exudation at the weight-bearing points of objects resting in storage. Also where there are snap fittings under compression, plasticizer can be lost. This leads to embrittlement. Examples of this are the location where a doll's arm snaps over a protruding socket at the shoulder, or where a hose fitting over a tube is often held by a hose clamp that adds more pressure and increases migration and subsequent embrittlement due to plasticizer loss. Plasticizer loss is usually accompanied by shrinkage resulting from loss of volume (i.e., that normally occupied by the plasticizer in the plastic). This leads to cracking, again exacerbated in areas of tension or compression.

Composition of PVC Plasticizers

All primary plasticizers for PVC are esters, functional groups that are reaction products of acids and alcohols. The acids may be cyclic (e.g., phthalic, benzoic, trimellitic, terephthalic) or linear (e.g., adipic, azelaic, sebacic, ethylhexanoic, isodecanoic). The alcohols may be monohydric (e.g., 2-ethylhexanol, isodecanol, butanol) or polyhydric (e.g., propylene glycol, ethylene glycol, pentaerythritol). Furthermore the alcohol may be linear or branched. Aryl (cyclic) and alkyl (linear) esters of phosphoric acid are also common.

Secondary plasticizers for PVC include various aromatic and mixed aromatic-aliphatic oils, chlorinated paraffins, some poly(alpha-methyl styrene) derivatives, and inexpensive esters of high molecular weight alcohols and organic acids that have marginal compatibility with PVC.

The most common general purpose plasticizers are cyclic dialkyl phthalates. As the alkyl side chain of the plasticizer increases in molecular weight volatility decreases, water extractability decreases, oil extractability increases, efficiency decreases, processing becomes more difficult, and specific gravity decreases. Trimellitate esters (i.e., derived from trimellitic acid) with branched or linear alkyl side chains having 7 to 10 carbons are cyclic plasticizers of higher molecular weight, which have low volatility and low water extractability. Major applications are in high temperature wire and non-fogging automotive compounds for upholstery and panels in car interiors. (Note: Fogging plasticizers are those that evaporate from plastic components inside automobiles then condense as the bluish oily film on the inside of the car windows.)

Linear plasticizers have improved low temperature performance. Their linear structure (no rings) make them less compatible with PVC and they tend to exude. Substitution of alkyl groups by aryl groups (rings) improves performance. Alkyl benzyl phthalates are high solvating plasticizers with increased compatibility with PVC. For example, butyl benzyl phthalate is used in vinyl asbestos floor tiles because it has less tendency to migrate from the tile into the flooring adhesive, thus preventing adhesive softening caused by the plasticizer. Citrate esters are approved for food products.

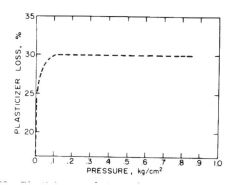

Figure 5 Loss of plasticizer due to pressure on PVC. Note that the pressure of 0.1 kg/cm² (which is equivalent to that exerted by a stack of 100 dimes or quarters) can be easily achieved on objects in storage, if the entire weight of the objects rests on small area bearing points. (from Darby and Sears 1976)

Phosphate plasticizers impart flame resistance. Triaryl (tricresyl, cresyl diphenyl, triphenyl) phosphates dissolve easily and are low in volatility. As aryl groups are substituted by alkyl groups, the properties of the plasticized plastic tend to become less useful. For example, tri-2-ethylhexyl phosphate is only good at low temperatures, has high oil extractability, high volatility, and poor heat stability (needs stabilizer).

Polymeric plasticizers (polyesters) are usually based on linear dibasic acids plus polyols (especially glycols). Their permanence improves with increased molecular weight. They generally have low volatility, good to very good extraction resistance to aqueous and hydrocarbon solvents, but have poor low temperature performance and are inefficient and difficult to process. Epoxy plasticizers are generally epoxidized oils (linseed and soya bean) and alkyl epoxy esters (tallates, oleates, linseed oil acids) with performance properties like polyesters. The presence of the oxirane group allows these to also serve as auxiliary heat and light stabilizers. Some soya and linseed oil epoxies are also FDA approved.

Aliphatic and aromatic hydrocarbons and chlorinated paraffins are generally not compatible with PVC. These are used as minor components of a plasticizer system as extenders to reduce cost in those few applications where they provide advantageous end-use properties.

Plasticizers for Plastics Other Than PVC

The amorphous character of PVC allows pasticization over a wide range of plasticizer concentrations, whereas the higher crystallinity of other polymers means that the region in which plasticizing is possible is smaller. This means that plasticizer compatibility must be critically evaluated. Plasticizers must be chosen with care.

Generally the plasticizers used for poly(vinyl chloride) work well for cellulose nitrate, cellulose acetate propionate, cellulose acetate butyrate, and ethyl cellulose. Cellulosics are best plasticized with dibutyl phthalate, alkyloxy phthalates, triaryl phosphates, and sulfonamides. Cellulose acetate requires lower alkyl phthalates, such as dimethyl and diethyl phthalate, for plasticization. Triacetin may also be used. Such materials have greater volatility than dioctyl phthalate (which is typically used in PVC) and are more subject to loss by evaporation leading to embrittlement and cracking due to shrinkage.

Plasticizers with high solvating power for PVC are suitable for poly(vinyl acetate), PVAC. Dibutyl and butyl benzyl phthalates, and glycol dibenzoates are widely used in PVAC. Phthalates and dibenzoates have been detected in several PVAC adhesives (white glues) analyzed in the Adhesive Testing Project at CCI (Down and Williams 1988).

Toluene ethyl sulfonamides are used to soften some grades of nylon. Poly(vinyl butyrals) are most often plasticized with glycol derivatives, some adipates, and some phosphates. Alkyl benzyl phthalates and phosphates are used in acrylics. Polyurethanes can be plasticized with many of the same compounds that are used for PVC.

Extraction of Plasticizers

Extraction of plasticizers from PVC by coatings, such as nitrocellulose, can mar finishes and cause discolouration and tackiness. This problem can be greatly reduced by the use of plasticizers with little or no affinity for the coating and by the selection of plasticizers with resistance to migration. Isophthalates (DIOP) and terephthalates (DOTP) have very low migration to nitrocellulose coatings and offer a marked improvement over all orthophthalate esters, but are very expensive.

As a consequence of these mutual compatibilities, it is essential that objects made of different polymers (such as these) be kept out of contact with each other. Plasticizer migration and plasticizer transfer will occur, usually with softening and increased tackiness of object surfaces. This also applies to the choice of storage materials. Storage materials must be carefully chosen to resist damage by plastic objects and their additives.

Conclusion

When collecting, displaying, and storing plastic objects it must be remembered that plastics are complex mixtures of polymers and additives. Changes in either the polymer or any of its additives will result in changes in the plastic, usually in a way that is described as degradation. This paper describes the wide variety of additives that are used and the delicate balance of properties that are required to ensure that all the ingredients are, and remain, compatible in a well formulated plastic. The effects of antioxidants, heat and light stabilizers, and plasticizers on the longevity of plastics has been discussed in some detail. Other additives not discussed here, such as colourants (pigments and dyes), mineral additives like fillers, extenders and reinforcing agents, and processing aids like anti-static agents, internal lubricants, mold release agents, and slip agents, also affect the longevity of a plastic, although probably not to the same degree as those discussed. Degradation profiles were introduced as an aid to understanding the states and stages of degradation of plastics as determined by the rates and extents of degradation processes occurring in aging plastics. The ways that additives and changes in additives can influence the shape of the degradation profile and thus the longevity of the plastic object were discussed.

Résumé

La composition des objets en plastique et leur longévité

Les objets en plastique sont généralement décrits d'après leur principal constituant polymérique — une feuille de polyéthylène, un revêtement en vinyle ou en polychlorure de vinyle, une sculpture en acrylique ou une boîte en polystyrène ou en styrène, par exemple. Or, tous les articles fabriqués en plastique sont constitués de préparations complexes de polymères, auxquels viennent s'ajouter les additifs nécessaires pour conférer au polymère de base les propriétés qu'exige son utilisation finale. Et les additifs — notamment les plastifiants, les stabilisants, les colorants, les agents favorisant le traitement, etc. — sont tout aussi importants que le polymère de base quand il s'agit de déterminer la durée de vie utile de tels objets ou la période durant laquelle ils pourront être conservés dans un musée.

Nous décrirons donc brièvement, dans le cadre de la présente communication, les principaux groupes de polymères auxquels appartiennent les plastiques qui entrent dans la composition des objets de musée les plus typiques, pour ensuite traiter dans le détail des additifs qui sont présents dans les plastiques fabriqués à partir de ces polymères. Les résultats d'analyses chimiques récentes, portant sur des objets en plastique dégradés, seront utilisés pour montrer l'incidence des additifs et des polymères de base sur la longévité des plastiques. Leur dégradation, de même que d'autres dommages qui leur sont causés — accrétion, cristallisation, craquellement, fissuration, décoloration, fragilisation, suintement, ramollissement, etc. —, est liée à une modification ou à une perte d'additifs. Et les conditions ambiantes ne sont en outre pas étrangères à de tels changements. Nous fournirons enfin des lignes directrices générales sur la mise en réserve des objets en plastique, qui permettront, d'une part, d'accroître leur longévité et, d'autre part, d'empêcher qu'ils ne causent des dommages aux matières environnantes

References

Barton, A.F.M. *CRC Handbook of Solubility Parameters and Other Cohesion Parameters* (Boca Raton, Florida: CRC Press, Inc., 1983).

Carlsson, D.J. and D.M. Wiles, "Degradation," in: *Encyclopedia of Polymer Science and Engineering, Volume 4* ed. H.F. Mark et al. (New York: John Wiley & Sons, 1986) pp. 630-696.

Darby, J.R. and J.K. Sears, "Theory of Solvation and Plasticization," in: *Encyclopedia of PVC, Volume 1, Chapter 10* ed. L.I. Nass (New York: Marcel Dekker, Inc., 1976) pp. 385-503.

Darby, J.R., N.W. Touchette and K. Sears, "Dielectric Constants of Plasticizers as Predictors of Compatibility with Polyvinyl Chloride," *Polymer Engineering and Science*, October 1967, pp. 295-309.

de la Rie, R., "Polymer Stabilizers. A Survey with Reference to Possible Applications in the Conservation Field," *Studies in Conservation*, vol. 33, no. 1, 1988, pp. 9-22.

Down, J.L. and R.S. Williams, "Report on Adhesive Testing at the Canadian Conservation Institute," *Symposium '88 Proceedings* (Ottawa: Canadian Conservation Institute, in press).

Feller, R.L., "Studies on the Photochemical Stability of Thermoplastic Resins," *Preprints of the 4th Triennial Meeting of the International Council of Museums Committee for Conservation Committee, Venice*, 75/22/4, 1975, pp. 1-11.

Feller, R.L., "Stages in the Deterioration of Organic Materials," in: *Preservation of Paper and Textiles of Historic and Artistic Value. Advances in Chemistry Series, No. 164* ed. J.C. Williams (Washington, D.C.: American Chemical Society, 1977) pp. 314-335.

Feller, R.L. and D.B. Encke, "Stages in Deterioration: The Examples of Rubber Cement and Transparent Mending Tape," in: *Science and Technology in the Service of Conservation. Preprints of the Contributions to the Washington Congress, 3-9 September 1982* ed. N.S. Brommelle and G. Thomson (London: International Institute for Conservation of Historic and Artistic Works, 1982) pp. 19-23.

Grattan, D.W., "The Oxidative Degradation of Organic Materials and Its Importance in the Deterioration of Artifacts," *Journal of the International Institute for Conservation - Canadian Group*, vol. 4, no. 1, 1978, pp. 17-26.

Grattan, D.W., "Degradation Rates for Some Historic Polymers and the Potential of Various Conservation Measures for Minimizing Oxidative Degradation," this volume.

Hedley, G., "Solubility Parameters and Varnish Removal: A Survey," *The Conservator*, vol. 4, 1980, pp. 12-18.

Horie, C.V., *Materials for Conservation: Organic Consolidants, Adhesives and Coatings* (London: Butterworths, 1987).

Nass, L.I., "Theory of Degradation and Stabilization Mechanisms," in: *Encyclopedia of PVC. Volume 1, Chapter 8* ed. L.I. Nass (New York: Marcel Dekker, Inc., 1976) pp. 271-293.

Nass, L.I., "Actions and Characteristics of Stabilizers," in: *Encyclopedia of PVC. Volume 1, Chapter 9* ed. L.I. Nass (New York: Marcel Dekker, Inc., 1976) pp. 295-384.

The Nature and Origin of Surface Veneer Checking in Plywood

Mark D. Minor

Department of Objects Conservation
The Metropolitain Museum of Art
New York, N.Y.
U.S.A.

Abstract

Plywood is a material occurring with greater frequency in both decorative and fine arts collections. While fundamentally wood, its structure and characteristics fall into a completely different realm than solid timber. One degradation problem evident in many pieces of furniture and painting supports are longitudinal surface veneer checks. These cracks are disfiguring to the display surface, they break up the continuity of the surface coatings, and they expose the underlying layers and adhesives to air, moisture and grime. As a precursor to responsible treatment of these objects, the nature and mechanism of these checks need to be understood by conservators.

The study to be discussed attempted to show a tangible connection between an inherent vice in rotary-peeled plywood veneer (lathe checks) and the formation of surface checking in plywood panels. It consists of two sections: a survey of research literature on the mechanics of the veneer cutting process combined with a microscopical examination of plywoods cycled to equilibrium at different moisture contents. A sample group of plywoods was cycled through two differing moisture extremes, representing an acceptable and an extreme climatic change, for 20 weeks. Periodic samples were taken and examined microscopically in cross-section to assess any changes to the wood structure.

Damage to the wood structure occurred much more quickly than expected, even in the acceptable 35% to 59% relative humidity (RH) cycle.

By the third week, checks extending from the original lathe checks had extended to approximately 75% to 80% of the veneer thickness. By the ninth week, several cracks had reached the surface of the panels. At week 20, a majority of the cracks had extended to the surface, regardless of the severity of the moisture change.

A model for formation of checks is suggested, based on compressive damage to the wood cells caused by moisture driven expansion, followed by tensile stress in subsequent shrinkage. The concept that plywood is not an inherently stable material but a fragile one is stressed. Implications for conservation are discussed, in particular the potential dangers of surface stabilization and reintegration.

Introduction and Objective

Plywood is a material showing up with greater frequency in decorative arts collections. While plywood is fundamentally wood, its structure and characteristics make it completely different from solid timber. One problem evident in many pieces of 19th- and 20th-century objects that incorporate plywood is longitudinal surface veneer checking. These checks are disfiguring to the surface, they break up the continuity of the surface coatings, and they expose underlying layers and adhesives to air, moisture and grime.

To devise optimal treatment methods and preventive conservation measures, the nature and origin of veneer checks need to be fully understood. Specifically, it needs to be ascertained whether (and to what extent) the checks are a result of relative humidity (RH) fluctuation. (RH fluctuation could cause mechanical damage on the cellular level, which would be observed as checks and these checks could be augmented by processing methods, such as rotary lathe checking.)

The purpose of this study is to provide empirical information on the nature and origin of surface checks in plywood. The study will seek a connection between rotary-peel lathe checks in tangentially cut veneer, and surface check formation in plywood panels composed of such veneer. This will be shown by exposing plywood to numerous high/low extremes of RH, and subsequently examining it in cross-section. The study will underscore the misconception that plywood is an inherently stable material. It will also help in the construction of a plausible model that explains the propagation of surface checks in plywood, in relation to the veneer cutting process, and the hygromechanical properties of wood. It is hoped that the study will create interest in plywood degradation among other conservators, and provide some preliminary recommendations on approaches to the conservation of plywood.

Consider some examples of surface checks in plywood objects (Figures 1 and 2). The first is a 1936 table by Marcel Breuer. The surface checks are evident on this piece, and have exacerbated a condition of brittle delamination of the cellulose nitrate finish. A similar but less

severe situation can be seen in a close-up of the chair by Charles Eames (Figures 3 and 4) which he termed "DCW" (Dining Chair Wood). Also, the effects of surface checking can be seen on many painted plywood panels, both new and old. Obviously, where ground and paint layers are not flexible enough to remain intact over a developing check, they will crack, in some cases much to the detriment of the pictorial effect of the painting.

Figure 2 Detail of surface veneer checking, Breuer table. Note the accompanying finish film cleavage.

Figure 3 DCW Chair, Charles Eames, 1946. Collection of the Fine Arts Museum of San Francisco (1987.62.1).

Figure 1 Nesting Table, Marcel Breuer, 1936. The Metropolitan Museum of Art, Gift of Daniel and Suzanne Geller in memory of Bert and Phyllis Geller (1989.52).

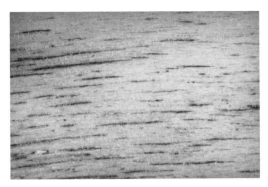

Figure 4 Detail of surface veneer checks, DCW Chair.

Plywood as an Art Material

Plywood has a diverse history of usage, which can be seen as a response to its unique characteristics. Plywood embodies at least three key advantages. The first advantage lies in its strength properties, which show remarkable advantages over solid wood of equivalent dimension.[1] Since plywood, by definition, consists of an odd number of veneer plies bound at 90° angles to one another, the weakness inherent in a thin piece of wood — that of stiffness or modulus of elasticity perpendicular to the grain direction — is mitigated. Plywood has virtually isotropic (i.e., directionless) strength properties in its "sheet" or planar dimension. Obviously, a thin sheet of plywood, when incorporated into a seat, will support a much greater load than a piece of solid wood of similar size; a distinct advantage, elegantly exploited by such designers as Alvaar Aalto in the 1930s.

A second advantage is the ability of plywood to be formed. Again, it is the fundamental precondition of being laminated that allowed users to modify plywood from flat sheets to fantastically curved forms like the *Arabesque* table of Carlo Mollino.

Such curved forms rely on the adhesive bond between laminae to "set" the shape upon curing. Solid wood could be processed to equivalent shapes, but at great effort, and again, would maintain its unfortunate perpendicular-to-grain weakness. In addition, solid wood shaped into tight curves would incorporate areas of "short grain," wherein the far weaker shear strength of solid wood perpendicular to

grain direction would render such designs useless.

The third advantage, of greatest interest here, is the dimensional stability of plywood. Plywood is widely considered by non-specialists to be ultimately stable, that is, absolutely immune from dimensional movement, since its alternating layers effectively lock each other into place. In truth, it is not dimensionally stable. In going from the green state, or with moisture content at fiber saturation point, to the oven-dry condition, plywood experiences a dimensional change that is but a fraction of that of solid wood. The shrinkage is 0.2% compared to 8.0%,[2] smaller by a factor of 40. Because of its significantly reduced potential for hygroscopic dimensional changes, plywood panels can be effectively glued to perpendicular or cross-grain frame elements. Such construction is either dangerous or impossible in solid wood, as can be seen in numerous furniture case constructions, where drawer rails and leg posts have been fastened tight across the width of the sides. Inevitably, such constructions lead to compression set of the panel as relative swelling, caused by moisture absorption, exceeds the proportional limit in compression of the wood. (Concise descriptions of the nature of compression set are given by Hoadley[3] and Stamm.[4]) Since longitudinal compressive and tensile strengths exceed those perpendicular to the grain direction, subsequent shrinking results in tensile cracking across the grain.

Plywood gains in strength and stability relative to solid wood through its cross-banded structure. Forced stability in plywood is not without its drawbacks, however. The restricted dimensional change (i.e., compared to solid wood) in relation to moisture content change is the cause of many of the problems apparent in art and artifacts incorporating plywood.

Lathe Checking and the Veneer Cutting Process

Surface checking can be found on weathered solid wood as well as plywood.[5] The mechanisms involved in either case are not obvious. For plywood, it is also not obvious from which direction (i.e., surface downward, or from the underneath working upwards) the checks evolve. The obvious culprits are lathe checks.

Since the 1890s, rotary lathe cutting has been the preferred manner to obtain the large sections of veneer needed to form sheets for making plywood.[6] A log or "blank" of wood, first boiled or steamed for softening, is spun against a large fixed knife, cutting a carefully controlled thickness of continuous veneer. Such veneer will obviously be sliced as a tangential spiral from the blank. Unfortunate by-products of this cutting action are lathe checks, which form on the downward or knife side of the veneer being formed. Lathe checks are periodic, radially oriented cracks in veneer, resulting from a complex interaction of compressive and tensile stresses during rotary lathe cutting[7] (Figure 5). From early on, lathe operators learned to optimize the settings of the lathe and the pre-conditioning of the wood to minimize lathe checking. Refinements such as the nosebar, a pre-compression apparatus, further reduced the formation of lathe checks.[8]

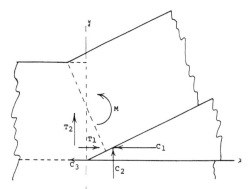

Figure 5 Stress distribution during veneer cutting. "C" denotes compression, "T" tension, and "M" moment. (After Leney 1960).

Theoretical work begun in the 1940s continues to shed a great deal of light on the origin of lathe checks. There are a number of studies on this topic that are noteworthy.[9-13] This research proved the phenomenon to be extremely complex. Based on these findings, a very idealized and simplified veneer cut can be summarized here. As a knife enters a block of wood (Figure 5), various compressive and tensile stresses become apparent. Wood cells are forced both

upward and forward as a result of the cutting wedge entering the tissue. Since the resulting chip is effectively levered upward, there is a noteworthy compression on the upper surface of the wood blank.

The combined stresses form a shear force, resulting from the very complex mixture of tension and compression. The shear plane is oriented at approximately 60° to the direction of cut. At some point in the cutting process, the shear stress will exceed the tensile strength of the wood cells, and failure (i.e., a lathe check) will occur. At this moment, the stresses are relieved by the rapid increase in strain (deflection upward of the veneer). The stresses will be cyclic, since both the tension and compression will increase as a chip is forced up the knife face, and be released somewhat after failure, only to increase again as the cut continues.

The result is a sheet of veneer with periodic checking on its under (or loose) side. Even with modern refinements, production of rotary-cut veneer without knife checks is a theoretical possibility, and in practice, all such veneer will contain checks to some extent.

The Hygromechanical Properties of Plywood

How might the hygromechanical properties of plywood affect its degradation? As can be seen in the following data, there is a notable difference in the equilibrium moisture content (EMC) of plywood in comparison to that of solid wood up to the fiber saturation point.[14]

Plywood EMC	RH%	Solid Wood EMC
6%	40	~8%
10%	70	~13%
28%	100	~28%

In simple terms, plywood is less hygroscopic than solid wood. It is prudent to consider what might cause this phenomenon. A ready explanation is the volumetric presence of a great deal of adhesive. For a given volume of plywood, compared to an equal volume of solid wood, more water-impervious material, in the form of adhesives, is present. But this is only part of the answer.

A more interesting explanation is that of reduced hygroscopicity: wood under high compressive stress experiences a small but significant reduction in hygroscopicity, known as the Barkas effect.[15] Obviously, individual plies, being cross-laminated, are restrained from swelling in the tangential direction by the adhesive bond to the adjacent ply (or plies).

We can deduce a situation in which hygroscopicity reduces as RH and, therefore, moisture content (MC) increases. It follows from general principles that as long as there is any degree of hygroscopicity in wood, *any rise in RH must be accompanied by a certain degree of swelling*. It is easy to see the somewhat canceling effects that further swelling would have on further hygroscopicity. But the reduction in hygroscopicity will not be enough to account for the reduction in swelling seen in plywood as compared to solid wood.[16]

Where does the swelling go? This is not a naive question. On a cellular level, one theory hypothesizes "inward swelling," where restrained wood is forced to expand "inside" into the cell lumen, or the empty space at the center of vessels, fibers, and tracheids.[17] Theoretically, on a molecular level, enough compression might induce a physical/chemical change in the wood tissue, with a redistribution of bonds between polymeric cellulose chains within the lignin matrix. Both models imply permanent set (this phenomenon is known in the world of wood technology as compression set). As compressed wood shrinks in a decreasing RH, it will do so from its compressed dimension, effectively trying to further reduce its size. But plywood is bound, one layer to another. Eventually, the compression of the swelling surface veneer will become a tension that exceeds the tensile strength of the shrinking veneer. In this manner, through numerous MC cycles, we can hypothesize that tensile cellular failure might occur in the surface veneer. This failure may perhaps eventually become a full-fledged check.

An Empirical Demonstration of Check Formation

As a means of visually gauging the onset and propagation of surface checks in plywood, a demonstration was devised to enable a cross-sectional viewing of wood cells in plywood through numerous cycles of RH changes. Conditions of extreme RH that an artifact might actually be exposed to were established. (The soaking, freezing and boiling associated with industrial standards were avoided. For an interesting critique of industrial test standards in plywood, see Carroll.[18]) Two relative humidity regimes were chosen: a moderate one of 33% to 59% RH, and a more drastic yet still realistic one of 12% to 85% RH. Small chambers were constructed, using saturated salt solutions to create the two regimes. (The following saturated salt solutions were used: lithium chloride 12%, magnesium chloride 33%, sodium bromide 59% and ammonium sulfate 85%.)

By monitoring the equilibrium moisture contents (EMCs) of the samples, it was decided that a 3.5 day changeover time (i.e., a complete low-high cycle took one week) was adequate. Weights were recorded at both the low and high EMCs to determine whether a significant gain or loss in weight occurred during the test. At the end of the exposure period to low humidity (EMC at minimum, shrinkage at maximum) several circular samples (6 mm in diameter) were removed from each test piece.

Two types of plywood samples were used in this demonstration. The first, representing a "new" piece of plywood, was commercial Baltic birch plywood. This consisted of nine plies of rotary-cut birch veneer, glued with a hot-press urea-formaldehyde adhesive. The second, representing an "old" or historic plywood, was taken from an early 20th-century object. It consisted of three plies of tangentially cut birch veneer, with a casein or soya adhesive.

All the samples were embedded, and examined microscopically, in both reflected visible light and long-wave ultraviolet illumination (UV exciter wavelength 365 nm, splitter wavelength 395 nm, barrier wavelength 420 nm). The condition(s) of the surface veneers were noted and photographed. Long-wave UV has been previously used in wood research to examine the wood-adhesive interface and the onset of fungal degradation.[19,20] It has the advantage of showing the lignin-rich areas of wood structure, and in this work aided the detection of check proliferation and cell wall breakage.

Results of Demonstration

1. The direction/evolution/resolution of lathe checks.

The lathe checks in the new plywood, while quite variable in nature, extended approximately one-third of the veneer thickness (Figure 6). The dark lumens seen in the photomicrographs are those completely infused with embedding medium, and tend to indicate increased cellular permeability due to damage. Lathe checks occur with a spacing that is roughly equal to the thickness of the veneer, and extend upward at an angle of approximately 45°. There appears to be a great tendency for lathe checks to resolve or end at some barrier point, such as a ray, a row of latewood cells, or a vessel element. Figure 7 shows a lathe check zone in the old plywood sample, the lower check resolving at a ray/vessel intersection.

Figure 6 Typical lathe check in the uncycled "new" plywood, extending to the left at an angle, then changing direction towards vertical. Note extent of adhesive layer penetration. (N.B.: all photomicrographs are at 150 x.)

2. Checking evolves from lathe checks, much more quickly than would be expected.

An original goal of this study was to visually determine from which direction, up or down, veneer checks originated and evolved. By the completion of the first humidity cycle, it was evident that the primary change occurring with

Figure 7 Typical lathe check in the uncycled "old" sample. Note the non-tangential orientation of the upper veneer, as well as the compression visible in vessel elements.

the samples was the extension of existing lathe checks (Figure 8). After this first cycle, the lathe checks had extended a great distance into the veneer, in some cases to within 10 cells of the surface. But most noteworthy was that the degree of damage was largely independent of the amplitude of RH variation. Note the damage to the sample in the "extreme" cycle seen in Figure 8, compared to the sample from the "moderate" or regime more likely to be seen in a museum, in Figure 9. There is an alarmingly similar degree of damage. This very pointedly underscores the sensitivity of plywood to swings in RH in the early stages of its life. The sample shown in Figure 10 again demonstrates the possibility of extreme damage in one cycle. Note the crushed layer of cells at the top of this sample — they are a result of compression and

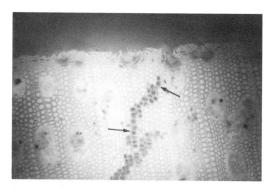

Figure 8 Cycle #1, extreme RH range ("new" ply). Note extension of crack system, and middle lamella (inter-cellular) failure in vertical section at lower arrow. The check terminates at a ray, near the surface.

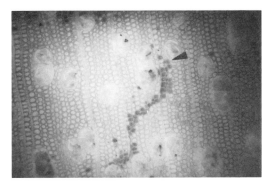

Figure 9 Cycle #1, moderate RH range ("new" ply). Photo shows relative damage after one cycle in the moderate RH range. Top margin of photo corresponds to surface of the veneer.

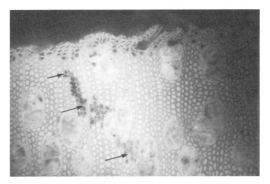

Figure 10 Cycle #1, extreme RH range ("new" ply). Extension of crack system to within 10 cells of surface. Note crushed cells at surface infused with embedding medium.

machine surfacing during manufacturing, and are not directly related to MC cycling.

3. Very little change occurs after the initial damage.

Aside from a slight "widening" of the area of damage within a crack system, and a gradual increase in the length and definition of the cracks, very little change was noted in 18 humidity cycles for both plywoods. Figures 11 to 16 show a series of cross-sections of plywood samples exposed to an increasing number of RH cyclic changes. In cycle 9 (Figure 12) the crack has reached the surface, while another sample (Figure 13) exposed to 18 cycles shows a check resolved at a ray somewhat further down, albeit near the surface. In the aged plywood sample

shown in Figure 14, virtually no damage that can be directly ascribed to this humidity cycling occurred, since extant surface coating material can be seen penetrating the check. This indicates that it is an old check. The great degree of variation (Figure 15) in damage to the older samples makes it difficult to connect any damages noted with this demonstration with particular causes. Since lathe/surface checks of many different lengths and widths were noted at the start, it became impossible to attribute any widening or lengthening to further RH cycling. It was apparent, however, that the frequency of checking did not increase, that is, it did not appear that any new cracks developed during the demonstration in either type of sample. This strongly suggests that checks are only associated with original lathe checks, since no new checks developed, either from above or below.

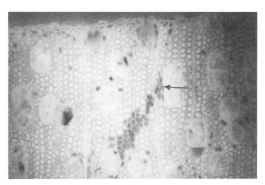

Figure 11 Cycle #2, moderate RH range ("new" ply). This sample shows no more damage than that of the first cycle.

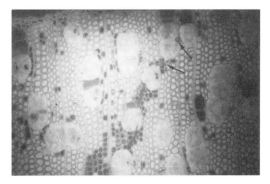

Figure 12 Cycle #9, moderate RH range ("new" ply). Typical damage after nine cycles. Check is effectively to surface. Note wider "footprint" of crack system.

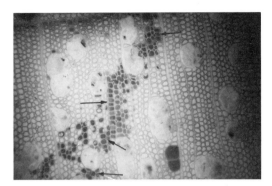

Figure 13 Cycle #18, extreme RH range ("new" ply). Note long, vertical, middle lamella failure, as well as severe and abrupt changes of direction.

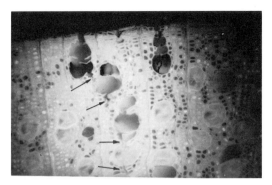

Figure 15 Cycle #18, moderate RH range ("old" ply). No extended lathe checks are visible in this sample; only surface damage in conjunction with vessel elements can be seen.

Figure 14 Cycle #6, moderate RH range ("old" ply). Note the surface coating material penetrating the check at the surface.

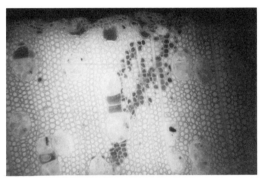

Figure 16 Cycle #18, extreme RH range ("new" ply). Full check extension.

Two or three moderate humidity cycles provided enough compressive stress to extend a lathe check nearly to the surface, yet another 16 cycles caused, at most, the crack to be barely complete and visible only under high magnification (Figure 16). Since the percentage of weight gain did not change noticeably with further cycling, the amount of expansion due to adsorption must remain virtually constant as shown in the data below.

Weight Gain Due to Moisture Uptake by Plywood	
Sample Group	Weight Gain % (Mean)
new ply, extreme cycle	2.56
old ply, extreme cycle	3.58
new ply, moderate cycle	0.74
old ply, moderate cycle	0.84

(Note the difference in moisture uptake between the "new" and "old" sample groups.) One

plausible explanation of the decline in crack propagation with increasing RH cycles is that the lengthened crack becomes its own expansion "release valve." Cracks provide a space to absorb expansion before it causes compressive stress leading to further failure. It follows that as the crack lengthens or widens, the relative degree of expansion needed to induce compressive damage would increase. Hence the slow progress of the crack after its initial extension.

4. Checks do not typically evolve at ray interfaces on the surface and work downward.

One theory of check propagation predicts that differing cellular orientation would make the interface of rays with vessels and fibers the primary location of check formation.[21] The reasoning is that any tangential or radial shrinkage in vessel or fiber tissue would be restrained by the radially orientated rays, causing a localized stress zone. No downward extending checks were ever noted at a ray/fiber or ray/vessel interface. After 18 "extreme" cycles, the new plywood showed no surface damage (i.e., damage other than the crushed outer layer of cells, an occurrence that is independent of humidity cycling). In the old sample only, however, a small number of surface checks of varying sizes were noted from the start. These were always associated with a vessel element (Figure 15). The fact that these checks often extended fairly deep implied that they were not merely a phenomenon caused by mechanical surfacing. The frequency of these checks did not change throughout the demonstration; in no instance was a surface check seen to connect with a lathe check to become a full-thickness check. While surface checking *proper* on plywood does exist, its frequency of occurrence is far less than that of surface damage resulting from the extension of a lathe check. This latter damage seems more in line with the explanation of weathering offered by Feist and Hon for solid wood.[5] No other explanation of the origin of these checks can be offered.

Conclusion and Conservation Recommendations

It should be evident that plywood is far from a perfectly stable material. In view of its potential for checking, we must conclude that plywood is not as stable as solid wood from a conservation point of view. Plywood was regarded as a panacea on its inception, and as a material that allowed artistic freedom for designers in the 1920s and 1930s. We as conservators, however, must now consider plywood as a product fraught with inherent problems. This insight demands a departure from the intuitive understanding held by most in favor of a new understanding: plywood is not stable, not inert, and is not able to survive the most demanding environmental conditions.

If plywood surface checks are considered to be disfiguring to objects, then pieces in decorative arts collections composed of plywood should and must be considered to be as fragile or perhaps more fragile than those constructed of solid wood. It has been shown that even a mild

degree of RH change will be enough to propagate checks that extend throughout the thickness of plywood veneers, and in a short period. On the bright side, it also has been shown that while damage may develop quickly, it occurs on a relatively minor scale, and the propagation of damage is slow. While checks were generated during the test, at no time were any gaping checks produced, such as those on the Breuer table.

It is hoped that the importance of paintings in most collections will help to underscore this point, for we only have to look at a small sampling of the many paintings executed on plywood grounds to see the effects of surface veneer checking. For paintings on plywood, it is not only the wood surface that is disfigured, but the decorative paint layers as well, quite possibly to the great disfigurement of the picture. Just as furniture finishes tend to give way with the evolving check, so do the ground and color layers in paintings.

This leads to an important point with respect to recommendations. What do we do when we are "too late"? As long as the RH variability that causes checks continues, any filling of these checks *will* exacerbate the crack. The fill provides a wedge for further compression, which negates the "release valve" potential. It is unknown at this time how great an effect filling will have. It is also unknown whether or not the filling of an applied decorative layer (such as paint) with differing mechanical properties will have a subsequent effect on the underlying plywood veneer. The object's environment, and the mechanical properties of the fill material, will play an important role in determining the extent of further damage. These are important areas for further study of plywood conservation.

Checks also provide a receptacle into which dust and airborne grime may settle. Covering plywood objects, whenever possible, is therefore a more important preventive conservation measure than it is for solid wood objects. Not only do years of accumulated grime begin to pose the same, inadvertent potential harm as a fill, but dirt-filled cracks have the added effect of becoming "beautiful black lines" across blonde wood, a problem known and loved by all who have tried to deal with it.

Further investigations will perhaps yield encouraging treatment possibilities. For now there are no easy answers. Surface veneer checking is in large part a classic "inherent vice" problem. Although latent, it is a difficulty we must unfortunately live with.

Résumé

Une étude préliminaire de l'origine et de la nature des craquelures qui se produisent dans le placage des contreplaqués

Le contreplaqué est un matériau qui se retrouve de plus en plus souvent dans les collections d'art décoratif et de beaux-arts. Bien que ce produit soit fondamentalement fait de bois, sa structure et ses caractéristiques le placent dans une catégorie totalement différente de celle des pièces de bois massif. Les craquelures longitudinales qui se produisent dans le placage de nombreux meubles ou supports de peinture constituent un exemple des problèmes de dégradation que peut présenter ce matériau. De telles craquelures défigurent la surface exposée, elles brisent la continuité des revêtements de surface et elles font que les couches sous-jacentes et les adhésifs entrent en contact avec l'air, l'humidité et la saleté. Pour qu'un traitement éclairé puisse être appliqué à ces objets, il faut d'abord que les spécialistes de la restauration comprennent la nature de ces craquelures et les mécanismes qui président à leur formation.

La présente communication fait état d'une étude qui visait à établir l'existence d'un lien réel entre un vice présent dans le placage (des craquelures de déroulage) et la formation de craquelures à la surface du contreplaqué. Elle comportait deux volets : l'établissement d'une liste de documents de recherche portant sur la mécanique du déroulage des placages et un examen au microscope de contreplaqués qui avaient traversé un cycle, en équilibre stable, à diverses teneurs en humidité. Un échantillon de contreplaqué a ainsi été soumis, pendant vingt semaines, à deux cycles de taux d'humidité différents, représentant respectivement un changement de conditions ambiantes acceptable et extrême. Des prélèvements ont été faits périodiquement, qui ont été examinés, en coupe, au microscope pour évaluer toute modification de la structure du bois.

Les dommages touchant la structure du bois sont apparus beaucoup plus rapidement que prévu, même dans le cas du cycle représentant un changement de conditions ambiantes acceptable (de 35 à 59 % d'humidité relative). Dès la troisième semaine, les craquelures qui partaient de la craquelure de déroulage originale atteignaient une profondeur de quelque 75 à 80 % du placage. À la neuvième semaine, nombre d'entre elles avaient atteint la surface du panneau. Et, à la vingtième semaine, la majorité s'étaient étendues à la surface, indépendamment de l'ampleur du changement d'humidité.

Un modèle est proposé pour expliquer la formation des craquelures. Il se fonde sur les dommages résultant de la compression que subissent les cellules de bois lorsque l'humidité, qui a favorisé une expansion du matériau, finit par se retirer, lui imposant ainsi un effort de tension. On insiste sur le fait que le contreplaqué est un matériau non pas stable mais fragile. Et l'on traite de l'incidence de ces découvertes sur la conservation de ce matériau, notamment en ce qui a trait aux risques éventuels que peuvent présenter la stabilisation et la réparation de la surface.

References

1. Forest Products Laboratory, Forest Service, U.S. Dept. of Agriculture, *Handbook of Wood and Wood-Based Materials for Engineers, Architects, and Builders* (New York: Hemisphere Publishing Corp., 1989) pp. 11-17.

2. Schniewind, A.P., ed., *Concise Encyclopedia of Wood and Wood-Based Materials* (Oxford: Pergamon Press, 1989) p. 224.

3. Hoadley, Bruce, *Understanding Wood* (Newtown, CT: The Taunton Press, 1980).

4. Stamm, A.J., *Wood and Cellulose Science* (New York: Ronald Press, 1964).

5. Feist, W.C. and D. Hon, "Chemistry of Weathering and Protection," in: *The Chemistry of Solid Wood, ACS, Advances in Chemistry Series*, Roger Rowell, ed. (Washington D.C.: American Chemical Society, 1984).

6. Susan Klim, "Composite Wood Materials in Twentieth Century Furniture," *Preprints of the Wooden Artifacts Group, American Institute for Conservation Annual Meeting*, 1990.

7. Leney, L., *Mechanism of Veneer Formation at the Cellular Level*, Research Bulletin No. 744, University of Missouri Agricultural Experiment Station, 1960.

8. McMillan, C.W., "The Relation of Mechanical Properties of Wood and Nosebar Pressure in Production of Veneer," *Forest Products Journal*, vol. 8, no. 1, 1958, pp. 23-32.

9. Fleischer, H.O., "Experiments in Rotary Veneer Cutting," *Forest Products Research Society Proceedings*, vol. 3, no. 20, 1949.

10. Kivimaa, E., "Investigating Rotary Veneer Cutting with the Aid of a Tension Test," *Forest Products Journal*, vol. 6, no. 7, 1957, pp. 251-255.

11. Feihl, O., "Peeling Defects in Veneer: Their Causes and Control," *Canadian Forest Products Research Bureau Technical Note* No. 25.

12. Cumming, J.D. and B.M. Collett, "Determining Lathe Settings for Optimum Veneer Quality," *Forest Products Journal*, vol. 20, no. 11, 1970, pp. 20-27.

13. Chih, L.C., *Fundamental Analysis of the Veneer Cutting Process*, unpublished dissertation (University of California at Berkeley, 1970).

14. Schniewind, *Concise Encyclopedia*, 1989, p. 224.

15. Barkas, W.W., "The Swelling of Wood Under Stress," *Forest Products Research Bulletin (G.B.)*, 1946.

16. Kollman, F.P., E.W. Kuenzi and A.J. Stamm, *Principles of Wood Science and Technology Vol. II: Wood Based Materials* (New York: Springer Verlag, 1975) p. 116.

17. Skaar, C., "Wood-Water Relationships," in: *The Chemistry of Solid Wood, ACS, Advances in Chemistry Series*, Roger Rowell, ed. (Washington, D.C.: American Chemical Society, 1984) p. 143.

18. Carroll, M.N., "We Still Don't Boil Houses: Examination of the Boil-Dry-Boil Test in Plywood Standards," *Forest Products Journal*, vol. 28, no. 5, 1978, pp. 23-27.

19. Murmanis, L. and B. River, "Microscopy of Abrasive-Planed and Knife-Planed Surfaces in Wood-Adhesive Bonds," *Wood and Fiber Science*, vol. 15, no. 2, pp. 102-115.

20. Krahmer, R., "Detecting Incipient Brown Rot with Fluorescence Microscopy," *Wood Science*, vol. 15, no. 2, pp. 78-80.

21. Schniewind, A.P., "Mechanism of Check Formation," *Forest Products Journal*, vol. 13, no. 11, 1963, pp. 475-480.

Case Studies and Specific Problems with Materials
Études de cas et problèmes particuliers posés par les matériaux

Deterioration of Cellulose Nitrate Sculptures Made by Gabo and Pevsner

Michele Derrick, Dusan Stulik

Getty Conservation Institute
Marina del Rey, California
U.S.A.

Eugena Ordonez

The Museum of Modern Art
New York, New York
U.S.A.

Abstract

Three sculptures by Naum Gabo and Antoine Pevsner in The Museum of Modern Art's collection exhibit varying degrees of deterioration and range from very good to poor in overall condition. The sculptures are made of thermally shaped pieces of cellulose ester (cellulose nitrate) attached together with an adhesive also based on cellulose ester. The translucent cellulose nitrate pieces, which originally may have been uncolored, are now shades of brown. The opacified pieces, which were colored white or black, have most likely also changed in tone. Some of the pieces exhibit finely spaced cracks while others have small drops of a clear to light-brown liquid present on the surface. Corrosion products are frequently found where metallic components are near the deteriorated cellulose nitrate. The process of deterioration of these works as well as works from other collections were studied using Fourier transform infrared microscopy (FTIR), X-ray diffraction (XRD), scanning electron microscopy coupled with X-ray spectrometry and backscatter electron imaging (SEM-EDS) and light microscopy. Information obtained about the possible deterioration mechanisms and the role that fillers and plasticizers may play is presented and proposed conservation treatments are discussed.

Introduction

Naum Gabo moved to Oslo in 1914 where in 1915 he created his first constructions. These consisted of flat and curved planes joined together to create open structures in which the interior space of the sculptures actively interacted with the exterior space. That is, Gabo started constructing sculpture in terms of space instead of volume or mass. A few years later, Gabo's older brother, Antoine Pevsner, a painter, also began to create three-dimensional constructions. Actually, Gabo described their works as four-dimensional because time as expressed through rhythm was also an element (Lassaw 1957, 160). The works of these two brothers highlight the formal vocabulary of the constructivist tradition for which conventional methods and materials were no longer applicable. Although Gabo and Pevsner did not ascribe to the utilitarian, propagandistic agenda that the Russian constructivists, such as Vladimir Tatlin and Alexander Rodchenko, pursued in their art, there are formal similarities in these artists' work, including their unconventional use of modern materials. (See Lodder 1983 for an in-depth study of Russian constructivism.)

The manufacture of new materials, such as plastics, allowed artists to explore new territories technically. The modern plastics of the early 1900s provided sculptors with a medium that was lightweight, easily cut and molded into a variety of shape-maintaining forms. The plastic could be made either transparent or opaque and in many colors. The versatility of this new material of the 20th century appears to have been perfect for their sculptures of the future except for one problem, the plastics in the early works of Gabo and Pevsner were cellulose esters. The early cellulose-derived plastics are inherently unstable and undergo slow, spontaneous degradation under normal room conditions.

This study incorporates the results of the examination and analysis of three sculptures in The Museum of Modern Art's (MoMA) collection in New York as well as the general findings on several works by Gabo and Pevsner in other museums. In all six works studied, covering a period of about 10 years (1917 to 1926), cellulose-based plastics were an integral part of the construction. The range and degree of deterioration that these plastics have undergone reflect numerous factors, including the composition of the starting material for the plastic and the environmental history of the work of art.

Cellulose Nitrate Preparation and Deterioration

Pullen and Heuman (1988) found that a number of Gabo's sculptures from the 1920s in the Tate Gallery were made from cellulose nitrate and that "most were in good condition." Their study showed that the problematic plastic sculptures were those made from cellulose acetate. Interestingly though, all four works by Pevsner in the present study were found to be made from cellulose nitrate and these works showed serious overall or local deterioration. Prior to discussing six works by Gabo and Pevsner, a brief background on cellulose nitrate, its manufacture and degradation processes, will be given.

Thermal, hydrolytic and photochemical processes are the primary decomposition mechanisms for the degradation of cellulose nitrate. (For a thorough description of these processes see Selwitz 1988.) In addition, secondary mechanisms due to reactions of additives and impurities in the cellulose nitrate also influence the degradation rates. Even when prepared under the best conditions, cellulose nitrate undergoes slow, spontaneous degradation in which the NO_2 groups split off to form nitrogen oxide gases. This thermal degradation is accelerated by ultraviolet light. Upon exposure to water and oxygen, the nitrogen oxides form nitric and nitrous acids, which then catalyze hydrolytic decomposition reactions. The autocatalytic cycle,

which is usually responsible for the fast deterioration of a work, is dependent on the presence of oxygen and water because the nitrogen oxides themselves do not react with the cellulose nitrate polymer.

Nearly every step in the production of cellulose nitrate has an effect on the final stability of the material. Cellulose nitrate is prepared by treating purified cellulose with nitric acid in the presence of sulfuric acid. The starting cellulose needs to be lignin-free since lignin is unstable and can photodegrade to produce a complex mixture of acidic materials that will promote degradation of the cellulose nitrate (Yarsley 1964). However, because pure cellulose was expensive at the turn of the century, many companies bought cheaper material, then cleaned and bleached it. This processing usually left residual acids and chlorine in the cellulose, which in turn could speed up the deterioration of the cellulose nitrate. Thus, to regain some stability, additional materials, such as sodium bisulfite and triphenyl phosphate, were put in as scavengers of the acids and chlorine.

In the nitration step, sulfuric acid was incorporated to safely control the rate and extent of the reaction. However, this resulted in small amounts of sulfate esters in the polymer, which later produced sulfuric acid and initiated rapid deterioration. The early remedy for this was to add alkaline additives to the polymer. But when added in small amounts, the alkalis were used up rapidly while large amounts of added alkali attacked the cellulose nitrate itself.

The nitrated cellulose (pyroxylin) was combined with necessary solvents and plasticizers to form a clear, plastic material. A variety of plasticizers were tried for the production of cellulose nitrate, such as phosphates, phthalates, oils, resins, gums and camphor. Camphor was considered the best and was the most commonly used since it not only acts as a plasticizer but also as a stabilizer. It forms hydrogen bonds with the unsubstituted hydroxyl group producing a non-crystalline, solid solution of cellulose nitrate that is strong and flexible. Cellulose nitrate with camphor as its plasticizer is referred to as celluloid.

Although camphor was the best plasticizer available it caused some problems. Impurities in the camphor are one of the causes of the yellowing of cellulose nitrate objects. Also, because it forms hydrogen bonds with the cellulose nitrate, the proportion of camphor in the final product is important. Too little camphor results in a brittle material subject to crazing. On the other hand, excess camphor slowly sublimes from the object, leaving a porous or cracked material that is more susceptible to oxidation and hydrolysis and thus to accelerated deterioration. Even in materials that have the optimum proportion of camphor (20% to 40%), the camphor will slowly sublime from the exposed surfaces promoting deterioration, and when the object degrades, more surface is usually exposed and camphor is lost more rapidly. (For further information on the use of camphor in celluloid see Reilly 1991.)

Stabilizers were often added to scavenge free radicals and unwanted acids. Urea and diphenyl amine were found to be effective initially, but later crystallized out and became more harmful than beneficial. Zinc oxide was commonly used as a filler and opacifier. It also acts as a stabilizer by rapidly consuming nitric acid to form zinc nitrates.

Sample Analyses

The decomposition of cellulose esters has been documented and studied extensively and the instability of these materials is generally acknowledged (Sirkis 1982). What is intriguing in the case of these sculptures, however, is the type and extent of degradation that occurs from work to work and from location to location within a sculpture. To obtain a better understanding of the relation between various deterioration mechanisms and the material composition, chemical analyses were performed on samples from several sculptures and from several sites within each sculpture whenever possible.

The samples, acquired as broken fragments or removed as scrapings, cross-sections and exudates, were analyzed by FTIR microscopy at the Getty Conservation Institute and by light microscopy, SEM-EDS and X-ray diffraction at The Museum of Modern Art. These methods

were used to identify and quantify additives in the polymer as well as identify the principal component of the plastic.

Sculptures

The earliest sculpture included in the present study is *Head of a Woman* by Naum Gabo, shown in Figure 1 and in the collection of The Museum of Modern Art. It is generally believed to have been made in Russia after the artist's return there in 1917, although the exact date of execution is not known. Nash and Merkert (1985) give arguments for possible dates of 1917 to 1920 as well as circa 1923.

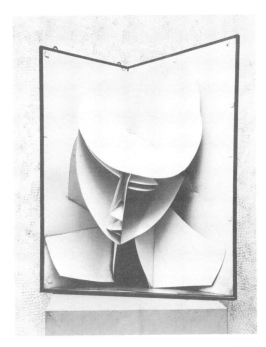

Figure 1   Naum Gabo, Head of a Woman *(ca. 1917 to 1920, after a work of 1916). Construction in celluloid and metal, 62.2 cm x 48.9 cm x 35.4 cm. Collection, The Museum of Modern Art, New York, Purchase. 397. 38.*

The work was formed from thermally shaped, cream-colored pieces of opacified cellulose nitrate. Frequently Gabo would make models of a work in materials, such as cardboard or wood, prior to executing the sculpture in metal. In a letter from 1948, Gabo described MoMA's *Head of a Woman* as being "finished and complete" but "in fact, the original model which I always make before executing a work in a proper and solid material. In the case of this head...the material is celluloid and therefore unstable..." (Nash and Merkert 1985, 202). In 1957 and 1964 Gabo borrowed the head to use as a model for a bronze version now in the collection of Gabo's family.

Since its acquisition in 1938, the sculpture has been frequently exhibited at the Museum. When on display, it has been hung above eye level in a corner with no vitrine in a similar fashion to the way it was presented in the Van Diemen Gallery in 1922. (See Nash and Merkert 1985, 27 for a photograph of the 1922 exhibition showing this work. It should be noted that Nash believes the object shown in this photograph is actually an earlier metallic version and not this celluloid version as other scholars believe.) In contrast to some other works done about this time by Gabo and Pevsner, to be discussed, this work is in very good condition. Nonetheless, by 1947, Gabo objected to the work being exhibited in its "present condition" (Richards 1947). It appears that the damage included at least two pieces of plastic that had fallen off. The work was not repaired by the artist in time for the Gabo-Pevsner Exhibition in 1948 and therefore was not included. It may have been this sculpture that Gabo is indirectly quoted as describing as "an early celluloid model, now in the collection of Alfred Barr, [which] has cracked and discolored severely, but was not intended to be permanent" (Siegl and d'Harnoncourt 1968).

Currently, there are long, fine cracks especially in the forehead area, some broken or missing pieces and separation of a few pieces from the main body, for example, the right proper shoulder has separated along the join line. Most of the damage appears to have resulted from mechanically induced stresses caused by handling the work or environmental factors. The pieces are a creamy-white except for three that are distinctly yellow, namely the proper right shoulder and two pieces near the chin area. FTIR analysis of the discolored pieces showed them to be cellulose nitrate (as were the other pieces). X-ray diffraction analysis indicated that zinc oxide was the principal opacifying pigment both in the yellow and cream-colored pieces. The cause of discoloration has not been determined.

In Alexi Pevsner's biography of his two brothers (1964), Naum and Antoine, he mentions that Gabo taught Pevsner "how to handle metal and plastic materials." *Head of a Woman* (Figure 2) made by Antoine Pevsner is dated 1923 (inscribed under the artist's signature in the lower left corner) and is in the collection of the Hirshhorn Museum, Washington, D.C. The work is in extremely poor condition and is no longer exhibited. The sculpture's pieces were made from translucent cellulose nitrate except for the creamy-white base that was opacified with zinc oxide. As shown in Figure 3 the translucent pieces have yellowed and cracked severely, joined pieces have separated and forms have fallen off. The pieces have also distorted out-of-plane by forming bubbled areas.

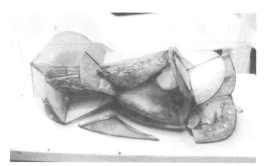

Figure 2   Antoine Pevsner, Head of a Woman *(1923) Hirshhorn Museum and Sculpture Garden (Photo taken in 1991).*

When the work was acquired in the early 1970s, it was placed in a wall-mounted vitrine case. By 1982 the sculpture had darkened, cracks had formed along the join lines and "beads of clear oily liquid" were present on the surface of the sculpture (Aks 1991). These drops were analyzed in 1983 and found to be an aqueous basic zinc nitrate solution (Erhardt et al. 1983). The 1983 analytical report further states that "zinc nitrate is a result of attack of nitric acid on the zinc oxide pigment of the celluloid on which the drops form....It was only when the object was sealed up that the generated acid was confined so that reaction with the available alkali (zinc oxide) became inevitable." After cleaning the sculpture, it was placed in storage in its vitrine and an effort was made to minimize exposure to light by covering the case with brown paper. By 1988 the sculpture was in a "severe state of deterioration....A clear

Figure 3 *Antoine Pevsner,* Head of a Woman, *detail of bottom portion.*

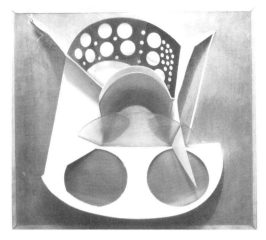

Figure 4 *Antoine Pevsner,* Bust *(1923 to 1924). Construction in metal and celluloid, 53 cm x 59.4 cm. Collection, The Museum of Modern Art, New York, Purchase. 396. 38.*

residue has reformed over the entire sculptural surface mostly in the form of oily beads" (Aks 1988). It was also noted that the cracking had worsened significantly and that "several plastic panels had collapsed and separated from the sculpture" (Aks 1988). For a while the work was kept in a fume hood where it was well ventilated and currently it is kept in an uncovered plywood box in storage. When the work was examined recently for this study, only a small amount of the oily drops was observed.

The presence of a liquid exudate has been noticed on other works such as Pevsner's *Bust* (shown in Figure 4) completed between 1923 and 1924. This relief sculpture, acquired by MoMA in 1938, is in relatively good condition even though it also has problems. It is made out of translucent and opacified cellulose nitrate pieces, the latter primarily opacified with zinc oxide. The cellulose nitrate has deteriorated in a variety of ways, including cracking, discoloration of translucent pieces, spotting (the presence of small, roundish areas slightly whiter in

color, as shown in Figure 5), as well as the formation of light-brown drops of liquid over several of the pieces. There is also localized corrosion of the metal in areas where the deteriorated cellulose nitrate contacts metallic pieces, such as the copper background or iron bolts.

Figure 5 *Antoine Pevsner,* Bust, *detail of upper portion showing extensive cracking of a translucent piece and spotting on an opaque piece (Photo taken 1991).*

Until 1980 this work was frequently exhibited at MoMA. Exhibition photographs show that it was hung without a vitrine on a wall. In 1989, for as yet undetermined reasons, the sculpture started producing a liquid exudate especially on the opacified cellulose nitrate pieces, such as the topmost curved piece. A small portion of the liquid was analyzed with FTIR

Figure 6   Calcium sulfate dihydrate crystals precipitated out of liquid degradation product, 500 times magnification.

spectroscopy and determined to be primarily composed of inorganic nitrate(s). Over several months, while the liquid was stored in a covered well-slide, crystal formation took place. With slight heat more crystals formed. Several chemical species appear to be present in the exudate and have only been partly identified at this time. X-ray diffraction of a large cluster of crystals showed these to be calcium sulfate dihydrate. Figure 6 is a secondary electron image of these crystals magnified approximately 500 times. Energy-dispersive spectrometric analysis (EDS) of the same crystals showed that along with calcium and sulfur, zinc was also present (though apparently not as a crystalline compound since it was not distinguished by XRD). SEM-EDS examination of a cross-section from an area where excessive liquid had accumulated indicates that there is about a 20 micron depletion of higher atomic weight elements from the surface of the piece as indicated in Figure 7. (Because of the sample size required for cross-sections and the delicate nature of the sculpture, confirmation of these preliminary results will have to be carried out on cellulose nitrate artifacts exhibiting similar symptoms.) Macroscopically, this effect was observed by an increased translucency at the surface, albeit exhibiting a slightly browner tonality. It thus appears that zinc salts as well as other compounds (such as calcium salts) are leached out as part of the degradation process. EDS analysis on a number of small scrapings of cellulose nitrate from this work as well as the two other

works at MoMA showed that potassium, chlorine, silicon, calcium and sulfur are usually present in both the opacified and the translucent cellulose nitrates.

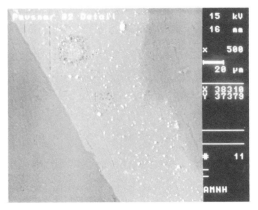

Figure 7   Higher atomic weight elements appear brighter. Top surface of the cross-section is diagonally across the lower left corner, 500 times magnification.

A third piece at MoMA, *Torso* (illustrated in Figure 8) dated 1924 to 1926, was also made by Pevsner. This work consists primarily of translucent cellulose nitrate pieces that are often attached with metal hardware to similarly shaped copper pieces. (Figure 9 is a detail of the proper right hand showing the copper and cellulose nitrate held together with a screw.) *Torso* was exhibited for many years on a pedestal and without a vitrine. In December 1954, the sculpture was accidently knocked over while on view, resulting in several broken pieces. The treatment report states that the physical effects of the fall were exacerbated by the deteriorated condition of the cellulose nitrate (which was incorrectly identified as cellulose acetate in the report). The treatment consisted of replacing a number of the pieces, mostly around the lower head area. After being repaired, the work was heavily exhibited until 1968 when it was removed after the black cellulose nitrate base (which had been progressively deteriorating since at least 1964) was too buckled and fragmented. For most of the time between 1968 and 1978 the sculpture was kept in storage. Part of the reason for storing this object, as well as other cellulose nitrate objects, was the fear that they would spontaneously

Figure 8   Antoine Pevsner, Torso *(1924 to 1926). Construction in plastic and copper, 74.9 cm x 29.4 cm x 38.7 cm. Collection, The Museum of Modern Art, New York. Katherine S. Dreier Bequest. 185. 53.*

Figure 9   Pevsner, Torso, *detail of hand (Photo taken in 1991).*

combust. Although it was unlikely that the objects would combust since the percent nitrate in polymers (10%) is lower than that in explosives (13% to 14%) or film (12%), suggestions were made to put them in airtight vitrines filled with nitrogen or to store them in explosion-proof steel cabinets. It appears instead that *Torso* was kept in storage with a plastic film draped over it. The present policy at MoMA is to keep air freely circulating around these objects while on exhibition and to lightly drape them with paper to keep dust off if they are not on view.

Torso was once described as being able to "exploit light through the various densities and directions of the planes" (Read 1948). The transparency of the plastic was also used to set up a "rhythmic dialogue" with the curved copper backing (Rankin 1988). The photograph of the sculpture presented in this paper was taken in 1933 and indeed shows how light could have penetrated the cellulose nitrate forms and reflected off the copper pieces. It no longer is able to do this as effectively because the cellulose nitrate pieces are all now discolored and some have cracked badly enough to form essentially opaque layers. A detail of the head area (illustrated in Figure 10) shows what is left of a cellulose nitrate piece and how corroded some of the copper pieces have become.

Figure 10 Pevsner, Torso, *detail from head area (Photo taken in 1991).*

At present there is only a slight amount of liquid formation on the cellulose nitrate surface. FTIR analysis of the liquid, which in this case crystallized out instantly on contact with a microscope slide, showed it to be inorganic nitrates (Figure 11 is an FTIR spectrum of these crystals). The XRD pattern indicated the presence of ammonium nitrate as one of the components (JCPDS 8-452). The copper pieces have also corroded to various degrees forming a blue-green, very fine-grained powder. Figure 12 is a backscatter electron image of the powder showing the general size distribution of the particles. Analyses so far indicate that it is a form of copper nitrate, possibly gerhardite. The same corrosion product was found on the copper backing in Pevsner's *Bust.*

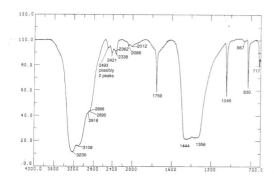

Figure 11 FTIR spectrum of crystallized liquid exudate from Pevsner Torso.

Figure 12 Corrosion product from the Pevsner Torso, 2,000 times magnification.

FTIR analysis of condensed fractions collected from heating cellulose nitrate pieces show that camphor was used as a plasticizing agent along with an additional oil. There is a direct correlation between the absence of camphor and severe degradation of the sample as shown in Figure 13. The top infrared spectrum is of cellulose nitrate in good condition and the bottom one is of the nitrate salt degradation product. Two stages of the deterioration are shown in between. Noticeable in the spectra is the increase in the intensity of a nitrate salt band at 1340 cm^{-1}. There is a corresponding decrease in the intensity of the carbonyl band at 1735 cm^{-1}, which is due to decreasing amounts of camphor, the plasticizer. (See Figure 14 for reference spectra of cellulose nitrate and camphor.)

Cross-sections taken from broken fragments of the sculpture were examined to assess the

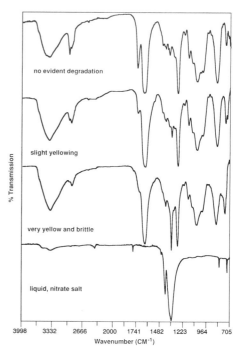

Figure 13 Infrared spectra for cellulose nitrate at various stages of degradation.

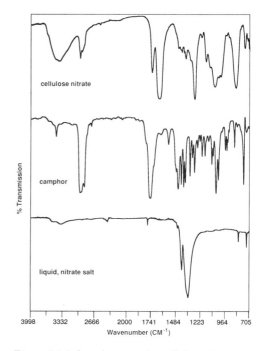

Figure 14 Infrared spectra for cellulose nitrate, camphor and liquid obtained from the Pevsner Torso.

extent of deterioration into the pieces of cellulose nitrate (i.e., depth-wise). Figure 15 shows an infrared spectrum produced by analyzing the surface of the cellulose nitrate piece. The other spectra were collected further into the sample, specifically at 1 mm and 2 mm. The spectra show that while the surface of the sculpture contains cellulose nitrate with a diminished amount of plasticizer, the celluloid 2 mm into the sample is in good condition.

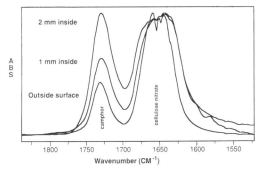

Figure 15 Overlay of infrared spectra collected at different depths in a cross-section sample from the Pevsner Torso. *The spectra obtained from the outer area of the cross-section show that there is a depletion of camphor near the surface.*

Another work of this period by Pevsner is the *Portrait of Marcel Duchamp* in the Yale University Art Gallery collection, which was commissioned in the spring of 1926 and completed in the summer of the same year. This work, like the *Bust* mentioned above, is a relief attached to a metallic backing. The artist used both clear and opaque plastic for this sculpture including pieces colored purple and black. By 1941, when the Yale University Art Gallery acquired the work, conservation records indicated that pieces were already warped and discolored. It was restored in 1957 by the artist after it was smashed en route to an exhibition. At that time the artist replaced broken pieces and changed the backing (originally a zinc plate) to copper because the latter harmonized better with the discolored pieces (Herbert 1984). Figure 16 shows the work after the 1957 repair. Within a few years the copper backing started corroding as the plastic pieces kept deteriorating. By 1979, a replica in plexiglass had been made for the gallery by a former assistant of Pevsner (Herbert 1984).

Figure 16 Antoine Pevsner, Portrait of Marcel Duchamp, *Yale University Art Gallery, Gift of Collection Société Anonyme.*

The sculpture is undergoing degradation processes, such as excessive liquid production on the surface (illustrated in Figure 17), cracking and buckling of the cellulose nitrate pieces and extensive corrosion of metallic parts. These metallic parts include the copper backing, which is now covered with a blue-green corrosion product, an iron-based strip of metal, which is now a pile of rust and the copper- and iron-based hardware, which have also corroded. The Yale University Art Gallery files indicate that at least since 1984 until now the work has been kept in storage in an essentially airtight vitrine. Andrew Petryn, former conservator at Yale, thought that the work might have been kept in a vitrine for a much longer period of time, although an exact date was not known (personal communication, 1991).

A detailed photograph from late 1984 shows an active corrosion problem but for the most part the pieces of cellulose nitrate do not appear badly cracked or out of plane. As mentioned earlier though, the pieces are now badly

Figure 17 Pevsner, Portrait of Marcel Duchamp, *detail of bottom edge of sculpture (Photo taken in 1991).*

cracked, many of them exhibiting widely spaced cracks with the plastic in between the cracks badly buckled, as shown in Figure 18. It thus appears that a significant amount of the cracking and buckling has occurred in the last few years. As will be discussed further in the following paragraphs, this type of damage appears to occur when the objects are kept in a sealed vitrine and then suddenly exposed to a new environment when the vitrine is opened. This change in environment allows the immediate loss of volatile degradation byproducts. This in turn appears to create internal stresses subsequently released by crack formation. It is known that the vitrine of the *Portrait of*

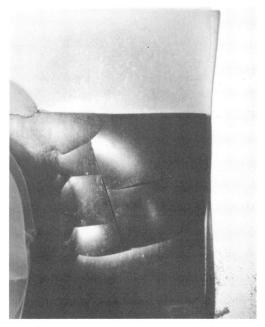

Figure 18 Pevsner, Portrait of Marcel Duchamp, *detail of plastic in upper right portion of sculpture (Photo taken in 1991).*

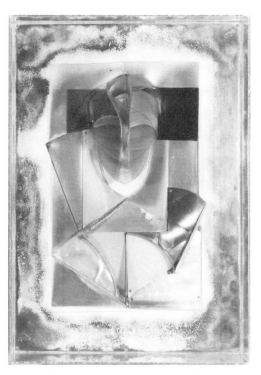

Figure 19 Antoine Pevsner, Portrait of Marcel Duchamp, *Yale University Art Gallery, Gift of Collection Société Anonyme.*

Marcel Duchamp was opened in 1986 to remove some fragments that had fallen off*. Rapid deterioration appears to have followed as shown by comparing the photograph in Figure 19 (taken around the mid-1980s) with the recently photographed details pictured in Figures 17 and 18.

When Gabo was asked how the invention of plastics affected the course of his works, he replied, "I did a great deal of work in plastics for only one reason: to accentuate the transparent character of space" (Kuh 1962, 102). The cones in *Construction in Space: Two Cones* (1927) in the Philadelphia Museum of Art exemplify Gabo's use of plastic for its transparent qualities. The artist also used opaque plastics though, in white, black and red for some of the pieces in this work, thus emphasizing their

*These fragments were analyzed for this study and found to be cellulose nitrate. It is not known what piece(s) they are from or if they are from the original 1926 pieces or the last 1957 restoration by the artist.

planes and curves. In its present condition, as the detail shown in Figure 20 indicates, both transparency and form have been seriously compromised with the deterioration of the plastics. (For an earlier photograph, see Nash and Merkert 1985, 215.)

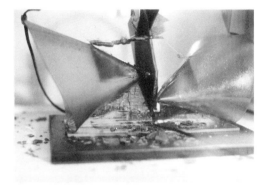

Figure 20 Naum Gabo, Construction in Space: Two Cones, *detail (Photo taken in 1991).*

For the most part, since the work was acquired in 1952 it has been kept in a sealed vitrine. Serious physical damage occurred after the sculpture was removed for study from its airtight vitrine in 1960 when condensation was noticed on the glass (Siegl 1966). Upon opening the case "a strong odor escaped from the case, then cracks developed in some parts of the construction, and on the following day the plastic base and the thick center stem were fractured to bits" (Siegl 1966). Figure 21 shows the fragments of the center stem. These have been identified as a cellulosic material possibly a regenerated cellulose*. (Based on the appearance of the work, it seems highly likely that other types of plastics were also used, but no further analysis has been done yet.) After replacing some of the broken pieces the sculpture was put back in its vitrine because it seemed that there was little that could be done. It continued to crack and sag and in 1968 it was taken to Gabo's home in Connecticut for possible repair. The artist suggested that it was how the object had been kept rather than the materials themselves that had enhanced the deterioration, since he had early works, including a model for this work, that were in much better condition (Gabo 1968). Gabo produced several pieces of old plastic (believed by the artist to be as old as those in

Figure 21 Fragments from Naum Gabo's Construction in Space: Two Cones *(Photo taken in 1991).*

the 1927 work), which he had in his studio and which were still in good condition (Siegl and d'Harnoncourt 1968). These were analyzed and all were found to be cellulose acetate (Miklas 1968). As described by Pullen and Heuman (1988) though, when Gabo used cellulose acetate in 1968 to make a replica of this work for the Tate Gallery, rapid deterioration again occurred. Unfortunately, as had been the case for the Philadelphia Museum of Art work, the Tate Gallery version had also been stored and exhibited in a closed vitrine.

During an interview in 1953, Gabo was asked if his constructions, which seemed so delicate, were permanent like traditional sculpture. Gabo replied, "There is nothing really permanent in the world. To base a work of art on permanency is to base it on something which does not exist" (Chanin 1953). Although some of the works described above attest to the considerably less permanent nature of the early plastic sculptures, other works have survived surprisingly well. It is clear that albeit the inherent instability of the materials used, the environment plays a significant role in extending or drastically reducing the life of the works.

---

*The fragments were sampled by Dr. Robert Feller in 1968 who found them to be "a generated cellulose or methylcellulose." Dr. Feller expressed surprise at these findings because "I had no idea that [these materials] could be fabricated into sheets" (Feller 1968). The samples were reanalyzed in 1992 at the Philadelphia Museum of Art by Beth Price who agreed with the 1968 findings.

Conservation Implications

The primary goal of conservation is to halt the deterioration without altering the appearance or structural integrity of the object. However, several studies have shown that with movie films the only way to stop degradation in cellulose nitrate is to freeze the object (Allen et al. 1988). Since this is not practical, a solution must be devised that at least minimizes the damage and extends the lifetime of the work.

Environmental control is critical to the stability of the work. Since temperature and humidity fluctuations may cause stresses, particularly at the join lines, it is important to keep the fluctuations to a minimum. The deterioration processes can be both thermally and photolytically induced, so lowering the temperature of the storage or display room is advisable and protecting the piece from ultraviolet light is crucial.

One inherent cause of degradation is the acid content of the object. Studies have looked into the effects of removing the accumulated acids by washing the object along with introducing acid neutralizers into the polymer (Green and Bradley 1988). Water, however, can have an extremely deleterious effect on the structural integrity of degraded cellulose nitrate and its use should be avoided on such sculptures. (Various other solvents, e.g., acetone, may also affect the object's appearance as well as increase the degradation rate.) Although the results have not yet been promising, one suggested method worth further study has been the vapor phase addition of ammonia to the object (Sirkis 1982). But caution must be taken not to induce any base-catalyzed degradation of the cellulose nitrate.

Studies have also been undertaken to devise methods for dealing with the effects of the deterioration process. Preliminary attempts have been made to consolidate cracked or powdery cellulose nitrate with adhesives likewise based on cellulose nitrate, for example, HMG (Green and Bradley 1988). This type of treatment probably would not be reversible, might change the appearance of the object and would interfere with future analytical work, but it might be one of the few options available for providing the object with some structural integrity. Methods for reintroducing the lost plasticizers and stabilizers have also been investigated by Green and Bradley. They attempted to reintroduce a plasticizer by soaking the object in dibutyl phthalate. The procedure was unsuccessful though because the cellulose nitrate was found not to be porous enough to permit penetration of the liquid into the bulk of the object. While further work is being done to determine future treatment procedures, it is imperative that measures be taken now to minimize further degradation of the works. For example, our study has shown that the degradation is directly related to the loss of camphor, therefore it is important to minimize its sublimation. One possible method to do so is given below.

The degradation processes become autocatalytic in the presence of oxygen and water vapor. Thus, attempts have been made to create a closed environment for cellulose nitrate objects by placing them in sealed containers. Unfortunately, this has frequently resulted in serious degradation of the sculptures. Considerable work needs to be carried out in designing display cases that can maintain a low relative humidity, provide protection from ultraviolet light and minimize the degradation processes. For example, such a case might contain vapor-phase camphor to prevent further camphor sublimation and consequent depletion of this stabilizing plasticizer. The case might also include an air circulation system that incorporates acid scavengers and/or nitrogen oxide specific absorbers. Each case should be designed specifically to prevent or counteract the sculpture's deterioration problems and to this extent one needs to take into account the work's material composition and condition. Until such display cases can be constructed, it has been recommended that it is best to place the sculpture in an area with adequate ventilation to prevent the nitrogen oxides from accumulating. Low relative humidities are also recommended, but studies need to be done to determine the optimum value, since a relative humidity that is too low may also cause problems. Further work is being carried out by the authors to try to determine general environmental parameters. This work involves the detailed material identification of various cellulose ester artifacts exhibiting serious degradation and the exposure of these artifacts to various environmental conditions.

Conclusion

The cellulose nitrate sculptures examined in this study exhibit various types and degrees of degradation. These range from surface crazing to cracking, discoloration, liquid production on the surface, and major structural damage. The process of deterioration was studied using FTIR spectroscopy, light microscopy, X-ray diffraction and SEM-EDS. The authors found that the various states of degradation relate to three factors:

- past storage and display conditions
- composition of additives and impurities within the piece
- physical construction of the work

At present there are no established treatments for reversing some of the degradation processes that these objects have undergone. Conservation treatment of the objects will try to minimize further degradation by direct control of the environment. It is imperative that the temperature, relative humidity and ultraviolet light exposure be controlled. This may eventually require building specifically designed display cases.

Acknowledgement

The authors thank the following individuals for their assistance: Kristen Hoerman of Yale University Art Gallery, New Haven; Lee Aks of the Hirshhorn Museum and Sculpture Garden, Washington, D.C.; Andrew Lins, Melissa Meighan and Beth Price of the Philadelphia Museum of Art; and Derrick Pullen of the Tate Gallery, London. Special thanks are given to Patricia Houlihan of The Museum of Modern Art, New York, for her numerous contributions in studying MoMA's sculptures. The authors also thank Keith Lauer of Massachusetts for his generous contribution of cellulose ester objects to be used for future experimentation.

Résumé

La dégradation de sculptures en nitrate de cellulose exécutées par Gabo et Pevsner

Trois sculptures de la collection du Museum of Modern Art de New York exécutées par Naum Gabo et par Antoine Pevsner présentent différents degrés de dégradation, leur état variant de très bon à médiocre. Ces sculptures sont constituées de pièces d'ester de cellulose (nitrate de cellulose) qui, thermiquement formées, sont collées ensemble avec un adhésif également à base d'ester de cellulose. Les pièces translucides en nitrate de cellulose, qui étaient probablement incolores à l'origine, ont maintenant pris une coloration qui tire à divers degrés sur le brun, tandis que les pièces opaques, blanches ou noires à l'origine, n'ont vraisemblablement plus le même ton. De fines craquelures se sont formées sur certaines pièces, alors que d'autres présentent, sur leur surface, des gouttelettes de liquide variant entre le clair et le brun clair. Bien souvent, des produits de corrosion se sont déposés aux points où le nitrate de cellulose se trouve à proximité d'éléments métalliques. Le processus de dégradation de ces œuvres et d'objets provenant d'autres collections a été étudié en ayant recours à la spectrométrie infrarouge à transformée de Fourier (IRTF), à la diffraction des rayons X, à la microscopie électronique à balayage associée à la spectrométrie de rayons X et à l'imagerie électronique de rétrodiffusion (microscopie électronique à balayage-diffraction électronique des rayons X) et à la microscopie photonique. Il est fait état, dans la présente communication, des mécanismes qui ont pu contribuer à la dégradation de ces objets et du rôle que les charges et plastifiants auraient joué à cet égard. On y effectue enfin une analyse des traitements de conservation qui sont proposés.

References

Aks, Lee, Conservation Report, Hirshhorn Museum and Sculpture Garden, Smithsonian Institution, 1988.

Aks, Lee, Reply to questionnaire sent by the authors to Mr. Aks, 1991.

Allen, N.S., M. Edge, C.V. Horie, T.S. Jewitt and J.H. Appleyard, "The Nature of the Degradation of Archival Cellulose-ester Base Motion Picture Film," *Journal of Photographic Science*, 36, 1988, pp. 34-39.

Chanin, A.L., "Gabo Makes a Construction," *Artnews*, vol. 52, November 1953, pp. 34-46.

Erhardt, David et al., Smithsonian CAL Analytical Report # 4111, Conservation Analytical Laboratories, Smithsonian Institution, 1983.

Feller, Robert to Theodor Siegl, April 5, 1968, Philadelphia Museum of Art Conservation Files, [letter].

Gabo, Naum to Ted Siegl, April 7, 1968, Philadelphia Museum of Art Conservation Files, [letter].

Green, Lorna and Susan Bradley, "An Investigation into the Deterioration and Stabilization of Nitrocellulose in Museum Collections," *Preprints of Contributions to the Modern Organic Materials Meeting*, Edinburgh, Scottish Society for Conservation and Restoration, 1988, pp. 81-95.

Herbert, Robert et al., eds., *The Société Anonyme and the Dreier Bequest at Yale University: A Catalogue Raisonne* (New Haven: Yale University Press, 1984).

JCPDS Powder Diffraction File, JCPDS International Center for Diffraction Data, Swarthmore, Pennsylvania, 1980.

Kuh, Katherine, *The Artist's Voice: Talks with 17 Artists* (New York: Harper and Row, 1962).

Lassaw, Abram and Ilya Bolotowsky, "Russia and Constructivism," in: *Gabo: Constructions, Sculpture, Paintings, Drawings, Engravings*, trans. Lund Humphries (Massachusetts: Harvard University Press, 1957).

Lodder Christina, *Russian Constructivism* (New Haven and London: Yale University Press, 1983).

Miklas, Helen, Analytical Report from Rohm and Haas, Bristol, Pennsylvania, 1968.

Nash, Steven and Jorn Merkert, *Naum Gabo: Sixty Years of Constructivism* (New York: Prestel-Verlag, 1985).

Petryn, Andrew, personal communication, 1991.

Pevsner, Alexi, *A Biographical Sketch of My Two Brothers, Naum Gabo and Antoine Pevsner* (Amsterdam: Augustin and Schoonman, 1964).

Pullen, Derek and Jackie Heuman, "Cellulose Acetate Deterioration in the Sculptures of Naum Gabo," *Preprints of Contributions to the Modern Organic Materials Meeting*, Edinburgh, Scottish Society for Conservation and Restoration, 1988, pp. 57-66.

Rankin, Elizabeth, "A Betrayal of Material: Problems of Conservation in the Constructivist Sculpture of Naum Gabo and Antoine Pevsner," *Leonardo*, vol. 31, no. 3, 1988, pp. 285-290.

Read, Herbert (introduction), Ruth Olson and Abraham Chanin (text), *Constructivism: the Art of Naum Gabo and Antoine Pevsner* (New York: The Museum of Modern Art, 1948).

Reilly, J.A., "Celluloid Objects: Their Chemistry and Preservation," *Journal of the American Institute for Conservation*, vol. 30, no. 2, 1991, pp. 145-162.

Richards, Monawee to Dorothy Dudley, December 16, 1947, The Museum of Modern Art, Painting and Sculpture Files, [letter].

Selwitz, Charles, *Cellulose Nitrate in Conservation* (Los Angeles: The J. Paul Getty Trust, 1988).

Siegl, Theodore, *Bulletin of the Philadelphia Museum of Art*, vol. 62, no. 291, 1966, p. 153.

Siegl, Theodore, Memo, April 7, 1968, Philadelphia Museum of Art Conservation Files.

Siegl, T. and A. d'Harnoncourt, Memo, January 25, 1968, Philadelphia Museum of Art Conservation Files.

Sirkis, Linda, "The History, Deterioration and Conservation of Cellulose Nitrate and Other Early Plastic Objects," Master's Thesis, Institute of Archaeology, London, 1982.

Yarsley, V.E., W. Flavell and N.G. Perkins, *Cellulose Plastics*, Plastics Institute, London, 1964.

Zimmer, Fritz, *Nitrocellulose Ester Lacquers: Their Composition, Application and Uses* (London: Chapman & Hall Ltd., 1934).

A.W. McCurdy's Developing Tank: Degradation of an Early Plastic

Robert D. Stevenson

Historic Resource Conservation Laboratory
Canadian Parks Service — Atlantic Region
Dartmouth, Nova Scotia
Canada

Abstract

A prototype of a daylight film developing tank, of the collection of the Alexander Graham Bell National Historic Park in Baddeck, Nova Scotia, is presented as an example of the problems associated with early plastics.

The tank was signed and dated by its maker (E. Schneider, Nov. 1899), and was presented to Mrs. Mabel Bell by A.W. McCurdy, its designer and Alexander Graham Bell's secretary for many years (and the father of J.A.D. McCurdy, the pilot of the first heavier-than-air flight in Canada).

The tank was discovered in its display case covered with droplets of a liquid, which, upon analysis, turned out to be sulphuric acid. The difficulties encountered during conservation are presented as a case study. Reference is made to techniques used in the conservation of two Marconi artifacts that contain similar plastics.

Introduction and History

This paper is about the plastic-bodied prototype of a daylight film developing tank. This tank is of interest because of its association with famous people, its precise dating and its spectacular deterioration.

The tank was designed in the late 1800s by A.W. McCurdy. Until I saw this object I knew of A.W. McCurdy only as the father of J.A.D. McCurdy, who piloted the first heavier-than-air flight in Canada. But A.W. McCurdy was for many years secretary to Alexander Graham Bell. Mabel Bell, Alexander's wife, was a great supporter of A.W. McCurdy and invested in his company while he was perfecting the tank, even borrowing to do so. No doubt this is why the prototype tank was presented to her on November 25, 1899. (Details of the presentation, including the date, are inscribed on the back of the tank, as shown in Figure 1.)

Figure 1 The developing tank as it appears today. Photo: Canadian Parks Service.

The tank is also signed and dated "E. Schneider, Nov. 1899" on the inner bevel of the window area of the removable top. The signature is that of the tank's maker I presume. This dating gives the object unique value as a record of the state of the art of plastics work during that period.

At the Alexander Graham Bell National Historic Park in Baddeck, Nova Scotia, there is a large and wonderful collection of papers relating to Bell's work and life, amongst which are letters to him from his wife. In her letters from the spring, summer and fall of 1899, Mabel Bell often mentions A.W. McCurdy's work on the developing tank. To my intense frustration the last letter in the files to mention this work is dated five days before McCurdy presented the prototype tank to her. And I cannot find mention of such a presentation elsewhere in the files.

The only mention of the tank material in Mabel Bell's letters would lead one to believe it is made of hard rubber (ebonite). She refers several times to Mr. McCurdy's search for hard rubber for producing the tank:

from a letter dated May 20, 1899:
> Mr. McCurdy found hard rubber boxes the size he will require for sale at a dollar and a quarter, the roll of celluloid [presumably for the film type he was working on] would cost only a few cents, ...

from a letter dated May 29, 1899:
> Meantime Mr. McCurdy is investigating the best and cheapest material for the box. Hard rubber will do, but it is expensive, and he thinks something else might be better.

from a letter dated June 2, 1899:
> He thinks that he must first have the box made of hard rubber and have the whole thing complete as a practical working machine — though rough and capable of further improvement before offering it to capitalists.

During this same period A.W. McCurdy patented various aspects of the design; showed the tank to George Eastman (of Kodak fame), who declared it not practical; made further modifications; and eventually sold the patent rights to Eastman for a small fortune.

Observation and Discovery

The material of the tank bears a striking resemblance to the materials found in two Marconi artifacts at our laboratory, parts of which were identified as hard rubber (ebonite). Testing by Fourier Transform Infra-red Spectroscopy (FTIR) has determined that the body and lid of the tank are also ebonite.

This developing tank is a beautifully made example of the plastic technology of the day, but it was in poor condition when it first came to my attention in the summer of 1988. There were droplets of a liquid distributed on all exposed surfaces of the artifact (Figure 2). The artifact was inside an unsealed display case constructed from wood, plywood and glass. As soon as I opened the case and smelled the acrid odour of acid I knew there was a problem! The liquid on the artifact's surface was brown and sticky, did not feel greasy and, strangely, had no apparent odour when isolated from the artifact.

Figure 2 The top of the tank showing the droplets of liquid on its surface as found on site.

I wrapped the artifact in acid-free tissue and transported it to our regional conservation laboratory. The liquid left a brownish stain on the tissue. This started me thinking that a layer of colour on the artifact was being washed off by the liquid. To ascertain what was in the liquid, I briefly put the artifact — which was drying out — in a sealed chamber to raise the RH. I then removed a few drops of the liquid by pipette and sent them off for analysis. I dipped a pH test strip in a droplet and got a rather startling reading of pH 0.5— the artifact should have been smoking! The result was confirmed when the liquid was identified as sulphuric acid.

I removed the developing tank from the chamber and let it acclimate to the ambient RH. I made one brief and regrettable attempt to wipe off the residue of liquid. Having tested the bottom of the artifact and noticed no problem, I then wiped one side of it. This left streaks, and I stopped the attempt (Figure 3).

Figure 3 Streaks caused by the initial wiping of the tank.

A Conservation Dilemma

Why did I get streaking on the side but not on the bottom? This remained a mystery until the following year when a conservator at our laboratory worked on two artifacts for the Marconi exhibit at Glace Bay, Nova Scotia. These artifacts contained hard rubber (ebonite) parts that had similar dull brown surfaces and showed shiny black where they were not exposed to light, just like the developing tank. To remove dirt and stains from these ebonite parts a method of swabbing the surface was developed using solvents such as acetone, ethanol, water and Varsol.

I used a modified version of this method to remove streaks I had caused on the developing tank, following the sequence below (which only took a few minutes):

1) wiping with an alcohol-saturated, soft cotton pad
   result: streaks of whitish-yellow colour
2) wiping with a water-saturated, soft cotton pad
   result: less streaking, pale whitish colour overall
3) wiping with an acetone-saturated, soft cotton pad
   result: faint streaks, surface dull
4) wiping with a small amount of alcohol on a soft cotton pad
   result: no more streaks, surface dull
5) wiping with a dry, soft cotton pad
   result: surface less dull (A dragging sensation was noted with this step, perhaps due to the slightly rough nature of the tank's surface.)

The cotton pads used in the initial alcohol swabbing picked up quite a lot of yellowish material, which is presumably composed of the plastic and its breakdown products. Lesser amounts were collected by the acetone pad and water pad, though perhaps this is due to the sequence of operations rather than to the differing solubilities of the various solvents. It would not be wise to prolong this process as obviously it removes material from the surface.

One point that should be noted about this procedure is that it was not possible to predict the solvents required or the order in which they were used. The method I used on the tank was the same as that used on the Marconi artifacts, but the sequence I followed was different. It was noticed (while working on the Marconi artifacts) that different pieces of the same artifact required different treatments. Some parts required only alcohol, for example, while others seemed to be unaffected by any of the solvents. Working on such artifacts makes for an exciting day!

When I first saw the artifact covered in droplets I was very concerned about the metal parts. However, they showed no apparent corrosion at the time, even though they were surrounded by sulphuric acid! I am sorry to report that in the three years the artifact has been at the laboratory, corrosion has started (Figure 4). The metal

Figure 4 Corrosion beginning on the metal parts of the tank. All metal parts were similarly affected.

parts have not been treated yet, but I plan to remove and treat them and insert Mylar washers or some other protective barrier under them before they are reinstalled. Yet this is not a wholly satisfactory solution because the metal parts all screw into the plastic, making direct contact unavoidable.

Another problem area involves a sandwich of at least two layers of red-coloured plastic (probably cellulose nitrate) in the centre of the lid. This sandwich is covered by two hinged panels of ebonite and may have been for viewing the film development process without exposing the film to damaging levels of light (Figure 5). There is a yellow powdery accretion growing between the layers.

Figure 5 A front view of the tank shows the wording EBEDEC. This is McCurdy's brand name, which is Greek for "out of Baddeck." Photo: Canadian Parks Service.

As well, there is a roll of clear plastic (also probably cellulose nitrate) inside the tank. In several of the historical papers, both in the laboratory notes and in Mabel Bell's letters, reference is made to A.W. McCurdy trying to invent a new way to hold a roll of film so that it could be processed without the adjacent layers touching each other. In one laboratory note he describes and draws a thick edging (probably leather) sewn onto the film. This is exactly the appearance of the roll in the tank at present, as pictured in Figure 6. McCurdy considered this idea to be more valuable than the developing tank, but it did not turn out that way.

Figure 6 A film separator invented by McCurdy, which has remained in the tank throughout its life, so far as is known. Photo: Canadian Parks Service.

Although these parts are deteriorating, I have made no attempt to treat them. Stabilization of the storage/display environment as noted below should be sufficient for the roll of film. However, it is not possible to treat the plastic sandwich because it cannot be removed from the tank's lid without causing further damage.

Plans are being made to create a refrigerated storage/display environment for the tank that will maintain cool, dry conditions using silica gel to buffer the RH and activated charcoal to protect against the various vaporous breakdown products. It may be necessary to create an oxygen-free atmosphere as well.

For a more detailed discussion of the deterioration of ebonite see the summary of the paper by Louise Bacon listed in the Bibliography.

Acknowledgement

The author thanks scientists at the Historic Resource Conservation Laboratory, Canadian Parks Service Headquarters, Ottawa, for their analysis of the surface liquid and for the FTIR work that identified the plastics.

Résumé

La cuve de développement d'A.W. McCurdy : un exemple de la dégradation des premiers plastiques

Un prototype de cuve de développement pour pellicule exposée à la lumière du jour, qui fait partie de la collection du parc historique national Alexander Graham Bell, à Baddeck (Nouvelle-Écosse), est présenté pour illustrer les problèmes que posent les premiers plastiques.

Signée et datée par le fabricant (E. Schneider, Nov. 1899), la cuve a été présentée à Mme Mabel Bell par son concepteur, A.W. McCurdy. Secrétaire d'Alexander Graham Bell pendant de nombreuses années, ce dernier est en outre le père de John A. D. McCurdy, qui sera le premier à piloter un « plus lourd que l'air » au Canada.

On a découvert la cuve, dans sa vitrine, couverte de gouttelettes — des gouttelettes d'acide sulfurique, comme l'ont révélé des analyses ultérieures. Nous présentons les problèmes rencontrés sous la forme d'une étude de cas et faisons état des techniques qui ont été utilisées au cours de la restauration de deux objets de Marconi contenant des plastiques semblables.

Bibliography

Adams, John V., *Plastics Arts Crafts*, ISBN 08492a15, (Toronto/New York/London: Van Nostrand, 1948).

A brief history of plastics technology and usage.

Bacon, Louise, "The Deterioration of Four Giorgi Flutes Made of Ebonite and a Possible Method for Their Conservation," ed. Victoria Todd, *Preprints for the UKIC 30th Anniversary Conference*, 1988, pp. 96-100.

Describes how the surface of ebonite undergoes severe decomposition through the action of light, air and moisture. The surface acid formed by this process can be wiped away, but in extreme cases neutralization may be necessary. This can be done with a dilute solution of sodium bicarbonate, rinsing and quick drying in industrial methylated spirit. For storage and display, light levels should be reduced to a minimum and UV eliminated. RH must be kept low. If possible, oxygen should also be eliminated.

Brydson, J.A., *Plastics Materials*, ISBN 0 408 00142 9, (London/Boston: Newnes-Butterworths, 1975).

Green, H. Gordon, *The Silver Dart* (Fredericton, New Brunswick: Brunswick Press, 1959).

A book about the first heavier-than-air flight in Canada, and the people involved in the event. These people include the inventor, Alexander Graham Bell, the pilot, J.A.D. McCurdy, and his father, A.W. McCurdy.

Sparke, Penny, ed., *The Plastics Age — From Modernity to Post Modernity*, ISBN 1 85177066 6, (London: Victoria and Albert Museum, 1990).

Essays that examine the history of plastic products from the late 19th century up to the present within the changing cultural climate of the period.

Degradation of Polyurethanes in 20th-Century Museum Textiles

Nancy Kerr and Jane Batcheller

Department of Clothing and Textiles
University of Alberta
Edmonton, Alberta
Canada

Abstract

The term "polyurethane" applies to a diverse group of materials used in 20th-century textiles. They may be fibres (spandex), adhesives or consolidants found in synthetic suedes, foams in bonded/laminated fabrics, surface foams of imitation suedes and water-repellant coatings or leather-look surfaces on some fabrics. There is much for conservators to learn about polyurethanes, including the variety of ways they are used in textiles, how to assess the condition of the material and what form degradation will take. This presentation will address these factors. The mode of degradation of polyurethanes will be discussed, based on a review of the extensive literature on this topic.

Photo-oxidation is particularly damaging to polyurethanes and is the most common cause of damage in the textiles we have examined. Polyurethanes based on aliphatic diisocyanates and polyester soft segments are more resistant to photo-oxidation than those formed from aromatic diisocyanates and polyether soft segments. Micro-organisms can grow on polyurethanes in such forms as cracked films. As growth proceeds, enzymes are secreted which can cause random chain cleavage at the polyurethane linkages or scission at chain ends.

A number of garments containing polyurethane as fibers, foams, films or adhesives will be shown, and the damage they exhibit will be discussed. In many of these garments, no evidence of photo-oxidative damage was visible until the garment was commercially dry-cleaned. Saturation with dry-cleaning solvent (perchloroethylene) and the mechanical agitation of the cleaning cycle caused the oxidized polyurethane component to break down. Suggestions will be given for the safe cleaning of polyurethane-containing garments.

Introduction

Polyurethanes are a very diverse group of polymers with many textile applications. The name polyurethane comes from the periodic urethane links (-NHCOO-) in the polymer "backbone," however, this name may be misleading because polymers are prepared from polyester, polyether or other short-chain polymers, and contain a variety of other links as well. Because polyurethanes do not always form the exposed surface of a fabric or garment, curators and conservators may not realize that many 20th-century textile collections contain polyurethanes. Polyurethanes appear in textiles primarily as elastomeric fibres and yarns (spandex), and as films, coatings and foams supported by traditional fabric structures. These materials are sensitive to a variety of degrading influences and require care in storage, display and cleaning if they are to be preserved.

Polyurethanes have been produced for commercial use since the early 1950s. Research on these polymers began before the Second World War. While Wallace Carothers was developing polyamides in the United States in the 1930s,

Otto Bayer and his associates at Farbenfabriken were experimenting with the polymerization of isocyanates and produced linear polyurethanes in 1938 (Hepburn 1982). The commercial production of polyester-based polyurethane foam began in the 1950s and was followed by the worldwide production of rigid and flexible foams, coatings, moldings and adhesives (Backus 1977, 642-643). Elastomeric fibres, intended to replace rubber, were commercially available as spandex fibres around 1960 (Joseph 1986, 142). Museum textiles collected since the early 1960s may include polyurethane in the form of spandex elastomers in foundation garments, foam layers in foam-bonded and laminated fabrics, foam paddings in tailored garments, water-repellent or waterproof coatings on textiles, coatings on synthetic leathers, the foam layer in artificial suedes, and as poromerics in shoe uppers. The most recent use of polyurethane is as a microporous breathable coating on rainwear.

The objectives of this paper are (1) to describe the formation and textile-related uses of polyurethanes, (2) to review the literature on the degradation of polyurethanes and present examples of degradation in polyurethane-containing garments and (3) to describe the degradation in four new polyurethane fabrics, which have been exposed to sunlight through glass for 63 days. The outdoor exposures were conducted in order to determine whether sunlight (through glass) would cause damage similar to that seen often in polyurethane-containing garments analyzed by the Textile Analysis Service.* Four new types of polyurethane fabric were chosen for testing because little information is available on their structure, physical or mechanical properties. These fabrics included a very realistic synthetic leather and suede and two polyurethane-coated fabrics. Suggestions for the conservation of textiles containing polyurethanes will also be given.

Formation of Polyurethanes

A number of authors have discussed in detail the formation of polyurethane polymers (Hepburn 1982; Backus 1977, 642; Lenz 1967, 180; Rosthauser and Nachtkamp 1987, 121). Perhaps no other polymer offers the versatility of polyurethane. Through molecular tailoring it is possible to make many different polyurethanes with a variety of physical and mechanical properties (Figure 1).

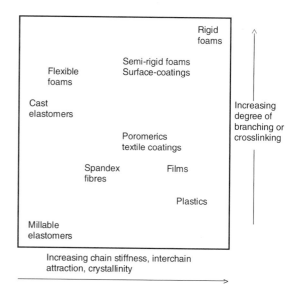

Figure 1 Structure/property relationships in polyurethanes (Hepburn 1982). Used with permission of Elsevier Applied Science Publishers.

The usual way to prepare polyurethanes is in two steps (Figure 2). The starting material is most often a short polymer of polyester or polyether with hydroxyl groups at each end (polyol), although other polymers, such as polycaprolactone, may be used (Carter 1971, 174). The polyester or polyether polyol is reacted with an excess of a diisocyanate to form a prepolymer (molecular weight approx. 15,000 to 20,000). Two of the most frequently used diisocyanates (Figure 3) are 4,4'-diphenylmethane diisocyanate (MDI) and a mixture of 2,4- and 2,6-toluene diisocyanate (TDI) (Backus 1977, 649). The prepolymer is a low melting point solid or liquid unsuitable for most applications, thus, the second step involves linking the prepolymers into long-chain polymers by reaction with a chain extender, usually a diol or diamine (Lenz 1967, 191). When the chain extender is a

---

*The Textile Analysis Service was set up in the Department of Clothing and Textiles in 1970. Its purpose is to analyze and resolve problems encountered during the use and care of garments, household and industrial textiles, furs and leathers.

diol, the polyurethane polymer contains urethane links; if it is an amine, urea links are formed (Figures 2 and 3). If carbon dioxide is released during the reaction, a polyurethane foam is made. Polyfunctional starting materials will produce polymers with branching or crosslinking. These polymers are more rigid than uncrosslinked polymers and are well suited for rigid foams and surface coatings (Figure 1). At this point, the polymers are either extruded as fibres, a continuous film or molded. Elastomeric textile fibres are formed by wet spinning into a coagulation bath, dry spinning after dissolving in a solvent, or melt spinning (Carter 1971, 177).

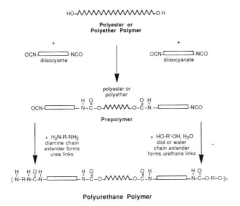

Figure 2 Two-step formation of polyurethane polymers. A polyester or polyether polyol reacts first with a diisocyanate, then with a chain extender (Hepburn 1982). Used with permission of Elsevier Applied Science Publishers.

When polyurethane is produced for elastomeric fibres it has a unique molecular structure that confers high elongation under stress and excellent elastic recovery. Hepburn (1982) gives structural formulae for a variety of polyesters and polyethers, isocyanates and chain extenders used in making elastomers. The polyester or polyether oligomer provides a long flexible amorphous "soft" segment that stretches easily under stress. The nature of the soft segments affects response to low temperatures, hardness, tear strength and modulus. Hepburn (1982, 73) states, "Polyethers generally give elastomers having a lower level of physical properties than the polyester-based materials due to the weaker inter-chain attractive forces." The "hard"

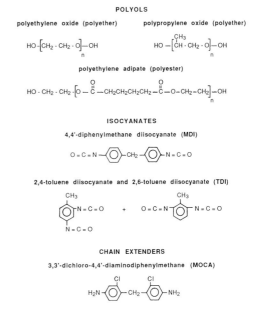

Figure 3 Starting materials frequently used in the production of polyurethanes (Hepburn 1982). Used with permission of Elsevier Applied Science Publishers.

segments or rigid domains in an elastomer consist of urethane, urea and other links formed from the diisocyanate and chain extender. They are held to neighbouring molecules by H-bonding, dipole-dipole interactions or Van der Waal's forces. In effect, the hard segments act as tie points or reinforcing "fillers" in the soft matrix. They affect properties, such as response to high temperatures and strength (Hepburn 1982, 69; Carter 1977, 174).

In recent years, water-borne polyurethanes or aqueous dispersions of polyurethanes have become increasingly important because they can be made into adhesives and coatings with little or no co-solvent (Rosthauser and Nachtkamp 1987, 121). This has reduced solvent emissions and lowered production costs. The films do not harm plastic surfaces and adhere well to many surfaces. Water serves as the chain extender, reacting with isocyanate groups on the prepolymer and forming urethane links. Hydrophilic groups, ionic groups (SO_3-Na^+) or water-soluble segments may be incorporated into the main chains.

Textile Uses of Polyurethanes

When the word polyurethane is mentioned, many people imagine foam materials or injection-molded plastics, however, museum collections have a great variety of other artifacts containing polyurethanes. Collections of 20th-century textiles include garments containing spandex or elastane fibres (generic names in North America and Europe respectively) (Textile Institute 1975). These spandex or elastane fibres made of either polyether- or polyester-based polyurethanes appeared as a replacement for rubber yarns in 1962 in women's foundation garments and bathing suits.

In another form, polyurethane was used in the 1960s for foam-bonded and laminated fabrics (Mansfield 1985). In *bonded* fabrics, a thin layer (1 mm to 3 mm) of polyurethane foam was used to hold together a face fabric and backing fabric, usually a tricot knit. The foam was flame-heated on both sides to melt it and bond it to the two exterior fabrics; alternatively, an adhesive was used with the foam as a bonding agent. Fabrics *laminated* with foam were similar to foam-bonded fabrics, however, no backing fabric was used. The face fabric was simply adhered by flame or adhesive to a thick layer (3 mm to 5 mm) of foam. A very lightweight, sometimes inferior fabric, was thus given body and stability so that it would be suitable for dress-wear, coatings and upholstery.

In the late 1970s and early 1980s polyurethane foams were used in the production of imitation suede fabrics. In the simplest fabric structures, a warp knit fabric is coated on one surface with a fine polyurethane foam to give a soft suede-like fabric (e.g., Suede 21 by Kanebo, Japan). If the foam is extremely fine grained, it produces a "handle" or "feel" very much like suede. Very fine polyester fibres may be embedded in the foam, or the fibers from the base fabric may be brushed or raised and incorporated into the foam to give a fibrous surface texture. The foam/fibre mixture may cover both surfaces of a woven or knitted fabric base, producing a reversible material with the appearance of suede on each surface. (e.g., Cavsuede by Collins and Aikman or Ultrana). The most expensive and possibly the most realistic synthetic suede fabrics, Ultrasuede, Supersuede, Clarino and

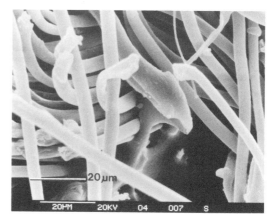

Figure 4 Imitation suede fabric (Supersuede) consists of fine (4 μm) polyester fibres embedded in a polyurethane foam base.

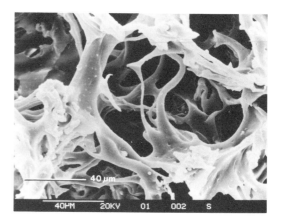

Figure 5 Polyurethane foam, which forms the base of Supersuede.

Belleseime, do not have a woven or knit fabric base. They are composed of a random web of extremely fine polyester or nylon bi-constituent fibres (60%), within a polyurethane foam matrix (40%) (Figures 4 and 5).

One of the most important uses for polyurethanes is for coating textiles to produce novelty fabrics, such as synthetic leather, or to produce fabrics with improved water or wind resistance. The coating may be applied to the face or the reverse side of the fabric. It may be very thin (Figure 6) or a rather thick (1 mm) foamed layer with an embossed surface resembling leather (Figure 7). In the transfer coating process, which is used to produce many coated fabrics and most leather-like materials, the

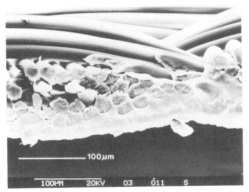

Figure 6 Arctic Armour is an example of a woven fabric undercoated with a 15 μm to 60 μm layer of polyester-based polyurethane.

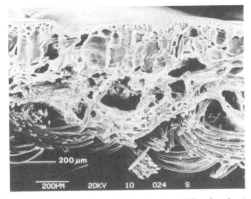

Figure 7 A realistic synthetic leather (Ultraleather) is shown in cross-section. The 15 μm polyurethane skin with leather-like grain is denser than the 300 μm polyurethane foam layer beneath it. A tricot knit stabilizes the fabric.

polyurethane is first spread in a thin layer over an embossed or smooth silicone-release paper. This "skin" layer will eventually form the film coating or leather-look surface of the fabric. A tie coat is applied, which laminates a backing fabric to the skin. After drying and curing, the silicone-release paper is removed to reveal the leather-like surface (Durst 1985).

The newest polyurethane-coated fabrics are advertised as waterproof or water-repellent and breathable (Mansfield 1985; Reagan 1990). The "breathability" is achieved in a solid polyurethane film by incorporating hydrophilic groups in the polymer. The films may also be breathable because of a microporous structure that allows water vapour but not liquid water to diffuse through (Table I).

Polyurethanes are also used as a finish on real leather. A split leather, for example, can be improved greatly by using an aqueous polyurethane-sizing treatment in the tanning process (Hepburn 1982, 151). A completely artificial leather, Corfam, was developed by Du Pont de Nemours and called a poromeric. This material was used for shoe and boot uppers. It consisted of polymer-impregnated non-woven nylon fabric, a layer of cellular structured polyurethane foam and a tough outer skin layer of polyurethane. The polyurethane is either a polyether- or polyester-based material (Webster 1985). Polyurethane uppers on shoes or boots were not as breathable as manufacturers had advertised. Du Pont ceased production of Corfam poromerics, but they are still produced in Poland under the trade name Polfam (Backus 1977).

Degradation of Polyurethanes

Polyurethanes are degraded by exposure to light, heat, and chemicals that cause hydrolysis, and micro-organisms. Each of these agents will be discussed and referenced to recent literature. The weak points on a polyurethane molecule are the various reactive bonds in the main polymer chains, such as urethane, ester, ether, amide, urea, and biuret. These bonds vary in their resistance to hydrolysis and oxidation.

Light: Some authors suggest that polyurethanes have good resistance to photo-oxidation caused by visible and ultraviolet (UV) radiation (Iyer 1989; Hepburn 1982) and others indicate that light resistance is a problem (Du Pont 1976; Gardette and Lemaire 1984; Abu-Zeid et al. 1984).

Photodegradation by UV and visible light produces a variety of breakdown products (Rek et al. 1988; Rånby and Rabek 1975). Photodegradation is accelerated by the presence of moisture and ammonia (Rånby and Rabek 1975). Residual catalysts, such as tertiary amines or divalent tin, left from the polymerization of rigid polyurethane foams appear to accelerate degradation of the foam by UV light and heat (Abu-Zeid and Nofal 1986). Ions from metals, such as Cu, Al, and Zn, form chelates with some polyurethanes and sensitize the polymers to UV light degradation (Rånby and Rabek 1975).

Table I

Polyurethane Coatings Used on Outdoor, Medical and Industrial Fabrics

Trade Name (Manufacturer)	Fabric Structure and Characteristics
Thintech (3M Insulation and Special Fabrics)	Introduced in 1987 as a garment insert, then in 1989 as a fabric laminate. Microporous olefin matrix impregnated with polyurethane making it a solid film. Film is bonded to various fabrics. Waterproof, breathable (see Table II).
Neozoic, Vapor Road (Teijin America)	Neozoic introduced in 1988 as a heavy microporous polyurethane membrane, laminated to various fabrics. Vapor Road introduced in 1986 in USA. Microporous polyurethane coating.
Bion II (Goldschmidt Labs)	Solid laminate or coating, breathable through hydrophilic groups within the polyurethane.
K-cote (Kenyon)	Microporous polyurethane coatings on underside of face fabrics.
Celtech (Unitika America)	Face fabric coated with microporous layer; waterproof, breathable, windproof.
Aqua-Guard (Schoeller/Rotofil)	Hydrophilic polyurethane coatings made in Switzerland, bonded to any face fabric.
Dermoflex and Radient (Consoltex Inc. Canadian Mill)	Microporous polyurethane coatings bonded to various fabrics. Also used as a garment liner. Radient is microporous polyurethane coating with carbon/ceramic particles for heat retention.
Entrant Sunlock (Toray Industries)	Microporous aqueous emulsion polyurethane coating bonded to various face fabrics. Entrant Sunlock has carbon or ceramic particles for heat retention.
Laytek, L-Therm, A, C, or Z (Asaki Chemical)	Microporous polyurethane coating. L-Therm, A, C, or Z is microporous polyurethane with aluminum, carbon or zirconium particles embedded. The added particles reflect, conduct or radiate body heat.
Microtech (Travis Textiles)	Solid polyurethane coating, breathable because film is hydrophilic.
Ucecoat 2010 (UCB Chemicals)	Solid polyurethane coating, breathable because of hydrophilic nature. Films applied by transfer coating from silicone-release paper.
Vent-X (Ventflex Fabrics)	British solid polyurethane coating, breathable through hydrophilic chemistry.

References: Mansfield 1985; Reagan 1990.

Initially both chain scission and crosslinking occur (Rek et al. 1986). When scission of the urethane link occurs, new amino groups and carboxyl groups are formed in the polymers (Rek et al. 1988). Carbon monoxide and carbon dioxide are given off when the -N-C- and -C-O- bonds break. When oxygen is present during light exposure hydroperoxides are formed (Rånby and Rabek 1975). Since peroxy groups absorb in the UV and visible regions, both UV and visible light will degrade polyurethanes. Over a period of time crosslinking prevails (Rek et al. 1986). Coatings become weak, and brittle instead of elastic; flexing or stretching causes them to break down completely (Holker 1988; Hepburn 1982).

The yellowing of polyurethanes from exposure to light is an inherent problem, particularly in foams, elastomers or coatings made from aromatic diisocyanates (Iyer 1989). The yellow colour is related to the formation of at least two types of structures: quinone-imides derived from the isocyanate MDI and photo-Fries products (Figure 8) (Abu-Zeid et al. 1984; Gardette and Lemaire 1982 and 1984; Rånby and Rabek 1975). Gardette and Lemaire (1984) state that excitation of aromatic chromophores by light of short wavelength up to 330 nm to 340 nm induces a photo-Fries rearrangement and the corresponding products absorb in the range 300 nm to 400 nm.

Considerable research has focused on the structure or composition of polyurethanes, which are

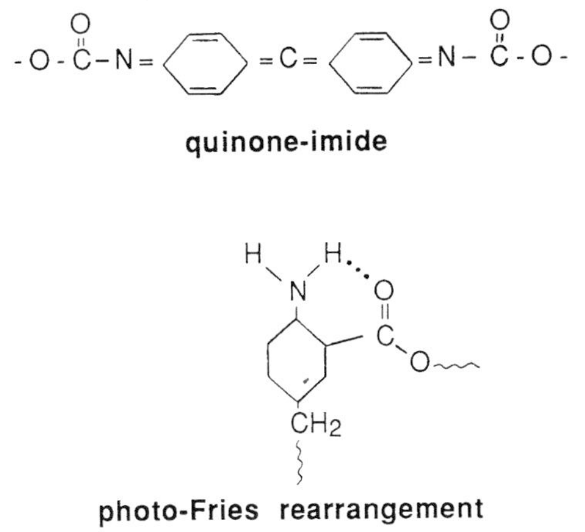

quinone-imide

photo-Fries rearrangement

Figure 8 Yellowing of polyurethanes is related to a photo-Fries rearrangement and to the formation of a quinone-imide group from the diisocyanate, MDI.

most sensitive to photo-oxidation. Light sensitivity depends on the structure of the isocyanate and the polyol used to form the polyurethane. The most *unstable* configuration is a polyurethane made from an aromatic diisocyanate (especially MDI) and a polyether polyol (Rosthauser and Nachtkamp 1987). Polyester polyols used to form the soft segments of a polyurethane molecule and aliphatic diisocyanates are most resistant to UV light (Rek et al. 1988). Rånby and Rabek (1975) report that photo-oxidation depends on the diisocyanate used in forming the polymers. The stability of three common diisocyanates to UV light follows the order: diphenylmethane diisocyanate < toluene diisocyanate < hexamethylene diisocyanate.

It is possible to stabilize polyurethanes to light degradation by incorporating antioxidants. Increased resistance of polyurethanes to weathering and radiation can be achieved by incorporating benzotriazole UV absorbers and hindered amine light stabilizers (HALS) (Gabriele et al. 1983; Stohler and Berger 1988). If a light-sensitive aromatic diisocyanate must be used in formulating a polyurethane, it is preferable for the isocyanate group (-NCO) to be separated from the benzene rings by one or more methylene groups (Iyer 1989).

Thermal: Because polyurethanes vary considerably in structure and composition, they also

vary in their sensitivity to heat. For many polyurethane elastomers, 80°C represents a maximum use temperature (Hepburn 1982, 351). At 70°C to 80°C, the tear strength of a polyurethane elastomer may only be about 50% of its room temperature value. Du Pont Bulletin L-86 (1976) includes the results of a test involving 50 cycles of machine washing (60°C) and tumble drying (82°C) on fabrics containing Lycra spandex or rubber thread. After the wash/dry test, the Lycra spandex fabrics withstood 10,000 cycles of repetitive elongation to 50% on a Zwick Flex Tester, whereas half the rubber specimens failed at 5,000 cycles. The International Fabricare Institute recommends that polyurethane-coated fabrics, imitation leathers or suedes and foam laminates be dried at a temperature not exceeding 50°C in order to minimize heat damage (Oehlke 1980; Scalco 1989; Rising and Scalco 1991). The temperature at which appreciable degradation occurs varies from about 180°C to 220°C (Iyer 1989; Abu-Zeid et al. 1983; Grassie et al. 1980).

Barendregt and Van den Berg (1980) suggest that two successive reactions play a role in the aging of polyurethanes. Both reactions have approximately the same activation energies (102 kJ/mole and 106 kJ/mole), but the first reaction is the most important below 100°C. They found that heat-induced aging was accelerated by oxygen and moisture. Hepburn (1982, 351) indicates that heat causes oxidative cleavage of ether and ester linkages in polyurethanes, although the ester linkages are considered more stable. Grassie and co-workers (1980) used thermal volatilization analysis (TVA) and thermo-gravimetry (TG) to study heat degradation mechanisms in a series of polyurethanes made from polyester soft segments and methylene bis(4-phenyl isocyanate) (MBPI). They demonstrated that the threshold degradation temperature increases as the content of the polyester soft segment increases. A proposed reaction sequence for the polyester-based polyurethanes is presented. Degradation in rigid polyurethane foams has been noted at temperatures as low as 60°C (Abu-Zeid et al. 1983). Specimens were heated for 15 minutes at 60°C, 80°C, 100°C, 150°C, 200°C and 250°C and their photo-acoustic spectra were analyzed. At 200°C and thereafter a major peak was noted and assigned to the quinone-imide group. This is one group considered responsible for the yellowing or darkening of polyurethanes on aging.

Chemical: One of the limitations of certain polyurethanes is their ease of hydrolysis (Hepburn 1982, 345). In order to determine whether a particular polyurethane is sensitive to hydrolysis, it is necessary to know its chemical makeup. It has been well established, for example, that polyester-based polyurethanes are more easily hydrolyzed than polyether-based polyurethanes (Du Pont 1976; Pavlova et al. 1985; Rosthauser and Nachtkamp 1987; Chapman et al. 1990). The three main polyols used in preparing elastomers are generally ranked for hydrolytic stability as follows: polyether > polycaprolactone > polyester (Hepburn 1982, 345).

Pavlova et al. (1985) state that polyester-based polyurethanes are hydrolyzed by alkalies that cause saponification of the ester group. When an ester link in the polymer backbone is broken, new carboxyl and alcohol groups are formed; the carboxyl group catalyzes further hydrolysis. Polyether-based polyurethanes, on the other hand, are subject to acid hydrolysis according to the accepted mechanism, and have very good stability in alkaline solutions. The rate of hydrolysis depends not only on the chemical composition of a polymer, but also on the diffusion properties of the polymeric matrix. In their search for polyurethanes with improved resistance to hydrolysis and thermo-oxidation, Chapman et al. (1990) have developed experimental polyurethanes that lack both ester and ether links in the soft segments. They contain non-self-associating polyamide blocks and yield polyurethane films that are more hydrolytically stable than polyester polyurethanes and less readily oxidized than polyether polyurethanes.

The resistance of polyurethanes to a wide variety of reagents can be found in a number of references (Hepburn 1982, 355-356; Du Pont 1976). In general, when polyurethanes are new and in good condition, they have excellent resistance to solvents used for solvent scouring, finishing and dry-cleaning, such as aliphatic, aromatic and chlorinated hydrocarbons. They also have good resistance to mildly polar solvents, such as acetone, methanol and diethyl ether. The strength of polyurethane elastomers is lowered as solvents become more polar. Solvents of very high polarity, such as dimethyl formamide and metacresol, will generally dissolve polyurethanes.

Microbial: Although most synthetic polymeric materials are not readily attacked by micro-organisms, polyurethanes are unusual in their susceptibility to microbial degradation, especially by fungi (Wales and Sagar 1991). As referred to in Webster (1985) and Shuttleworth and Seal (1986), when a polyurethane film or foam has been damaged by microbial growth, evidence of the damage will include the following:

- loss of mass
- surface peeling or flaking
- surface crazing or deep cracking
- staining of the cracks from the growth of fungal hyphae
- matting of the interstices of foam
- surface discolouration (bloom) from fungal growth beneath
- the formation of holes in films

Darby and Kaplan (1968) determined that polyester-based polyurethanes are more easily degraded by micro-organisms than polyether-based polyurethanes. In their study, 100 polyether- and polyester-based polyurethanes of known formulation were challenged with a mixed fungal inoculum (*Aspergillus niger, A. flavus, A. versicolor, Penicillium funiculosum, Pullalaria pullulans, Trichoderms sp.* and *Chaetomium globosum*). The polyester polyurethanes supported excellent growth after three weeks whereas the polyether polyurethanes showed only light to moderate attack. Enzymes were able to attack only if the polyether or polyester segment had at least three $-CH_2$ groups in a straight carbon chain (Kaplan et al. 1968). They emphasized the need to know the exact formulation of a polyurethane in order to make meaningful evaluations. Other researchers have confirmed that polyester-based polyurethanes are most susceptible to fungal damage (Filip 1978; Webster 1985; Shuttleworth and Seal 1986). Shuttleworth and Seal (1986) found that the most extensive deterioration of polyester-based polyurethanes was caused by *Gliocladium roseum*, although fungi belonging to other genera (*Alternaria, Fusarium, Penicillium* and *Ulocladium*) were able to produce similar results over a longer period of time. A major study of the mechanism of polyurethane biodeterioration is being conducted by researchers at the British Textile Technology Group (Wales and Sagar, 1985, 1988, and 1991).

Degradation in Garments Analyzed by the Textile Analysis Service

Many garments containing polyurethanes have been examined by the University of Alberta, Textile Analysis Service during the past 20 years. These include coated fabrics used in rainwear, imitation suedes, imitation leathers and foam-bonded or laminated fabrics. The garments belong to individuals and are not museum artifacts, but they exhibit typical signs of degradation that may be present in polyurethane-containing garments within museum collections. The garments examined in the laboratory have developed problems within the first few years of manufacture. As with many materials, the degraded condition of the polyurethane may not be readily apparent or discernible by casual examination.

The most frequent cause of deterioration in these garments is light damage. It is most evident in imitation suede garments in which the surface is a layer of fine polyurethane foam. These fabrics often exhibit loss of foam in areas of the garment that received the most light exposure: the shoulders, outer sides of the sleeves, and top of the collar and lapels. When dry-cleaned, the light-damaged foam crumbles and is lost from the fabric base, since it is not able to withstand immersion in the cleaning solvent and abrasion from commercial dry-cleaning cycles (Figure 9).

On one occasion, the most severe loss of foam occurred *under* the collar and lapels where light had not degraded the polyurethane foam. It is possible that residual catalyst or a breakdown product from the foam was trapped under the collar and lapels and accelerated the degradation of the foam in this area.

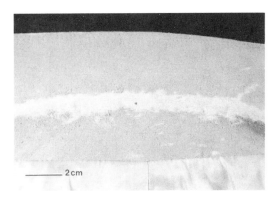

Figure 9 When this imitation suede garment was dry-cleaned, loss of polyurethane foam occurred on the collar, shoulders, and cuffs, areas subject to light exposure and abrasion during use.

In luxurious imitation suedes like Ultrasuede, Belleseime, and Supersuede, the polyurethane foam forms the base of the fabric in which the suede-like polyester fibres are embedded (Figures 4 and 5). When the foam deteriorates from exposure to light or oxides of nitrogen, the fabric shreds easily in areas of stress, such as across the shoulders, at the "armseye" seams, or buttonholes. These fabrics also deteriorate at collar and cuff edges from abrasion during wear. In addition, the dry-cleaning process causes fabrics to soften and lose body (Figure 10).

In the deterioration of imitation leather or polyurethane-coated fabrics used in rainwear, light damage is sometimes, but not always, evident. During dry-cleaning, the polyurethane film may separate from the base fabric to which it is bonded because of swelling of the film in perchloroethylene or softening of the adhesive or tie layer holding the film to the base fabric. The film balloons away from the backing fabric and often tears in its weakened, swollen condition. During solvent extraction and drying, the separated film may stick to itself or re-adhere to the base fabric in a wrinkled and distorted manner (Figure 11). Often film separation *only* occurs where light has damaged the polyurethane.

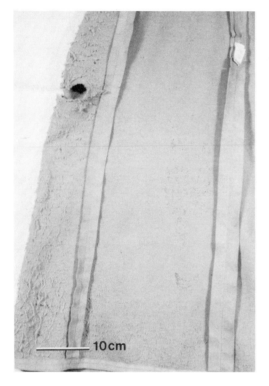

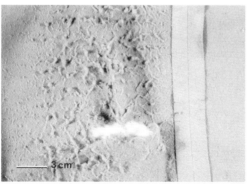

Figure 10 Ultrasuede skirt, turned inside out, exhibits severe pilling and a hole where the polyester fibres have shredded from stress.

Figure 11 The thin polyurethane film coating the surface of this imitation leather garment has separated from the backing fabric during dry-cleaning. In its weakened condition, the film has torn and adhered to itself.

Bonded and laminated fabrics having a layer of foam beneath a surface fabric created many problems for manufacturers during the late 1960s and early 1970s. If a face fabric was loosely woven or knitted, it often appeared to change colour as the foam layer beneath it yellowed from light and atmospheric fumes. Another common problem during washing or dry-cleaning was the separation of the foam layer from the face or backing fabric. This localized separation of layers gave the garment a bubbled appearance, as shown in Figure 12. The separation often occurred in light-damaged areas. There are several causes for the separation: insufficient softening of the foam before adhering it to the face and back layer, or weakening of bond due to deterioration of the foam as it ages.

The Textile Analysis Service has also examined bathing suits reinforced with spandex that has stretched and lost its elasticity after several months of continuous use in a chlorinated pool. Polyurethanes are damaged by chlorine in pool water or hypochlorite bleaches.

Experimental

Four new polyurethane fabrics were chosen for testing because they are typical of synthetic suede, synthetic leather and coated water-repellent fabrics. The fabrics are described in Table II. They were subjected to aging in sunlight outdoors in order to determine whether sunlight would produce degradation similar to that seen in polyurethane garments analyzed by the Textile Analysis Service. The polyurethane fabrics and a set of AATCC Blue Wool Light Fastness Standards were exposed to daylight through glass as described in AATCC Test Method 16C-1988 (AATCC 1989). The temperature in the ventilated exposure cabinets was not monitored continuously but was known to reach at least 45°C when the air temperature was 30°C. After exposure for 63 days during June and July 1991, Blue Wool Standard L-8 showed a colour change equivalent to Step 4 on the Gray Scale for colour change. This amount of daylight exposure is equivalent to 320 AATCC Fading Units (AFU) (AATCC 1989, 35). Following exposure to daylight, changes in fabric colour, stiffness (flexural rigidity), mass and bursting strength were

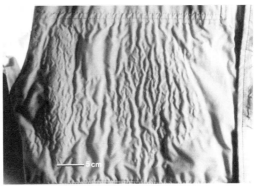

Figure 12 The dry cleaner was unaware of a water-repellent polyurethane film bonded to the underside of this rain jacket. During dry-cleaning, the film in one panel partially separated and shrank causing puckering of the face fabric.

determined. Colour difference was determined on a Hunter Lab D25M-9 Tristimulus colorimeter following AATCC Test Method 153-1985. The CIE 1976 L*a*b* system was used to determine the difference in colour between the unexposed fabric and the exposed fabric. Changes in flexibility were determined according to ASTM Test Method D1388-64 - Cantilever Test (ASTM 1990). Fabric mass was measured as specified in CAN/CGSB-4.2 No. 5.1-M90 (CGSB 1990). Changes in bursting strength

Table II

Fabrics Used in Experimental Study

Fabric Structure (Sample Number)	Fibre Content	Cost (1991)
Supersuede Springs Industries Extremely fine fibres (4 μm) embedded in polyurethane foam (1 and 2)	60% polyester fibres 40% polyurethane foam (polyether based)	$85/m
Ultraleather Plus Springs Industries Polyurethane skin-foam coated on a tricot knit (3 and 4)	face—polyurethane (polyester based) back—70% cuprammonium rayon/30% nylon	$95/m
Arctic Armour Plain weave face fabric undercoated with white polyurethane layer (15 μm to 60 μm) (6, 7, and 8)	face—nylon back—polyurethane (polyester based)	$8/m
Thintech garment liner 3M Corporation Tricot knit coated with transparent polyurethane layer on a microporous olefin matrix (9, 10, and 11)	knit—nylon coating—75% polyurethane (polyether based)/ 25% olefin matrix	$19/m

following aging were determined according to CAN/CGSB-4.2 Method No. 11.2-M89 (CGSB 1990). Bursting strength was measured on an Instron Universal tester. Changes in surface topography and fabric structural details were examined with the aid of a Cambridge Stereoscan 250 scanning electron microscope after specimens were sputter-coated with gold.

Results and Discussion

The four experimental polyurethane-containing fabrics were examined frequently during the 63-day exposure period. The turquoise blue Supersuede faded rapidly, as expected. It was assigned an AATCC lightfastness rating of L-4, which is the minimal lightfastness rating recommended for most clothing. The pink Arctic Armour nylon fabric coated with polyurethane also faded rapidly, even though the polyurethane layer rather than the nylon was exposed to the light. The fading may have been caused by radiation that penetrated the opaque polyurethane film or atmospheric fumes in the exposure cabinet. The polyurethane coating on

the Thintech fabric became opaque during light exposure and the fabric shrank from heat. The olefin matrix that makes up 25% of the coating layer is very heat sensitive. During the June and July exposure period, the outdoor temperature reached a maximum of about 30°C and the temperature in the cabinet reached 45°C to 50°C in full sun.

Colour Change: Ultraleather, Thintech, and Arctic Armour all showed visible yellowing of the polyurethane layer after light exposure for 63 days (Table III). The greater change showed by Thintech (Δ E=12.4) than by Ultraleather (Δ E=5.3) or Arctic Armour (Δ E=3.3) is to be expected because the polyurethane component in Thintech is ether-based whereas the other two fabrics contain ester-based polyurethane coatings (Rek et al. 1988). The colour change shown by Supersuede (Δ E=29.1) does not represent a change in the polyurethane foam because it is hidden by polyester fibres comprising the fabric surface; rather, it represents fading of the turquoise-dyed polyester fibres on the surface of the fabric.

Table III

Changes in Physical Properties of Polyurethane-containing Fabrics after Exposure through Glass to 63 Days of Sunlight

Fabric Structure and Composition	Flexural Rigidity % change[a]	Color Difference ΔE (CIE1976 L*a*b* units)	Mass[d]		Bursting Strength % change
			(g/m^2)	% change	
Supersuede nonwoven 60% polyester fibers 40% PUR foam	+ 24	29.1[b]	246	- 0.94	- 13
Ultrateather Plus PUR foam-coating tricot knit backing	+ 28	5.3	254	- 0.53	- 10
Arctic Armour Woven nylon PUR coating	+ 13	3.3[c]	140	+ 5.10	- 75
Thintech 3M tricot knit PUR coating	- 27	12.4	89	- 2.65	- 78

[a] + = stiffer; - = more flexible
[b] represents fading of turquoise fabric
[c] represents colour change of polyurethane coating and fading of the pink fabric beneath
[d] mass before outdoor exposure

Bursting Strength: Two fabrics, Arctic Armour and Thintech, were extremely weak after exposure to light. Their loss of bursting strength after a 63-day exposure period, 75% and 78% respectively, demonstrates how sensitive some polyurethanes are to light. The failure of Arctic Armour, which has an ester-based polyurethane film, is due, in part, to the poor light resistance of the nylon face fabric. During the bursting test, the nylon fabric shred under minimal pressure. The ester-based urethane film on this fabric, although expected to have good light resistance, was not sufficiently strong to hold the degraded nylon fabric together. The formation of crosslinks during irradiation could contribute to the observed loss in bursting strength. Bursting strength is controlled by the least extensible fibres or yarns in a fabric; they reach their maximum extension and break before the more extensible fibres or yarns have been stretched to their limit.

Flexural Rigidity: The flexural rigidity or stiffness of both the Supersuede and Ultraleather fabrics increased 24% and 28% respectively. The increase in stiffness is a recognized change in polyurethanes exposed to light and oxygen and is caused by crosslinking of the polyurethane molecules (Rek et al. 1986). Both chain scission and crosslinking are induced by light exposure, but crosslinking eventually

predominates (Rek et al. 1986). The Thintech fabric was more flexible after light exposure. During outdoor exposure the fabric shrank slightly and curled at the edges probably because of the olefin matrix. The specimens curled and twisted during testing, making it difficult to measure flexural rigidity accurately.

Scanning Electron Microscopy: Polyurethane films are known to become crazed, cracked and pitted during outdoor exposure to light, oxygen, air pollutants and micro-organisms (Gabriele et al. 1983). The polyurethane surfaces of the Ultraleather, Thintech and Arctic Armour fabrics were examined with the aid of an electron microscope. Figure 13 shows the original appearance (left) and appearance after 63 days of outdoor exposure (right). There is little visual difference in the Ultraleather (Figure 13a), or the Arctic Armour (Figure 13b). This finding is not surprising since both have ester-based urethane coatings and Ultraleather showed little loss of mass (-0.53%) after exposure. Since the exposure cabinet was covered with glass and only filtered air entered the cabinet, fabrics did not become soiled with particulate. The Thintech fabric (ether-based urethane) (Figure 13c) shows more surface change than the other two specimens. There appears to be some pitting of the surface; these pits are consistent with the loss of mass measure (-2.65%). The surface of

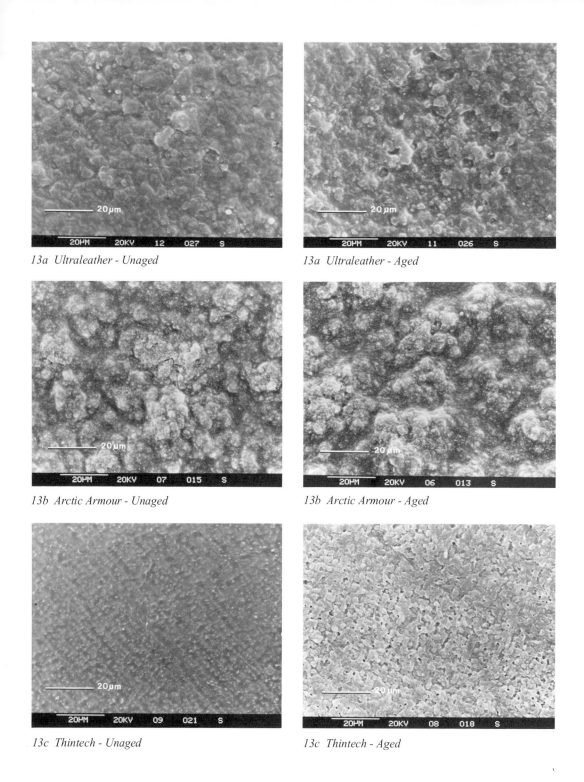

13a *Ultraleather - Unaged*

13a *Ultraleather - Aged*

13b *Arctic Armour - Unaged*

13b *Arctic Armour - Aged*

13c *Thintech - Unaged*

13c *Thintech - Aged*

Figure 13 After outdoor exposure through glass for 63 days (420 AATCC fading units) Ultraleather (a) and Arctic Armour (b) show no surface change, whereas Thintech (c) shows evidence of pitting. Left: unexposed. Right: exposed.

the Thintech specimen was analyzed with energy dispersive X-rays. No change in elements on the surface was observed after exposure.

In conclusion, after a brief 63-day exposure period behind glass, the four specimens containing polyurethane showed physical changes that are typical for ester- and ether-based urethanes. Yellowing, increased brittleness and loss of bursting strength were expected and occurred in most specimens. The woven nylon component of Arctic Armour degraded much faster than the polyurethane coating. In addition, the heat-sensitive olefin matrix in Thintech added a complicating variable that made it difficult to assess the changes in the polyurethane film in this fabric.

Conservation of Polyurethanes

In general, the conservation considerations for textiles containing polyurethane are the same as for other textiles. During storage and display, light exposure must be minimal, UV light excluded, relative humidity in the range of 50% to 55%, and high temperatures avoided. Storage and display areas should also have adequate ventilation to dissipate any volatile products of degradation. Polyurethane-containing artifacts should be stored separately from other textiles. Layers of foam, films or coatings should not be left in direct contact in storage as they may stick together. For example, sleeves should not rest directly on the sides of a garment and collars and lapels should be lifted slightly or separated from the body of the garment with inserts of fabric or acid-free tissue.

Standard wet-cleaning procedures used in textile conservation are suitable for cleaning polyurethane. The wash water should remain in the neutral range of pH 5 to 8. It is important to minimize the agitation, flexing and manipulation of the garment during the cleaning process, particularly when the textile contains polyurethane foam. Aged foams are frequently brittle and readily crumbled with too much handling. Textiles containing polyurethane should not be bleached, and they should not be heated to dry, or pressed.

Dry-cleaning solvents do not damage polyurethane and may be used for hand cleaning; however, adhesives used to bond polyurethane films and foams to fabrics are sometimes soluble in dry-cleaning solvents (Figure 11). Commercial dry-cleaning is not recommended for cleaning garments containing polyurethane as the process involves a considerable amount of mechanical action and cannot be considered safe for aged polyurethane films, coatings or foams (Figures 9, 10, and 11).

Polyurethane can be identified and distinguished from other similar materials by burning tests and chemical solubility tests (Textile Institute 1975). Elastomeric polyurethane fibres (spandex or elastane) are easily distinguished from rubber fibres by their microscopic appearance (round cross-section) or by burning. The characteristic odor of burning rubber will identify rubber. Synthetic suedes and leathers used in textile applications since the 1960s will be made of either polyurethane or poly(vinyl chloride). Imitation leathers and suedes composed of polyurethane can sometimes be quickly distinguished from products made of poly(vinyl chloride) by a Beilstein copper wire test (Textile Institute 1975, 227). Poly(vinyl chloride) produces a green flame in this test while polyurethane does not. Solvents to dissolve or disintegrate polyurethane coatings and foams include boiling dimethyl formamide and boiling NaOH (10%) (Textile Institute 1975, 160).

Acknowledgement

The authors thank several people who provided assistance in the preparation of this paper. Catherine Jacobsen, a Clothing and Textiles student, gathered material for the literature review and helped perform physical tests on the experimental fabrics. George Braybrook, Dept. of Entomology, took the scanning electron micrographs, Linda Turner took the photographs of Textile Analysis Service garments, and Diana Parsons typed the manuscript.

Résumé

La dégradation des polyuréthannes présents dans les textiles du XXᵉ siècle conservés dans des musées

Le terme « polyuréthanne » s'applique à un groupe diversifié de matières qui entrent dans la fabrication des textiles du XXᵉ siècle. Au nombre de ces matières, figurent les fibres (spandex), les adhésifs et les agents de consolidation des suèdes synthétiques, les mousses des tissus contre-collés, les mousses de surface des simili-suèdes ainsi que les revêtements hydrofuges ou les surfaces imitant le cuir de certains tissus. Il incombe aux spécialistes de la restauration de se familiariser avec les diverses facettes de ces matières — depuis leurs multiples modes d'utilisation dans les textiles jusqu'à l'évaluation de l'état d'un tissu ou de la forme sous laquelle se manifestera leur dégradation. Tous ces aspects seront traités dans le cadre de la présente communication, au cours de laquelle nous étudierons en outre le mode de dégradation des polyuréthannes, en passant en revue les nombreux documents qui existent sur le sujet.

La photo-oxydation est particulièrement dommageable pour les polyuréthannes, et elle demeure la première cause des dommages subis par les textiles que nous avons examinés. Les polyuréthannes à base de diisocyanates aliphatiques et de segments souples en polyester résistent mieux à la photo-oxydation que ceux qui sont formés à partir de diisocyanates aromatiques et de segments mous de polyéther. Des micro-organismes peuvent croître sur les polyuréthannes, sous forme de pellicule craquelée. Au fur et à mesure de la croissance, des enzymes sont sécrétées, qui peuvent couper les chaînes au hasard à la liaison uréthanne ou près de leurs extrémités.

Un certain nombre de vêtements renfermant du polyuréthanne sous forme de fibres, de mousses, de pellicules ou d'adhésifs seront présentés, avec une description des dommages qu'ils ont subis. Dans nombre de cas, les vêtements n'ont présenté aucun signe de dommage photo-oxydatif avant d'être nettoyés à sec dans un établissement commercial. Leur saturation avec le solvant de nettoyage à sec (perchloroéthylène) et l'agitation mécanique à laquelle ils ont été soumis pendant le cycle de nettoyage ont fait que le polyuréthanne oxydé s'est décomposé. Nous fournirons enfin des suggestions sur la façon de nettoyer, en toute sécurité, les vêtements renfermant du polyuréthanne.

References

Abu-Zeid, M.E., E.E. Nofal, F.A. Abdul-Rasoul, M.A. Marati, G.S. Mahmoud and A. Ledwith, "Photoacoustic Study of Thermal Degradation of Polyurethane," *Journal of Applied Polymer Science*, vol. 28, no. 7, 1983, pp. 2317-2324.

Abu-Zeid, M.E, E.E. Nofal and L.A. Tahseen, "Photoacoustic Study of UV, UV-thermal and Weathering Degradation of Rigid Foam Polyurethane," *Journal of Applied Polymer Science*, vol. 29, no. 8, 1984, pp. 2443-2452.

Abu-Zeid, M.E. and E.E. Nofal, "Effect of Catalyst Residues on the Degradation of Rigid Foam Polyurethane," *Journal of Applied Polymer Science*, vol. 31, no. 8, 1986, pp. 2407-2415.

Allen, N.S. and J.F. McKellar, "The Role of Luminescent Species in the Photo-oxidation of Commercial Polymers," in: *Developments in Polymer Degradation-2*, N. Grassie, ed. (London: Applied Science Publishers, 1979) pp. 145-148.

American Association of Textile Chemists and Colorists, *Technical Manual of the AATCC*, Vol. 64 (Research Triangle Park: AATCC, 1991).

American Society for Testing and Materials, *1990 Annual Book of Standards*, Vol. 7.01 (Philadelphia, P.A.: ASTM, 1990) pp. 361-364.

Backus, J.K., "Polyurethanes," in: *Polymerization Processes*, C.E. Schildknecht and I. Skeist, eds. (New York: J. Wiley & Sons, 1977) pp. 642-680.

Barendregt, R.B. and P.G Van den Berg, "The Degradation of Polyurethane," *Thermochima Acta*, vol. 38, 1980, pp. 181-195.

Canadian General Standards Board, *Textile Test Methods, Can/CGSB-4.2* (Ottawa: CGSB, 1990).

Carter, M.E., *Essential Fiber Chemistry* (New York: Marcel Dekker, 1971).

Chapman, T.M., D.M. Rakiewicz-Nemeth, J. Swestock and R. Benrashid, "Polyurethane Elastomers with Hydrolytic and Thermo-oxidative Stability. 1. Polyurethanes with N-alkylated Polyamide Soft Blocks," *Journal of Polymer Science: Part A: Polymer Chemistry*, vol. 28, no. 6, 1990, pp. 1473-1482.

Darby, R.T. and A.M. Kaplan, "Fungal Susceptibility of Polyurethanes," *Applied Microbiology*, vol. 16, no. 6, 1968, pp. 900-905.

Du Pont de Nemours & Co. (Inc.), "Lycra Spandex Fiber," *Du Pont Technical Information Bulletin L-86* (Wilmington: Du Pont, 1976).

Durst, P., "PU Transfer Coating of Fabrics for Leather-like Fashion Products," *Journal of Coated Fabrics*, vol. 14, 1985, pp. 227-240.

Filip, Z., "Decomposition of Polyurethane in Garbage Landfill Leakage Water and by Soil Micro-organisms," *European Journal of Applied Microbiology and Biotechnology*, vol. 5, 1978, pp. 225-231.

Gabriele, P.D., J.R. Geib, R.M. Iannucci and W.J. Reid, "Photochemical Degradation and Biological Defacement of Polymers," in: *The Effects of Hostile Environments on Coatings and Plastics*, D.P. Garner and G.A. Stahl, eds. *ACS Symposium Series 229* (Washington, D.C.: American Chemical Society, 1983) pp. 317-330.

Gardette, J.L. and J. Lemaire, "Oxydation photothermique d'élastomères de polyuréthannes thermoplastiques, Partie 2: Influence de la longueur d'onde et des conditions d'irradiation sur le jaunissement des polyuréthannes à structure aromatique," *Die Makromolekulare Chemie*, vol. 183, no. 10, 1982, pp. 2415-2425.

Gardette, J.L. and J. Lemaire, "Photo-Thermal Oxidation of Thermoplastic Polyurethane Elastomers: Part 3 - Influence of the Excitation Wavelengths on the Oxidative Evolution of Polyurethanes in the Solid State," *Polymer Degradation and Stability*, vol. 6, 1984, pp. 135-148.

Grassie, N., M. Zulfiqar and M.I. Guy, "Thermal Degradation of a Series of Polyurethanes," *Journal of Polymer Science: Polymer Chemistry Edition*, vol. 18, no. 1, 1980, pp. 265-274.

Hepburn, C., *Polyurethane Elastomers* (London: Applied Science Publishers, 1982).

Holker, J.R., "Weathering," *Textiles*, vol. 17, no. 3, 1988, pp. 64-71.

Iyer, S.B., "Recent Developments in Polyurethanes - XXI," *Man-made Textiles in India*, vol. 32, no. 4, 1989, pp. 158-160.

Joseph, M.L., *Introductory Textile Science* (New York: Holt, Rinehart & Winston, 1986).

Kaplan, A.M., R.T. Darby, M. Greenberger and M.R. Rogers, "Microbial Deterioration of Poly-urethane Systems," *Developments in Industrial Microbiology*, vol. 9, 1968, pp. 201-217.

Lenz, R.W., *Organic Chemistry of Synthetic High Polymers* (New York: Interscience Publishers, 1967).

Mansfield, R.G., "High Performance Coatings and Finishes Expand Uses," *Textile World*, May, 1985, pp. 58-60.

Oehlke, N., "Polyurethane Coated Fabrics," *IFI Bulletin FF288* (Silver Spring, M.D.: International Fabricare Institute, 1980).

Pavlova, M., M. Oraganova and P. Novakov, "Hydrolytic Stability and Protective Properties of Polyurethane Oligomers Based on Polyes-ter/Ether/Polyols," *Polymer*, vol. 26, no. 11, 1985, pp. 1901-1905.

Rånby, B. and F.F. Rabek, *Photodegradation, Photo-oxidation and Photostabilization of Polymers* (London: John Wiley, 1975) pp. 241-243.

Reagan, E., "Examining the Moisture Managers," *Outside Business*, April, 1990, pp. 37-46.

Rek, V., H.J. Mencer and M. Bravar, "GPC and Structural Analysis of Polyurethane Degradation," *Polymer Photochemistry*, vol. 7, 1986, pp. 273-283.

Rek, V., M. Bravar, T. Jocić and E. Govorcin, "A Contribution to the UV Degradation of Polyurethanes," *Die Angewandte Makromolekulare Chemie*, vol. 158/159, 1988, pp. 247-263.

Rek, V., M. Bravar, E. Govorcin and M. Suceska, "Mechanical and Structural Studies of Photo-degraded Polyurethane," *Polymer Degradation and Stability*, vol. 24, 1989, pp. 399-411.

Rising, J. and M. Scalco, "Ultraleather®," *IFI Bulletin FF386* (Silver Spring, M.D.: International Fabricare Institute, 1991).

Rosthauser, J.W. and K. Nachtkamp, "Waterborne Polyurethanes," in: *Advances in Urethane Science and Technology*, Vol. 10, K.C. Frisch and D. Klempner, eds. (Basel: Technomic, 1987) pp. 121-161.

Scalco, M., "Foam Laminates," *IFI Bulletin FF364* (Silver Spring, M.D.: International Fabricare Institute, 1989).

Shuttleworth, W.A. and K.J. Seal, "A Rapid Technique for Evaluating the Biodeterioration Potential of Polyurethane Elastomers," *Applied Microbiology and Biotechnology*, vol. 23, 1986, pp. 407-409.

Stohler, F.R. and K. Berger, "New Results Upon the Stabilization of Polyurethane Systems Against Photo-oxidative Influences," *Die Angewandte Makromolekulare Chemie*, vol. 158/159, 1988, pp. 233-246.

Textile Institute, *Identification of Textile Materials*, 7th edn. (Manchester: Textile Institute, 1975).

Wales, D.S. and B.F. Sagar, "The Mechanism of Polyurethane Biodeterioration," in: *Biodeterioration of Plastics and Polymers*, K.G. Seal, ed. (Kew, Surrey: Biodeterioration Society, 1985) pp. 56-69.

Wales, D.S. and B.F. Sagar, "Mechanistic Aspects of Polyurethane Biodeterioration," in: *Biodeterioration 7*, D.R. Houghton, R.N. Smith and H.O.W. Eggins, eds. (London: Elsevier Applied Science, 1988) pp. 351-358.

Wales, D.S. and B.F. Sagar, "Effect of Structure on Susceptibility of Polyurethanes to Biodegradation," *Biodeterioration and Biodegradation 8*, H. Rossmore, ed. (London: Elsevier Applied Science, 1991) pp. 241-248.

Webster, R.M., "A Case Study of the Biodeterioration of Some Boot Uppers Made From a Polyurethane Poromeric," *Journal of the American Leather Chemists Association*, vol. 80, no. 6, 1985, pp. 172-183.

Treating Early Regenerated Cellulose Textiles: Two Case Histories

Emma Telford

Textile Conservation Studio
The National Trust
Aylsham, U.K.

Abstract

This paper focuses on the positive and negative aspects of some conventional and less conventional textile conservation treatments to regenerated cellulose textiles.

The effects of wet-cleaning and different forms of de-acidification treatments are discussed in relation to two case histories. The aim is to make practical judgements about potential treatments, drawing from both scientific evidence and personal experience.

The first case history, essentially a non-treatment, concerns a piece of a costume ca. 1912. The costume is composed of silk and cuprammonium rayon fabrics. Discussion focuses on the need to de-acidify or remove acid soiling from this textile, bearing in mind the effect of water on regenerated cellulose fibres and their consequent reduced wet strength. The decision not to wet-clean is argued.

The second case history concerns part of a costume from the 1920s. An attempt to quantify the effect of water on degraded regenerated cellulose is made by conducting the following analyses both before and after wet-cleaning: 1) surface pH to establish the extent of removal of acid soiling; and 2) tests to identify any reduction in tensile strength.

In addition, experiments are conducted with ammonia vapour to establish its efficiency as an alternative in reducing acidity. Specifically, a combined treatment of ammonia vapour followed by wet-cleaning is done to see whether conversion to salts renders acids more easily removable.

Introduction

In the final year of training at the Textile Conservation Centre, Hampton Court Palace, students are required to select and treat a textile object. This paper describes the conservation of a piece of an early 20th-century costume that incorporated a manufactured fibre element.

Twentieth-century material and manufactured fibres in particular had been entirely overlooked in the teaching programme at the time, and little had been researched or documented on this topic from the point of view of conservation.

The artefact was privately owned and the client gave an almost entirely open brief, with the request that the artefact be made safe for storage and occasional display for study purposes.

Description and Attribution

The artefact was a dress composed of a pink silk underdress and a black gauze overdress made from cuprammonium rayon (or cupro as it is also known). This latter fibre was identified by microscopic examination and solubility tests. This makes the dress an early example of this fibre, which only came into general use ca. 1910.[1] The gauze and silk layers of the dress were stitched together and were not separable.

It was dated to ca. 1912 by costume experts from the Victoria and Albert Museum, the Museum of London and the National Museums of Scotland. The rough and ready construction of the dress originally suggested that it had been manufactured later than 1912, but in the style of that period perhaps for drama or fancy dress purposes. However, apparently such poor workmanship was in fact quite typical of even haute couture clothing of the period. Other features typical of the period that helped to date the dress were the following: the very popular colour combinations of the time, pink and black; a short filmy overdress over a longer underdress; heavy surface decoration; and large clumsy fastenings.

However, the dress does have a history of theatrical use, having been part of a university drama department wardrobe for some years. This would account for some of the damage (e.g., heavy sweat-staining), which is more consistent with it being worn as a theatrical costume rather than as a dress.

Condition

The poor condition of the dress probably resulted from its use in the theatre. It was generally soiled, badly stained underarm and ripped at the shoulders and around the hem. Both gauze and silk fabrics were also badly creased and worn in places. The cuprammonium rayon appeared to be fairly degraded and brittle, being particularly weak in the weft. In order to establish in greater detail the condition, and also study and gain familiarity with the fibre characteristics under very high magnification, fibre samples from the hem area of the gauze and the braid were examined by scanning electron microscope. On examination of the photomicrographs and with the help of the useful Hearle et al.[2] reference it was possible to determine the following characteristics:

- The fibres exhibit typical cuprammonium rayon cross-sectional and longitudinal features, that is, kidney-like cross-section, no lengthwise striations, smooth, featureless. In comparison with ordinary viscose rayon, which has a much more lobal cross-section giving rise to numerous lengthwise striations, it is easily distinguishable.

- The fibres appear moderately brittle and some evidently suffer the type of break known as brittle break. This is identified by the angular nature of the broken end, which has a step-like feature. Other types of failure occurring in the fibres are tensile breaks, which occur when the fibre is still strong and which is recognizable by the granular nature of the broken end; and axial failure, where the fibre is fractured along its axis probably as a result of the wear process.

- Dark spots that sometimes show up on the fibres may be attributable to static charging under the scanning electron micrograph in areas that have insufficient gold covering. However, the dark, pitted features evident on some fibres may be due to a number of other things. Bacterial, fungal, or acid attack (during spinning or subsequently) may be responsible, and depending on the dyestuff used, it may be a dyestuff attack. Early examples of cuprammonium rayon (such as this) are likely to have been left acid after manufacture, as early washing techniques were ineffective and any acidity would not have been neutralized.

Treatment Options

The most effective treatment method from the point of view of stabilization would have been wet-cleaning. This would have removed much soiling, creasing and also acidity, and was believed to be beneficial to the cuprammonium rayon, which is particularly susceptible to acid degradation. In investigating this possibility a variety of tests, including one for dye fastness, were conducted. It transpired that the pink silk dye and also the black braid dye were not wet-fast, and this eliminated the possibility of wet-cleaning. However, the likely effect of wet-cleaning on the degraded cuprammonium rayon also needed to be investigated.

The major drawback of cuprammonium rayon is its poor tensile strength. This is due largely to the highly amorphous polymer system that prevents sufficient hydrogen bonding between polymer chains to impart strength.[3] This amorphous structure (60% to 65% of the polymer) also accounts for its reduced wet strength, which is roughly half that of the dry. Water can penetrate easily and force the polymer chains apart, thus reducing further the inter-polymer hydrogen bonding. These hydrogen bonds will rarely re-form in their original positions, which is why the fibre is so susceptible to deformation during and following wet treatments, and also why distortion and creasing is likely to remain even after strains have been removed in the dry state.

Cuprammonium rayon consists almost entirely of pure cellulose. However, the polymer chains are short, on average having a degree of polymerization of 250 to 300 — low compared to other cellulosics, such as cotton (5,000) and flax (18,000). Thus, the polymers contain a high number of reactive end groups, making the fibre more susceptible to attack by acids. Hence the need to remove acid soiling. In addition, the cuprammonium rayon contains some aldehyde, ketone and carboxylic acid groups, which are created during manufacture, making it prematurely slightly degraded. Cuprammonium rayon in a degraded condition would naturally have an increased susceptibility to acid attack. It is also reasonable to argue that any wet treatments applied to cuprammonium rayon in that state may damage the textile substantially by breaking the inter-polymer bonds that may not re-form.

Threads removed for testing to water showed no apparent deterioration. However, a sample large enough to test the strength before and after wetting could not be removed. In the event, fugitive dyes precluded any wet treatment as previously mentioned, but it was still important to know whether the benefits of removing acidity would outweigh the possible disadvantages of wet-cleaning.

Treatment

The treatment of the textile was essentially non-interventionist.

Underdress: Work commenced on the silk underdress, starting with the hem area, and involved relaxation by means of a cold poultice, followed by stitching to a dyed silk fabric support. The underarm areas were treated in the same way, although because of access problems to the underarm areas, caused by the gauze, it was unfortunately necessary to undo original seaming in the gauze in order to adequately support and stitch the silk. Worn, fragile areas of silk, such as the pleated cuffs, buckle and sash, were covered with a protective layer of silk crepeline.

Gauze Overdress: Structural damage to the bodice part or the gauze was also given a full support with silk crepeline. The open leno weave structure of the gauze allowed stitching without creating even tiny holes, or any damage. A pink support was chosen to minimize reduction in the transparency of the gauze. The gauze was not relaxed with humidity prior to supporting, because it may be inadvisable to introduce moisture to an acidic textile without first rinsing away acidic products. The short period during which the textile is damp may be sufficient for acids to start attacking the textile. Damage caused during this time could be extensive.

In wet-cleaning, the acids are released, but are diluted immediately and washed away quickly. Due to the acid-sensitive nature of cuprammonium rayon a treatment involving humidity was not used.

Issues Arising from Treatment

The project raised some issues that were worth investigating further.

- What were the possibilities of neutralizing acidity in regenerated cellulosic materials without wet-cleaning?

- What likely effect would wet and other treatments have on the tensile strength of such textiles?

Experiments: Some simple experiments were conducted on a kimono dated to the 1920s that could be sacrificed for this purpose. The textile had a plain weave structure and a printed floral design. The fibre was identified by microscopy and solubility tests as viscose rayon.

The condition of the textile appeared to be generally good and fairly typical of this age. However, on close examination the weft threads seemed extremely weak and the textile had to be handled with care.

The aim of the experiment was to try an ammonia vapour treatment as a means of de-acidifying the textile without wetting it. A subsidiary aim was to investigate whether conversion of the acids to ammonium salts would render the acids more easily removable in wet-cleaning, which would allow a shorter wet process to be used. Thus a sample was treated with a rapid wet process (i.e., wash) after exposure to the ammonia vapour.

Tensile Strength Measurement: A sample of untreated textile was tested to determine its tensile strength. The test was carried out according to British Standard BS2576:1986 on an Instron apparatus. The weft in particular was found to be extremely weak, with a mean strength of 6.7 kg/denier. The warp was stronger with a mean strength of 30 kg/denier.

pH Measurements: pH tests on the untreated textile showed it to be acidic, pH 4.5. For the purposes of these tests this was considered sufficiently acidic to show clearly any change resulting from treatment.

Test Treatments: One section of textile was given standard wet-cleaning with a solution of 0.1% Synperonic 'N' (non-ionic detergent) and 0.05% sodium carboxy methylcellulose in softened water at a temperature of 19°C. The sample was subjected to a series of three baths, which involved soaking initially and sponging. This was followed by a series of rinses in softened water, with a final rinse in deionized water. The pH of the rinsing was monitored throughout, and this gradually increased through repeated changes of water to pH 6.

It was noted that once wetted out, the textile contracted quickly in both warp and weft directions. It thus required some manipulation to reshape it when laying it out to dry. This was

difficult due to the very fragile nature of the weft. Once dry, the textile was visibly cleaner and more lustrous.

Two other samples were placed in a desiccator in the presence of a small amount of aqueous ammonia solution (15%), and the humidity was gradually raised with an ultrasonic humidifier to 95% over a period of almost four hours. The relative humidity was monitored constantly in the chamber, and the pH of the textile, once every hour. At the end of the process the pH readings of the textiles were around pH 8.

One piece was given a minimal wet treatment that involved rinsing in deionized water.

Results: Following these three treatments the samples were tested for tensile strength and the results were as follows:

Untreated	6.7 kg/denier in weft	30.0 kg/denier in warp
Wet-cleaning only	7.75 kg/denier in weft	30.3 kg/denier in warp
NH$_3$ vapour only	7.8 kg/denier in weft	27.7 kg/denier in warp
NH$_3$ vapour plus wet rise	6.17 kg/denier in weft	27.5 kg/denier in warp

Discussion

These data suggest that the textile has been slightly strengthened by the wet-cleaning and also by the ammonia vapour treatment in the weft direction, although the change is minimal. The only loss of strength, again minimal, was caused by the treatment with NH$_3$ vapour followed by a wet rinse. In the warp direction also the results seem favourable, with slight decline in strength for the two NH$_3$ vapour-treated samples and no real change for the wet-cleaned sample.

Thus it would appear that the wet treatment on this textile certainly has no harmful effects. However, the NH$_3$ vapour treatments seem to have been as effective at reducing acidity. The pH readings on all the samples remain neutral.

Concerning the sample treated only with ammonia vapour, the question remains as to whether the salts in the textile will remain stable over time, or whether they will convert back to the acid state. This depends on the sort of environment to which the textile is exposed. It has been suggested that the de-acidification will last only for a matter of months before conversion back to acids occurs.[4] If so, then there is an argument for rinsing out the salts before they have a chance to convert back. The use of buffers, such as sodium bicarbonate, however, may render these salts more stable. This possibility has not been investigated.

Another disadvantage of ammonia vapour treatments is that the textile is humidified in its soiled state, which as mentioned previously is certainly a cause for anxiety.

It is worth remembering that wet-cleaning is not used solely as a means of de-acidifying a textile. It also allows the relaxation and realignment of the threads and fibres, and often improves the appearance and handle of a textile, generally restoring some of the physical fibre properties. Alternative treatments cannot do this.

Conclusion

Although each textile must be considered according to its structure and condition when devising treatments, the data obtained indicate that wet processes can be applied to early regenerated cellulosic fibres. Extra care needs to be taken when handling such textiles in the wet state. Ammonia vapour has also been shown to work as a de-acidifying treatment on regenerated cellulosic textiles. From these simple experiments, however, it is not possible to establish whether the effects are too ephemeral to make it worthwhile. In any case, the aesthetic effects of wet-cleaning are far superior.

Acknowledgement

Instron tensile test measurements were conducted at the Scottish Textile and Technology Centre, and photomicrography was conducted at the English Heritage Laboratories in Fortress House.

Résumé

Le traitement de textiles anciens en cellulose régénérée : deux études de cas

La présente communication porte sur les aspects positifs et négatifs de certains traitements de conservation, classiques ou plus inhabituels, qui sont appliqués aux textiles de cellulose régénérée.

Les effets du lavage et de différentes formes de traitement de désacidification sont abordés dans le cadre de deux études de cas. Et, notre démarche vise à porter des jugements pratiques sur divers traitements éventuels, en nous fondant, d'une part, sur des faits scientifiques et, d'autre part, sur des expériences personnelles.

La première étude de cas, qui est essentiellement un exemple de non-traitement, porte sur un costume datant de 1912 environ. Ce costume est constitué de tissus en soie et en rayonne au cuproammonium. Notre exposé portera surtout sur l'éventualité de désacidifier ce textile ou d'y enlever les taches d'acide, en tenant compte de facteurs comme l'effet de l'eau sur la cellulose régénérée et la diminution subséquente de sa résistance au mouillé. Nous débattrons en outre de la question de savoir s'il faut ou non laver ce textile.

La deuxième étude de cas porte sur un costume des années 20. Nous tenterons de fournir des données quantitatives sur l'effet de l'eau sur la cellulose régénérée dégradée à partir des analyses suivantes, qui ont été effectuées avant et après le lavage :

1. une évaluation du pH à la surface, afin de déterminer dans quelle mesure les taches d'acide ont été éliminées;

2. divers essais, afin de déterminer la résistance à la tension.

Des expériences sont en outre effectuées avec de la vapeur d'ammoniac, afin d'établir si cette substance permet aussi de réduire l'acidité. Et, ce genre de traitement, suivi d'un lavage, est notamment employé pour déterminer si, une fois transformés en sels, les acides s'éliminent plus facilement.

References

1. Gordon-Cook, J., *Handbook of Textile Fibres, Vol. 2, Man-made Fibres*, 4th edn. (London: Merrow Publishing Co. Ltd., 1968).

2. Hearle, J.W.S., B. Lomas, W.D. Cooke and I.J. Duerdon, *Fibre Fracture and Wear of Materials — An Atlas of Fracture, Fatigue and Durability*, Ellis Horwood Series in Polymer Science and Technology (Chichester: Ellis Horwood Ltd., 1989).

3. Cockett, S.R., *An Introduction to Man-made Fibres* (London: Pitman, 1966).

4. Sykas, Philip, personal communication, Manchester City Art Galleries, February, 1991.

Treatment of 20th-Century Rubberized Multimedia Costume: Conservation of a Mary Quant Raincoat (ca. 1967)

Clare Stoughton-Harris

The Textile Conservation Centre
Hampton Court Palace
East Molesey, Surrey
U.K.

Abstract

This paper is based on a 20-week project that was submitted in part fulfillment of a postgraduate diploma in textile conservation awarded by the Courtauld Institute of Art, University of London. The project investigated the care of rubberized costume at The Gallery of English Costume, Platt Hall, Manchester, England.

The paper demonstrates the problems of conserving 20th-century rubberized costume by looking in depth at a Mary Quant raincoat (ca. 1967). This is a composite garment comprising wool, cotton, acrylic, viscose rayon, cellulose acetate rayon, two rubberized finishes, plastic buttons, metal fastenings and adhesives.

The raincoat is of importance as an excellent example of Mary Quant's work in the late 1960s, and because it is handled frequently for study purposes. It had become soiled and showed signs of deterioration, and thus required attention to remain an important study piece. The project is of importance on a wider scale because of its multimedia nature. It illustrates many of the inherent problems associated with rubberized composite costume.

The paper sets out full characterization of all the materials concerned and assesses the deterioration mechanisms caused by: 1) inherent instability and the interaction of the component parts; 2) use, both from wear and study; and 3) environmental conditions.

Problems and solutions are evaluated in relation to treatment of other rubberized objects from the same museum collection. The technological and industrial backgrounds of such objects are investigated to allow a better understanding of the materials and degradation processes, and to support the conservation treatment that seeks to clean, reform, stabilize and support the object for storage, study and display.

Introduction

In 1985 a rubberized raincoat, designed by Mary Quant, was donated by its owner to The Gallery of English Costume, at Platt Hall in Manchester. By 1990, the raincoat's condition and stability was giving some cause for concern. This initiated an investigation into the care of rubberized objects collected at Platt Hall, which was carried out as a postgraduate research project. The Mary Quant raincoat was treated and thus formed the basis of a case study.

Platt Hall primarily houses collections of costume made or worn in England or by English people. It also has a special objective to collect examples of costume from the Manchester region, which has been the centre of the rubberized rainwear industry since its beginnings.[1] It is therefore natural that the Platt Hall collection has come to include a number of rubberized garments and accessories.

Objects range from a late-19th century rubberized cotton bathing cap (from the Cunnington collection) to a rubberized cotton raincoat designed by BIBA in the early 1970s.

The Problem

Four main areas of concern over the waterproof rubberized items of costume were identified:

• Many of the rubberized objects were of unknown materials; the waterproof coatings had not been identified.

• Some of the rubberized coatings were deteriorating: they were starting to crumble, dry out, or go sticky. Many rubberized objects had distorted and partially set, making them liable to further damage.

• Storage of the objects was a problem in that, as with all museums, space is limited and the potential harmful interaction of rubberized and other materials stored in close proximity is not well understood.

• The collections are all available to researchers on request and may be required for temporary display from time to time.

The Mary Quant raincoat served as a good illustration of these points and its treatment forms a case study. The objective of the treatment was to allow the raincoat to remain accessible to researchers and to restore as far as possible the original intended appearance of the coat. This required that the stability of the raincoat be ensured and the rate of deterioration be reduced where possible.

Description and Analysis

The raincoat (Figure 1) is of simple cut and made of black and white houndstooth fabric that has a rubberized waterproofing layer on the inside. Textile fibres were identified by microscopy.[2] Natural fibres were recognized by their morphology in longitudinal section, and the synthetic components by their interference colours when viewed between crossed polars at 45° (i.e., between the extinction positions)

Figure 1 Front view of the Mary Quant raincoat before conservation.

through a first order red plate. Solubility tests were used to substantiate the identification.[2]

The white (warp and weft) was identified as a blend of cotton, acrylic and viscose rayon, and the black (warp and weft) as a chrome dyed blend of wool, acrylic and cotton. The dye was identified by examination of a black wool fibre using a scanning electron microscope with energy dispersive X-ray analysis. The rubber layer on the inside of the houndstooth textile was identified as neoprene (polychloroprene, one of the earliest synthetic rubbers) using pyrolysis-gas chromatography (P-GC). Both natural and synthetic rubbers are usually blended with other ingredients to give specific properties. Using a scanning electron microscope with X-ray analysis, the main inorganic components of the neoprene were identified as calcium, probably in the form of calcium carbonate, and silicon or magnesium oxide, which were probably used as curing agents. Titanium was also identified, and was probably added as an oxide for brightening[3] even though, in this case, the rubberized coating was not intended to be seen.

214

The collar is faced with a black twill weave cotton that also has a rubberized coating on one side. This was identified as natural rubber using P-GC. As the rubber was black it was assumed to be filled with carbon black.

Both rubberized fabrics used in the raincoat's construction are known as single textured fabrics because the waterproofing is applied to one side of a single layer of cloth. (A double texture is the alternative type of waterproofing, and in this, two layers of fabric have a layer of rubber between them.) Both types, double and single textured rubberized fabrics, were found in objects from the collection at Platt Hall.

The whole raincoat is lined with green/brown tabby weave fabric (Figure 2), which was identified with solubility tests as cellulose acetate. *In-situ* electrolytic spot tests, as described by Townsend,[4] identified the metallic non-textile parts of the raincoat. These included coated brass underarm eyelets, a brass press-stud fastener, and a zip fastening that is composed of such metals as zinc alloy, brass, iron and nickel plate. There were also three plastic buttons. The button material was identified as casein by its

Figure 2 Inside upper back: cellulose acetate lining, rubberized cotton collar and labels.

infra-red spectrum. Analysis was carried out using an infra-red transmitting microscope attached to an FTIR spectrometer.

The raincoat was constructed using a combination of machine stitching and sticking with rubber solution.

This complex mixture of materials is typical of 20th-century material culture. The raincoat is not unique; it is a mass-produced object and like many fashion items from the 1960s, not particularly well made. There are many faults in construction. The back panel, for example, is not cut straight, which causes one shoulder to be higher than the other. Tucks are taken in the facings to prevent them from hanging below the hem, and the collar is permanently distorted by its crooked attachment.

Condition

Externally, the instability of the coat was not immediately apparent. However, it was distorted into heavy (i.e., large, deep) vertical folds and the whole coat was discoloured. On the inside of the coat where the neoprene layer was visible, the full extent of the degradation was evident.

The neoprene coating on the houndstooth fabric appeared to be in a worse state than the black rubber used on the collar. In unexposed areas, such as inside the facings, the neoprene coating was still supple and had not cracked. However, in exposed areas and areas of wear, such as around the shoulder region, it had disintegrated to leave behind a much weakened textile structure.

The difference in the state of the neoprene and the black natural rubber coatings was not just due to the fact that one was synthetic and the other was natural rubber; much was due to the compounding. The natural rubber filled with carbon black is more resistant to deterioration, whereas the white neoprene is much more vulnerable as it contains white or pale pigments and fillers. The polymer matrix is eaten away leaving behind the chalk filler. Light is unable to penetrate carbon black-filled rubbers and thus they are less vulnerable to the effects of light, particularly photo-oxidation.

No trace of antidegradents was found in the neoprene. If antidegradents had been added during the original compounding it is thought that they would have been of the phenolic type, which are non-toxic and often non-staining. They are thus suitable for rubber used in clothing. However, they are volatile, can be leached out by water, and are not particularly stable to light. They are therefore lost easily. This loss would be exacerbated in a coat exposed to heavy rain.

Because the neoprene coating was a structural stiffening element as well as a waterproof layer, its deterioration was the predominant reason for the coat's poor condition.

Distortions in the coat, caused by wear and hanging in storage (and which had become set), were clearly visible in the side panels; here the textile weave hangs on the bias. The textile weave had distorted and the neoprene had deformed by slowly flowing to the new position and then setting. This is possible at room temperature as the glass transition temperature of neoprene is -50°C. At the centre-back hem a heavy fold had also developed.

Neoprene is known to be less resistant than natural rubber to water[5] and there is evidence to suggest that when wet, neoprene becomes fairly tacky. This was apparent in the form of deposits of neoprene particles on the coat's cellulose acetate lining. The lining had also adhered lightly to the neoprene in some areas.

There was evidence of "metal poisoning" where copper might have acted as a catalyst for rubber ageing.[6] This can be seen in the underarm area around the brass eyelets (Figure 3) and behind the press-stud fastener in the centre front. However, heat and the build-up of moisture in the underarm area are thought to have been the predominant degrading factors.

The houndstooth fabric was abraded in areas of wear, such as around the cuff and centre-front opening. The discolouration of the white yarns was thought to have occurred as a result of the following three factors, which may have been linked and/or self-perpetuating:

- The presence of general soiling deposited during wear; it was established that the raincoat had never been wet- or dry-cleaned.

- Further analysis indicated that the cellulose fibres were considerably degraded and yellow/brown cellulose degradation products, resulting from acid hydrolysis and the production of aldehydes, were present. (The presence of aldehyde groups resulting from acid hydrolysis was established by a Fehlings reagent test on the cellulose fibres.) The average pH of the textile surface was in the region of pH 5.

- Although no antidegradents were found in the neoprene, it was possible that some other compounding residues had been absorbed into the textile fabric, accounting for some of the discolouration.

As mentioned before, the lining had a number of neoprene particles stuck to it, and it had also developed a rippled effect (Figure 2). It was as if the acetate had been pressed against the rubberized houndstooth fabric so that the impression of the weave was transferred onto the lining material. It then transpired, in talking to the original owner, that the coat had been dried in front of a central heating hot air vent. This would have forced the lining material against the outer fabric, thus forming the impression and in some areas making the lining stick to the neoprene. Furthermore, the cellulose acetate had discoloured as a result of gas-fume or acid fading, possibly induced by the acidity created

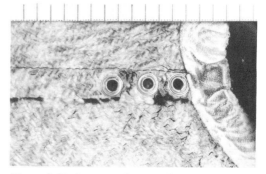

Figure 3 Underarm eyelets punched through the neoprene-coated houndstooth fabric and showing resultant degradation of the rubberized layer.

by the degrading rubber components and general soiling. There were also rips in the lining in both underarm areas.

Investigations into Possible Treatment

Preventive conservation was not considered adequate and thus a procedure involving the following actions was investigated:

- Reduce acidity and therefore limit the potential for acid hydrolysis of the textile components and reduce the possibility for further fading of the cellulose acetate

- Remove degradation products

- Remove body dirt, grease and general soiling

- Enhance the aesthetic quality of the object by removing the folds and distortions

Following the treatment, passive conservation would be implemented to improve storage and reduce damage through handling.

A cleaning treatment was investigated. It was realized that one treatment might be capable of removing the damaging factors and also reducing the distortion. A wet-cleaning treatment, known to be safe for the textiles, was proposed (the dyes were tested for wet fastness and found to be non-fugitive) with the proviso that it would only be employed if tests indicated that the natural rubber and neoprene would not be unduly affected. While investigating the reaction of the natural rubber and neoprene to a wet treatment it was realized that, like the textile elements, they might be plasticized and allow for relaxation of the folds and realignment of the raincoat to its ideal shape. It was thought that the neoprene especially would plasticize to some degree.

It became possible, therefore, to devise a treatment whereby the coat could be cleaned and reshaped in the same process. There were, however, risks involved in the wet-cleaning treatment. Whilst it was expected that the textile elements of the coat would swell in water and the neoprene would soften, the manageability of a wet raincoat was an unknown quantity.

Also, there was a minor concern that any remaining antidegradents might be lost in the wet-cleaning process; however, if any were still present, they were probably non-functioning.

Treatment

After surface cleaning with a low-powered vacuum suction unit the coat was stuffed with nylon net until it became quite rigid. The purpose of the stuffing was to help maintain the three-dimensional quality and to prevent the neoprene and textile from moving apart when wet.

In addition, a layer of non-woven spun-bonded polyester Reemay was inserted between the cellulose acetate lining and the surface of the neoprene on the main body of the coat. This was to act as a barrier layer and prevent the neoprene from sticking to the lining fabric while wet.

During the wet-cleaning process, the coat was supported on nylon mesh screens. These were also used to turn the coat.

The coat was wet-cleaned in soft water with a 0.1% non-ionic Synperonic 'N' detergent and 0.05 g per litre of sodium carboxymethyl cellulose as a suspending agent. Final rinsing was carried out using deionized water.

After about 30 minutes in the wash bath the neoprene started to plasticize. The coat was gently sponged on the front and back surfaces. A fair amount of soiling was removed in the wash water. The heavy folds in the coat relaxed with no additional manipulation. However, the weave of the back and side panels needed easing back into place.

To dry the coat, muslin was draped over it to absorb as much dirt and degradation products as possible. This proved very efficient although the constituents of the brown stain that resulted on the muslin were not identified.

Having improved the appearance and removed some possible degrading elements, further stabilization of the houndstooth fabric was required to prevent further loss of the neoprene, particularly in the shoulder region (Figure 4) and to

Figure 4 Inside shoulder region illustrating considerable loss of the neoprene surface and remaining weakened textile structure.

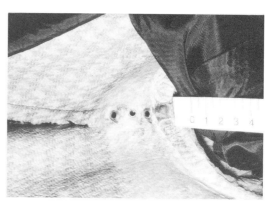

Figure 5 Underarm eyelet area after application of the spun-bonded polyester Reemay and Klucel G.

maintain the shape established in the wet treatment.

The reapplication of antioxidants, which has been suggested as a treatment for degrading rubber,[7,8] was considered for the neoprene, but abandoned at an early stage due to the unknown response of the textiles. Coatings and consolidants were considered, but a less drastic treatment was adopted. A water-soluble adhesive was used to attach a support to the textile.

The non-woven spun-bonded polyester, Reemay 2250 (of weight per unit area 17 g/m^2, i.e., the finest grade), was used as a support and adhered with a 5% solution of Klucel G (hydroxy propylcellulose) in water. Patches of the Reemay were adhered over the degraded areas of neoprene and a 5% Klucel G solution was brushed over them. The Klucel G penetrated between the patch and the object where it formed an adhesive bond. Support was given to areas where the textile was most vulnerable, which generally corresponded with the areas from which the coat would be hung. In effect the Reemay patches acted as barriers between the neoprene and the cellulose acetate lining (Figure 5).

The ripped lining in the underarm areas was supported with suitably dyed medium-weight Habutai silk held in place with stitching. A couching technique and fine polyester thread were used.

A hanging system was made to provide maximum support; to allow the object to be stored, studied and displayed; and to limit the degree of handling. The hanging mechanism was based on a system used at Platt Hall, but with some modification. It consists of an armature for the shoulders, covered with polyester wadding and cotton lawn, and a second armature to which the main body support is attached. Both armatures slide onto a vertical pole that has a hook at the top. This can be hung in the gallery cupboard, but when required for study, it can be unhooked and placed on a stand. This reduces the handling and means the researcher can view the object in the round. Detachable sleeve supports, which are secured with velcro at the shoulders, limit the manipulation necessary to remove the raincoat from its support. A case cover made with ties at the side keeps the raincoat in position while hanging. Figure 6 shows the raincoat after conservation.

The Collection of 20th-Century Costume

The treatment of the Mary Quant raincoat has brought to light some issues that need to be addressed when collecting not only rubberized costume but all costume from the 20th century.

Identification

When objects are accessioned by the museum their composition is not usually known. Whilst the identification of natural fibres and most synthetics is comparatively straightforward, the

Figure 6 Three-quarter view of the raincoat after conservation.

non-textile synthetic components are not so easily characterized, thus conservation needs may not be obvious. Simple methods can be used to identify plastics,[9] but full and reliable identification can only be carried out with instrumental methods, which are usually not within the scope of a museum conservation department.

Without the help of The Malaysian Rubber Producers' Research Association, it would not have been possible to identify and analyse the rubber compounds. It seems that staff of museums with smaller collections will have to continue to rely on the goodwill of such establishments.

With contemporary objects, information on the materials originating from the manufacturer may be available when the object is accessioned. In retrospect, it is unfortunate that such information was not recorded at the time of the raincoat's acquisition in 1985. This is particularly unfortunate because the London

Waterproof Company, which produced the coat, was dissolved in 1984.

Inherent Instability

The majority of modern costume acquisitions are mass produced. In the 1960s, it seems that the original purpose of such garments was not longevity. The decade saw the development of a fast-growing fashion business relying on built-in obsolescence. Thus garments were not made to last a lifetime, but perhaps one season only.

Some general conclusions can be drawn with specific reference to rubberized costume as a result of the survey of such objects at Platt Hall and from the treatment of the Mary Quant raincoat. Any object containing rubber is prone to fairly rapid deterioration through shelf ageing or normal oxidation of the rubber components. Oxidation is initiated by thermal, photochemical or mechanical stimuli. The behaviour of such materials is not well understood by most conservators. It may seem that the most desirable treatment is to eliminate oxygen by the use of oxygen absorbers and scavengers. However, this could be slightly impractical for costume where the object is fairly large and requires support.

The use of either double or single textured rubberized fabrics has an effect on the vulnerability of the garment to degradation. It was evident that the double textured fabrics were in better condition probably because the rubber layer was protected on both sides.

With regard to the use of dark and light rubbers, it was noted that the Mary Quant raincoat had suffered as a result of the light coloured neoprene. This can be compared with a cotton windcheater from 1956, which has a similar rubber proofing and is degrading. However, a utility cape, also single textured but proofed with a black rubber, is in very good condition.

The cut of the textile in a rubberized garment affects the stresses and hence the subsequent mechanical degradation of the rubberized coatings. Components, such as copper (in the fastenings), have a local degradative effect on the rubber. Copper acts as a catalyst for oxidation of rubber.

Environmental Observations

The behaviour of the objects in the cooler stores and the warm office, where objects are studied, was particularly apparent. When removed from the stores, most of the objects seemed fairly inflexible. However, once they had acclimatized to the warmer environment, they could be handled with greater ease. Therefore, it was proposed that the objects should have a conditioning period and not be handled immediately when removed from the stores.

Conclusion

The treatment carried out on the Mary Quant raincoat has gone some way towards seeking a solution to the problems identified at the outset of the project. However, identification of the varying materials required extensive use of external resources and an assessment of the deterioration mechanisms indicated the complexities involved in a multimedia object. The treatment initially appears successful and any immediate concern over the coat's storage is now limited. However, the long-term effects of the cleaning, reshaping and stabilization technique will require monitoring, and an assessment should be made of the storage, display and handling to which the object will be subjected. The object can be studied by researchers with minimal handling and manipulation by its new hung-storage method.

With regard to the other rubberized garments in the collections at Platt Hall, a more detailed report on their condition has been documented[10] and areas of concern pin-pointed with the possibility of conducting some minimal treatments based on those carried out on the Mary Quant raincoat. However, it is clear that preventive rather than risky active conservation methods be implemented to give adequate support and limit manipulation, so as to prevent further distortions and subsequent stress damage. It is impossible to prevent the deterioration of the rubber coatings unless oxygen is eliminated. On a more positive note, it is hoped that by giving some attention to the rubberized costume, further consideration will be given to collection policy, material identification and special handling procedures.

Acknowledgement

The author thanks the Malaysian Rubber Producers' Research Association (Hertford, England) for analysis of the rubber; The Ancient Monuments Laboratory for help; English Heritage, London, for dye identification; and The Rubber and Plastics Research Association (RAPRA), Shropshire, for analysis of casein plastic.

Résumé

Le traitement d'un costume multimédia caoutchouté du XXe siècle : la conservation d'un imperméable Mary Quant datant de 1967 environ

La présente communication se fonde sur un projet d'une durée de vingt semaines présenté en vue de l'obtention d'un diplôme d'études supérieures en conservation des textiles offert par le Courtauld Institute of Art de l'University of London. Des travaux de recherche, portant sur l'entretien des costumes caoutchoutés conservés à la Gallery of English Costume de Platt Hall, à Manchester (Angleterre), ont été effectués dans le cadre de ce projet.

Nous chercherons à montrer les problèmes que pose la conservation de costumes caoutchoutés du XXe siècle en examinant en profondeur un imperméable Mary Quant datant de 1967 environ. Vêtement créé à partir de plusieurs matériaux, il est constitué de laine, de coton, d'acrylique, de rayonne de viscose, de rayonne d'acétate de cellulose et de deux revêtements caoutchoutés, et il comporte des boutons en plastique, des attaches en métal et des adhésifs.

Cet imperméable, qui constitue un excellent exemple du travail de Mary Quant à la fin des années 60, sert souvent d'objet d'étude, et il est donc souvent manipulé. Il s'est sali et il a commencé à se détériorer avec le temps, si bien que des mesures ont dû être prises pour lui conserver son importante fonction d'objet d'étude. Le projet a par ailleurs une portée plus vaste du simple fait de la nature multimédia de cet objet, qui permet ainsi d'illustrer nombre de problèmes inhérents aux costumes caoutchoutés constitués de plusieurs matériaux.

Nous procéderons, dans le cours de notre communication, à une caractérisation complète des matières qui constituent cet objet, et nous évaluerons les mécanismes de détérioration attribuables aux facteurs suivants :

1° son instabilité inhérente et les interactions entre ses diverses parties;
2° son utilisation, résultant tout aussi bien d'une usure normale que de sa fonction d'objet d'étude;
3° les conditions ambiantes.

Nous procéderons enfin à une évaluation des problèmes soulevés et des solutions qui auront été trouvées pour y remédier, en tenant compte des autres objets caoutchoutés qui font partie de la même collection. Les antécédents technologiques et industriels de ces objets seront en outre analysés pour acquérir une meilleure connaissance des matériaux qui les composent et de leurs processus de dégradation, ainsi que pour établir les bases des traitements de conservation qui seront appliqués à ces objets pour les nettoyer, leur redonner une forme, les stabiliser et les soutenir en vue de leur mise en réserve, de leur étude et de leur exposition.

References

1. Levitt, S., "Manchester Mackintoshes: A History of the Rubberized Garment Trade in Manchester," *Textile History*, vol. 17, no. 1, 1986, pp. 51-70.

2. *The Identification of Textile Materials* (Manchester: Textile Institute, 1985).

3. Loadman, J., personal communication, Malaysian Rubber Producers' Research Association, 1991.

4. Townsend, J.H., "The Identification of Metals: Chemical Spot Tests," in: *Modern Metals in Museums*, eds. R.E. Child and J.H. Townsend (London: Institute of Archaeology Publications, 1987).

5. Blow, C.M. and C. Hepburn, *Rubber Technology and Manufacture*, 2nd edn. (London: Butterworths, 1982).

6. Buist, J.M., *Ageing and Weathering of Rubber* (Cambridge: Heffer, 1956).

7. Grattan, D.W., "Rubber Deterioration: Can Antioxidants Save Artifacts?" *International Institute for Conservation - Canadian Group Newsletter*, vol. 12, no. 4, 1987.

8. Murray, W.A.E., *The Deterioration and Conservation of Natural Rubber: A Preliminary Report*, unpublished diploma report, Durham University, 1988.

9. Mossman, S., "Simple Methods of Identifying Plastics," in: *Preprints of The Modern Materials Meeting*, Edinburgh, Scottish Society for Conservation and Restoration, 1988, pp. 41-45.

10. Stoughton-Harris, C., "The Conservation of a ca. 1967 Raincoat Designed by Mary Quant," unpublished diploma report, The Textile Conservation Centre, Hampton Court Palace, in conjunction with the Courtauld Institute of Art, University of London, 1991.

Spacesuits: NASA's Dream — Conservator's Nightmare

Mary T. Baker

Conservation Analytical Laboratory
Smithsonian Institution
Washington, D.C.
U.S.A.

Ed McManus

National Air and Space Museum
Smithsonian Institution
Washington, D.C.
U.S.A.

Abstract

Human spaceflight was a pivotal achievement in U.S. history, and the spacesuits used are testimony to the technological advances involved in reaching this goal. Unfortunately, the materials in these suits are deteriorating rapidly, endangering the only records of some stages of the space race technology. Some materials, such as certain neoprene/natural rubber blends, are degrading due to poor manufacturing techniques necessitated by the accelerated pace of the space program. Other materials, such as plasticized PVC tubing, pose a threat to the rest of the artifact. Still others are deteriorating due to conditions to which they were exposed by the National Aeronautics and Space Administration (NASA) testing and use. Present methods of display and storage of these artifacts are not sufficient to delay the degradation process and, in many cases, are accelerating it.

Treatment and storage decisions for these objects are not simple, as the suits contain a variety of materials, including metals, synthetic and natural textiles, synthetic and natural plastics, rubber and adhesives, as well as paints and varnishes; clearly, an interdisciplinary approach to their conservation is needed.

This paper will discuss the results of testing some proposed storage conditions for these materials, which were designed with large collections and low budgets in mind. Recent research on the acceleration of aging in some materials by the conditions encountered in NASA's use and testing of the suits will be reviewed. In addition, treatment considerations, with a focus on the treatments currently used on the suits, will be discussed.

Introduction

Modern materials show up in virtually every museum. However, air and space museums, unlike traditional museums, primarily collect artifacts of relatively recent manufacture. Despite the advances made in materials engineering and processing since the dawn of the space age, there is much to be learned, especially with regard to how such materials will age. Spacesuits are an example of a product of the space age, made of materials that held up to extreme conditions, that are now endangered by very ordinary environments.

It cannot be assumed that new objects and new materials require less care than the more traditional museum objects. At this time, unfortunately, it is suspected that the Smithsonian's National Air and Space Museum (NASM) may be losing some historically significant space artifacts because of a casual approach to modern materials and objects of recent manufacture. Although, for example, Apollo spacesuits worn during the first lunar mission compare in significance to the Wright Flyer, they received far less attention and storage care. It became apparent that storage, display and treatment guidelines were needed if the suits were going to survive for future generations.

Spacesuit Acquisitions[*]

On March 3, 1967, the National Aeronautics and Space Administration (NASA) and the National Air and Space Museum created an agreement. Called "Agreement between the NASA and the Smithsonian Institution concerning custody and management of NASA historical artifacts," it is registered under NASA Management Instruction 1052.85. The National Air and Space Museum was essentially given first refusal on space hardware and equipment that was retired from active service.

In 1968, the spacesuit worn by Project Mercury astronaut Alan Shepard was acquired by NASM; it was the first spacesuit of the collection. Between 1968 and 1976, many more suits were acquired due to increased activity in human spaceflight programs and the race to the moon. There was no collections rationale or preservation planning for the new space age acquisitions. Many of the suits that were collected by NASM were placed on loan to other museums, and in some instances back to NASA for exhibit in their visitor centers.

Prior to 1975, spacesuits not on exhibit or loan were stored in a warehouse in the Georgetown section of Washington, D.C. They were packed in boxes or suitcases. In 1975 the spacesuits were relocated to the Garber Facility, where they were hung on hangers and placed in tall, cedar-lined cases. It is not known whether the cedar-lined cases were used because they were available, or because the cedar lining was considered to be a preservation measure. At that time, there were no storage buildings with museum quality environmental control at the Garber Facility. Many buildings were unheated.

One of the primary reasons for accepting suits was for exhibit; the spacesuits were treated as exhibit props. Back-up suits and training suits were collected for spare parts. No thought was given to exhibit conditions, such as light levels, temperature and relative humidity, or the length of time suits could be safely exhibited. The suits were stuffed with ill-fitting department store mannequins. Spacesuits were removed from exhibit when they began to "look bad." There were no investigations into why the changes in the suits were made. Some spacesuits were used in demonstrations and were considered to be expendable.

In the absence of a collections rationale, and a collections maintenance program, a rather interesting consensus developed regarding the significance of the various types of suits. Flown suits (suits that were actually worn by astronauts on space missions) were considered to be historically significant and therefore worthy of preservation. Unflown suits (suits worn in training or intended as back-up suits) were much less significant, and were considered to be expendable. The perceived categories of significance provided a convenient excuse for tolerating poor storage conditions and consumptive use, and scavenging for spare parts.

Spacesuit Development[**]

Long before the space program was a reality, suits were being designed to keep humans alive in low pressure environments. Early achievements were made in the early 1930s, when altitude records were being made and broken by balloonists and pilots. During the 1930s and 1940s, pressure suits were developed for short-term emergency use by jet pilots. None were very mobile when used in low pressure, nor were they comfortable. In the early 1950s the U.S. Air Force set out to fulfill a requirement that a pressure suit be developed for pilots of the B-52 plane. The suit had to be comfortable enough to be used for many hours at a time and flexible enough to allow the pilot sufficient movement for flying. At the same time, the U.S. Navy was developing its own high altitude suit with similar requirements. Thus, in the early 1960s, when John F. Kennedy proclaimed the need for a space program that would eventually put a man on the moon, decades of research on spacesuit development had already been completed.

---

* A more complete discussion of the acquisition and treatment philosophies has been given by Baker and McManus elsewhere.[1]

** There are few histories of spacesuit development; the most complete is that of Mallan.[2] Another helpful resource comes in the person of Lillian Kozloski at the Smithsonian Institution.[3]

The suits for the first missions (Mercury) were modified Navy high-altitude suits with a ventilated undergarment developed by the Air Force. They consisted of a rubberized cloth suit that could be pressurized, an outer garment and a close-fitting helmet. They were very difficult to move in, especially when in use in a vacuum, but this was considered a minor problem, since the Mercury astronauts would complete their missions sitting in their capsules. The suit was mainly an emergency protection from accidental loss of pressure during the mission. The outer layer of the suits was an aluminized cloth, which, it was hoped, would protect the astronaut from radiation and extremes of heat during orbit and especially during atmosphere re-entry (Figure 1).

Figure 1 *Mercury spacesuit, worn by L. Gordon Cooper. Notice the aluminized cloth exterior and foam padded helmet. Photo courtesy of NASA.*

The next set of missions (Gemini) put a new demand on the suits. The astronaut needed to be able to perform work in the spacesuit inside and outside the capsule. Previously, attempts had been made to solve the problem of bending a suit that was inflated, but none of the designed systems were satisfactory. The inflated suits, like balloons, were very difficult to bend, causing near immobility of the astronaut. The solution for the Gemini suits was to use a similar rubber-coated fabric bladder to that used in the Mercury missions, which covered most of the astronaut like a loose wet suit. This bladder was restrained from expanding under pressure by a net (originally Dacron, later Teflon), which decreased the ballooning effect, but was still flexible, allowing bending of the joints. The aluminized outer garment used in Mercury was used only in the prototype Gemini suits; it was replaced by Nylon and Nomex outer layers and aluminized Mylar inner layers. The Gemini suits had increased abrasion resistance and mobility, and could be used for the first spacewalks (Figure 2).

Figure 2 *Gemini spacesuit, once worn by Edwin White, now on display in NASM. The outer layer is a facsimile, made by David Clark Company; the original was damaged by exhibit and has been retired. Photo by Virginia Pledger.*

The Apollo missions were the culmination of the race to the moon; the suits needed not only to protect the astronaut on the surface of the moon, but also to allow travel far from the capsule or lunar lander. Modifications on the suits included improved helmet design and a liquid coolant garment (LCG) for temperature control. The LCG was a union suit with tubing running throughout; water flowed through the tubes, carrying away excess heat from the astronaut's body. The LCG was a great improvement over the Gemini method, which used air circulation for cooling. The improved helmet design eliminated the close-fitting foam cushion around the head that had been used in Mercury and Gemini helmets; this allowed for more mobility inside the helmet (Figure 3).

Figure 3 Apollo spacesuit.

Shuttle suits had added requirements, which included greater ease of donning and the capacity for reuse. The previous suits were made for one-time use only, and for a particular astronaut. Now, the suits were to be made in generic sizes, with, it was hoped, a long shelf life. The traditional zipper construction was abandoned for teflon seals, which were more flexible and allowed the astronauts to dress themselves and to dress in less time.

The above evolution of suits is a mere outline of all the changes that took place in spacesuits over the course of years. While the changes can be followed by examination of the flown suits, this does not tell the whole story. Many ideas and improvements were tested on prototype suits; some of these changes were adopted for the final suits, others were not. Some suits were of a completely different design, having been part of a contract bid from a new company. A collection of only the suits used on missions does not give a complete story of the inventiveness that went into suit design.

Research is required at this time to gather historic information about the design, construction and testing of spacesuits. Time is of the essence because some of the companies that were involved with spacesuit research and development no longer exist, and researchers who were involved are growing older. Research is also important to the understanding of the deterioration process. That information will enable us to develop better exhibit and storage techniques.

Research on the NASM Suits

The materials in the spacesuits that were showing the most degradation are the soft rubber pieces, such as gloves, boots, linings and gaskets, and the adhesive used to laminate the aluminized fabrics. The rubber parts were softening and flowing, then hardening irreversibly into distorted shapes. The adhesive used in laminating the aluminum to the fabric was becoming very brittle and flaking off, along with the aluminum. Other problems included the poly(vinyl chloride) tubing on the LCGs, which was starting to weep plasticizer; the foam inside the Mercury and Gemini helmets was hardening, and the textiles showed wear spots and discoloration.

The initial work on this project had centered around following the free radical population, in an attempt to determine if there were still reactive sites in the materials. This was a matter of concern since, in the presence of oxygen, free radicals cause oxidation and chain scission, but in the absence of oxygen, free radicals cause crosslinking, as has been discussed in more detail by Schnabel.[4] This information could be important in choosing an oxygen-free storage atmosphere. Electron Spin Resonance (ESR) had been used to show very high populations of free radicals in the glove materials, which were determined to be very stable; most likely they were the result of the antioxidant in the gloves having scavenged the radicals. Since these stable radicals are not likely to be a threat to the suit materials, other causes for their breakdown were investigated.

It was noted in a survey of the suits that many of the unflown suits were in much worse condition than the flown suits. Some of this difference was attributed to the respectful handling of the flown suits by NASA and NASM, yet some of the problems could not be explained by poor handling alone. Some background research showed that extensive artificial aging testing had been conducted on the natural rubber/neoprene blends as well as on the aluminizing adhesive, the results of which predicted that the materials should have fared better than they did, even after storage at high temperatures.

More background research revealed that most of the unflown suits were used in training the astronauts for space; some of this training included wearing the suits in a swimming pool to simulate maneuvering at low gravity. These pools were kept chlorinated; some sources recalled using calcium hypochlorite. (Such pools are still being used for the same purpose by the present manufacturer of space shuttle suits.[5])

Since hypochlorite is a strong oxidizer, it seemed likely that residues from the swimming pool tests could be accelerating the degradation of the spacesuit materials. Since natural rubber seemed to be the suit material that was suffering the most from aging, it was a logical choice for the first material tested. The natural rubber was cast on aluminum foil sheets from solution and allowed to dry. These films could then be monitored by Fourier Transform Infrared Spectroscopy (FTIR), using a microscope attachment in reflectance mode. The dried films were very irregular; they were examined under the microscope and the smoothest areas were chosen. These areas were marked with the tip of a disposable pipette, which coincidentally is the same size as the analysis area of the FTIR-microscope. (In-depth information on the FTIR-microscope theory and methods as they relate to conservation has been given by Baker, von Endt, Hopwood and Erhardt.[6]) With this mark as a guide, the microscope could be set to analyze the exact same spot each time; the spectra taken from such a spot on a given day would overlay perfectly with spectra taken from the same spot one week later.

Several natural rubber/aluminum foil sheets were dipped in simulated pool water, while others were dipped in plain distilled water. The oxidation of the samples was monitored hourly during artificial aging at 60°C, 70°C, 80°C and 90°C for various periods. The FTIR spectra were collected, and the absorbance of the carbonyl band was measured. The spectra showed the greatest difference between pool and distilled water at 90°C and no significant difference at 60°C (Figure 4).

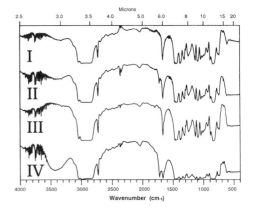

Figure 4 FTIR-microspectra of polyisoprene: (I) dipped in distilled water, unaged; (II) dipped in distilled water, aged at 80°C for 3.5 hours; (III) dipped in pool water, unaged; (IV) dipped in pool water, aged at 80°C for 3.5 hours. Note the peak at 1725 cm[-1] is equal for the two unaged samples, but is much greater for the pool-dipped aged sample than the distilled-water aged sample, indicating greater oxidation at that point, due to the hypochlorite in the pool water. Also note the growth of the broad peak at around 3400 cm[-1], which suggests formation of peroxides.

While this is an interesting phenomenon, if the increased oxidation rate of the rubber chain is not causing a like increase in chain scission, then the mechanical properties of the rubber are unlikely to have been changed by the hypochlorite residue. In other words, the additional oxidation seen by the FTIR could be in the form of stable carbonyls on the rubber chain, and no extra chain scission would actually be happening. Molecular weight determinations would be necessary to monitor the chain scission, as well as any other molecular weight changes, such as crosslinking. These molecular weight changes were monitored by the use of a Size Exclusion Chromatograph (SEC), made up of a multi-angle laser light scattering detector

(MALLS) and ultrastyragel columns. The columns included a linear, mixed bed column, able to separate molecules by molecular size for a range of molecular weights from 500 to 20,000,000. An additional column, useful for low molecular weight molecules, was added to increase the sensitivity on the low end of this range.

The pool-treated and distilled water-treated rubber samples were analyzed by the SEC-MALLS set-up and the results indicated a difference in the molecular weight distribution between the distilled water- and pool-treated rubber samples. Not all of the samples have been analyzed to date, so there are no correlations that can be made with time or temperature, as yet.

Conclusion

These experiments show that exposure to calcium hypochlorite will accelerate the oxidation of rubber, apparently both by decreasing the induction time and increasing the rate of reaction. Ramifications of these findings pose the following questions: Will storage in nitrogen slow or stop this process (or will it favor another reaction, such as crosslinking)? Is there another way to stop it (such as cold storage or chemical treatment)? These areas will be studied in the future. Other future plans include studying some of the other materials that are in trouble, such as neoprene, the nitrile adhesive used in making the aluminized fabric, and the foam inside the helmets.

In summary, NASA has a collection of historically important spacesuits, most of which have not received the best handling in the past. In this collection, a subgroup exists of suits that have not been considered important because they were not used on missions. However, many of them contain intermediate stages of development, which also appeared in the mission suits; considering the amount of records that have been destroyed by NASA and the suit manufacturers, these non-mission suits may be the only record of the course of these developments. Most of these suits have probably been exposed to a strong oxidizer in the form of calcium hypochlorite in addition to the careless handling they received before the recent

reappraisal. While this work may have found an answer to why the non-mission suits are deteriorating faster, the need to look for possible ways to stop this deterioration still exists. In addition, work will continue to test storage methods for all the suits not on exhibit; at present, they are housed at low temperature, in the dark, with internal support and an air filtering system. Questions of interest that have come about include the following: Will it be cost-effective to contain the suits in bags with an oxygen-free atmosphere? Can NASM demand proper mannequins (Figure 5) for the entire collection? What restoration, if any, should be allowed of the suits?

These questions apply to the suits on exhibit, as well. Would it be possible to acquire air-tight, oxygen-free, UV-screening, temperature-controlled display cases? While this goal may be unrealistic, NASM is reviewing its loan policy

Figure 5 Virginia Pledger (right) and Lillian Kozloski installing mannequin head in Gemini suit helmet. Virginia Pledger designed and constructed mannequins (under contract for NASM) that fit the new criteria for display of spacesuits as given by Baker and McManus.[1]

and recalling some of its suits for re-evaluation. The idea is to display the suits for public education of the history they represent without further endangering the only surviving artifacts of the human space race.

An interesting development, as a result of this project, has been the contacts that have been established with companies currently manufacturing spacesuits. We are concerned with the preservation of historic spacesuits while the manufacturers have a desire to extend the useful working life of spacesuits currently in service. Both of us are, for once, very much interested in the same goals; the next generation may, as a result, have more comprehensive and stable documentation of the advances being made in human spaceflight today.

Résumé

Les combinaisons spatiales : un rêve pour la NASA, mais un cauchemar pour les sécialistes de la restauration

Le lancement d'engins spatiaux habités a été un événement marquant de l'histoire des États-Unis, et les combinaisons spatiales que portaient alors les astronautes témoignent des progrès technologiques sur lesquels reposait cette réussite. Néanmoins, les matériaux qui entrent dans la composition de ces combinaisons se détériorent très rapidement, menaçant ainsi l'existence même des seuls objets qui témoignent encore de certaines étapes de la course technologique de l'espace. La dégradation de ces matériaux — des amalgames de caoutchouc naturel et de néoprène, par exemple — s'explique tantôt par la mauvaise qualité des techniques de fabrication auxquelles on a dû, dans la course effrénée du programme spatial, avoir recours. Tantôt, comme dans le cas des tubes de polychlorure de vinyle plastifié, ils constituent une menace pour le reste de l'objet. Et dans d'autres cas encore, ils se détériorent à cause des mauvaises conditions auxquelles ils ont été soumis, lors de leur mise à l'essai ou de leur utilisation, à la National Aeronautics and Space Administration (NASA). Les méthodes qui sont actuellement mises en application pour l'exposition et la mise en réserve de tels objets ne sont pas suffisantes pour retarder la dégradation et, dans nombre de cas, elles l'accélèrent. Or, il n'est par ailleurs pas facile de déterminer le genre de traitement ou le mode de mise en réserve qui leur conviendra le mieux, car ces objets contiennent des matériaux très variés, dont des métaux, des textiles synthétiques et naturels, des plastiques synthétiques et naturels, du caoutchouc, des adhésifs, des peintures et des vernis; et il conviendra donc, de toute évidence, d'adopter une approche multidisciplinaire pour assurer leur conservation. Nous traiterons donc, dans la présente communication, des résultats de l'essai de diverses propositions qui, visant de grandes collections tout en tenant compte d'un budget restreint, définissaient les conditions de mise en réserve de ces matières. Nous passerons ensuite en revue les plus récents travaux de recherche sur le vieillissement accéléré de certaines matières qui serait attribuable aux conditions dans lesquelles elles sont mises à l'essai ou utilisées à la NASA. Enfin, nous traiterons de certaines considérations relatives aux traitements de conservation, en mettant tout particulièrement l'accent sur ceux qui sont actuellement appliqués aux combinaisons spatiales.

References

1. Baker, M.T. and E. McManus, "History, Care, and Handling of America's Spacesuits: Problems in Modern Materials," *Journal of the American Institute for Conservation*, vol. 31 (1992) pp. 77-85.

2. Mallan, Lloyd, *Suiting Up for Space: The Evolution of the Spacesuit* (New York: The John Day Company, 1971).

3. Kozloski, L., *Suited Up for Living and Working in Space: U.S. Spacesuits of the National Air and Space Museum*, NASM Artifact Series, Smithsonian Press, unpublished manuscript.

4. Schnabel, W., *Polymer Degradation, Principles and Practical Applications* (Munich: Hasner International, 1981) pp. 86-89.

5. Gomes, Cheryl, personal communication, ILC Dover, March, 1991.

6. Baker, M., D. von Endt, W. Hopwood and D. Erhardt, "FTIR Microspectrometry: A Powerful Conservation Analysis Tool," *Preprints of the 16th Annual AIC Meeting*, June 1-5, 1988, New Orleans, Louisiana (Washington, D.C.: American Institute of Conservation, 1988) pp. 1-13.

Conservation of Paintings on Delaminated Plywood Supports

Donald C. Williams

Conservation Analytical Laboratory
Smithsonian Institution
Washington, D.C.
U.S.A.

Ann Creager

National Museum of American Art
Smithsonian Institution
Washington, D.C
U.S.A.

Abstract

As industrial production of modified wood materials developed in the early 20th century, plywood panels and other composites were used by artists as substitutes for more traditional art materials. Nowhere was this more evident than in painting, where artists employed plywood as a cheaper, more uniform, and versatile replacement for solid lumber substrates in panel paintings. Now, a half century or more later, as these modern substrates begin to deteriorate, those caring for these artifacts are faced with an entirely new set of problems.

These problems became evident in a group of paintings by the American artist William H. Johnson (1901 to 1970) in the collections of the National Museum of American Art. Johnson, who was active in both the U.S. and Europe between 1926 and 1946, was academically trained but chose to paint in a style approaching the vernacular. Probably for reasons of economy, Johnson executed several paintings on plywood sheets between 1939 and 1944. Near the end of his life, ill health forced his hospitalization. At that time and after his death, a dispute over the disposition of his belongings led to the abandonment of several of these paintings for approximately 10 years. For some of this period the paintings were probably on the docks of New York City. Extended exposure to the unregulated outdoor environment functioned as an accelerated aging test on the paintings and their substrates, resulting in gross delamination, buckling, and fracturing of the plywood laminae.

A planned exhibition of Johnson's work forced conservators at the National Museum of American Art and the Conservation Analytical Laboratory of the Smithsonian Institution to explore treatment options for the paintings. Several procedures were conceived and designed specifically for the treatment of the painting supports, but could be applied to any wood laminar structure. The two primary options for the treatments were to either reintegrate the existing artifact as a whole, or to remove the lamina bearing the paint layer.

This paper discusses the ethical and technical issues surrounding the artifacts and their treatments, reviews the models for each of the major options and subsequent variants considered, and illustrates the treatments as they were finally executed.

Introduction

In late 1989, the final checklist of paintings for the major show of William H. Johnson's later works was received in the National Museum of American Art laboratory. Of the 39 paintings from the collection that were requested for the show, 10 were on plywood supports. They were in various states of delamination and structural deterioration. Deletion of any of these works from the show was not a consideration, since they all were crucial images, and included several of the artist's masterworks from the period. We knew that this show would travel, probably extensively, and that although venue selection might be subject to our opinion, selection would not rest on conservation standards alone. Therefore, for the most severely damaged paintings, major treatment was the only option.

Before discussing the specific problems, materials and treatments, it is worth taking a brief look at the life of the artist. It is not easy to understand how such a powerfully original painter has achieved little recognition to date unless it is due to the fact that he was black and he was not a part of any movement, school or group. However, it is easy to understand, from the sequence of events in his life, how a large body of his innovative and spiritually lyrical works came to fall into such profound disrepair.

William H. Johnson was born in the small town of Florence, South Carolina in 1901. His schooling was intermittent and although his talent was recognized and encouraged by several teachers, he was unable to realize his ambitions in the segregated South. At 17, he moved to New York and eventually entered the five-year program at the National Academy of Design. The artist Charles Hawthorne was his teacher, mentor, and friend, and upon his graduation in 1926, Hawthorne personally raised enough money to send him to Europe for three years.

Johnson spent one year in Paris, where he was influenced by Soutine, the European Expressionist, and had several one-man shows. He then settled in the south of France and painted while traveling extensively through Europe. He returned to the United States and set up a studio in Harlem, but went back to Denmark in 1930 and married Holcha Krake, a Danish weaver and ceramicist. It was during this time in Denmark that he painted many of his most boldly beautiful works, depicting eruptive force scenes of harbors, fjords, mountains and people, with a wildly rich palette. Because poverty was always with him, most of these paintings were executed on a coarse burlap feed bag material, which is now in a very fragile and damaged condition.

After eight years of traveling and painting through Europe and North America and with World War II looming, Johnson and his wife returned to New York. There he began his series of interpretations of black life in Harlem and the rural South, depicted in a simple flat style. The paintings on plywood are from this period between 1939 and 1944.

In the early 1940s, Johnson's life took on tragic proportions. A fire burned his studio apartment and, in 1943, Holcha died of cancer. Johnson, who had already started to show signs of erratic behavior, now began to clearly manifest the beginnings of a debilitating mental illness. He made at least one return trip to Denmark with all his paintings and possessions in tow but was eventually sent back to New York in 1947, and was immediately placed in a mental hospital on Long Island. He never painted again. He remained in the hospital for 23 years until his death in 1970.

It can only be imagined how those paintings were transported back and forth between continents or how they were stored in a dockside warehouse following Johnson's committal to the institution. It is this more than nine-year period of extended exposure to an unregulated environment that has functioned as an accelerated aging test on the paintings and their substrates, resulting in loss, delamination, buckling and fracturing of the plywood laminae and the generally sad condition of all of these works.

In 1956, all of Johnson's works were turned over to the Harmon Foundation, an organization that had long sought to make Johnson a recognized artist. When the Foundation closed in 1967, over 1,100 paintings, drawings and prints were given to the National Collection of Fine Arts, now known as the National Museum of American Art, which is part of the Smithsonian Institution.

Since the collection was acquired, many of the Johnson paintings have been treated. This most recent show consists of works from his last active years. Ten of the paintings on plywood support required treatment. Of these, four required removal of the back plies and major structural work with attachment to new supports. Four others received localized structural treatment without removal of the original plies. The remaining two paintings had been remounted and treated 21 years ago with subsequent structural failure. These required reversal of the old treatment and employment of the current one.

Some generalizations of the artist's materials and techniques can be made. All 10 paintings are in oil medium. Handling and application of the medium vary from those where it is simple and direct to those where paint is thickly applied with brushed or palette knife impasto. This variance of application bears no relation to subsequent structural condition. There is some cracking, cleavage and paint loss on both thinly and thickly applied surfaces, although generally the paint layers remain in good condition.

By the time these paintings were done, Johnson seemed to have abandoned the use of his more traditional lead white and calcite grounds. These panels are all primed with a pinkish-brown or dark-brown paint layer on both sides of the support. This preparation layer is gritty on some paintings, and on others it is thinly applied and does not obscure the texture of the wood.

While most of the paintings had no varnish layer, several had a dull streaked, slightly discolored coating that had been randomly applied. On all, there was a substantial layer of embedded dirt and grime as well as fibers and chips of paint stuck to the surfaces from other paintings that had leaned and pressed against them in storage.

It is in the choice of plywood supports for each of these paintings where a more direct correlation can be made between the quality and type of material and the resulting vulnerability and ultimate damage sustained. The construction of each of the plywood panels was balanced, in that they consisted of an odd number of plies (this is almost always true for plywood). The two-face plies were oriented in the same direction while that of the core ply was at a right angle to them. (Note: There were only three-ply panels). The flanking-face plies were of the same kind and quality of wood, and presumably had the same moisture content. However, those panels that sustained less distortion and separation between plies were of a uniformly thick three-ply construction. Their thickness was a total of 5 mm. Those panels with the most severe delamination, buckling and

warping were ones with a total thickness of just over 3.5 mm: these thinner panels were also of much poorer grade and fabrication quality, and contained knots and surface imperfections.

For purposes of brevity, only one painting from each of the three categories of treatment is discussed.

Local Structural Treatment: *Folk Family* (1939 to 1944)

This painting was on a 5 mm-thick plywood support. Both sides of the support were primed with a brown gritty paint layer. The paint was generously applied with considerable impasto. There was no varnish or surface coating. The condition of the support was poor, with broad convex warps creating planar distortion. All corners had delaminated and there were losses in one or more of the ply layers at all corners. The top horizontal edge was completely delaminated and buckled and it was broken up by several vertical cracks and splits in the uppermost half. The splits varied from 1.3 cm to 15 cm. There were losses of support and design layers along the top edge as well. Despite the poor condition of the support, the paint layers remained in good condition. Although some vertical hairline cracks were present in the upper half of the painting, most of the paint was stable and secure. The surface texture was rough, due possibly to the gritty priming layer, and the paint was unevenly matte and glossy. There were small damages and gouges randomly throughout, some surface abrasion, and numerous scattered edge losses. The surface had paint spatters and a substantial layer of heavily embedded dirt and grime.

Treatment
The surface dirt was removed with a 5% solution of di-ammonium citrate in distilled water followed with a distilled water rinse. Overall planar distortions were reduced by placing the painting face up over moistened blotters, then covering it with a sheet of glassine, a thick felt blanket and finally a sheet of masonite and heavy weights. The delamination along the upper edge was consolidated with hot liquid hide glue (315 g) injected between the plies, and then the edge placed between padded clamps

for flattening. A filling compound of sawdust mixed with CM Bond M3 [poly(vinyl acetate) emulsion] was used to replace the missing corners and other sections. On the front of the painting these fills were subsequently covered with a layer of gesso. A thin brush coat of Soluvar Matte Varnish was applied as an isolating layer and the inpainting carried out with dry pigments and AYAC [poly(vinyl acetate) resin] in ethanol over a base of watercolor. This painting and the three others treated in the same way will continue to be monitored for any further planar distortion or delamination, but it is our hope that more drastic treatment will never be necessary.

Major Structural Treatment: *Going to Market* (1939 to 1944)

This panel painting, shown in Figure 1, represents those paintings that were most severely warped, buckled, split and delaminated. There was no question of a partial or remedial approach to treatment. The fragility and thinness of the combined plies made these paintings difficult even to turn and handle. Typical examples of damages common to each are described in the following paragraphs.

The support was of three-ply construction, the grains of the face plies extending in the same direction while that of the core ply was at a right angle to them. All three plies were of the same thickness and kind of wood. The total combined thickness of plies was less than 3.5 mm. The quality or grade of wood was very poor, each ply having numerous inherent defects, such as knots and voids. There was overall warping of the panel as a unit and inter-ply warping and buckling. (The condition of the panels is shown in Figures 2 and 3.) These warps and buckles were running with the grain of each ply. The paint-layer face ply was completely split down the middle, the edges of the split forming a cupped ridge at the apex. Four vertical splits, 2.5 cm to 5.1 cm in length, ran from the bottom upward on the right side and each individual split was severely warped in a convex manner. There was complete loss of face and back ply along the right side, up to 10.2 cm of image, exposing the buckled core ply. In several areas, the core ply had split and pushed up on the painted top ply, causing it to split and sustain splintered losses.

Figure 1 Going to Market *by William H. Johnson. Raking light shows central split and complete loss of face plies exposing buckled and split core plywood.*

Figure 2 Detail of Going to Market *showing washboard-like warping of vertical splits and ply loss.*

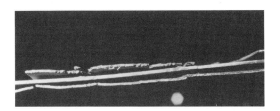

Figure 3 Cross-sectional view of typical inter-ply delamination found on all the paintings in varying degrees.

The thinly applied priming layer was a pinkish-brown paint with a somewhat gritty texture. The paint was of moderate thickness with some areas of brushed and palette knife impasto. There was random abrasion and small paint losses, and a thin, streaked surface coating that was gritty and uneven in its application. Dirt and grime were embedded in this coating as well as on the paint surface, giving an overall gray appearance.

Treatment
The painting was cleaned and areas of insecure and semi-detached paint were infused with Beva 371 [poly(ethylene-vinylacetate)] and set down with heat. We decided that the plies of this painting support were too thin to attempt delamination first, so the entire panel was pre-flattened as a unit. The painting was placed face down on a 10 mm-thick sheet of closed-cell neoprene. A sheet of glassine separated the neoprene and the painting surface. The back of the panel was misted generously with water and blotters were laid on top. Plexiglass sheets were placed over this and weighted. This process was repeated over many days with misting, blotter changes, and gradually increasing weights. In some areas of closely-spaced warps, large padded clamps were used.

When the painting was as flat as seemed possible and completely dry, it was placed face up. The surface was then faced with Tosa Tenjugo Japanese tissue and wheat flour paste and when this was dry, another facing with cheese cloth was applied with an Acryloid B-67 emulsion composed of 10% water, 1% aerosol OT (a clear liquid containing 10% diacetyl sodium sulfosuccinate, water and mutual solvent), and 89% Acryloid B-67 stock solution. The painting was again placed face down on the same

cushioned surface and a large spatula used to remove the back and core plies one layer at a time.

Treatment of Remounted Paintings

The next two paintings to be treated were those in which treatments carried out more than 20 years ago had failed (as a result of a number of factors combined). Like those described above, these older treatments had also involved removal of two plies, but unlike the current approach no flattening of warped or buckled areas was carried out. In the original treatment each painting had been mounted with a wax-resin adhesive to different supports. One painting was adhered to a strainer-supported masonite board, and the other to an aluminum-honeycomb panel. The wax adhesive also served to fill the voids where the warped original support did not make contact with the new support. In some places the wax was almost 5.5 mm thick. Failure of the bond between materials on these paintings had been accelerated due to an active lending program that allowed the paintings to travel to venues having inadequate temperature and humidity controls.

Treatment
These paintings were removed from their supports and the wax-resin scraped off and leached from the plywood with solvent until clean. Imperfections were sanded, and warps and buckled areas were flattened with moisture and pressure.

It was at this point in treatment that the Conservation Analytical Laboratory of the Smithsonian Institution was called upon to help work out a new support system with careful attention and debate given to the choices of adhesives.

General Treatment Considerations for Plywood Artifacts

Degraded artifacts constructed of plywood pose a vexing conservation problem that requires careful consideration of several factors. If the problem with the artifact is not defined accurately, the proposed or executed treatments can range from those that are inspired and successful to those that are based on ignorance and therefore doomed to fail.

The major considerations are the history, technology and character of the original raw material and its subsequent utilization in the artifact. Klim's recent article on composite wood materials includes a review of plywood history.[1] An understanding of the nature of plywood is vital to responding appropriately to its deterioration.

Next to consider is the artist's motive or intent in using the material in question. Why was this particular material selected rather than another? There are several probable "correct answers," which take account of cost, convenience, availability of materials, uniformity, and stability of materials. Usually, all of these factors play a role in the artist's selection of material, and plywood paneling is considered like all other artists' materials. Plywood was (and is) a cheap, easily worked, planar alternative to solid or joined-wood panel supports for painters and also serves the more widespread needs of cabinet-making and related crafts.

Another critical step for paintings on plywood supports is careful evaluation of the object: how delaminated is the structure, how stable is that which remains, and how did the damage occur?

Finally, how does the presence or lack of plywood as a raw material affect the interpretation of the object? For three-dimensional objects, such as furniture or sculpture, the answer is pretty clear — the plywood is an integral part of the object and without it there is no artifact. For paintings on plywood, however, the answer may be very different. Traditionally, art historians and restorers have considered that the painted image *is* the artifact and the plywood is simply the support for that image. Therefore, while the plywood substrate for a painting may remain important for ancillary reasons, it may not necessarily be inviolable, as would be the case with most three-dimensional objects constructed of plywood.

Removal Versus Reintegration

There are two main directions for treatment of delaminated plywood. The plywood support can be considered expendable and the important lamina (i.e., that containing the painted image), can be removed from the degraded structure and remounted onto another substrate. Alternatively, the plywood support may be considered integral to the artifact and be reintegrated with the important lamina into a single unified element. Both general approaches are justifiable based on the specific circumstances of the treatment.

In the case of the Johnson paintings, there were degrees of damage that varied from virtual delamination and complete loss of structural integrity to minor, localized separations. In keeping with this range of deterioration, a number of specific treatment options were formulated within the two major directions already mentioned. These treatment options were tempered by cost and time limitations and by the possibility that the paintings conservators conducting the treatments would be more familiar, more comfortable and more skilled with manipulating paint and canvas than wood and the adhesive systems best suited to wood. This possibility fostered a desire for a "low-tech" approach requiring little woodworking expertise yet allowing for control over the process. By "low-tech" we mean that the process should be straightforward with simple steps and with little chance for error in preparation and over the course of the treatment. In addition, there were the usual concerns over "retreatability." Finally, as would be expected in treating painted wood, there were requirements for minimizing encroachment by water and organic solvents into the object. Introducing water-based adhesives into a hygroscopic material raised the risk of extreme stress through swelling and shrinking, and solvent-based adhesive systems have negative effects on the paint film and on the conservators.

Testing Treatment Methods with Sample Panels

In order to explore our ideas for treatment, a group of mock painting-on-plywood panels were created for sacrificial testing. A sheet of plywood similar to that used in the paintings to be treated was purchased, cut into 60 cm squares and painted. These squares were then subjected to extremely harsh environmental conditions in order to induce the delamination observed in the Johnson paintings. Unfortunately, the quality of the plywood purchased for the mock-up panels clearly surpassed that used by Johnson. It is a credit to modern adhesive and plywood technology that after 15 cycles of 72 hours of submersion in water followed by 72 hours in the oven at 60°C, the panels were still in generally good condition. There was widespread cracking and cupping on the surface and some localized delamination, but nothing approaching the damage expected. The panels were nevertheless extremely useful in evaluating the physical manifestations of our ideas. A number of treatment processes using these panels are described below.

Remounting the Decorated Lamina

In the instances where the painting support was badly damaged or mutilated, remounting the painted surface on a new support was a viable option. The main questions were: 1) onto what material will the painting be mounted? and 2) how will the painting be adhered to the new support?

Several supports were considered for remounting the painting once it was removed from the remaining fragments of original substrate. Much of the decision making for this option was influenced by the earlier failure of a remounting treatment onto aluminum honeycomb that was used for one of the Johnson paintings. Having little experience with aluminum honeycomb and a dislike of superimposing materials of greatly dissimilar properties, we decided to limit the choice of new substrate materials to wood or wood-like materials, which were sympathetic to the original fabrication, nature, and intent of the artifacts. The paintings were on wood, albeit a modified form of wood, and in our opinion, the best solution to the problem was to approach it as a wood problem — we wanted to remain with a system that was based on wood-glued-to-wood. This led to our process and material selections.

We narrowed our scope of options for new supports to include only materials with the same properties as plywood. This was not only because the original artifacts were made of plywood, but also because plywood has many inherent benefits. These benefits, which have been mentioned previously, include cost, availability, ease of manipulation, the ability to work quickly or slowly and dimensional stability. To use these properties to their fullest, the new supports were designed around high-quality plywood.

Torsion-box Support Panels

One of the earliest proposals we considered was to remount the lamina onto a solid plywood sheet. However, the weight of plywood thick enough to maintain planarity proved to be excessive for safe handling and exhibition. We then turned to the idea of improving the properties of plywood by utilizing "torsion-box panels." These have been used for some time in the fabrication of custom furniture. Torsion boxes are constructed of ribs and thin-facing laminae that act together as a panel comprised of a series of tiny I-beams. The weight of the support panel is reduced greatly but the panel is still nearly as strong as a solid plywood substrate. Our hollow-core torsion boxes were designed and fabricated using marine/aircraft grade mahogany and poplar plywood faces over wooden ribs (Figure 4). The structure of these support panels conceptually is remarkably similar to that of aluminum-honeycomb panels, that is, their strength, stiffness and lightness are outstanding and they can be built to any size. (They were made as 60 cm squares for the

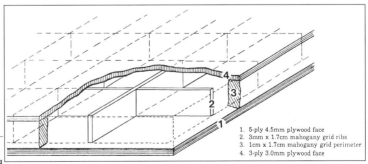

1. 5-ply 4.5mm plywood face
2. 3mm x 1.7cm mahogany grid ribs
3. 1cm x 1.7cm mahogany grid perimeter
4. 3-ply 3.0mm plywood face

Figure 4 A cutaway diagram of the torsion-box support panel.

mock-paintings.) The torsion-box panels had the additional advantages of being easy and cheap to build and made from material very similar to that of the original plywood supports. In overall construction, however, the torsion-box panel was quite different.

Construction of the Remounting Panels

Probably the most critical factor for assuring a high quality panel is to make sure that the vertical dimension of all ribs (i.e., the rib dimension determining the thickness of the panel) is identical. The easiest way to achieve this is by surfacing a board using a power planer and cutting thin strips from this board for all rib-stock. Since mahogany, *Swietenia spp.,* has long been highly regarded for its dimensional stability, it was selected for the ribs and prepared to a thickness of 12 mm. Interior ribs of 3 mm and perimeter ribs 25 mm wide were cut from the 12 mm-thick prepared stock using a table saw with a fine-tooth blade.

In most small-scale wood construction the notion of "balanced lamination" is an important one for the long-term stability of the object. In other words, what is done to one side or component must be done to the other side. With that in mind, one of the plywood faces selected for the panel was 3 mm thick and the other 4.5 mm. Later adhesion of the painted lamina from the mock-painting to the 3 mm-thick face brought the total face thickness to approximately 4.2 mm. The difference in thickness of the two faces is practically undetectable. (In Figure 5 a side view of the torsion box is shown. Note that the top face ply is thinner than the bottom ply so that later adhesion of the painted lamina will make both top and bottom facing plies approximately equal in thickness.)

For convenience, the panel was fabricated using hot glue (315 g). The 4.5 mm face was placed on a very flat work table and the perimeter ribs were rub-joined to it using full-bodied hot hide glue. (It is *extremely* important to choose the assembly work surface carefully — the panel will adopt the contour of that surface during fabrication and maintain it afterwards. The new panel will not be planar if the assembly surface is not planar.) The hot glue gels

Figure 5 Torsion-box panel, side view. Top face ply is thinner than bottom ply, so that later adhesion of painted lamina to the top will bring the two face-ply thicknesses almost exactly equal.

extremely quickly, precluding the need for clamping the ribs while they set. Interior ribs were cut from the 3 mm-wide strips and attached in the same manner to form a grid of ribs approximately 10 cm apart. (This measurement is not critical.) The top edges of the ribs and the underside of the 3 mm face were then coated with the hot hide glue and the face was placed on the panel and weighted or clamped.

As mentioned, these panels were remarkably strong and light. Before mounting the painted lamina, the 60 cm x 60 cm x 19.5 mm panels weighed 3 kg. Strength was tested by securing opposite edges of the panel and then loading it with approximately 80 kg at the center — there was no discernible deflection.

Similar support panels that substitute a paper honeycomb for the internal rib grid are also an excellent option and provide nearly the same strength characteristics without the need to actually fabricate the interior of the panel. The perimeter ribs are attached and the paper grid is cut from a stock sheet to fit the opening formed by the perimeter ribs, then glued as described above. The perimeter ribs must be exactly the same thickness as the paper core.

The Adhesive System for Remounting Paintings on Plywood

From an adhesion-strength perspective, the best adhesive for wood is a protein adhesive, or a hot, animal-derived glue. It is easily prepared in water, it is quite stable and is relatively easily reversed. One of the mock-paintings was remounted successfully onto a thin plywood support using hot hide glue. Nevertheless, we were concerned about introducing substantial quantities of moisture into the painted lamina. This, combined with the desire for minimal use of organic solvents, restricted us to heat-activated adhesives for the remounting. AYAA and Beva 371 were flocked onto separate sheets of Japanese tissue paper, which were then used as heat-activated "dry mount" adhesives. The painted lamina was glued by the tissue interleaf to the new support on a heated table with a mylar vacuum membrane. Some success was achieved but the results were not satisfactory enough to select either of these adhesives without further experimentation.

We kept returning to the notion that hide glue was the best adhesive if we could reduce the amount of moisture in the system. The solution was to manipulate the hide glue in a manner similar to that used for the AYAA and Beva 371. However, since hide glue cannot be flocked it was introduced to the tissue as a liquid and later used as a solid. Sheets of tissue paper were laid flat on a sheet of mylar and prepared hot hide glue was brushed onto the tissue until it was thoroughly impregnated, and allowed to dry overnight. Hot hide glue films can be cast onto mylar, but the tissue functions as a means of handling the hide glue (and other adhesives) more easily. It also acts as a release agent should the interface need to be removed in a future treatment.

Using the tissue impregnated with hide glue as a heat-only activated adhesive did not prove successful, but heat in combination with a light water misting of the tissue yielded a remarkably strong adhesive material. The support panel was placed on the heated work surface with the 3 mm-thick face exposed. This face was sprayed lightly with water, and the impregnated tissue was then placed on the support face and treated in the same way. The

mock-painting lamina was placed immediately on the tissue and a vacuum was pulled, clamping the entire unit in place. The result was exactly what we wanted — a very strong bond with the amount of water reduced by about 75%. This method was selected as the treatment procedure for the Johnson paintings that needed complete remounting (Figure 6).

One alternative to this process would be using hot hide glue with gel suppressants, such as salt or urea, to give the glue an indefinite working time. In this manner, the pressure of time limitations for assembly would be removed.

Reintegrating the Separated Laminae

Three reintegration schemes were defined, attempted on models and found to be acceptable for this circumstance. (This does not imply that there were only three methods. These were the ones tried that satisfied our requirements.)

The first method was the most straightforward. Adhesive was injected or poured into the void left by the delamination and the object was clamped between release films and two flat cauls until the adhesive had set thoroughly.

The second method also involved the introduction of liquid adhesive, although to our knowledge, the technique is specific to hot hide glue. This process is most useful on a cracked and cupped surface that has not significantly detached. The hot hide glue is brushed generously onto the surface, and a transparent membrane (e.g., thin polyethylene) is placed over the liquid glue. A warm lamp shining on the surface keeps the glue fluid under the membrane. By massaging the polyethylene film with the fingertips, the glue is forced into the delamination voids (the film acts as a hydraulic membrane). Once sufficient glue has been squeezed into the voids, the membrane is removed, the excess glue cleaned off the surface, and the object

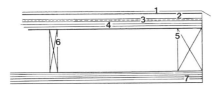

1. Suction membrane
2. Painted lamina
3. Glue-impregnated tissue
4. 3-ply, 3.0 mm plywood face
5. 1 cm x 1.7 cm mahogany grid perimeter
6. 3 mm x 1.7 cm mahogany grid ribs
7. 5-ply, 4.5 mm plywood face

Figure 6 A cross-section diagram of the remounted paintings.

clamped as described above. The primary factor in choosing this technique is that it should be attempted only on surfaces that are very stable.

The third method involved a modified version of the glue-impregnated tissue described above. The stiff, dry impregnated tissue was cut to fit an individual void. It was then sprayed lightly with water and placed in a deep-freeze chest at about -30°C. Once the tissue had frozen solid it could be inserted into even deep voids like a stiff blade. The frozen adhesive tissue sweated naturally as it warmed, and the condensed moisture combined with the thawed water to reactivate the glue. The addition of gentle heat followed by clamping pressure yielded an entirely satisfactory bond between the delaminated strata.

Remounting the Johnson Paintings

Once the treatment of the painting was underway sufficiently so that the painted lamina was completely stable, the support panel was constructed to fit. The specifications were given to the museum cabinet shop, and the craftsmen did an excellent job of executing our design (Figure 7). If there is no access to in-house fabrication, any competent commercial cabinet shop can do the same. While the panels were being built, the hide glue tissue was prepared in the manner described previously.

Figure 7 During construction of interior grid of torsion-box panel. (Panels were constructed in the workshop at the National Museum of American Art, Smithsonian Institution.)

The treatment in remounting a painting is a very rapid process that needs extensive and accurate preparations. We conducted all our treatments on a heated vacuum table, on which a membrane envelope was partially prepared by adhering two edges to the table. The support panel was placed on the heated table, and once the panel was warmed, the mounting surface was misted lightly with water from a spray bottle. The tissue was immediately put in place on the panel and misted with water to reactivate the glue, and the moistened tissue was smoothed out by hand. The painted lamina was then placed on the panel and the vacuum envelope taped shut. Once the air was evacuated, felt blankets were placed on top to retain heat in the unit and to allow full adhesive flow to occur, the heat was turned off and the remounted painting allowed to cool slowly. The vacuum was left on until the glue had set. The elapsed time from first misting to membrane evacuation was about four minutes.

The remounted painting was removed from the table and placed under gentle weight or clamping overnight (usually with "sausage" weights around the perimeter). This final step was probably overkill to a certain degree, but it did result in the paintings being well-adhered to the new supports. The only problem we encountered was that the combination of heat and vacuum led to a too-rapid drying of the glue at the very edges of the painting. This was alleviated simply by wicking small amounts of water at the edge of the remounted painting. This immediately reactivated the glue and was followed by gentle weighting or clamping.

Figure 8 Going to Market after delamination of core and back plies and attachment to torsion-box panel.

Following the implementation of the new mounting system, the final aspect of treatment was the compensation of the losses (Figure 8).

Conclusion

Plywood is certainly a modern material by definition, but fortunately for us, its technology is well known. In addition, the technology of assembling wood veneers is one familiar to most wood conservators. Ironically, this modern material may be best manipulated using ancient craft techniques, even when treating degraded artifacts. By combining traditional craft technique with the knowledge of this modern material, conservation treatments can be undertaken with considerable confidence.

Acknowledgement

Photographs by the authors, courtesy of the National Museum of American Art and the Conservation Analytical Laboratory, Smithsonian Institution, Washington, D.C.

Résumé

La conservation de peintures sur supports de contreplaqué décollés

Au fur et à mesure que s'est développée la production industrielle de matériaux de bois modifié au début du XXe siècle, les panneaux de contreplaqué et d'autres matières mixtes en sont venus à se substituer au matériel d'artiste classique. Et ce principe vaut tout particulièrement pour le domaine de la peinture, où les artistes préféraient le contreplaqué, moins cher et plus uniforme et versatile, aux supports de bois massif pour exécuter leurs peintures sur panneau. Aujourd'hui, soit environ un demi-siècle plus tard, ces supports ont commencé à se détériorer, ce qui n'est pas sans poser toute une série de problèmes inédits aux responsables des œuvres peintes sur de tels matériaux.

Des problèmes de cet ordre se sont posés pour la première fois dans le cas d'une série de peintures de l'artiste américain William H. Johnson (1901-1970) faisant partie de la collection du National Museum of American Art. Johnson, qui a peint aux États-Unis et en Europe entre 1926 et 1946, a, en dépit de sa formation académique, choisi de peindre suivant un style quasi-vernaculaire. Probablement pour des raisons d'économie, entre 1939 et 1942, il a peint nombre de ses tableaux sur des panneaux de contreplaqué. Il a dû être hospitalisé vers la fin de sa vie, si bien que ses œuvres sont tombées dans l'oubli pendant une dizaine d'années, soit durant son hospitalisation puis, à cause d'un litige relatif à la disposition de ses biens, pendant la période qui a suivi sa mort. Ses tableaux ont probablement passé certaines de ces années sur les quais de la ville de New York. Leur exposition prolongée à un environnement extérieur non contrôlé a eu, sur les peintures et sur leurs supports, des effets semblables à ceux d'un essai de vieillissement accéléré, de sorte que les diverses couches du contreplaqué ont fini par se décoller, par se boursoufler et par se casser.

Or, la mise sur pied prochaine d'une exposition des œuvres de Johnson a amené les spécialistes de la restauration du National Museum of American Art et du Conservation Analytical Laboratory de la Smithsonian Institution à étudier les divers traitements qui pourraient être appliqués à ces peintures. Plusieurs méthodes spécialement adaptées au traitement du support des peintures ont ainsi été conçues, qui peuvent aussi être appliquées à toute structure de bois constituée de plusieurs couches. Deux options principales s'offraient alors, à savoir remettre ces objets de musée entièrement en état ou enlever la couche portant la peinture.

L'article porte sur les diverses questions d'ordre éthique et technique qui peuvent se poser face aux objets de musée et à leur traitement. Il fait en outre état de chacune des principales options qui ont été envisagées et de ses variantes subséquentes, tout en fournissant une illustration des traitements qui ont finalement été appliqués.

Reference

1. Klim, S. "Composite Wood Materials in Twentieth-Century Furniture," *AIC Wooden Artifacts Group, Richmond meeting 1990* (Washington, D.C.: American Institute for Conservation, 1990).

Chicken Bones and Cardboard: The Conservation
of a Collection of Eugene Von Bruenchenhein's Art

Anton Rajer

Madison, Wisconsin
U.S.A.

Emil L. Donoval

John Michael Kohler Arts Center
Sheboygan, Wisconsin
U.S.A.

Abstract

Eugene Von Bruenchenhein (1910 – 1983), a self-trained artist, created art from found objects and household materials. Living in Milwaukee, Wisconsin, he supported himself and his wife, Marie, on the modest salary of a baker and created his works at night and on weekends.

His materials ranged from the typical — oils, enamel, watercolors — to the unconventional — chicken and turkey bones, oven-baked clays, cardboard and plywood, house paint, and concrete. Many other materials that he used, such as PVAC glue, are unique to the 20th century.

After Von Bruenchenhein's death, more than 300 of his 1,500 total works were acquired by the John Michael Kohler Arts Center (JMKAC) in Sheboygan, Wisconsin. This paper discusses the Center's conservation efforts on a collection of Von Bruenchenhein's works.

Von Bruenchenhein's art falls into three categories: paintings, sculptures, and photographs. Before treatment, all objects were inventoried and a conservation survey was prepared. The objects were cleaned superficially by dusting, as the artist's home had been heated by a coal stove and all objects were covered with a thick layer of soot. Then, conservation priorities were established for the Center's collection with two major goals in mind: to stabilize the collection and to prepare most of it for the JMKAC and Milwaukee Art Museum exhibitions. Severely damaged objects were set aside for treatment at a future date.

Solvent cleaning tests on most of the paintings indicated that the thick, discolored resin varnish applied by the artist had a solubility parameter close to that of the paint film. Varnish removal was not attempted because there was no viable system to remove the varnish without possible damage to the paint and because of the tight scheduling of exhibitions. Instead, the varnished paintings were coated with a thin layer of Acryloid F-10 and Acryloid B-67 to retard further yellowing of the varnish. Those paintings that had not been varnished originally by the artist were left unvarnished. All paintings were cleaned with a mild soap solution.

Treatment of the sculptures ranged from light cleaning to repairs and inpainting. Repairs were made with PVAC emulsion. Inpainting was done with acrylics and watercolors. Some items required only cleaning.

The photographs needed the least attention. The artist had frequently photographed his wife, developing black-and-white montage prints in the bathroom sink of their home. Hundreds of these photographs from the 1950s and 1960s were dusted, inventoried, and placed in storage envelopes.

The conservation challenges posed by this collection were overcome with curatorial assistance, a minimalist approach to intervention, and respect for the artist's intent. The treatment of this collection underscored the realization that today's conservation methods do not have all the answers in caring for such a unique collection by a 20th-century artist.

Introduction

Twentieth-century art historians have documented and described a type of isolated creative individual known as the "naive" or "outsider," whose artistic style is highly individualistic and divorced from major artistic movements. One such individual, Eugene Von Bruenchenhein (1910 - 1983), a self-trained artist, created his works from found objects and household materials. He was self-taught and relied on his family and friends for supplies and moral support. He received minor recognition for his relentless creative efforts during his lifetime. Despite his poverty, a lack of recognition, and many other obstacles, Von Bruenchenhein created more than 1,500 artworks over a 40-year period. He also wrote poetry and essays on the nature of art, life and the universe and developed theories and inventions he hoped would aid humanity.

Von Bruenchenhein lived in Milwaukee, Wisconsin, and supported himself and his wife, Marie, on a modest salary, creating his works in the evenings and on weekends. He worked at a local bakery for many years, and according to rumor took an early retirement because of health difficulties. His income had been modest to begin with; his retirement left him and Marie nearly penniless.

He had no studio, pursuing his artistic vision in the living or common area of his tiny home. He never exhibited or sold a work in his lifetime. He was regarded in his neighborhood as a strange man and some of his artworks, such as the large concrete masks he installed outside the house, were periodically vandalized. Nevertheless, he continued to create his works with a persistence and dedication that might be best characterized as obsessive. His unique vision and arrangement of materials qualify him as an artist.

After the artist's death, and following the settlement of his estate, more than 300 of his works passed into the collection of the John Michael Kohler Arts Center (JMKAC) in Sheboygan, Wisconsin. The Center sponsored the conservation of Von Bruenchenhein's collection, a book about the artist, and an exhibition that was shown at the Center in 1984 and at the Milwaukee Art Museum in 1988. This paper discusses the conservation of Von Bruenchenhein's works in the JMKAC collection.

Materials and Techniques

Working outside the traditional aesthetic circles usually associated with art schools and the artistic establishment of his time, Von Bruenchenhein supported his art both with his small salary and his personal resourcefulness.

Von Bruenchenhein fashioned artist's tools from a variety of items, including combs, leaves, sticks, and other found objects. He made his own paintbrushes from tufts of his wife's hair, bound with string and glued into the end of plastic soda fountain straws, which he then painted with aluminum paint to give them the appearance of commercially made brushes.

His choice of materials likewise reflected his resourcefulness. These ranged from typical ones, such as oils, enamel, and watercolors, to unconventional ones. Many of the materials he used, such as PVAC solvent-based model airplane glue and PVAC white glue, are unique to the 20th century. Other materials included chicken and turkey bones, from which he constructed miniature thrones and towers (Figure 1); oven-baked clay, from which he fashioned crowns and pots in the shape of animals; cardboard and plywood, from which he made painting supports and non-functioning musical instruments; and house paint, with which he created paintings and painted some of his sculptures and concrete pieces, which he fashioned into bas-relief sculptures.

A few crowns were fabricated from glass Christmas ornaments (one of the few instances in which Von Bruenchenhein used ready-made objects in his artworks) and twisted aluminum salvaged from beer cans. Miscellaneous items, such as a painted and incised fiberglass plaque and Indian arrowheads, chipped out of bottle-glass, were also among the *oeuvre*.

Inventory Phase

After acquiring the collection, the JMKAC removed it from the artist's home

Figure 1 Chair by Eugene Von Bruenchenhein. Chicken and turkey bones, glued and painted. 6 3/4 in. x 4 1/2 in. x 4 in. (17.1 cm x 11.4 cm x 10.2 cm) No. 84.VB.B.68. Photo courtesy of the John Michael Kohler Arts Center.

for inventory and conservation. Because the Von Bruenchenhein home was heated with coal, the artworks, like the interior of the house itself, were covered with a fine layer of soot. All objects were inventoried and assigned a number according to the category they represented.

During the inventory phase, an informal conservation survey was prepared for the entire collection. Many objects, such as the bone towers, were extremely fragile and showed evidence of having been repaired by the artist himself. As mentioned earlier, many of the paintings were covered with soot, as well as a thick, discolored resin. Fortunately, the artist's photographs appeared stable; he had boxed these himself. Conservation and curatorial priorities were established to stabilize the works, to prepare the objects for two exhibits, and to publish a book on the collection.

Treatment

Von Bruenchenhein's art falls into three categories: paintings, sculptures, and photographs.

Treatment of the collection took about 18 months. It was conducted by a team comprising a conservator and three technicians, who carried out the work in phases, which corresponded with the three categories of works.

First, the surfaces of all the works were cleaned by dusting with a soft brush and canned air.

All paintings were cleaned with mild soap and water. The artist had chosen to protect some paintings by placing a layer of newspaper between them. Where newsprint stuck to the paintings, the conservation team dampened it with water before attempting to remove it. Flaking paint was stabilized with BEVA 371. Inpainting, where necessary, was accomplished with acrylic emulsion paints and watercolors.

Solvent cleaning tests on most of the paintings indicated that a thick resin varnish had been applied by the artist. The varnish was also discolored. Unfortunately, this varnish had a solubility characteristic close to that of the paint film. Varnish removal was not attempted because there was no viable system to remove the varnish without possible damage to the paint and because of the tight scheduling of exhibitions. Instead, the varnished paintings were coated with a thin layer of Acryloid F-10 and Acryloid B-67 in the hope that the synthetic resin would retard further yellowing of the varnish.

Out of respect for the artist's intention, the paintings that had not been varnished originally were left unvarnished.

The conservation team attempted to duplicate the artist's original surface effects using the Acryloid F-10/Acryloid B-67 varnish mixture.

A five-degree scale of surface texture/reflectivity was developed, ranging from gloss to matte. No gloss meter was used; the five categories were subjectively constructed by determining five grades of gloss/matte on Von Bruenchenhein's paintings. The categories ranged from high gloss (like a plate of glass) to none at all. Varnish formulas were designed to reproduce the degrees. The surface of each original painting was rated according to this scale, and the conservation team duplicated the appropriate effect.

Research on the suitability of the new cleaning methods, such as the Wolbers' techniques (i.e., utilizing surfactants or industrial enzymes in gel systems), is still in progress. Cross-sectional microscopy has revealed that, for most paintings analyzed thus far, the artist applied thick, white grounds and followed these with applications of very thin layers of paint. Thus the paint layer was applied in a fashion much like a glaze. Von Bruenchenhein frequently incised this top layer, in this way achieving a greater depth and luminosity.

Previously unframed paintings in the collection were framed, with curatorial input as to the style and aesthetic of the frames Von Bruenchenhein himself had made. Color schemes were selected to harmonize with those in the paintings.

Several details of Von Bruenchenhein's paintings are noteworthy. First, he serialized his paintings, often incising a number and his signature into the painting while it was still wet. This is unusual because it breaks the established practice of signing a painting when finished, not while in progress. And, many of his paintings from the 1950s deal with the subject of nuclear holocaust. Swirling, kinetic mushroom clouds, some with demonic faces, as shown in Figure 2, ascend into glowing atomic skies.

Treatment of the sculptures ranged from light cleaning to repairs and inpainting. Broken clay crowns, animal pots, and objects fabricated from chicken or turkey bones were repaired with PVAC or cyanoacrylate adhesives.

Of all items in the collection, the photographs required the least attention. The artist had frequently photographed his wife (Figure 3), developing the black-and-white montage prints in the bathroom sink of their home. Hundreds of these photographs from the 1950s and 1960s

Figure 2 Untitled # 673 by Eugene Von Bruenchenhein, 1958. Oil on cardboard. 28 1/4 in. x 22 1/4 in. (71.8 cm x 56.5 cm) No. 84.VB.p.401. Photo courtesy of the John Michael Kohler Arts Center.

Figure 3 "Portrait of artist's wife Marie", Eugene Von Bruenchenhein. Gelatin-silver print, (21.9 cm x 13.2 cm) No. 84.VB.PH.2696. Photo courtesy of the John Michael Kohler Arts Center.

were dusted, inventoried, and placed in storage envelopes. Among the photographic collection are some prints that were hand tinted by the artist.

Conclusion

The art of Eugene Von Bruenchenhein has posed significant curatorial and conservation challenges over the past nine years. Conservation efforts have been grounded in respect for the artist's intent and have been marked by minimal intervention. In short, it is clear that today's conservation methods cannot solve all the problems raised by this unique collection. Ongoing conservation research has raised possibilities, such as the use of the Wolbers' techniques for cleaning paintings, which may prove useful in the future conservation of the collection.

Von Bruenchenhein's unique contribution to 20th-century art is finally being recognized and his visionary legacy preserved for future students of the "naive" or "outsider" aesthetic.

Acknowledgement

The authors thank the John Michael Kohler Arts Center for helping them prepare this paper and for providing the photographs of Eugene Von Bruenchenhein's work.

Résumé

Les os de poulet et le carton ou la conservation d'une collection d'œuvres d'Eugene Von Bruenchenhein

Eugene Von Bruenchenhein (1910-1983), artiste américain autodidacte, créait des œuvres d'art à partir d'objets trouvés et de produits domestiques. Établi à Milwaukee (Wisconsin), il assurait sa subsistance et celle de sa femme Marie grâce à un modeste salaire de boulanger, et il s'adonnait à son art les soirs et les fins de semaine.

Pour exécuter ses œuvres, il avait recours tantôt à des matériaux usuels — peinture à l'huile, émail et aquarelle — tantôt à des matières plutôt inusitées — os de poulet ou de dinde, argile cuite, carton, contreplaqué, peinture domestique et béton. Nombre de ces autres matières qu'il employait — telle la colle de polyacétate de vinyle (PAV) pour la confection d'avions miniatures — sont des produits particuliers au XXe siècle.

À la mort de l'artiste, plus de 300 de ses 1 500 œuvres ont été acquises par le John Michael Kohler Arts Center (JMKAC) de Sheboyan (Wisconsin), et la présente communication fait état des efforts qu'a déployés le JMKAC pour conserver ces œuvres.

Les œuvres de Von Bruenchenhein se classent parmi trois catégories : la peinture, la sculpture et la photographie. Avant d'amorcer le traitement de conservation, on a dressé un inventaire de tous ces objets, et préparé une évaluation des traitements qui leur seraient appliqués. La surface des objets a ensuite été dépoussiérée car, comme la maison de l'artiste avait été chauffée au bois, ils étaient couverts d'une épaisse couche de suie. Enfin, un ordre de priorité a été établi pour le traitement des objets de la collection du JMKAC, traitement qui aurait deux grands objectifs, à savoir stabiliser, dans un premier temps, la collection et préparer, dans un second temps, le plus grand nombre possible de ces œuvres en vue de leur exposition au JMKAC et au Milwaukee Art Museum.

Les essais de nettoyage avec solvant effectués sur les tableaux ont montré que, dans la plupart des cas, l'épais vernis de résine décoloré qu'avait appliqué l'artiste présentait une solubilité approchante de celle de la couche picturale. On n'a donc pas tenté de débarrasser ces œuvres de leur vernis car on ne disposait alors d'aucune technique qui aurait permis de le faire sans risque pour la couche picturale, et à l'intérieur de l'échéancier prévu pour leur exposition. On a donc plutôt opté pour l'application, sur les tableaux ainsi vernis, d'une mince couche d'Acryloid F-10 et B-67 pour retarder leur jaunissement ultérieur, tandis que les autres, non vernis à l'origine par l'artiste, ont été laissés tels quels. Tous ont néanmoins été nettoyés avec un savon léger.

Les sculptures ont, pour leur part, fait l'objet de niveaux variables de traitement — depuis le simple nettoyage jusqu'aux réparations ou retouches. Les réparations ont été effectuées avec une émulsion de PAV, et les retouches, avec de l'acrylique et de l'aquarelle. Certaines œuvres n'ont exigé qu'un léger nettoyage.

Ce sont les photographies qui ont exigé le moins de soins particuliers. L'artiste, qui photographiait souvent sa femme, développait ses épreuves en noir et blanc destinées au montage dans l'évier de sa salle de bain. Des centaines de ces photographies, des années 50 et 60, ont été dépoussiérées et glissées dans des enveloppes avant d'être mises en réserve.

Les problèmes de conservation qu'a posés cette collection ont été résolus en faisant appel à l'aide de conservateurs et en adoptant une approche qui, fondée sur le principe d'un minimum d'interventions, respecte l'intention de l'artiste. Le traitement de ces œuvres a par ailleurs permis de constater que les techniques de conservation actuelles ne permettent pas toujours de résoudre toutes les difficultés que pose la préservation d'une collection d'œuvres du XXe siècle aussi unique.

Ensuring a Future for Our Present High-Tech Past: Lessons from the ENIAC for the Conservation of Major Electronic Technology

Jon Eklund and Beth Richwine

Division of Conservation
Smithsonian Institution
Washington, D.C.
U.S.A.

Abstract

In March of 1990, the National Museum of American History opened the largest technology exhibition in the Smithsonian's history: The Information Age. *The largest and one of the most historically significant of the objects in the exhibition was a partial re-creation of the first successful, electronic, general-purpose computer: the* Electronic Numerical Integrator And Computer (ENIAC). *Occupying several hundred cubic feet and weighing several tons, the 15 exhibited units varied widely in their conservation problems. Choices among classical inpainting, complete repainting and component replacement had to be made according to such competing factors as exhibit schedule constraints, conservation standards and experiments on the behavior of available modern versions of finishes. Before conservation was completed some 15 people, including the object's curator, had put in over 180 hours of treatment under the coordination of a conservator who is a coauthor of this paper. Such close collaboration between curators and conservators is not as common as it should be. Because of the joint effort here, however, information about this artifact that came to light during the conservation effort stimulated further curatorial research on the wrinkle finishes used on the ENIAC and research on other electronic instruments of the 1940s and 1950s. These finishes produced a particular "look" and "feel" to these instruments, which were noticeably different from both their predecessors of the 1920s and successors of the post-Sputnik era. The analysis, conservation and restoration aspects of the ENIAC finishes will be presented in this paper, as well as the historical implications of the work.*

Introduction

In March of 1990, the National Museum of American History (NMAH) opened the largest and most expensive technology exhibition in the Smithsonian's history: *The Information Age*. Behind the 1,300 square metres (14,000 square feet) of communications and computer history developed by the curatorial team was a massive effort by the NMAH Conservation Department to preserve and prepare some 750 historic artifacts and a similar number of graphics from America's high-technology past. Of these, the largest and one of the most significant was a partial re-creation of the first successful, electronic, general-purpose computer: the *Electronic Numerical Integrator And Computer* (ENIAC). Occupying several hundred cubic feet and weighing several tons, the units varied widely in conservation problems. Before conservation was completed, some 15 people had worked on the project under the supervision of Conservator Beth Richwine of the Smithsonian Division of Conservation. The variety of conservation solutions chosen were a function of exhibit schedule constraints as well as conservation standards and research into the paint technologies used for electronics during the era of World War II.

Conservation always has an intrinsic historical component; even if the objects to be treated have little historical significance, the conservator must know something of the object's specific history as an artifact (what it was made of, how it was made and what its present condition is) in order to properly treat it. In view of this, it is surprising that there have been so few direct collaborations between curators and conservators in museum projects that study or exhibit artifacts. In the case of the conservation of the ENIAC for *The Information Age*, however, the strong time pressures and the importance and complexity of the artifact made such a collaboration particularly useful, and a member of the Smithsonian curatorial team, Jon Eklund, Curator of the History of Information Technology and of Chemistry, elected to devote much of his efforts to working with the Division of Conservation in this task. In turn, information about this artifact that came to light during the conservation effort stimulated further curatorial research on the finishes used on the ENIAC and other electronic instruments of the period. These finishes produced a particular "look" and "feel" to these instruments that were noticeably different from both their predecessors of the 1920s and successors of the post-Sputnik era. The analysis and the treatment of the ENIAC finishes will be presented in this paper, as well as the historical implications of the work.

First we will outline the historical background of this important artifact, then say something about its history and situation *as an object* from a curatorial and conservation standpoint. We will follow this with a discussion of the treatment strategies and particularly about the conservation decisions that had to be made singly and jointly by the conservator and the curator.

History

Surprisingly, perhaps, most early computational devices were not intended for daily use. The motivation and end product for most such machines were tables of numbers to be used in hand calculations. The best known examples are the tables of logarithms and the trigonometry tables long remembered by the pre-electronic calculator generation. Table production was the motivation for the ENIAC. The tables for which people lusted in this case were firing tables for World War II artillery pieces. Thus the ENIAC, like so many other technological achievements over the centuries, was encouraged and funded by the government, and specifically the war department.

The problem of aiming artillery is complex. There is a specific path called a trajectory for each projectile or firing. The trajectory varies for each type of loading, shell, gun, and each angle that the gun is tilted (e.g., in hard or soft ground in a breeze of "x" miles per hour and a barometric pressure of "y" mm of mercury). During World War II each of these trajectories required a complex set of calculations (Figure 1). With aptitude and intensive training, and the use of an electrically driven mechanical calculator, a "computer" (i.e., a person who computes) could calculate one of these paths or trajectories in about 20 hours. With the many developments in new guns and shells in World War II, the Ballistic Research Laboratory of the U.S. Army was falling further and further behind in meeting the demands for tables. Faster methods were needed.

SHARPLY POINTED PROJECTILE MOVING THROUGH THE AIR

$$(a^2 - u^2)\frac{\partial u}{\partial x} - u\,v\left(\frac{\partial u}{\partial y} + \frac{\partial v}{\partial x}\right)$$
$$+ (a^2 - v^2)\frac{\partial v}{\partial y} + \frac{a^2\,v}{y} = 0,$$
$$\frac{\partial v}{\partial x} - \frac{\partial u}{\partial y} = 0$$

IN THESE EQUATIONS, AT ANY POINT (X,Y)

IN SPACE

u = COMPONENT OF VELOCITY OF AIR IN x DIRECTION

v = COMPONENT OF VELOCITY OF AIR IN y DIRECTION

a, THE VELOCITY OF SOUND, IS GIVEN BY

$$a^2 = \frac{\partial P}{\partial s}$$

P = PRESSURE

s = DENSITY

Figure 1 An example of a differential equation used by the ENIAC to calculate a trajectory.

In the late thirties and early forties, an electro-mechanical calculating device called a *differential analyzer* was developed and built at the Massachusetts Institute of Technology in Cambridge, Massachusetts, and a similar one at the Moore School of Electrical Engineering, a part of the University of Pennsylvania in Philadelphia. It could solve a trajectory using about 20 minutes of calculating time and perhaps half of that to do a simple change or two for the next path. Though an impressive achievement providing a considerable savings in time, it still wasn't fast enough.

By 1942, a physicist named John W. Mauchley was on the staff of the Moore School and had become friends with a brilliant graduate student, J. Presper Eckert. They had many discussions about the possibilities of building computing machinery out of ultra-fast electronic components. Mauchley even wrote a short paper entitled "The Use of High-Speed Vacuum Tube Devices for Calculating." He theorized that such a machine could calculate paths every 100 seconds.

In early 1943 the U.S. Army sent out a mathematician, Lt. Herman H. Goldstine, to the Moore School and other research installations associated with the Army's Ballistic Research Laboratory program. His task was to see if there were machines or ideas for speeding up the process of making firing tables. Hearing of Mauchley and Eckert's work, Goldstine reviewed their ideas and arranged for a presentation at the Aberdeen Proving Ground in Maryland. Their project was approved, and construction of an electronic computer started May 31, 1943 at the Moore School with Mauchley in charge of the general or conceptual design and Eckert in charge of the designs for the specific circuits. The ENIAC design grew from a device that used about 500 electron tubes to a completed machine that, astoundingly, used close to 18,000 electron tubes. Even the lower number of 500 was phenomenal for that time, since

electron tubes were unstable and changed their working characteristics over their lifetimes; it was a challenge to get a dozen to work together over a long period of time. For the ENIAC, this meant great care had to be taken to match tubes wherever necessary and to watch carefully for signs of change or malfunction. In the end, the original ENIAC had 40 rack units plus three rolling "function tables" on wheels. It was arranged in a "U" shape in a large room (Figure 2). In November 1946, ENIAC was disassembled and moved to Aberdeen Proving Ground. Strictly speaking, World War II was over before ENIAC produced many ballistic tables. It was used on post-war calculations for the H-bomb for the war department. On the civilian side, it produced calculations for weather forecasting models, number theory, and fluid flow in hydrodynamics. After ENIAC was moved to Aberdeen it was put to work on firing tables and produced them for the Korean War. By that time, it could calculate a path in 20 seconds. ENIAC was used until October 2, 1955 when it was shut down and gradually dismantled. All told, nearly 30 of the rack units survived and most were donated to the Smithsonian in the late 1950s and early 1960s.

Physical Description

Fourteen of the fifteen ENIAC electronic rack units in the exhibition are vertically oriented and generally similar in appearance (Figure 3). Each of the vertical units is

Figure 2 ENIAC as it looked in the 1950s at Aberdeen Proving Ground.

approximately 213 cm x 76 cm x 61 cm deep (7 ft x 2.5 ft x 2 ft). Several of these have hundreds of antique vacuum tubes attached in the back. The fifteenth unit, a "function table," is horizontally oriented and measures 183 cm x 30 cm x 152 cm (6 ft x 1 ft x 5 ft). It contains over 900 knobs. The units vary in weight from about 68 kg (150 lb) to 136 kg (300 lb), depending on the types of fittings contained in the rack.

Figure 3 Interface unit for function table #3, before conservation. The non-original "feet" were added to allow it to stand by itself.

The units are made of mild steel, but there are also knobs, sockets and other accessories on the units that are made of smooth plastics. The majority of the knobs and sockets appear to be a phenol formaldehyde (Bakelite) plastic. Behind the knobs, small plates of an unknown soft, white metal are painted flat-black or dull-gold with white or black lettering. These indicate the name of the unit.

In addition to the large units there are numerous horizontal flat units in three lengths from 61 cm to 183 cm (2 ft to 6 ft). Called "buses," these were used to make connections among the rack units during operation of the ENIAC and were stacked across the bases with cables and plugs leading to the units.

The Kyoto Exposition

The first conservation treatment on the ENIAC was not done for *The Information Age* exhibition. In the fall of 1987, five ENIAC units were sent to Kyoto, Japan, for a cultural exchange festival, the *World Expo of Historical Cities*.

One of the most noted features of the ENIAC was the large number of tubes (Figure 4). For the original exhibit in the NMAH, the curatorial decision was to show the vacuum tubes. However, for the Kyoto trip, the tubes were too fragile and rare to travel. Every tube had to be taken out by hand and packed separately and then reinstalled when the pieces were returned from Japan. In 1988 these pieces were moved again and put into storage when the Math Hall was taken down for building renovations.

Figure 4 Looking over a few hundred of the ENIAC's 18,000 electron tubes in the late 1940s is Army liaison Lt. Herman H. Goldstine, who originally brought the government's attention to the Eckert-Mauchley project.

The conservation on the five units sent to Japan taught much about the ENIAC to both curatorial and conservation staff. The decisions made at that time meant that several of the units were in rather good shape and all but ready to install in a new exhibit. Thus this early project served as a model for the later and larger effort to re-create a portion of the ENIAC in *The Information Age* exhibition.

The Washington Exposition

In May 1990, *The Information Age* exhibit was to open at NMAH. To give visitors a clear sense of the size of the early mainframe computers, the design called for a walk-through re-creation of about 40 percent of the ENIAC using 15 of the surviving units. In January of that year, the five ENIAC units that had gone to Japan along with the 10 more that were taken from one of the Smithsonian off-site storage areas were gradually brought down to the Objects Conservation Laboratory for treatment. The large size and weight of the units made their moving and handling difficult, but the problems were too complex and the storage site too confining to try to conserve them in the field.

Problems

The units varied widely in the conservation problems they presented. Often the solutions had to be worked out between the department of conservation staff and the curatorial staff. Problems included the following:

A) Overall structural instability of the free-standing units

B) Gross damage, including missing panels and parts

C) Surface damage, including instability of the paint surfaces and the need to integrate paint losses and treat other visual defects

There was also a need to give the units long-term protection from dust and from the public.

A) Structural Instability
Originally, the ENIAC units were bolted together on special bases made for the site. Since vertical rack units no longer had their original bases new ones had to be made so that the units could stand alone with stability.

B) Gross Damage
Dents, Bends, and Torquing
There were scattered dents and bends in the metals on some pieces. In the past, when many of the units had been moved, the frames had become torqued*. Because of this many of the screw holes in the panels no longer lined up exactly with screw holes in the frames.

Missing Parts and Pieces
There were many missing screws in the frames. There were also more than 10 missing upper panels and three missing grills from the frames' lower halves that needed to be replaced. The missing panels were primarily flat in the center with side flanges that were bent over on two sides to fit between the two major vertical supports. The original grills measured about 61 cm x 76 cm (2 ft x 2.5 ft).

C) Surface Damage
Paint Losses and Instability
The painted surfaces of the major elements from the original ENIAC were covered with a black wrinkle paint. Samples of this paint, analyzed using infrared spectrometry and gas chromatography, were found to contain an alkyd resin (Figure 5). Alkyd resin is made by chemically combining a natural ester-based oil with a resin. The wrinkle finish was first developed during the 1920s but did not actually start to become popular until the early 1940s. The two major active ingredients for the wrinkling process were generally a natural ester-based oil such as Tung oil and a natural ester resin such as Congo copal. Two fairly thick coats of wrinkle paint needed to be applied in fairly quick succession. The basic mechanism is one of

---

* As normally understood and as scientifically defined, torque is the *moment* of a system of forces causing rotation rather than the rotation of twisting itself. However, we have used the term here because "twisting" is not adequate to describe what is happening to the frames. We use torquing to mean that moments of force were applied that caused the cabinets or frames to become out-of-square.

differential shrinkage of the two layers with rapid evaporation of the solvents. Other additives affected the pattern and size of the wrinkle. The wrinkle paint was advertised for use to increase grip, lessen eye strain because of decreased reflection and reduce finishing of the metal before painting.

Figure 6 Accumulator unit #19 illustrates the kind and extent of paint damage and loss in many of the ENIAC sections.

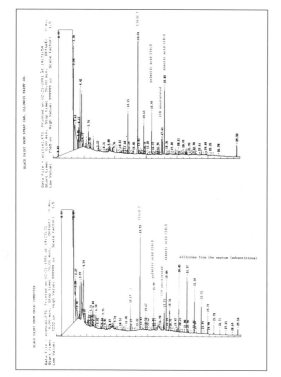

Figure 5 Gas chromatographs show comparisons of the original ENIAC wrinkle paint with the modern version used in the conservation effort.

The conditions of the wrinkle paint ranged from good to fair depending on each unit. Many of the units had varying degrees of past restoration and conservation. Two of the units had severe loss of the wrinkle paint due to rust and improper surface preparation. Other units had losses of paint on single parts, scratches, chips and abrasions. There were numerous small areas of flaking finish and loss primarily due to rust. The areas of rust on the panels were very scattered and appeared as groupings of small dots or large irregular areas of fine rust (Figure 6).

Defects Subsequent to the ENIAC's Working Lifetime

Many of the panels had rough identification labels scrawled on the front. Most were marked with orange grease-pencil but some were marked with white paint. We do not know for certain if these markings were made during the working lifetime of the machine. Some of the units also had thick adhesive residues in areas where a fiber-reinforced tape label had been applied.

Treatment

Specific aspects of treatment are organized under similar subheadings to those cited in the discussion of problems.

In general the units were first vacuumed to remove a thick accumulation of dust and dirt — all were very dusty. Plastic knobs were cleaned using soft cloths or cotton swabs and distilled water.

Stabilizing the Units

Feet, composed of 7.6 cm x 7.6 cm (3 in. x 3 in.) angle-rolled steel were made to allow units to stand alone. These new bases allowed the units to be moved and installed individually in the exhibit area as their conservation treatments were completed. Three units that were bolted together had a special base made, allowing them to stand as a triple unit. Bases were also designed so that the units could be bolted together in groups as they were in the original installation.

Removal of Dents and Bends

The dents and distortions in the panels were fairly minor. One or two panels had to be straightened somewhat to make them fit, but the dents and other distortions were left untouched.

Torquing Problems

Over the years, the panel frames had torqued slightly due to moving and incautious storage. As a result, the screw holes in many of the old panels and almost all of the new ones had to be custom drilled or enlarged to allow them to fit.

Replacement of Missing Parts and Pieces

We decided that the missing panels should be replaced so that the units appeared as complete as they were during the ENIAC's working lifetime. New panels for the units were constructed out of 26-gauge galvanized steel sheet. They were then measured for the screw positions, drilled, and the smaller replacement pieces were painted. The two large bases that held the ENIAC's connecting buses were painted in black wrinkle varnish thinned to work in spray guns.

The new panels were fastened to the units using new screws painted with black acrylic paint to better integrate them with the existing screws. Further inpainting and integration with the resin-varnish mixture was done as needed after installation of the units. Because of the difficulty in matching the texture and the surface sheen, the inpainted losses are still somewhat evident. Thus it is fortunate that the most inpainted areas are not highly lit.

In addition to the 15 basic units there were the numerous horizontal flat units or "buses" that were stacked across the bases of the basic units once the ENIAC was assembled.

Equally important, many of the original cables and plugs were missing. Even though the ENIAC units were not being restored back to functional use, both the conservation staff and the curator felt it important to restore these as closely as possible to their in-use appearance. New plugs and cable components were obtained at an electronic supply store. They were similar in appearance to the originals but made of modern plastics. Even though they were not painted and did not have quite the same texture as the originals, they blended in nicely.

Surface Instability and Consolidation

In order to try to save the remaining finish on the panels, the rusted surfaces were coated with a resin to act as a consolidant by, in essence, binding the finish and the corrosion products to the surface of the metal. The consolidant was either painted on with a small brush around the areas of loss or sprayed on, depending on the severity of the flaking.

Inpainting with Acrylics

On the panels where the paint was in relatively good condition the losses were isolated with an acrylic resin and inpainted with acrylic paints. The isolating resin is easily soluble so it enables removal of any inpainting in those areas in the future. The initial treatments provided a solid base so that the units could travel to the exhibit site needing at most a few minor aesthetic touch-ups later on.

A major problem for surface reconstruction arose because some of the ENIAC units also had thick adhesive residues in areas where a fiber-reinforced tape label had been applied. We were unable to find a solvent mild enough to remove these residues without damaging the paint. Where possible the residues were scraped off and overpainted with acrylic paints. The problem with this treatment was that the adhesive residues along with the acrylic overpaint produced a smooth surface with a reflectance different from that of the surrounding surface. The only way to blend in these areas was to painstakingly dot them in with a glossy resin.

Orange Grease-pencil Markings

At first, the orange grease-pencil letters on one panel were removed with solvent. It was very difficult to prevent the solvent from carrying the orange residues of the grease-pencil outward into the surrounding wrinkle finish and creating ugly orange halos. Because of the finish it was impossible to remove all of the grease-pencil in the interstices without damaging the paint underneath. This required stronger solvents or poulticing, which meant that a solvent had to remain on the paint surface for a long time. At the same time some controversy arose over whether or not the markings were put on while in original use, in storage or even later by the Smithsonian. We decided to only remove or overpaint those areas that would be most visible and visually disturbing while on exhibit.

White Paint Markings
The writing in insoluble white paint on some of the panels was carefully picked out using a scalpel, and any remaining white paint was covered over with a black acrylic paint. Unfortunately, there was still a considerable amount of paint that remained in the interstices of the wrinkled areas. This smoothed out the finish but made the areas more obvious. In order to visually break up the smooth surfaces caused by acrylic inpainting and remaining white paint, a glossy resin was dotted on. This process was satisfactory for many of the small scattered areas of loss, but the smoothness of the finish or lack of texture, such as in the original paint, had made the larger areas of inpainted losses obvious. We decided to try to alleviate this problem by using wrinkle paint for inpainting.

Modern Wrinkle Finish
Initially we were able to purchase black Ruf-Koat Wrinkle Varnish (made by the Illinois Bronze Powder and Paint Co.) at an electronics supply store. This type of finish is still used by the electronics industry and comes in a small selection of colors. The wrinkle paint would wrinkle on its own if merely left to dry overnight, but the wrinkles were large and often areas would not wrinkle at all. Normally in a commercial establishment the panels would have been baked in an oven after painting. Our small oven in the laboratory was not nearly large enough so we decided to try to get the same effect using infrared heat lamps.

Often, after applying the wrinkle paint, we would position the heat lamps long enough at one end of the piece to start the wrinkling process. Then we would gradually move them down the length of the piece to heat the metal and the paint surface as the wrinkling progressed (Figure 7). Occasionally we would still end up with small areas that would not wrinkle even after leaving them exposed to the heat lamps for a

Figure 7 An example of the heat lamp arrangements used to induce the wrinkle effect in the finish. Note the wrinkle boundaries spreading out from two areas at the top of the panel.

while. We do not know exactly what caused this, but there seems to be many possibilities, including dirt, mixing of paint, film thickness, amount of time between heating and spraying, and temperature of the heat lamps.

Close examination showed that generally our wrinkles were not as fine as those of the original finish. Perhaps a commercial establishment's equipment could control the variables more closely and produce better results on average. However, on further examination, we did find that some areas of the original wrinkle finish on the ENIAC and other instruments of the period seemed to have some of the same problems that we experienced. Thus overall the repainting process went remarkably well and could be done in most facilities.

We found the manufacturer, Illinois Bronze Powder and Paint Co., very cooperative when we explained our project and problems. Local supplies of this product were often limited, but we were able to get the product directly. We were also able to get advice on usage of the paint.

Inpainting with Wrinkle Finish
In order to inpaint the wrinkle paint in small areas with a fine brush, the paint was sprayed from aerosol cans into a small metal tin and used quickly and in small amounts before the rapid evaporation of the solvent made the paint

too thick to paint easily. The texture and sheen of the applied wrinkle paint were slightly different than the original wrinkle finish. Care had to be taken not to paint over the edges to avoid thick build up; the effect was much more successful than acrylic or any other substitute paints tried. Even the bulk wrinkle paint in the can had different surface effects. No matter how much it was thinned, the wrinkle effect was not as fine grained. Ultimately only the paint from the aerosol spray can gave really good inpainting results.

Repainting and Overpainting

The original literature on wrinkle finishes claimed that the paint adhered very well to bare metal. However, as the condition of the ENIAC proved, this did not always hold true. While a few of the units appeared to be in very good condition, most had mild to severe paint loss. Much of this could have been due to the improper storage conditions that promoted rust. Initially we tried to inpaint only in the losses on some of the badly rusted panels, but the appearance was not satisfactory. We thus decided to repaint them entirely with the black wrinkle paint. Thereafter, wherever flaking paint was severe and wherever the losses would be visible while on exhibit, we brushed or scraped all of the remaining paint off and repainted entirely.

The knobs and other areas not to be painted were blocked out or covered. For large areas, painters' masking tape and brown paper were used (Figure 8). At first the many small set-in plastic sockets were covered with tape and then the edges were further sealed by painting on artists' liquid latex masking fluid. In tests this seemed to work well but after painting one of the large panels we decided that it was too difficult to paint the latex on evenly around the tape. The tape seemed to work well if it was carefully cut, applied, and sealed by pressing with our fingernails around the edges. This was also a lot less time-consuming than painting around each of the hundred or so sockets. The tape was, of course, removed soon after painting.

In hopes that the newly applied paint would adhere better, the panels were painted first with grey Rust-oleum Auto Primer spray paint and

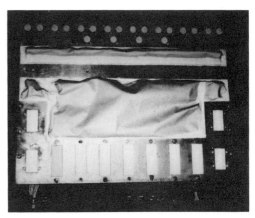

Figure 8 Accumulator unit #19 at a later stage shows blocking arrangements just prior to painting. The original paint was too badly damaged in many areas of this object to be reliably consolidated.

then with two coats of the black wrinkle paint. The presence of primer indicated which units were scraped and repainted since the originals were never primed. We then painted the panels with the wrinkle paint and positioned the heat lamps to cause fine wrinkles.

Finally, in order to better integrate the fresh and glossy appearance of the repainted panels with the original panels, which were blanched or appeared lightened from dirt, both were coated with a wax-resin mixture. This acted like a varnish to produce a satin-gloss appearance.

Protection from Dust and the Public

Because the plugs could easily be pulled out and knobs twisted until broken off, we felt it necessary to protect the ENIAC units from prying hands and souvenir hunters. The design concept of the exhibit was to be as open as possible so a plexiglass barrier was placed in front of the units. While generally protecting the units, this type of barrier unfortunately still allows the units to accumulate dust and dirt and at the same time makes cleaning access difficult.

Conclusion

The 15 or so people who worked on the conservation of the ENIAC together contributed over 520 hours of time. This project was a challenge because of the size of the artifact, the time constraints and also the nature of the primary problem: the unusual finish. Over a year's worth of time could have easily been taken to treat the ENIAC considering the size and number of units, but one has to be realistic when working with large, multi-unit objects. Also, visitors to history museums, as opposed to fine or decorative art museums, expect the functional objects on display to look used. Thus it is often not only unrealistic but undesirable to return an historic object to its original condition (Figures 9 and 10).

Figure 9 Accumulator unit #19 after conservation.

Figure 10 A bank of eight of the original ENIAC units on display in The Information Age *exhibition at the National Museum of American History. At right is a video clip selector featuring the ENIAC's chief engineer, Presper Eckert, in a 1988 interview explaining key aspects of the computer.*

Even a partial restoration of the electronic apparatus that so pervade 20th-century science and technology will pose continuing challenges as such artifacts are collected and exhibited. For example, preliminary research shows that the pervasive black wrinkle finishes were challenged, giving way to other color variants and metallic glazes. There were definite preferences for color and appearance of finishes at various periods that might even be characterized as fashions or at least fads.

Manufacturers of laboratory furniture and apparatus in the late 1950s and early 1960s moved quickly to take advantage of increased funding during the immediate post-Sputnik period. Brightly colored, "modern" metallic finishes graced power supplies as well as automobiles. In the late 1960s and 1970s, flat-beige and blue-matte finishes were fashionable for a while and even the dull-black of military gear was used a bit, though it caught on much more with consumer electronics. Similarly, some manufacturers experimented with brushed aluminum, though, it too, was more popular for high-fidelity gear.

In future cases, conservators will face finishes composed primarily of one type of polymer, but there may be formulations with several polymers, as this was common practice in the past. Each of these trends in finishes will present specific problems for the conservator, depending on the degree to which the curators and designers want the surface to be restored or simply stabilized and consolidated.

The close collaboration between curator and conservator made this project run much more smoothly when it came to making decisions on the different treatment options. It is crucial to have the curatorial staff help with treatments of major artifact systems like the ENIAC not only because it leads to faster decision making and easier solutions to problems, but because it leads to learning more about the objects. And isn't that what a museum is for?

Résumé

Garantir l'avenir des vestiges de notre haute technologie : les leçons à tirer de l'expérience de l'ENIAC pour assurer la conservation des grandes techniques de l'électronique

Au mois de mars 1990, le National Museum of American History présentait, sous le titre de The Information Age *(L'ère de l'information), la plus grande exposition technologique de l'histoire du Smithsonian. Le plus volumineux des objets exposés, et le plus important au point de vue historique, était une reproduction partielle du premier ordinateur électronique tout usage, l'Electronic Numerical Integrator And Computer (ENIAC). Occupant un volume total de quelques centaines de mètres cubes et pesant plusieurs tonnes, les 15 unités exposées posaient des problèmes de conservation très diversifiés. On a ainsi eu à choisir, pour les composants, parmi la retouche classique, la repeinture complète et la substitution de pièces, en tenant compte de facteurs concurrents comme les contraintes du calendrier d'exposition, les normes de conservation et les données d'expériences effectuées pour étudier la réaction de versions modernes de revêtements. Avant la fin des travaux de restauration, environ 15 membres du personnel, dont le conservateur responsable de l'objet, avaient consacré 180 heures aux opérations de traitement, sous la coordination de l'un des auteurs de la présente communication. Des expériences de collaboration aussi étroite entre spécialistes de la restauration et de la conservation méritent d'être répétées. Les données recueillies dans le cours des travaux de restauration ont mené à des recherches en conservation plus poussées sur le revêtement vermiculé de l'ENIAC, ainsi qu'à des études portant sur d'autres appareils électroniques des années 40 et 50. Un tel revêtement donne à ces appareils un aspect particulier, à la vue comme au toucher, qui est sensiblement différent de celui de leurs prédécesseurs, des années 20, et de leurs successeurs, de la période postérieure au* Spoutnik. *La présente communication portera sur l'analyse, sur la conservation et sur la restauration du revêtement de l'ENIAC, tout en traitant des répercussions historiques des travaux qui ont été effectués.*

Bibliography

Hopwood, Walter, "Paint Samples from the ENIAC," *Smithsonian CAL Analysis Report*: February, 1990.

Stern, Nancy, *From ENIAC to UNIVAC* (Bedford, Massachusetts: Digital Press, 1981).

Waldie, W.A., *The Science of Wrinkle Finishing* (Dayton, Ohio: Research Press, Inc., 1949).

Williams, M.R., *A History of Computing Technology* (Englewood Cliffs, New Jersey: Prentice Hall, 1985).

Modern Metals in Museum Collections

Lorna R. Green and David Thickett

Department of Conservation
The British Museum
London, U.K.

Abstract

It is well known that materials used for the storage and display of antiquities can emit harmful gases that initiate corrosion and cause other deterioration processes. Since 1972 conservation scientists at the British Museum have been using an accelerated ageing test known as the Oddy test to evaluate the potential of materials to cause corrosion of metals. The test has been used to evaluate the corrosive effect on silver, copper and lead, the metals that have shown the greatest potential to corrode in the Museum. The introduction of the testing procedure dramatically reduced the number of instances of objects corroding in exhibition cases. It also reduced the rate at which silver tarnished.

In common with many museums, the British Museum has continued to collect into the 20th century, bringing modern metals into the collection. Artefacts, coins and medals made of aluminium, zinc and magnesium and their alloys form a small but significant part of the collection. Such metals are commonly found in galleries of modern art. These metals are no less susceptible to corrosion than the metals of antiquity. Aluminium artefacts have exhibited both localized pitting corrosion and the formation of a thin layer of white corrosion. Zinc money from the First and Second World Wars has been found to corrode completely when stored in wooden coin cabinets. Magnesium has also been found to corrode forming a white surface corrosion layer. These observations have caused concern to curators and conservators. As a result, a study was undertaken to identify the cause of the corrosion; to develop the Oddy test for materials to be used in the storage and display of these metals; and to produce guidelines for their storage and display.

The corrosion processes involved have been investigated by identification of the corrosion products and a survey of the corrosion literature. Using this information as a basis, a series of corrosion experiments was carried out to investigate the effects of the known common pollutants in the museum environment on these metals. Guidelines for the storage and display of these metals were prepared.

Introduction

It is well known that materials used for the storage and display of antiquities can emit harmful gases that initiate corrosion and cause other deterioration processes.[1] Since 1972, the British Museum has been using an accelerated ageing test, the Oddy test, to evaluate the potential of materials to cause corrosion of metals in the Museum's collection.[2] This test has been used to evaluate the corrosive effect of materials on the common metals of antiquity, silver, copper and lead, which are most readily corroded in a museum environment. The introduction of the testing procedure resulted in a dramatic reduction in the number of objects corroding in exhibition cases. In common with many museums, the British Museum has continued to collect into the 20th century. This has brought modern metals into the collection. Artefacts, coins and medals made of metals, such as aluminium, magnesium and zinc, and their alloys, now form a small but significant part of the collection.

Aim

The aim of this study was twofold: first, to assess the condition of modern metals in museum collections, and second, to identify materials often used for storage and display purposes in museums, which are potentially corrosive to zinc, aluminium and magnesium.

Modern Metals and Their Corrosion Processes

Zinc

Although zinc was known as a distinct metal in India in the 14th century and probably earlier in China, it was not until 1740 that the first commercial zinc extraction plant was built in Europe.[3] Hence, when compared with metals of antiquity, silver, lead and gold, zinc may be considered a "modern" metal.

In damp air, in the absence of carbon dioxide, zinc hydroxide $Zn(OH)_2$ forms. However, where carbon dioxide is present, a thin grey-white covering of carbonate possibly $ZnCO_3$ and $ZnCO_3.Zn(OH)_2$ forms, which protects against further corrosion.[4] In the presence of sulphur dioxide, zinc sulphate $ZnSO_4$ forms.[5,6] Zinc corrodes in the presence of acetic acid, formic acid and formaldehyde.[7] Gaseous and aqueous hydrogen halides also affect zinc.[8] As with most metals, the corrosion rate of zinc increases with increasing relative humidity. It has been reported that zinc-tin alloys have shown greater corrosion resistance than zinc. Previous tests undertaken in differing climates have shown that zinc corrodes in the presence of drying oils, such as tung oil in plywood packing cases, and with formaldehyde adhesives.[7]

Aluminium

Aluminium was discovered in 1820. Marked growth of the aluminium industry occurred in the years 1914 to 1918.[9]

In pollution-free conditions, aluminium is resistant to corrosion due to the formation of a protective film of aluminium oxide, Al_2O_3. Formic acid, however, peptizes this oxide film, producing a gelatinous layer that is no longer protective. Organic chlorides and hydrogen chloride also disrupt the oxide layer. Particularly in outdoor environments, aluminium is sensitive to sulphur dioxide. Surface analysis of aluminium from an indoor environment has shown that it accumulates adherent particles of chloride and sulphate. Pitting corrosion is characteristic of chloride and carboxylic acid corrosion.[10,11] In general, addition of alloying metals, such as copper, reduces the corrosion resistance of aluminium.[12] Previous tests have shown that aluminium corrodes in an enclosed environment containing urea-formaldehyde adhesive, in tropical conditions. Drying oils and painted plywood had no effect.[7]

Magnesium

Magnesium was isolated in 1808. Industrial production commenced on a modest scale towards the close of the 19th century.

Indoors, the primary reaction of magnesium is to form a hydroxide, $Mg(OH)_2$. This film becomes protective by secondary reactions, resulting in the formation of hydrated carbonates and sulphates. The most severely corroding environments for magnesium and its alloys are dilute chloride solutions and dilute acids, particularly mineral acids and organic acids, such as acetic and tartaric acids.[13] Alloying metals, such as manganese and zinc, reduce the electrode potential from that of pure magnesium, and the corrosion rate increases accordingly. It has been recommended that red lead or white lead paints should not be used with magnesium and its alloys, as traces of lead are precipitated electrolytically and cause pronounced local cell corrosion.[14]

Magnesium ribbon, stored in the laboratory, acquired a dense black covering where it had been exposed to the air. Tests with materials used to make packing cases showed that magnesium alloys corroded in wooden boxes of pine, beech and birch plywood. As a result recommendations were made that wood should be avoided when packing magnesium alloy parts.[7]

A Survey of Modern Metals in Museum Collections

The first stage was to assess the condition of modern metals in ambient museum environments. Objects in the collections of the Tate Gallery, Victoria and Albert Museum, Royal Air Force Museum and the British Museum were examined for signs of corrosion. Corrosion products were found on some objects containing zinc, aluminium and magnesium. However, many objects made from these metals exhibited no signs of corrosion.

Sculpture
A sculpture in magnesium consisting of 144 squares was found to have a white powdery deposit around the edges of the squares. This corrosion was identified as a mixture of magnesium oxide, MgO_2, and magnesium borate hydrate, $Mg_5(BO_3)O(OH)_5.2H_2O$. It is thought that this may have formed as a result of boric acid being used as a fire retardant,[15] or from cleaning agents around the sculpture.

In a sculpture by Beuys, comprising a zinc box containing fat resting in a painted wooden showcase, extensive zinc corrosion was observed. The zinc was in good condition in 1989. However, the showcase is part of the composition and the artist had instructed that the paint be maintained in good order. Following repainting in August 1990, the zinc developed a thick, white corrosion crust over its entire exposed surface. Analysis by X-ray diffraction (XRD) has shown this to be zinc formate hydrate, $C_2H_2O_4Zn.2H_2O$.

A screen-printed aluminium alloy sheet, by Longo, approximately five years old had developed elongated patches of white corrosion, corresponding to the direction of printing. This piece had been on open display and has been stored in wooden packing cases. Because of difficulty in obtaining a sample, analysis of the corrosion was not undertaken in this instance.

Bidri Ware
Bidri ware, made from a zinc alloy, was found to be corroding. The corrosion was identified as simonkolleite, $Zn_5(OH)_8Cl_2$.[16]

Aircraft Parts
Aircraft parts are generally made of aluminium and magnesium alloys for their low density and high strength. A number were examined and sampled at RAF Cardington, which holds part of the reserve collections of the Royal Air Force Museum at Hendon, London. Corrosion of some artefacts had occurred prior to collection, as they were often retrieved from wreckage after many years in the sea or outdoor environments. In one instance, a gearbox casing was found to be composed of a zinc-copper alloy, with corrosion products containing chlorides.

The majority of the artefacts are stored on open shelving in heat-sealed polyethylene bags. The "bagging-up" is carried out during periods of low humidities. This appears to be very successful, and no signs of further degradation of the metal pieces are visible.

Coins
The largest concentration of modern metals was found to be in the Department of Coins and Medals at the British Museum.

All coins are stored in non-lacquered mahogany coin trays in traditional wooden cabinets with tight-fitting wooden doors, thus the storage environment has negligible air exchange.

German coins issued during the years of 1914 to 1918 and 1939 to 1945 were found to be corroding, in most cases, producing a bulky white corrosion product.

More recent currency was observed to have a thin surface layer of white corrosion. Several of these coins had been retrieved from a small fountain in one of the Museum galleries, where visitors throw their loose change. The chloride level (58 ppm), conductivity (0.7 S cm^{-1} [where S represents Siemens]) and pH (8.3) of the water from the fountain were similar to levels found in tap water.

Ten coins in varying states of preservation were selected for further examination (Figure 1).

Figure 1 Corrosion on zinc coins stored in wooden cabinets. Photo: Department of Conservation, British Museum.

Analysis of Selected Coins

The coins were analysed using the scanning electron microscope with energy dispersive X-ray analysis SEM (EDXA). On most of the coins, it was possible to analyse a non-corroded and corroded area. The corrosion was further analysed by powder XRD. Results are shown in Table I.

Discussion of Coin Analysis

Most of the coins analysed were identified as zinc. In most cases the corrosion appeared to be active. Zinc formate hydrate was identified on one coin, and its formation was apparently due to exposure to formaldehyde, or formic acid, both of which can be emitted by wood and wood composites.

Although chlorides were present on the surface of the other zinc coins, only one chloride-containing corrosion product was identified, simonkolleite, $Zn_5(OH)_8Cl_2$. The most likely source of these chlorides is from handling the coins.

Table I

Condition of Coins and Analysis of Corrosion Products

NA = not analyzed
tr = trace

Coin	Condition	Elements Detected SEM (EDXA)		Corrosion Product (XRD)
		Metal	Corrosion	
German, 5 Gelder Stadtmark, circa 1920	General white surface thin corrosion layer	Zn, (tr: Cl, Ca)	Zn, Cl, (tr: Fe, Ca)	Amorphous
German, 10 Mark, 1919	General white thin corrosion layer, patches of thicker white corrosion	Zn, (tr: Pb, Cl)	Zn, (tr: Fe, Cl, Si, K)	Zinc formate hydrate $C_2H_2O_4Zn. 2H_2O$
German, 50 Pfennig, 1920	Localized patches, white corrosion	Zn, (tr: Cl, K, Ca)	Zn, Cl, (tr: Fe, Pb)	Simonkolleite $Zn_5 (OH)_8Cl_2$
German, 50 Pfennig, 1917	Small patches, white corrosion, generally good condition	Zn, (tr: Pb, S, Cl, Si, Al)	NA	NA
Czech, 2 Haleru, circa 1920	General white surface thin corrosion layer	NA	Zn, Cl, (tr: S, Fe)	Zinc carbonate hydroxide $Zn_5(CO_3)_2(OH)_6$
Icelandic, 5 Øre, 1954	Thick white surface corrosion	Zn, Cu, (tr: Cl, Si, Al, K, Ca)	Zn, Cl, (tr: Si, S, Al, Co)	Zinc carbonate hydroxide
French, 1 Franc, 1949	General white surface thin corrosion layer, with thicker patches	Al, (tr: Ag, Cl, Si, Ca, K, Sn, Cu)	Al, (tr: S, Cl, Ag, Si, Fe, Cu)	Unidentified
German, (Dresden), 20 Pfennig, circa 1920	Few white patches of corrosion	Ni, Zn, Cu, (tr: Mg, Ca, Fe, Cl)	Zn, Ni, Cl, (tr: Cu, S, Fe)	Zinc carbonate
German, 10 Mark, 1943	Some small patches of corrosion	Mg, (tr: Si, Al, Ca, Mn, S)	Mg, (tr: Fe, S, Ca, Cl, Si, K)	Magnesium carbonate hydroxide hydrate $Mg_5(CO_3)_4(OH)_2 .5H_2O$
Japanese, 1 Yen, 1986	Thick surface corrosion layer	Al, (tr: Ag, Si, Ca, K)	Al (tr: Si, Ag, Fe)	Unidentified

The corrosion product on the aluminium coin contained chloride, but was not positively identified as it gave a poor XRD pattern. Again the source of the chloride is probably handling. The magnesium corrosion, a carbonate, is probably due to reaction with atmospheric carbon dioxide. This reaction may be catalysed by the presence of organic acid vapours.

Ethnographic Artefacts

In the Department of Ethnography, a group of approximately 40 objects was examined. Most have been in the Museum since the beginning of this century. All are loosely wrapped in acid-free tissue and stored in boxes made from resin-bonded fibre. Several zinc objects were found to have patches of corrosion, though many pieces were in good condition. Zinc corrosion was also noted on some Indian anklets stored in wooden drawers. In general the aluminium was in good condition, even where it was in direct contact with wood. Nevertheless, two instances of corrosion of aluminium were observed and samples were taken for analysis.

Analysis of Ethnographic Artefacts

Simonkolleite, $Zn_5(OH)_8Cl_2$, was found on the edge of a zinc frame holding a museum label. The corrosion on the anklets was identified as basic zinc carbonate. Both these corrosion products, which are similar to those found on the coins, may have formed due to handling and the presence of volatile organic acids in the atmosphere. Two of the aluminium corrosion products were amorphous. Although the others remain unidentified, they were found, using the SEM (EDXA), to contain chlorides, presumably from handling.

Survey Conclusion

From this limited survey it appears that zinc presents the greatest problem. This was expected as zinc is known to corrode in the presence of common museum pollutants, such as organic acids.

Aluminium objects showed fewer instances of corrosion, but in general, they may be susceptible to a build-up of gases in an enclosed showcase or storage area.

As pure magnesium corrodes on exposure to moist air, it is unlikely to be encountered in pure form in museum objects. Only one magnesium alloy coin and one sculpture were identified in the survey. Magnesium alloys are more stable, but not fully resistant to pollutants potentially present in a museum environment.[17,18]

Materials Corrosive to Modern Metals Identified by the Oddy Test

In the British Museum, the corrosive effects of all materials to be used in the storage and display of silver, copper, lead and their alloys are assessed using the Oddy test.[2] This involves enclosing the material under investigation in a boiling tube with a clean, degreased coupon of metal, chosen to represent the composition of the artefacts to be stored or displayed, in close proximity to the material. To avoid contact with the test material, the metal coupon is suspended in the tube using nylon monofilament. To accelerate corrosion reactions, a small volume of water is added to create a high humidity. Solid carbon dioxide is added when lead is used to accelerate corrosion, as carbonates are formed as corrosion products. The boiling tube is sealed and placed in an oven at 60°C (see Figure 2).

The condition of the metal coupon is examined after 28 days and used to evaluate the suitability of the test material. The method of conducting the tests is under review and will be the subject of a later publication.[19]

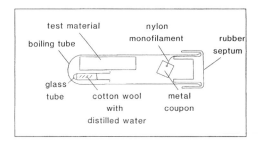

Figure 2 Diagrammatic representation of the Oddy test.

This test procedure was used to assess the corrosive effects of common materials used in storage and display in museums on zinc, aluminium and magnesium and their alloys. Tests were carried out with and without solid carbon dioxide added, to evaluate its effect.

The metals used in the tests were zinc, from a sheet already in the Museum; aluminium foil; Duralumin, an aluminium alloy containing a few percent of copper; magnesium sheet; and AZ31,* a magnesium alloy with small concentrations of aluminium, manganese and zinc.

Common materials used in storage and display in museums and known to be potentially corrosive to metals of antiquity were selected for the tests. These included wood, wood composites, paint, plastic and wool. The last was selected because wool-based fabrics, such as felt, are often used to dress display cases or in storage even though wool is known to evolve sulphur-containing gases that are corrosive to silver and other materials.

Tests with oak and plywood were set up in duplicate, one set having carbon dioxide ($CO_2(s)$) added, in order to investigate whether its presence is necessary to promote corrosion reactions of the metals and alloys under test. Controls were set up in ambient conditions, and, as in an Oddy test, with only water or water with $CO_2(s)$. Because of limited time and availability of some sample materials all of the samples were tested against zinc and aluminium, but only some were tested against magnesium, AZ31 magnesium alloy and Duralumin.

The metal coupons were examined after 28 days. Several samples of corrosion were taken and analysed using XRD. The results of the tests and the analysis are shown in Tables II, III, IV, V and VI.

Discussion of Oddy Tests

Zinc

Zinc showed slight corrosion in the presence of water, and water and carbon dioxide. However, the wood and wood composites caused much more severe corrosion. The zinc coupon with oak was so extensively corroded that it was beginning to laminate. Addition of carbon dioxide did cause increased corrosion with oak and plywood, but it is not considered to have had an effect on the outcome of the test, that is, the classification of the test material as unsuitable for use, or suitable for temporary or permanent use.

Zinc oxide was identified as the major corrosion product with the oak and plywood tests, even when additional carbon dioxide had been added. Later analysis showed that zinc carbonates were also present. This suggests that there had been reaction with atmospheric carbon dioxide after removal of the zinc pieces from the tests. Similar results have been reported by other workers.[4]

Formic acid attacked the zinc, producing a thick corrosion crust. Paints had some deleterious effect on zinc. Corrosion occurred in the presence of wool, but the resultant corrosion did not appear to contain sulphur.

Aluminium

Aluminium corroded only in the presence of formic acid. Some wood and wood composites did cause a slight dullness to the surface of the test pieces, but no corrosion product was formed. Similarly, wool and woollen felt produced a dull surface, which was yellow/brown in places. The latter is possibly due to deposits from the wool condensing on the metal.

Duralumin showed more evidence of surface dulling and discolouration in the tests. Corrosion formed on Duralumin in the tests with plywood and with formic acid, the latter producing both aluminium and copper corrosion. The corrosion products produced weak but similar XRD patterns. Although they were compared

---

* Specification, Magnesium Elektron Ltd. Report Serial No: ML11561

Zn	Al	Si	Cu	Mn	Fe
0.75	2.7	<0.01	<0.01	0.23	0.003

Ni	Ca	Zr	Others	Mg
<0.005	<0.01	<0.01	0.3	Rem

(units in percent)   Rem = Remainder

with known XRD patterns of common aluminium corrosion products, they were not identified. They appeared to be different from the unidentified patterns obtained from samples of aluminium corrosion from objects in the ethnographic collection in the British Museum. Addition of CO_2 to the tests had little effect on the aluminium or Duralumin.

Magnesium

Magnesium was particularly susceptible to corrosion under the test conditions. The "control" conditions, that is, with water alone, and water with carbon dioxide, caused slight corrosion of the test pieces with corrosion products being white in all cases. However, some of the materials under test caused considerably more corrosion. Only the degrading PVC and the paints did not cause corrosion of the pure magnesium test pieces.

The magnesium alloy AZ31 was also susceptible to corrosion. However, although it had acquired a thin corrosion layer in many of the tests, the samples were not as extensively attacked as the pure magnesium samples. Carbon dioxide did not affect the outcome of tests with magnesium or AZ31.

Conclusion from Oddy Tests

The results suggest that the Oddy test can be used to evaluate the corrosive effects of storage and display materials on zinc, aluminium, magnesium and their alloys. The addition of carbon dioxide is not necessary as it does not affect the results of the test. A control, with the metal and water only, should always be carried out and used for comparison with other tests.

It should be borne in mind that wood may vary according to its age, storage and seasoning. This in turn may affect its corrosive nature. Wood composites, such as chipboard and plywood, can also have variable effects because of variability in composition. The drying period

Table II

Condition of Zinc and Major Corrosion Products after the Oddy Test with a Range of Materials

NC = no change	NA = not analysed	
Test Conditions	**Condition after Test**	**Corrosion Product (XRD)**
Control (window sill)	NC	-
Material in Oddy Test		
-	Darkening of surface	ZnO
CO_2	Darkening of surface, light thin corrosion layer on low edge	ZnO
Oak	Extensive white corrosion	ZnO
Oak, CO_2	Thick white corrosion, lamination of metal	NA
Plywood	Extensive white corrosion	NA
Plywood, CO_2	Extensive white corrosion	$ZnO + Zn_4CO_3(OH)_6.H_2O$
Formic acid (1 drop)	Thick white corrosion	zinc formate hydrate $Zn(COOH)_2.2H_2O$
Cardboard	Slight white surface corrosion	NA
Gloss paint	Yellow/white thin corrosion layer on surface	NA
Vinyl matt paint	Slight surface corrosion layer	NA
Scoured, unspun wool	Heavy yellow/white corrosion	NA
Degrading PVC	Slight corrosion layer	NA
Mahogany	Light surface corrosion layer	ZnO
Pine	Thick white corrosion, lamination of metal	ZnO
Medium-density fibreboard (MDF)	Thick white corrosion	ZnO
Chipboard	Entire surface covered with white corrosion	possibly $Zn_5(CO_3)_2(OH)_6$

Table III

Condition of Aluminium and Major Corrosion Products after the Oddy Test with a Range of Materials

NC = no change

Test Conditions	Condition after Test	Corrosion Product (XRD)
Control (window sill)	NC	-
Material in Oddy Test		
-	NC	-
CO_2	NC	-
Oak	Dulling of surface	-
Oak, CO_2	Dulling of surface	-
Plywood	Dulling of surface	-
Plywood, CO_2	Dulling of surface	-
Formic acid (1 drop)	Off-white surface, metal disintegrating	-
Cardboard	NC	-
Gloss paint	NC	-
Vinyl matt paint	NC	-
Scoured, unspun wool	Some yellow/brown patches but no corrosion	-
Degrading PVC	NC	-
Mahogany	NC	-
Pine	NC	-
Medium-density fibreboard (MDF)	NC (resinous deposit)	-
Chipboard	NC (resinous deposit)	-
Woollen felt	Dulling of surface, yellow/brown in places	

Table IV

Condition of Duralumin, an Aluminium Alloy, and Major Corrosion Products after the Oddy Test with a Range of Materials

NC = no change   NA = not analysed

Test Conditions	Condition after Test	Corrosion Product (XRD)
Control (window sill)	Slight dulling	-
Material in Oddy Test		
-	Dulling of surface	-
CO_2	Small patch of white corrosion on lower edge	NA
Oak	Small patch of white corrosion on lower edge	NA
Oak, CO_2	Small patch of white corrosion on lower edge	NA
Plywood	Few spots of corrosion	NA
Plywood, CO_2	Few spots of corrosion	Unidentified
Formic acid (1 drop)	Patches of white corrosion sometimes "watery," and some green corrosion	Unidentified
Cardboard	NC	NA
Gloss paint	Some dulling	NA
Vinyl matt paint	Some dulling	NA
Scoured, unspun wool	Yellowish thin corrosion layer	NA
Degrading PVC	Grey, powdery corrosion on lower edge	NA

268

Table V

Condition of Magnesium and Major Corrosion Products after the Oddy Test with a Range of Materials

NC = no change   NA = not analysed

Test Conditions	Condition after Test	Corrosion Product (XRD)
Control (window sill)	NC	-
Material in Oddy Test		
-	Darkened surface, white corrosion lower edge	NA
CO_2	Darkened surface, white corrosion lower edge	NA
Oak	Heavy corrosion	Magnesium carbonate hydroxide hydrate $Mg(CO_3)_4.5H_2O$
Oak, CO_2	Thick voluminous corrosion	$Mg(CO_3)_4.5H_2O$
Plywood	Extensive corrosion	$Mg(CO_3)_4.5H_2O$
Plywood, CO_2	Several spots of corrosion	NA
Formic acid (1 drop)	Metal eaten away, white corrosion	$Mg(CO_3)_4.5H_2O$
Cardboard	Heavy outbreaks, white corrosion	NA
Gloss paint	Slight corrosion, lower edge	NA
Vinyl matt paint	Some corrosion on lower half	NA
Scoured, unspun wool	Heavy corrosion over entire surface	$Mg_5(CO_3)_4(OH)_2.4H_2O$
Degrading PVC	Some corrosion on lower half	amorphous

Table VI

Condition of AZ31, a Magnesium Alloy, and Major Corrosion Products after the Oddy Test with a Range of Materials

NC = no change   NA = not analysed

Test Conditions	Condition after Test	Corrosion Product (XRD)
Control (window sill)	NC	-
Material in Oddy Test		
-	Black surface, white corrosion, lower edge	NA
CO_2	Black surface, white corrosion, lower edge	NA
Oak	Spots of white corrosion over entire surface	NA
Oak, CO_2	Spots of white corrosion over entire surface	Magnesium carbonate hydroxide hydrate $Mg(CO_3)_4(OH)_2.5H_2O$
Plywood	White thin corrosion layer over entire surface	NA
Plywood, CO_2	White thin corrosion layer over entire surface	$Mg(CO_3)_4(OH)_2.5H_2O$
Formic acid (1 drop)	Metal eaten away, white corrosion	Magnesium formate hydrate $Mg(COOH)_2. 2H_2O$
Cardboard	White thin corrosion layer and spots of corrosion	NA
Gloss paint	White "watery" corrosion	NA
Vinyl matt paint	White thin corrosion layer over entire surface	NA
Scoured, unspun wool	Heavy off-white thin corrosion layer	$Mg_5(CO_3)_4(OH)_2. 5H_2O$
Degrading PVC	Black surface, white corrosion lower edge	NA

should be considered when dealing with paints, as the rate of emission of corrosive gases usually decreases with increased drying period.

Recommendations for Storage and Display of Modern Metals

Aluminium and Duralumin appear to be stable towards the gases of common materials used in storage and display in museums, with the exception of high concentrations of formic acid. It is therefore recommended that since formaldehyde may oxidize to formic acid at the metal surface, high formaldehyde emitters and materials that can give off formic acid should not be used in conjunction with aluminium and its alloys. Such materials may include urea-formaldehyde and phenol-formaldehyde adhesives and composite wood products whose wood and adhesive content may vary from batch to batch. Although PVC did not cause corrosion in these tests it is not recommended for use.

Zinc and magnesium corrode in the presence of organic acids. Thus woods, wood composites, paints and adhesives that evolve organic acids should not be used in the storage and display of these metals and their alloys. Since high humidity will promote the corrosion reactions, these metals should be kept in a relatively dry environment, for example, below 50% RH. Storing artefacts made from these metals in stove-enamelled or epoxy-coated metal cabinets will provide a stable environment.

Conclusion

This study has shown that modern metals, particularly zinc and magnesium, are susceptible to corrosion by common atmospheric pollutants in museums. However, if care is taken when selecting materials for use in storage and display, these metals should not present more of a problem than the metals of antiquity.

Acknowledgement

The authors thank W.A. Oddy, Keeper of the Department of Conservation, for editing and permission to publish; S. Bradley for guidance and advice; C. Enderly and P. Attwood for help with coins and medals collections; J. Osborn for help with ethnography collections; J. Heumann of the Tate Gallery and D. Heath and G. Martin of the Victoria and Albert Museum for permission to examine parts of their collections and undertake analysis on corrosion products; P. Whelan of Magnesium Elektron Ltd. for generous donation of samples of magnesium and magnesium alloy and for experimental work; staff members at the Royal Air Force Museum at Hendon; R. Funnell, curator at the Royal Air Force Museum's Cardington outstation, for information regarding the use of modern metals in aircraft and help and permission to examine parts of the collection and to take samples; V. Tremain and B. Burr for typing; T. Springett and K. Lovelock for photography; and the Conservation Unit for helping finance the trip to Ottawa to present this paper.

Suppliers

Magnesium Ribbon
Merck Ltd., Broom Road, Poole, Dorset, BH12 4NN, U.K.

Magnesium Alloy AZ31
Magnesium Elektron Ltd., P.O. Box 6, Swinton, Manchester M27 2LS, U.K.

Nylon Monofilament
Available as fishing line from fishing tackle shops or as nylon thread from haberdashers.

Résumé

Les métaux modernes dans les collections de musée

Il est bien connu que les matières utilisées pour la mise en réserve et l'exposition d'objets anciens peuvent libérer des gaz nocifs qui sont à la source de divers processus de dégradation, dont la corrosion. Aussi, pour évaluer jusqu'à quel point ces matières peuvent causer de la corrosion chez les métaux, les spécialistes de la restauration du British Museum se servent-ils, depuis 1972, d'un essai de vieillissement accéléré qui, connu sous le nom de « test Oddy », a été utilisé pour mesurer leur effet corrosif sur l'argent, sur le cuivre et sur le plomb, soit les trois métaux qui ont le plus tendance à se corroder. De telles mesures ont d'ailleurs permis de réduire de façon marquée le nombre des objets qui se corrodent dans les vitrines d'exposition, et de ralentir le ternissement de l'argent.

À l'instar des autres musées, le British Museum continue, en ce XXe siècle, de collectionner des objets, de sorte que divers objets — des pièces de monnaie ou des médailles, entre autres — faits à partir de métaux modernes — l'aluminium, le zinc, le magnésium ou des alliages de ces métaux — forment désormais une partie importante de ses collections. Ces métaux se retrouvent d'ailleurs souvent dans les galeries d'art moderne, et ils ne risquent pas moins de se corroder que les métaux anciens. On a ainsi constaté que des objets en aluminium présentaient une corrosion localisée par piqûres ou une mince couche blanche de corrosion. Que des pièces de monnaie en zinc datant de la première et de la seconde guerre mondiale, qui avaient été mises en réserve dans des armoires en bois, s'étaient complètement corrodées. Et qu'une couche blanche superficielle de corrosion s'était formée sur du magnésium. Ces constatations ne sont pas sans préoccuper les spécialistes de la restauration, qui ont donc entrepris une étude en vue de déterminer les causes de la corrosion, mettre au point des tests Oddy pour les matières que l'on voudrait employer pour la mise en réserve et l'exposition d'objets faits à partir de ces métaux et énoncer des directives pour la mise en réserve et l'exposition d'objets faits à partir de ces métaux.

Pour mieux comprendre ces divers processus de la corrosion, on a d'abord commencé par identifier les matières qui en sont à la source, et par passer en revue les documents qui existent sur le sujet. Une série d'expériences a ensuite été menée en se fondant sur ces données, afin d'étudier l'incidence qu'ont, sur ces métaux, les substances polluantes connues qui se retrouvent dans les musées.

Les directives pour la mise en réserve et l'exposition d'objets faits à partir de ces métaux ont été préparées.

References

1. Blackshaw, S.M. and V.D. Daniels, "The Testing of Materials for Use in the Storage and Display in Museums," *The Conservator*, vol. 3, 1979, pp. 16-19.

2. Oddy, W.A., "An Unsuspected Danger in Display," *Museums Journal*, vol. 73, no. 1, 1973, pp. 27-28.

3. Smith, E., ed., *Monographs on Industrial Chemistry* (London: Longman Green and Co., 1918).

4. Haynie, F.H., "Theoretical Air Pollution and Climate Effects on Materials Confirmed by Zinc Corrosion Data," in: *Durability of Building Materials and Components*, Proc. of the 1st International Conference, Ottawa, 1978, pp. 157-175.

5. Skerry, B.S. et al., "Corrosion in Smoke, Hydrocarbon and SO_2 Polluted Atmospheres - III The General Behaviour of Zinc," *Corrosion Science*, vol. 28, no. 7, 1988, pp. 721-740.

6. Rance, V.E. and H.G. Cole, *Corrosion of Metals by Vapours from Organic Materials: A Survey* (London: Her Majesty's Stationary Office, 1958).

7. Mellor, J.W., *A Comprehensive Treatise on Inorganic and Theoretical Chemistry* (London: Longmans Green and Co., 1923), vol. IV, p. 476.

8. Duncan, S., "Aluminium: Its Alloys, Coatings and Corrosion," in: *Modern Metals in Museums* (London: Institute of Archaeology Publications, 1988) pp. 27-32.

9. Graedel, T.E., "Corrosion Mechanisms for Aluminiums Exposed to the Atmosphere," *J. Electrochem. Soc.*, vol. 136, no. 4, 1989, pp. 204C-212C.

10. Gorson, M.G., *Aluminium and Its Alloys* (New York: Van Nostrand Reinhold, 1926).

11. Farmer, H. and C. Porter, "Corrosion of Metals in Association with Wood. Part 3. Corrosion of Aluminium in Contact with Wood," *Wood*, vol. 28, 1963, pp. 505-507.

12. Roberts, Sheldon, *Magnesium and Its Alloys* (New York: John Wiley and Sons Inc., 1960).

13. Beck, A., *The Technology of Magnesium and Its Alloys*, 3rd edn., A translation from German by the technical staffs of F.A. Hughes & Co. Ltd. and Magnesium Elektron Limited of Magnesium und seine Legierungen (London: F.A. Hughes & Co. Ltd., 1943) p. 298.

14. Beck, A., *The Technology of Magnesium*, p. 308.

15. Bradley, S.M., personal communication, 1991.

16. La Niece, S. and G. Martin, "The Technical Examination of Bidri Ware," *Studies in Conservation*, vol. 32, 1987, pp. 97-101.

17. Brimblecombe, P., "The Chemistry of Museum Air," *Environmental Monitoring and Control*, SSCR Dundee, pp. 56-64.

18. Brimblecombe, P., "The Composition of Museum Atmospheres," *Atmospheric Environment*, vol. 24B, no. 1, 1990, pp. 1-18.

19. Thickett, D. and L.R. Green, "Re-evaluation of the Testing Procedures for Materials for Storage and Display in The British Museum," *The British Museum Conservation Research Section Internal Report* 1991, 22.

Finishes on Aluminium — A Conservation Perspective

Chris Adams and David Hallam

Conservation Section
Australian War Memorial
Canberra, Australia

Abstract

In terms of volume of production, aluminium is the world's leading non-ferrous metal. Because of its lightness and unique physical and chemical properties, its suitability for the construction of aircraft was recognized early this century.

Concurrent with the development of aluminium and its alloys as a construction material arose the need for stable and resistant surface finishes. Surface finishing techniques developed rapidly in both Europe and the United States. Today several important classes of finishes are used.

The Australian War Memorial (AWM) has an extensive collection of aluminium aircraft. In this paper these aircraft are used to illustrate the development of aluminium alloys as structural materials and of the associated coating technologies. Particular emphasis is placed on oxide conversion coatings.

In museums, it has been our observation that these finishes have, to a large extent, been ignored — to the detriment of objects, their history and conservation in general. These coatings can offer important historical and technical information. As intrinsic parts of the object, every effort should be made to devise conservation strategies to retain them. Further, it is only through an understanding of the construction of an object and its deterioration that appropriate treatments can be developed.

Methods of categorization and analysis developed and used at the AWM are discussed, including the reproduction of various coatings from the original formulations. Some conservation strategies have been developed, some are proposed. The implications of this methodology and future prospects conclude the discussion.

This paper attempts to initiate debate on the above through a discussion of the relevance of surface coatings studies to the museum.

Introduction

Most conservation projects have a logical beginning. In July 1982 we decided to restore our Messerschmitt Me 262A-1 aircraft. The Conservation Section of the Australian War Memorial (AWM) was given the task of writing the specification for the project. We found this task was not easy, but it did provide us with a good introduction to aircraft technology. Our attention was soon drawn to the grey-green "anodizing" on the aluminium surfaces of unpainted portions of the aircraft.

Before treatment commenced, we wanted to know more about the materials on which we were to work. Communication with other museums with similar aircraft uncovered a large gap in their knowledge of aluminium surface coatings used in the construction of aircraft. Some had stripped the coatings during restoration, others had no idea that coatings were indeed present. The lack of understanding within the museum community as to the importance of metal surface modification was obvious. The need to conserve the metal surfaces as well as the body of the object was not appreciated by those working with technology collections.

We decided to use aluminium oxide coatings as an example of a modified metal surface and undertake investigations from historical and conservation points of view. (The same sort of study is needed for ferrous metals, magnesium, zinc, copper, and all other modern metals and their alloys.)

Fortunately the Me 262A-1 restoration project was aborted and the aircraft was returned to storage for further study and a more sympathetic treatment was undertaken 10 years later. Our approach to aircraft is now quite different in that it is based firmly in the conservation ethic.

Aims

In this study we aimed to confirm historical sources of information about the treatment of aluminium and the manufacturing of aircraft. We also wanted to confirm or add to the information on the technology transfer between the Germans and Japanese during the 1930s and 1940s.

As conservators we wanted to understand more about the history and technology of finishes on aluminium; the chemistry of the aluminium surface and its interactions with the environment; and the effects of any possible treatment on the aluminium surface and its long-term stability.

This work is by no means complete, but we hope that it will go some way towards a better understanding of the behaviour of aluminium so that we may develop conservation approaches that maintain an object's integrity. In museums the general approach to aluminium is to assume that it is unstable. Thus any treatment commences with the stripping of the unstable natural oxides along with the synthetic conversion coating, followed by the application of inhibited or uninhibited organic coatings.

Eventually data on oxide coating types, combined with information on the alloy composition and paint types should assist in studies of the authenticity and provenance of objects.

So far, we have carried out literature and historical searches on aluminium finishes, history and technology. We have also developed analytical approaches to characterize and identify the coatings used on aircraft in the AWM collection.

Historical Information

In order to understand finishes on aluminium we must first gain an appreciation of aluminium as a structural material. It has been argued that it did not supersede wood as the main aircraft construction material until its corrosion behaviour was understood and control processes had been developed.[1] This was accomplished independently in several countries. In the United States, Alclad was developed by Alcoa.[2] The English developed anodizing.[3] The Europeans, particularly the Germans, developed the use of oxide conversion coatings.[4] The Japanese developed the oxalic acid anodizing process.[5]

Aluminium finishes can be divided into the following classes: mechanical finishes; chemical finishes; metallic coatings; organic and inorganic coatings; anodizing; and chemical conversion coatings. In our study we are primarily interested in the chemical conversion coatings, but we will also briefly consider the other classes.

Aluminium Surface Finishes

The oxide film on aluminium forms immediately on exposure to the atmosphere. (Oxide film thicknesses are shown in Table I.) It has a molecular volume of 1.5 times that of the metal. It is thus under compressive stress, and covers the metal continuously. Furthermore, it can cope with substantial deformation without rupture. As the film grows naturally, it breaks from the metal surface to form its own structure, and this reduces the stress on the film. Imperfections develop in this transition, and these accelerate the breakdown of the film. Breakdown is also accelerated by the solubilization

Table I
Thickness of Oxide Coatings on Aluminium

Coatings	Thickness in nm
Natural oxide on Al or Al-Mg alloy (formed below 300°C)	1 to 3
Natural oxide on Al (formed above 300°C)	30
Natural oxide on Al-Mg alloy (formed above 300°C)	3,000
Normal chemical oxide coating (e.g., MBV, Alrok, etc.)	2,500 to 5,000
Normal barrier layer anodizing	250 to 750
Normal protective anodic coating (e.g., Sulphuric acid anodizing)	5,000 to 30,000
Hard anodic coatings (e.g., for engineering purposes)	25,000 to 150,000

of the film by aggressive anions, such as chlorides and sulphates.

By growing the films in a controlled manner during the manufacture, thicker, compact films with a higher corrosion resistance can be formed. Although this was realized in the 19th century[6] it was not developed until 1916 in Germany.[4]

Mechanical Finishes

Mechanical finishes[7] are created by cutting and milling. These mechanical processes work the upper layers of the metal and impose stress. Mechanical finishes may either increase or decrease susceptibility to corrosion. The more stressed the surface, the more likely corrosion is to occur. Hence a polished surface should be more stable than a rough milled surface. The basic mechanical finishes are as follows:

Grinding and Dressing: This is done with emery wheels or abrasive belts with an open abrasive structure to prevent clogging. It is normally undertaken as part of a rough fitting or finishing process.

Abrasive Blasting: Normally this is done to produce an even finish on castings or forgings and to remove the thick oxide layer formed during the manufacturing process.[8]

Scratch Brushing: Wire scratch brushes are used to produce a matt surface. The bristles move at 90 m to 120 m per min (300 ft to 400 ft per min). The surface may also be pickled to enhance the effect. Parts so treated are normally decorative and are lacquered. Unlacquered components can be cleaned with an eraser.

Burnishing and Polishing: The same type of methods are used for aluminium as for other metals.

Ball Burnishing: Rotating barrels filled with metal balls and a silicate detergent are used to produce a burnished surface on small parts.

Rough Polishing: This is used as a preliminary step to other finishing techniques to remove the scratches from dressing and remnants of the casting skin. Normally the abrasive (silicon carbide or alumina) is belt- or wheel-mounted, and runs at speeds of 1,800 m to 2,400 m per min (6,000 ft to 8,000 ft per min).

Polishing or Buffing: Mops with polishing compound of alumina, tripoli, and chrome oxides are used. The compound is applied to the mop as a wax mix, for example, one part montane wax and three parts alumina. The part is held against the mop until the glazing scratches are removed. Final polish is done on a loose mop after removing the previous polish residue. Tints can be produced by using a final polish that is coloured.

Chemical Finishes

Frosting: Frosted finishes are normally produced in either a 20% hot (50°C to 80 °C) caustic soda solution or a mix of nitric and hydrofluoric acid. Both processes involve controlled corrosion of the object and produce a surface full of micro-pits.[8]

Acid Cleaning: This practice primarily in mineral acid by immersion or application is a common pre-treatment for aluminium in the fabrication of a component. Acid cleaning is used in the following ways: cleaning with little or no etch prior to organic coating or electroplating; removing smut and neutralizing after alkaline etching; removing oxides; matt or bright etching for decorative finishes; deep etching of pattern or relief; very deep etching for chemical milling or contouring; undercut etching for application to teflon (PTFE); and electrolytic etching for lithographic printing processes.

Etching: Aluminium can be etched using a bituminous relief and an etchant composed of 100 mL of 10% copper sulphate, 20 mL of concentrated hydrochloric acid, and glycerine as a thickening agent.

Chemical Milling: Developed in the U.S. in 1949, this is also a form of controlled etching that is now used to machine material without stress.

Acid Treatments of Aluminium: Early treatments of aluminium seem to have used non-etching chromic acid, since traces of chromate have been found on the aluminium engine cowl skin from the SPAD aircraft at the National Air and Space Museum in Washington, D.C. during restoration treatment. A typical chromic acid solution is composed of: chromic acid 5%, sulphuric acid 15% and water 80%. The earliest reference we have found is Bengston.[9]

Hydrofluoric[10] and phosphoric acid based[11] solutions are used widely to remove oxides and etch the alloy surface. Typical formulations are the following:

hydrofluoric acid (40%)	10%
nitric acid (specific gravity 1.42)	10%
water	80%
or:	
phosphoric acid	10%
butyl alcohol	40%
isopropanol	30%
water	20%
wetting agent (i.e., naphthalene sulphonic acid)	trace %

Metallic Coatings

Chemical: Baths have been used to cement thin coatings of copper to aluminium before electroplating, without the use of electricity.[12]

Electroplate: Aluminium can be electroplated. In the AWM we have examples of nickel, chrome and copper plating. Most of the electroplated objects are of Japanese origin, and none have survived well.

Applied Metal Coatings

Spray: Spray coating of pure aluminium onto castings is a rare type of treatment that predates Alclad.[13]

Roll-on: Work by Dix[14] at Alcoa to create Alclad changed the use of aluminium in aircraft and resulted in the demise of wooden structures. As a rule, the outer pure aluminium coating is 5% to 10% of the total cross-sectional area. Duralplat, Alplat, Albondur, Avionalplat, and Chitonal are but a few of the trade names used in the late 1930s by other firms throughout the world producing clad aluminium.

Anodizing: At present 5% of all aluminium manufactured is anodized.[15] In the 1930s and 1940s it was used most extensively on naval aircraft and in particular on seaplanes. Anodizing processes can be identified visually, although at times process colouring can make this more difficult. Anodized surfaces are stable except when exposed to industrial and saline environments for periods longer than 40 years. Most of the processes are based on chromic acid, sulphuric acid or oxalic acid.

Chromic Acid: The process of anodizing was first introduced as the Bengough-Stuart[16] chromic acid process in 1927 for the protection of Duraluminium seaplanes. The process is still widely used in Britain under specification DEF 151. In the U.S. this process was modified by the Battle Memorial Institute[17] using more concentrated solutions, a constant voltage and additions of sulphuric acid.

Sulphuric Acid: The use of sulphuric acid for anodizing was developed in the U.S. and patented in Britain in 1927 by C.H.R. Gower and S.O. O'Brien.

Oxalic Acid: The oxalic acid process was first developed in Japan. The Germans adopted it under the name Eloxal during the 1930s and 1940s (note: German authors also use the name Eloxal GS to denote a direct-current process employing sulphuric acid). A second oxalic acid based process called Ematal was developed in 1935 in Switzerland.

Electro-brightening: Bright anodizing is used to produce such items as reflectors on lights and automotive trim (e.g., Volkswagen logos and Volvo bumper bars). Two processes were patented in 1936 in England and the U.S. The English Bytal process[18] patented by the British Aluminium Company is based on sodium carbonate and tri-sodium phosphate solutions. The American Alzak[19] process uses a fluoroborate solution. The finishes resulting from these processes have a high reflectance but do not have outstanding corrosion resistance.

Chemical Conversion Coatings

These can be classified and described as follows:

Boiling: This process is used in the production of capacitors,[20] but was used early this century as a general finishing method on aluminium.

Acid Treatment: The finishes produced by phosphoric acid and chromic acid mixtures used during manufacture can be considered to be conversion coatings, as they leave aluminium chromate and phosphate residues on the surface. These residues have a slight grey colour and some iridescence. Often these treatments were done as part of the foundry or fabrication shop process to clean the metal and were not applied specifically for corrosion resistance. Thus they differ significantly from the later (post 1945) conversion coatings.

Oxide Films

These tend to be derived from alkaline based treatments containing chromates. The main types are as follows:

Bauer Vogel (BV): The aluminium is immersed in a boiling solution of alkaline carbonate and chromate for about an hour.[4]

Modified Bauer Vogel (MBV): This modification on the original process[21] reduces the treatment time to five minutes and produces a light-to dark-grey film. The intensity of the colour depends on the time of immersion. The coating can be sealed with sodium silicate. Colour can vary with immersion time, surface state and alloy composition, as shown in Table II.

Erftwek (EW): This[22] was based on the MBV process but contained silicate and could be used on alloys of high copper content, giving a much lighter colour than the MBV process. The solution contains fluoride, chromate and carbonate. The related LW[23] process produces a clear coating.

Alrok: This American version of the MBV process was developed by Alcoa and used potassium carbonate and sodium dichromate. The protective film was sealed with a potassium dichromate solution.

Pylumin: This process[23] is based on di-sodium phosphate and was used by the British.

Table II
Effects of Surface State and Alloy Composition on Appearance of MBV Coatings

Alloy Composition %		State of Surface	Appearance with Casting Skin Intact	Removed
Al	99.8	Fine	Green/grey	Green/grey
Si	0.08			
Fe	0.11	Coarse	Spotty	Green, metallic, spotty
Al	99.2	Fine	Green/grey	Dark grey
Si	0.36			
Fe	0.41	Coarse	Spotty	Green/grey, local light spotting
Al	99.5	Fine	Milky grey	Light grey
Si	0.16			
Fe	0.22	Coarse	Spotty	Light grey

Acid Processes Conversion Coatings

The principal acid-based processes were developed in the 1940s in the U.S. Immersion times are typically 30 seconds to five minutes at room temperature. The main types are as follows:

Phosphate Conversion Coatings: The solutions contain phosphate, chromate and fluoride ions. Films produced are greenish in colour and consist of chromium and aluminium phosphates. Common trade names are Alodine and Alocrom.

Chromate Conversion Coatings: More recently, solutions containing chromate fluoride and nitrate have been used to produce a golden brown coating containing chromate as a major constituent (e.g., Alocrom 1200 and its derivatives).

As environmental legislation restricts the use of chromium, manufacturers are now avoiding its use and tending towards the use of phosphates and an Australian-developed cerium-based coating.[24]

Analytical Techniques to Characterize and Identify Coatings on the AWM Aircraft

Before any analytical techniques were investigated, we considered it appropriate to reproduce known coatings using original formulations and procedures obtained from original sources. We considered three processes, Bauer Vogel, Modified Bauer Vogel and Erftwerk, to be appropriate. These would provide a good representation of the processes likely to be found on the aircraft to be studied.

In all the original formulations we recognized that immersion time was the major variable in producing coatings of appropriate thicknesses that possess sufficient adherent properties. These times were varied significantly by the original formulators either intentionally to obtain certain properties or effects[25] or accidentally as a result of poor quality control.

Therefore, a certain amount of experimentation was necessary initially to replicate the homogeneous coating that could occur on the objects to be investigated. Figures 1 and 2 show scanning electron micrographs of MBV coatings produced by immersion for 25 minutes and 5 minutes respectively. The 25-minute sample shows that the adherent properties of the layer have been lost. The 5-minute sample adheres and is, apparently, quite homogeneous in nature.

Samples were then taken from three aircraft from the Second World War period, namely, a Messerschmitt Me 109G-6 (1945), a Messerschmitt Me 262A-1 (1944), and a

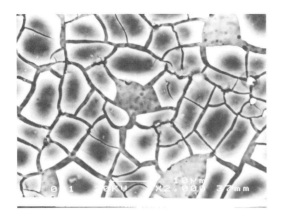

Figure 1 MBV coating produced by immersion for 25 minutes.

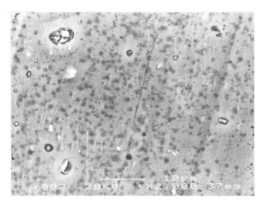

Figure 2 MBV coating produced by immersion for 5 minutes.

Mitsubishi A6M2 Zero (1942). These were chosen because they had a high treatment priority and because they represented typical examples of the mass-produced fighting aircraft of two nations. Also, these aircraft were considered to be in their original condition, as their histories were known.

Our primary aim was to investigate and, if necessary, develop techniques by which we could categorize and compare surface coatings in detail.

Examination Techniques

Visual Examination: This type of examination of an alloy surface can quite often reveal the presence of some sort of inorganic surface coating or other surface finish.[26] With

experience, it is sometimes possible to differentiate between chromate coatings, anodization and chemical conversion coatings by noting interference fringes and colour differences. Although visual examination is useful, we require far more specific information than it can provide.

Optical Microscopy: Information obtained by cross-sectioning, polishing, etching, and visual examination under a high-powered optical microscope can provide useful information for the identification of the base alloy.[27] The nature of the base metal is of significance, as historically it is known that only certain classes of coatings were used with certain types of alloys.[4]

Structure samples taken from the three aircraft studied are shown in Figures 3, 4 and 5. Although they have similar chemical compositions, the grain structure of these samples are somewhat dissimilar and display the fact that their manufacturing processes were not the same. For example, it is apparent that although all the samples have been hot- or cold-rolled, the more rounded nature of the grains in the Me 109G-6 sample indicate that an extensive process of annealing has occurred. Conversely, the very elongated grains exhibited in the other two samples indicate that no annealing was undertaken. It was further noted that the only non-clad alloy was that of the Zero fabrication sheet.

Optical microscopy can also be used to reveal the presence of a surface coating, although no information as to its composition can be gained. In some instances microchemical techniques have revealed the presence of

Figure 3 Me 109G-6 fabrication sheet, base metal structure (1,000x).

Figure 4 Me 262A-1 fabrication sheet, tail section base metal structure (1,000x).

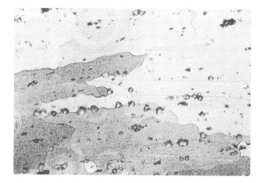

Figure 5 Mi A6M2 Zero fabrication sheet, drop tank base metal structure (1,000x).

chromium and other metals associated with oxide coatings.[28]

Scanning Electron Microscopy and Energy Dispersive X-ray Analysis (EDXA): When combined with information obtained from the optical microscope regarding grain structure, qualitative and quantitative elemental analysis of the base metal will aid in classification. The equipment used for these studies was a Cambridge Stereoscan 360 fitted with a Tracor Northern EDXA analyser using a standardless semi-quantitative analysis program. A summary of base alloy analysis from the three study aircraft is presented in Table III.

These results indicate that all were aluminium/copper alloys, which would place them in the modern categorization of the 2,000 series of copper-containing aluminium alloys. It should be noted that aluminium and magnesium concentrations are combined because the aluminium Ka peak and the magnesium Ka peak are close in energy distribution at the concentrations encountered, and differentiation is impossible. To identify positively a particular alloy, the magnesium content should be known.

Problems arise however, when the composition of the surface coatings are to be studied. Typically the film thickness of a chemical conversion coating will range from 0.5 microns to 5 microns. Figure 6 shows a SEM image of the conversion coating on the sample taken from the Zero drop tank. Operating at a 20 KeV energy level, that which is required for an analysis of this type, the electron beam has a penetration into aluminium of around 1.0 micron to 3.0 microns, depending on circumstances and a minimum diameter of approximately 1.0 micron.[29] Thus, the ability to detect elements that are perhaps present in small proportion from a thin layer is severely hampered. The analysis obtained in most cases is that of the underlying base metal rather than that of the surface coating. Some success has been achieved, however. Figure 7 indicates an EDXA trace of the analysis of the drop tank

Table III

Standardless Quantitative EDXA Analysis of Base Metal Alloys

| | % by weight composition | | | |
	Al & Mg	Mn	Cu	Fe
Zero drop tank	96.93	0.45	2.39	0.22
Zero fabrication sheet	96.54	0.40	2.98	0.08
Me109G-6 fabrication sheet	96.90	0.51	2.44	0.14
Me262A-1 tail	96.83	0.41	2.43	0.34
Me262A-1 main plane	96.71	0.49	2.58	0.22

Figure 6 Scanning electron micrograph showing thickness of typical chromate conversion coating (Zero drop tank).

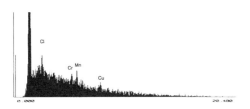

Figure 7 EDXA analysis of Zero drop tank conversion coating.

from the Zero where chromium has been detected.

Obviously the thicker the coating, the easier it is to detect chromium. Although it was determined that coatings were present in some instances they could not be specifically identified.

To date, experiments of mounting the sample with different orientations to increase the response from the surface, both in cross-section and plane-section, have proved to be of little advantage.

X-ray Diffraction (XRD): XRD of surfaces treated with the MBV process indicated the presence of an aluminium oxide polymorph. No chromium species were detected, probably because if there were any, they would be in an amorphous form. If any crystalline species were present, they would have a peak probably masked by the large aluminium peak. This technique therefore does not appear to be very useful.

X-ray Photoelectron Spectroscopy (XPS):
XPS analysis uses low-energy X-rays (from aluminium or magnesium targets) to produce a spectrum of photoelectrons and Auger electrons. This non-destructive technique yields quantitative data regarding chemical state, oxidation state and elemental composition of the surface. Argon-Ion-Depth-Profiling is a technique that uses a focussed beam of argon ions to etch material at controlled rates. XPS is then used to analyse the exposed surfaces. Data obtained include percentages of atomic concentrations. The equipment used for these studies was a Kratos IXSAM 800 from the University of New South Wales.

Table IV is a summary of the analysis of a sample taken from the Me 109G-6. Data were obtained with surface contamination removed and depth profiling at 2 nm intervals down to a maximum depth of 100 nm. The high carbon and silicon content might suggest surface contamination. However, as the silicon is present as the oxide, it is unclear if this arises from a water-glass over-coating[15] or due to plasticizer contamination from polymeric storage containers. It was only after surface etching that the true composition of the conversion coating was revealed. Since chromium was found in significant amounts (shown in the 100 nm analysis) it is obvious that a chromate conversion coating is present.

The presence of chromium and aluminium in the oxide form was demonstrated, together with sodium and chlorine in significant amounts in the bulk material of the surface coating. The former confirms the existence of a chromate-based coating.

As yet we have not progressed to the stage of being able to differentiate between surface coatings produced by similar processes (e.g., BV, EW and MBV). A far larger sample base will be needed for this. Indications are that a sufficiently accurate procedure can be developed.

Summary

All the alloys examined so far have been found to be copper-containing, equivalent to the 2,000 series. All samples, except that from the Zero drop tank, were of the clad type,

Table IV
XPS Analysis of Surface of Me 109G-6 Fabrication Sheet

ELEMENT	CONCENTRATION (% by atomic weight)		
	As Presented	With Removal of Surface Contamination	100 nm into Bulk
Aluminium	10.83	30.04	50.07
Chromium	0.11	0.77	1.09
Silicon	1.57	0.00	0.00
Sodium	0.16	0.10	0.22
Oxygen	22.12	33.82	34.23
Carbon	63.62	34.41	13.57
Chlorine	0.48	0.85	0.81
Nitrogen	1.10	0.00	0.00

where the copper-containing core has been covered with a more corrosion-resistant layer of almost pure aluminium. Grain structures vary, indicating somewhat different methods of manufacture and/or variations in post-manufacture treatment processes.

The Zero drop tank and the Me 109G-6 fabrication sheet both revealed the presence of a chromate chemical conversion coating. We could not fingerprint the type of oxide coating nor could we attribute it to a particular process.

The aim of this preliminary investigation, to devise a practical and effective strategy to differentiate and identify coatings, has not proved to be a simple task. We have demonstrated that no single technique provides all the information necessary to be able to reach positive conclusions as to the treatments used on the aluminium.

Optical Microscopy combined with EDXA analysis provides information enabling the identification of the base alloy and manufacturing processes, but falls down when examining the added surface coating (EDXA is not a true surface analysis technique). The preferred method of approach for examining these surface coatings is to use X-ray Photoelectron Spectroscopy (XPS). This technique can provide the composition analysis of a surface and when combined with Argon-Ion-Depth-Profiling, it

can enable identification of the chemical elements at known depths within the bulk material.

The results so far fall somewhat short of our goal of obtaining specific chemical compositions and differentiating between similar processes. Notwithstanding, enough encouragement and information has been gained to suggest the detail of information that we might expect in the future.

On the down side, XPS analysis requires sophisticated and expensive equipment and is time consuming in its implementation. The minimum sample size ($2 \ mm^2$) needed for this technique is also of concern, posing both practical and ethical problems.

This exercise demonstrates that both technical and historical information must be combined with accurate material analysis in order to obtain a balanced perspective when studying the deterioration of the object and developing subsequent conservation strategies.

Conservation of Aluminium with Oxide Films

Stability of Aluminium: Any conservation strategy depends on the stability of the material and the environment to which the material was exposed in the past. Aluminium objects that have not been exposed to an aggressive environment are quite stable. Oxide-coated objects are even more stable. Generally speaking, aluminium exposed to clean environments should need little treatment. Dust, sulphates, chlorides and high relative humidity (greater than 80%) will break down the stable natural oxide film. The porous oxide coating that results is non-protective and traps pollutants, hence accelerated corrosion begins.

Environmental Corrosivity: This can be measured[30] and quantified. If objects are stored indoors in dry climates (e.g., Canberra or Arizona with an average relative humidity (RH) below 55%) corrosion will be minimal, unless the object has been previously rendered unstable.

Stabilization of Aluminium Oxide Films: Merely placing an object indoors reduces its corrosion rate by a factor of $1,000$[31] and the use of a cloth cover will reduce this another 20 times. A further simple step in reducing corrosion is the use of dehumidification to reduce RH. It has been a standard military practice for some time[32] and could easily be adopted by museums. It should be noted that the use of dehumidifiers will extend the lifetime of any corrosion inhibitor.

Use of Inhibited Wax Coatings: Although inhibited wax coatings (based on petroleum sulphonate and tertiary amines) are used on operational aircraft, their use in a museum needs thorough investigation. (At the AWM, Dinol-inhibited wax coatings are used. The Duxford branch of the Imperial War Museum uses the same compounds in an annual maintenance program on outside display items.) The concern is that these products are being used without enough basic information or knowledge of their long-term effectiveness.[33]

Stabilization by Altering the Aluminium Surface: Traditional abrasive surface cleaning methods, such as glass beads at 3.1×10^5 Pa (45 psi) to 6.9×10^5 Pa (100 psi), remove the oxide coatings. By using plastic abrasives[34] and low pressures (below 1.0×10^5 Pa [15 psi]), porous oxides can be removed and the conversion coating left intact. Care must be exercised in the choice of the abrasive grade and delivery pressure. The treated surface should be coated with an inhibited wax.

Electrolysis: This technique is described by C. Degrigny elsewhere in this publication.

Use of Cerium-based Coatings: Cerium-based coatings[35] have been used by McLeod to treat the hull of the 12-metre yacht *Australia 2*, and they appear to work well.

Conclusion

The sand-blasting approach to the conservation of large technological items should be made extinct. Armed with the knowledge obtained from historical sources and the data provided by modern analytical procedures (that are now within the reach of every major conservation establishment) there is no longer any real excuse for the destruction of object integrity during conservation treatment. An integrated approach that involves the development of the following four main strategies must be adopted:

- A sound understanding of the nature of the surfaces of modern metal objects, which includes base metal chemical coatings and overlying organic coatings.

- An understanding of the interactions of modern metals with their environment. For example, we know that clean aluminium will not corrode in a clean environment at anything less than 80% RH. At the other extreme we know that aluminium removed from saline environments will continue to corrode actively even at low RH values. We need to study other types of environments in order to develop strategies for protection.

- A study of the nature and effectiveness of post-treatment organic coatings, such as Water Displacing Corrosion Preventatives (WDCP). Electrochemical methods of evaluation also appear to hold promise.

- The development of techniques for the differential removal of non-original organic coatings. Working from the premise that the integrity of the original surface should be maintained, it is imperative that less aggressive techniques are developed for the removal of overlying layers. Recent developments by

Richard Wolbers for the treatment of works of art and furniture using gel and emulsion technology should be investigated further. The use of low velocity, plastic-bead blasting for the removal of aluminium oxide corrosion products should also be studied in detail.

Acknowledgement

The authors thank the Australian War Memorial; the National Air and Space Museum of the Smithsonian Institution; and the Canadian Conservation Institute. Scanning Electron Microscopy and Energy Dispersive X-Ray Analysis (EDXA) were performed at the Electron Microscopy Unit of the Australian National University, Canberra, Australia. X-ray Photoelectron Spectroscopy was performed at the Surface Analysis Facility, University of New South Wales.

Résumé

L'application de revêtements sur l'aluminium : un point de vue axé sur la conservation

L'aluminium demeure le métal non ferreux le plus produit dans le monde. Dès le début du siècle, on a constaté que, du fait de sa légèreté et de ses propriétés physiques et chimiques uniques, il convenait bien à la construction des aéronefs.

Or, avec la mise au point de l'aluminium et d'alliages d'aluminium utilisables comme matériau de construction, est né le besoin de créer des revêtements de surface qui soient à la fois stables et résistants. Ces revêtements de surface se sont développés rapidement en Europe et aux États-Unis, si bien qu'aujourd'hui plusieurs grandes catégories de revêtements de ce genre sont utilisées.

L'Australian War Memorial possède une collection importante d'aéronefs en aluminium. Et ce sont ces aéronefs qui sont utilisés pour illustrer, dans la présente communication, l'évolution des alliages d'aluminium servant dans la construction, ainsi que les techniques connexes de revêtement, dont, d'une façon toute particulière, les revêtements constitués d'une couche d'oxyde.

Aux musées, nous avons constaté que, dans une large mesure, l'on n'a pas tenu compte du revêtement. Cette lacune a pu avoir des répercussions négatives tant sur le plan de l'historique et des objets eux-mêmes que sur celui de la conservation en général. Nous demeurons fermement convaincus que ces revêtements peuvent fournir d'importants renseignements d'ordre tant historique que technique. Et, comme ils font partie intégrante de l'objet, il devient impérieux d'élaborer des stratégies qui permettront d'assurer leur conservation. Qui plus est, la mise au point de techniques de traitement appropriées passe nécessairement par une connaissance du mode de construction des objets et des facteurs qui tendent à les détériorer. Nous décrirons les méthodes de catégorisation et d'analyse qui y ont été mises au point et utilisées, dont la reproduction de divers revêtements à partir des préparations originales. Après avoir élaboré ou proposé certaines stratégies de conservation, nous conclurons en traitant des répercussions d'une telle méthodologie et en fournissant un aperçu des perspectives d'avenir.

References

1. Schatzberg, E., Dissertation; Excerpts Related to Dural Corrosion (Philadelphia: University of Philadelphia, June 30, 1989).

2. Dix, E.H., "Aluminium Clad Products," in: *Engineering Laminates* ed. A. Dietz (New York: John Wiley and Sons, Inc., 1949) pp. 382-402.

3. Bengough, G.D. and H. Sutton, "The Protection of Aluminium and Its Alloys against Corrosion by Anodic Oxidation," *Engineering* no. 122, August 27, 1926, pp. 274-277.

4. Bauer, O. and O. Vogel, *International Zeitschrift fur Metallographie,* vol. 8, 1916, p. 101.

5. Setoh, S. and A. Miyata, "Electrolytic Oxidation of Aluminium and Its Industrial Applications," in: *Proceedings World Engineering Congress Tokyo 1929*, vol. 22, 1931, pp. 73-100.

6. Buff, H., *Liebigs Annalen der Chemie,* vol. 102, no. 3, 1857, p. 265.

7. Samuels, L.E., "The Effects of Mechanical Finishing Processes on Metal Surfaces," in: *The Finishing of Aluminium* ed. G.H. Kissin (New York: Reinhold Publishing Corporation, 1963) pp. 192-214.

8. Von Zeerleder, A., *The Technology of Aluminium and Its Light Alloys* (Amsterdam: Nordemann Publishing Company, 1936).

9. Bengston, H., "Methods of Preparation of Aluminium for Electroplating," *Transactions of the Electrochemical Society*, vol. 88, 1945, p. 307.

10. Bullough, W. and G.E. Gradam, *Journal of the Electrodeposition Technical Society*, vol. 22, 1947, p. 169.

11. Bowen, E.W., *Aluminium and Non-Ferrous Review,* vol. 3, 1938, p. 16, as cited in Wernick et al., 1987.

12. Wernick, S., R. Piner and P.G. Sheasby, *The Surface Treatment and Finishing of Aluminium and Its Alloys* (Teddington, England: Finishing Publications Ltd., 1987).

13. Ministry of Defence, "Protection of Aluminium Alloys by Sprayed Metal Coatings." *Defence Standard* 03-3(1), December 28, 1970.

14. Dix, E.H., *"ALCLAD": A New Corrosion Resistant Aluminium Product* (Washington D.C.: Metallurgist, Research Bureau, August 1927).

15. Gabe, D.R., *Principles of Metal Surface Treatment and Protection* (Oxford: Pergamon Press, 1978).

16. Bengough, G.D. and J.M. Stuart, British Patent 223994, 1923.

17. Slunder, C.J. and H.A.H. Pray, *Metal Finishing*, vol. 44, 1946, pp. 479-483, as cited in Wernick et al., 1987.

18. Pullen, N.D., "Protection from Corrosion of Aluminium and Its Alloys," *Metal Industries (London)*, vol. 44, 1934, pp. 133-136, 187-188.

19. Mason, R.B., U.S. Patent 2108603, 1938, as cited in Wernick et al., 1987.

20. Altenpohl, D.G., "Use of Boehmite Films for Corrosion Protection of Aluminium," *Corrosion. A Journal of Science and Engineering*, vol. 18, no. 4, April 1962, pp. 143-153.

21. Eckert, G., *Aluminium*, vol. 19, 1937, p. 608, as cited in Kissin, G.H., 1963.

22. Vereinigte Aluminium Werke A.G., German Patent 678119, 1937, as cited in Wernick et al., 1987.

23. "Pylumin Process," British Patent 441088.

24. Arnott, D.R., B.R.W. Hinton and N.E. Ryan, "Cationic-film-forming Inhibitors for the Protection of AA 7075 Aluminium Alloy against Corrosion in Aqueous Chloride Solution," *Corrosion*, vol. 45, no. 1, January 1989, pp. 12-18.

25. Kissin, G.H., *The Finishing of Aluminium* (New York: Reinhold Publishing Corporation, 1963).

26. Gailer, J.W. and E.J. Vaughan, *Protective Coatings for Metals* (London: Charles Griffin & Company Limited, 1950).

27. Greaves, R.H. and H. Wrighton, *Practical Microscopical Metallography* (London: Chapman Hall, 1960).

28. Biestek, T. and J. Weber, *Electrolytic and Chemical Coatings, A Concise Survey of Their Production, Properties and Testing* (Redhill: Portcullis Press, 1978).

29. Goldstein, J.I. and H. Yakowitz, *Practical Scanning Electron Microscopy* (New York: Plenum Press, 1977).

30. Berndt, H., "Measuring the Rate of Atmospheric Corrosion in Microclimates," *Journal of the American Institute for Conservation*, vol. 29, 1990, pp. 207-220.

31. Rice, D.W., R.J. Cappell, W. Kinsolving and J. Laskowski, "Indoor Corrosion of Metals," *Journal of the Electrochemical Society*, vol. 127, no. 4, April 1980, pp. 891-901.

32. Cargocaire Inc., *The Dehumidification Handbook* (Amesbury, Massachusetts: Cargocaire Engineering Corporation, 1988).

33. Tromans, D., "Effect of Organic Adsorbents on the Aqueous Stress Corrosion Cracking of AA 7075-T651 Aluminium Alloy," *Corrosion. The Journal of Science and Engineering*, vol. 42, no. 10, October 1986, pp. 601-608.

34. *Non-Chemical Depainting Compounds, Equipment Technology. Suggestion for Dry Blast Paint Removal on Aircraft* (Notre Dame, Indiana: Aero-Blast Products Inc., 1984).

35. Hinton, B.R.W. and R. Arnott David, "The Characteristics of Corrosion Inhibiting Films Formed in the Presence of Rare Earth Cations," *Microstructural Science*, vol. 17, 1986, pp. 311-319.

Radiation Hazards in Museum Aircraft

John Ashton

Conservation Section
Australian War Memorial
Canberra, Australia

Abstract

A survey of the possible radioactivity hazards associated with museum aircraft and their components was carried out on the Australian War Memorial collection. The survey was performed using a portable contamination monitor to detect the presence of radioactive material and an ionization chamber survey meter to show the dose rate measurements.

The survey results show a large number of radioactive sources both in aircraft and in individual instruments in storage. Some of the instruments indicate an exposure rate of over 300 mR/h, and one switch in a German aircraft indicates 60 mR/h. The types of instruments, parent aircraft, and exposure rate readings for surface and 100-mm distances are listed.

The different types of radioactive material used in aircraft, the terminology used in radioactivity measurement, and the safe handling, storage and labelling of radioactive aircraft components are discussed. Suggestions for methods of protecting the public and museum staff from exposure to radiation are offered.

Introduction

In 1990 I was alerted to the possible danger of radiation hazards in the Australian War Memorial (AWM) aircraft collection. Upon return to Australia from the United States, David Hallam brought a copy of a document published by the U.S. Department of Defence Air Force Museums Program. This document mentioned U.S. Federal and Air Force directives that dealt with the possession, use and precautions of radioactive material and it also described workable radiation hazard policies. One of the most telling paragraphs in that document warns "we must all recognize our obligation to minimize the potential for inadvertent radiation exposure to the public and the workforce."[1]

Although radium-painted dial faces are the best known sources of radiation in aircraft, several types of radioactive materials have been used in aircraft, including tritium, promethium-145, radium-226, krypton-85, magnesium-thorium, and depleted uranium. For example, the Dassault Mirage III-0 jet aircraft (built under license in Australia) is equipped with an Atar engine that has the compound magnesium-thorium in the compressor halves and centre castings. A special fatigue and creep inhibitor in light alloys of the Mirage, known as ZT1 and also containing magnesium-thorium, was used in the 1970s and later. This material was considered a hazard and thus the castings, foundry pieces and grindings were stored in dispersed areas, although the material stock had very low radiation readings. The air intake castings of the Mirage have rare earth alloys in their composition.[2] In March 1991, the Australian Nuclear Safeguards Authority was in the process of identifying the concentrations of these materials (magnesium-thorium, ZT1 and rare earth alloys) around the country.

Radioactive materials have been used in igniter plugs, counterweights, aircraft structural components near engine exhaust areas, gearboxes, windshield drains, circuit breakers, switches, exit signs, flight-instrument dials and engine fluid-level gauges, compasses, camera lenses, and aircrew wrist-watches. Nucleonic oil gauges containing krypton-85 have been cited as needing specific storage requirements.[1]

Certain luminescent safety devices on aircraft may contain up to 10 curies of tritium or up to 300 millicuries of promethium-145 as sealed sources.[1] (These amounts seem higher than would be expected; perhaps the readings should be millicuries and microcuries respectively.) Instrument radiation surveys cannot detect tritium and may not detect some promethium-145 sources because of their low energy beta emissions. Items exhibiting luminescence that do not give a reading on the survey meter should be suspected of containing one of these radionuclides and managed accordingly. These materials are dangerous in the long term. The half-life of radium for radioactive decay is 1,620 years whereas the half-life for elimination from the body is 45 years.[3]

Literature Survey

Quite often the technical publications issued by the various authorities that use aircraft do not mention radiation hazards. They only mention aircraft instruments in the context of their use by aviators and their basic fitting to the aircraft by technicians.

The U.S. Army Air Corps Technical Orders[4] has several relevant paragraphs in different sections describing the use of radioactive material. Of the 18 General Electric tachometers tabled in section AN 05-5-4, three are listed as having luminous scale markings, while the others have phosphorescent or fluorescent markings and pointers. The luminous material is radium paint, which emits light without any external source of excitation. The fluorescent material emits light when exposed to ultraviolet (UV) radiation. The phosphorescent material emits light when exposed to UV and in addition continues to emit light for a period of time after the removal of the UV source. The light emitted by the fluorescent material is pale yellow in colour while that emitted by the luminous and phosphorescent materials is pale green.

In section AN 05-10-1, the Pioneer Instrument Company air speed indicators and one cabin air flow gauge are described by type numbers and the dials' graduations and divisions are listed according to their type of material. Radium paint was used on seven out of 10 of these instruments and some fluorescent lacquer was also used. A suction gauge also made by Pioneer is shown as having a "radium-painted dial and pointer." Technical order 05-20-27 in the same publication deals with the Kollsman Instrument Division Type C-2 rate-of-climb indicator, which has the pointer hand, major graduations, numerals (except 0.5) and the arc between the 6,000 ft graduations painted with luminous material. The remainder of the lettering and numerals are treated with fluorescent lacquer.

Thermocouple thermometers made by Lewis Engineering are covered in Technical order 05-40D-2. In this section the use of luminous material is only mentioned as an "as required" entry indicating that some of these instruments are likely to contain radioactive material and should be treated accordingly. The overhaul of fuel contents gauges manufactured by the Liquidometer Corporation is covered in section AN 05-65A-6, in which there is no mention of the dial-painting medium.

A "three element nucleonic fuel quantity system" referred to in an engineering paper describes its radiation source as consisting of coiled stainless steel or aluminium tubing containing krypton-85, a radioactive gas.[5]

The Kollsman Instrument Handbook[6] mentions the use of radium paint on pointers as a cause of balancing problems if the paint is newly applied and still wet. Page 16 of the same document deals with the application of radium paint to dials. The information is of historical interest only, and the methods of application and denials of danger are not supported by the present understanding of radiation hazards.

Most old luminous paint contains radium-226 at much higher concentrations than is now usually used.[3] Another source of radioactive material, which may be overlooked, is the fluid inside a compass, which is in contact with the luminous paint on the dial. Although the fluid (normally an alcohol solution) may not dissolve the radium oxides, it may carry loose particles that are hazardous to health.

The loss of tritium from luminous aircraft exit signs has been examined.[7] Although only about 2% of the tritium was present in the oxide form, (with the remainder as tritium gas) tritium oxide was measured because the biological effect is greater than that of the elemental tritium. About 99% of the tritium released from a broken exit sign escapes in the first 1.75 hours.

According to Harley, "a radiation protection program must consist of two parts — evaluation and control. Evaluation consists of the measurements required to estimate possible radiation exposures and the necessary interpretation of these measurements. Control consists of taking actions required to reduce radiation exposure."[8]

Surveying the Collection

Monitoring Equipment
Determining if an aircraft component is a radiation hazard may be achieved by using an inexpensive radiation monitor capable of measuring ionizing radiation by means of a Geiger-Muller (G-M) tube with a thin mica end window. When a ray or particle of ionizing radiation strikes the fully enclosed G-M tube it is sensed electronically and displayed by a pointer on an analogue dial face. The instrument may be set to respond to each ionizing event with a flashing light and an audible beep. Alpha and beta radiation are usually measured in counts per minute (cpm) or in mSv/h in SI units while mR/h is commonly used to measure gamma radiation. About 5 to 25 cpm at random intervals (depending on the monitoring location) can be expected from naturally occurring background radiation. The instrument should have a range switch to change the scale of the readings, for example, 0 to 0.5 mR/h (0 to 500 cpm), 0 to 5 mR/h (0 to 5,000 cpm) or 0 to 50 mR/h (0 to 50,000 cpm).

The inexpensive monitors have some inherent faults.[4] The readings in mR/h are not accurate (the accuracy factor stated by the manufacturers is usually plus or minus 10% of full scale for the calibrating source, commonly cesium 137) and if the count rate is excessively high the monitor may be prone to "runaway" or "paralysis." A much more expensive type of monitor has an ionization chamber. This type of instrument can provide a reliable measurement over a wide range of incident energies.

The AWM uses an inexpensive monitor[9] to do an initial check for radiation sources. If any readings above background are observed, a reliable measurement is then sought from the local Radiation Safety Section of the Department of Health (government experts who offer an accurate measuring service for $A60/hr — the most effective and prudent method of surveying for the presence of radioactive materials).

The AWM survey[10] was conducted using a portable contamination monitor (Nuclear Enterprises PCM5/1 with beta/gamma probe BP1/4 Geiger-Muller Counter) to detect radioactive material. According to the manufacturer the accuracy rate is plus or minus 25%. Dose rate measurements were made using the low energy mylar window (1.7 mg/cm^2 density) of a Victoreen 450 Ionization Chamber Survey Meter. The accuracy stated for this instrument is plus or minus 10%, exclusive of energy response.

The presence of radon gas was determined by using a Nuclear Enterprises Radioactive Gas Monitor RGM1/1. Accuracy is stated at plus or minus 20%. The check for radon was thought necessary because of the accumulation of stored instruments loose in cardboard boxes on a mobile shelving system. The shelves were left closed for four days after which the activity was read as the shelves were opened. Radon was detected but the amount was insignificant.

Although no mention was found in the U.S. military literature of the use of radioactive material in temperature and fuel gauges, the AWM survey indicated the use of radium in all gauges monitored.

The results of the survey follow, listing complete aircraft first (Table I), then individual instruments in storage (Table II). The instruments are listed by their common names along with the radioactivity readings, which are taken at the surface of the instrument glass (or just above the surface of paint if there is no glass) and also at a 100-mm distance from the surface. Figure 1 shows the relationship between the two readings of a sample of American instruments. A general background reading taken in the cockpit area of each aircraft and in the storage areas proved to be between 0.1 mR/h and 0.2 mR/h in most cases, and is listed as BG in the aircraft tables and as a figure of 0.15 mR/h in the stored instrument tables.

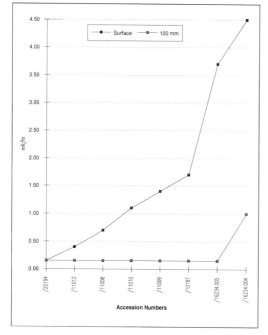

Figure 1 The relationship between surface and 100-mm radiation activity readings of individual American aircraft flight instruments.

Discussion of Survey Results

Messerschmitt Me 163B-1
This aircraft has an almost complete instrument panel and cockpit fittings and it appears to be quite representative of the type of German aircraft for the period. The background radioactivity reading is a little on the high side and some of the surface readings are 20 times the background readings.

Messerschmitt Me BF 109G-6
This aircraft from the same period as the Me 163B-1 would be expected to have the same levels of radioactivity. This is not reflected in the recorded readings, as the aircraft is in a dismantled state and has no instrument panel fitted. The instruments are stored and are listed amongst the German ones. The one reading obtained from two radio frequency selector buttons was very high. This was a case where radium oxide paint had been applied quite thickly in a groove around the perimeter of each button with a central accumulation of paint about 4 mm in diameter. These buttons did not appear to have any lacquer or other coatings on them.

Mitsubishi A6M2 Zero
This fully restored aircraft shows only two instruments as having radioactivity readings.

Commonwealth CA-5 Wirraway
This aircraft was built as a training aircraft and has about 80% of its complement of instruments, none of which appear to be hazardous at reasonable distances.

Link Flight Simulator Trainer
The Link simulator exhibited a single radiation reading from one instrument which, because of its construction, did not allow a surface measurement. The background reading in the seat area was almost three times the norm.

Commonwealth CA-12 Boomerang
This early World War II Australian aircraft showed fairly normal readings except for one engine manifold pressure gauge.

English Electric Canberra B20 (built by Government Aircraft Factory)
This Australian built Canberra from the 1950s was from a period when the hazards of radioactive emissions from instruments were becoming unacceptable and the use of non-radioactive materials was becoming more prevalent. Only one item on the pilot's panel indicated any radioactivity (a low reading) and the navigator's area had only one switch on one side panel that registered quite high on the monitor.

Avro Lancaster MK I

The Lancaster is a large aircraft with multiple instrument positions. Most were found to be fairly average in radioactive readings with a few notable exceptions, mainly the engine performance instruments. The 100-mm readings were found to be distorted by the mass of instruments side by side, and were considered not worth recording.

North American B25 J Mitchell

This North American aircraft, although built later than the others, still showed a few instruments with high readings. The most obvious hazard in this aircraft was the multitude of switches with heavy deposits of radioactive paint, all very prominent and easy to touch.

Supermarine Spitfire MK IIa

The Spitfire readings are included, but only as a guide. The Turn and Bank indicator, which has no protective glass front, probably interfered with all the other readings from this aircraft's relatively small instrument panel. Further readings will be taken once the glass has been replaced, but in the meantime the aircraft cockpit is out-of-bounds.

Stored Instruments

The individual readings of stored instruments taken at the surface and at 100-mm distances revealed some alarming statistics. One evident trend is that all instruments with broken, cracked or no glass are likely to be very hazardous to health. In addition, the British aircraft instruments seem to have more, and slightly higher, readings than aircraft from other countries.

Reducing Exposure to Radiation

All types of radiation share the property of energy loss by absorption in passing through matter. The degree of absorption depends on the type of radiation and the absorbing material. This absorption process results in ionization, which is the removal of an extra nuclear electron from an atom of the absorbing material.

The intensity of radiation decreases with the inverse square of the distance (d) on moving away from the radiation source (Figure 2). Thus the intensity 10 m away is only 1% of the intensity at 1 m.[4] Therefore the further away one is from the source of radiation, the better.

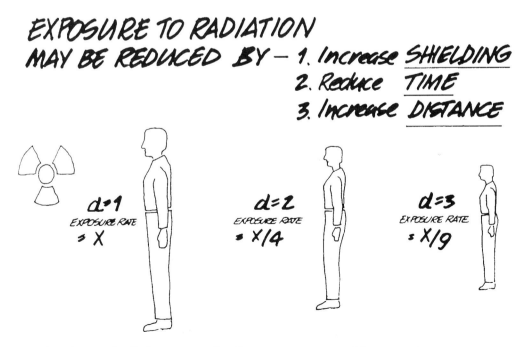

EXPOSURE TO RADIATION MAY BE REDUCED BY – 1. Increase SHIELDING 2. Reduce TIME 3. Increase DISTANCE

d=1 EXPOSURE RATE = X   d=2 EXPOSURE RATE = X/4   d=3 EXPOSURE RATE = X/9

Figure 2 Reduction of radiation exposure (d = distance; x = exposure rate).

Since radiation dose to a worker is directly proportional to exposure time, it is obvious that reducing the exposure time by half (by working quickly) is not as effective a safety measure as increasing the distance from the radioactive source (e.g., by using tongs or similar tools). Notwithstanding, nothing should be done to an aircraft component by non-radiation-trained museum staff that would release or disturb the radium-based paint.

Storage of Radioactive Materials

Individual radioactive instruments should be stored in two or more strong plastic bags and then in boxes clearly labelled to warn that radioactive luminous compounds are present.[4] In the case of instruments with missing or broken glass faces, an aluminium or lead lined box may be advisable as an extra precaution. Seek expert advice from local radiation safety organizations to clarify such situations. Some switches and selector buttons in aircraft have had radioactive luminous paint applied. These items can be removed if they are in an area where physical damage to the paint is likely to occur, or they can be sealed with a clear acrylic lacquer.

Marking Radioactive Components

The U.S. Air Force Museum Program Handbook states that red adhesive dot labels are to be used to identify radioactive commodities in aircraft or in display cases — this being to alert maintenance personnel of the dangers present. A green dot is to be used to identify non-radioactive instruments. This system ensures that all aircraft instruments or suspect materials are surveyed and appropriately identified. The AWM is not using this method of marking instruments, as the aircraft in the collection are neither open for public inspection nor maintained by aircraft technicians. Conservation maintenance of the collection does include cleaning inside aircraft, but this is only performed by staff aware of the hazards of disturbing radioactive materials. The instruments in storage are identified with standard radioactive material warning labels.

Disposal of Radioactive Materials

In the Australian Capital Territory where the AWM is situated, there is no legal disposal method of alpha-emitting radiation material. This policy means that any instruments or switches with radium paint that are considered too hazardous to display must be stored by the AWM. Other states and territories in Australia may have different regulations regarding this type of material disposal. A national repository for radioactive waste disposal may be built in the future. Until then, these materials remain our responsibility.

Conclusion

Museum collections containing aircraft most likely have some radioactive sources. The most prominent sources of ionizing radiation are radium-painted instruments and switches. Approximately 30% of the AWM collection of aircraft instruments and other components indicated radioactivity above normal background levels.

Exposure to radiation may be reduced by the following three barriers:

- Increasing the shielding between the source and the subject

- Reducing the time of exposure of the source to the subject

- Increasing the distance between the source and the subject

The most economic barrier that can be raised against overexposure is the third one.

Specific advice on radiation safety is limited in this paper both because of my lack of expertise in this area and the various legislations by council, state, and country on the management of ionizing radiation. I can only stress that collection managers, be they curators or conservators, seek the assistance and advice of their local radiation safety experts.

Appendix A. Glossary

Radiation is a form of energy and may be explained as the emission and propagation of energy through any material in the form of waves.

Radioactivity is the spontaneous disintegration of atomic nuclei with emission of corpuscular or electromagnetic radiation. All elements of atomic number greater than 83 exhibit radioactive decay.

Nuclear radiation emissions are, most commonly, alpha (α), beta (β) and gamma (γ) radiations.

Gamma radiation is electromagnetic — similar properties to visible light or ultraviolet, but more penetrating, and may traverse several centimetres of lead.

Beta and alpha radiations are particulate — extremely small particles moving at very high velocity.

Alpha particles are emitted by many of the heavy artificial and naturally radioactive elements. The particle is the same as the nucleus of the helium atom (2 protons and 2 neutrons). The particle is heavy and slow moving and dissipates energy easily — most are completely absorbed by a few centimetres of air, or less than 0.005 mm of aluminium, or a sheet of paper. They are not considered a very serious health hazard external to the body, although internally they are most serious owing to their very short range and great ionizing power. They are among the most radiotoxic nuclides. The decay of the alpha particles in radium results in the transformation to radon (gas).

Beta particles are composed of electrons (positrons and negatrons) emitted by both heavy and light radioactive elements. These particles possess kinetic energy because of their high emission speed. The more energetic beta particles approach the speed of light. The range in air may be more than a metre and they can penetrate several millimetres of aluminium or plastic, however the particles emitted from tritium or carbon-14 may be stopped by a few centimetres of air.

Gamma emission is a secondary process following certain alpha or beta decays. The nucleus may be left in an unstable state as a result of the alpha and beta emissions and the excess energy is released in the form of gamma radiation. Gamma radiation can be very penetrating and absorbing material only reduces the intensity. Gamma radiation from a radium source is reduced to 50% of its incident value by 25.4 mm of lead.

Bremsstrahlung is secondary radiation arising from collision or deviation between fast-moving electrons and atoms.

Appendix B. Radioactive Materials

Radon: heaviest noble gas, radioactive, half-life 3.82 days. Symbol for radium emanation or radon is RaEm.

Emanations: heavy inert gases resulting from decay of natural radioactive elements; e.g., radium —> radon, thorium —> thoron, actinium —> actinon. These are short lived and decay to other radioactive elements.

Tritium: radioactive isotope of hydrogen with a half-life of 12.5 years. Very rare as naturally occurring material. It is used as a radioactive tracer or label and is very important in radiobiology. It has also been used as a substitute for radium oxides on instruments to provide luminescence. It produces low energy beta radiation that cannot penetrate beyond the glass lens of the instrument.

Promethium-145: rare earth, no known stable isotopes in nature. Half-life greater than 20 years. Emits medium energy beta particles.

Krypton-85: rare gas, colourless, odourless, forms one millionth of the atmosphere.

Radium-226: one of the alkaline-earth metals, emits alpha, high-energy beta, gamma and Bremsstrahlung.

Radioactive Luminous Compounds: These consist of a phosphor, such as zinc sulphide, intimately mixed with a radioactive material, such as radium-226, the radiation from which activates the phosphor to emit light. The alpha particles emitted by a material, such as radium, destroy the phosphor more quickly than the beta particles emitted by promethium-145 or tritium. When the phosphor is destroyed the luminous compound becomes ineffective, but most of the radioactivity remains.

Appendix C. Measurement of Radiation

There are many different but related terms used to provide measurement data on radiation. Some of the most commonly used terms are the following:

Electron volts (eV): The measurement of the energy of any radiation (and hence its ability to penetrate biological tissue) is expressed in electron volts. This is the energy gained through the acceleration of an electron by an electrical potential of one volt. This is sometimes expressed in SI units as 1.602×10^{-19} Joules; because of the small size of this unit the energies are usually given in thousands or millions of electron volts (keV or MeV).

The usual range of energies for single particles or rays of common radiations are the following:

Alpha particles	4 MeV to 8 MeV
Beta particles	0 MeV to 4 MeV
Gamma rays	0 MeV to 2 MeV

Activity: Radioactive isotope activity was formerly expressed in terms of the curie (Ci), the millicurie (μCi) or the microcurie (μCi) (after the famous Polish-born pioneer of radioactivity). One curie is the activity associated with any radioactive isotope when it is undergoing 3.7×10^{10} nuclear disintegrations per second, historically equivalent to one gram of radium. The current SI unit is the becquerel (Bq), which equals one nuclear transformation per second.

Physical Half-Life (T_p): the time during which an aggregate of radioactive atoms decays to half its number.

Biological Half-Life (T_b): the time during which the number of atoms of a stable nuclide ingested into the body is reduced to one half (this depends on the radioactive element and the excretion rate).

Effective Half-Life (T_e): always less than both physical and biological half-lives. Time during which the activity in a particular biological system is reduced to half by both radioactive decay and biological excretion. The physical and biological half-lives of a radioactive isotope can be combined to find the effective half-life in the body by:

$$1/T_{\text{effective}} = 1/T_{\text{physical}} + 1/T_{\text{biological}}$$

Dose: the quantity of ionizing radiation to which a sample has been exposed.

Dose Equivalent: the biological effect corrected for certain factors measured as sieverts (Sv) in SI units and rem (rem) in conventional units (1.0 rem = 0.01 Sv).

Dose Equivalent Rate: shown as sievert per second (Sv s^{-1}) or rem per second (rem s^{-1}) (1.0 rem s^{-1} = 0.01 Sv s^{-1}).

Exposure: measured in coulomb per kilogram (C kg^{-1}) in SI units. Roentgen (R) was the old (and probably better known) unit of exposure (1 R = 2.38×10^{-4} C/kg).

Absorbed Dose: measured in Joule per kilogram (J kg^{-1}) known as gray (Gy) in SI units. The rad was the former measurement of the amount of energy deposited by radiation in the human or animal body (1 Gy = 100 rads). A more realistic understanding of the gray may be seen in the two following observations of the rad, which has only one hundredth of the gray's value:

1. The normal background level of radiation (from radioactive rocks, cosmic rays and internal deposits, such as potassium ^{40}K) is about 0.2 rad per year.

2. A dose of about 700 rad delivered in a short time to the whole body has a 95% probability of causing death. The same dose delivered to only a small part of the body is less serious.

Quality Factor: The concept of the absorbed dose has to be applied with caution as it makes no allowance for the different types of radiation. Equal doses measured in grays of 5 MeV alpha particles and 220 keV X-rays would give very different biological effects. An approximate weighting factor called the quality factor has been ascribed to each type of radiation without specifying the biological effect.

Rem: the acronym for Roentgen equivalent man. It is the amount of ionizing radiation that produces the same damage to a human as one roentgen of about 200 keV X-rays.

The still commonly used value of the millirem (m rem) appears to be interchangeable with milliRoentgen (mR). The dose equivalent in rem is the product of the absorbed dose in rad and the quality factor. Equal doses of different types of radiation measured in rem produce approximately the same biological effect.

Reliable measuring instruments indicate the exposure in milliRoentgen per hour (mR/h) or in counts per minute (cpm). Radiation types that have a quality factor of one may be approximately equated for biological materials: Exposure measured in Roentgen = absorbed dose measured in rad = dose equivalent measured in rem.

Radioresistant: able to withstand considerable radioactive doses without injury.

Radiosensitive: this normally refers to organs quickly injured or changed by irradiation. The gonads, the blood-forming organs and the corneas are biologically most radiosensitive in humans.

Résumé

Les risques d'exposition aux radiations provenant d'aéronefs exposés dans les musées

Une étude, portant sur les risques éventuels d'exposition aux radiations provenant des aéronefs exposés dans les musées et de leurs composants a été menée à l'Australian War Memorial. Pour déceler la présence de matières radioactives, on s'est alors servi d'un détecteur portatif de radiation, tandis qu'un appareil de mesure à chambre d'ionisation a été utilisé pour évaluer la dose absorbée.

De nombreuses sources radioactives, tant à l'intérieur des aéronefs que parmi les composants mis en réserve individuellement, ont été découvertes. Certains instruments atteignent ainsi un taux d'exposition supérieur à 300 mR/h, tandis qu'un interrupteur, placé à l'intérieur d'un aéronef allemand, indique, à lui seul, un taux de 60 mR/h. Le taux d'exposition a été mesuré en surface et à une distance de 100 mètres de hauteur. Les taux sont indiqués selon le type d'instrument et d'aéronef.

À ces données s'ajoutent une description des différents genres de matières radioactives qui sont utilisées dans les aéronefs, un lexique des termes en usage dans le domaine de l'évaluation de la radioactivité, ainsi qu'une définition des méthodes sûres de manutention, de mise en réserve et d'étiquetage des composants radioactifs. On suggère enfin certains moyens qui permettront de protéger tant le personnel que le public des musées d'une exposition aux radiations.

References

1. *United States Air Force Museum Program Handbook* (Ohio: USAFM, Wright-Patterson AFB, Ohio, 1988).

2. Baker, Dennis, personal communication, Historical Projects Group, Hawker de Havilland, 1991.

3. *Code of Practice for the Safe Use of Radioactive Luminous Compounds* (Canberra: Australian Department of Health, 1971).

4. Chamberlain, K.B., ed., *Australian National University Ionizing Radiation Safety* (Canberra: Australian National University, Canberra, 1989).

5. Walker, W.P. and F.J. Steinbrenner, "Design and Testing of Aircraft Nucleonic Fuel Quantity System," *Society of American Engineers* paper 690673, 1969.

6. *Handbook of Airplane Instruments* (New York: Kollsman Instrument Division of Square D Co., 1940).

7. Niemeyer, R.G., "Tritium Loss from Tritium Self-luminous Aircraft Exit Signs," *Isotopes and Radiation Technology*, vol. 7, no. 3, 1970.

8. Harley, J.H., *Dangerous Properties of Industrial Materials*, 3rd edn. (New York: Reinhold, 1968).

9. *Operation Manual for the Radiation Alert Monitor 4*, Extech Equipment Pty Ltd., Victoria, Australia.

10. Evans, V., *Report to Australian War Museum on Radiation Survey of Aircraft Collection*, AWM File 90/0534(14), 11 Dec. 1990.

Table I
Radiation Survey of Aircraft (ca. 1917 to 1960s)

Instrument/Location	Surface	100 mm	Instrument/Location	Surface	100 mm
Messerschmitt Me 163B-1 (1945)			**Avro 504K (1918)**	no instruments fitted	
Air Speed Indicator	0.6	BG			
Altimeter	4.0	0.4			
Chronometer	4.0	BG	**Airco DH9 (1918)**	BG	
Oxygen Supply	1.0	BG			
Air Temperature	1.0	BG	**Bell 47G-3B Sioux (1960s)**	displayed out of reach	
VHF Radio Buttons	3.0	0.25			
			Pfalz D XII (1918)	no readings	
Cockpit area background reading 0.2					
			Royal Aircraft Factory SE5A (1917)	no readings	
Messerschmitt Me/BF 109G-6 (1945)					
			Albatros D Va (1917)	no readings	
VHF Radio Buttons (Stbd)	60.0	1.0			
			Messerschmitt Me 262A-1 Jabo (1944)	no instruments fitted	
Cockpit area background reading 0.1					
			Gloster Meteor F8 (early 1950s)	BG	
Mitsubishi A6M2 Zero (1942)					
			Bell UH-1B Iroquois (1960s)	BG	
Variometer	2.0	BG			
Air Temperature	0.34	BG	**Avro Lancaster Mk I (1942)**		
Commonwealth CA-5 Wirraway (1942)			Pilot's Panel		
			(Stbd side reading at 300 mm 1.0)		
Rate of Climb	0.8	BG	(Port side reading at 600 mm 0.6)		
Turn and Bank	0.3	BG	Trim	5.5	
Air Speed Indicator	0.3	BG	P4 Compass	1.1	
Manifold Pressure	0.34	BG	Undercarriage Indicator	2.7	
Oil Temperature	0.9	BG	Flaps Position	1.3	
Fuel Oil Temperature	0.6	BG	Beam Approach	12.0	
Air Temperature	1.1	BG	Altimeter	5.0	
			Air Speed Indicator	6.5	
Cockpit area background reading 0.1			Artificial Horizon	8.3	
			AFN Direction	8.5	
Link Flight Simulator Trainer (1950s)			Turn and Slip	4.5	
			Rate of Climb	17.0	4.0
(Readings 20 mm from surface 2.5)			Engine Boost: 1	10.0	
(Readings at seat distance 0.6)			2	10.0	
			3	3.0	
Commonwealth CA-12 Boomerang (1942)			4	3.0	
			Engine RPM: 1	20.0	2.5
Manifold Pressure	20.0	1.0	2	20.0	2.5
Air Temperature	3.5	BG	3	20.0	2.5
Oil Temperature	2.0	BG	4	20.0	2.5
Voltage (at 20 mm)	2.5	BG	Flaps Position	8.0	
Others (unidentified)	1.0	BG	Air Temperature	6.0	
			DF Indicator	1.0	
English Electric Canberra B20 (1950s)			DR Compass Repeater	0.8	
			Oxygen Regulator	1.6	
Pilot's panel (Stbd)			Oxygen Contents	1.5	
Fuel Transfer Switch	1.0	BG	Brakes Pressure	1.8	
Navigator's area					
Stbd of seat, lower of two rear components	23.0	1.2			

Note: All the readings are given in milliroentgens per hour (mR/h). The surface and 100-mm readings used in the survey are given in mR/h as they are more manageable in that format. To convert the readings to counts per minute multiply by 1,000. If the reading is undetectable from the background radiation level it is denoted by BG (background).

Table I (continued)

Radiation Survey of Aircraft (ca. 1917 to 1960s)

Instrument/Location		Surface	100 mm	Instrument/Location	Surface	100 mm
Engineer's Panel				Brakes Pressure	0.45	BG
(Panel at 300 mm 1.6)				Hydraulic Pressure	0.4	BG
Radiator Temperature:	1	8.0	BG	Oxygen Flow Indicator	4.0	BG
	2	12.0	BG			
	3	10.0	BG	Centre Switch Panel		
	4	14.0	BG	Lights, Fuel Transfer,		
Fuel Contents: No. 3 Stbd		1.4	BG	Prime Pumps, etc.	4.0	1.0
No. 2 Stbd		3.0	BG	Armament Panel Switches	2.2	1.0
No. 2 Port		12.0	BG	Electrics Panel Switches		
No. 3 Port		10.0	BG	Navigator Lights, Master Right,		
No. 1 Stbd		1.2	BG	Gear Warning Horn, Pilot,		
No. 1 Port		1.4	BG	Battery Left, etc.	4.5	1.0
Oil Pressure: Rear		8.0	BG			
Front		4.5	BG	Emergency Compass	BG	BG
Oil Temperature (x 4)		2.5	BG			
				Supermarine Spitfire Mk IIa (1941)		
Navigator's Table/Panel						
Altimeter		1.0	BG	(Background radiation level (BG) 0.15)		
Air Speed Indicator		7.0	1.8	(300 mm from panel 0.7)		
North American B25 J Mitchell (1945)				Brakes Pressure/Supply	3.2	BG
				Oxygen Regulator/Gauges	3.0	BG
Background in cockpit 0.02				Navigation Light Switch	2.0	1.5
				Air Speed Indicator	10.0	2.0
Oxygen Flow Indicator		4.0	BG	Altimeter	25.0	3.0
Air Speed Indicator		BG	BG	Compass Direction Indicator	10.0	
DR Compass Repeater		1.0	BG	Turn and Bank (No glass)	50.0	
Artificial Horizon		2.6	BG	Rate of Climb	15.0	
Rate of Climb		BG	BG	Artificial Horizon	14.0	
Turn and Bank		BG	BG	Engine RPM	10.0	
Altimeter		BG	BG	Fuel Pressure	10.0	
				Fuel Suction	20.0	
No. 2 Engine				Oil Pressure	10.0	
Manifold Pressure		0.1	BG	Radiator Temperature	8.0	
Speed in RPM		0.1	BG	Air Temperature	7.0	
Oil Pressure		0.1	BG	Fuel Contents	7.0	
Fuel Pressure		0.1	BG	Gun Sight Dimmer Switch	4.5	
Undercarriage Indicator		0.2	BG	Generator Supply and Switch	2.0	
Oil Temperature		0.1	BG			
Cylinder Temperature		0.1	BG			
Carburetor Air Temperature		0.15	BG	All these readings may be suspect due to the influence		
Suction		0.4	BG	of the unglazed Turn and Bank Indicator; further		
Air Temperature		0.1	BG	readings should be made when the offending		
				instrument is reglazed.		
Fuel Contents: Front		0.2	BG			
Rear		0.35	BG			
Auxiliary		50.0	1.0			

Note: All the readings are given in milliroentgens per hour (mR/h). The surface and 100-mm readings used in the survey are given in mR/h as they are more manageable in that format. To convert the readings to counts per minute multiply by 1,000. If the reading is undetectable from the background radiation level it is denoted by BG (background).

Table II

Stored Instruments

(Background (BG) reading 0.15 mR/hr)

Accn. No.	Instruments	Country	Condition	Readings in mR/hr	
				Surface	100 mm
/16015	Air Pressure (0-100 kg/cm^2)	Japan	OK	0.15	0.15
/6350.001	Air Speed Indicator	Germany	OK	0.70	0.20
/11504	Altimeter	Britain	OK	0.80	0.15
/16016.001	Altimeter	Japan	OK	4.50	0.60
/16016.002	Altimeter	Japan	OK	3.00	0.40
AWM34872	Altimeter	Germany	OK	0.50	0.15
AWM34822	Altimeter (0-5 km)	Germany	OK	0.80	0.15
/8073	Artificial Horizon	Japan	OK	0.15	0.15
/11009	Air Speed Indicator	America	OK	1.40	0.15
/11017	Air Speed Indicator	Britain	OK	2.50	0.15
/12177	Air Speed Indicator	Japan	Broken glass	200.00	11.00
/16002.002	Air Speed Indicator	Britain	OK	4.50	1.50
/16016.002	Air Speed Indicator	Japan	OK	4.00	1.10
/6350.002	Air Speed Indicator	Germany	OK	0.70	0.20
/7152	Air Speed Indicator	Britain	OK	11.00	1.00
/7319	Air Speed Indicator	Germany	Broken glass	50.00	1.00
/8144	Air Speed Indicator	Britain	Broken glass	2.50	0.50
AWM34863	Air Speed Indicator	Germany	OK	0.70	0.15
/20194	Autopilot Altitude	America	OK	0.15	0.15
/8096	Chronometer	Germany	OK	3.00	0.50
/8482	Chronometer	Japan	OK	1.60	0.15
/11012	Compass	America	OK	0.40	0.15
/8074	Compass	Japan	OK	2.00	0.50
/8464	Compass	Germany	OK	0.60	0.15
/8424	Compass E2A	Britain	OK	2.00	0.15
/8376	Compass P8	Britain	OK	6.50	1.00
/16413	Compass Type 96	Japan	OK	0.50	0.30
/7346	Drift Indicator	Germany	No glass	100.00	8.00
/16937	Engine Boost Pressure	Japan	OK	4.20	100
/7321	Engine Boost Pressure	Germany	OK	0.70	0.15
/8139	Engine Boost Pressure	Britain	OK	80.00	2.00
AWM34884(x2)	Engine Boost Pressure	Germany	OK	11.00	0.40
/10187	Engine Manifold Pressure	America	OK	1.70	0.15
/11010	Engine Manifold Pressure	America	OK	1.10	0.15
AWM34873	Engine Oil Temperature	Germany	OK	1.50	0.15
/16047.001	Engine Speed (RPM)	Japan	Broken, no glass	400.00	20.00
/12179	Exhaust Temperature	Japan	OK	7.00	1.60
OL 18	Exhaust Temperature	Japan	Cracked glass	0.15	0.15
/8134	Flap Position Indicator	Britain	OK	3.40	0.80
/5460.001	Fuel Contents	Britain	OK	7.00	1.50
/5460.002	Fuel Contents	Britain	OK	7.00	1.50
AWM34877.002	Fuel Contents (0-3800 ltr)	Germany	OK	0.50	0.15
AWM34877.003	Fuel Contents (0-3800 ltr)	Germany	OK	0.50	0.15
AWM34877.001	Fuel Contents (0-400 ltr)	Germany	OK	0.50	0.15
/8132	Fuel Flow (No. 1 & 2 Eng)	Britain	OK	6.00	2.00
/16234.004	Fuel Pressure (0-25)	America	OK	4.50	1.00
/16234.005	Fuel Pressure (0-25)	America	OK	3.70	0.15
/AWM34851	Oil Pressure (0-10 kg/cm^2)	Germany	OK	0.80	0.15
/7245	Oxygen Flow	Germany	OK	1.30	0.15
AWM34844	Oxygen Flow	Germany	OK	2.60	0.15
/12896	Oxygen Pressure	Germany	No case, no glass	18.00	2.50
/8138	Oxygen Regulator	Britain	OK	2.90	0.40
/20198	Hydraulic Pressure (0-22 kg/cm^2)	Germany	OK	1.00	0.15
AWM34842(x2)	Hydraulic Pressure (0-3,0-15 kg/cm^2)	Germany	OK	0.70	0.15
/7238	Hydraulic Pressure (0-160 kg/cm^2)	Germany	OK	0.40	0.15
/7345	QNH Indicator (Air Pressure in Millibars)	Germany	No glass	340.00	30.00
/7347	QNH Indicator (Air Pressure in Millibars)	Germany	No glass	200.00	20.00

Table II (continued)
Stored Instruments

Accn. No.	Instrument	Country	Condition	Readings in mR/hr Surface	100 mm
/7325	Rate of Climb	Germany	OK	0.50	0.15
/16047.001	Rate of Climb	Japan	OK	1.00	0.15
/10184	Engine RPM	Britain	OK	0.80	0.15
/7219	Engine RPM	Britain	OK	7.00	1.00
/7351	Engine RPM	Germany	OK	0.40	0.15
/8143	Engine RPM	Britain	No case, no glass	7.00	1.00
AWM34841	Engine RPM	Germany	OK	0.80	0.15
AWM34878	Engine RPM	Germany	OK	0.50	0.15
/11008	Suction	America	OK	0.70	0.15
/10194	Suction (0-10" Hg)	Britain	OK	400.00	6.00
/8072	Temperature (0-150°C)	Japan	OK	0.15	0.15
/8429	Temperature (0-350°C)	Japan	OK	4.00	1.00
AWM34892	Thermal Self-trip Switch	Germany	No glass	55.00	1.00
/8076	Turn & Bank	Britain	Broken glass	4.00	1.00
AWM34846	Turn & Bank	Germany	OK	3.50	0.15
AWM34889	Turn & Bank	Germany	OK	3.50	0.15
OL 17	Turn & Bank	Japan	Broken, no glass	85.00	14.00
AWM34881	Variometer	Germany	OK	0.50	0.15

Conservation of One of Alexander Calder's Largest Mobiles

Albert Marshall and Shelley Sturman

Department of Conservation
National Gallery of Art
Washington, D.C.
U.S.A.

Abstract

Alexander Calder began making his moving sculpture, the mobiles, in the 1930s. As long as these sculptures were small and light, the grinding of one metal surface against another was minimal, but as size and weight increased, so did the issue of wear. The 23 m (76 ft), 418 kg (920 lb) mobile Untitled (1976), commissioned for the grand atrium of the East Building of the National Gallery of Art in Washington, D.C., was enlarged and fabricated from Calder's 30.5 cm (1 ft) maquette.

When the mobile was lowered for cleaning and inspection after 10 years of exhibition, an appreciable loss of metal was observed at certain points of contact on the sculpture. These losses are representative of a common problem in our industrial society. Over the years, various methods of lubrication have been developed to slow the inevitable progression of wear. In a sculpture that moves, the effect of wear is not always taken into account, and the object can slowly grind itself away. If a lubrication system is not built into an art object, it cannot be accomplished easily within the ethical constraints of the conservation profession.

This paper presents the problems encountered in making such a large sculpture that hangs from a single point and moves in air currents without a motor. The construction eventually involved use of advanced materials, such as aircraft specification aluminum and plasma-spray application of molybdenum to the probable points of wear.

The paper also discusses the conservation measures needed to restore proper movement to the mobile. These measures included the tungsten-inert-gas welding of losses to the aluminum and a surface hardening with a spray of titanium dioxide to the contact surfaces of the sculpture.

The Development and Construction of Calder's Mobile

Alexander Calder's grand mobile has become the unofficial mascot of the East Building of the National Gallery of Art. Upon entering the museum, one is immediately engaged by the expansive space frame and the slowly rotating, colorful mobile. In the late 1960s when architect I.M. Pei was making drawings for the East Building, plans for commissioning artworks to complement the architecture were set in motion. In June of 1973, Alexander Calder was commissioned to design, fabricate and install a large mobile sculpture for the central, interior court of the National Gallery's East Building. This sculpture became the ultimate example of Calder's art, and the study of its manufacture and its conservation provided an outstanding opportunity to understand and work with late-20th-century art materials (Figure 1).

Calder, who referred to the piece only as "my object," produced a maquette of the mobile shortly after his initial meetings with gallery officials. Engineers at the Biemont Iron Works in Tours, France, who had helped Calder create

Figure 1 Alexander Calder: Untitled, *1976. National Gallery of Art, Washington, D.C., Gift of the Collector's Committee, (1977.76.1). NGA photograph by Philip Charles.*

many of his earlier outdoor stabiles and mobile/stabile combinations, determined the projected weight of the mobile to be more than three tonnes. This estimate assumed that the mobile would be 32 times larger than the maquette and that it would be constructed from traditional steel and solid metal plates. Structural elements necessary to support the mobile's weight and the motor required to rotate it within the large open area would affect the design of the dramatic space frame. The massive sculpture being developed at the Biemont foundry was far removed from the artist's delicate, almost weightless model that responded to the slightest puff of air.

At this point Paul Matisse, an artist and engineer, was consulted. Matisse, who is the grandson of the artist Henri Matisse and who knew Calder from childhood, proposed a novel idea. His suggestion to construct the mobile from aluminum-skinned honeycomb, a high-strength, lightweight, aircraft material, solved the weight problem, retained the qualities of Calder's original, and received the artist's blessing. In May of 1975 Calder wrote to Matisse: "You go ahead and build the thing — I will come to see it when you've finished it."[1] By November 1976, Matisse had the huge mobile ready for inspection. Eight days after he had seen the mobile in the large warehouse that Matisse had rented for its construction, Calder died.

With Matisse planning and supervising every step, the mobile was completed at one-sixth the weight originally projected by Biemont. In its finished state, the mobile consisted of 13 panels and 12 arms, weighing 418 kg (920 lb) and spanning approximately 23 m (76 ft). It was constructed of aluminum-skinned honeycomb for the flat panels (planes, blades and wings), with filled and shaped epoxy edges. These were hung on aircraft specification 2024 aluminum tubes. In anticipation of heavy wear at the contact points, five of the loops bearing the most weight were made of steel, 12 intermediate weight-bearing loops were made of surface treated aluminum, and the remaining loops were made of untreated aluminum. Matisse used a plasma-spray application of molybdenum to surface harden the intermediate weight-bearing aluminum loops.

Figure 2 shows a loop with plasma-sprayed molybdenum hardfacing intact. Plasma spray is an industrial technique that applies molten metal to the workpiece by passing powdered material through an inert gas plasma at temperatures as high as 15,000°C. According to Herbert Herman, plasma spraying "can melt and apply a variety of materials, including refractory ceramics, at a high rate. The technique carries much less risk of degrading the coating and substrate than many other high-temperature processes do, because the gas in the plasma flame

Figure 2 Exposed area on aluminum loop showing molybdenum plasma-sprayed hardfacing. NGA photograph by Philip Charles.

is chemically inert and the target can be kept fairly cool."[2]

The loops were attached to the arms with epoxy construction adhesive (Tracor, Trabond 2101). The arms had been carefully bent by Matisse to show the exact curvature under load as the arms of the maquette produced by Calder. Once all of the arms were assembled and the panels made, the sculpture was painted in Calder's trademark colors, matt surface black, blue and red, in a silicone modified alkyd binder developed by Keeler and Long of Connecticut.

Today, the mobile rotates slowly around the central court, moved only by air passing through vents high up in the walls. It was Alexander Calder's last major work of art, though he did not live to see it installed in the National Gallery of Art.

The Condition of the Mobile in 1988

In 1988, the mobile was removed from exhibition for the first time since it was originally installed in the newly completed East Building more than 10 years earlier. This gave the object conservation department, working in concert with Paul Matisse, an opportunity to examine the entire sculpture and treat existing conditions as well as one unforseen condition.

Three components of the sculpture's condition were addressed in the treatment: cleaning the dirt, grime and finger marks; correcting a manufacturing defect; and attending to the loss of material caused by wear at the contact points of the loops. The first two components were anticipated before examining the disassembled mobile; the last component was discovered only after the mobile's lowering and disassembly.

All of the upper surfaces of the horizontal panels had a thick accumulation of dirt and dust. This had collected from the construction that occurs during the special exhibitions and the general dust in the building's atmosphere. Condensation

drops from the skylight frame modified the paint on the top surfaces of the panels. Some of the arms had a white precipitate on their undersides, possibly from the dripping condensate. Dark finger marks could be seen on the bottom portions of the red blades, which are within reach of tall museum visitors.

The mobile was delivered with a manufacturing defect. This went unnoticed because the mobile could not be completely assembled until it was permanently installed in the East Building. Therefore a slight twist in the orientation of the wing arm assembly loop of cross arm #1 caused wing assembly #4 to hang almost perpendicular to cross arm #1 instead of nearly parallel (see Figure 3 for numbering of mobile panels). In the interest of time, Matisse, together with gallery engineering staff, effected a temporary solution to the misalignment in April 1978: a steel pin was placed in a newly drilled hole in the loop of cross arm #1 so that wing arm #4 would hang in its proper orientation. Sometime during August 1988, this pin dislodged, causing the misalignment of the arm to recur and two of the black panels to cross over each other.

These two conditions were already known and their solutions were straightforward. The third problem was more of a surprise. Upon disassembling the work we found that in five of the loops the aluminum had worn, creating small depressions of up to 3 mm (1/8 in.). As conceived, the mobile not only rotates on its main axis, but the individual arms also pivot as they

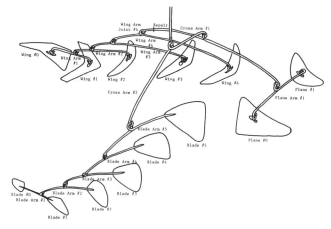

Figure 3 Schematic drawing of the mobile with parts labeled.

hang from the loops. (Figure 4 shows a loop with a depression from wear.) The depressions restricted movement of the loops, because the two loops keyed into one another. Continued wear would aggravate this arm locking problem and eventually cause more problems for the sculpture and the public walking beneath it.

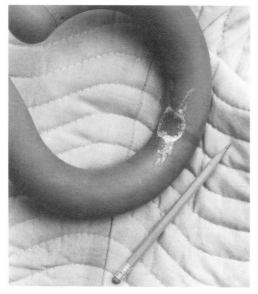

Figure 4 Depression, approximately 3 mm, in aluminum loop, caused by wear. NGA photograph by Philip Charles.

Conservation Treatment of the Mobile

The first part of the treatment involved an elaborate "choreography" of lowering and disassembling the sculpture. Matisse had a very detailed script for installing and de-installing the piece. As the sculpture is lowered the pieces land on different floor levels, and when a part is removed it must be replaced with an equal weight to keep the rest of the mobile level. Once all was disassembled, a cursory washing was undertaken with Orvus (an anionic detergent made by Proctor and Gamble) and water to remove most of the dirt. All of the pieces were dried and taken to a storage area. (A drawing of the mobile with parts labeled and repair to cross arm #1 indicated is seen in Figure 3.)

The manufacturing defect mentioned above was rectified by cutting cross arm #1 105 cm

(42 in.) from the end that holds the wing section. Next, a 30.5 cm (12 in.) joint bar of 6061-T6 aluminum tube was machined by Paul Matisse to fit precisely into the cross arm allowing space for adhesive. The arm was temporarily fitted together and hung by the center loop. A loop representing wing arm #4 was placed on the short end loop and weights equal to the normal loads of 90.5 kg (199 lb) and 116 kg (255 lb) were applied to each end of the arm. The cut end of the cross arm was then rotated about its axis until the proxy loop for the wing arm came to its proper orientation. The rotation turned out to be about five degrees. This position was marked, the arm was disassembled and then reassembled with the same epoxy construction adhesive as was originally used.

Once we discovered the losses of aluminum in the loops, it was Matisse's wish that they be filled with aluminum and hardfaced in a similar manner to his original surface treatment. As mentioned above, Matisse had originally applied molybdenum by plasma spray. While plasma spray was not commercially available at the time, we found that thermal spray, a similar technique, was used in the area. (Discussions with the welding firm led us to their supplier, Eutectic Corporation of Flushing, New York. Their representatives and engineers recommended Eutectic MetaCeram 25040, a titanium dioxide [typical hardness: Rb 57] with Eutectic MetaCeram 21031 for the bond coat.)

Thermal spray has been used industrially since the 1940s. It involves spraying a material through an oxy-acetylene flame onto the workpiece at temperatures lower than those used for plasma spray.

The loops were restored by first removing the paint from nine pairs of loops. The original molybdenum on the loops of wing arm joint #1 (the one bearing the least amount of weight) was found to be intact leaving 16 surfaces that required a new hardfacing. First, the five loops with aluminum losses were filled by aluminum tungsten-inert-gas welding. Then these five loops and the remaining 11 loops were grit blasted with steel pellets to further clean and texture their surfaces. All of these areas were thermal sprayed with a bond coat of Eutectic

Figure 5 *During treatment, before inpainting. NGA photograph by Philip Charles.*

MetaCeram 21031, a nickel/aluminum/molybdenum alloy in a 90:5:5 ratio. (Figure 5 shows a loop with thermal-sprayed hardfacing before inpainting.) Then, a topcoat of Eutectic MetaCeram 25040, titanium dioxide, was applied by thermal spray. The surface of the thermal spray coat and the edge ridges were smoothed. All of the areas that had lost paint were repainted with the same formula paint as the original, a poly-silicone. The sculpture was given a thorough cleaning with dilute Vulpex (potassium methyl cyclohexyl oleate) and water.

After months of collaborative effort among conservators, engineers, machinists, and fabricator, the restored mobile was reinstalled following the original script prepared by Matisse. The awaited rehanging coincided with the celebration of the 10th anniversary of the opening of the East Building.

Résumé

Les restauration d'un des plus grands mobiles d'Alexander Calder

Alexander Calder a commencé à faire ses sculptures en équilibre instable, ses mobiles, dans les années 30. Lorsque ces sculptures étaient petites et légères, le frottement des surfaces métalliques entre elles était minimal mais, avec le temps,

l'artiste a réalisé des œuvres de plus en plus grandes et lourdes, accroissant d'autant le problème de leur usure. Le mobile de 23 m, pesant plus de 400 kg, Sans titre *(1976), qui a été commandé pour le grand atrium de la National Gallery of Art de Washington, D.C. a été agrandi et fabriqué à partir d'une maquette de quelque 30 cm réalisée par Calder.*

Lorsque, après dix ans, il a fallu descendre ce mobile pour le nettoyer et l'inspecter, on a constaté une usure appréciable du métal à certains points de contact. Et cette usure témoigne d'un problème que l'on rencontre fréquemment dans notre société industrielle. Au fil des ans, diverses méthodes de lubrification ont été mises au point pour ralentir l'inévitable progression de l'usure. Or, dans le cas plus particulier d'une sculpture en équilibre instable, l'usure n'est pas toujours prise en compte, et il se peut donc que ses effets graduels finissent par compromettre l'existence même de l'œuvre. Si l'artiste n'a pas intégré un système de lubrification à l'œuvre au moment de sa création, les spécialistes de la restauration pourront difficilement décider, à cause de considérations liées aux règles de la profession, de l'ajouter par la suite.

Dans le cadre de la présente communication, nous décrirons les problèmes entourant la fabrication d'une sculpture aussi grande qui, accrochée en un seul point, doit se mouvoir sous l'action des courants d'air, sans moteur. Sa construction a éventuellement exigé l'utilisation de matériaux de pointe, tel l'aluminium employé en aéronautique et du molybdène pulvérisé, qui a été appliqué sur les points d'usure probables.

Les mesures de conservation nécessaires pour assurer le bon mouvement du mobile seront également abordées. Au nombre de ces mesures, figurent la réparation de l'aluminium par le procédé TIG (Tungsten Inert Gas) et le durcissement de la surface par la pulvérisation de dioxyde de titane sur les points de contact.

References

1. Calder, Alexander, Letter to Paul Matisse, May 3, 1975, Archives of the National Gallery of Art, Washington, D.C.

2. Herman, Herbert, "Plasma-sprayed Coatings," *Scientific American*, September 1988, p. 112.

Conservation of Weathering Steel Sculpture

John Scott

Sculpture Conservator
New York Conservation Center
New York, N.Y.
U.S.A.

Abstract

After a long history in decorative arts and architecture, steel has perhaps become the predominant material of 20th-century sculpture. Its design and production now engage sculptors much as carving, modeling and the foundry. Accordingly, today's conservators of sculpture are interested in the history, technology, deterioration, preservation and restoration of steel.

This paper focuses on high-strength, low-alloy weathering steel commonly known as "corten," after the United States Steel Corporation product "USS COR-TEN," which appeared in contemporary sculpture in the mid-1960s and continues in use today. Some weathering steel sculptures have deteriorated severely, sometimes within a short period after installation. Others weather well for many years despite being given little care.

A brief historical discussion of the development and general adoption of weathering steel is concluded with an account of the material's adoption as a sculptural medium. That introductory account situates the matter of weathering steel's appearance and special corrosion resistance in a historical context of metallurgy, economics and art. A chronological review of scientific theories about the protective patina is presented, including the most current accounts. A discussion of conservation methods focuses on ad hoc practices now in widespread use, which are evaluated with respect to practical effectiveness as well as aesthetic and historic appropriateness. A concluding discussion of ethics presumes the considerable understanding and practical ability that any conservator active in this area should possess, and that the preceding sections sketch.

Introduction

The care of contemporary art often includes the care of steel sculpture. Special problems are encountered in the conservation of the many sculptures in "weathering steel" (e.g., Cor-Ten, discussed below), a material that develops a remarkable appearance and corrosion resistance through outdoor weathering. Thus, we conservators and our colleagues in the field of contemporary art need historical information on the development and design requirements of weathering steel, its marketing history and the circumstances surrounding the adoption of weathering steel as a sculptural medium. Good conservation planning requires, as well, some basic understanding of weathering steel's distinctive corrosion process. This introductory exposition addresses these topics, then presents preservation and maintenance methods and ethical considerations.

Development and Design Requirements

Iron-copper alloys have interested Western metallurgists since at least the early 17th century. Throughout the 19th century such alloys received increasing attention, and the earliest useful work on the mechanical properties of wrought "copper steel" appeared around the last decade of the century. ("Steel" is a general term for iron alloys containing less than 2% carbon. Late 19th and early 20th century copper steel contained from 1% to 2% copper in addition to carbon and other alloying elements.)

Corrosion characteristics are always of interest in materials science, and early in the 20th century, systematic data were collected on the corrosion resistance of copper steel. While some copper steel was found to be as much as 25% more corrosion resistant than most copper-free steel, other similar steel containing only about 0.20% to 0.25% copper was found to have even better resistance to atmospheric corrosion.

In submerged or buried conditions, however, the presence of copper in any amount proved of little benefit. It was recognized early that frequent repetition in wetting and drying the exposed metal surfaces was an important factor in maintaining exceptional corrosion resistance.

Beginning in 1916, the American Society for Testing Materials (ASTM) conducted tests that clarified the benefit of incorporating 0.2% to 0.5% copper and phosphorus into steel. In 1929, the United States Steel Corporation (U.S. Steel) started developing proprietary corrosion resistant "low-alloy" steel (having special properties imparted by small additions of certain elements). In 1933 U.S. Steel introduced its "low-alloy high-tensile" steel product Cor-Ten A, and later, Cor-Ten B.

Today similar weathering steel (meeting ASTM specifications A242, A325 or A588) is provided by several manufacturers.

U.S. Steel continued testing low-alloy steel compositions, and in 1961 its researchers Larrabee and Coburn published corrosion rate data on 15.5-year trials of 270 types of steel with systematic variations in the copper, nickel, chromium, silicon and phosphorus composition. Alloy variation also affects strength, hardness, working and other properties. Weathering steel was the earliest type of today's "high-strength low-alloy" (HSLA) steel.

The design requirements specific to weathering steel are not complex. To weather and endure

outdoors as intended, weathering steel must drain well and dry quickly after wetting. Size is important: small structures can be less susceptible to destructive corrosion than larger structures if they are more effectively dried by sun and wind.

When weathering steel drains poorly or remains wet, it develops no protective rust, and under such conditions rapid destructive corrosion proceeds unless wetting is prevented. Added to steel's usual structural requirements, drainage and quick drying are fundamental for good design and fabrication in weathering steel.

Marketing

Soon after 1933, U.S. Steel strongly promoted its new "low-alloy high-tensile" product Cor-Ten for the manufacture of railroad equipment. Subsequently many diverse applications have been developed, and with close attention to design constraints, weathering steel is now widely employed in architectural and civil engineering applications. Cor-Ten is still marketed by U.S. Steel's successor, U.S. X Corporation.

A 1937 U.S. Steel marketing booklet promotes the use of Cor-Ten through three basic themes, which are still persuasive to the present day. First and second are the economic benefits of Cor-Ten due to its exceptional strength and significant maintenance reduction. Cost savings are promised based on using less Cor-Ten than a given strength specification would require in carbon steel, and also based on the elimination of protective painting, due to Cor-Ten's very low corrosion rates. The third marketing theme is that a well developed rust layer on Cor-Ten steel is aesthetically pleasing.

When used properly, weathering steel is indeed economically beneficial due to its exceptional strength and minimal maintenance. The dark, tightly adherent rust patina that develops through weathering is protective, given suitable conditions, and is compatible with a broad range of contemporary styles.

In the early 1960s Cor-Ten was promoted in the architectural and civil engineering literature as combining structural and aesthetic utility, and its adoption led to sculptural applications within a few years. In 1966, Coburn promoted unpainted Cor-Ten steel for use in highway applications, transmission towers and architecture. He confirmed that Cor-Ten had been tested with regard to atmospheric corrosion resistance for 30 years, and stated that it had proved four to six times as resistant as carbon steel. Coburn wrote that about 80 percent of weathering steel's corrosion takes place during the first two or three years of exposure, with a loss of about 38 μm (1.5 mil) metal thickness, and that the expected total loss of metal thickness during the subsequent 20 years is only about 12.5 μm (0.5 mil). These figures were for urban and semi-rural atmospheres, as marine and industrial atmospheres had proved quite aggressive to weathering steel.

Perusal of diverse marketing and design literature published during the period 1934 to present indicates that before the mid-1960s very little mention was made of the special design requirents for minimizing weathering steel corrosion. While steel industry scientific staff may have often advised designers directly, manufacturers' literature gave such information little place before the early 1970s. By the late 1970s and early 1980s, manufacturers' literature featured special design constraints and recommended specific fabrication materials and methods.

Highway designers readily adopted weathering steel in the early 1960s, but in many cases they neglected to provide for adequate drainage, so some parts of their structures retained moisture. As a result of disastrous consequences, civil engineers and steel industry scientists were re-evaluating the usefulness of weathering steel and discussing its special requirements by the mid-1960s. A similar development took place in architecture.

The birth of modern steel sculpture between World Wars was followed by tremendous development after 1945. David Smith and other sculptors through the 1950s and 1960s adopted the materials and techniques of iron-working. Soon, steel joined bronze and stone as the pre-eminent media of sculpture, and, influenced by architectural and other applications, sculptors began using weathering steel in the late 1960s.

For many contemporary artists keenly aware of relations between art history, art criticism and art patronage, long-term survival of artworks has been of great concern. According to conversational reminiscences from sculptors active in the mid-1960s and later, the advent of weathering steel seemed to permit iron-working artists to place sculpture outdoors with every expectation that it would last as long as bronze.

In fact, when sculptors "discovered" weathering steel in the mid-1960s, information was already being disseminated on its susceptibility to corrosion, and its consequent special design requirements.

Some artists and sculpture fabricators have understood these requirements and some have not. In 1970, U.S. Steel published *Steel In Sculpture*, making important information more accessible, but many artists remained uninformed. As is often the case, new developments were probably missed through lack of adequate communication among artists, manufacturers and technical professionals, and an unfamiliarity with existing literature. Certainly weathering steel has been enthusiastically adopted by many contemporary sculptors.

A Distinctive Corrosion Process

The modern technology of weathering steel is an outgrowth of earlier copper steel technology. Current understanding of weathering steel's protective rust follows a long history of hypotheses regarding similar phenomena.

The corrosion resistance of copper steel was actively investigated beginning in the late 19th century. Early explanations were based on galvanic cell chemistry and noted the importance of water and air. By 1900 and soon after, observation had established that copper steel in buried or submerged conditions showed no special corrosion resistance. It was recognized that complete drying-out at frequent intervals was necessary to maintain copper steel's best corrosion resistance. These observations have subsequently proved applicable to weathering steel's corrosion resistance.

In 1934 Gregg and Daniloff reported the theories (1929 to 1931) of Carius, a German scientist. Carius postulated barrier mechanisms closely related to earlier galvanic theories of corrosion protection. Carius taught that a virtually impervious copper surface layer was formed by dissolution of copper from the copper steel, followed by galvanic redeposition of the copper at the steel surface, and formation of a layer of cupric oxide over the copper. According to Carius, corrosion was controlled by the dual copper/copper oxide layer, which effectively prevented air and water from reaching the steel surface. Gregg and Daniloff mentioned that iron oxides forming simultaneously with the copper and copper oxide film must prevent formation of a completely protective film, but otherwise accepted Carius' theory. While it would appear that well developed light microscopical methods widely available in Carius' era had actually revealed the presence of copper layers on copper steel, Horton and Goldberg later stated that Carius' copper film had never been observed, and that copper films artificially applied to steel had not resulted in the degree of corrosion resistance observed in copper steel. Carius' galvanic and barrier mechanisms were ignored by pre-eminent weathering steel corrosion and passivation researchers little more than a decade later, but more advanced models of electrochemical processes and barriers to corrosive agents remain fundamental in explaining steel corrosion and passivation.

In 1945, Copson proposed that HSLA steel containing copper, nickel and chromium forms sulfates of these elements during the corrosion process. He suggested that these compounds, less soluble than iron sulfates, precipitate and clog pores in rust (apparently still regarded as steel's most commonly occurring rust, comprised mainly of magnetite, Fe_3O_4), thus restricting water and air access to steel surfaces. Hence the rust is a protective barrier.

Schikorr proposed in 1964 that in steel corrosion the reaction of iron with dissolved atmospheric oxygen and sulfur dioxide produces ferrous sulfates, which then react autocatalytically with water and dissolved oxygen to produce iron hydroxide and sulfuric acid. The acid reacts with iron to produce more sulfates and water, and the cycle continues. According to Schikorr, copper, chromium and nickel in weathering steel participate in the corrosion

process, but form water-insoluble sulfates, thus removing sulfate ions needed for autocatalysis and slowing the generation of corrosive iron sulfate. A similar article by Fyfe in 1969 adds that the precipitated sulfates help to consolidate a protective rust.

In 1966 Horton and Goldberg published eight excellent photomacrographic black-and-white images detailing cross-sections of the protective rust, noted a two-layer structure, described layer compositions, and identified the predominant constituents as alpha- and gamma-FeOOH. However, despite a competent review of pertinent literature, Horton and Goldberg were unable to suggest formation or functional mechanisms for the protective rust.

Our current understanding of weathering steel rust derives from work published in two 1969 articles. In that year, Schmitt and Gallagher of U.S. Steel critiqued the Copson and Schikorr approaches as too simple to fully explain "the many effects of alloying element combinations," as indicated by U.S. Steel research presented in 1961 by Larrabee and Coburn. Schmitt and Gallagher mention a model, "cathodic control," in which the rate of anodic iron oxidation depends on the rate of cathodic oxygen reduction. They suggest that the alloying elements have some unexplained effect on the physical and electrical properties of the rust films, properties that keep the rate of oxygen reduction very low. This critique of earlier thinking introduced modern electrochemical concepts to the dialogue on weathering steel corrosion.[*] The Schmitt and Gallagher

---

[*] These concepts are also fundamental to cathodic protection methods for corrosion control, which first drew attention around 1929 and which by 1949 were in wide use and under enthusiastic developmental research. The basic mechanism of cathodic protection is the sacrificial corrosion of a metal anode electrically joined to a cathodic structure being protected. Electrochemical potential, derived from the reduction of a surrounding electrolyte as the anode corrodes, is applied to the cathodic structure, where the excess of potential passivates the structure's surface.

Today cathodic protection and protective coating are our major tools against corrosion of buried and submerged metals.

discussion also showed that the time was ripe for a contribution of major significance from Okada et al., also published in 1969.

Okada and his colleagues made electrochemical measurements of the polarization characteristics of rusted weathering steel, and used polarized light microscopy in conjunction with the electron microprobe to examine rust formed in atmospheric corrosion. They reported a two-layered structure: an inner layer of "spinel-type" iron oxide under an outer layer of iron oxyhydroxide (FeOOH). They suggested that the amorphous oxide next to the steel surface is a kind of oxide polymer with unit structures linked by hydroxide bridges, and that this structure acts as a barrier to oxygen and water. Okada also reported that prolonged exposure to moisture without intermittent drying results in the loss of the apparently protective inner layer.

Subsequently, Misawa et al. studied weathering steel rust using infrared (IR) and far-IR spectroscopy, X-ray diffraction, and scanning electron microscopy (SEM). They suggested in 1974 that the inner layer is an amorphous ferric oxyhydroxide, $FeO_x(OH)_{3-2x}$ (which has much bound water), which can transform to alpha-FeOOH. They inferred that formation of amorphous oxyhydroxides could be catalyzed by copper, chromium and phosphorus.

A succinct 1975 article by Pourbaix and de Miranda summarized the then current understanding of the structure and the formation mechanisms of protective rusts on weathering steel. Omitting earlier theories, they reviewed the work of Okada and of Misawa, then presented results from their own electrochemical investigations, which modeled formation of the protective rust. By analogy to the surface films of corrosion products, which they had produced on weathering steel in galvanic cells at their laboratory, Pourbaix and de Miranda identified the protective rust's inner layer as alpha-FeOOH, goethite. They stated that when the rust is wet, alloying elements, particularly copper, dissolve from metal into crevices, where they inhibit the formation of magnetite, Fe_3O_4 (non-protective rust) and catalyze the formation of additional goethite, which consolidates the inner protective layer. (Incidentally, in 1983 Pourbaix and Pourbaix announced an

ongoing worldwide study of exposed samples of weathering steel.)

Recently, Kihira, Ito and Murata re-examined weathering steel rust structure using computer-aided X-ray microanalysis and laser Raman spectroscopy. They reported that a thin layer of phosphatic rust forms at the steel surface in the initial stage of rust formation, with subsequent gradual formation of mostly amorphous iron oxyhydroxide under the phosphatic layer and a mostly crystalline layer above.

Okada et al. laid the foundation for our current understanding of weathering steel's protective rust. Subsequent work has been concerned with discerning finer physical structures, more accurately characterizing components and explaining additional aspects of formation (and degradation) processes for the protective rust. In 1991 Wurth summarized current thinking on the subject:

> The protective iron corrosion products on weathering steels form a two-layer structure. The inner layer of this structure consists of fine, tightly adherent amorphous and poorly crystallized ferric hydroxides. Among these ferric species, the amorphous ferric oxyhydroxide [$FeO_x(OH)_{3-2x}$] is thought to be important in preventing both the flow of O_2 and corrosive anions to the metal surface and the flow of ferrous species into solution. The loose and often flaky outer layer is composed mainly of this two-layer structure.

> The sequence of reactions forming the two-layer structure changes, depending on the environment to which the steel is exposed. Parameters such as pH, presence of solution anions, and availability of oxidizers determine which species are formed and how quickly they decompose....

Sculpture Preservation and Maintenance

Important factors affecting the condition of weathering steel sculpture are design, fabrication, location of site, installation and ambient environment. The basic requirements for proper function of unpainted weathering steel surfaces are that they must have regular cycles of wetting and complete drying. Thus, all designs for unpainted HSLA steel must provide for good drainage, and all faying (i.e., closely fitted) surfaces and other features that tend to attract and retain moisture, such as interior surfaces and voids, must be well sealed. On the other hand, exposed surfaces that drain well and that are effectively dried by both sun and air currents do not require sealing. Notwithstanding the importance of technical aspects of media choices, the artist's primary responsibilities are to observe and communicate in exceptional ways. Physical properties of media chosen by contemporary artists often prove unexpectedly problematic, and so present new challenges for care and maintenance.

An ad hoc approach, using mostly local information and skills for preserving weathering steel sculpture, has prevailed among sculptors, sculpture fabricators, iron-working craftsmen, restorers, owners, curators and conservators since the mid-1970s. A variety of measures, some more effective than others, have been taken, sometimes with valuable advice from steel industry experts. It is useful to consider the most common measures, those we should adopt and improve, and others we should avoid. Common ad hoc measures include the following:

Cleaning: Careful cleaning using dry brush, broom, low-pressure water blast, organic solvents or detergent solutions will often remove paint, marker graffiti, or detritus, and these methods should always be tested first. Steam cleaning can be very effective. Blasting (high-pressure hydro-blast, or air-blast abrasion using fine grain silica, alumina or plastic blast media) is an ad hoc measure commonly used to eliminate marring by destructive rust, repair scars, graffiti, old paint, and so forth.

Stimulation of New Rust: Development of new, visually homogeneous rust on weathering steel sculptures is often stimulated by blast-cleaning. New rust normally appears within days after blasting begins on outdoor installations. At rates dependent on ambient conditions, the patina develops over several weeks from a bright orange-red to light red-brown. Within a few months, a dark brown color usually develops, which within a few years becomes very dark.

However, abrasive blasting is not always possible or advisable. For instance, in many municipalities, local law prohibits outdoor silica, alumina or similar abrasive blasting for reasons of public health and sanitation. The cost of blasting may also be a deterrent. Finally, complete blasting may unnecessarily disrupt enjoyment of well-weathered sculpture. In some instances, cleaned or repaired areas are small in relation to the sculpture as a whole, or they may not be visible in some views.

Rusting of newly fabricated or blast-cleaned weathering steel is sometimes stimulated or modulated by rinsing with salt solution. Avoid chloride ion, one of metal's worst enemies; chlorides are very detrimental to weathering steel's protective rust.

Painting and Clearcoating: Painting and coating of steel are also facilitated by blasting. Weathering steel sculptures are often painted, clearcoated or waxed in an ad hoc manner. However, coating originally unpainted weathering steel sculpture is an ineffective conservation measure because it adds the problems of weathered coatings to the usual problems of weathering steel. Thus, repair funds are consumed without optimum benefits, more effective drainage and sealing measures may be delayed or diminished and necessary maintenance becomes more difficult and frequent.

Both painting and clearcoating markedly alter surface appearance. Painting imposes non-original color, while clearcoats and wax saturate (darken) the patina color. Painting and clearcoating also alter surface texture. Although common in ad hoc preservation of weathering steel sculptures, such painting and coating are seldom appropriate. Well-meaning preservationists have compromised the historic and aesthetic integrity of many weathering steel sculptures.

However, some sculptures are located on unsuitable sites where local moisture persists or local activities invite graffiti or other destructive contamination. In such cases inobtrusive physical barriers should be installed to protect the sculpture. Following conservation, after new patina has developed, it may be necessary to clearcoat only the threatened areas in order to create a moisture barrier or to simplify frequent surface cleaning.

Refabrication: This practice is often necessary to reinforce or replace deteriorated parts or entire sculptures, or to allow sealing or elimination of corrosion-prone features. It is important to ensure that appropriate materials are used in refabrication. If possible, the weathering steel used for the repair should be the same type as that originally used in the sculpture.

Assembly hardware, such as screws, bolts, washers and nuts, must be compatible with the steel. Sometimes the original hardware is not compatible and this often results in corrosion of the hardware and surrounding metal. Currently, manufacturers recommend ASTM 316 stainless steel, or weathering steel ASTM A325 for bolts, washers and nuts. When possible, dissimilar metals should be isolated by electrically insulating hole liners and washers to avoid bimetallic corrosion. Hardware joints and holes must be sealed, since they otherwise tend to retain moisture and corrode.

Except in non-welded structures, arc welding is the appropriate method of repair joining, and should follow manufacturer's specifications. Generally, single-pass and structural welds may be made using E70-group, mild-steel covered electrodes, as long as the weld ensures proper composition enrichment from adjacent steel. More care must be taken, and different weld methods and fill materials used, when the exposed weld is broad or must closely match the surrounding surface in color and corrosion resistance. Manufacturer specifications should be obtained and followed; certified welders should be employed and closely supervised.

The heat of welding destroys weathering steel patina close to the weld. Heat from the front face of a steel plate will usually destroy patina on the back face. The resulting scars are quite unsightly and bright orange. After covered electrode welding, burnt patina will be obscured temporarily by a blotchy white welding fume residue. The burnt surface soon regenerates its protective rust under the darkening residue of the burnt patina, which separates from the surface in paper-thin fragments. Eventually the burnt material crumbles away; this may be hastened by hydro-blast or wire-brushing. Frequently the visual effect of weld repair is mitigated by abrasive blasting of the entire affected surface, or of the complete sculpture. Then the entire blasted area weathers together and regains its patina, and the appearance of the weld area matches the rest of that surface. As discussed above, blasting is not always advisable.

Although the bright contrast of welds with adjacent unaffected mature patina is alarming at first, the appearance of properly welded areas improves quickly. After four to six months of normal weathering in urban atmospheres, welded areas are quite dark. After a year, it may be difficult to pick out a weld on the surface of a large structure. As time goes on the welded area blends very well.

Sealing Corrosion-prone Sites

Before sealing at all edges, faying surfaces prone to corrosion must be cleared as completely as possible of loose or impacted matter (very high pressure hydro-blasting can give a reasonably thorough effect), and dried thoroughly by compressed air or heat. Joints and gaps can often be sealed effectively using weather-resistant, flexible and long-lasting caulks, such as RTV silicones. When necessary and appropriate, deteriorated sculptures may be taken apart. The faying surfaces are then cleared thoroughly by blasting and are well sealed with appropriate paint, which also serves as primer for joint sealant. Sculptures are reassembled with "formed in place gaskets" of caulk sealing the joints. Sometimes instead of priming and caulking, faying surface edges are sealed by welding.

Drainage Enhancement: This is a common strategy for dealing with water pooling, which causes destructive corrosion. It is important that the sculpture's foundation site be well drained, and that an effective moisture barrier exists between the base of the sculpture and the surface beneath it. In the sculpture itself, weep-holes or slots allow water to drain away rather than to pool. Such drains must be properly located and of correct size: large enough to avoid clogging yet small and inobtrusive. Weep-holes and slots that tend to collect detritus must be cleared regularly to promote proper drainage.

Corrosion-prone surfaces in areas of water pooling that cannot be drained may need to be sealed with a clear, water-excluding coating. When such areas are out of sight, the aesthetic impact of coatings is minimal. Of course, such coatings must be maintained in good condition.

It is also very important to frequently clear away accumulations of rust, dirt, dust and other detritus, which tend to build up in gaps, corners and on horizontal surfaces of weathering steel structures. Such accumulations become slow-drying poultices, which keep weathering steel surfaces actively corroding.

Appropriate conservation requires thorough and periodic examination, condition evaluation, documentation and reporting by a qualified conservator. The conservator should specify and implement effective treatment procedures and a regular maintenance program for cleaning, drainage enhancement, dry sealing of faying surfaces, and structural repair as necessary. Localized clearcoating, though sometimes unavoidable, should be limited. Complete painting or clearcoating should be strictly avoided. It may be possible to protect grade-level or buried features by cathodic means. The conservator should also supervise or personally carry out both the recommended treatment procedures and maintenance program.

Ethics in Conserving Contemporary Art

Simplistic problem-solving measures, such as sandblasting, painting, relocating or removing, characterize the ad hoc approach to caring for weathering steel sculpture. Unfortunately, destruction of deteriorating artworks is another ad hoc solution, efficient in eliminating problems, but incompatible with the conservator's most fundamental responsibilities. Ethically minded conservators will refuse the often-offered roles of arbiter, facilitator or confessor in the alteration or disposal of art. To help us transform destructive attitudes and educate decision makers through our own practice of responsible conservation, conservators must understand why inappropriate measures are often proposed.

Public art may suffer popular or official rejection; this is especially true of modern or contemporary art if the public or the government associate the art with an unfamiliar or elite taste. A display site may seem ill chosen. Safety issues often are important in dealing with deteriorating structures. The daunting prospect of an artwork's conservation may overwhelm those entrusted with its care. Curators, planners, and administrators can easily lose enthusiasm for conservation projects that require substantial amounts of time and money. Planning often omits consultation with expert conservators, relying exclusively upon local administrators, committees, tradespersons, architects or engineers. In these and similar situations, the worst of the ad hoc measures are sometimes employed. Unfortunately, many weathering steel sculptures and other contemporary artworks with apparently severe condition problems have been altered, removed from context or destroyed due to inadequate consideration and triage.

To enhance appropriate and effective conservation planning and implementation it is very important to obtain genuine expertise and practical understanding concerning specific art media, and appropriate technology for preservation, restoration and maintenance. Planners must also draw upon historically and technically accurate assessments of aesthetics, significance, structure and condition. The conservator's role in consulting or project management encompasses developing knowledge and providing information, guiding and developing conservation specifications, supervising conservation activities, and helping all concerned to maintain firm commitment to the preservation and integrity of each work of art.

Conclusion

In most cases weathering steel sculpture can be preserved by proper cleaning, replacing deteriorated parts, enhancing drainage, sealing moisture-prone features and following a regular program of maintenance. These measures, when planned and implemented with a good understanding of weathering steel, can stabilize the sculptural structure and patina. The appearance of a stable and well-maintained weathering steel sculpture is enhanced with the passage of time.

It seems that the surface and other remarkable qualities of weathering steel are being closely studied by corrosion scientists outside the conservation field. In addition to this research, it would be really useful for conservation scientists to undertake sustained studies on the care of weathering steel. For now however, conservators with some rudimentary under-standing of weathering steel must employ provisional solutions to pressing conservation problems.

Notes for Figures 1, 2, 3 and 4

Atmosphere and Environment X by Louise Nevelson (1970), shown in Figures 1, 2 and 3,

Figure 2 Atmosphere and Environment X *Louise Nevelson, Fairmount Park, Philadelphia. Photo: J. Scott (detail).*

comprises 30 boxes of 12.5 mm (0.5 in.) weath-ering steel plates screwed and bolted together with a welded base, all on a concrete footing. This open structure incorporates many water catchments and faying surfaces both broad and narrow. The boxes were originally held to-gether by unsealed, uninsulated screws of mild steel, which corroded rapidly. At the edges of broad faying surfaces considerable gaps devel-oped within several years of installation, due to rust expansion in continually moist interiors. Adjacent narrow (12.5 mm) faying surfaces dry well, so edges remain in close contact. Non-conserved exemplars of this edition located in Philadelphia, New Haven and elsewhere are in very poor condition after 20 years of exposure.

Night Presences IV by Louise Nevelson (1972), shown in Figure 4, comprises several smooth closed forms fabricated of weathering

Figure 1 Atmosphere and Environment X *Louise Nevelson, 1970, Princeton. The John B. Putnam Jr. Memorial Collection. Photo: The Art Museum, Princeton University.*

Figure 3 Atmosphere and Environment X *Louise Nevelson, 1970, Princeton. Photo: The Art Museum, Princeton University. Y.L. Kim.*

steel with all seams welded and no faying surfaces, all set on a concrete footing. The entire structure drains very well, except that detritus collects and expansive rust forms at the bottom of a few narrow gaps between vertical elements. While there has been some restoration of the horizontal surface of the base, the sculpture is today in fine condition after 20 years of exposure.

⌐ 1 micron

Figure 5 Weathering steel and patina. PLM brightfield, no analyzer. Photo taken by J. Scott at the N.Y. Conservation Center, Inc., New York City.

the light path, the patina region becomes two: a bright and largely birefringent outer area next to the mounting medium, at the patina's surface, and a dark, largely isotropic inner area, next to the steel (Figure 6). These exemplify weathering steel patina's characteristic two-layer structure, which alternates mostly amorphous oxyhydroxides with more crystalline ferric hydroxides (Figure 7). Also visible are parallel strata comprising these layers, and tiny faults running through the strata.

The patina in another mounted sample is examined using the scanning electron microscope (SEM), magnified 1,000 times (Figure 8). Note that darker regions are more dense than lighter regions. Stratification is evident, with many faults, but next to the metal at left is a very continuous dense layer.

Figure 4 Night Presences IV Louise Nevelson, Park Ave. at 92 St., New York City. Photo: J. Scott (detail).

Notes for Figures 5, 6, 7, 8, 9 and 10

Polished cross-sectional surface samples of long-exposed weathering steel illustrate the structure of protective patina.

Examination is through the use of metallograph and brightfield polarized light. The patina in a mounted sample ca. 65 μm wide at center is a somewhat striated grayish region next to the bright steel (Figure 5). The darkest region, on the other side of the gray band, is the mounting medium. Examined with the analyzer placed in

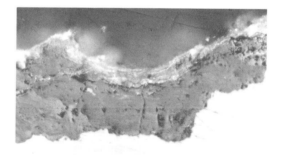

⌐ 1 micron

Figure 6 Weathering steel and patina. PLM brightfield, crossed polars. Photo taken by J. Scott at the N.Y. Conservation Center, Inc., New York City.

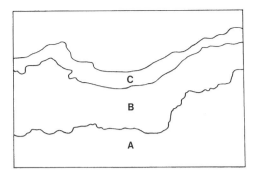

Figure 7 Weathering steel and patina. A) steel, B) patina inner, and C) patina outer. (Diagrammatic representation of Figure 6). Diagram: J. Scott.

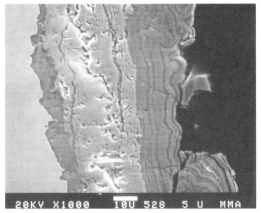

Figure 8 Weathering steel and patina. SEM 1,000x. Photo: J. Scott/Mark Wypyski (Wypyski is a Research Associate, Department of Objects Conservation, The Metropolitan Museum of Art, N.Y.).

The corner of an unmounted sample is examined using SEM, magnified 750 times (Figure 9). The corner between the polished face and the outer surface of the patina is viewed directly, at an angle about 135° from each surface. The jagged profile of the interface between steel and patina on the polished face appears in the lower half of the image. Above the dark (dense) inner patina layer is the lighter (less dense) outer layer, and the outer surface is seen above the corner.

Examining the unmounted sample with SEM, magnified 200 times, the viewing angle is moved past the corner, away from the polished face, which appears in the lower part of the image (Figure 10). The balance of the image depicts a richly textured and fissured outer patina surface.

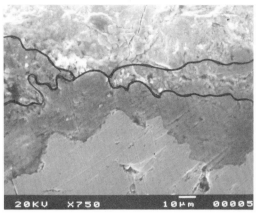

Figure 9 Weathering steel and patina. SEM 750x. Photo taken by J. Scott at Lucius Pitkin, Inc., New York City.

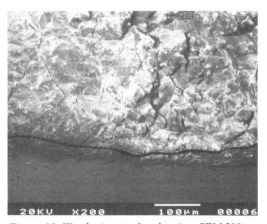

Figure 10 Weathering steel and patina. SEM 200x. Photo taken by J. Scott at Lucius Pitkin, Inc., New York City.

Appendix

A Note on Terminology
Certain terms and ideas are introduced in the forms they actually took in the articles discussed. This is to emphasize the chronological nature of the account of weathering steel.

For instance, U.S. Steel originally referred to their weathering steel product as "Cor-Ten," and later as "CorTen." More recently the term "USS CORTEN" has appeared, probably to avoid possible loss of trademark status with the product name's slide into the generic. Today we use the term "weathering steel," while during the 1930s to the 1960s technical parlance favored "CorTen" or sometimes "high-strength low-alloy steel" or "HSLA steel." Today not all HSLA steel is weathering steel.

Weathering steel had its genesis in the technology of "copper steel," a term still current, which predates the 20th century in common use and which refers to a specific type of industrial product. Another current term, "copper-bearing steel," has a broad meaning, but it is more recent and was not seen in the technical literature of the 19th or early 20th centuries.

Acknowledgement

Field examinations and consulting assignments, together with major conservation projects for Princeton University (The Putnam Collection of Modern Sculpture) and for the Board of Education of the City of New York (Public Art for Public Schools), have helped the author to learn, develop, apply and evaluate conservation methods for weathering steel sculpture.

Résumé

La conservation de sculptures en acier

Utilisé depuis longtemps dans les arts décoratifs et en architecture, l'acier en est sans doute venu à constituer le matériau principal des sculptures du XXe siècle. Les sculpteurs travaillent désormais à sa conception et à sa production, au même titre qu'ils s'intéressent de longue date aux techniques de la sculpture, du moulage et de la fonte. De même, les spécialistes de la restauration des sculptures d'aujourd'hui se préoccupent-ils de mieux connaître l'histoire et la technologie de l'acier, et de mieux comprendre le phénomène de la dégradation de ce matériau, ainsi que les techniques permettant de le préserver et de le restaurer.

Dans le cadre de la présente communication, nous parlerons surtout de l'acier patinable à haute résistance faiblement allié, mieux connu sous le nom de « corten » (du « USS COR-TEN » de la U. S. Steel) qui, ayant fait son apparition dans la sculpture contemporaine au milieu des années 60, continue d'être utilisé aujourd'hui.

Certaines sculptures faites à partir de ce matériau se sont sérieusement détériorées, parfois peu de temps après leur installation, tandis que d'autres résistent fort bien aux intempéries pendant de nombreuses années, et ce, même si elles ne font l'objet que de peu de soins.

Nous décrirons brièvement l'histoire de la technique du corten, ainsi que la commercialisation de ce produit et ses applications, tout en soulignant l'intérêt qu'il suscite, de façon parallèle ou divergente, au sein de l'industrie et chez les artistes. Nous fournirons, d'autre part, des explications quant aux connaissances scientifiques que l'on possède actuellement sur la nature de la surface d'oxyde protecteur, connaissances qui aideront à mieux comprendre le vice inhérent et manifeste que présente le corten. Les problèmes usuels de conservation que pose ce matériau sont clairement dus à des facteurs liés à sa conception et à des facteurs environnementaux.

Nous ferons, par ailleurs, quelques suggestions au sujet des méthodes de conservation les plus pertinentes. Et, nous fournirons une illustration des mesures de restauration ponctuelles qui sont actuellement très répandues, tout en évaluant tant leur efficacité sur le plan technique que leur pertinence du point de vue esthétique et historique. Ces propos seront étayés d'études de cas portant sur des objets qui sont actuellement en traitement.

Une bibliographie à jour de documents scientifiques, techniques et critiques portant sur le sujet accompagnera enfin cette communication.

References and Bibliography

A sampling of pertinent literature regarding weathering steel was compiled for this paper. Not all references are cited in the text.

Aitchison, L. and W.I. Pumphrey, *Engineering Steels* (London: Macdonald & Evans, 1953).

Boyer, H.E. and T.L. Gall, eds., *Metals Handbook*, 10th edn. (Metals Park, Ohio: ASM International, 1990).

Brockenbrough, R.L. and B.G. Johnston, *Steel Design Manual* (Pittsburgh: U.S. Steel Corp., 1968).

Buck, D.C., "Influence of Very Low Percentages of Copper in Retarding the Corrosion of Steel," *Proceedings of ASTM*, vol. 19, no. 2, 1919. (Abstracted in *Iron Age*, 104, 1919, p. 44).

Cathodic Protection, a Symposium by the Electrochemical Society and the National Association of Corrosion Engineers (New York: NACE, 1949).

Chizhmakov, M.B. and M.B. Shapiro, "Use of Physical Methods for Investigation of Corrosion Resistant Steel and Alloys," *Chemical and Petroleum Engineering*, vol. 23, nos. 11-12, July 1988, pp. 625-628.

Coburn, S.K., "A Low-Cost Maintenance-Free Structural Steel for Highway Applications," *Highway Research Record*, 110, Washington, D.C., 1966.

Coburn, S.K., "Increasing Container Service Life with Painted USS CORTEN Steel," *Proceedings, Second Container Technology Conference*, Brighton, England, Dec. 1978, p. 177.

Coburn, S.K., *Corrosion Sourcebook* (Houston, Texas/Metals Park, Ohio: ASM/NACE, 1984).

Copson, H.R., "A Theory of the Mechanism of Rusting of Low Alloy Steels in the Atmosphere," *Proceedings of ASTM*, vol. 45, 1945, pp. 554-580.

Cor-Ten, the Low-Cost, High-strength, Corrosion-resisting Steel of Many Uses (New York: United States Steel Corporation, 1937) [Copious listings of USS researchers' and marketers' articles and lectures on USS Corten, 1933.]

Dinkaloo, J. "The Steel Will Weather Naturally," *Architectural Record*, Aug. 1992, pp. 148-150.

Dinkaloo, J. "Bold and Direct Using Metal in a Strong Basic Way," *Architectural Record*, July 1964, pp. 135-142.

Duennwald, J. and A. Otto, "Investigation of Phase Transitions in Rust Layers Using Raman Spectroscopy," *Corrosion Science*, vol. 29, no. 9, 1989, pp. 1167-1176.

Eichhorn, K.J. and W. Forker, "The Properties of Oxide and Water Films Formed during the Atmospheric Exposure of Iron and Low Alloy Steels," *Corrosion Science*, vol. 28, no. 8, 1988, pp. 745-758.

Evans, U.R., *Metallic Corrosion, Passivity and Protection*, 2nd edn. (New York: Edward Arnold & Co., 1946).

Forker, W. et al., "Untersuchungen zur ausbildung von deckschichten auf niedriglegierten staehlen und baustahl mit einem wechselt-archverfahren," *Neue Huette*, vol. 18, no. 4, April 1973, pp. 235-240.

Fromhold, A.T. and S.J. Noh, "The Transport of Ions and Electrons through Microscopically Inhomogenous Passive Films; Breakdown Implications," *Corrosion Science*, vol. 29, nos. 2-3, 1988, pp. 237-255.

Fyfe, D. et al., "Atmospheric Corrosion of Fe-Cu Alloys and Cu-containing Steels," *4th International Congress on Metallic Corrosion*, Amsterdam, Sept. 7-14, NACE, Houston, 1969.

Glueck, G., "Sculptor's Ordeal With Steel: It's Pretty but Temperamental," *New York Times*, August 23, 1991, pp. C13, C17.

Gregg, J.L. and B.N. Daniloff, *Alloys of Iron and Copper* (New York/London: McGraw-Hill, 1934) [N.B.: good bibliography 1627-1934.]

Hayes, J.M. and S.P. Maggard, "Economic Possibilities of Corrosion Resistant Low Alloy Steel in Short Span Bridges," *Proceedings of National Engineering Conference*, Denver, CO, May 5-6, 1960, pp. 59-60.

Hayne, F.H., J.W. Spence and J.B. Upham (Environmental Protection Agency Environmental Research Center in Research Triangle Park, N.C., U.S.A.) "Effects of Air Pollutants on Weathering Steel and Galvanized Steel: A Chamber Study," *Materials Performance*, vol. 15, no. 4 (Houston: National Association of Corrosion Engineers) April 1976, p. 48.

Heidersbach, R. and F. Purcell, "Analysis of Corrosion Products with the Use of the Raman Microprobe," *Microbeam Analysis 1984*, Proceedings of the 19th Annual Conference of the Microbeam Society, July 16-20, 1984, Bethlehem, PA, Ronig, A.D. and J.I. Goldstein, eds. (San Francisco: San Francisco Press, Inc., 1984).

High Strength Low Alloy Steels Publication ADV 1809R3-5M-274B (Cleveland: Republic Steel, 1974).

Honzak, J.G.V., "Macroscopic Structure of the Rust Layer Formed in the Atmospheric Corrosion of Steel," *British Corrosion Journal*, vol. 8, no. 4, July 1973, pp. 162-166.

Horton, J.B. and M.M. Goldberg, "Distribution of Alloying Elements in the Rust Layers Formed Naturally on Corrosion Resistant Low-Alloy Constructional (Weathering) Steel," *4th International Congress on Metallic Corrosion*, Amsterdam, September 7-14, 1969 (Houston: NACE, 1969).

Horton, J.B. and M.M. Goldberg, "The Rusting of Low-Alloy Steels in the Atmosphere," *American Iron and Steel Institute Regional Technical Meetings 1965* (New York: American Iron and Steel Institute, 1966) pp. 171-195.

HSLA Steel for Architectural Applications U.S. Steel Publication ADUSS-88-6659-02 (Pittsburgh: United States Steel Corporation, 1977).

Kandeil, A.Y. and M.Y. Mourad, "Effect of Surface Texture on Corrosion Behavior of Steel," *Surface & Coatings Technology*, vol. 37, no. 2, 1989, pp. 237-250.

Kawasaki River Ten Atmospheric Corrosion Resistant Steels (Tokyo: Kawasaki Steel Corporation, 1977).

Keane, J.D. et al., *Remedial Painting of Weathering Steel: A State-of-the-Art Survey* (Pittsburgh: Steel Structures Painting Council, 1984).

Keiser, J.T. et al., "Characterization of the Passive Film Formed on Weathering Steels," *Corrosion Science*, vol. 23, no. 3, 1983, pp. 251-259.

Kihira, H., S. Ito and T. Murata, "Quantitative Classification of Patina Conditions for Weathering Steels Using a Recently Developed Instrument," *Corrosion*, vol. 45, no. 4, April 1989, pp. 347-352.

Kihira, H., S. Ito and T. Murata, "Behavior of Phosphorus During Passivation of Weathering Steel by Protective Patina Formation," in: *Passivation of Metals and Semiconductors*, Proceedings of the Sixth International Symposium on Passivity, Sapporo, Japan, September 24-28, 1989, Part 1 (of 2), *Corrosion Science*, vol. 31, part 1, 1990, pp. 383-388.

Kim, Y.L., "Problems in Cor-Ten Steel Sculpture," *Preprints*, AIC 7th Annual Meeting, May 30-June 1, 1979, Toronto, pp. 59-65.

Komp, M.E., "Atmospheric Corrosion Ratings of Weathering Steels — Calculation and Significance," *Materials Performance*, vol. 26, no. 7, July 1987, pp. 42-44.

Kruger, J, "The Nature of the Passive Film on Iron and Ferrous Alloys," *Corrosion Science*, vol. 29, nos. 2-3, 1988, pp. 149-152.

Kukurs, O. et al., "Structure of Rust Layer on Low-Alloy Steels," *Protection of Metals*, vol. 21, no. 3, May-June 1985, pp. 349-353.

Larrabee, C.P. and S.K. Coburn, "The Atmospheric Corrosion of Steels as Influenced by Changes in Chemical Composition," *First International Congress on Metallic Corrosion*, (London: Butterworth, 1961) pp. 276-285.

Leidheiser, H. Jr., "Corrosion Behavior of Steel Pretreated with Silanes," *Corrosion*, vol. 43, no. 6, June 1987, pp. 382-387.

Leiderheiser, H. Jr. and I. Czako-Nagy, "Mossbauer Spectroscopic Study of Rust Formed During Simulated Atmospheric Corrosion," *Corrosion Science*, vol. 24, no. 7, 1984, pp. 569-577.

Lloyd, B. and M.I. Manning, "Episodic Nature of the Atmospheric Rusting of Steel," *Corrosion Science*, vol. 30, no. 1, 1990, pp. 77-85.

Materials Handbook, 13th edn. (New York: McGraw Hill, 1991).

Metals and Alloys: Steel, Weathering Publication 5, Folder 2424 (Bethlehem, PA: Bethlehem Steel Co.).

Misawa, T. et al., "Mechanism of Atmospheric Rusting and the Protective Amorphous Rust on Low-Alloy Steel," *Corrosion Science*, vol. 14, no. 4, April 1974, pp. 279-289.

Misawa, T. et al., "Corrosion Science in Rusting of Iron and Weathering Steel," *Boshoku Gijutsu*, vol. 37, no. 8, 1988, pp. 501-506.

Modern Steels and Their Properties, 6th edn., Handbook 268-E (Bethlehem, Pennsylvania: Bethlehem Steel Co., 1961).

Okada, H. et al., "The Protective Rust Layer Formed on Low-Alloy Steels in Atmospheric Corrosion," *4th International Congress on Metallic Corrosion*, Amsterdam, September 7-14, 1969 (Houston: NACE, 1969).

Paint Lasts Longer on USS COR-TEN Steel U.S. Steel Publication ADUSS-87-2133-02 (Pittsburgh: United States Steel Corporation, 1975).

Performance of Weathering Steel in Highway Bridges (Washington, D.C.: American Iron & Steel Institute, 1982).

Popova, V.M. et al., "Corrosion Resistance of Low-Alloy Steels in the Atmosphere," *Protection of Metals*, vol. 18, no. 2, March-April 1982, pp. 129-133.

Pourbaix, M. and L. de Miranda, "On the Nature of the Rust Layers Formed on Steels in Atmospheric Corrosion as a Function of Alloy Composition, Environmental Composition, Temperature and Electrode Potential," in: *Passivity and Its Breakdown on Iron and Iron Base Alloys*, Staehle, R.W. and H. Okada, eds. (Houston: NACE, 1976) pp. 47-48.

Pourbaix, M. and L. de Miranda, "Weathering Steel's Performance and the Effect of Copper," *ATB Metallurgie*, vol. 29, no. 4, 1983, pp. 7.1-7.18.

Pourbaix, M. and A. Pourbaix, "Recent Progress in Atmospheric Corrosion Testing," *Corrosion*, vol. 45, no. 1, 1989, pp. 71-83.

Pourbaix, M. (J.A.S. Green, trans., R.W. Staehle, trans. ed.) *Lectures on Electrochemical Corrosion* (New York/London: Plenum Press for CEBELCOR, Brussels, 1973).

Priest, H.M. and J.A. Gilligan, *Design Manual for High-Strength Steels* USS #ADVL-215-54 (Pittsburgh: U.S. Steel Corporation, 1954).

Products and Publications of United States Steel Corporation (New York: U.S. Steel Corp., 1929). [This pamphlet includes an extensive bibliography of publications by U.S. Steel and its affiliates on copper steel.]

Raman, A., "Characteristics of the Rust from Weathering Steels in Louisiana Bridge Spans," *Corrosion*, vol. 42, no. 8, Aug. 1986, pp. 447-455.

Raman, A., "Atmospheric Corrosion Problems with Weathering Steels in Louisiana Bridges," *Degradation of Metals in the Atmosphere*, ASTM Technical Publication STP no. 965 (Philadelphia: ASTM, 1988) pp. 16-29.

Raman, A., S. Nasrazadani and L. Sharma, "Morphology of Rust Phases Formed on Weathering Steel in Various Laboratory Corrosion Tests," *Metallography*, vol. 22, no. 1, January 1989, pp. 79-96.

Raman, A. and S. Nasrazadani, "Packing Corrosion in Bridge Structures," *Corrosion*, vol. 46, no. 7, July 1990, pp. 601-605.

Riederer, J., "Rostender Stahl: Materialverhalten und Restaurierungsprobleme," *Nur Rost* (Munstger und Marl: Landschaftsverband, Westfalen Lippe, 1986) pp. 26-29.

Ruth, U., "Aussenskulptur und Umwelt heute— zu den praktischen Aspekten," *Museumkunde*, vol. 51, no. 3, 1986, pp. 144-148.

Sakai, T. and S. Tokunaga, "Maintenance-Free Service of Weathering Steel by Rust Stabilization Accelerating Treatment," *Corrosion/79* (Houston: NACE, 1979).

Scharnweber, D. et al., "Electrochemical and Surface Analytical Investigation of Weathering Steels," *Corrosion Science*, vol. 24, no. 2, 1984, pp. 67-82.

Schmid, E.V., "The Weatherability of CorTen Steel," *Applica*, vol. 87, no. 12, 1980, pp. 10-13.

Schmitt, R.J. and W.T. Gallagher, "Unpainted HSLA Steel for Architectural Applications," *Material Protection*, vol. 8, no. 12, December 1969.

Schwitter, H. and H. Boehn, "Influence of Accelerated Weathering on the Corrosion of Low Alloy Steels," *Journal of the Electrochemical Society*, vol. 127, no. 1, June 1980, pp. 15-20.

Shastry, C.R., J.J. Friel and H.E. Townsend, "Sixteen-year Atmospheric Corrosion Performance of Weathering Steel in Marine, Rural and Industrial Environments," *Degradation of Metals in the Atmosphere*, ASTM Technical Publication STP no. 965 (Philadelphia: ASTM, 1988) pp. 5-15.

Shikorr, *Werkstoffe u. Korrosion*, 15, 1964, p. 457.

Staehle, R.W. and H. Okada, eds. *Passivity and its Breakdown on Iron and Iron Base Alloys* (Houston: NACE, 1976).

Steel in Sculpture U.S. Steel Publication ADUSS-88-4830-01 (Pittsburgh: United States Steel Corporation, 1970).

Storad, A.S., "Coating Systems for High Strength Low Alloy Steel, Are They Necessary?" *Corrosion/83*, Paper 288 (Houston: NACE, 1983).

Strekalov, P.V., "Wind Regimes, Chloride Aerosol Particle Sedimentation and Atmospheric Corrosion of Steel and Copper," *Protection of Metals*, vol. 24, no. 5, May 1989, pp. 630-641.

Szaver, T. and J. Jackobs, "Pitting Corrosion of Low Alloy and Mild Steels," *Corrosion Science*, vol. 16, no. 12, 1976, pp. 945-949.

Tamba, A. and G. Bombara, "Die Porositaet und Hydrophiliedes Rostes von niedriglegierten staehlen." *Archiv Fuer das Eisenhuettenwesen*, vol. 43, no. 9, Sept. 1972, pp. 713-719.

Thomas, N.L., "Protective Action of Coatings on Rusty Steel,*" Journal of Protective Coatings and Linings*, vol. 6, no. 12, Dec. 1989, pp. 63-69.

Tosto, S. and G. Brusco, "Effect of Relative Humidity on the Corrosion Kinetics of HSLA and Low Carbon Steels," *Corrosion*, vol. 40, no. 10, Oct. 1984, p. 507.

The Use of Unpainted Low Alloy-High Strength Steel Publication 33 (Ottawa: Canadian Good Roads Association, 1968).

USS COR-TEN High-Strength Low-Alloy Steel U.S. Steel Publication ADUSS-88-7888-01 (Pittsburgh: United States Steel Corporation, 1980).

Vedenkin, S.G., "Effect of Composition on Atmospheric Corrosion of Low Alloy Structural Steels," *Protection of Metals*, vol. 11, no. 3, May-June 1975, pp. 259-270.

Wurth, L.A., "The Role of Chromium in Weathering Steel Passivation," *Materials Performance*, vol. 3, no. 1, January 1991, pp. 62-63.

Testing and Development of Conservation Processes
Élaboration et mise à l'essai des méthodes de conservation

An Evaluation of Eleven Adhesives for Repairing Poly(methyl methacrylate) Objects and Sculpture

Don Sale

Assistant Keeper (Conservation)
Sainsbury Centre for Visual Arts
University of East Anglia
Norwich, England

Abstract

Perspex or Plexiglas, poly(methyl methacrylate) (PMMA), is found in collections ranging from fine art and design to social history. First used for aircraft glazing in the Second World War, PMMA is suitable for sculpture, furniture, jewelry, clothing and industrial objects because of its optical and physical properties. When PMMA objects are broken it is difficult to choose an appropriate adhesive because the material is often transparent and susceptible to stress-crazing or cracking when exposed to adhesives or degreasing solvents. Since PMMA may be stressed in the manufacture of the sheet and/or the fabrication of an object, crazing is highly probable.

A series of tests were performed investigating the properties of 11 adhesives from five categories:

- *Two-component all-acrylic cold setting*
  Tensol 70 and Acrifix 90

- *Two-component epoxy resin cold setting*
  Ablebond 342-1 and HXTAL NYL-1

- *Single-component ultraviolet light curing*
  Norland OA65 and Norland OA68

- *Polymer in solvent*
  Tensol 12, Acryloid B-72 and a 1:1 mixture of Acryloid B-67 and Acryloid F-10

- *Cyanoacrylates*
  Loctite 406 and Loctite 460

Stress-crazing due to adhesive contact was investigated following the American Society for Testing and Materials (ASTM) tests F 791-82 and F 484-83. The tensile strength of butt-joints was determined. The effects of detergent (0.5% Synperonic 'N' non-ionic) and solvent (petroleum spirit, boiling range 100°C to 120°C) degreasers on the tensile strength of adhesives were compared. PMMA test specimens were taken from a 3 mm clear cell-cast (non-directional) ICI Perspex sheet.

HXTAL NYL-1, Norland OA65 and a 1:1 mixture of Acryloid B-67 and Acryloid F-10 may be suitable for repairing certain types of damage.

Introduction

The widespread use of poly(methyl methacrylate) (PMMA) in functional as well as decorative objects guarantees its presence in museum collections; hence its significance for conservators. Soon after commercial availability in 1934 this thermoplastic was applied as aircraft glazing material superior to glass due to its light weight, optical and physical properties. By the late 1930s and early 1940s sculptors such as Naum Gabo and Moholy-Nagy were machining and thermoforming this material into numerous shapes. The many colors and surface decoration techniques possible (i.e., engraving, frosting or printing) extend the application potential of this material. Furniture, jewelry, lamp fittings, illuminated signs, juke boxes, thermoformed prints and architectural models illustrate a few examples of objects made of PMMA. A partial list of commercial names includes Perspex (ICI) and Plexiglas (Rohm and Haas), and molding powders, such as Diakon (ICI), Lucite (Du Pont) and Vedril (Montecantini).

Properties of PMMA

The many applications of PMMA result from the optical and physical properties of the polymer. The refractive index is approximately 1.49, which is slightly lower than some glasses, while the light transmission capability is 92%, which is slightly higher than glass.[1] A property that is frequently exploited is that of total internal reflection; this allows the transmission of light around corners as well as light enhanced designs made by releasing light at cuts made into the material.[2]

The physical properties allow production in a number of forms including sheet, block, moldings, rod, tubing and unusual castings. As it is a rigid material with a glass transition temperature (Tg) of 104°C many shapes can be cut with hand-held or power saws, drills and lasers. Cut edges can be highly polished. A multitude of non-planar forms can also be created by heating due to the wide temperature range over which softening is observed.[2] In order to achieve sharp forms, air and mechanical pressure as well as vacuum assistance are used.

PMMA can vary in additive content, purity, molecular weight and polymer arrangement. Dyes and pigments, ultraviolet light absorbers and plasticizers can be added to PMMA and it may be coated to resist surface abrasion. Differing purities are also available (e.g., specialty medical and inexpensive grades). PMMA can also differ in internal stress levels as a result of manufacturing processes (i.e., stresses caused while setting/curing in sheet or rod form).[3] Stresses may be introduced by techniques, such as cutting, drilling or thermoforming. Due to the high coefficient of thermal expansion, stresses may also result from material being tightly bound with inadequate allowance for dimensional changes.[3] In addition, adhesives can introduce stresses in PMMA by solvent absorption or heat production as a result of exothermic reactions.[2]

Strength in PMMA depends on manufacturing technique as well as molecular weight and molecular orientation. PMMA is annealed or "normalized" to reduce internal stresses, making it more resistant to stress-related damage, such as crazing.[4] In addition, annealing produces a more highly polymerized product, with a very low content of free monomer. This improves resistance to ultraviolet light induced degradation.[3]

Differences in physical properties of PMMA result from the two main methods of manufacture, casting and extrusion. PMMA may also be injection molded but the material so produced has similar properties to extruded material. A higher molecular weight polymer (molecular weight = 10^6) is used for casting. When cast, the material forms a three-dimensional network of interlocking polymer chains, which means that it has no directional preference in strength. It is a stronger and more "forgiving" material than the extruded material.[3,5] Sheets and blocks, and unusual shapes or even rods (specifically those over 76 mm in diameter) are cast.[5] Extruded material is made of lower molecular weight polymers (molecular weight = 10^5). The shorter polymer chains have a linear alignment.[3,5] This material allows the production of sharp-edged thermoformed objects at lower temperatures than the higher molecular weight resin would allow. However, the extruded material is more susceptible to failure and weaker in the direction perpendicular to the molecular orientation.[2] It is also more easily stressed and more susceptible to crazing by solvents and adhesives.[3,6] Rods, tubes and moldings are generally extruded, but sheets can also be produced by extrusion. While extruded and injection molded material have similar properties and behavior, extruded material is made from monomer-polymer syrups and injection molded material is made from rigid pellets of PMMA.

Cast and extruded PMMA in objects cannot be easily distinguished by conservators. However, extruded rod and tubing has only been available since the 1970s[5] and extruded sheet since 1978.[7] One method of determining if a sheet is extruded is to pass a beam of light from a fluorescent tube through the edge of a sheet and view the sheet from the opposite edge while facing the light. If the sheet is extruded the viewer should see parallel ridges, which have resulted from the material passing between calender rollers during manufacture. Likewise, if a light beam is projected through the material at the correct angle, the ridges may produce lines on a wall.[5] The only reliable method of differentiation between cast or extruded material involves burning and is thus destructive. Extruded material drips, burns quietly and smells like acrylate due to the low molecular weight and orientation. Cast material ignites but does not drip and the flame makes a crackling sound due to the extensive molecular entanglements.[5,8] Gel permeation chromatography may also distinguish the two forms.[5] According to PMMA manufacturers, polarized light will show stress but cannot differentiate between cast and extruded material.[5,8]

Repair Difficulties

The conservator faces a number of problems when repairing PMMA objects. The three main difficulties arise from the transparency, the thermoplastic properties and the susceptibility of the material to stress-craze or crack when in the presence of solvents and adhesives. The difficulties of making strong, visually satisfactory joints also confront commercial manufacturers. Generally, monomer-polymer solutions make the best "weld-joins." These contain either a photocatalyst that induces hardening by ultraviolet light or a promoter containing a peroxide to catalyze polymerization.[2] While materials and procedures for repairing transparent glass are well documented in the conservation literature, many of these materials are unsuitable due to the thermoplastic properties of PMMA. In addition, it is suggested in the plastics and adhesives literature that many adhesives would probably damage stressed PMMA. There are few suggestions for adhesives in the conservation literature that directly relate to plastics.[2,9] Further, many thermosetting adhesives, such as epoxies that bond adequately to PMMA, can cause damage in application or upon removal.[10] An additional problem is that it can be difficult to remove old adhesives; mechanical removal appears to be the safest option.

As mentioned earlier, the susceptibility of PMMA to stress-crazing or cracking when exposed to adhesives or degreasing solvents is perhaps the major concern of the conservator. While there are published charts in the technical literature of damage resulting from solvents and adhesives on stress-free material, no publication could be found giving materials suitable for stressed PMMA.[11,12] Older material is more likely to be damaged when exposed to solvents because it absorbs moisture from the environment (0.4% to 0.5% at ambient RH), which increases the likelihood of crazing.[4] Solvent vapors surrounding objects in enclosed environments, as well as vapors within a closed form, can also cause crazing. A further problem is that internal stresses are not generally detectable or quantifiable until relieved by crazing and/or cracking, when it is too late. Adhesive and material manufacturers advise annealing in order to relieve potential stress prior to adhering; numerous charts outlining annealing procedures are available.[4] Annealing might decrease the potential of crazing, however, there are many practical and ethical considerations concerning annealing artifacts.

Only two solvents typically used by conservators are safe to use on PMMA; these are water and petroleum spirits. Solvents to avoid (because they dissolve material) have Hildebrand solubility parameters close to that of PMMA (18.8 MPa$^{1/2}$),[2] as shown in Table I.

Table I

Hildebrand Solubility Parameters of Solvents that Cause Problems for PMMA

Solvent	Hildebrand Solubility Parameter (MPA $^{1/2}$)	Likely to Dissolve PMMA
ethyl acetate	18.6	yes
ethylene dichloride	20.0	yes
toluene	18.2	yes
acetone	20.2	yes
methyl ethyl ketone	19.0	yes
methanol	29.6	no, craze
ethanol	26.0	no, craze
isopropanol	23.5	no, craze

Such ketones as acetone and methyl ethyl ketone will also dissolve the polymer. Aliphatic alcohols and those typically used by conservators, such as methanol, ethanol, isopropanol and industrial methylated spirits or IMS (95% ethanol and 5% methanol) are known to cause crazing.[2,11,12] Aliphatic hydrocarbon solutions will cause crazing after long exposure;[11] those with high aromatic contents, such as VM & P Naphtha and Stoddard Solvent, will cause damage in a shorter time.

Another consideration when choosing an adhesive is that the glossy surface of the material is easily disfigured. This is a difficult problem to overcome because adhesives that adequately bond will also damage the surface. As a result a surface-protecting masking material, such as pressure-sensitive or water-based adhesive tape, is required when joining with adhesives. There are concerns about adhesive residues left from masking tapes and an investigation is warranted. Finally, since the surface is easily scratched, it is difficult to remove excess rigid adhesive.

Cyanoacrylates, Acryloid B-72 in acetone and Weld On Number 3 (which contains methylene chloride and trichloroethylene) are examples of potentially damaging adhesives that have been successfully used. Time may prove that these adhesives cause damage and the risks preclude their use when conserving historic objects.

Study Aims

The aims were to find and evaluate adhesives that would: not cause crazing or cracking of stressed PMMA; form load-bearing bonds; make joins with a good appearance. (Join appearance is dependent on join integrity, refractive index and transparency.) In addition, the physical properties of the adhesives would include ease of use, having a lower Tg than PMMA, and, ideally, being reversible or at least detectable by analysis.

Adhesive bond strength was one of the important issues in the evaluation, and thus tensile properties of the PMMA test material were investigated. They were determined mainly for three reasons: to compare data to the technical literature, to review the effect of the sample preparation procedure and to compare the data for the adhesives.

Materials

PMMA
The PMMA chosen for this study was clear cell-cast (non-directional) ICI Perspex sheeting, 000 .[11] It was 3 mm in thickness, although there was slight variation in this. The material was chosen because it has no preferred direction in strength and therefore should give reproducible test results. In addition, it is a high quality, additive-free material that has been annealed by the manufacturer to remove internal stress. It is reported to contain less than 1% free monomer. Finally, the surface-protecting material is pressure-bound polyethylene with no adhesive coating that could affect the testing.

Adhesives
Eleven adhesives, representing five categories, were evaluated. The choice was based on recommendations from PMMA manufacturers, adhesives and conservation literature. Many of the adhesives tested did not fit all study aims (e.g., reversibility). Two adhesives of each type were tested for comparative purposes. The adhesives tested are those shown in Table II.

Table II
Adhesives Used in the Testing Program

Adhesive Categories	Adhesive Tested
Two-component all acrylic cold setting	Tensol 70 (ICI, U.K.)
	Acrifix 90 (Rohm, U.K.)
Two-component epoxy resin	Ablebond 342-1
	HXTAL NYL-1 (U.S.)
Single-component ultraviolet light curing	Norland 0A65 (U.S.)
	Norland 0A68 (U.S.)
Polymer in solvent	Tensol 12 (ICI, U.K.)
	Acryloid B-72
	1:1 mixture of Acryloid B-67 and Acryloid F-10
Cyanoacrylate	Loctite 406 (U.K.)
	Loctite 460 (U.K.)

Water-based adhesives, such as poly(vinyl acetate) or ethylene vinyl acetate copolymer emulsions or dispersions, were not evaluated because they are not transparent. The wider range in variables of the polymer-in-solvent adhesive group warranted the inclusion of three adhesives.

Properties of the Adhesives

Two-component All-acrylic Cold Setting

The two-part Tensol 70 and Acrifix 90 are composed of a mobile solution of monomer in polymer in which a liquid catalyst is added to initiate polymerization.[12] ICI designed the Tensol adhesives to attack surfaces rapidly, which may indicate that the methacrylate monomer acts as a solvent or that a solvent is present. It was assumed that Acrifix 90 would behave similarly to Tensol 70. A significant point about Acrifix 90 is that it has a low refractive index (1.44), well below that of the other adhesives evaluated and the ICI Perspex (1.49).[13] These adhesives were expected to cause stressed PMMA to craze.

Two-component Epoxy Resin

Ablebond 342-1 and HXTAL NYL-1 are familiar to most objects and sculpture conservators; they have been extensively tested and have refractive indices of 1.56 and 1.52 respectively.[14] They contain no solvents but before polymerization, epoxy resins may act as solvents for some plastics.[9]

Single-component Ultraviolet Light Curing

There is no documented use in conservation of the ultraviolet light curing adhesives tested in this study, although two similar adhesives (Norland optical adhesives OA61 and OA63) have been tested for glass repair.[15] Norland adhesives OA65 and OA68 were tested because they contain no solvents. They have been described as urethane-related prepolymers,[16] and are presumed to be thermosetting in character, because of their lack of solubility.

These adhesives were chosen for investigation after consideration of manufacturers' technical information. They differ in their flexibility, strength in bonding to plastic, and refractive indices (1.52 and 1.54 respectively).[17]

Polymer in Solvent

There are considerable differences among the three adhesives in this category. Tensol 12 is a commercial product, produced specifically for joining PMMA. It is composed of an acrylic polymer dissolved in dichloromethane and methyl methacrylate monomer. It works by polymer deposition as solvent evaporates and is absorbed into the PMMA. It contains a solvent known to attack PMMA and it will extract soluble colorants; it was expected to cause stressed PMMA to craze.[12]

The Acryloid acrylic resins (refractive indices 1.48 and 1.49) have a history of use and testing in conservation.[14] Acryloid B-72 was applied in a 3:1 solution of ethanol and xylene and it was anticipated that this would cause stressed PMMA to craze. Xylene was added to the solution because Acryloid B-72 would not dissolve in ethanol alone. Of the solvents acetone, toluene and xylene, xylene seemed the most appropriate to add. In a previous study it was found that xylene caused less weight loss than toluene and it therefore appeared to be a less effective solvent.[18] Also, Horie classes toluene as a solvent and xylene as a non-solvent for PMMA.[19]

The 1:1 mixture of Acryloid B-67 and Acryloid F-10 was evaluated as an adhesive, even though it has no documented use as such, because these resins are soluble in petroleum spirits (a 'safe' solvent) and can be combined with each other.[20] The refractive indices are 1.49 and 1.48 respectively.[14] Preliminary testing indicated that Acryloid B-67 in petroleum spirit was brittle and bonded weakly to PMMA. It was assumed that this behavior was a consequence of the relatively high Tg of 50°C. The Acryloid F-10, with a Tg of 20°C, was added to decrease the brittleness and increase adhesion. In addition, the manufacturers' literature suggests that Acryloid F-10 is good for solvent-sensitive finishes. The Acryloid B-67 was used in petroleum spirit with a boiling range of 100°C to 120°C and the Acryloid F-10 was used as supplied at 40% solids in a 9:1 solution of mineral spirits and Aromatic 150.[20]

Cyanoacrylate

Cyanoacrylates are used in industry to join plastics and have been considered as potential adhesives by conservators. Loctite 406 is recommended for joining rubbers and plastics, and forms strong bonds rapidly. Loctite 460 is a low-bloom, low-odour adhesive of a high molecular weight, which is suitable for bonding dark shiny plastics that will be critically damaged if crazing occurs.[21,22]

Degreasers

The effect of degreasers on adhesive tensile strength was compared using 0.5% Synperonic 'N' non-ionic detergent in deionized water and 'AnalaR' petroleum spirit with a boiling range of 100°C to 120°C. The petroleum spirit has an aromatic content of up to 1%.[23] These very different degreasers were chosen to represent the two potentially safe solvents that could be used on PMMA.

Sample Preparation and Testing Procedures

Four tests were carried out with the intention of measuring the following effects:

• Stress-crazing due to adhesive contact

• Tensile properties of the PMMA test material

• Tensile properties of the adhesives on tension-loaded butt-joined samples

• The effect of degreasers on the tensile properties of the butt-joined samples

Crazing of PMMA Stressed at Specific Loads

This test procedure was intended to identify adhesives that damage PMMA by causing crazing or cracking; it was modelled on two ASTM methods, namely, F 791-82 and F 484-83.[24,25] PMMA samples were stressed with a load, and adhesive was applied to the critically stressed area. The primary purpose was to determine if an adhesive would cause a stressed sample of PMMA to craze, crack or break. The secondary purposes were to determine if a critical amount of stress resulting from the load was required for an adhesive to cause crazing or cracking and if an adhesive caused damage to PMMA at any level of stress.

Sample Preparation

Seven randomly chosen PMMA test specimens were prepared for each adhesive. Samples were cut to the dimensions of 178 mm long by 25.4 mm wide from the 3 mm test material. The rough sawn edges were not smoothed and

samples were not annealed. A hole was drilled in one end of each sample to hold the load. The samples were conditioned in the laboratory for at least a week before testing. Laboratory conditions during all the testing were 20°C ± 1.5°C and 48% ± 5% RH.

Test Procedure

The apparatus for testing the adhesives was constructed to accommodate a group of seven samples exposed to one adhesive (Figure 1). The samples, numbered one to seven, were placed on the apparatus approximately 125 mm apart. Samples numbered one were controls and had no load applied. Samples numbered two through seven were stressed with specific weights: samples two and three with 250 g, samples four and five with 500 g, and samples six and seven with 1,000 g.

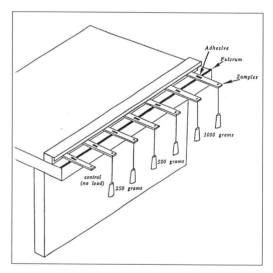

Figure 1 Stress-crazing testing apparatus.

A light source was used to highlight crazing; this is because light readily passes through PMMA unless there is a disruption, such as a gap caused by a craze. The light was placed at a 45° angle below the horizontal plane of the sample being examined. Crazing was observed at a 45° angle above the samples (i.e., at 90° to the light path of the source below) with the unaided eye, and with 30 times magnification (Figure 2).

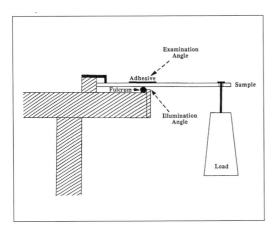

Labels in figure: Examination Angle, Adhesive, Fulcrum, Sample, Illumination Angle, Load

Figure 2 Testing apparatus showing observation of stress-crazing.

Ten minutes after loading the samples, they were examined for crazing and adhesive was applied with a brush or pipette to the surface above the fulcrum; the area of application was approximately 13.9 mm by 25.4 mm. Following this, the samples were examined for crazing. Sample examination times were immediately after adhesive application and at intervals of 10 minutes, 30 minutes, 1 hour, 2 hours, 4 hours, 8 hours and 24 hours.

Most of the sample groups were removed from the loading apparatus 24 hours after adhesive application. However, Ablebond 342-1 and HXTAL NYL-1 samples remained in place and loaded for 72 hours, to ensure that the adhesives were cured. The samples used to evaluate Norland OA65 and Norland OA68 were exposed to ultraviolet light for 30 minutes to cure them. This was 10 minutes longer than specified by the manufacturer to ensure a complete cure. (N.B. The lights were removed when examining the samples and were kept in place until 30 minutes of exposure had been achieved.) The bulbs were positioned 76 mm above the sample surfaces to cure the adhesive. The light source consisted of two 15-watt fluorescent black lights.

Tensile Strength of PMMA Test Material

An Instron Tensile Testing Machine Model 1026 was used for determining the tensile strength of the test material and the butt-joined samples. It was set with a cross-head distance of 127 mm, a cross-head speed of 2 mm/minute and a chart speed of 100 mm/minute. A 500-kilogram load cell was used for the testing. Laboratory conditions were the same as above.

Samples, 178 mm by 25.4 mm, were cut from the 3 mm sheet of Perspex. (These dimensions equalled those of the adhesive joined samples.) Before placing the samples in the cross-head of the tensile tester, the samples were marked across the breadth with lines, 25.4 mm from each end, which left a central region, 127 mm in length, equal to the cross-head distance.

Tensile strength of butt-joined PMMA and the effects of degreaser on the tensile properties of butt-joined Perspex samples were determined following, in part, ASTM test method D 3163-73.[26] Butt-joints were investigated because it was felt that they more closely resembled the types of repairs anticipated for objects.

The tensile properties for the cyanoacrylates were not measured because crazing of samples took place at the lowest applied load. The adhesives were also spread under the masking tape protecting the surface, and did not wet the rough join surfaces.

Twelve randomly selected pairs of Perspex samples were joined with each adhesive. Samples were 89 mm by 25.4 mm and thus joined samples were 2 x 89 mm = 178 mm in length. The join surfaces were equally roughened with circular saw marks; sample sides were jagged due to the band-saw cuts. As above, the samples were not annealed.

Join surfaces were degreased before adhesive application. For each adhesive tested, six pairs of surfaces to be joined were degreased with 'AnalaR' petroleum spirit (100°C to 120°C) and the other six pairs with 0.5% Synperonic 'N'. The samples degreased with the latter detergent were then rinsed twice with deionized water. The samples were air-dried under a dust cover for two days in ambient conditions.

In order to protect the glossy surfaces of the Perspex from the adhesives, transparent pressure-sensitive tape was applied adjacent to the join surfaces. The tape was burnished to ensure a strong bond. The lengthwise edges of the samples were not masked. Two kinds of masking tapes were compared and little difference in effectiveness was observed. Prior to adhesive application, the degreased, masked joint ends were butted together and secured on one side with a tape hinge placed over the masking tape.

The adhesives, prepared following manufacturers' instructions, were applied with a brush or pipette to the join surfaces. After application, samples were placed on a flat surface and excess adhesive was allowed to remain on the surface of the masking tape. When bonds were secure according to the manufacturers' instructions, the masking tapes were removed. The joined samples were marked with a line 25.4 mm from each end similarly to the procedure described above.

The ultraviolet light curing adhesives were treated following the procedure outlined in the section "Crazing of PMMA Stressed at Specific Loads."

Before joining the samples with Acryloid B-72 and the 1:1 mixture of Acryloid B-67 and Acryloid F-10, two dilute layers of the adhesives were applied to the join surfaces. Solvents were allowed to evaporate for two days between applications and before the final concentrated adhesive solution was applied. After final application, the solvents from these adhesives were allowed to evaporate for three weeks before removing the tape.

Results and Discussion

The results indicate that crazing or cracking of stressed PMMA after adhesive contact depends first, on the amount of stress applied and second, on the composition of the adhesive. None of the adhesives caused the unloaded control samples to crack even though the samples were probably weakened with internal stress caused by the preparation procedure. The relative extent or density of the crazing or cracking was not evaluated.

It is interesting that the low-bloom, low-odour cyanoacrylate, Loctite 460, took longer to

Table III
Crazing of PMMA Stressed at Specific Loads

Adhesive	No Load	250 g	500 g	1,000 g
Ablebond 342-1	none	none	none	none
HXTAL NYL-1	none	none	none	none
Norland OA65	none	none	none	none
Norland OA68	none	none	none	none
1:1 mixture of Acryloid B-67 and Acryloid F-10	none	none	none	none
Acryloid B-72	none	none	one crazed one hour	both crazed two hours
Tensol 70	none	none	both crazed 10 min.	both crazed immediately
Tensol 12	none	both crazed 10 min.	both crazed immediately	both crazed immediately
Acrifix 90	none	both crazed one hour	both crazed immediately	both crazed immediately, broke 10 min.
Loctite 406	none	both crazed one hour	both crazed 10 min.	both crazed immediately, broke 10 min. and 4 hours
Loctite 460	none	both crazed, one hour and four hours	both crazed 30 min.	both crazed immediately, broke 30 min.

Stress-crazing of cell-cast PMMA (ICI Perspex) due to adhesive contact at specified loads. Each adhesive was applied to seven samples: one unloaded and two at each of the three loads. In some instances the two samples at one load behaved differently.

cause damage; perhaps it contains a less active solvent. It was surprising that the Acryloid B-72 solution caused so little damage because ethanol and xylene are known to attack PMMA.

In summary, the 500 g load appeared to be the critical load in the testing. When assessing the data, a trend was evident: the five adhesives that did not cause damage at this load did not damage samples at the heavier load of 1,000 g.

Samples stressed by the heaviest load, 1,000 g, crazed when exposed to six adhesives; the same adhesives also damaged samples loaded at 500 g.

While three of the adhesives weakened the samples to breaking point, it is interesting to note that those exposed to Tensol 12 did not break even though samples exposed to this adhesive crazed at the stress level induced by the lowest test load of 250 g. Nevertheless, five of the adhesives tested did not damage the samples at the 1,000 g load; these were the two epoxies, the two ultraviolet light curing adhesives, and the 1:1 mixture of Acryloid B-67 and Acryloid F-10. These should be further investigated.

It is unknown whether the differing times of sample damage in equally loaded pairs resulted from different amounts of internal stress. However, when two samples at the same loads behaved differently after adhesive application, a trend appeared; the second sample to receive adhesive cracked before the first one. This may indicate that the second sample was weakened by an increased volume of solvent vapor released from the adhesive in the test environment. This observation raises an important consideration when using adhesives in the vicinity of PMMA objects: objects can become stressed by adhesive vapors and crazing or cracking could occur without contact.

Evaluation of Test

The test methods used to determine which adhesives caused crazing of stressed PMMA were useful, but the sample size required is large. If samples had been annealed or aged either naturally or artificially, different results might have occurred.

Tensile Strength of PMMA Test Material

The load at break of the test material was difficult to compare with that reported by the manufacturer.[11] There were two reasons for this. First, it was too difficult to prepare the samples in the manner specified by the manufacturer's standard and it was felt that the sample size, preparation and test procedure should model the one chosen for testing the adhesives. A second consideration was that the samples, which were probably weakened by stresses induced during preparation, were not annealed. The data obtained from 12 randomly chosen samples of test material were:

- mean load at break 336 ± 10 kg

- nominal ultimate tensile strength 43.88 ± 3.07 MN/m^2

- extension at break 3.97 ± 0.19 mm

- (UTS, see Appendix 1)

- (relative error, see Appendix 2)

Tensile Strength of Butt-joined PMMA

The load at break, the ultimate tensile strength and extension at break were determined for samples butt-joined with the nine adhesives shown in Table IV. In Figure 3 a plot of these data (the load at break versus the extension at break) is shown. Useful extrapolations, such as estimations of bond strength and the impact of degreaser, can be made from the data. However, as with all tensile testing there were large deviations. This is due to the small number of samples being tested; typically six per group.

All samples broke at the adhesive join at a load well below the tensile strength determined for the Perspex (336 ±10 kg). Tensol 70, Acrifix 90 and Tensol 12 were strong, but despite being specifically manufactured for joining PMMA, they were not the strongest according to these tests. The samples joined with the epoxy resins, Ablebond 342-1 and HXTAL NYL-1 broke at similarly high loads but with smaller deviations from the mean. The samples

Table IV

Tensile Strength of Butt-joined PMMA and Degreaser Impact

Adhesive	Load at Break (kg)		Ultimate Tensile Strength (MN /m^2)		Extension at Break (mm)	
	Petroleum Spirit	Synperonic N	Petroleum Spirit	Synperonic N	Petroleum Spirit	Synperonic N
Ablebond 342-1	143 ±16 (5)	101 ± 7 (6)	18.74 ± 2.44	13.15 ± 1.18	1.48 ± 0.17	1.05 ± 0.09
HXTAL NYL-1	82 ± 17 (6)	65 ± 15 (6)	10.76 ± 2.26	8.44 ± 2.11	0.81 ± 0.19	0.62 ± 0.14
Norland OA65	42 ± 13 (4)	42 ± 7 (6)	5.48 ± 1.70	5.45 ± 0.98	0.23 ± 0.2	0.22 ± 0.02
Norland OA68	51 ± 5 (5)	44 ± 5 (6)	6.62 ± 0.73	5.77 ± 0.75	0.48 ± 0.07	0.42 ± 0.05
1:1 Mixture of Acryloid B-67 and Acryloid F-10	15 ± 2 (6) not dry	13 ± 2 (6) not dry	2 ± 0.34	1.73 ± 0.26	0.21 ± 0.01	0.21 ± 0.02
Acryloid B-72	12 ± 6 (6) not dry	9 ± 3 (6) not dry	1.54 ± 0.85	1.11 ± 0.38	0.21 ± 0.05	0.19 ± 0.02
Tensol 70	68 ± 15 (6)	69 ± 18 (6)	8.87 ± 2.04	8.98 ± 2.43	0.74 ± 0.21	0.70 ± 0.18
Tensol 12	80 ± 26 (5)	86 ± 11 (6)	10.39 ± 3.53	11.20 ± 1.57	0.84 ± 0.27	0.89 ± 0.12
Acrifix 90	98 ± 25 (5)	101 ± 27 (6)	12.77 ± 3.45	13.17 ± 3.69	1.02 ± 0.29	1.04 ± 0.31

Load at break in kg, ultimate tensile strength (nominal) or UTS in MN/m^{2*} and extension at break in millimeters of butt-joined PMMA samples; the effect of two degreasers used before adhesive application, petroleum spirit and 0.5% Synperonic 'N' in deionized water is compared. Mean of data group is presented, plus or minus sample standard deviation.[27] The relative error[**28] is presented with the UTS. The quantity of samples used for each measurement is given in parentheses.

*See Appendix 1.   **See Appendix 2.

---

degreased with petroleum spirit and joined with Ablebond 342-1 had a considerably higher bond strength than any other adhesives.

The adhesives not produced by PMMA manufacturers broke in four fairly distinct ranges. The epoxies formed the strongest bonds breaking at two different load ranges; of these Ablebond 342-1 formed considerably stronger bonds. The ultraviolet light curing adhesives broke at loads only slightly greater than half those of the epoxies. Though they broke at similar weights, Norland OA68 broke at slightly higher loads than Norland OA65; this was not surprising as the manufacturer's literature indicated that OA68 formed stronger bonds to plastic. The acrylic polymers in solvent, Acryloid B-72 and the 1:1 mixture of Acryloid B-67 and Acryloid F-10 formed very weak bonds. This was anticipated but the load at break was probably lower because the solvents had not evaporated from the adhesives, even after three weeks; these bonds stretched while the other adhesives broke cleanly.

It was anticipated that the Acryloid B-72 would form stronger bonds than the 1:1 mixture of Acryloid B-67 and Acryloid F-10 because the 3:1 ethanol and xylene solution was expected to attack the PMMA more than the petroleum spirit mixture. Solvent retention may have been responsible for masking this difference.

The extension at break of the two epoxies, Ablebond 342-1 and HXTAL NYL-1, varied significantly depending on the degreaser. An explanation of this probably relates to the impact of degreaser as will be discussed. Of the ultraviolet light curing adhesives, Norland OA65 extended approximately half that of Norland OA68. This difference was not anticipated because Norland OA65 is manufactured to be more flexible than Norland OA68. Perhaps Norland OA68 was not fully polymerized.

However, the extension at break is mainly a function of the load at break as shown in Figure 3.

Degreasers

With the exception of the epoxies, the two degreasers appeared to have little impact on the adhesive bonds. The epoxy-joined samples degreased with petroleum spirit broke at significantly higher test loads and extended more than the detergent-degreased samples; this suggests that the detergent solution had some impact on join integrity. This might be because detergent remained on the surface forming a barrier, or that the detergent attracted moisture to the surface, thereby reducing bond strength. It should also be considered that petroleum spirit may be a more effective degreaser. (It may be significant that the epoxies are the only adhesives that exhibited a significant difference in bond strength resulting from the degreaser.) This finding reiterates the cautions that have been suggested about the use of detergents on plastics.[10,18]

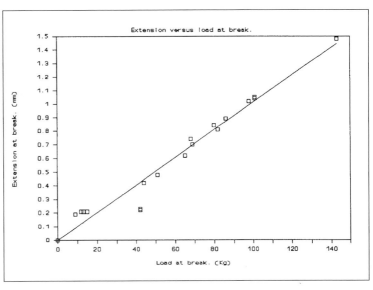

Figure 3 *Extension at break as a function of load at break.*

Evaluation of Test

The tensile testing procedure could be modified or a much larger number of samples could be tested in hopes of reducing the high errors in the data. In addition, it should be noted that as a result of the join surfaces being slightly irregular due to the circular saw marks, stronger bonds may have been created than would have occured on smooth surfaces; this is because the adhesives may have been physically bound to the surfaces. However, breaks on objects are generally not planar or devoid of surface irregularity.

Conclusion

Though it is anticipated that PMMA found in artifacts and objects may not behave the same as new cell-cast PMMA, useful extrapolations can be made from this test data. The PMMA manufacturer-produced adhesives should not be used to conserve historic objects because they caused stressed PMMA to craze. Five of the adhesives tested did not damage PMMA stressed at any of the test loads; these were the two epoxies, the two ultraviolet light curing adhesives and the 1:1 mixture of Acryloid B-67 and Acryloid F-10. Of these, it appears that three may produce satisfactory joins with differing requirements based on their refractive indices (1.52 to 1.49) and the test data; these are HXTAL NYL-1, Norland OA65 and the 1:1 mixture of Acryloid B-67 and Acryloid F-10 in petroleum spirits. It is important to match refractive indices when joining transparent materials, and Ablebond 342-1 and Norland OA68 were eliminated for clear material because they have refractive indices that differ significantly from PMMA.

Differing applications are possible with the three favored adhesives due to the distinct ranges of load at break observed, as well as their other properties. For example, the thermoset HXTAL NYL-1 was similar in strength to the commercially produced adhesives for PMMA and could be used for load-bearing bonds. However, although HXTAL NYL-1 is detectable it could only be removed mechanically. Norland OA65, also presumed to be a thermosetting resin, would be useful for quickly "tacking" difficult joins. The testing also indicated that it is rubbery and new adhesive could be pulled off the PMMA. More investigation is warranted concerning this property and the aging behavior of this adhesive.

The 1:1 mixture of Acryloid B-67 and Acryloid F-10 made very weak bonds that may be suitable for repairing delicate objects, such as jewelry, sculptors' maquettes and architectural models. This was the only adhesive tested that appears to be removable by solvents that will not attack PMMA. While it is known that Acryloid B-67 is often difficult to remove with petroleum spirits alone, requiring the addition of polar solvents or even heat, it is hoped that the addition of Acryloid F-10 will increase solubility.

It must be emphasized that the results of these tests are not conclusive because the PMMA tested is new material of a high quality with a high molecular weight and a homogeneous structure of extensive molecular entanglements. With the exception of the stresses caused by the sample preparation and testing procedures this material is strong and resistant. It is expected that old, extruded material, annealed material, or material cast in an artist's studio may behave differently. PMMA that is not totally polymerized, contains additives, such as colorants or plasticizers, or has a coating, may also act differently when exposed to these adhesives.

In summary, the three adhesives that met many of the five criteria used to evaluate the adhesives in this study were HXTAL NYL-1, Norland OA65 and a 1:1 mixture of Acryloid B-67 and Acryloid F-10. These adhesives did not craze or crack stressed PMMA, they formed load-bearing bonds at different ranges and they have refractive indices closer to PMMA than the two other adhesives that did not cause crazing. In addition, these adhesives have desirable physical properties including a lower Tg than PMMA.

Acknowledgement

Research was carried out in the Sculpture Conservation Department of the Tate Gallery. I would like to thank the following people from the Tate Gallery: Jackie Heuman, Senior Sculpture Conservator, Derek Pullen, Head of Sculpture Conservation and Joyce Townsend, Conservation Scientist, for continuous encouragement and assistance in all aspects of the study. I would also like to thank The Henry Moore Foundation for funding the post in which I carried out this research. A large part of this research would not have been possible without the assistance of the late Gerry Hedley, who showed me how to use the tensile tester and assisted in preliminary organization of the data, and The Courtauld Institute for allowing me to use their tensile testing machine. In addition, I would like to thank Dr. Jonathan Ashley-Smith, Department Head of Conservation at the Victoria and Albert Museum for allowing me time to work on the study while I was employed, and Graham Martin, Head of the Scientific Section, and Boris Pretzel, Conservation Scientist, for their assistance in using spread sheets for determining the statistical data of this study. Finally, I would like to thank The Gabo Trust and The Samuel H. Kress Foundation for the joint sponsorship that allowed me to present my research at this conference.

Appendix 1

UTS(N) or ultimate tensile strength (nominal) = F/A where:
F = the mean load at break of the group of samples tested
A = the initial cross-sectional area of the samples determined by multiplying the mean depth in millimeters times the mean width in millimeters of 10 randomly selected samples.

Appendix 2

The relative error of the UTS(N) was determined with the following formula:
$[(S_L/L)^2 + (S_W/W)^2 + (S_D/D)^2]^{1/2}$ where:
L = the mean load at break in kilograms of the sample group
W = the mean width in millimeters of 10 randomly selected samples
D = the mean depth in millimeters of 10 randomly selected samples
S = sample standard deviation of the sample group results

Suppliers of Materials

Ablebond 342-1, HXTAL NYL-1, Synperonic 'N' non-ionic detergent
  Archival Aids Ltd.,
  P.O. Box 5, Spondon, Derby,
  DE2 7BP, England.

Acrifix 90
  (Rohm Plastics) Righton Ltd.,
  Unit 4, Bush Industrial Estate,
  Station Road,
  London, N19 5UN.

Acryloid (Paraloid) B-72, B-67 and F-10
  (Rohm and Haas Ltd.) U.K. distributor,
  Chemicryl Ltd.,
  Hockerill Street,
  Bishop's Stortford, Hertfordshire,
  CM23 2DW, England.

Loctite 406 and 460
  (Loctite U.K.), Loctite Holdings Ltd.,
  Watchmead, Welwyn Garden City,
  Hertfordshire,
  AL7 1JB, England.

Norland Optical Adhesive OA65 and OA68
  Tech Optics Ltd.,
  Unit 6, Cala Industrial Estate,
  Tannery Road,
  Tonbridge, Kent,
  TN9 1RF, England.
  (In U.S.A. from Norland Products Inc.,
  695 Joyce Kilmer Avenue,
  New Brunswick, N.J. 08902.)

Perspex, Clear cell-cast sheet, 000, Tensol 70 and Tensol 12
  (ICI) Amari Plastics,
  2 Cumberland Avenue,
  Park Royal, London,
  NW10 7RL, England.

Petroleum Spirit 100°C to 120°C 'AnalaR'
  BDH Laboratory Chemicals,
  Freshwater Road, Dagenham, Essex,
  RM8 1RF, England.

Résumé

L'évaluation de 11 adhésifs en vue de leur utilisation pour la réparation d'objets et de sculptures en poly(méthacrylate de méthyle)

Les poly(méthacrylate de méthyle) Perspex ou Plexiglas se retrouvent tant dans des œuvres issues des beaux-arts ou du design que dans des objets qui témoignent de l'histoire sociale. D'abord utilisé comme revêtement d'avion, durant la seconde guerre mondiale, ce produit convient particulièrement bien, du fait de ses propriétés optiques et physiques, à l'exécution de sculptures et à la fabrication de meubles, de bijoux, de vêtements et d'objets industriels. Il est néanmoins fort difficile de trouver un adhésif pour réparer un objet en PMMA, car ce matériau, souvent transparent, devient plus sensible à la fissuration et au craquellement sous contrainte lorsqu'il est mis en présence d'adhésifs ou de solvants de dégraissage. De plus, tant la feuille de ce matériau (au moment de sa fabrication) que l'objet lui-même (au moment de son exécution) auront sans doute déjà subi de telles contraintes, ce qui augmentera d'autant le risque de fissuration.

Des essais ont été effectués pour évaluer les propriétés de 11 adhésifs relevant de l'une ou l'autre des cinq catégories suivantes :

- *la prise à froid à deux éléments tout acrylique : Tensol 70 et Acryfix 90;*

- *la prise à froid à deux éléments de résine époxy : Ablebond 342-1 et HXTAL NYL-1;*

- *la prise à un seul élément induite à l'ultra-violet : Norland 0A65 et Norland 0A68;*

- *un polymère dans un solvant : Tensol 12, Acryloid B-72 et mélange d'une partie d'Acryloid B-67 pour une partie d'Acryloid F-10;*

- *les cyanoacrylates : Loctite 406 et Loctite 460;*

La fissuration sous contrainte résultant d'un contact avec des adhésifs a été étudiée en ayant recours aux essais F 791-82 et F 484-83 dc de l'American Society for Testing and Materials (ASTM). La résistance à la tension des extrémités réparées a été mesurée. Et les effets des agents de dégraissage à détergent (0,5 pour 100 de Synperonic «N» non ionique) et à solvant (essence de pétrole dont l'intervalle de distillation se situe entre 100 et 120°C) sur la résistance à la tension des adhésifs ont été comparés. Les échantillons utilisés aux fins de ces essais provenaient d'un panneau de perspex de 3 mm transparent, fabriqué par les Imperial Chemical Industries (ICI) et moulé en cuve (non orienté).

L'HXTAL NYL-1, le Norland 0A65 et le mélange d'une partie d'Acryloid B-67 pour une partie d'Acryloid F-10 pourraient être utilisés pour réparer certains genres de dommages.

References

1. 'Perspex' Cast Acrylic Sheet for Glazing, PX TD236 (Welwyn Garden City, Hertfordshire: Imperial Chemical Industries PLC, 1986).

2. Brydson, J.A., Plastics Materials (London: Butterworth Scientific, London, 1982).

3. Cousens, D., "'Perspex' a Technical Appreciation," a one-day course, Imperial Chemical Industries PLC, Chemicals and Polymers Group, Welwyn Garden City, Hertfordshire, 1988.

4. Normalizing and Stress-Relieving of 'Perspex' Cell-Cast Acrylic Sheet, PX TD230, 9th edn. (ICI, Chemicals and Polymers Group, Welwyn Garden City, Hertfordshire: Imperial Chemical Industries PLC, undated).

5. Lombard, M. and others, Imperial Chemical Industries PLC, personal communications with staff of Acrylics, Technical Department, P.O. Box 34, Darwen, Lancaster, BB3 1QB, 1990 and 1991.

6. Chemical Resistance in General Use: 'Plexiglas' GS and 'Plexiglas' XT (Röhm GMBH Chemische Fabrik, Postfach 4242, Kirschenallee, D-6100, Darmstadt 1: Röhm Plastics, 1986).

7. Perspex: The First Fifty Years 1934-84 (P.O. Box 34, Darwen, Lancashire, BB3 1QB: Imperial Chemical Industries PLC, 1984).

8. RËhm, personal communication with staff of Technical Department, RËhm Ltd., Bradbourn Drive, Tilbank, Milton Keynes, MK7 8AU, 1990 and 1991.

9. Shields, J., Adhesives Handbook (London: Butterworths, 1984).

10. Blank, S., "An Introduction to Plastics and Rubbers in Collections," Studies in Conservation, vol. 35, 1990, pp. 53-63.

11. 'Perspex' Cell-Cast Acrylic Sheet: Properties and Fabrication Techniques, PX 127, 4th edn. (ICI, P.O. Box 34, Darwen, Lancashire, BB3 1QB: Imperial Chemical Industries PLC, 1989).

12. 'Tensol' Cements for 'Perspex' Acrylic Sheet, 6th edn. (ICI, P.O. Box 34, Darwen, Lancashire, BB3 1QB: Imperial Chemical Industries PLC, undated).

13. Technical Information, Acrifix 90, 2-Component Polymerization Adhesive (Röhm GMBH Chemische Fabrik, Postfach 4242, Kirschenallee, D-6100 Darmstadt 1: Röhm Plastics, 1989).

14. Tennent, N.H. and J.H. Townsend, "The Significance of the Refractive Index of Adhesives for Glass Repair," IIC Adhesives and Consolidants, Paris, 1984, pp. 205-212.

15. Robson, M., "Clear, Colourless Adhesives for Glass," Conservation News, vol. 30, 1986, pp. 14-16.

16. Robson, M., "A Comparative Study of a Range of Glass Adhesives," Poster Session Paper in: Recent Advances in the Conservation and Analysis of Artifacts, University of London, Institute of Archaeology, London, 1987.

17. Norland UV Curing Adhesives: Technical Data (Norland, 695 Joyce Kilmer Ave., New Brunswick, N.J. 08902.: Norland Products Inc., undated).

18. Sale, D. Jr., "The Effect of Solvents on Four Plastics Found in Museum Collections," in: *Modern Organic Materials*, Scottish Society for Conservation & Restoration, Edinburgh, 1988, pp. 105-114.

19. Horie, C.V., *Materials for Conservation* (London: Butterworths, 1987).

20. *Acryloid Thermoplastic Acrylic Ester Resins for Industrial Finishing* (Philadelphia: Röhm and Haas, 1987).

21. *'Loctite' Instant Adhesives* (Watchmead, Welwyn Garden City, Hertfordshire AL7 1J: Loctite U.K., 1988).

22. Loctite, personal communication with staff of Technical Department, Loctite U.K., Watchmead, Welwyn Garden City, Hertfordshire AL7 1JB, 1990.

23. BDH, personal communication with staff of Technical Department, BDH Laboratory Chemicals, Freshwater Rd., Dagenham, Essex, RM8 1RF.

24. "Standard Practice for Stress Crazing of Transparent Plastics," Standard No. F 791-82, *Plastics* (Philadelphia: American Society For Testing and Materials (ASTM), 1989).

25. "Standard Test Method for Stress Crazing of Acrylic Plastics in Contact with Liquid or Semi-liquid Compounds," Standard No. F 484-83, *Plastics* (Philadelphia: American Society for Testing and Materials, (ASTM), 1989).

26. "Standard Test Method for Determining the Strength of Adhesively Bonded Rigid Plastic Lap-Shear Joints in Shear by Tension Loading," Standard No. D 3263-73, *Plastics* (Philadelphia: American Society for Testing and Materials, (ASTM), 1989).

27. Quattro Pro, Spreadsheet Program with Statistical Analysis Functions, Boland, Scotts Valley, California, 95067-0001.

28. Pretzel, B., personal communication, Research Scientist, Victoria and Albert Museum, 1991.

Labelling Plastic Artefacts

Julia Fenn

Royal Ontario Museum
Toronto, Ontario
Canada

Abstract

The high risk of using inks, paints or varnishes when applying registration numbers to plastic artefacts is becoming increasingly apparent. Plasticizers, solvents, pigments and dyes can interact irreversibly with the plastic substrate, accelerating stress-cracking, deformation, discolouration and even complete disintegration. The long-term nature of much of the damage, which may take months to become visible, and the lack of information about conditions under which molecular complexes form, mean that damaging combinations cannot be identified by tests on an inconspicuous area of the artefact. As a result, the first step towards recording a plastic artefact for posterity could be the one that initiates its destruction.

Each type of plastic is susceptible to damage from a different range of materials. So, theoretically, damage could be avoided by using customized labelling solutions for each type of plastic. However, this depends on being able to identify the plastic accurately, which is very difficult without expensive analytical equipment. Even assuming a reliable identification system, there are still variables caused by manufacturing techniques, additives, contaminants and aging; several polymers are known to alter their solubility parameters with age.

Another aspect of this interaction that is not always considered is the effect of the plastic artefacts on the labels. Artefacts made from materials such as vulcanite, poly(vinyl chloride), cellulose acetate and cellulose nitrate are capable of bleaching or bleeding inks and attacking paint and varnish media so that in a surprisingly short time the numbers become illegible or crumble away. This type of attack affects not only traditional varnish and ink-marking systems but also attacks threads, wires and other materials used for tie-on labels or exhibition labels, which are adjacent to unstable plastics in display cases.

This paper will detail further experiments with combinations of different inks and polymers that appear to minimize the risk of attack on the artefact and show greater resistance to degradation products from the artefacts.

Introduction

When an artefact is acquired by a museum virtually the first treatment it receives is the application of a registration number. Unfortunately methods of labelling that are satisfactory for most museum materials are not safe for plastic artefacts. Solvents, dyes, plasticizers and pigments in the labelling materials can cause irreversible degradation, which may eventually destroy the artefact functionally and aesthetically. *So this very first step towards identifying a plastic artefact as a permanent record for posterity may be the very one that initiates its destruction.*

Common Labelling Techniques: Effects of Solvents and Plasticizers

The most common museum method of labelling is to apply the registration number to a small insulating patch of lacquer on the artefact, followed by another layer of lacquer to protect the ink from mechanical damage. Unfortunately it is not always possible to predict how, or when, a varnish will affect a plastic. Dissolution is only one of several types of irreversible damage that can be caused by contact with organic solvents or exposure to their vapours. Even if the lacquer does not immediately bond irreversibly to the plastic substrate, the artefact may gradually swell and distort. This type of damage is most often seen in flexible plastics, such as poly(vinyl chloride) belts and raincoats, but we also have examples of rigid cellulose nitrate knife handles that were labelled with an acrylic varnish in ethanol. This particular cellulose nitrate was not directly soluble in ethanol, but within a year the surface under and adjacent to the registration number had rippled (Figure 1). The varnish layer was easily removed mechanically because it had not fused to the substrate, but the distortion in the cellulose nitrate was permanent. Volatile solvents have been found to be retained for months, even years in an apparently dry varnish; it is sheer luck if they don't eventually interact with some part of the polymer substrate.

Figure 1 A 1950s' cellulose nitrate knife handle shows distortion that occurred within three months of applying the registration number.

Some cellulose nitrates are not soluble in either ethanol or ether, but dissolve readily in combinations of the two solvents. In the same way solubility of the plastic can be affected by infinitesimal amounts of absorbed plasticizers, which form molecular complexes with applied solvents. For example, plastics that have been stored in contact with other polymers, or modern pieces that have been kept in their original "shrink-wrap" packaging, may have absorbed plasticizers at the contact area, which can cause local alteration of their solubility. Testing the labelling solution on an inconspicuous area of the object will be inconclusive if the test area is not comparable with the rest of the artefact. Other possible causes of differential solubility are exposure to volatile corrosion inhibitors, mothballs, cleaning fluids or adhesives.

There is a cellulose nitrate comb in our teaching collection that had an old stain caused by a pressure-sensitive price tag. When an attempt was made to clean off the adhesive stain using isopropyl alcohol, which had already been tested without visible damage on other parts of the comb, the plastic instantly softened and blanched around the stain. Pressure-sensitive labels tend to be even more harmful to plastics than they are to other museum materials. Cellulose nitrates sometimes develop quite colourful stains especially from rubber-based pressure-sensitive materials (Figure 2). Even polyolefins, which resist most adhesives, can absorb pressure-sensitive adhesives so deeply that only the most drastic cleaning agents will (partially) remove them. The effects can be seen on polyethylene kitchenware where the commercial labels have been left in place too long.

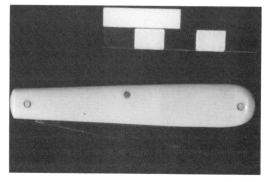

Figure 2 French ivory pocket knife with orange-coloured stain from contact with rubber-based adhesive.

Light damage is another common source of changes in solvent sensitivity. Ebonite (highly vulcanized rubber) is resistant to most solvents, but after photo-oxidation its surface can be disrupted by contact with any liquid. Casein is normally swollen and cracked by prolonged contact with water but its moisture sensitivity can be greatly increased if the artefact has been overexposed to ultraviolet light (Figures 3 and 4).

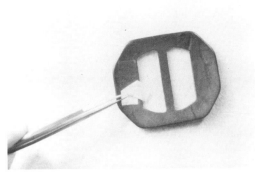

Figure 3 A 1950s' casein buckle shows surface damage caused by a paper label experimentally wetted with water adjusted to the same pH as Acryloid 33.

Figure 4 Same casein buckle shows detail of cracking within the wetted area.

It was disconcerting to observe in our experimental samples of coloured casein and urea-formaldehyde buttons that increased solubility often occurred well before there was any noticeable fading of the dyes or loss of surface gloss, indicating that it is not always possible to judge probable sensitivity by appearance. Light damage also appears to increase the solvent and moisture sensitivity of some natural plastics, such as oriental lacquer[1,2] and amber.[3]

Crazing or stress-cracking is another phenomenon associated with exposure to solvent vapours, especially in rigid plastics such as polystyrene, polycarbonate or poly(methyl methacrylate). Absorption of high, local concentrations of solvent vapours apparently encourages compression cracking and the release of strains already incorporated into the plastic during manufacture. The damage often does not become visible until most of the absorbed solvent has dissipated, days or even months later. We were able to demonstrate this delayed reaction by using the traditional labelling method on modern crystal polystyrene mugs (Figures 5 and 6). A small patch of Acryloid B72 in Camsco Super Hi-Flash (a commercial mixture of mineral spirits, which has just enough aromatic content to dissolve the acrylic varnish but not dissolve the polystyrene) was painted below the rim. Within a week small cloudy patches marred the translucency of the polystyrene; these appeared to be enhanced polishing marks. Shortly afterwards, small cracks appeared around the rim and the base. The cracking has continued, and now nearly three years later the polystyrene is virtually opaque.

The stress-cracking phenomenon is quite complex and is not fully understood as the following explanation illustrates. Solvents can apparently initiate stress-cracking in several ways: by encouraging the migration of plasticizers and antioxidants, or by removing or introducing moisture. Evaporation chill may also be a factor: some plastics such as poly(methyl methacrylate) expand and contract to a greater degree than metals; at the same time they have poor thermal conductivity so the rapid lowering of the temperature in one area by the evaporation of very volatile solvents could conceivably aggravate existing stress sufficiently to initiate crazing. However, not all plastics are affected by the same solvents regardless of their volatility, and it is doubtful if dimensional changes and loss of flexibility can be the sole cause of stress-cracking. A brittle plastic, such as polystyrene, may be remarkably resistant to dimensional changes caused by extreme temperature changes and nevertheless be extremely susceptible to stress-cracking when exposed to vapours from hydrocarbon solvents. Manufacturers use the weight changes in plastics caused by exposure to solvents as one means of predicting

Figure 5 A 1984 crystal polystyrene mug just after application of registration number.

Figure 6 Same crystal polystyrene mug three months later shows stress-cracking.

which solvents are likely to attack the polymer. However some plastics, such as poly(methyl methacrylate), when exposed to certain solvents, such as isopropyl alcohol, show no weight changes and yet have been found to suffer subsequent loss of impact resistance and crazing. *This unpredictability suggests that it is never wise to expose a plastic to any solvent vapour.* Testing a solution on an artefact, especially if several solvents are investigated in series, may itself initiate stress-cracking. Once crazing has begun it usually continues until the strain is relieved, by which time the artefact may be ruined.

Unfortunately, there seems to be no one solvent that can be safely used to make a varnish suitable for all plastics. Even aliphatic hydrocarbons, which seem to be promising because of their low solubility, cannot be recommended because they: 1) cause swelling distortion of poorly vulcanized ebonite, 2) leach plasticizers used in flexible vinyl-type plastics, and 3) craze polystyrene, which is one of the most common plastics. Alcohols are potentially harmful to polycarbonate, poly(methyl methacrylate) and some cellulose nitrate, cellulose acetate and polystyrene resins.

Most plastics are not damaged by a short exposure to cold water of neutral pH, but there are exceptions. One example is any plastic with a high proportion of poorly combined hygroscopic filler, such as wood flour. Early "composition" plastics, such as Bois Durci and many moulded shellacs, fall into this category. Degrading cellulose nitrates and acetates as well as light-damaged plastics, such as ebonite or urea-formaldehyde, are also potentially vulnerable to staining, distortion or accelerated degradation if wetted. Variations in the pH usually aggravate the damage: cellulose nitrate and acetate are susceptible to both acid and alkaline hydrolysis and casein and other "protein" plastics are particularly sensitive to alkalinity. In spite of these problems, water is often more satisfactory than organic solvents because its effects are more predictable.

Other Methods of Attaching Labels

There are several methods of numbering plastic artefacts that avoid the use of solvents, for example, by labelling the container and not the artefact. However, in museums where the artefact is so often separated from its storage container while on display or loan, this may not be satisfactory. Moreover several plastics, such as cellulose acetate, degenerate more rapidly when kept enclosed; storage in vented cabinets is preferable for such polymers. Possibly a more satisfactory method for exceptionally important pieces might be to label individually customized supports that can remain with the artefact at all times.

Methods of attaching registration numbers mechanically by sewing or tying numbered tags are also in common use, especially on garments or textile accessories made from sheet plastics, such as poly(ethylene terepthalate) (Mylar), plasticized poly(vinyl chlorides), and cellulose acetate. Some of these sheet plastics are notch-sensitive so tears can easily be initiated during subsequent handling from the points where the needle has punctured the sheet. If it is essential to attach a label this way, the danger of tearing can be reduced by using a very sharp leather punch to create tiny circular holes without ragged edges or by using a heated needle so the plastic at the edge of the needle hole melts. However, both methods are risky and irreversible. The type of thread also has to be taken into consideration; silk, wools, and cellulose threads are rotted by acid degradation products and certain plasticizers, nylon monofilament has a sharp cutting edge in addition to poor chemical resistance, and metal wires can catalyse polymer breakdown and leave ineradicable stains from corrosion products.

One private collector has solved the problem of attaching labels to artefacts such as bowls by drilling a tiny hole in the artefact so that a tag can be attached. It is doubtful if conservators could bring themselves to do this, but in fact it is probably less damaging than some other methods considered quite acceptable. Nevertheless such treatment will do nothing for the appearance of translucent plastics, such as poly(methyl methacrylate) or polystyrene, whose light-transmitting properties accentuate even minor flaws. It will also decrease the mechanical strength of notch-sensitive or highly stressed plastics. The development of tiny cracks around holes can sometimes be seen in museum vitrines made from polycarbonate or poly(methyl methacrylate) even after they have been annealed to reduce stress. Another related technique is the "scrimshaw" method where the identification number is scratched into the artefact's surface and may have ink or other colouring agents rubbed in to enhance visibility. The same objections apply to this method, although if the scratches are very shallow they can at least be mechanically removed by light abrasion, but direct contact with inks can be harmful.

Inks and Paints:
Damage Caused by Dyes and Pigments

Dyes and pigments in direct contact with plastics can act as catalysts or photosensitizers[4] or cause irreversible staining. Plastic manufacturers found that nigrosine, an azine dye still used in fabric marking pens and some newsprint, accelerates the evolution of nitrogen dioxide from cellulose nitrate.[5] Even melamine-formaldehyde, which is used as the surfacing material in counter-tops because of its excellent resistance to chemical attack, can be damaged by inks. The Royal Ontario Museum recently acquired a pink melamine bowl on which the ink stamp from a long-departed paper label had left a colourless etched copy of itself in the surface of the bowl (Figure 7).

Figure 7 Etched stamp mark in a 1960s' melamine-formaldehyde bowl.

Old numbering systems where inks or paints were applied directly to the surface of the object are no longer in favour because of corrosive acid inks and the difficulty in removing the number. But, on plastic artefacts, a varnish layer creates a larger area of solvent contact without offering any improved protection or reversibility so it seems an unnecessary complication. Providing that the inks or paints are very carefully chosen for compatibility, applying the numbering medium directly to the surface of the artefact (rather than to a plastic insulating layer) offers several advantages:

- a much smaller area of contact

- much less solvent

- better adhesion: the discontinuous lines forming the numbers often have much better resistance to flexing and dimensional changes than solid patches of relatively rigid varnish

- no unsightly patches of discoloured varnish

- easier mechanical removal

There are basically two types of ink that will adhere to plastics: *solvent dispersed dyes*, which adhere by dissolving slightly into the surface of the plastic, for example, freezer pen inks, and *particulate pigments suspended in a resin medium*, which bond to the plastic, for example, alkyd hobby craft paints or India inks made from carbon black dispersed in shellac.

In the dispersed dye inks, dark colours such as black are usually made up of several different colours, which tend to react differently to long-term contact with the various constituents of the substrate, resulting in bleeding or the development of a halo around the ink. Polyolefins, nylons and all highly plasticized polymers are particularly susceptible to this kind of damage. The dispersed dye inks are also prone to differential fading and occasionally the haloed area may become hard and brittle, probably because of the photo-tendering effect of the dyes. Although such inks may fade or bleed to illegibility over time, they usually leave some sort of stain or distortion.

Removal of dyes is a risky procedure requiring solvents. The longer the ink remains in contact, the more difficult it is to remove as it sinks further into the matrix. Casein, urea-formaldehyde and melamine-formaldehyde as well as light-coloured cast phenolic resins tend to be permanently stained with a shadow of the ink number unless it is removed within two to three years. This is something to consider when buying antique plastics because dealers seem to be almost as fond of ball-point pens and felt-tip pens as they are of pressure-sensitive labels. None of the dye inks, or wax crayons and china markers, which have a similar effect, can be recommended for labelling museum artefacts.

Particulate pigments in a suitable medium are more promising. Only black and white pigments were evaluated because either one colour or the other is legible on artefacts of any colour. Pure carbon black does not react harmfully with any plastic and has excellent chemical resistance, but the presence of contaminants depends on the source and type of combustion. Lamp black is often greasy and ivory/bone black may contain imperfectly burned organic material. Alkaline agents in these types of carbon pigments have been associated with the breakdown of cellulose nitrates.[5] The most commonly used carbon black in commercial hobby paints seems to be furnace black produced by high temperature thermal decomposition of petroleum products. Carbon in the form of graphite pencil lead is also used by some museums as a temporary marker for light-coloured plastics. The only disadvantages are a tendency to smudge and possible indentation of soft or degraded surfaces. Unfortunately pencils do not write well on soft elastomers or vinyl sheets. Other black pigments, such as those containing iron salts, catalyse degradation especially in cellulose plastics, and are often very acidic.

The white pigments are more of a problem; many of the white inks used on our collections in the past have deteriorated badly. Experimental samples of zinc oxide, calcium carbonate, titanium dioxide as well as lead carbonate and barium sulphate (both of the latter pigments are under restrictions because of their toxicity) were applied in various media to old samples of cellulose nitrate and ebonite for observation. Most of them proved to be unacceptable because of hygroscopic degradation products or incompatible pH.

Zinc oxide (Chinese white) was once widely used as an activator in vulcanized rubbers and a whitening agent in plastics. The comparatively good survival of celluloid ivory imitations, in comparison with translucent celluloid tortoise-shell imitations, is usually attributed to the superior acid-scavenging and light-screening properties of zinc oxide over aniline dyes. However, zinc oxide is chemically reactive and its behaviour when applied as an ink can be very damaging, especially if it is not well combined in a water-resistant medium. On cellulose nitrate, zinc oxide inks in media such as gelatine, gum Arabic and methyl cellulose were transformed into transparent wet patches on the surface. The rate at which this happened depended on the ambient humidity and how badly the cellulose nitrate was degrading. Even waterproof alkyd paints coloured with zinc oxide and exposed to emissions from degrading celluloid eventually discoloured and became hygroscopic (Figure 8). Similar results were obtained with calcium carbonate, which is often incorporated into inks and paints as an extender. Its acid-scavenging properties have usually been regarded as an asset, but in this context they accelerate degradation. Metallic aluminium pigments that had been used in an old repair on a cellulose nitrate artefact also liquified and the results were repeatable with oil-based aluminium inks. No such effects have occurred with titanium dioxides, even on badly degrading plastics, during the two years that they have been under observation.

On ebonite, all the white pigments discoloured to some extent, but at high relative humidities (above 68%), zinc oxide darkened rapidly until it was barely visible against the ebonite (Figure 9). Examples of lead white in a waterproof

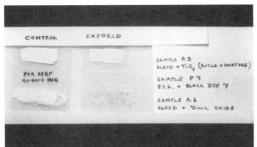

Figure 8 Effect of emissions from decaying cellulose nitrate on three typical labelling media for plastics.

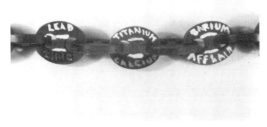

Figure 9 Various white pigments in gelatine medium on degraded ebonite show relative discoloration within one month at ambient humidity.

alkyd medium, which were applied to ebonite jewellery in the 1960s, have yellowed, but they are still perfectly legible and are adhering well. However, attempts to use the same type of ink to apply new registration numbers to the same artefacts caused major discolouration of the ink and disruption of the artefact surface because of changes in the properties of the ebonite during the last two decades of imperfect storage.

Photosensitization is another problem with some white pigments. Although zinc oxide and titanium dioxide can have a protective light-screening effect, they are also reputed to sensitize polymers to ultraviolet light, encouraging stress-cracking and embrittlement, especially in nylons and the polyolefins.[4,6] The effect has also been studied in paint films where the polymer medium erodes at an accelerated rate exposing the pigment to mechanical damage (chalking).[7] Chalking can be desirable in commercial outdoor paints because of the self-cleaning effect on grimy surfaces that constantly erode, revealing a clean undersurface (and increasing sales by the rapid attrition of the paint). However, it is not an advantage on museum artefacts where handling could dislodge registration numbers with degraded media. Of the two crystalline forms of titanium dioxide, anatase is the more photo-active. Rutile titanium dioxide is also available coated with silicone or non-porous inorganic minerals, which help to reduce photo-activity to some extent. It is probable that photo-actination would be more likely to affect the ink/paint medium than the artefact beneath, but there is no guarantee that harmful degradation products will not migrate to the substrate.

At present the best white pigment appears to be coated rutile titanium dioxide, but it is also advisable to keep the artefact protected from ultraviolet light, which is very harmful to most plastics regardless of the presence of photosensitizing inks. Most labelling media have some light-screening effects so it is advisable to apply the number in an area protected from light or there will be differential fading (Figure 10).

Aggressive Plastics

Labelling media can attack artefacts, but the effect of plastic artefacts on the labelling media

Figure 10 Differential fading on casein button where pigments have blocked the light.

also needs to be considered. Numbering systems must be able to accommodate dramatic dimensional changes caused by flexing, temperature and deterioration without flaking off; otherwise the registration numbers will quietly disappear from the artefacts in storage. Some of the old gelatine and gum Arabic inks used on our cellulose nitrate in the past have flaked to illegibility, whereas shellac-based inks are still legible even where the celluloid is disintegrating beneath them.

As plastics degrade, some of them become increasingly corrosive giving off volatile materials, such as nitrogen dioxide, sulphur dioxide, hydrogen sulphide, hydrogen chloride, formic acid, acetic acid and camphor. Such emissions inevitably attack labelling media, not only on the plastic artefacts but also on adjacent collections.

Various resins and labelling materials used in our own and other museums were applied to a mylar strip and enclosed (but not sealed) in a small Plexiglas display case with a piece of decaying cellulose nitrate from a 1930s' handbag. A set of controls was kept in a similar case in the same ambient environment. Materials that proved resistant to the emissions were subsequently tested in direct contact with decaying cellulose nitrate. A similar experiment was set up using an ebonite bracelet from the 1870s, which was emitting both hydrogen sulphide and sulphur dioxide.

Within six months many of the inks and paints exposed to cellulose nitrate had become brittle

and flaky and most of the black dye-based inks showed severe fume fading. There was severe discolouration of many of the resins, especially epoxy and polyurethane varnishes. Alkyd varnishes yellowed, but not to the extent of obscuring the legibility of the inks, and their adhesion was initially unaffected although some degraded before the end of the year. Not surprisingly, cellulosic resins, such as methyl cellulose and cellulose nitrate, showed very poor resistance as did archival paper labels. All metallic wires corroded rapidly, nylon monofilament was eventually weakened to breaking point by direct contact with both plastics, and cellulose threads were only slightly more resistant. Polypropylene sheet and cords seemed to be unaffected, but the manufacturers did not recommend its long-term use under such aggressive conditions. The severity of the damage in so short a time was surprising and horrifying since the decaying piece of cellulose nitrate was not very large and the conditions of the experiment were very similar to conditions in which some of our early cellulose nitrates are kept. Damage caused by the ebonite was less dramatic except where inks and tying materials were in direct contact with the acidic surface.

After two years of exposure, shellac, poly(vinyl acetate) resins (but not emulsions) and acrylic resins (both emulsion and solvent types) have neither embrittled nor discoloured.

These initial results suggest that neutral aqueous dispersions of acrylic polymers are the safest media in which to mix pigments that are to be applied directly to plastic surfaces. Colloidal dispersions with their finer particle size generally have superior properties and fewer additives than the emulsions,[8] but both dispersions and emulsions that have been thickened with organic solvents or cellulose ethers should be avoided because of the increased risk of solvent damage or decreased moisture resistance in the dried film. Dispersions are manufactured for the paint industry where requirements are continually changed and new lines are introduced and discontinued frequently. So it is advisable to assess dispersions carefully before using them. Desirable properties for labelling media are a neutral pH; a low organic solvent content; tough, slightly flexible films; and a glass transition temperature above room temperature. At present we are using Acrysol WS 68 (Rohm and Haas), which satisfies most of the conditions except that the film is rather soft.

Conclusion: Guidelines for Labelling Plastic Artefacts

Each plastic has its own sensitivities, which are affected by manufacturing techniques, additives, age and use. It is difficult for institutions without sophisticated analytical equipment to distinguish one type of plastic from another, since many simple tests are destructive and unreliable.[9] The staff responsible for applying registration numbers cannot be expected to spend a great deal of time devising separate methods for labelling each individual plastic artefact, taking its specific sensitivities into account. To simplify matters the following are suggested for labelling artefacts made wholly or in part from plastics:

Use tie-on tags made from Teflon tape where possible. Plumbers' tape, which comes in several grades, can be used as the tag or twisted to form the tie, and it is much cheaper than other forms of poly(tetra fluoroethylene) tape. Mylar D, chemically known as poly(ethylene terepthalate), can be used to make chemically resistant tags, but it has extremely sharp edges that may cut through the cord attaching it to the artefact.

Number the artefact directly without an intervening layer of varnish; use a suitable ink/paint of known composition. To avoid problems with constantly changing constituents in a commercial ink, it is safer to make one. Finely divided carbon black or coated rutile titanium dioxide without impurities can be mixed into a neutral acrylic dispersion, such as Acrysol WS 68. Homemade paints are more difficult to use than commercial mixtures because they lack the additives that control flow, homogeneous pigment dispersion and drying time. Nevertheless it is possible, with a little practice, to adjust the viscosity with water to permit small, neat lettering that will not spread into degraded surfaces and can, if necessary, be removed mechanically after drying. Shellac is the next best choice of medium for carbon and titanium pigments and it has the advantage of being much more available and easier to use, but the alcohol solvent poses a risk to highly stressed plastics as well as those that are soluble or partly soluble in alcohol. Some light-coloured plastics that will not be subjected to extensive handling can also be numbered safely using a soft (2B to 4B) graphite pencil.

There is still an element of risk that can be further minimized by careful placement of the registration number.

- Where possible apply the label to a non-plastic component of the artefact, preferably not directly adjacent to plastic components.

- Avoid the areas that are most likely to be exposed to light, abrasion or handling.

- Avoid areas that are already visibly degraded, that is, dulled, faded, cracked, distorted or excreting plasticizers.

- Avoid areas that are likely to be under stress, that is, adjacent to glue lines, repairs, interfaces between different plastics, areas that are constantly flexed, such as Tupperware lids or polypropylene-membrane hinges. Anything that might swell the polypropylene and relax the biaxial orientation of the molecules will reduce flex resistance. Knife handles also are usually under stress because the metal tang is inserted in the plastic while it is hot, so that as it cools, it shrinks around the metal to give a tight fit. The label in Figure 1 has been placed on the most stressed area of the artefact.

Finally, in case the numbering should initiate damage in spite of all precautions, avoid placing labels adjacent to the manufacturers' marks, where critical information can be destroyed first.

Résumé

La pose des numéros d'enregistrement sur les objets en plastique

Il est de plus en plus évident que la pose de numéros d'enregistrement sur les objets en plastique présente des risques élevés. Il peut en effet alors se produire une interaction irréversible entre, d'une part, les plastifiants, les solvants, les pigments et les teintures et, d'autre part, le support de plastique, et un tel phénomène pourrait fort bien accélérer la fissuration sous contrainte du matériau, sa déformation ou sa décoloration, voire sa désintégration complète. Le temps que mettront les dommages à apparaître — parfois des mois, ce qui les situe dans le long terme — et le manque d'informations sur les conditions présidant à la formation des complexes moléculaires font qu'il devient impossible d'effectuer ne serait-ce que des essais sur des parties cachées de l'objet pour tenter de déterminer les combinaisons dommageables. Ironie du sort, si l'on procédait à de tels essais, cette première étape du processus visant à conserver l'objet pour la postérité pourrait fort bien constituer l'amorce de sa destruction.

Chaque genre de plastique étant vulnérable à une série particulière de matières, il serait théoriquement possible d'empêcher qu'ils ne s'abîment en établissant, pour chacun, un mode d'étiquetage particulier. Reste néanmoins qu'il faudrait d'abord pouvoir les identifier correctement, et qu'il est fort difficile de le faire sans appareils d'analyse, qui sont par ailleurs coûteux. Et même si un tel système d'étiquetage, fiable, était mis en place, il faudrait aussi considérer l'incidence d'autres facteurs comme les techniques de fabrication, les additifs, les contaminants et le vieillissement. Sans compter que les paramètres de solubilité de plusieurs polymères se modifient avec le temps.

L'autre aspect de cette interaction, à savoir l'effet que peut avoir l'objet en plastique sur l'étiquette, n'est, par ailleurs, pas toujours pris en compte. Les objets qui comportent des matières comme la vulcanite, le polychlorure de vinyle (PCV), l'acétate de cellulose et le nitrate de cellulose risquent ainsi de faire blanchir ou couler les encres et d'attaquer la peinture et le vernis, si bien que, dans un laps de temps relativement court, les numéros deviendront illisibles, s'ils ne s'effritent pas complètement. De tels dommages seront non seulement causés aux éléments (encre et vernis) de marquage classiques, mais encore aux fils de textile ou de fer et aux autres matières qui, servant à attacher les étiquettes volantes et les étiquettes d'exposition, auront été placés dans les vitrines d'exposition à proximité de plastiques instables.

Dans le cadre de la présente communication, nous ferons état dans le détail d'expériences poussées portant sur différentes combinaisons d'encres et de polymères qui ne risquent pratiquement pas d'abîmer l'objet, tout en résistant mieux aux produits de dégradation qui en proviennent.

References

1. Umney, Nicholas, "Oriental Lacquer," *Conservation News*, vol. 32, March 1987, pp. 23-25.

2. Webb, Marianne, "Light Degradation of Oriental Lacquer," *IIC-CG Abstracts of the 13th Annual Conference,* Victoria, B.C., 1987, p. 55.

3. Williams, R. Scott, Janet Waddington and Julia Fenn, "Infra-red Spectroscopic Analysis of Central and South American Amber Exposed to Air Pollutants, Biocides, Light and Moisture," *Collections Forum*, vol. 6, no. 2, Fall 1990, pp. 65-75.

4. Allen, Norman S., "Effects of Dyes and Pigments," in: *Comprehensive Polymer Science*, ed. G. Allen, vol. 2, chap. 20, (London: Pergamon Press) pp. 579-595 .

5. *Nitrocellulose. The Chemical and Physical Properties*, Technical pamphlet (Wilmington, Delaware: Hercules Inc., 1979) p. 28.

6. Davidson, R.S. and R.R. Meck, "The Photodegradation of Polyethylene and Polypropylene in the Presence and Absence of Added Titanium Dioxide," *European Polymer Journal*, vol. 17, 1981, pp. 163-167.

7. Hoffman, E. and A. Saracz, "Weathering of Paint Films: I. Chalking Caused by Zinc Oxide in Latex Paints,"; "Weathering of Paint Films: II. Chalking Caused by Anatase Titanium Dioxide in Latex Paints," *Journal of the Oil and Colour Chemists Assoc.*, vol. 52, 1969, pp. 113-132; pp. 1130-1144.

8. Koob, Stephen P., "Consolidation with Acrylic Dispersions," *Preprints of the 9th Annual Meeting of the American Institution for the Conservation of Historic and Artistic Works*, May 1981, pp. 86-94.

9. Coxon, Helen C., "Practical Pitfalls in the Identification of Plastics," this volume.

Degradation Rates for Some Historic Polymers and the Potential of Various Conservation Measures for Minimizing Oxidative Degradation

David W. Grattan

Canadian Conservation Institute
Department of Communications
Ottawa, Ontario
Canada

Abstract

Polymers in the form of plastics, rubbers or textiles cause major headaches for museums. Their instability and unpredictability make the work of conservation, display and storage a difficult challenge. At the Canadian Conservation Institute, we are well aware of these difficulties and also of the limited nature of the options that we have to cope with them. For many polymers, degradation is caused by a chemical reaction with oxygen. There may be many factors that initiate this process and many complex stages involved but the outward signs are quite straightforward. Polymeric materials react with oxygen and become increasingly fragile. They may change in volume and colour and may also become acidic or release volatile products.

These effects, which result from chemical reactions, can be slowed down in several ways. The oxygen can be excluded, the temperature can be reduced, the active chemical species within the polymer can be trapped or destroyed chemically by antioxidants or stabilizers, and light (especially UV) can be excluded. This list is not exhaustive, but it does cover the main options.

Although a number of the above countermeasures have been explored, little is known about the actual rates of decay of historic materials. The first step to measuring the success of any conservation procedure appears to be the measurement of oxidation rates, and oxygen absorption measurements for ambient and low temperature studies are currently being used.

In this paper the results of these measurements are considered in relation to various conservation procedures, with special reference to refrigeration and the use of Ageless* oxygen absorber.

*Ageless is a trade name of the Mitsubishi Gas Chemical Company Inc. of Japan.

Introduction

Rubbers or plastics (i.e., materials composed of carbon chain polymers) degrade principally by oxidation. Although other forms of decay, such as depolymerization or the acidic breakdown of cellulose nitrate and cellulose acetate, do occur, for many polymers the principal pathway involves the absorption of oxygen from the atmosphere. Following this step, which is a chemical reaction, various oxidation products are formed, and the polymer backbone is often fragmented. As a result, the chemical and physical nature of polymers alter, and this affects the plastic or rubber materials of which they form the major component. There may be several diverse outward signs. Plastics may shrink, become brittle and decrease radically in strength. These changes result in distortion and cracking of objects. Materials may alter in colour either because dark-coloured oxidation products form or because the colourant oxidizes or fades. The production of oxidation products, such as acids, aldehydes, ketones and peroxides, causes polymers to become more polar. Thus, their solubility characteristics alter and this often means that plasticizers, originally dissolved within, come out of solution and migrate to the surface.

If oxidation can be stopped, many (although not all) of the degradation processes will cease. The simplest way to do this is to deny the polymer access to oxygen by using a nitrogen or argon atmosphere or placing the polymer under vacuum. Oxygen absorber sachets, such as Ageless (manufactured by Mitsubishi Gas Chemical Company Inc. of Japan) or Freshpax (marketed by the Ludlow Corporation of the U.S.), provide a simple way of removing oxygen from closed atmospheres, and the investigation of this approach forms the topic of this paper.

Oxygen absorbers do not, however, remove all the oxygen. A small proportion remains (with Ageless this is at minimum 0.01%) and it is vital to know whether this is sufficient to prevent significant oxidation. In addition, most containers leak over time; for instance, most oxygen-barrier films are slightly permeable. Thus, one of the functions of the absorber is to trap the oxygen that leaks in.

A short-term direct test demonstrating that materials stored in low oxygen conditions do not degrade would be most useful. This would have to be accomplished by measuring directly the accumulation of oxidation products or the alteration in properties. However, there are problems with this approach. For such an experiment, objects would be placed in oxygen-free conditions and attempts would be made to observe differences in the accumulation of oxidation products or alteration in properties compared to similar objects stored in air. But degradation is quite slow and the resulting changes slight. Analyses of these changes would have to be very sensitive to small differences and the test objects would also have to be homogeneous in condition (particularly in their state of deterioration). This direct approach was thus considered unlikely to prove fruitful.

One way of avoiding these problems might be to use rapidly deteriorating materials that would quickly show oxidative changes. However, since such materials have large appetites for oxygen, oxidation rates would certainly be reduced in the low oxygen levels created by Ageless, but would also probably be reduced in atmospheres in which some oxygen remained (i.e., ineffectually scavenged). The real question of whether the very low oxygen concentrations produced by Ageless would allow a slowly oxidizing material (i.e., a typical material) to continue degrading would remain unanswered.

It was concluded that the problem could only be tackled indirectly. To do this, the following information was required:

• The rate of oxygen absorption of historic polymeric materials under ambient and cold conditions

• The actual level of oxygen in a closed envelope containing an oxygen absorber, and how this level changes over time

• The leak rate of plastic envelopes

Experimental

Ageless Oxygen Absorber: This material is a mixture of finely divided iron, molecule sieves, sodium chloride and moisture that binds oxygen chemically in the presence of moisture. It is marketed in sealed paper sachets that are permeable to oxygen but less so to moisture. Different formulations are sold for various ranges of relative humidity (RH), and Ageless Z, the formulation used in these experiments, functions best in the RH range of 0% to 85%. Other formulations of Ageless are intended for higher humidity. Sachets are prepared in various sizes according to the volume of oxygen that can be absorbed.

Ageless Eye is an indicator that turns pink in less than 0.01% oxygen.

Ageless can create oxygen-free conditions in heat-sealed oxygen-barrier film enclosures. Flexible films allow the consumption of oxygen without pressure differences developing across the barrier. Films simply flex to take up the volume change as oxygen is consumed. In a rigid enclosure, a pressure difference develops, which encourages gas leakage.

Heat-sealed envelopes containing Ageless sachets were prepared from a number of barrier films. The gaseous contents were analyzed by gas-chromatography over a period of a few months. The aims were to measure oxygen depletion and moisture content. A series of experiments were carried out. At first, there was no control of RH, but in the later experiments, conditioned silica gel sealed in Remay pouches was added to produce a range of relative humidities within the envelopes.

Barrier Films: Du Pont Canada Inc. of Mississauga, Ontario, and Condor Laminations Ltd. of Agincourt, Ontario, supplied batches of films for testing. The Du Pont films included Oxybar 1, 2, 3 and 4. Oxygen permeance data (supplied by Du Pont and measured following ASTM D1434) for these films are shown in Table I. (N.B. Permeance is defined as the ratio of the gas transmission rate to the difference in partial pressure of the gas on the two sides of the film.)

Table I

Permeance of Barrier Films Supplied by Du Pont

Film	Permeance* at 50% RH	Permeance* at 0% RH
Oxybar 1	0.08	0.08
Oxybar 2	0.08	0.03
Oxybar 3	0.60	0.03
Oxybar 4	0.05	0.05

* Permeance units are in mL oxygen per 100 square inches of barrier film, per 1 atmosphere partial pressure difference from one side of the film to the other for 24 hours at 23°C.

Composition of Films: No composition data or permeance values are available for the Condor film. The Oxybar films were taken from batches produced for experimental purposes only, whereas the Condor film was taken from a standard production run.

Experiments

Ageless Z was tested in envelopes composed of each of the five types of barrier films. Two envelopes were prepared for each film type at each intended relative humidity. Relative humidities of 51%, 65% and 77% were regulated by placing silica gel in the envelopes, and one set of envelopes was prepared with no humidity control. Thus 40 envelopes, each varying in volume from around 150 mL to 200 mL, were prepared.

The sealed envelopes contained:

- An Ageless sachet

- Four sampling serum cap vials (there was only one vial per envelope of opaque Oxybar 4 film)

- Ageless Eye (not included in the opaque Oxybar 4 film envelopes)

- 15 g of conditioned silica gel in heat-sealed Remay pouches. The use and preparation of these is explained in more detail below.

Ageless: Samples of Ageless were received from Mitsubishi packed in heat-sealed envelopes composed of barrier film. The Ageless sachets were kept thus until needed for experiments. Envelopes were prepared in the open laboratory and were heat-sealed quickly with an Audion Elektro Sealmaster 420.

Ageless Eye: Indicator capsules of Ageless Eye (also received from Mitsubishi) were added to each envelope of transparent film.

Table II

The Composition of Oxygen Barrier Films (Information is based on data supplied by Du Pont.)

Film	Barrier	Sealing Layer
Oxybar 1	poly(vinylidene chloride)	polyethylene
Oxybar 2	poly(ethylene vinyl acetate)	polyethylene
Oxybar 3	oriented nylon	polyethylene
Oxybar 4 (opaque film)	aluminium metallized polyester	polyethylene

Silica Gel: A 50:50 mixture of 3-9 mesh grade 41, and 3-8 mesh grade 59 silica gel was conditioned for six months with saturated solutions of sodium chloride to give 77% RH, magnesium acetate to give 65% RH and calcium nitrate to give 51% RH. Portions of 15 g were heat-sealed in Remay (non-woven textile) pouches for inclusion in the envelopes with the Ageless.

Sampling Procedure: The atmospheres in the sealed envelopes (i.e., containing Ageless) were sampled at regular intervals using four 3.5 mL screw cap serum vials. At predetermined times, labelled vials were capped by screwing a neoprene/teflon membrane in place. The vials remained in the envelopes until time of analysis.

Measurement Procedure: All sampling and transfer operations were carried out in an oxygen-free atmosphere. For this purpose, a nitrogen glove bag was placed on top of the gas chromatograph with the injection port sealed within. To conduct an analysis, the envelopes containing Ageless were placed in the glove bag, which was then closed. The bag was inflated and purged with dry nitrogen, and to ensure that oxygen had been purged out, the atmosphere was sampled repeatedly by making injections into the gas chromatograph. This was carried out until the oxygen peak had almost disappeared in the gas chromatogram.

Analytical Procedure: Analysis was performed on a Hewlett Packard 5840 A dual column instrument with thermal conductivity detectors and, initially, with an Alltech concentric column model CTR-1. The outer column was 2 m x 63 mm activated molecular sieve, and the inner, 2 m x 32 mm "Porapak mixture." (This is presumably composed of two or more unspecified grades of Porapak.) This column is intended for the analysis of oxygen, water, carbon dioxide, nitrogen, carbon monoxide, etc. Conditions for the CTR-1 column: Column temperature 100°C, injection port temperature 80°C and detector temperature 135°C. Ultrapure helium carrier gas flowed at 45 mL per minute.

Unfortunately argon elutes at the same point as oxygen with this column, and thus oxygen was determined by subtraction of the argon. This proved to be very inaccurate because argon (0.934% of the atmosphere) is present in overwhelming amounts compared to oxygen and thus this method was discontinued. Some analyses of water were successful with the CTR-1 column and estimates of RH were carried out. They were very inaccurate.

In a second series of experiments a HayeSep A porous polymer column[1,2] (10 metres of 0.3 mm diameter HayeSep A, 80/100 mesh) separated oxygen from argon and nitrogen. A typical analysis is shown in Figure 1. Water analysis, and hence RH determination, was not possible with the HayeSep A column.

Conditions for the HayeSep A column were: Column temperature 0°C, injection port temperature 25°C and detector temperature 135°C, flow rate 17 mL per minute ultrapure helium carrier gas.

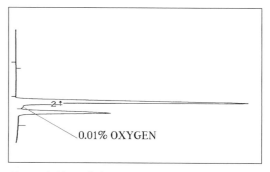

Figure 1 Typical chromatogram showing, in order of descent, (1) large nitrogen peak, (2) scale change to a more sensitive setting at 2↑, (3) small oxygen peak almost at detection limit, and (4) argon peak.

Calibration: This was performed by measuring response in area units, as given by the integrator function of the chromatograph, versus injection volume measured at about 757 torr pressure and 23.5°C. Calibration data is shown in Table III, and plots of peak area versus sample size for various gases are shown in Figures 2, 3, and 4.

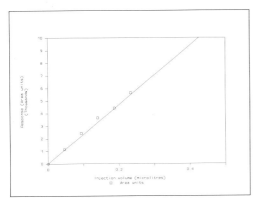

Figure 2 Calibration of HayeSep A column for argon.

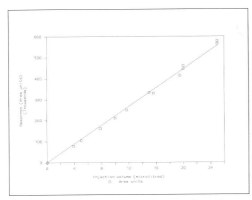

Figure 3 Calibration of HayeSep A column for nitrogen.

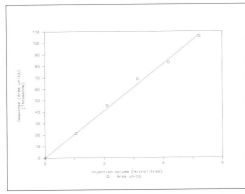

Figure 4 Calibration of HayeSep A column for oxygen.

The limit of detection was given by the height of the smallest observable peak. In practice this indicated a limit of about 0.003% oxygen. The value of argon was typically around 1.2%, as would be expected from a 20% reduction in volume (i.e., from loss of the oxygen).

Table III

Response of Gas Chromatograph in Area Units for Various Gases

Gas	Response (area units / microlitres)
Argon	23,498
Nitrogen	22,264
Oxygen	20,476

Results

The results of analysis by gas chromatography are shown in Table IV.

Table IV

Oxygen Content of Envelopes as Given by Gas Chromatography

Film	Intended RH	Average Percent Oxygen Analysis by HayeSep A *
Oxybar 1	51%	0.000%
	65%	0.000%
	77%	0.000%
	uncontrolled	(0.05 ± 0.03%)
Oxibar 2	51%	0.000%
	65%	0.000-0.003%
	77%	0.000-0.005%
	uncontrolled	(0.039 ± 0.03%)
Oxibar 3	51%	0.000%
	65%	0.000-0.004%
	77%	0.000-0.009%
	uncontrolled	(0.026 ± 0.03%)
Oxybar 4	51%	0.004-0.03%
	65%	0.007-0.02%
	77%	0.000%
	uncontrolled	(0.52 ± 0.03%)
Condor	51%	(0.017 ± 0.03%)
	65%	(0.018 ± 0.03%)
	77%	(0.013 ± 0.03%)
	uncontrolled	(0.026 ± 0.03%)

*Figures in parentheses denote CTR-1 readings.

Discussion of Oxygen Analysis

The oxygen analysis using the CTR-1 column was very imprecise because of the interference of argon with the oxygen peak. Thus the values quoted in Table IV are for the analysis with the HayeSep A column (except where these data are unobtainable). Oxygen analyses obtained with the CTR-1 column are shown in brackets. There is an uncertainty of at least ± 0.03% for all the values quoted above.

Those data obtained with the HayeSep A column (which does separate argon from oxygen) show very much lower oxygen levels, which are in most cases below the detection limit of 0.003%. The uncertainties in the values given in the HayeSep A column result from differences in the amount of oxygen measured. In some instances there was a small amount of oxygen in the glove bag and this may have contaminated the syringe during transfer operations: at these very low levels it could happen very easily. In most instances the oxygen content of all vials was about the same regardless of when sealing took place. It seems logical that oxygen cannot diffuse out of the sampling vials during transfer. Thus it also seems logical that the lowest reading for oxygen is always likely to be the most accurate.

This analysis was carried out one year after the vials had been sealed. Thus in most instances the level of oxygen was below the limit of detection (0.003%) and remained so for the period of the experiment regardless of the relative humidity.

The water analysis was found to be unreliable and it is thought that the control exercised by the silica gel — as conferred by the pre-equilibration with saturated salts — is a better guide to envelope humidity than is the measured water-peak area. This poor water analysis is not surprising since the water peak "tails" badly in the chromatograms.

Ageless Eye went pink in all sealed envelopes very rapidly and remained in that condition until analysis. The colour change was most rapid in the envelopes of higher humidity. It therefore has proven to be a reliable indicator of oxygen content so far.

It is clear that Ageless is capable of producing very low levels of oxygen. However, for this technique to be considered useful as a method of anaerobic storage, oxygen levels must be significantly lower than the oxygen consumption of a deteriorating object in air over a reasonable period of time.

Measurements of Oxygen Uptake of Some Historic Materials

Measurement of the rate of oxidation of historic materials has been performed with an oxygen absorption apparatus — namely the Warburg respirometer. Intended for use for determining the oxygen demand by living organisms, the Warburg has been successfully used here to measure the comparatively low rates of uptake of oxidizing polymers.

Experimental

The respirometer, shown in Figure 5, consists of a 25 mL conical flask connected to a mercury manometer. The oxidizing material is placed in the conical flask and the apparatus immersed in a thermostatically controlled bath at 25°C. After allowing time for equilibration the apparatus is sealed with the mercury level in the manometer set at a known point (15 cm on the 0 cm to 30 cm scale), and the atmospheric pressure noted. At intervals of about one month the manometer is carefully read (usually over a range of pressures to compensate for the inaccuracy of single point readings) and the reading corrected for atmospheric pressure variation. In this way (i.e., by measuring the reduction in total gas volume in the apparatus) the amount of oxygen absorbed can be calculated per unit weight of polymer. If a significant proportion of the oxygen is removed then it is relatively simple to restore the atmospheric gas composition by passing air through the apparatus. It can then be re-sealed for further measurements.

The apparatus was modified to enable oxygen uptake measurements to be made at lower temperatures (ca. -20°C). For this purpose, a tap that could be closed between measurements was inserted between the manometer and the conical flask. Without the tap, the reduction in pressure brought about by the lowering of temperature caused mercury to be sucked out of the manometer into the conical flask.

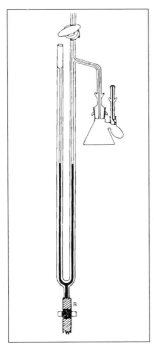

Figure 5 The Warburg respirometer.

Results

Figures 6 and 7 show the rate of oxygen uptake for a number of items of different polymeric materials. (Note that the graphs are labelled in descending order, and that more information can be found in Table V, which also gives quantitative oxygen absorption data. Note also that the oxygen uptake is estimated for a period of 100 days.)

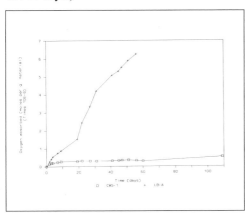

Figure 6 Oxygen uptake for lamp base (LB-A), rubber cape (CWS-1) (see Table V).

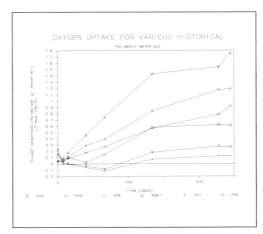

Figure 7 Oxygen uptake for shoe sole (NSA-1), PVC pad (FH-1), ABS cup (FH-4), polyurethane foam (FH-2) and (FH-5), ABS "spacer" (FH-3) (see Table V).

Discussion

For all samples, the amount of oxygen that would normally be consumed in a 100-day period is well in excess of the static amount of oxygen available in the sealed envelopes. There is a problem however, in that the concentration of oxygen within the envelopes results from a dynamic equilibrium. Oxygen diffusing through the film is consumed by the Ageless. More oxygen than is suggested by the static value of the percentage oxygen content enters the sealed bag and may therefore be available to the oxidizing object.

There are thus three main problems to resolve:

- The leak rate of different oxygen barrier films is an important factor. It is important to quantify how much oxygen actually flows through each type of barrier.

- The competition for oxygen between Ageless and an oxidizing organic object should be considered. If an object can compete success-fully for oxygen it will continue to decay.

- If a given bag leaks oxygen at a certain rate, how much extra Ageless is necessary to remove the leaked-in oxygen over a 10- to 20-year period?

Table V

Meaurements of Oxygen Uptake of Some Historic Materials
(It is assumed that at room temperature [25°C] one mole of oxygen occupies 24,450 cc.)

Sample	Polymer	Sample Code	Perriod of Test (days)	Amount of O_2 Consumed per Gram Polymer (moles)	Oxygen Absorbed as Percentage of Air Volume per 100 days
Rubber cape (WW II, 1940s)	Butyl rubber with TiO_2 filler	CWS-1	108	5.3×10^{-7}	0.40%
Plastic lamp base (1970s)	Polyethylene with TiO_2 filler	LB-A	48	5.4×10^{-6}	7.5%
Rubber shoe sole (1950s)	is-1,4-polyisoprene plus styrene-butadiene copolymer. Ca, Al silicates, TiO_2 filler	NSA-1	490	1.76×10^{-5}	2.9%
Plastic ear cup in pilot's helmet (1950s)	Poly (acrylonitrile/ butadiene/styrene with TiO_2 filler	FH-4	490	9.2×10^{-6}	1.5%
PVC pad from pilot's helmet (1950s)	Poly(vinyl chloride), di(2-ethyl hexyl) phthalate (plasticizer), trace TiO_2	FH-1	490	1.2×10^{-5}	2.0%
Grey plastic spacer from pilot's helmet (1950s)	Poly (acrylonitrile/ butadiene/styrene) with TiO_2 filler	FH-3	490	1.2×10^{-6}	0.2%
Black foam "rubber" from pilot's helmet (1950s)	Polyurethane	FH-2	490	2.6×10^{-6}	0.44%
Black foam "rubber" from pilot's helmet (1950s)	Polyurethane	FH-5	490	6.1×10^{-6}	1.0%

Leak Rate: Examinations of a number of bagged objects have led to a very rough rule-of-thumb that for every gram of object, we can normally expect about 6 square cm (1 square in.) of barrier wall (as objects become larger this value decreases) and about 3 mL of air space once the oxygen is consumed (as objects get larger this value tends to decrease). In practice this latter value of 3 mL per g may well vary from 1 mL to 10 mL depending on the shape of the object.

Thus for a 100-day period with Oxybar 1 film barrier, the leakage rate per gram of object (using the Du Pont permeance values quoted in Table I) would be calculated thus:

0.08 (permeance units, mL oxygen per 100 square inches of barrier film, per 1 atmosphere partial pressure difference from one side of the film to the other for 24 hours at 23°C)

x 1/100   (to correct the value for 1 square inch of barrier film)

x 100   (to correct the value for a 100-day period)

x 21/100   (to correct the value for the partial pressure of oxygen — approximately 21% of the atmosphere)

= 1.7×10^{-2} mL oxygen passing through the barrier in 100 days per gram of object.

But, as stated above, for each gram of object we have assumed there are 3 mL of gas space (after the initial oxygen is consumed), thus the percentage of oxygen that would leak in equals:

$$100 \times 1.7 \times 10^{-2} / 3 = 0.6\%$$

This means that if an average-sized envelope of Oxybar 1 (containing no Ageless) was to be filled with pure nitrogen, after 100 days it would contain 0.6% oxygen.

The values for the other Du Pont barrier films, calculated similarly, are shown in Table VI.

Table VI

Estimated Percentage of Leaked-in Oxygen for Envelopes Composed of Various Barrier Films at 23°C

Barrier Film	Percent Oxygen at 50% RH	Percent Oxygen at 0% RH
Oxybar 1	0.6	0.6
Oxybar 2	0.6	0.2
Oxybar 3	4.5	0.2
Oxybar 4	0.4	0.4

Competition for Oxygen: As shown above, the rate of oxygen leakage is such that if the organic material were to compete for it successfully, the oxidation rate would still be significant, despite the low oxygen concentration in the envelope and the presence of Ageless. The principal reaction by which oxygen is absorbed, the interaction of alkyl radicals with oxygen to form peroxy radicals, is very rapid. Other factors that play a part are the following:

• The overall oxidation rate of the stored object

• The concentration of oxygen-absorbing species in the stored object

• The rates of diffusion of oxygen into various materials

• The amount of Ageless added and its surface area

• The rate of reaction of Ageless plus oxygen

Of these, probably the most important consideration is the huge surface area of Ageless. This arises from its small particle size and porous nature. The alkyl radical, produced as a reactive intermediate in the degradation of organic materials, may compete with Ageless for oxygen. It is only ever present at very low concentration, but reacts with oxygen exceedingly rapidly. Despite this, it is thus quite reasonable to suppose that little of the leaked-in oxygen will end up in the oxidizing material, because the surface presented by the Ageless is so large and the reaction is also very rapid.

Capacity of Ageless: Ageless sachets are rated by the manufacturer in terms of the number of cc. of oxygen that can be absorbed. Mitsubishi suggests that the amount of Ageless to be employed in a given storage envelope should be based simply on the amount of oxygen initially present. Allowing for oxygen leakage is not suggested. Presumably this is because for food packaging, only a relatively short storage period is necessary. For conservation, however, leak rate is an important consideration.

Consider what might happen to a 100-g object in a sealed envelope composed of Oxybar 1.

According to the rule-of-thumb explained above, for an approximately 125-g object we expect 380 mL of air to be present initially. In this volume of air, 80 mL of oxygen is present, thus the volume becomes 300 mL after oxygen removal.

Over 100 days, we know from Table VI that 0.6% oxygen leaks in, which means that

$$(0.6/100) \times 300 = 1.8 \text{ mL} \quad \text{of oxygen enters the storage envelope.}$$

Over a year, it means that 6.6 mL of oxygen enters, and over 10 years 66 mL is expected to leak in. For an envelope intended for long-term use oxygen leakage is therefore significant and may overwhelm the Ageless capacity unless allowed for.

Conclusion

If Ageless can bring oxygen levels down to an amount that is significantly less than that consumed by decaying objects over a 100-day period, further oxidation is probably prevented or at least severely limited. Oxygen that permeates through the film will be competed for by the decaying object and the Ageless. It is probable that the Ageless will trap most of the leaked-in oxygen.

In order to maintain an environment with a very low level of oxygen, oxygen permeation into the envelope should be limited as much as possible. This can be achieved by placing the "object envelope" within an outer envelope. Each would contain an Ageless sachet. The outer envelope would maintain the oxygen level at a low level around the inner envelope so that oxygen diffusion into the inner envelope would be negligible. (The actual rate of permeation would be reduced by a factor of 840 compared to an envelope exposed directly to the atmosphere. This is because the oxygen partial pressure difference across the envelope wall would decrease from 2.1×10^{-1} atm to 2.5×10^{-4} atm.)

For the inner envelope the amount of Ageless to be added could be calculated in the manner suggested by Mitsubishi —that is, it would be governed by the amount of oxygen initially present with a small excess. On the other hand, for the outer envelope, it would also be important to consider the leak rate of the barrier film over a long period. This is shown for the films described in Table VII.

Table VII
Oxygen Permeation through Different Films for a 10-Year Period

Film	Permeation Over 10 years*, 50% RH (mL)	Permeation Over 10 years*, 0% RH (mL)
Oxybar 1	61	61
Oxybar 2	61	23
Oxybar 3	460	23
Oxybar 4	38	38

* mL oxygen per 100 square inches of barrier film, per 0.21 atmosphere partial pressure difference for 10 years at 23°C

Acknowledgement

The author thanks Elizabeth Moffatt of Analytical Research Services of CCI for the analysis of both plastic and rubber samples.

Résumé

Le rythme de dégradation de certains polymères d'importance historique et les diverses mesures de conservation qui permettraient de réduire au minimum la dégradation oxydative

Si ce n'est déjà clair pour les spécialistes de la restauration, il leur suffira de parcourir les présents résumés pour constater que les polymères — plastiques, caoutchoucs et textiles — posent des problèmes sérieux au personnel des musées. La conservation, l'exposition et la mise en réserve de ces matières instables et imprévisibles représentent ainsi un défi de taille. Et à l'Institut canadien de conservation, nous nous sommes bien rendus compte de ces difficultés, de même que du nombre limité de solutions qui peuvent être mises en œuvre pour tenter de les résoudre. La dégradation de nombre de polymères tient bien souvent à une réaction chimique avec l'oxygène. Si ce processus peut s'amorcer par suite de nombreux facteurs, et s'il comporte parfois plusieurs étapes complexes, il n'en demeure pas moins que ses signes extérieurs ne laissent aucun doute. Les matières polymériques réagissent avec l'oxygène, puis elles deviennent de plus en plus fragiles. Il leur arrive même parfois de changer de volume ou de couleur, de devenir acides ou de libérer des substances volatiles.

Il est néanmoins possible de freiner ces effets, qui résultent de réactions chimiques, en usant de diverses techniques — en éliminant l'oxygène, en réduisant la température, en captant les espèces chimiques actives présentes dans le polymère ou en les détruisant chimiquement avec des antioxydants ou des stabilisants, ou en bloquant la lumière (l'ultraviolet, tout particulièrement). Cette liste, qui n'est pas exhaustive, couvre néanmoins les principales options qui s'offrent aux spécialistes de la restauration.

Bien qu'un certain nombre des ces mesures aient été étudiées, on sait néanmoins peu de choses du rythme réel de dégradation des matériaux d'importance historique. Or, pour évaluer le degré de réussite de toute technique de conservation, il semble indiqué de mesurer d'abord les taux d'oxydation, et l'on a déjà commencé à se servir d'études portant sur des mesures de l'absorption de l'oxygène pour des températures ambiantes et faibles.

Dans le cadre du présent article, nous considérerons les résultats de ces mesures en tenant compte des diverses méthodes de conservation, dont la réfrigération et l'emploi de l'Ageless*, un absorbant d'oxygène.

*Ageless est une marque déposée de la Mitsubishi Gas Chemical Company Inc.

References

1. Catalogue, *Chromatographic Specialties '91* (Brockville, Ontario, Canada: Chromatographic Specialties, 1991) p. 43.

2. G.E. Pollock, D. O'Hara and O.L. Hollis, "Gas Chromatographic Separation of Nitrogen, Oxygen, Argon and Carbon Dioxide Using Custom-made Porous Polymers from High Purity Divinylbenzene," *Journal of Chromatographic Science*, vol. 22, 1984, pp. 343-347.

A Field Trial for the Use of Ageless in the Preservation of Rubber in Museum Collections

Yvonne Shashoua and Scott Thomsen

Department of Conservation
The British Museum
London, U.K.

Abstract

Rubber deteriorates when exposed to ultraviolet light, oxygen or ozone. The deterioration shows either as cracking and embrittlement or as softening and poor mechanical properties, depending on the environment.

Several approaches to the preservation of rubber have been investigated at The British Museum during the last two years. These have involved the use of consolidants, plasticizers and protective coatings. Since the results of these studies were not encouraging, it was decided to pursue a strategy based upon preventive conservation. The main constraint was that the objects concerned had to be kept in their existing storage areas. The most useful approach appeared to involve sealing the objects into an oxygen-depleted micro environment created by the use of Ageless, an oxygen scavenger.

A field trial was set up in the Museum's Ethnography store to determine whether storing rubber objects in an oxygen-depleted micro environment noticeably reduced their rate of deterioration and, if this was the case, whether such a procedure was practical. A laboratory trial involving natural and accelerated ageing suggested that Cryovac BDF 200 polyolefin barrier film was most effective at excluding oxygen when made into heat-sealed bags incorporating Ageless. Enclosing rubber bands in this manner considerably extended their useful lifetime. Based on these results, selected ethnographic artefacts were enclosed in oxygen-depleted micro environments

and returned to their storage areas. The same number of objects were enclosed without Ageless present to act as controls.

All objects will be visually examined and photographed regularly in order to monitor the rate of degradation.

Introduction

The Ethnographic Collections of The British Museum contain a number of rubber objects; these may be composed solely of rubber or may incorporate wood, metals or textiles. The rubber is present in the form of natural rubber bands, coloured balloons, rubber tubing or motor car tyres and inner tubes. Since rubber is largely composed of unsaturated polymers, that is, polyisoprene, polybutadiene, and poly(styrene-co-butadiene), it is susceptible to oxidation, which results in either softening or hardening of the substrate. Attack by ozone causes embrittlement and subsequent cracking of the objects. Prolonged, uncontrolled oxidation and attack by ozone results in disintegration of rubber and serious damage to objects.

There are several techniques that can be used to protect rubber against degradation. Physical methods that involve introducing a barrier between rubber and atmosphere include coating the surface with paraffin or microcrystalline waxes or an epoxy paint. However, this method dramatically alters the appearance of the object. Chemical antioxidants and antiozonants, such as dialkyl p-phenylenediamines, have been introduced into rubber formulations since the 1930s. Black rubber, such as that used in tyre manufacture, has good resistance to oxidation due to its ability to trap oxygen radicals. However, it is extremely difficult to introduce these inhibitors into finished rubber objects. For this reason, it seems unlikely that the introduction of additives shows much potential for museum objects. Previous research projects at The British Museum have investigated the use of consolidation to preserve the degraded rubber surfaces by impregnation of weakened rubber with plasticizers and by application of protective coatings to inhibit further attack.[1,2] Although some of the materials used proved effective at stabilizing the substrate, they tended to alter the appearance of the surface to an unacceptable degree. This was particularly noticeable when the surface was pigmented. It was felt that non-intervention in the method of conservation would be preferable.

Storage of rubber objects in an inert atmosphere has been recommended by Clavir.[3] This would minimize the exposure of susceptible objects to oxygen and ozone. However, the practicality and cost of purging a large storage or display area with an inert gas, and excluding oxygen for a prolonged period would be prohibitive.

In March 1990, David Grattan reported that oxygen-depleted environments could be effectively produced by enclosing a chemical oxygen scavenger known as Ageless*, in a sealed oxygen-impermeable film envelope.[4]

Ageless has found widespread application in the food industry for prolonging the shelf-life of dry foods and wines. The major ingredient of Ageless sachets is finely divided active iron, which forms iron oxides and hydroxides on absorption of oxygen.[5] It is claimed to reduce the oxygen concentration of an air-tight container down to 0.01% (100 ppm) or less. Ageless has been used in museums for the treatment of insect infestations, but little research has been

done into its efficiency at prolonging the life of organic artefacts by inhibiting the oxidation reaction. For this reason it was felt appropriate to conduct such a study in The British Museum.

The aim of the study was to determine whether storing rubber objects in an oxygen-depleted environment, achieved using Ageless, noticeably reduces their rate of deterioration. The work falls into two parts; a laboratory trial was used to select the most suitable materials and techniques for encasing rubber objects and monitoring the rate of degradation, and a pilot scheme that used the results of the trial to store a selection of rubber objects from the Ethnographic Collections. The findings of the laboratory trial will be the main concern of this paper.

Degradation of Rubbers

The mechanisms that govern the deterioration of rubbers are complex. All chemically unsaturated rubbers, synthetic as well as natural, are susceptible to oxidation by atmospheric oxygen, a reaction that is greatly accelerated by a rise in temperature, the presence of metallic ions, and by absorption of light, especially in the ultraviolet region of the spectrum. It is not thought that relative humidity is an important factor at room temperature.

Two types of ageing processes, defined by Buist,[6] are the most relevant to rubber objects stored in museums. Shelf ageing, which occurs at ambient temperatures in the dark, is autoxidation. Oxidation is carried out via a chain reaction mechanism that involves free radicals formed from attack on the rubber hydrocarbon. Free radicals are highly reactive molecular fragments that have one unpaired electron available for bonding. They can react with oxygen to produce peroxy radicals by which the oxidation process fuels itself. Ketones, aldehydes and acidic groups are likely to be formed as by-products of the oxidation process. Shelf ageing can result either in hardening or softening of rubbers depending on their formulation and on the conditions of storage.

Atmospheric cracking is the term applied to the reactions that occur when rubber artefacts are exposed to ultraviolet light. In addition to the oxidation mechanism described previously,

---

*Ageless is produced by the Mitsubishi Gas Chemical Company Inc. of Japan.

ozonolysis, or attack by ozone, takes place. Ozone is formed in the atmosphere by the chemical reaction between atomic and molecular oxygen. It is now thought that a concentration of less than five parts of ozone per hundred million is sufficient to cause ozonolysis.[7]

Ozone reacts with non-stretched rubber by adding to the double bonds to form ozonides (Figure 1). When all the surface double bonds are consumed the reaction ceases. A grey film or frosting, 10 to 40 molecular layers thick, may appear on the surface. If this film is disrupted by stretching the rubber, unsaturated molecules are exposed and the energy required to promote tearing and further crack growth becomes available.[8] Cracks form at right angles to the surface of the rubber and eventually cause failure.

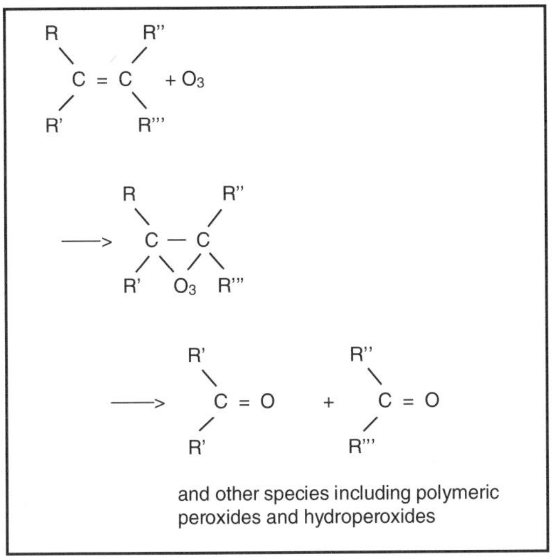

Figure 1 Attack by ozone on rubber.

Laboratory Evaluation of Ageless in the Preservation of Rubber

Selection of Ageless
Ageless is manufactured in the form of small sachets containing an oxygen absorbent that is based on finely divided iron. The iron is sealed within several layers of a gas-permeable plastic film that controls the rate of flow of oxygen and moisture to the absorbent. Iron oxide and hydroxides are formed on reaction with oxygen via the following half-reactions.[9]

$$Fe \longrightarrow Fe^{2+} + 2e^{-}$$

$$\tfrac{1}{2} O_2 + H_2O + 2e^{-} \longrightarrow 2OH^{-}$$

$$Fe^{2+} + 2 (OH)^{-} \longrightarrow Fe(OH)_2$$

$$Fe(OH)_2 + \tfrac{1}{4} O_2 + \tfrac{1}{2} H_2O \longrightarrow Fe(OH)_3$$

Different types of Ageless are available depending on the water activity of the material to be packaged. Ageless Z is recommended for the preservation of material that has a water activity (humidity divided by 100) of 0.85% or less, and so it is the most suitable grade for use with rubber. Ageless is also available in different sizes depending on the volume of oxygen to be scavenged. Ageless Z-200, which absorbs 200 mL of oxygen from 1 litre of air, was used in the laboratory trial.

Selection of Packaging Materials
Five main criteria were used to select a suitable packaging material.

- The material must be sufficiently stable so that it does not accelerate degradation of any component of the enclosed object, or lose cohesiveness during the period of the trial.

- The material must be highly impermeable to oxygen, and should buffer the object against extreme changes in relative humidity.

- The material must offer mechanical protection to the object.

- The material must be transparent so that study of the artefacts during the trial is possible without removing the object from its microclimate.

- The material must be amenable to resealing in order to facilitate regular examination of test pieces.

The materials that were considered to have suitable properties and to be readily available were glass in the form of air-tight Kilner preserving jars, poly(vinylidene chloride) (PVDC) film, self-closing polyethylene sample bags and Cryovac BDF 200 film. Cryovac BDF 200 film is a thin, multi-layered co-extruded polyolefin formulation, which is supplied for use with Ageless oxygen absorber.

In order to predict the chemical stability of the packaging materials under their proposed conditions of use, Oddy tests were used.[10] Samples of polyethylene bags were wrapped around coupons of freshly cleaned silver, copper, and lead. The test pieces were sealed in glass tubes with ground-glass stoppers and aged for 28 days at 60°C. In order to assess any adverse reactions between polymer films and rubber, an adaptation of the Oddy test was carried out. A strip of polyethylene film was wrapped around a piece of motor car inner tube and a rubber band, before sealing in a glass tube and ageing, as had been done with the metal coupons. The procedure was repeated with PVDC and Cryovac BDF 200. After ageing, all metal coupons and samples of rubber were examined by optical microscope for evidence of corrosion or other deterioration. None was detected and it was concluded that all the films were sufficiently stable for use in the trial.

In order to investigate the colour stability and retention of mechanical strength of the potential packaging materials, samples of PVDC, polyethylene sample bags and Cryovac BDF 200 films were light- and heat-aged. Glass was assumed to be sufficiently stable for the trial. Films were light-aged for 28 days in a Microscal light-fastness tester fitted with an MBTL 500 bulb. This exposed the films to an emission spectrum similar to that of daylight but approximately 100 times more intense. Heat-ageing was effected by sealing films in a test-tube with a ground-glass stopper, maintained at 70°C for 28 days. Aged and unaged films were examined by ultraviolet/visible spectroscopy and by human eye in order to determine the extent of discolouration of the films, and were tensile tested to quantify their loss in strength with age.

Ultraviolet reflectance spectroscopy is a technique by which the percentage of light reflected by the sample at each wavelength in the visible spectrum can be monitored. A change in the shape of the spectral trace produced indicates a change in hue and lightness of the material, the technique being more sensitive than the human eye to small changes. Reflectance spectra data

can be converted into CIE L* a* b* colour coordinates using a computer programme, where L* is a measure of the lightness of the sample, a* relates to redness/greenness, and b* determines yellowness/blueness.[11] None of the materials tested appeared to yellow after light- or heat-ageing. However, colour measurements suggest that Cryovac BDF 200 had a higher degree of colour stability, the greatest change in colour occurring in the b* (yellowness/blueness) value (Table I). The breaking strengths of aged and unaged strips of each film were determined in order to assess the suitability of the packaging materials to maintain a physical barrier between the objects to be enclosed and the environment of the store. Dumb-bell-shaped test pieces were conditioned at 65% RH and 22°C for two hours prior to tensile testing to breaking point on a J.J. Lloyd tensile tester. This procedure was carried out in accordance with the methods described in British Standard 2782 Part 3, 1976.[12] Elongation and breaking strength values for aged and unaged films were read from the trace.

Table I

Colour Measurements on Aged Packaging Materials for Rubber

Material	Colour Difference (Delta E)
Cryovac BDF 200	
Heat-aged	0.04
Light-aged	0.07
Polyethylene	
Heat-aged	0.11
Light-aged	1.17
PVDC	
Heat-aged	0.42
Light-aged	2.09

$$\text{Delta E} = [\,(\text{Delta } L^*)^2 + (\text{Delta } a^*)^2 + (\text{Delta } b^*)^2\,]^{1/2}$$

where L^* = lightness
a^* = redness/greenness
b^* = yellowness/blueness

PVDC lost approximately 27% of its elongation after light- and heat-ageing (Table II) compared with a loss of almost 5% by Cryovac BDF 200 and 7% by polyethylene. Breaking stress did not alter greatly on ageing. From these results it was concluded that either

Table II

Mean Elongation at Yield for Rubber Packaging Materials

	Elongation (mm)		
	Cryovac BDF 200	PVDC	Polyethylene
Unaged	44.9	37.0	27.8
Heat-aged	44.7	25.8	26.2
Light-aged	44.6	27.0	25.6

Cryovac BDF 200 or polyethylene films would be suitable for the field trial.

Selection of Sealing System for Oxygen Impermeable Films

In order to evaluate the most effective method for creating an oxygen-depleted environment in which to store a museum object, a series of encasing methods were examined. Enclosures were prepared using polyethylene self-sealing bags, poly(vinylidene chloride) film, glass Kilner jars and Cryovac BDF 200 film. Bags were prepared from PVDC and Cryovac BDF 200 films by heat-sealing the edges using a domestic heat-sealing device. Double seams with reinforcement seams at each corner were found to produce the strongest and most leak-resistant bags. A sachet of Ageless Z-200 was placed in the bag or Kilner jar and, in the case of double bags, a sachet was added between each layer.

The effectiveness of the containers to maintain an oxygen-depleted atmosphere was determined by measuring the time required for Ageless Eye, the oxygen indicator supplied with Ageless, to change from pale pink (less than 0.1% oxygen) to dark blue (greater than 0.5% oxygen). Ageless Eye is reusable. On moving from an oxygen-rich to an oxygen-free atmosphere it regains its pale pink colouration after two to three hours at 25°C. Bags and Kilner jars were either left unpurged (controls), flushed with oxygen-free nitrogen or vacuum packed. Bags were flushed or evacuated via a glass Pasteur pipette, which was inserted before the bag was heat- or self-sealed, and attached via silicon tubing to a nitrogen cylinder or

vacuum pump. The pipette was withdrawn after flushing or evacuation, and the last side of the bag was sealed. The time taken to heat-seal the films was critical. If the heat sealer was left in contact with Cryovac BDF 200 for more than two seconds, the film shrank, causing pinholes and tearing of the film. Kilner jars were evacuated or flushed by placing the jar in a self-seal polyethylene bag and using the pipette technique. The jar was closed while inside the bag. Ageless was put in some containers.

The time required for sufficient oxygen to penetrate the container (or inner bag where double bags were used) to change the colour of the Ageless Eye from pale pink to dark blue was recorded using a stopwatch (Table III).

The results suggested that all containers' systems maintained their low oxygen environment for longer when they were purged with nitrogen than if they were evacuated or left unpurged. Flushing with nitrogen prolonged the life of Ageless and did not produce the closely fitting packaging associated with using a vacuum, which can cause physical damage to a friable object.

Enclosing the inner, object-containing bag in a similar outer bag, also containing one sachet of Ageless, was found to prolong the useful lifetime of the oxygen absorber, reducing the rate of oxygen diffusion into the microclimate in which the object was to be stored. Cryovac BDF 200 proved to be the most effective barrier film from which to prepare bags. It proved most resistant to oxygen diffusion under all testing conditions. The Ageless contained within double Cryovac BDF 200 bags, which had been flushed with nitrogen, was still active after six months, the length of this trial. Kilner jars also provided an excellent barrier to oxygen, but would not be practical for large objects.

Many of the ethnographic objects in the collection contain wood, textile or metal components in addition to rubber. These secondary components are more sensitive to extreme changes in relative humidity than rubber, and may undergo dimensional changes resulting in the formation of undesirable stresses on the object, or in the acceleration of corrosion in the case of metals.

Table III
Efficiency of Enclosure Systems for Preventive Storage of Rubber

Barrier Material	Single (S) or Double (D) Layer	Atmosphere	Time for Ageless Eye to Detect Oxygen (Hours)
Polystyrene Box		Air	0.04
Cryovac BDF 200	S	Air	24.61
	D	Air	72.05
	S	Normal	144.16
	D	Normal	4336+
	S	Vacuum	96.02
	D	Vacuum	4336+
Polyethylene	S	Air	0.14
	D	Air	48.32
	S	Normal	96.77
	D	Normal	100.10
	S	Vacuum	24.03
	D	Vacuum	24.18
PVDC	S	Air	6.19
	D	Air	48.45
	S	Normal	24.52
	D	Normal	120.37
	S	Vacuum	53.21
	D	Vacuum	25.37
Kilner Jar		Air	4336+
		Normal	4336+

Since the Ethnography store is humidity controlled to 55% ± 5%, under normal circumstances there should be little cause for concern. However, if the enclosed objects were to be exposed to a dramatic rise in temperature then it would be possible for condensation to form inside the bags.

In order to assess the effects of a rapid rise in temperature on the relative humidity inside a bag containing an oxygen-depleted atmosphere, bags prepared from single layers of Cryovac BDF 200 and PVDC and self-seal polyethylene bags were examined. A sachet of Ageless Z-200 and a dial hygrometer were placed in the bags prior to sealing in the laboratory (20°C ± 2°C and 60% RH ± 5% RH). The prepared bags were placed in an oven at 40°C ± 1°C for one hour. At the end of this period the bags were returned to the laboratory environment, the dial hygrometer readings recorded, and the time for the relative humidity to equilibrate with the surroundings noted.

The results suggested (Table IV) that relative humidity increased in all the bags, and took longest to return to laboratory conditions in the PVDC enclosure, and least time to equilibrate in the polyethylene bag. This may be attributed to the very low moisture vapour transmission value of PVDC (1.5 g m^{-2} to 5.0 g m^{-2} per 24 h, for 25 μm films at 90% RH and 38°C) compared with that for polyethylene (15 g m^{-2} to 20 g m^{-2} per 24 h), which controls the rate of escape of excess moisture.[13] These results indicate that if large variations in relative humidity

Table IV
Effect of Exposing Packaging Bags to Sudden Temperature Increases

| | Packaging Material | | |
	Cryovac	Polyethylene	PVDC
RH after one hour at 40°C (1%)	77	70	80
Time for RH to return to 60% ±5% (minutes)	126	60	135

are of concern, buffering agents, such as silica gel, could be incorporated into the bagging system. However, it should be remembered that some moisture is required to activate Ageless to absorb oxygen.

Relating Accelerated Ageing to Natural Ageing

In order to quantify the effectiveness of enclosing rubber objects some further laboratory trials were made. Thick (1 cm wide) rubber bands were washed in the non-ionic surfactant Synperonic 'N' in order to remove any separating agents, such as talc. They were then stretched on a polystyrene former so that their length increased by 50%.

The rubber bands, still stretched on the formers, were sealed in double bags made from Cryovac BDF 200. One sachet of Ageless and an Ageless Eye was placed in each bag, and bags were either flushed with nitrogen or left unpurged. The enclosed rubber bands were light-aged until the first signs of deterioration were evident. Samples of rubber bands stretched in a similar manner but left unbagged were also light-aged in order to compare the rates of degradation between bagging and open storage. Stretched samples were also naturally aged.

The first signs of deterioration occurred after 336 hours. After this period of exposure, all bands were examined by Scanning Electron Microscopy (SEM) and their breaking stress determined using tensile testing. The procedure detailed in British Standard 903 Part A2 1989 was followed.

Light-Aged Rubber Band (mag. x 2000)

Light-Aged Rubber Band Plus Ageless (mag. x 2000)

Figure 2 Scanning electron micrograph of ozone cracking on a rubber band after light-ageing (normal atmosphere) compared to one aged in an oxygen-depleted atmosphere, created with Ageless.

SEM examination (Figure 2) showed severe ozone cracking to be present on the surface of the rubber band that had been light-aged under open conditions, compared with the unchanged surfaces of a band that had been light-aged in an oxygen-depleted atmosphere. The results of breaking stress measurements suggested that enclosing the rubber bands in an oxygen-depleted atmosphere significantly reduced the loss in strength caused by ozone attack. Optimum protection was afforded by flushing the Cryovac BDF 200 bags with nitrogen prior to sealing. The naturally aged band showed the first signs of degradation after 2,208 hours (92 days) compared with 130 hours for an openly light-aged band. Rubber bands light-aged in oxygen-depleted atmospheres have not shown visible signs of deterioration to date, six months into the trial.

Preventive Storage of Ethnographic Objects in an Oxygen-Depleted Atmosphere

In the stores, The British Museum Ethnographic Collections are arranged by geographic origin rather than on the basis of materials. Hence the rubber objects are to be found in numerous locations. Objects are kept in wooden drawers or boxes on a racking system and are only exposed to daylight when being studied or on display in the Museum. The store is humidity controlled (55% ± 5%).

The objects containing rubber were identified from the computerized catalogue of the collections. The conditions of the rubber artefacts were assessed. The earliest object was collected in 1855 and predates the discovery of vulcanization. The collections are still growing and consist mainly of toys, sandals and musical instruments. Those objects made from the sidewalls of motor car tyres, such as sandals, were in excellent condition, while those comprised of thin strips of inner tube stretched tightly around a wooden base, as in a child's catapult, showed signs of deterioration and of bloom. Objects that contained copper wire, for example, a cage for singing birds, were in a more advanced state of degradation. This may be attributed to the presence of the copper, which is known to catalyse attack by ozone.[14]

Twenty objects representative of the technology and types of rubber in the collections were selected for use in the pilot scheme. They ranged in types and levels of degradation. Half of the objects were selected for storage under oxygen-depleted conditions and half were stored in air so that comparisons of the rates and extents of degradation could be made. All objects were photographed using colour film and black-and-white film in order to record their condition prior to the trial. Pencil drawings of all objects were made in order to highlight details of deterioration, and micrographs were taken of the areas of concern using a reflectance microscope.

Laboratory trials showed Cryovac BDF 200 to be the most stable and efficient barrier film to oxygen, and heat-sealing to be the most convenient method of sealing the bags made from the film. The volumes of the objects to be stored in oxygen-depleted conditions were estimated in order to calculate the number of sachets of Ageless Z required in each case. Very small and fragile objects were placed in polystyrene boxes for mechanical protection prior to enclosing in Cryovac BDF 200 bags. Since polystyrene is highly permeable to oxygen, this would not reduce the exposure of the object to oxygen. Bags were prepared as described earlier, but using a larger commercial heat sealer in place of the small domestic equipment used for the laboratory trials.

Ten of the objects were enclosed in double bags, each of which contained the appropriate number of Ageless Z sachets and an Ageless Eye indicator. Each bag was flushed with oxygen-free nitrogen prior to heat-sealing. The concentration of oxygen was determined by the colour of the Ageless Eye. The remaining objects were enclosed in double bags containing air. All objects were returned to the store.

The bagged objects have now been put back in the Department of Ethnography store and they will be examined after three months using the optical microscope and photography. Examinations will be repeated every six months.

Conclusion

The technique of using oxygen-depleted microclimates to inhibit long-term degradation mechanisms for museum objects is new to The British Museum. It is a passive method of conservation that neither precludes the use of other treatments nor requires special materials. For these reasons the curatorial staff have been amenable to its use. Laboratory trials have shown it to be a relatively straightforward and inexpensive method of prolonging the useful life of rubber bands. Rubber objects selected from the Ethnographic Collections have recently been heat-sealed in bags made from Cryovac BDF 200 film, which were flushed with nitrogen in order to prolong the life of the oxygen absorber, Ageless. Their physical condition will be monitored regularly by optical microscopy and photography in order to assess the effectiveness of this technique. The effect of enclosing these objects and thus preventing accessibility for study and handling, particularly when they are required in the departmental student room, will also be evaluated. If successful, the use of oxygen-depleted microclimates may be applied to a wide range of materials stored in museums.

Acknowledgement

The authors thank Paul Aspill of W.R. Grace Ltd., for kindly providing samples of Ageless, Ageless Eye and Cryovac BDF 200. They appreciate the time taken by John Loadman and the staff at the Tun Abdul Razak Laboratory to discuss the analysis, deterioration of rubber, and developments in the rubber industry. They also thank their colleagues, Dr. John Mack, Keeper of the Department of Ethnography for permission to carry out the trial, John Osborn for assistance with locating the objects, Susan Bradley and Dr. Vincent Daniels for discussing the work and the paper, and Andrew Oddy, Keeper of Conservation, for permission to publish the paper.

Suppliers

Ageless, Ageless Eye and Cryovac BDF 200

W.R. Grace Ltd.
Northdale House
North Circular Road   Tel: 081-965 0611
London NW10 7UH   Fax: 081-961 6480
United Kingdom

Poly(vinylidene chloride) Film (Safeway Non-PVC Cling Film)

Safeway (Head Office U.K.)
6 Millington Road
Hayes
Middlesex UB3 4AY
United Kingdom

Polyethylene Self-Seal Bags

Supreme Plastics Ltd.
Supreme House
Vale Road
Harringay
London N4 1QB   Tel: 081-802 4202
United Kingdom

Polystyrene Boxes

Stewart Plastics
Purley Way
Croydon CR9 4HS   Tel: 081-686 2231
United Kingdom

Résumé

L'essai pratique de l'Ageless pour la conservation du caoutchouc dans les collections de musée*

Le caoutchouc se dégrade lorsqu'il est exposé aux ultraviolets, à l'oxygène ou à l'ozone. Cette détérioration se traduit, suivant le milieu, soit par son craquellement et sa fragilisation, soit par son ramollissement et par une perte de propriétés mécaniques.

Au cours des deux dernières années, le British Museum a étudié diverses méthodes pour assurer la conservation du caoutchouc, qui reposent notamment sur l'emploi d'agents de consolidation, de plastifiants et de revêtements protecteurs. Les résultats de ces études n'ont toutefois pas été très encourageants, et on a donc choisi de poursuivre une stratégie davantage axée sur la conservation préventive. La principale contrainte venait du fait que les objets devaient être laissés à l'endroit même où ils étaient mis en réserve. Parmi les techniques qui ont été envisagées, la plus utile semble être celle qui se fonde sur la création d'un micro-environnement autour des objets grâce à de l'Ageless, un désoxygénant.

On a donc effectué les préparatifs en vue de mener, dans la réserve d'objets ethnographiques du musée, un essai pratique qui permettrait, d'une part, d'établir si l'entreposage des objets en caoutchouc dans un milieu sans oxygène contribue effectivement à ralentir de façon marquée le rythme de leur détérioration et, d'autre part, d'évaluer l'incidence d'une telle technique sur le fonctionnement de la réserve — en particulier, lorsque les objets doivent être utilisés dans la salle des étudiants du département.

Les objets et les sachets d'Ageless ont été déposés dans des boîtes en polystyrène transparent, puis scellés dans des sacs étanches faits d'une pellicule de polyoléfine. Pour cet essai, 50 objets de la collection ont été retenus. Après les avoir ainsi scellés, on a cherché à élaborer une technique qui permettrait de déceler leur dégradation. On a alors puisé à diverses méthodes, au nombre desquelles figuraient, parmi celles qui apparaissaient comme les plus prometteuses, l'examen à l'œil nu ou au microscope classique ou électronique à balayage — quoique cette dernière méthode exige le prélèvement d'échantillons, ce qui ne pourrait pratiquement pas se faire dans le cas d'objets de musée — et la spectrométrie infrarouge à transformée de Fourier (IRTF). Les observations faites lors d'expériences avec des échantillons de caoutchouc scellés suivant la méthode susmentionnée et exposés à une lampe donnant le spectre de la lumière visible, dans un dispositif de vérification de la résistance à la lumière, permettront d'établir la méthode qui convient le mieux pour un musée. Ces échantillons serviront en outre de groupe témoin lors de l'essai pratique, et des échantillons scellés avec de l'Ageless et non scellés avec ce produit seront placés dans la réserve.

L'étude des méthodes à utiliser pour sceller les objets et pour surveiller le déroulement de l'essai sera menée à terme, et l'on connaîtra les résultats des essais de vieillissement accéléré. Un rapport intérimaire sur le déroulement de l'essai sera présenté.

*Ageless est une marque déposée de la Mitsubishi Gas Chemical Company Inc.

References

1. Shashoua, Y., "Inhibitive Treatments for Rubber," *Newsletter of the ICOM Working Group on the Conservation of Modern Materials*, July 1991.

2. Shashoua, Y., "Evaluation of Adipate Plasticizers and a Protective Coating as Inhibitors for Natural Rubber," *The British Museum Internal Report*, No. VII33, February 1989.

3. Clavir, M., "An Initial Approach to the Stabilization of Rubber from Archaeological Sites and in Museum Collections," *Journal of the IIC-Canadian Group*, vol. 7, nos. 1 and 2, 1982, pp. 3-10.

4. Grattan, D.W., personal communication to Dr. V. Daniels, March, 1990.

5. *Ageless Oxygen Absorber: A New Age in Food Preservation* (Tokyo: Mitsubishi Gas Chemical Corporation, 1987).

6. Buist, J.M., *Ageing and Weathering of Rubber* (London: W. Heffer and Sons Ltd., 1955) p. 24.

7. Layer, R.W. and R.P. Lattimer, "Protection of Rubber Against Ozone," *Rubber Chemistry and Technology Rubber Reviews* No. 3, July-August 1990.

8. Lewis, P.M., "Protecting Natural Rubber Against Ozone Cracking," *NR Technology, Rubber Developments Supplement* Part 1, 1972, p. 2.

9. Nakamura, H. and J. Hoshiro, *Techniques for the Preservation of Food by Employment of an Oxygen Absorber Sanitation Control for Food Sterilizing Techniques* (Tokyo: Sanya Publishing Co., 1983).

10. Oddy, W.A., "An Unsuspected Danger in Display," *Museums Journal*, vol. 73, June 1973, pp. 27-28.

11. Billmeyer, F.W. and M. Saltzman, *Principles of Colour Technology* (New York: Wiley Interscience, 1966).

12. British Standard, *Tensile Strength, Elongation and Elastic Modulus of Plastics* British Standard 2782 Part 3, Methods 320A-F, 1976.

13. Bristow, J.H., *Plastics Films* (London: Longman Group Ltd., 1974).

14. Naunton, W.J.S., *The Applied Science of Rubber* (London: Edward Arnold Ltd., 1961) p. 103.

La mise au point d'un traitement cathodique de stabilisation de vestiges aéronautiques immergés en alliages d'aluminium

Christian Degrigny

Groupe Valectra
Direction des études et recherches
Électricité de France
Saint-Denis
France

Résumé

Afin d'éviter la dégradation à l'atmosphère de pièces en alliages d'aluminium provenant de vestiges aéronautiques immergés depuis une longue période en eau douce, un traitement de conservation a été mis au point. Il consiste en l'extraction d'ions dangereux pour le métal, sous polarisation cathodique.

Dans un premier temps, des tests de corrosion accélérée ont permis d'établir que, en l'absence de traitement, les alliages d'aluminium précorrodés subissent une dégradation rapide au cours de leur remise à l'air libre. Les ions chlorure, contenus dans les matériaux, sont responsables de l'accélération de la corrosion, qui est en outre activée par la présence de produits de corrosion instables.

L'extraction des ions chlorure est réalisée en solution tamponnée sous polarisation cathodique à potentiel imposé, mais des corrosions associées peuvent aussi se produire. On pourra ainsi noter, entre autres, l'existence d'une corrosion par piqûres, due aux ions chlorure extraits, ainsi qu'une corrosion cathodique.

Le domaine de piqûration a été défini à partir des valeurs caractéristiques des potentiels de piqûre et de l'aération du milieu.

Les mécanismes et la cinétique de la corrosion cathodique ont été étudiés en détail au moyen d'essais potentio-statiques menés avec une microcellule d'observation. En milieu tamponné, tout phénomène d'alcalinisation local au voisinage de la surface est impossible; la corrosion provient donc de la modification des propriétés de la couche passive d'alumine sous polarisation cathodique. Le rôle majeur des précipités intermétalliques dans l'initiation de la corrosion et leur évolution au cours des processus ont été mis en évidence.

On a pu ainsi déterminer, en solution d'ions citrate, un ensemble de conditions à respecter au cours du traitement pour éviter des corrosions indésirables (désaération et agitation de la solution, maintien d'un pH faiblement acide et du potentiel cathodique au-dessus de la zone de corrosion cathodique). La cinétique d'extraction des ions chlorure sous polarisation a alors été étudiée et les paramètres ont été optimisés afin d'accélérer le traitement. Un prétraitement complexant, assurant une meilleure efficacité d'extraction, a été également considéré.

L'application du procédé à des pièces réelles provenant d'épaves aéronautiques a donné des résultats reproductibles. Ainsi, l'extraction des ions chlorure sous polarisation cathodique est rapide et efficace. Des traitements adaptés, pour les cas où des alliages ferreux sont associés aux alliages d'aluminium, sont également proposés.

Introduction

Une quantité non négligeable d'épaves aéronautiques se trouvent immergées en eau de mer ou en eau douce. Or ces pièces immergées présentent parfois une valeur historique indéniable, et devraient donc être en partie ou totalement remontées si l'on veut qu'elles retrouvent la place qui leur revient dans la mémoire du public. Tel est effectivement le cas, par exemple, des hydravions de l'étang de Biscarrosse (dans les Landes, en France), qui sont les symboles d'une époque révolue de l'histoire de l'aéronautique.

Souvent métalliques, ces vestiges sont, pour la plupart, constitués d'alliages ferreux et d'alliages d'aluminium. Durant leur période d'immersion, des corrosions intenses par contact entre ces métaux se sont établies, aux dépens des alliages d'aluminium. Et puisque ce phénomène est évolutif, il remet en cause la conservation *in situ* et à long terme de ceux-ci, et donc des pièces qui en contiennent.

Des tentatives de nettoyage ont été menées afin de mettre un terme à ces corrosions irréversibles mais elles ont toutes révélé que, sans traitement ultérieur, les pièces en alliages d'aluminium continuent de se dégrader à l'atmosphère, habituellement dans les zones précorrodées[1].

Contacté à ce propos par le musée de l'Air du Bourget (Paris), le groupe Valectra d'Électricité de France, spécialisé dans les techniques électrolytiques de conservation-restauration, s'est chargé de proposer une procédure de traitement. La nocivité des espèces chlorurées présentes dans les alliages d'aluminium ayant été démontrée, Valectra a opté pour une déchloruration de ces alliages sous polarisation cathodique. Puisque certaines formes de corrosion associées à ce traitement pouvaient se produire au cours de l'opération, des conditions de protection ont été définies, et une optimisation des paramètres expérimentaux a permis d'assurer un traitement plus efficace[2].

La description des alliages et le choix du traitement

Toute intervention visant la conservation future d'un objet dégradé nécessite une étude qui, axée sur les causes de la corrosion initiale, permettra de mieux prévoir son évolution ultérieure, lorsque l'objet sera exposé à l'atmosphère.

Les alliages d'aluminium sont aussi variés par leur composition que par les formes de corrosion qu'ils présentent. Dans le secteur aéronautique, les alliages les plus courants sont sans doute ceux qui contiennent du cuivre comme principal élément d'addition. Leurs très bonnes propriétés mécaniques, connues dès les années 1912-1913, en ont fait les alliages idéaux pour les fuselages et les structures. Ils sont toutefois très sensibles aux différentes formes de corrosion, de sorte qu'ils sont recouverts d'un placage d'alliage plus résistant aux agressions extérieures. Au nombre des autres alliages habituels, figurent ceux qui contiennent, comme élément d'addition, du manganèse ou du magnésium, ou encore une combinaison de magnésium et de silicium; ces matériaux peuvent; du fait de leur meilleure résistance à la corrosion, être utilisés à diverses fins bien précises (voir le tableau I).

Après un séjour prolongé en milieu subaquatique, ces alliages présentent, au moment de leur sortie de l'eau, des états de surface plus ou moins différents. Ainsi, les alliages aluminium-cuivre auront subi des corrosions intergranulaires et par piqûres — celles-ci étant profondes et de type transgranulaire —, tandis que les alliages aluminium-manganèse et aluminium-magnésium-silicium n'auront été sensibles qu'à des formes de corrosion par piqûres de type hémisphérique.

La couche de corrosion est particulièrement complexe sur les alliages aluminium-cuivre. Elle est formée, en fait, d'une double couche : une couche adhérente, de faible épaisseur (0,2 μm), et une couche couvrante, sur laquelle s'étendent des produits de corrosion issus de l'action de l'environnement (voir la figure 1). On note ainsi la présence de sulfates à l'intérieur de cette dernière couche, composée essentiellement d'alumine hydratée $Al(OH)_3$. Cette couche de corrosion est de plus polluée, à l'extérieur, par du fer (à cause de la présence de pièces en acier à proximité) et par des ions chlorure mais surtout, dans le fond des piqûres, par du cuivre et, là également, par des ions chlorure. Quant aux autres alliages, on ne trouve, sur la surface métallique, que des pustules d'alumine hydratée recouvrant les piqûres qui se sont formées, au fond desquelles des

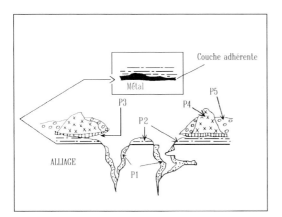

Figure 1 : La nature de la couche de corrosion présente à la surface d'un alliage aluminium-cuivre immergé depuis une longue période en milieu subaquatique.

P1 *Silicate de calcium et d'aluminium et Al(OH)$_3$ pollués (Cu, Cl)*
P2 *Al(OH)$_3$ pollué (S)*
P3 *Peinture*
P4 *Sulphate ferrique, silicates et Al(OH)$_3$ pollués (Fe, Cl)*
P5 *Concrétions amorphes*

ions chlorure peuvent encore être très actifs. Des tests de corrosion accélérée, en atmosphère naturelle à Biscarrosse, ont été menés avec des échantillons dégradés; ils visaient à obtenir des données sur la stabilité à l'atmosphère de ces états de corrosion à long terme. Ils ont tous montré que l'état de corrosion initial évolue plus ou moins vite à l'atmosphère, et que toute l'épaisseur peut, dans les cas extrêmes, être

touchée. Ce phénomène se développe, en fait, à partir des zones précorrodées, sous la couche d'altération et sutout dans le fond des piqûres, là où il y a une quantité importante d'ions chlorure. La présence de nombreux produits de corrosion — dans le cas d'un alliage aluminium-cuivre, par exemple — peut accentuer les processus.

Il est donc nécessaire d'appliquer un traitement de conservation aux alliages d'aluminium précorrodés. Pour extraire rapidement les ions chlorure insérés dans les matériaux, il est proposé d'avoir recours à la polarisation cathodique, mais on pourra aussi envisager des dissolutions partielles ou globales des produits de corrosion.

Les conditions du traitement

En se référant au diagramme d'équilibres potentiel-pH de l'aluminium en eau pure — et donc dans des conditions idéales — défini par Pourbaix[3], on constate que, si le pH se situe entre 4 et 9, la surface métallique est protégée (voir la figure 2). Or, lors du traitement cathodique, dans cette zone de pH, d'alliages d'aluminium dégradés et pollués par des ions chlorure, deux formes de corrosion peuvent apparaître, à savoir :

- la **corrosion par piqûres**, due aux ions chlorure extraits durant le traitement, qui peuvent se refixer en surface;

Tableau I

Les principales familles d'alliages trouvés dans les vestiges aéronautiques

Système	Série	Teneur de l'élément d'addition principal	Caractéristiques et utilisation
Al non allié	1XXX		faibles propriétés mécaniques : peu utilisés
Al-Cu	2XXX	Cu : 2 à 6 %	recouverts d'un placage d'Al 1XXX (fuselages)
Al-Mn	3XXX	Mn : 0,5 à 1,5 % Mn : 4 %	pour alliages corroyés pour alliages moulés
Al-Si	4XXX	Si : 3 à 22 %	pour alliages moulés (moteurs et appareils de bord)
Al-Mg	5XXX	Mg : 0,5 à 7 %	pour structures et fuselages
Al-Mg-Si	6XXX	Mg : 0,5 à 1,5 % Si : 0,5 à 1,5 %	pour structures et fuselages

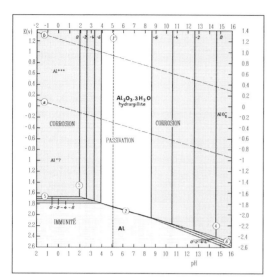

Figure 2 : Le diagramme d'équilibres potentiel-pH *de l'aluminium en eau pure à 25° C selon Pourbaix*[3].

• la **corrosion cathodique**, due à l'affaiblissement des propriétés isolantes du film d'oxyde superficiel sous polarisation cathodique.

On a donc cherché à délimiter la zone qui, dans le diagramme d'équilibres potentiel-pH précédent, permettrait d'assurer une protection réelle aux alliages durant le traitement.

La sensibilité des alliages d'aluminium à la **corrosion par piqûres** est définie, en utilisant

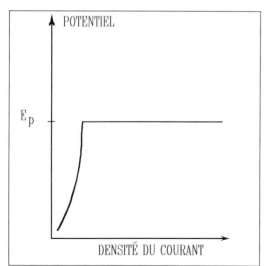

Figure 3 : La corrosion par piqûres : définition du *potentiel d'amorçage des piqûres.*

des échantillons non corrodés, à partir de deux paramètres : le potentiel d'amorçage des piqûres (E_p), caractéristique du processus d'initiation, et le potentiel de corrosion (E_{corr}), qui, par son évolution au cours de l'immersion, caractérise la phase de propagation. E_p est défini suivant les courbes densité de courant-potentiel obtenues à partir d'études potentiodynamiques (voir la figure 3). Sa valeur n'étant pas reproductible, on la détermine pour un ensemble d'échantillons, ce qui permet de définir un domaine de probabilité de piqûration (voir la figure 4), qui par ailleurs variera selon le pH (voir la figure 5).

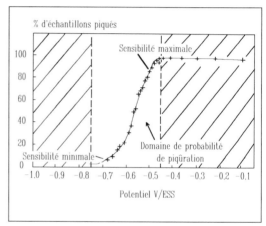

Figure 4 : La détermination du domaine de pro-*babilité de piqûration pour l'alliage 3003 en milieu tamponné de citrate de sodium : pH = 5,4; T = 10° C; vb = 10 mV/min; [NaCl] = 10^{-3}M.*

vb : vitesse de balayage

Le tracé de l'évolution de E_{corr} des alliages d'aluminium en fonction de la durée de leur immersion montre que, après un certain temps, cette valeur pénètre dans la zone où l'alliage devient sensible à la corrosion par piqûres (voir la figure 6). Selon l'alliage, cette corrosion se développera plus ou moins rapidement. Il a ainsi été démontré que, après deux à trois semaines en eau déminéralisée, une pièce précorrodée en alliage aluminium-cuivre se recouvre de pustules qui témoignent de la présence de nouveaux phénomènes de piqûration, tandis qu'il faut quelques mois pour que ce phénomène se produise dans le cas d'alliages sans cuivre qui sont placés en milieu désaéré.

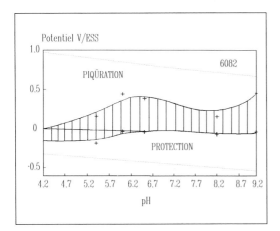

Figure 5 : L'influence du pH sur la sensibilité de l'alliage 6082 (Al-Mg-Si) à la corrosion par piqûres : T = 10° C; [NaCl] = 10^{-3}M.

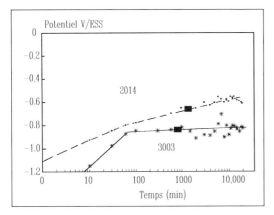

Figure 6 : L'évolution de E_{corr} des alliages d'aluminium en fonction de la durée de leur immersion en solution de citrate de sodium : pH = 5,4; T = 10° C; [NaCl] = 10^{-3}M.

■ : limite inférieure du domaine de piqûration.

Sous polarisation cathodique, les alliages d'aluminium peuvent être le siège d'une **corrosion cathodique** qui prendra, selon les cas, la forme de piqûres ou d'une corrosion généralisée. Afin d'éviter le risque majeur de corrosion due à des alcalinisations locales de la solution à proximité de la surface métallique, notre étude a été menée en milieu faiblement acide et tamponné de citrate de sodium. L'évolution de l'état de surface sur des échantillons non dégradés initialement peut alors être suivie

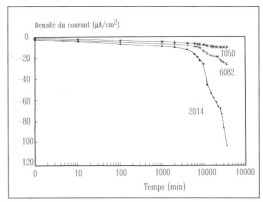

Figure 7 : La polarisation cathodique à -1,4 V/ESS (électrode au sulphate mercureux) pour différents alliages d'aluminium en solution tamponnée de citrate de sodium : pH = 5,4; T = 10° C; [NaCl] = 10^{-3}M.

à partir d'essais potentiostatiques (voir la figure 7). Deux étapes apparaissent, en fait, sur les courbes densité de courant-temps (appelées « courbes de polarisation ») obtenues. La première, caractérisée par une évolution lente des densités du courant, correspond à l'hydratation progressive du film d'oxyde initial à la suite de l'incorporation des ions H^+ du milieu. Cette incorporation des H^+ est d'ailleurs plus rapide au voisinage des inclusions qui, contenant des éléments nobles tels que le cuivre ou le fer, sont présentes dans les alliages d'aluminium. Le film ainsi modifié localement permet alors, dans une seconde étape, l'activation de la corrosion des inclusions : la matrice environnante est consommée et, au terme du processus, les inclusions sont éliminées (voir la figure 8). Ce phénomène étant plus ou moins important selon l'alliage, l'aération du milieu et le potentiel cathodique, l'augmentation correspondante des densités de courant sera, elle aussi, plus ou moins prononcée (voir la figure 7).

Après quelques jours de polarisation, la surface est habituellement recouverte de piqûres isolées ou en amas. La corrosion est particulièrement développée lorsque les bulles d'hydrogène, formées sur la surface métallique, ne sont pas évacuées, car des phénomènes d'alcalinisation locale apparaissent alors sous celles-ci. Une agitation conséquente de la solution permet de parer à cet inconvénient.

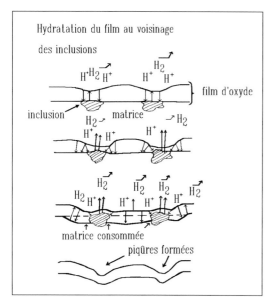

Figure 8 : Le mécanisme de la corrosion cathodique
des alliages d'aluminium en milieu tamponné.

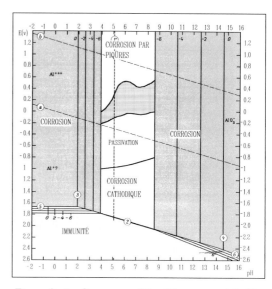

Figure 9 : Le diagramme d'équilibres potentiel-pH
expérimental intégrant la sensibilité des alliages
d'aluminium (l'alliage 6082, dans ce cas) à la
corrosion par piqûres et à la corrosion cathodique.

**Au terme de cette étude, le diagramme
d'équilibres potentiel-pH expérimental,
adapté à nos conditions opératoires, a pu
être tracé. La zone qui permettra d'assurer
la protection des alliages d'aluminium
durant le traitement de déchloruration a
dès lors été délimitée (voir la figure 9).**

L'optimisation de la déchloruration

Une polarisation cathodique contrôlée à potentiel imposé, en milieu faiblement acide et tamponné de citrate de sodium, agité et désaéré,
est proposée afin d'extraire rapidement les
ions chlorure présents dans les alliages d'aluminium. Avant cette étape, ces alliages sont
toujours immergés dans une solution complexante (et sans polarisation), afin de dis-
soudre les produits de corrosion gênants qui,
contenant des éléments tels que du cuivre ou
du fer, peuvent se réduire facilement sur les
surfaces métalliques. De plus, on extrait ainsi
les ions chlorure superficiels qui n'exigent
aucun traitement électrolytique pour
passer en solution.

La polarisation cathodique qui est appliquée
par la suite, grâce à un générateur de tension
dont la borne positive est reliée à une tôle

déployée en acier inoxydable, permet en
fait d'extraire les ions chlorure insérés profondément dans les matériaux. Le potentiel
cathodique et l'agitation peuvent être optimisés
pour augmenter l'efficacité de cette technique,
mais c'est la sensibilité des alliages à la corrosion cathodique qui délimitera les valeurs
réellement utilisables. La déchloruration sous
polarisation cathodique obéit à la loi d'extraction $\log(C_{Cl^-}) = at^{1/2}$, où a = constante, plus
rapide que les lois habituelles rencontrées
sans polarisation[4,5], ce qui confirme l'effet
bénéfique du potentiel qui est appliqué lors du
nettoyage (voir la figure 10).

Des exemples de traitement

Les objets à traiter sont, pour la plupart, composites, de sorte que la stabilisation des alliages
d'aluminium doit se situer dans un cadre de
restauration plus général. Les systèmes fer-
aluminium exigent ainsi deux phases sup-
plémentaires dans la procédure de traitement
qui est préconisée ci-dessus : un dégangage
des pièces ferreuses en solution basique et in-
hibitrice de corrosion pour les alliages d'aluminium (métasilicate de sodium 0,5 N), d'une
part, et, d'autre part, un nettoyage des surfaces
métalliques en eau courante mais sous

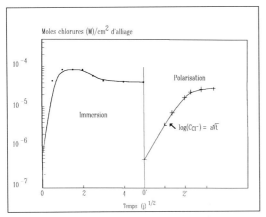

Figure 10 : La courbe de déchloruration
d'une plaque précorrodée en alliage aluminium-
cuivre 2014 sans polarisation, puis avec polarisation
en solution de citrate de sodium, l'anode étant en
acier inoxydable 316.

protection cathodique. Ces deux nouvelles
étapes se situent entre la phase initiale d'immersion en solution complexante et le traitement de
déchloruration de la pièce (entière) sous polarisation cathodique.

Conclusion

Centré initialement sur le problème de la stabilisation des alliages d'aluminium, le traitement
des vestiges aéronautiques conduit à considérer
la conservation-restauration de matériaux composites, dont les alliages d'aluminium ne forment qu'une partie. Des méthodes existent
aujourd'hui pour les systèmes fer-aluminium
ou cuivre-aluminium mais le cas des composites métal-matériau organique, que l'on trouve
autant sur les épaves les plus anciennes que sur
les plus récentes, reste posé.

Abstract

An Electrolytic Treatment for Stabilizing Submerged Aluminium Alloy Aircraft Fragments

Once retrieved, after long periods of immersion
under water, aluminium alloy artifacts (i.e., aircraft fragments) must be given conservation treatment. Our method consists of the extraction of
"threatening" ions using cathodic polarization.

It has been established using accelerated corrosion tests that without treatment, pre-corroded
aluminium alloys are subject to rapid corrosion
on exposure to the open atmosphere. The chlorides contained in the materials are responsible
for the acceleration of corrosion, but the presence of unstable corrosion products may also
activate the processes.

The extraction of chlorides is achieved in a buffered solution under cathodic polarization at constant potential, but different forms of corrosion
may occur. Those observed are pitting corrosion
caused by extracted chlorides and cathodic
corrosion.

The pitting field has been determined from the
characteristic pitting potentials and the degree of
aeration of the solution.

The mechanisms and the kinetics of the cathodic
corrosion have been studied in detail by means of
potentiostatic measurements. In a buffered solution, localized alkalinization close to the surface
is impossible, thus the corrosion arises from
the loss of the oxide layer's passive properties,
which, in turn, is caused by cathodic polarization.
The major role of the intermetallics in the initiation of corrosion has been determined and the
way in which they change with time during the
process has been revealed.

Conditions required for the treatment and which
ensure the protection of the alloys may be established in a de-aerated, stirred citrate solution
with a stable, slightly acid pH and with a
cathodic potential above that at which cathodic
corrosion takes place. The kinetics of extraction
of chloride ions under polarization has been studied and the conditions have been optimized to accelerate it. A pre-treatment employing chemical
complexation to make the extraction more effective is also described.

The application of this treatment to samples from
sub-aquatic aircraft remains has given reproducible results. It has been found that the extraction
of chloride ions under cathodic polarization is
rapid and effective. Where iron alloys are combined with aluminium alloys, specific treatments
have been proposed.

Références

1. Lacoudre, N., *Électricité et Archéologie*,
Paris, Admitech-Électricité de France,
1991 (ISBN 2-7240-0015-3).

2. Degrigny, C., Thèse de doctorat, Université de Paris-VI, novembre 1990.

3. Tiré de l'*Atlas of Electrochemical Equilibrium in Aqueous Solutions*, M. Pourbaix, traduit par J. A. Franklin, National Association of Corrosion Engineers, 1974, avec la permission de NACE.

4. North, N. A., et C. Pearson, « Washing Methods for Chloride Ion Removal from Marine Iron Artifacts », *Studies in Conservation*, vol. 23 (1978), p. 174-176.

5. MacLeod, I. D., « Corrosion of Corroded Copper Alloys: A comparison of new and traditional methods for removing chloride ions », *Studies in Conservation*, vol. 32 (1987), p. 25-40.

The Discoloration of Acrylic Dispersion Media

James Hamm, Ben Gavett, Mark Golden,
Jim Hayes, Charles Kelly, John Messinger,
Margaret Contompasis and Bruce Suffield

Art Conservation Department
Buffalo State College
Buffalo, N.Y.
U.S.A.

Abstract

An uncharacteristic yellow/brown discoloration[1]
in the background of a color-field painting (1970)
by Robert Goodnough initiated the present investi-
gation of acrylic dispersion media. The owner re-
calls that the yellowing had become objectionable
as early as the mid 1970s, suggesting that the
problem had occurred fairly early in the life of
the painting. During recent telephone conversa-
tions, the artist indicated that, in this period, he
typically would coat his cotton duck canvas over-
all with Liquitex matte medium before applying
any paint.

At present, the color of the Liquitex matte me-
dium closely resembles deposits from cigarette
smoke. Initial tests have shown that although
cigarette smoke residue may have contributed
somewhat to the appearance of the painting, this
is not the major cause for the yellow/brown
discoloration.

Evidence obtained from mock-ups created to du-
plicate discoloration caused by natural aging is
discussed. Remarkably, this discoloration occurs
over a relatively brief period of time under ordi-
nary environmental conditions of temperature,
relative humidity, and light. The discoloration
can occur in any brand of acrylic media or gel,
but is most noticeable in the unpigmented gels,
matte, and gloss media. It is the result of a detri-
mental interaction between the support and
the media.

Heat and ultraviolet induced aging of mock-ups
were also separately pursued. Further testing has
shown that the changes obtained with these meth-
ods are not as significant to the study of the Good-
nough painting as those obtained by natural
aging under ordinary environmental conditions.

Introduction

Since the early 1930s, various new synthetic
resins have been employed by artists for reasons of increased durability, rapid drying, ease
of handling, new application techniques, or to
achieve different effects. Since its introduction
around 1953, acrylic emulsion paint[2], as it has
been popularly described, has gradually become accepted as a viable painting medium
by professional artists. In relatively few years,
manufacturers have introduced a wide variety
of products for use with acrylic paints, such as
clear gels of varying viscosity, matte and gloss
media, modeling pastes, drying rate retarders,
and varnishes. The gels and media are often
used independently of the paint for textural
effects, coatings, collage adhesives, or as
transparent gel colors, slightly tinted with
acrylic paints.

Some artists have used these clear drying,
acrylic dispersion media as coatings or size
layers on bare canvas, over which a painting
is then executed. An example of the use of
Liquitex matte medium as a coating or sizing
on bare canvas, and the resultant discoloration

that occurred, can be seen in a Robert Good-nough painting done in 1970, titled *Development MC* (Figure 1). In 1990, during telephone conversations, the artist indicated that he had sized the entire canvas with Liquitex matte medium before applying the paint. The original and current owner noticed that the yellowing had become objectionable by the early- to mid-1970s. By comparing this painting with other paintings and serigraphs done by the artist at about the same time, but without the matte medium sizing, we can easily imagine how this painting once looked originally.

Figure 1 Development MC, *a color-field painting by Robert Goodnough (1970), measuring 61 cm x 122 cm (24 in. x 48 in.), from the collection of Mr. and Mrs. Charles M. Liddle the Third.*

It shouldn't be too surprising that changes in color might have occurred, since the composition of acrylic dispersion media is quite complex, and some of the individual components may not age well on their own. Besides the acrylic resin itself, we may find residual (unpolymerized) monomer, surface active agent (emulsifier), protective colloid (thickener), water-soluble initiator, plasticizer, pH buffer, anti-foaming agent, coalescing agent (film former), preservative, drying retarder, freeze-thaw stabilizer, ultraviolet (UV) inhibitor, optical brightener, matting agent, and water.

Suggestions that the raw acrylic dispersions may be susceptible to yellowing or discoloration, especially during thermal aging tests, have been made by a few authors. However, as discussed by Howells, Burnstock, Hedley, and Hackney thermal aging tests cannot be related to the aging produced naturally over time, unlike those changes induced by light aging.[3] Thermal aging tests (at temperatures of 59°C

and 83°C) may be useful indicators of relative stability, when compared with other samples experiencing the same conditions, but evidence of discoloration produced at elevated temperatures does not imply that the same discoloration can ever occur at normal temperatures.

Presumably, the Goodnough painting has not experienced thermal aging tests. The question then is: why has it discolored and, furthermore, why in such a relatively brief time? Could it be contaminated medium, tobacco smoke (or other atmospheric pollutants), or an apparent yellowing tendency of the medium itself? Is this problem localized to paintings by this particular artist or medium, or is it broader, encompassing other artists or other acrylic media?

Background

The laboratory work at Buffalo State College involved testing Liquitex acrylic matte and gloss media under harsh environmental conditions with the hope of duplicating the appearance of the discolored Goodnough painting. Contompasis, and later Suffield, created canvas mock-ups, using washed and unwashed cotton and linen, coated with the Liquitex media. Testing occurred under conditions of 90°C and 50% RH for a period of seven days using the *Blue M Humid Flow Temperature and Relative Humidity Cabinet*. A control support of glass was also used for the media tests.

The testing showed that the gloss medium discolored slightly more when applied to cotton as compared to linen, but overall less than the matte medium applied to either support. Some discoloration occurred in the unaged matte medium applied to linen. Generally, the matte acrylic medium discolored the most, even when the substrate was glass.

With respect to the latter finding where glass is the substrate, the testing conditions were not the same as those described in the Howells et al. article, which may explain why an apparently greater degree of discoloration was obtained by them. Howells et al. ran tests for 50 days with presumably no RH control, as none was mentioned, while Contompasis and Suffield ran tests for seven days at 50% RH.

In 1989, the Research Laboratory at Golden Artist Colors, Inc. tested several raw acrylic dispersions and several brands of acrylic gel media (from Aquatec, Golden, Hunt, Lascaux, and Liquitex) in a QUV Weathering Tester. The test exposed the materials to 400 intermittent hours of UVA exposure at ambient humidity and temperatures of 30°C to 35°C. The raw dispersion samples were prepared by pouring them into plastic trays, and the gels by applying 2.5 mm (100 mil) wet thicknesses over gessoed canvases. Major discoloration was observed and attributed primarily to the UV exposure. Indeed, a medium formulated with UV inhibitors, tested under similar conditions but drawn-down[4] on an alternative support (posterboard), resulted in the elimination of most of the discoloration relative to the control. However, further tests with UV-inhibited formulations revealed they were capable of discoloring just as dramatically under a few weeks of *ambient* conditions, when applied to canvas, as they had in the initial test under accelerated conditions. The conclusion: something other than UV radiation and heat was causing the discoloration.

The first clear indication of a problem possibly originating with the supports came from one of these test panels where a small section on the edge had pulled away from the canvas before complete drying had occurred. This section remained clear while the rest of the test strip discolored. If the discoloration problem resided solely in the medium, then why did this small section remain clear? If the problem originates with the support, then why did the rest of the test strip discolor, irrespective of whether it was over the canvas or the gesso?

This "accident," combined with the previous observations, raised some important questions:

- How effective is acrylic gesso as a barrier?

- What effect would washing the support have?

- How do different types of supports compare?

- How do different brands of acrylic media compare?

- Does thickness of application affect the degree of discoloration?

- Are tinted gels, used as glazes, affected by discoloration? What effect does pigmentation of the gel have on the degree of discoloration?

With these questions in mind, a series of tests was designed in order to isolate pertinent factors.

Experimental

The mock-up materials and conditions created in the following experiments closely parallel those normally used by artists. We avoided using enhanced conditions of artificial aging in order to restrict the study to those phenomena that would occur under normal environmental conditions.

Effectiveness of Acrylic Gesso as a Barrier between Support and Media

The test was designed to show whether or not the acrylic gesso would provide a barrier to any discoloration derived from the canvas, and also whether or not some discoloration could be expected to occur in the gel regardless of the nature of the barrier layer.

Heavy linen canvas was stretched over a 30.5 cm x 45.7 cm (12 in. x 18 in.) wooden stretcher and stapled in place. The surface was divided into four equal areas and treated in the following manner: the first area was brush coated with two layers of acrylic gesso, the second with five layers of the same gesso, the third area was protected by a 25.4 μm (1 mil) mylar barrier, and the fourth was left uncoated. A 3.81 mm (150 mil)-thick coating of Golden Regular acrylic gel was applied across all four areas with a 10.2 cm (4 in.) Gardner/Neotec adjustable film casting knife. The coated canvas was stored under indoor ambient conditions and evaluated after two weeks.

Effect of Pre-washing the Support

This test was designed to determine to what extent, if any, washing fabric supports would subsequently reduce discoloration in gels.

Pieces of heavy linen, #12 cotton, and #10 cotton were cut in half. One piece of each was machine washed using a household washing machine on normal cycle (warm-water wash, cold-water rinse) without detergents. After air drying, the washed and unwashed samples were stretched on individual wooden stretchers 15.2 cm x 15.2 cm (6 in. x 6 in.) and coated with gesso according to the following procedure: each support was coated with three 0.254 mm (10 mil) layers of Golden Acrylic Gesso, applied with a 10.2 cm (4 in.) Gardner applicator. During the application only, the fabrics were supported from beneath with a block providing a firm, flat base. This ensured that all applied coatings would be of uniform thickness.

We continued to use acrylic gesso as the priming layer of choice for consistent spectrophotometric readings of color changes, realizing that it provided very little impediment to the movement of discolored material.

After allowing 10 days for the final gesso coat to dry, Golden Regular Gel was then applied to each piece at a thickness of 3.81 mm (150 mil), (Figures 2a and 2b). The gel was allowed to dry for five days before testing began, sufficient time to allow it to become clear. All prepared pieces were tested under indoor ambient conditions for 90 days.

Spectrophotometric measurements were taken at frequent intervals and recorded using

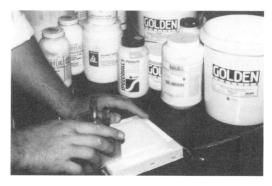

Figure 2b Application of acrylic gel using the Gardner/Neotec film casting knife.

a Pacific Scientific model TCM 8800 spectrophotometer configured with a 10 degree observation angle under D6500 illumination, using the CIELab color scale (Figure 3). Color differences were obtained by comparing the measurements of the test samples with measurements taken from identically prepared polyester supported samples of the same age. Color differences were calculated using the CIELab color difference equation.[5] Ongoing measurements were periodically recorded and the calculations plotted against time.

Figure 3 Pacific Scientific model TCM 8800 spectrophotometer.

Comparisons were made with a polyester supported gel because the polyester had previously proven to have minimal effect on the coloration of the gels over time. This allowed color differences resulting from aging of the gel alone to be separated from those resulting from the support. The color difference of the gel over the polyester support was calculated from the initial measurements taken after the gel had

Figure 2a A 10.2 cm (4 in.) Gardner/Neotec adjustable film casting knife.

dried sufficiently to become clear, an average period of five days.

Comparison of Manufacturers' Acrylic Dispersion Gels over Different Supports

Individual wooden stretchers, measuring 15.2 cm x 15.2 cm (6 in. x 6 in.), were assembled and covered with supports that are marketed for artists' use: woven polyester 0.475 kg/m^2 (14 oz./yd^2), heavy linen 0.364 kg/m^2 (10.75 oz./yd^2), and #10 cotton. Untempered Masonite panels measuring 15.24 m x 15.24 cm x 0.635 cm (6 in. x 6 in. x 1/4 in.) were also prepared. All materials were selected from single pieces to minimize variability. Each support was coated with three 0.25 mm (10 mil) layers of Golden Acrylic Gesso according to the procedure described previously.

After allowing 10 days for the final gesso coat to dry, each type of support received a 3.81 mm (150 mil) wet film application of each of six different commercially available acrylic gels, yielding a total of 24 test pieces. The gels were allowed to dry for five days before measurements began. The overall test period lasted for 90 days under indoor ambient conditions, as before (Figures 4 to 6). The gels included in this discussion are: Golden Regular, Grumbacher, Lascaux, Liquitex, Speedball, and Utrecht.

Figure 4 Some of the test materials on display.

Spectrophotometric measurements were taken at frequent intervals and recorded as before. For the purpose of making the calculations, gels over the cotton, linen, and Masonite samples were compared to the same gels over polyester of the exact same age, as described previously.

Figure 5 Eight brands of acrylic gel on an acrylic gesso coated cotton support showing various discoloration at 56 days.

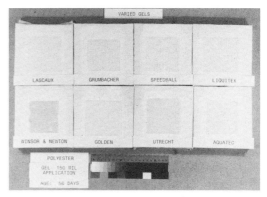

Figure 6 Eight brands of acrylic gel on an acrylic gesso coated polyester support showing minor discoloration at 56 days.

Thickness Variations

To determine the amount of discoloration occurring in a gel due to its thickness of application, a test was conducted by preparing individual 15.24 cm x 30.48 cm (6 in. x 12 in.) supports of Masonite and #10 cotton. The supports were prepared with the same techniques employed earlier. A Gardner/Neotec adjustable film casting knife was then used to apply gel in a stepped down application ranging from 3.81 mm to 0.635 mm (150 mil to 25 mil) wet film thicknesses, in 0.635 mm (25 mil) increments. CIELab measurements and color differences were periodically recorded.

Effect of Gel Pigmentation on Degree of Discoloration

This test was designed to determine the effects of discoloration associated with different supports upon pigmented gels. Five different supports were used: polyester, heavy linen, #10 cotton, Masonite 0.635 cm (1/4 in.) untempered, and lauan plywood 0.635 cm (1/4 in.). All supports were prepared following the conventions described above.

Golden Regular Gel, tinted in the following ratios with Golden Heavy Body Ultramarine Blue Acrylic Artist Paint, was applied in 3.8 mm (150 mil) applications to each type of support in the following ratios: 500:1, 100:1, 10:1, and 0:1 (Gel:Paint). CIELab measurements and color differences were recorded periodically through the 90-day test period. Color differences were calculated by comparing the polyester to the other supports at points of identical ages.

Results

Effectiveness of Acrylic Gesso as a Barrier between Support and Media

It is clear that discoloration did not develop in the section of acrylic gel applied over the mylar barrier, thus indicating that within the limits of this experiment, the gel does not have a tendency to rapidly discolor when separated from the canvas (Figure 7).

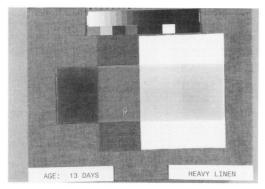

Figure 7 Linen support brush-coated in two areas with two layers and five layers of acrylic gesso, the third area protected by a 25.4 μm (1 mil) mylar barrier, and the fourth left uncoated.

In the other three areas, discoloration has occurred whether the acrylic gel is over two, five, or no layers of acrylic gesso. Consequently, the acrylic gesso here is generally ineffective at providing a barrier to discoloration. Other tests

using linen, Masonite, and other brands of acrylic gesso have given similar results. Not all gessos behave the same; however, all allow at least some discoloration to pass through from the support.

Effect of Pre-washing the Support

Washing the fabric supports was clearly effective at reducing the extent of discoloration, as the curves indicate (Figure 8). Discoloration of the gels over the two cotton supports (#12 and #10 weights) was reduced from 18.9 and 12.9 units to 0.76 and 0.9 units respectively at 84 days aging.

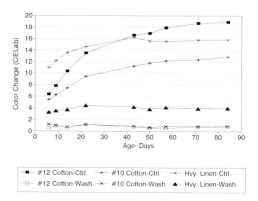

Figure 8 Relative color change of Golden Regular Acrylic Gel applied over acrylic gesso on three washed and three unwashed cotton and linen canvas supports.

Washing the linen also reduced the amount of available discoloring agent, but not to the same extent as for the two cotton fabrics. Apparently, these materials from linen are not as easily removed by a single-water wash. It may be that they are more readily released with the application of emulsifiers, solvents, or one of the other numerous additives found in acrylic dispersions.

Comparison of Manufacturers' Acrylic Dispersion Gels over Different Supports

The four graphs in Figures 9 to 12, which show the performance of all the acrylic gels over each of the four supports, reveal that discoloration depends more on the support used than on the brand of gel selected. Polyester performed the best, with discoloration at 80 days ranging between 0.45 and 2.1 units. It was not determined if this discoloration was related to the

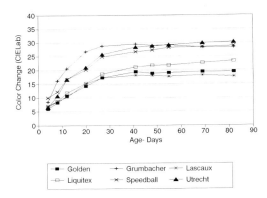

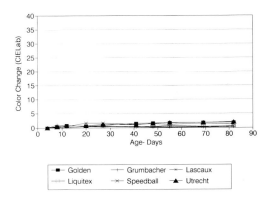

Figure 9 Discoloration of various acrylic gels over #10 cotton.

Figure 12 Discoloration of various acrylic gels over polyester.

polyester, or if it was inherent in the gels themselves. The other supports in the test resulted in much more discoloration: Masonite 23.7 to 33.5 units, heavy linen 16.2 to 27.5 units, and #10 cotton 17.7 to 30.2 units.

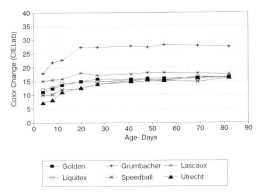

Figure 10 Discoloration of various acrylic gels over heavy linen.

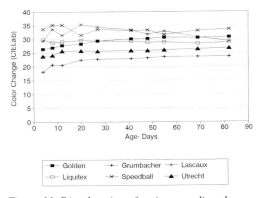

Figure 11 Discoloration of various acrylic gels over Masonite.

The shape of the curves, as they reflect the rate of change, appear consistent for each support, regardless of the gel used. Over Masonite, at least 75% of the discoloration occurred within the first four days, over heavy linen, within 20 days, and over cotton, within 27 days.

While the extent of discoloration may vary significantly among different gels over the same support, the rank of the gels, in terms of most to least discoloration, varied between supports. For example, over Masonite at 82 days of age, Speedball exhibited the most discoloration, followed by Golden, Lascaux, Liquitex, Utrecht, and Grumbacher. However, Grumbacher discolored the most (27.47 units) when the gels were applied over heavy linen, with the other gels tightly grouped between 16.2 and 17.5 units.

The graphs in Figures 13 to 18 group the data by gel manufacturer, showing the relative impact of each of the supports on any one gel. These graphs also illustrate an interesting variation in the rankings of the extent of discoloration from gel to gel. With four of the six gels, the Masonite support showed the most discoloration, while cotton showed the most in the other two gels.

Thickness Variations
Figures 19 and 20 show that increasing the thickness of the gel does increase the discoloration.

Appearances suggested that perhaps the thicker areas of gel discolored even more than the thinner areas, beyond simply a proportional

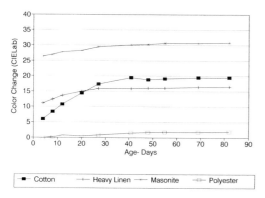

Figure 13 *Effects of support on discoloration: Golden Regular Gel.*

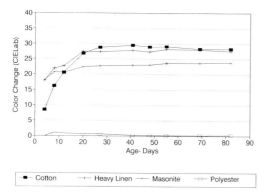

Figure 14 *Effects of support on discoloration: Grumbacher Gel.*

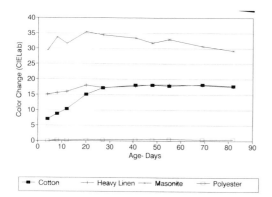

Figure 15 *Effects of support on discoloration: Lascaux Gel.*

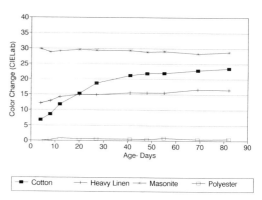

Figure 16 *Effects of support on discoloration: Liquitex Gel.*

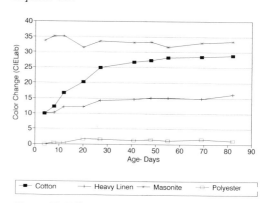

Figure 17 *Effects of support on discoloration: Speedball Gel.*

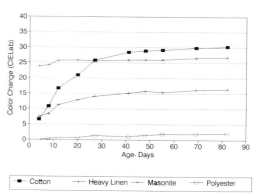

Figure 18 *Effects of support on discoloration: Utrecht Gel.*

increase. However, comparing gel thicknesses of 0.625 mm and 2.54 mm (25 mil and 100 mil) at day eight, the CIELab units are respectively 1.2 and 9.7, a difference of approximately 8 times, while at day eighty-two the units are respectively 2.1 and 18.0, a difference of

approximately 8.5 times. Since the discoloration remains closely proportional between thicknesses at widely different moments in time, then the extent of discoloration is simply proportional to the thickness of application only.

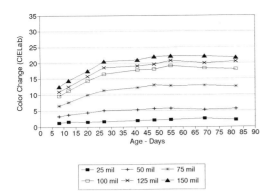

Figure 19 Discoloration related to gel thickness over #10 cotton.

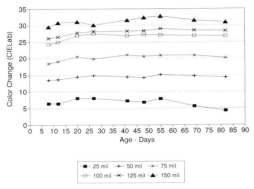

Figure 20 Discoloration related to gel thickness over Masonite.

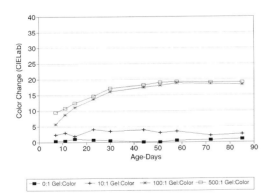

Figure 21 Discoloration of colored glazes Ultramarine Blue Acrylic Paint: Golden Regular Gel mixed in various ratios and applied to acrylic gesso primed cotton.

Effect of Gel Pigmentation on the Degree of Discoloration

Figures 21 to 24 indicate that measurable, hence visible, discoloration generally increases as the concentration of pigment decreases.

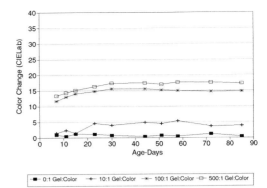

Figure 22 Discoloration of colored glazes Ultramarine Blue Acrylic Paint: Golden Regular Gel mixed in various ratios and applied to acrylic gesso primed heavy linen.

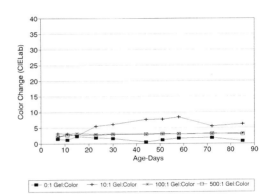

Figure 23 Discoloration of colored glazes Ultramarine Blue Acrylic Paint: Golden Regular Gel mixed in various ratios and applied to acrylic gesso primed lauan plywood.

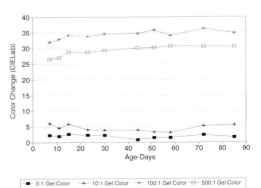

Figure 24 Discoloration of colored glazes Ultramarine Blue Acrylic Paint: Golden Regular Gel mixed in various ratios applied to acrylic gesso primed Masonite.

On the cotton support, the two higher proportions of gel do in fact discolor at an increasing rate, displaying curves similar to those seen earlier. The surprising difference between these two higher proportions is that the curves closely follow one another, even though there is five times more gel in one than in the other.

As we might have predicted, the curves for Masonite indicate the greatest degree of discoloration in the higher gel content samples. However, Masonite's curves are fairly similar to those of cotton and linen when gel proportions are low.

In general, at gel:paint proportions over 10:1, noticeable discoloration can be expected when the support is linen, cotton, or Masonite. The results recorded for lauan plywood are somewhat inconsistent with the other findings and therefore require further inquiry.

Conclusion

The graphs clearly show that supports typically used by artists can create significant discoloration of acrylic media. Modern paintings, especially color-field paintings, or any painting incorporating the acrylic media described, may show a discoloration originating from the interaction between the acrylic dispersion medium and the support.[6] This phenomenon is most noticeable in the unpigmented gels, matte, and gloss media, but can occur in acrylic paint containing these media. It is a characteristic that can be expected to occur regardless of the brand of acrylic medium used. This phenomenon should be distinguished from changes in color, which are due to atmospheric/environmental pollution, or a possible inherent tendency for a given acrylic dispersion to discolor.

The graphs also indicate that the discoloration can occur quite rapidly over a few weeks, but generally levels off after a few months. Long-term measurements should be pursued in order to determine whether or not the discoloration curves remain flat or gradually change (increase or decrease) over the years.

The commonly used acrylic gesso does not significantly inhibit the Support Induced Discoloration (SID).[7] However, the washing of a fabric support before stretching markedly reduces the potential for discoloration of the acrylic media, whether gesso is used or not.

A likely mechanism for SID is the following: immediately after the application of an acrylic medium, water and other ingredients[8] move into the support, allowing unidentified soluble components in the support to migrate back into the medium as the water evaporates, thus creating the discoloration. The unknown components are most likely finishing materials used by yarn and/or fabric manufacturers,[9] dirt, or other contaminants from crop growing, fiber storage, or mill operations. They may also include components of the plant from which the fiber is produced.

Some questions remain:

- At what point during the drying process of the acrylic medium does the discolored material become extracted?

- Does discoloration change continually over time?

- Can the extractable discolored material be identified more specifically?[10]

- How can paintings that have already discolored be treated?[11]

Endnotes

1. The term *discoloration* is used here to mean an undesirable change in color.

2. It is worth mentioning that the terms *emulsion* and *dispersion* often used to describe these paint media are not interchangeable, although they are related. The resins used in the manufacture of these media are commonly marketed as "acrylic emulsions." They are, in fact, according to the Paint/Coatings Dictionary of the Federation of Societies for Coatings Technology, produced by emulsion polymerization. This is a process whereby the monomeric material present as the discontinuous phase of an emulsion is polymerized *in situ*. However, according to the same source, "after polymerization, a latex

[acrylic emulsion] is a solid dispersed in water and, therefore, is not an emulsion."

Emulsion is defined as a two phase, all liquid system in which small droplets of one liquid (the internal phase) are immiscible in, and dispersed uniformly throughout, a second continuous liquid phase, the external phase. The term *dispersion* has broader meaning, encompassing any composition or state related to a heterogeneous system of solids, liquids, gases, or immiscible liquids. Therefore, an emulsion qualifies as a special type of dispersion. In the topic at hand, the polymerized acrylic resin solids comprise the internal phase, while water comprises the continuous external phase of a heterogeneous system. Technically, the materials we are discussing are called acrylic dispersions, even though they are marketed as acrylic emulsions.

3. In the Howells, Burnstock, Hedley, and Hackney 1984 IIC Paris Preprints article "Polymer Dispersions Artificially Aged," six acrylic dispersions in a field of 14 polymer dispersions were subjected to enhanced environmental conditions using sunlight, fluorescent light, and elevated temperatures. The dispersions were then tested for changes in weight, color, solubility, mechanical properties, softening to heat, submersion in water, and pH. Only one resin showed no significant changes throughout all the tests. The most common change among the others was yellowing, a characteristic that did not seem to impact any of the other physical properties of the dispersions.

4. American Society for Testing and Materials (ASTM), "Standard Practice for Preparing Drawdowns of Artists' Paste Paints," (Designation D 4941-89) *ASTM Standards*, Philadelphia, P.A. (1990) pp. 916-917.

5. ASTM, "Standard Test Method for Calculation of Color Differences from Instrumentally Measured Color Coordinates," (Designation D 2244-89) *ASTM Standards*, Philadelphia, P.A. (1990) pp. 297-300.

6. Coverings or coatings on the back of the canvas, such as stretcher bars contacting the canvas, engaged panel stretchers, or paint on back of the canvas, can worsen the discoloration. Any of these will retard or prevent the evaporation of water from the reverse, thus forcing all moisture to migrate to the surface of the painting in order to evaporate. This one-sided evaporation of moisture apparently enhances the movement of extractable materials from the support to the surface of the painting, thus intensifying the discoloration.

7. A new acronym proposed by the authors to reference this phenomenon.

8. Some likely candidates include emulsifier, surfactant, coalescing solvent, stabilizer, or these (and other ingredients) working in concert.

9. Monie (1908) described fabric sizings (many of which are still used today) containing several types of starches (farina, wheat, or rice), fats, waxes, or glycerine, which may interact with acrylic dispersions media unfavorably.

10. Suffield (1991) described the identification of components of the soluble extract. Cotton and linen canvases were examined using microchemical tests. The tests indicated the presence of starch and lignin in the linen samples and primarily starch in the cotton. Subsequent thin layer chromatography and infrared spectrophotometry also indicated proteins were present in both canvases. After tagging the hydrolyzed proteins with dansyl chloride in order to visualize the chromatographs with UV light after development, the results indicated the presence of a mixture of casein and other proteins in both cotton and linen canvases.

11. Contompasis and Hamm have tested treatment options on the Robert Goodnough painting in Figure 1 using UV filtered fluorescent light as a bleaching tool (Tahk 1979). Results have shown an improvement in appearance, but not to a degree sufficient to warrant recommendation as a viable treatment option in this case. (See Watherston 1972, p. 838 for a more aggressive approach.)

Résumé

La décoloration des médias de dispersion acryliques

*Une décoloration jaune-brun plutôt exception-
nelle, sur le fond d'une peinture par champs de
couleurs de Robert Goodnough (1970), est à
l'origine de l'étude sur les médias de dispersion
acryliques qui est décrite dans la présente communication. Tant le premier propriétaire du tableau que le propriétaire actuel se souviennent
que ce jaunissement avait déjà atteint le stade
d'une coloration indésirable au milieu des années 70, ce qui signifie qu'il se serait produit
assez tôt après l'exécution de la peinture. L'artiste a pour sa part indiqué, lors d'une conversation téléphonique récente, qu'il avait l'habitude,
durant cette période, de couvrir ses toiles (en
coton) avec du Liquitex mat avant d'appliquer
toute peinture.*

*À l'heure actuelle, le Liquitex mat ressemble de
très près à la couleur que laisseraient des dépôts
de fumée de cigarette. S'il est effectivement possible que de la fumée de cigarette ait quelque peu
contribué à donner à la peinture son aspect actuel, de premiers essais ont néanmoins révélé
qu'elle ne saurait être considérée comme la
principale source de cette décoloration
jaune-brun.*

*Il est fait état, dans la présente communication,
des résultats d'expériences qui ont permis de
reproduire, à l'aide de maquettes, des décolorations causées par un vieillissement naturel. Il est
à noter que ces décolorations se produisent assez
tôt dans un milieu ambiant normal — où la température, l'humidité relative et la lumière sont
normales. Si toutes les marques de médias ou de
gels acryliques sont susceptibles de se décolorer,
cette décoloration sera plus apparente dans le
cas d'un gel pigmenté, mat, et d'un médium lus-
tré. Il s'agit d'une interaction indésirable entre
le support et le médium.*

*Des expériences distinctes, à l'aide de maquettes
également, ont été menées pour évaluer la décoloration causée par la chaleur et l'ultraviolet.
Néanmoins, des essais ultérieurs ont révélé que
les modifications obtenues à l'aide de telles techniques n'étaient pas aussi significatives, aux fins
de l'étude du Goodnough, que celles qui avaient
été obtenues au terme d'un vieillissement naturel,
dans un milieu ambiant normal.*

References

LeSota, S. et al., *Paint/Coatings Dictionary*
(Philadelphia: Federation of Societies for
Coatings Technology, 1978).

Howells, R., A. Burnstock, G. Hedley and S.
Hackney, "Polymer Dispersions Artificially
Aged," *Adhesives and Consolidants*, Preprints
of the Contributions to the Paris Congress,
2-8 September 1984 (London: International
Institute for Conservation, 1984) pp. 36-43.

Monie, H., *Sizing Ingredients, Size Mixing
and Sizing* (Manchester, England: Abel
Heywood & Son, 1908).

Suffield, B., "An Investigation into the
Discoloration of Acrylic Dispersion Media,
Seventeenth Annual Conservation Training
Programs Conference (New York: The Institute
of Fine Arts Conservation Center, New York
University, 1991) pp. 152-166.

Tahk, C., "The Recovery of Color in Scorched
Oil Paint Films," *Journal of the American
Institute for Conservation*, vol. 19, no. 1, 1979,
pp. 3-13.

Watherston, M., "Problems Presented by
Color Field Paintings. Cleaning of Color Field
Paintings," *Conservation of Paintings and the
Graphic Arts*, Preprints of Contributions to
The Lisbon Congress 1972, 9-14 October 1972
(London: International Institute for Conserva-
tion, 1972) pp. 831-845.

Methods of Analysis and Identification
Méthodes d'analyse et d'identification

Practical Pitfalls in the Identification of Plastics

Helen C. Coxon

Royal Ontario Museum
Toronto, Ontario
Canada

Abstract

The plastic artefacts now making their way into museums and private collections represent a new field for the conservator, one in which research is only just beginning, and there are few, if any, guidelines for treatment. Unlike materials such as ceramics or metal, which if stored properly will remain stable for long periods of time, plastics can and will continue to degrade, sometimes with startling rapidity. The initiating agent for such deterioration can be as apparently insignificant as the application of a layer of lacquer before applying an accession number.

Plastics vary widely in their reaction to factors such as heat, light, cleaning agents and other environmental conditions, and can also have drastic effects on each other. Before we can begin to set up treatments for specific polymers, we need to be able to identify those polymers with accuracy.

While infra-red spectroscopy provides the best means of identification, there is also a need for simpler identification methods, preferably applicable by conservators and collectors on a routine basis. Many such methods are suggested in plastics literature, some scientific, some more empirical. Float tests attempt to distinguish plastics using solutions of known density; burn tests use smell and behaviour when heated or ignited; chemical spot-tests rely on colour changes in response to a particular experimental procedure. Identification by trade name (if known) or by stylistic design and/or type of object represent the more subjective approach. Several years of work with plastic artefacts, and with plastics both old and new collected for experimental purposes, have shown quite clearly that there are limitations in the use of such methods. Thus, it is essential to be aware of these limitations if identifications are to be made with any degree of certainty.

The principal problem appears to be that literature regarding plastic often presents tests that work well on samples of pure polymer, whereas manufactured plastic items are rarely unmodified. Fillers and pigments affect the density and appearance of plastics, and interfere with colour reactions. Plasticizers also alter the properties in unpredictable ways, and chemical alteration as a result of degradation cannot be ignored. Using art history texts as a means of identification also has its difficulties.

These problems will be illustrated with reference to actual experience in trying to set up a coherent identification scheme for plastics.

Introduction

The so-called "age of plastics" is conventionally dated from the late 1860s, when Alexander Parkes in the U.K. and John and Isaiah Hyatt in the U.S. developed and marketed very similar semi-synthetic materials, known as Parkesine on one side of the Atlantic and Celluloid on the other.

These days the number of plastics available seems almost infinite, their properties can be tailored to meet specific criteria, and if we look around us, more items than not in our everyday lives are made wholly or partially of plastics. Correspondingly, plastics in an artefactual context are increasingly becoming a part of the museum world. Initially they often appeared in museum collections more or less accidentally, as incidental components of artefacts collected for other reasons, for example, cellulose nitrate fan sticks, an ebonite pistol grip, or an early composite book cover. Now, however, plastics are being collected in their own right.

Some six years ago the European department of the Royal Ontario Museum began a deliberate collection of plastics, both art objects and more utilitarian items. The collection currently includes items made from cellulose nitrate, acrylic, melamine-formaldehyde, urea-formaldehyde and phenol-formaldehyde, poly(vinyl chloride), ebonite, cellulose acetate, and casein. Many of these newly accessioned objects are now on display in the 'Lifestyles' section of the European Gallery. With the creation of the Institute for Contemporary Culture within the museum, we can expect the number of plastic artefacts in the collections to increase.

There is probably no need to stress the fact that it is going to be some time before we have many definitive answers to the problems we are facing in treating these materials. As a new type of material in the museum field, conservators, curators and collectors are only just beginning to come to grips with the reactions of plastics to light, heat, atmospheric pollutants and repair materials, and their effects on each other and on other materials associated with them.

In the past few years of working with various aspects of plastics, particularly their identification, a number of difficulties and anomalies have become apparent, which it seems appropriate to bring to the attention of others working in the field.

Why Identify?

First of all, why identify? At a very basic level, we need to know what material we are dealing with in order to be able to attempt to devise a suitable treatment. Where plastics are concerned, we need to know more than that, however. It is not enough just to look at an artefact and say "plastic." Since plastics vary widely in their response to factors such as heat, light, airborne pollutants and potential conservation treatments, it is important to be able to identify them accurately. For example, the wrong choice of solvent, or even the use of a solvent at all, can be disastrous, since, unlike artefact materials such as glass or metal, some plastics are inherently solvent-soluble. This has profound implications for other types of treatment — repair, infill, and to a certain extent inpainting — as many adhesives and repair materials either will not adhere well, or will do so by partial dissolution of the plastic surface.

There are other reasons for identification also. It enables us to separate out items that may give off breakdown products harmful to other materials. We are used to testing display materials with such a reason in mind, but we must now apply it also to plastic artefacts. Cellulose nitrate, for example, gives off acidic nitrogen dioxide as it ages, which can cause bleaching or fading of pigments and dyes, corrosion of metals, and discolouration, distortion or accelerated breakdown in other polymers in direct contact or in an enclosed space, such as a display case or storage drawer.

Identification also enables us to discover plastics masquerading as natural materials, among the most obvious being cellulose nitrate imitating ivory or tortoiseshell.

Identification

Information on the identification of polymers can be found mainly in publications dealing with the history of plastics, industrial chemistry journals, books on polymer science, organic chemistry, fine art, and the food industry,[1-4,16,20] as well as more specific publications.[5-8] Suggested properties and means of identification can be broadly grouped into four areas (Table I).

Analytical methods such as Fourier Transform Infra-red Spectroscopy (FTIR) and Gas

Table I
Suggested Identification Methods for Plastics

Visible Characteristics:
- comparison with reference literature
- trademarks
- function
- design
- date
- colour
- feel: surface texture, weight, etc.

Simple Physical Characteristics:
- taste and smell
- folding, tearing, etc. (sheet materials only)
- density

Chemical Reactions:
- pyrolysis
- pH
- solubility
- colour change reactions

Instrumental Methods:
- Fourier Transform Infra-red Spectroscopy (FTIR), Gas Chromatography (GC), etc.

plastics, and are used as references for the identification of plastic objects by means of visible characteristics.[1,4,11,12]

At the outset it seemed as though identification would not be too much of a difficulty with regard to the museum's holdings, since the initial selection of objects for purchase was more or less picked straight from the pages of various books on the art history of plastics.

However, it can be unwise to rely completely on art history or dealer identifications. The museum acquired a small box in black plastic, designed by René Lalique in the 1930s, the design being identical to that in a photograph in one of the aforementioned books on the art history of plastics, except that the pictured box is red. The author of the book identifies the box as "probably made from celluloid," that is, cellulose nitrate, and ours was labelled as such by the dealer from whom it was bought, probably on the basis of a photograph such as this. However, our box is actually made from cellulose acetate — this was indicated by the strong smell of acetic acid coming from it, and confirmed by means of a chemical spot-test. This may be a case of the same design having been used with different plastics, or it may be an example of the use of the term 'celluloid' generically, since in the early years of the development of cellulose acetate as a replacement for cellulose nitrate in certain applications, cellulose acetate was often referred to as "non-flammable celluloid." Either way, the discovery of the discrepancy does give an indication of the kind of problem that may be encountered.

An acrylic display head, also purchased with reference to a photograph, gives us another case in point. It was accepted that it was acrylic, that is, poly(methyl methacrylate), without question, having no information to the contrary, until a colleague, while visiting a plastics factory in France, discovered in the course of a casual conversation that students in plastics training schools in Paris were often required to duplicate that particular piece as an exercise... in polyester.

Other problems with relying on reference literature include frequent lack of agreement on dates, and a bias towards the history of plastics

Chromatography (GC) are frequently referred to as essential means for identifying the complex mixtures of components present in many plastics, especially more recent plastics.[9,10] However, many conservators do not have ready access to such equipment, and would therefore have use for simpler identification methods.

The initial focus of the identification work, before plastics became a real presence in the collections, was on sheet materials and adhesives. However, it became very apparent that manufactured artefacts are much less straightforward. "Case histories" of some identification problems will demonstrate some of the problems or anomalies that may be encountered, and show that a certain degree of caution in the interpretation of results is advisable.

Identification by Visible Characteristics

Reference Literature for Identification
Dealing first with what is sometimes called reference literature, these publications usually describe the history or art history of plastics. They often include lists of trade names and information on properties, illustrations of typical designs, and typical functions for the various

in one particular country, with corresponding gaps in the record. Identification by date also assumes either that the date is stamped on the piece, or that its history is sufficiently well-documented to be fairly certain of its date of manufacture.

Identification by Trade Name

Identification by trade name should also be handled warily. Strictly speaking, the name Celluloid should be used only for the cellulose nitrate products of the Albany Dental Plate Corporation, to whom the name was originally registered in 1869 to 1870, followed by the Celluloid Manufacturing Corporation and, more recently, the Celanese Plastics Corporation. However, just as we tend to call all photocopiers Xerox machines, so the name has become generically associated with all cellulose nitrate products.

Bakelite was the trade name originally given to the resin produced from phenol and formaldehyde by means of a process involving heat and pressure, patented by Leo Baekeland in 1909. The final product gave a characteristic dark, mottled appearance to manufactured items such as electrical fittings. However, it would be a mistake to assume that everything labelled Bakelite is phenol-formaldehyde, since that trade name now applies to polyethylene, polypropylene, epoxy, phenolic, polystyrene, phenoxy, polysulphone, ethylene copolymer, ABS, acrylic and vinyl plastics, among others. Conversely, despite some texts that will try to convince you that phenol-formaldehyde plastic was only available in dull, dark colours, the same resin, used unfilled for items made by casting rather than moulding, could be all colours of the rainbow, and was used to imitate jade, amber, onyx, and similar materials. Nor is everything dark and mottled brown necessarily phenol-formaldehyde.

Where plastics are concerned, appearances can be deceiving. The visible attributes of a piece — colour, design, function, feel — may indeed hold clues to the identity of the material, but we should also remember that plastics were often deliberately fabricated to resemble other materials, and a wide range of surface finishes was possible.

Identification by Physical Properties

The second group of identification possibilities is based on physical properties. As shown in Table II, non-artefactual sheet materials can be initially assessed by means of a range of physical properties:
- appearance
- flexibility
- whether the material holds a crease
- the degree to which it can be stretched
- how easy it is to tear

These properties are often useful in the identification of plastic storage materials. However, this kind of test is difficult to perform on three-dimensional pieces, and although some collectors routinely use the smell and taste of plastics as a guide to identification, such methods have obvious negative implications.

Identification by Chemical Reactions

Density Test: One readily performed test can be used to distinguish the polyolefins, that is, polyethylene, polypropylene, polyisobutylene, from other materials, at least in fairly pure forms. The polyolefins have a density less than one, so if a small sample is dropped into a beaker of water to which a few drops of detergent have been added to negate the surface tension, it will float, while all other materials will sink, provided there are no air bubbles clinging to the sample.

By extension, it is possible to devise a theoretical system of separating plastics into groups based on density, or specific gravity, which is assessed according to whether the material sinks or floats in solutions of known specific gravity, such as saturated sodium chloride. In practice, however, additives and fillers in artefact materials may alter the density to the extent that this method becomes, at the best, very unreliable. Tables III a and III b show values for various plastics compared with the specific gravities of saturated solutions. It is noticeable that several plastics have a wide range of possible density, some of which bracket the saturated solutions. It is also possible for moisture-absorbent fillers to affect the flotation response by absorbing water from the solutions. Out of a group of casein and melamine-formaldehyde

Table II

Physical Characteristics of Sheet Materials

Material	Appearance	Stretch Characteristics	Tear Characteristics
Cellophane	Transparent, very flexible; crackling sound when crumpled. Coated films are water-resistant and will mist if breathed on. Uncoated films become limp when wet. Holds a crease well.	Fairly hard to stretch, medium extensibility. Permanent deformation.	Easily torn, tears in an undulating line. Tear may be hard to initiate.
Cellulose acetate or triacetate	Transparent, medium flexibility. Does not crumple. Holds a crease well.	Hard to stretch. No permanent deformation.	Easily torn. Tear is initiated easily from a cut edge, less easily from a torn edge.
Polyamide	Transparent, very flexible. Holds a crease well.	Hard to stretch. No permanent deformation.	Hard to tear, even when initiated with a scissor cut. Edges of tear stretch.
Polycarbonate	Transparent, usually as a sheet several millimetres thick.		
Polyethylene	Slightly cloudy. Flexibility depends on thickness. Slightly waxy feel. Holds a crease moderately well.	Easy to stretch, depending on thickness. Permanent extension.	Fairly hard to tear, even when tear initiated with a scissor cut. Edges of tear stretch.
Poly(ethylene terephthalate)	Transparent. Very flexible to moderately flexible, depending on thickness. Holds a crease moderately well; thinner grades better than thicker.	Hard to stretch. No permanent extension.	Tears with difficulty, and only if initiated with scissor cut. Thinner grades tear more easily. Characteristic rough edge to tear, especially in thicker grades, which separate within the thickness as if laminated.
Poly(methyl methacrylate)	Transparent. Used as sheets several millimetres in thickness.		
Polypropylene	Transparent, hard, and relatively inflexible. Does not hold a crease well.	Hard to stretch. No permanent extension.	After initiation with scissor cut, tears easily in a straight line with a cloudy edge to the tear.
Polystyrene	Transparent, relatively inflex-ible. Characteristic metallic sound when flexed. Holds a crease well; crease line shows white crazing.	Very hard to stretch. No permanent extension.	Very easy to initiate and propagate. Tears cleanly but not straight with a cloudy edge to the tear.
Poly(vinyl chloride) (rigid)	Transparent. Softer feel and more flexible than polypropylene or polystyrene. Holds a crease well; crease shows a small amount of white crazing.	Hard to stretch. No permanent deformation.	Requires a scissor cut to initiate. Fairly hard to tear. Slightly ragged tear with some stretching of edges.
Poly(vinylidene chloride)	Transparent, very flexible. Softest of the sheet materials. Easily crumpled and holds a crease well. (May depend on grade.)	Fairly easy to stretch. Medium extensibility (less than polyethylene.)	Tear is hard to initiate. Tears easily, but not in a straight line.

samples, some floated in saturated magnesium chloride, some sank, and some progressed from one state to the other over a period of time.

Manufactured plastic objects also present a considerable problem in terms of their chemical structure. The vast majority of literature references apply to the testing of plastics in a fairly pure form. Unfortunately, plastics are very seldom pure, unaltered materials. They may contain not only the original base plastic, but also structures altered by breakdown and crosslinking, copolymers, similar chemical structures, and plasticizers and other additives, all of which combine to make the task of identification a more complex one, since removal of such additives is usually difficult, if not impossible, by simple means. The failure of a test to work on a plastic that it is supposed to identify then raises the question as to whether an unknown

element within the plastic is blocking or skewing the result, or whether there is a problem in experimental method.

Burn Tests: Pyrolysis, or 'heat and burn' tests, can be applied to plastics in all forms. These tests aim to identify plastics by their reactions to heat and flame, based on observations such as whether a sample melts or decomposes, whether it will continue to burn after being ignited, what colour the flame is, and the odour of any fumes given off.

With the exception of the Beilstein Test,[13] which identifies poly(vinyl chloride) or poly(vinylidene chloride), the results of such tests are of limited practical value, for several reasons. Observations have to be made very rapidly, especially in the burn test, and judgements, for example on the colour of the flame, are very subjective. This is reflected by the lack of agreement between published sources, as demonstrated in the comparative data in Table IV, so that interpretation of the results becomes something of a guessing game.

Experimentation revealed fewer easily identifiable differences between flames than the sources would suggest, and though the results usually agreed fairly well with one source or another, they did not agree with the same source consistently. These procedures also required the removal of larger samples than would usually be acceptable for museum artefacts.

One variation of this identification method often suggested, which may be of more use when dealing with plastics in the sense that it is not necessary to remove a sample, is to apply a hot needle in an inconspicuous place, observe the behaviour of the plastic, and sniff the odour of the fumes given off. A number of difficulties are apparent here, though the method is useful as a basic means of distinguishing between thermosets and thermoplastics.

Using buttons as experimental samples for the most part, this method was successfully used on casein, shellac, phenolics, acrylic and what appear to be two grades of polystyrene. However, there were instances where the identification was uncertain. For example, it was difficult

---

Table III a

Specific Gravity of Selected Plastics

Specific Gravity Ranges of Plastics

ABS	1.04 - 1.10	
Casein	1.26	Pure
	1.35	Plastic
Cellulose acetate	1.25 - 1.35	
Cellulose nitrate	1.34 - 1.38	Plastic
	1.45	Film
Ebonite	1.08 - 1.25	Unfilled
	1.25 - 1.80	Filled
Nylon	1.01 - 1.16	
Phenol-formaldehyde	1.27 - 1.30	Unfilled
	1.36 - 1.46	Cellulose Filled
	1.54 - 1.75	Mineral Filled
	1.75 - 1.92	Mineral or Glassfibre Filled
Polycarbonate	1.20 - 1.22	
Polyethylene	0.91 - 0.95	
Poly(ethylene terephthalate)	1.38 - 1.41	
Poly(methyl methacrylate)	1.16 - 1.20	
Polypropylene	0.85 - 0.92	
Polystyrene	1.04 - 1.08	
Poly(vinyl chloride)	1.19 - 1.35	Plasticized
	1.38 - 1.41	Rigid
Urea- and Melamine-		
formaldehyde	1.50	Pure
	1.80 - 2.10	Filled

Specific Gravities of Saturated Aqueous Solutions

Water	1.00
Sodium Chloride	1.20
Magnesium Chloride	1.34
Calcium Chloride	1.45
Zinc Chloride	2.01

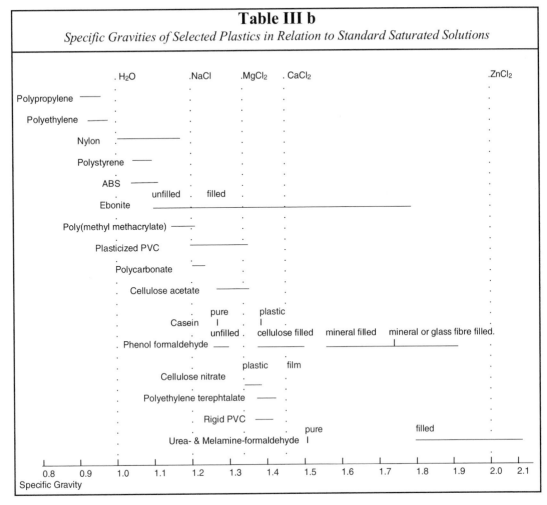

Table III b

Specific Gravities of Selected Plastics in Relation to Standard Saturated Solutions

. H₂O   .NaCl   .MgCl₂   . CaCl₂   .ZnCl₂

Polypropylene

Polyethylene

Nylon

Polystyrene

ABS

Ebonite

Poly(methyl methacrylate)

Plasticized PVC

Polycarbonate

Cellulose acetate

Casein — pure, plastic, unfilled, cellulose filled, mineral filled, mineral or glass fibre filled.

Phenol formaldehyde

Cellulose nitrate — plastic, film

Polyethylene terephtalate

Rigid PVC

Urea- & Melamine-formaldehyde — pure, filled

0.8   0.9   1.0   1.1   1.2   1.3   1.4   1.5   1.6   1.7   1.8   1.9   2.0   2.1
Specific Gravity

to distinguish among urea-formaldehyde, melamine-formaldehyde and casein plastics, as they all smelt similar.

There was one type of button identified, or rather separated from the rest, only by the smell of burnt caramel and the fact that it squeaked when touched with the hot point. Nowhere in the reference material was there mention of burnt caramel as an identifying odour, let alone the squeak, which left a large question mark. Sometime later, when a batch of samples was analysed by infra-red spectroscopy, it was discovered that these buttons were made from vegetable ivory, and that such buttons were rather common at a certain point in time, due to the use of vegetable ivory nuts as ballast in cargo vessels.

The squeak seems to be due to a small amount of moisture being turned into steam, and can be heard also from other water-absorbing plastics such as urea-formaldehyde and casein. Vegetable ivory closely resembles a cellulose nitrate plastic in visual appearance, and also tests negative for both starch and cellulose. This is a very specific example, and vegetable ivory is unlikely to be found in large pieces, but it demonstrates a potential problem.

It is obvious, both from these tests and from previous experience, that assessment and description of flame colour and odour is very subjective, and this is corroborated by the fact that published lists often disagree, or are incomplete. Odour identification can be made more reliable by having a series of reference samples,

401

Table IV
Heat and Burn Tests: A Comparison of Results

Material Source (films and sheets)	Source* Krause and Lange[5]	Sauders[7]	Other**
Cellophane	a. easy b. continues c. light like paper d. burns quickly and completely e. burnt paper f. neutral	a. n/a b. n/a c. n/a d. n/a e. n/a f. n/a	a. n/a b. n/a c. n/a d. n/a e. n/a f. n/a
Cellulose acetate or triacetate	a. easy b. extinguishes c. dark yellow, sooty d. melts, forms drops e. acetic acid f. acidic	a. n/a b. continues c. yellow d. n/a e. acetic acid f. acidic	a. n/a b. continues[19] c. yellow-green edge[20] d. burns slowly[21] e. n/a f. n/a
Fluorocarbon	a. non-inflammable b. n/a c. n/a d. n/a e. hydrogen fluoride or chloride f. strongly acidic	a. n/a b. extinguishes c. yellow d. burns with difficulty, chars slowly e. none f. acidic	a. no flame b. n/a c. n/a d. sample deforms slowly[22] e. n/a f. n/a
Polycarbonate	a. difficult b. extinguishes c. luminous, sooty d. melts, decomposes, chars e. non-characteristic f. neutral, weakly acidic initially	a. difficult b. continues c. yellow, smoky d. n/a e. phenolic f. n/a	a. n/a b. n/a c. n/a d. n/a e. n/a f. n/a
Polyethylene	a. difficult or easy luminous b. n/a c. blue centre d. melts, forms drops e. like extinguished candles f. neutral	a. n/a b. continues c. yellow with blue base d. clear when molten e. burning candle wax f. n/a	a. n/a b. n/a c. no smoke, blue flame[22] d. n/a e. n/a f. n/a
Poly(ethylene terephthalate)	a. difficult b. continues c. yellow-orange, sooty d. softens, melts, drips e. sweet, aromatic f. n/a	a. n/a b. continues c. yellow with blue base d. melts sharply to free-flowing liquid that can be drawn into a fibre e. sweet f. n/a	a. n/a b. ignites but extinguishes[22] c. n/a d. n/a e. n/a f. n/a
Poly(methyl methacrylate)	a. easy b. continues c. luminous yellow, blue edge, slightly sooty d. softens e. sweet, fruity f. neutral	a. n/a b. continues c. yellow with blue base d. n/a e. methyl methacrylate f. n/a	a. n/a b. n/a c. white tip?, blue flame d. n/a e. odour sweet, fruity, floral[20] f. n/a
Polypropylene	a. difficult or easy b. continues c. luminous with blue centre d. melts, forms drops e. like extinguished candles f. neutral	a. n/a b. continues c. yellow with blue base d. becomes clear when molten e. burning candle wax f. n/a	a. n/a b. n/a c. no smoke, blue flame[22] d. n/a e. n/a f. n/a
Polystyrene	a. easy b. continues c. luminous, sooty d. softens e. sweet (styrene) f. neutral	a. n/a b. continues c. yellow with blue base d. very smoky e. styrene f. n/a	a. n/a b. n/a c. n/a d. melts into clear liquid e. smells like marigolds[21] f. n/a
Poly(vinyl chloride), poly(vinylidene chloride)	a. difficult b. extinguishes c. yellow-orange, green border d. softens, decomposes to black e. hydrogen chloride f. strongly acidic	a. n/a b. extinguishes c. yellow with green base d. n/a e. acrid f. acidic	a. n/a b. n/a c. n/a d. n/a e. n/a f. n/a

Table IV (continued)

*Results from the two major sources are paraphrased to save space. The letters in the Table represent the categories given in the legend below. In some instances information or findings may not be available for a particular category and thus will be marked n/a.

        a. ease of ignition
        b. whether samples continue burning after removal from flame
        c. flame colour
        d. behaviour during burning
        e. odour
        f. vapour acidic or alkaline

** Other sources are quoted only when their results differ significantly from the major sources.

The numbering of Table sources corresponds to the main list of References.

    5. Krause and Lange, 1969, pp. 4-8.
    7. Saunders, 1966, pp. 15-19.
   19. Briston, 1974, p. 289.
   20. Nechamkin, 1943.
   21. Taylor, 1985.
   22. Bird, 1963.

but it is impossible to tell how fillers and additives will affect the odour, and furthermore, from a health and safety point of view it does not seem sensible to be inhaling fumes, many of which are toxic.

Last but not least in the list of negative comments, a fair degree of damage can be caused to plastics by a hot needle.

pH Tests: The one aspect of these tests that proved both fairly accurate and potentially useful for preliminary identification of sheet materials was the pH determination. Good results were obtained using Merck non-bleeding pH indicator strips, dampened with distilled water and hooked over the lip of the test-tube during heating. Results ranged from a pH of 0.0 to 0.5, given by poly(vinyl chloride) and poly(vinylidene chloride), to a pH of 9.0 to 10.0 given by polyamide (Table V). Here again, the presence of additives in manufactured items makes this a suspect method for artefacts. As a footnote, since the Merck strips are supported by a poly(vinyl chloride) backing, it is important to avoid heating the strips themselves, or the resulting pH may be too low.

Solubility Tests: Some initial consideration was given to the identification of plastics by solubility, but an elimination scheme such as that in Table VI requires a considerable number of different solvents, some of which are carcinogenic, such as tetrachloromethane and benzene, and generally no longer found in conservation laboratories. As in the case of the pyrolysis tests, sample sizes would also be prohibitively large.

Overall, then, various aspects of the test methods mentioned so far may be of some use in preliminary identification of plastics, but it must be emphasized that the results are often subjective and, as such, should be interpreted with caution.

Table V

pH Values of Vapours Released from Sheet Materials During Heating

Material	Approximate pH
PVC/PVDC	0.0 to 0.5
Cellulose triacetate	2.5
Polyethylene/Polypropylene	3.0 to 4.0
Poly(ethylene terephthalate) (Mylar)	4.0
Polycarbonate	4.5 to 5.5
Polystyrene	5.5
Polyamide (nylon)	9.0 to 10.0

Spot-Tests: Moving onward to colour change reactions, it is important that the tests be as simple as possible (i.e., ideally they should involve: only basic laboratory equipment, such as test-tubes and pipettes; as few reagents as possible; and uncomplicated procedures). Otherwise a certain degree of investment in time, money and equipment is required. In doing early research into published plastics identification methods, the aim was to find a spot-test for each material, along the lines of spot-tests used to identify metals. These self-imposed limitations rule out a considerable number of published tests that require complex apparatus or esoteric or expensive reagents, but even so-called "simple" tests may not be so simple in practice. As with all the other identification methods mentioned so far, some of the results have been good, and some have been most puzzling.

One procedure that generally gives good, definite results is a test for the presence of acetates that requires the application of four pre-mixed reagents in succession (Table VII). The Lalique box mentioned earlier was identified using this test after the smell of acetic acid alerted us to the likelihood that it was not cellulose nitrate. The positive colour may vary from pale pink to burgundy red, depending on the size of the sample relative to the volume of reagent.

To date only one problem has occurred when using this test. One pair of spectacle frames smelt strongly of acetic acid, implying cellulose acetate, but showed breakdown patterns characteristic of cellulose nitrate, and the plastic tested positive for cellulose nitrate and negative for cellulose acetate. As yet, no answer to this apparent contradiction has been found.

The Diphenylamine Test for Cellulose Nitrate[14]**:** The reagent is a solution of diphenylamine in concentrated sulphuric acid. The acid liberates nitrogen oxides from the surface of a cellulose nitrate object, and these oxidize the diphenylamine to a dark blue dye, which appears virtually instantaneously on applying the reagent. This does indeed work very effectively on cellulose nitrate. However, any oxidizing agent will give the same result. A surface contaminated with normal museum dust can give a very convincing positive result. A dusty polypropylene lid, partly cleaned, gave a negative result on the clean area, but as the solution came into contact with the dust on the other half of the lid, the characteristic blue colour appeared. The point here is that for reliable results, the surface to be tested must be clean, and it is entirely possible for a cracked surface, or one that is oozing plasticizer, to give a positive result due to the presence of dust or other contaminants in the cracks or adhering to the surface, even after wiping.

The test is extremely sensitive, requiring only a tiny sample, and it is essential to beware of cross-contamination. A pipette accidentally touched to the surface of a cellulose nitrate object can subsequently produce a false positive if used for a non-cellulose nitrate object. A side-effect of this sensitivity is that the presence of cellulose nitrate as a component of an object, even in tiny quantities, can result in a mistaken identification.

This can lead to ambiguities in the identification of early film materials. One piece that was sent to us for identification gave a positive result with the diphenylamine test around the edges of the sample, but not on the flat surfaces. Removal of the emulsion from the base plastic and retesting revealed that the base plastic was cellulose acetate. The cellulose nitrate was eventually tracked down to a thin sublayer between the emulsion and the base plastic.

Another drawback to the diphenylamine test is the mark left on a glossy surface, and even the potential for a colour change.

It is also worth noting that this test is mentioned by a variety of sources,[7,15,16] but there is considerable disagreement as to the concentrations of diphenylamine and sulphuric acid required. Given concentrations range from 0.5% diphenylamine in 90% acid to 20% diphenylamine in 100% acid. Trying a range of solution concentrations revealed some very inconsistent results. The best, most consistent results were obtained from a 5% solution of diphenylamine in 75% to 85% sulphuric acid.

Table VI
Scheme for Identification of Polymers by Solubility (After Briston [19])

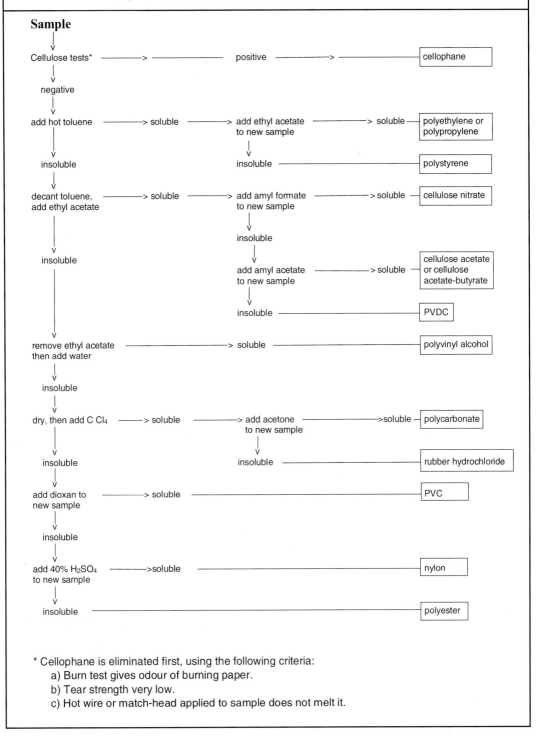

Sample
↓
Cellulose tests* ——→ —— positive ——→ —— cellophane
↓
negative
↓
add hot toluene ——→ soluble ——→ add ethyl acetate ——→ soluble — polyethylene or polypropylene
↓ to new sample
↓
insoluble ↓
↓ insoluble —— polystyrene
↓
decant toluene, ——→ soluble ——→ add amyl formate ——→ soluble — cellulose nitrate
add ethyl acetate to new sample
↓
↓ insoluble
↓
insoluble add amyl acetate ——→ soluble — cellulose acetate or cellulose acetate-butyrate
to new sample
↓
insoluble —— PVDC
↓
remove ethyl acetate ——→ soluble —— polyvinyl alcohol
then add water
↓
insoluble
↓
dry, then add C Cl₄ ——→ soluble ——→ add acetone ——→soluble — polycarbonate
↓ to new sample
↓
insoluble insoluble —— rubber hydrochloride
↓
add dioxan to ——→ soluble —— PVC
new sample
↓
insoluble
↓
add 40% H₂SO₄ ——→soluble —— nylon
to new sample
↓
insoluble —— polyester

* Cellophane is eliminated first, using the following criteria:
    a) Burn test gives odour of burning paper.
    b) Tear strength very low.
    c) Hot wire or match-head applied to sample does not melt it.

Conclusion

It is true of all the wet-chemical tests that they identify one component of a polymeric substance without revealing whether it is a pure substance or a copolymer. To identify a copolymer requires deliberate testing for both polymers, with the added complication that the presence of one may mask the other. A positive test result for one particular plastic tends to lead to the assumption that it is unnecessary to test for other plastics in the same sample. In reviewing the literature there is no mention of a tested plastic giving results that seem to indicate the presence of two polymers, but there is, for example, a publication from the 1920s that states that casein compounded with cellulose nitrate was actually being used more often than celluloid.[17] Whether or not this is accurate, most of us would look no further than the positive result for cellulose nitrate. The question of copolymers complicates analysis to the extent that modern, multi-component plastics are essentially unidentifiable by such methods.

A further problem is discovered in cases where the applied reagent solution produces a colour change on the sample rather than in the solution itself. A spot-test for protein, using 2% copper sulphate solution followed by 10% sodium hydroxide solution, gave dubious results when used on a sample from a casein plastic button, though the same test performed on a casein in-painting medium gave a positive result. The strong purple colour seen on the gelatin sample was present on the casein, but only faintly, probably due to the treatment of casein with formaldehyde to create the plastic. Pigmentation in the casein totally obscures the result, since the colour is developed on the plastic surface, not in the solution, so that the test can only be performed effectively on pale-coloured objects.

Another factor that can interfere with correct identification is the assumption that a trade name product will always have the same composition. This problem arose in connection with Saflip coin holders for the storage of coin collections. According to the manufacturer's information, and a 1982 analysis, the Saflip holders were made from poly(ethylene terephthalate), better known as Mylar, but in terms of physical properties and solvent testing, they behaved unlike any identified sample of Mylar. Based on tearing and folding tests, and solvent susceptibility, the best guess was that they were a laminate of cellulose acetate on the inside and

---

Table VII

Test for the Presence of Acetates

Requirements: a) solution of 6% potassium hydroxide in methanol
                      b) saturated solution of hydroxylamine hydrochloride in methanol
                      c) solution of 1% ferric chloride in water
                      d) solution of 10% hydrochloric acid

1. Place sample in test-tube. Add 1 mL of solution a), then 1 to 2 drops of solution b). Shake gently and leave to stand for at least 3 minutes. Volume of solutions added should be altered in proportion to amount of sample.

2. Add 1 drop of solution c) and shake again.

3. Add solution d), one drop at a time, shaking gently after each addition. Up to 25 drops may be required in some cases. A burgundy-red colour indicates the presence of cellulose acetate or poly(vinyl acetate). Pale yellow is a negative result. Pale purple-red is either a dilute positive result (repeat test, if possible, using smaller quantities of reagents), or may indicate cyanoacrylate or cellulose nitrate.

Alternative Procedure: some forms of this test suggest warming the mixture gently after the addition of solution b). This step probably has the same effect as leaving it to stand for a few minutes.

polystyrene on the outside. A second and more recent instrumental analysis revealed that Saflip holders are made from glycol-modified poly(ethylene terephthalate); a small change, seemingly, but enough of an alteration that the plastic was not correctly identifiable by simple means.

One question yet to be addressed is that of sample taking. Here arises the same dilemma as with the identification of any material from which a sample must be taken. Modern analytical equipment allows the removal of ever smaller portions of the object under study, or in some cases none at all, but the grosser identification methods outlined earlier require rather larger amounts for accurate results. The diphenylamine test for cellulose nitrate is extremely sensitive and can be performed under a microscope with a tiny sample. Other tests may require a small shaving from an inconspicuous place. Spot-testing on the surface, as we might do for metal spot-tests, is risky, since many of the reagent solutions will mark a plastic surface. On the other hand, it does not involve removing any part of the object. In many cases it may well be possible to further refine the tests to reduce the quantities involved. The important point is not to drown a small sample in reagent, or the colour may be indeterminate.

In finishing, having made all the foregoing negative comments, it is necessary to redress the balance a little. From everything said, it would be natural to think that the conclusion is that instrumental analysis is the only way to go. However, along with the problems, some of which have been outlined, there have also been some very good results from using the kind of spot-tests and simple physical determinations discussed earlier. Certainly it is not the claim that these methods can replace full instrumental analysis, but if all we need to know is what the base plastic is, and particularly if we have a good idea of what the plastic might be on stylistic or visual grounds, then it may well be possible to prove it with a specific test. Working towards an elimination scheme for the identification of complete unknowns is a project currently underway that may also prove useful. Overall, the experience has been that many of the outlined methods are of assistance in the identification of plastics, but we should be wary of relying on them solely or implicitly.

Résumé

Les difficultés pratiques liées à l'identification des plastiques

Les objets en plastique qui sont maintenant conservés dans les musées et dans les collections privées définissent une discipline nouvelle pour les spécialistes de la restauration, un domaine dans lequel les recherches ne commencent qu'à peine et où il n'existe que fort peu — s'il en est — de directives de traitement. Or, contrairement à ces matières qui, tels la céramique ou le métal, resteront stables pendant longtemps si elles sont mises en réserve dans un milieu approprié, les plastiques risquent de se dégrader, parfois avec une rapidité étonnante. Et le facteur qui amorcera une telle dégradation sera parfois, en apparence, aussi anodin que cette couche de laque que l'on applique avant d'apposer le numéro d'enregistrement.

Les plastiques réagiront de façon très variée face à la chaleur, à la lumière et à d'autres facteurs liés aux conditions ambiantes ou aux agents de nettoyage, et ils auront parfois eux-mêmes des effets marqués les uns sur les autres. C'est donc dire toute l'importance de bien identifier les polymères avant d'amorcer tout traitement.

Si la spectroscopie infrarouge demeure la meilleure méthode pour identifier de tels matériaux, il n'en demeure pas moins que l'on doit aussi disposer de méthodes d'identification plus simples, qui puissent être couramment appliquées tout aussi bien par les spécialistes de la restauration que par les responsables des collections. Les documents portant sur les plastiques offrent nombre d'exemples de telles méthodes, dont certaines sont scientifiques et d'autres, plus empiriques. Les essais de flottation se fondent ainsi sur des solutions de masse volumique connue pour distinguer les divers genres de plastiques; les essais de combustion, sur l'odeur qu'ils dégagent et sur leurs réactions à la chaleur et au feu; les analyses chimiques ponctuelles, sur les changements de couleur que provoque le procédé expérimental qui est utilisé. L'identification d'après la marque de commerce (si elle est connue) ou d'après le style ou le genre particuliers de l'objet demeure une approche plus subjective. Et, l'expérience acquise au terme de plusieurs années de travaux portant sur des objets en plastique, ainsi que sur des plastiques tant anciens que nouveaux qui sont conservés à des fins expérimentales, démontre assez clairement les limites de telles méthodes, limites qu'il est essentiel de connaître si l'on veut faire des identifications qui seront un tant soit peu certaines.

La principale difficulté tiendrait au fait que les documents portant sur les plastiques présentent souvent des essais qui s'appliquent bien à des échantillons de polymère pur. Et il est plutôt rare que l'on trouve des articles fabriqués en plastique qui n'aient subi aucune modification. Qui plus est, les charges et les pigments influent sur la masse volumique des plastiques et sur leur apparence, et interfèrent donc avec les essais qui se fondent sur les changements de couleur, tandis que les plastifiants modifient les propriétés des polymères de manière imprévisible. Sans compter que la dégradation elle-même produit des modifications chimiques.

Par ailleurs, le recours aux textes d'histoire de l'art pour identifier les plastiques n'est pas sans poser des difficultés d'un tout autre ordre.

Dans la présente communication, nous aborderons ces problèmes en faisant référence à des expériences réelles qui ont été faites en vue d'établir un système d'identification cohérent pour les plastiques.

References

1. Katz, S., *Classic Plastics* (London: Thames and Hudson, 1984).

2. Baer, N.S. and M.J.D. Low, "Advances in Scientific Instrumentation for Conservation," in: N.S. Brommelle and G. Thomson, eds., *Science and Technology in the Service of Conservation: Preprints of the Contributions to the Washington Congress*, 3-9 September (London: IIC, 1982).

3. Delmonte, J., "Effect of Solvents upon Organic Plastics," *Journal of Industrial and Engineering Chemistry*, vol. 14, no. 6, 1942.

4. Sparke, P., ed., *The Plastics Age* (London: Victoria and Albert Museum, 1990).

5. Krause, A. and A. Lange, *Introduction to the Chemical Analysis of Plastics*, trans. J. Haslam (London: Iliffe Books Ltd., 1969).

6. Braun, D., *Simple Methods for Identification of Plastics*, 2nd edn. (Munich: Hanser, 1986).

7. Saunders, K.J., *The Identification of Plastics and Rubbers* (London: Chapman and Hall, 1966).

8. Haslam, J., H.A. Willis and D.C.M. Squirrell, *Identification and Analysis of Plastics*, 2nd edn. (London: Iliffe Books Ltd., 1972).

9. Baker, M., D. von Endt, W. Hopwood and D. Erhardt, "FTIR Microspectrometry: A Powerful Conservation Analysis Tool" in: *Preprints of the 16th Annual Meeting of the American Institute for Conservation of Historic and Artistic Works*, 1988.

10. Cardamone, J.M., "Reflectance Absorption Fourier Transform Infra-red Spectroscopy for Nondestructive Chemical Analysis," in: *Proceedings of the 14th Annual IIC-CG Conference, 27-30 May* (Toronto: IIC-CG, 1988).

11. Newman, T.R., *Plastics as an Art Form* (Philadelphia: Chilton Book Co., 1969).

12. Kaufman, M., *The First Century of Plastics* (London: The Plastics & Rubber Institute, 1963).

13. Williams, R.S., "The Beilstein Test," *CCI Notes* No. 17/1 (Ottawa: Canadian Conservation Institute, 1989).

14. Williams, R.S., "The Diphenylamine Spot Test for Cellulose Nitrate in Museum Objects," *CCI Notes* No. 17/2 (Ottawa: Canadian Conservation Institute, 1988).

15. Browning, B.L., *Analysis of Paper*, 2nd edn. (New York: Marcel Dekker Inc., 1977).

16. Shaw, T.P.G., "Systematic Procedure for Identification of Synthetic Resins and Plastics," *Journal of Industrial and Engineering Chemistry, Analytical Edition*, vol. 16, no. 9, 1944.

17. Tague, E.L., *Casein, Its Preparation, Chemistry and Technical Utilization* (New York: D. Van Nostrand Co., 1926).

18. Coxon, H.C., "An Evaluation of Tests for the Identification of Polymeric Materials Used in Conservation," 1986, unpublished.

19. Briston, J.H., *Plastics Films*, Plastics Institute Monograph (New York: Halstead Press, John Wiley and Sons, 1974).

20. Nechamkin, H., "A Schematic Procedure for Identification of Common Commercial Plastics," *Journal of Industrial and Engineering Chemistry*, vol. 15, no. 1, 1943.

21. Taylor, Thomas O., "The Use and Identification of Plastic Packaging Films for Conservation," in: *The Book and Paper Group Annual*, American Institute for Conservation of Historic and Artistic Works, 1985.

22. Bird, V., "How to Identify Plastic Films," *Plastics Technology*, vol. 9, no. 9, 1963.

The Identification and Characterization of Acrylic Emulsion Paint Media

Carol Stringari

The Museum of Modern Art
New York, N.Y.
U.S.A.

Ellen Pratt

Conservation Center
Institute of Fine Arts, New York University
New York, N.Y.
U.S.A.

Abstract

An ongoing project to study the properties of acrylic emulsion paints is underway at The Museum of Modern Art, New York. Approximately 150 paintings in the collection were surveyed to study the medium and assess condition. Routine examination and testing were done in the laboratory and a body of standards was prepared for comparison. Three case studies were chosen to explore more specific methods of identification. These methods included microscopic analysis and staining, Fourier Transform Infrared Spectroscopy (FTIR), and Pyrolysis-Gas Chromatography (Py-GC).

Introduction

Marcel Duchamp, when asked about his decision to stop painting and pursue chess as an art form, stated:

> I have not stopped painting. Every picture has to exist in the mind before it is put on canvas, and it always loses something when it is turned into paint (Schwarz 1969).

During the twentieth century, creative expression was redefined and existing notions of aesthetics were challenged. Modern works often require analysis beyond material characterization, and in the case of conceptual works, there are no existing materials to identify. Nonetheless, conservators are faced with the task of understanding physical attributes in order to make informed decisions about preservation where this is appropriate.

The range of materials used in this epoch is limitless. The manufacture of synthetic products for industrial use escalated after World War II and artists began to experiment with these materials in their creative endeavors. Acrylic emulsion paints as an artist's medium became widely available in the late 1950s to early 1960s and were fundamental in resolving some contemporary aesthetic concerns. Color-field painters, pop artists, and hard-edge minimalists gravitated quite naturally towards this medium.

The availability of acrylic paints directly coincided with a prevalent rejection of traditional values and romantic notions, and an increased interest in rational objective geometry. Some of the properties of the emulsion paints germane to artistic production during this period were their immediacy (fast drying and water soluble), flexibility, and ability to achieve a hard edge and a slick "contemporary" surface not prone to cracking.

Artists such as Kenneth Noland, Jules Olitski, and Ellsworth Kelly rejected the lyrical expressionist work of artists such as Willem de Kooning and Jackson Pollock, stressing objectivity and pure visual configuration. These artists utilized acrylic paints to realize their formalist concerns.

Concurrent to formalism was an inclination for mass media and pop culture, where art was produced and simultaneously called its role into question. These ideas were embodied in the work of artists such as Andy Warhol and Roy Lichtenstein.

Although materials ultimately act as vehicles, subservient to ideas, their properties and limitations can often influence the realization of a concept. Acrylics facilitated the evolution from heavy paint and gestural brushwork to sharp clean surfaces and precise outlines.

This study investigates the acrylic emulsion paints manufactured for use as artists' materials during this revolutionary period of the 1960s and early 1970s.

Composition of Acrylic Emulsions

The base acrylic emulsions are composed of homopolymers or copolymers of acrylate and/or methacrylate monomers (Figure 1), which undergo free radical emulsion polymerization (Bennett et al. 1968). By varying proportions of these monomers a resin can be tailored for specific properties, such as adhesion, glass transition temperature, tensile strength, and elongation (Bondy 1968). For example, the

substitution of a methyl group for the alpha-hydrogen in the acrylate monomer produces a methacrylate monomer. The polymer formed by methacrylate monomer has more steric hindrance than a poly-acrylate and therefore forms a harder polymer with higher tensile strength (Figure 2). Since the polymers are insoluble in water and must be suspended in a water phase, a surfactant, which is essentially a soap, is used to facilitate this dispersal (Becher 1983). (See footnote for monomer abbreviations.) Base emulsions, such as Rhoplex (or Primal in the U.K.) AC-234 (66% PEA/34% PMMA), Rhoplex AC-33 (66% PEA/33% PMA/1% acrylic acid), Rhoplex AC-22, or Rhoplex AC-507 (PnBMA/PMA), or any of a wide range of acrylic emulsions with varying specificity and properties, are purchased by paint manufacturers.

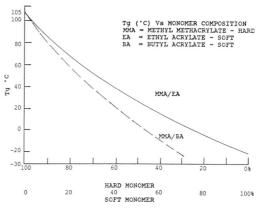

Figure 2 Copolymer composition and its relation to glass transition temperature.

Abbreviations used for monomers:

MA	=	methyl acrylate
EA	=	ethyl acrylate
MMA	=	methyl methacrylate
EMA	=	ethyl methacrylate
iBMA	=	iso-butyl methacrylate
nBMA	=	n-butyl methacrylate

Polymers are distinguished from monomers by the prefix P, thus PMA is poly(methyl acrylate).

Figure 1 Acrylate and methacrylate monomers.

412

These base emulsions require a number of additives to disperse the pigment, to create a homogeneous mixture with specific film forming and levelling properties, and to ensure the shelf life of the product (Martens 1968). These numerous additives are present in quite small percentages and are being constantly re-evaluated and changed by manufacturers, without regulations or standards.

Earlier formulations contained higher concentrations of fillers, surfactants, and colloids, which were water-soluble and resulted in low gloss (van de Wiel and Zom 1981). More recent formulations include surfactants that perform optimally at very low concentrations and internal plasticizers that do not migrate through the film.

Methods of polymer production have been improved to obtain high specificity in the properties of the emulsion without the need for excessive alterations with additives. Nonetheless, no precise information is given about the constituents, and this seems to be problematic. Little is known about the long-term properties of the additives and how they ultimately affect the aging of the films. It is clear that some of these materials act as humectants and have an affinity for moisture and particulate matter in the environment (Brendley and Erhard 1973). Cleaning an acrylic film with moisture can often result in foaming, indicating that there are materials being leached. Yet it is not clear whether this will have a deleterious effect on the paint film by leaving it more porous, or perhaps even an advantageous one, by removing hydrophilic components.

The drying mechanism of the acrylic paints is vastly different from traditional oil binders, which auto-oxidize and crosslink. The acrylic emulsions form a film by evaporation of the water phase. Strong capillary tensions draw the water out of the acrylic film, forcing the long polymer chains to deform and stack together in a tightly packed polyhedral arrangement (Bondy and Coleman 1970). The emulsions are suspensions of spherical resinous particles that are very close in size to the pigment particles incorporated in the film (Figure 3). The critical pigment volume concentration (CPVC) plays

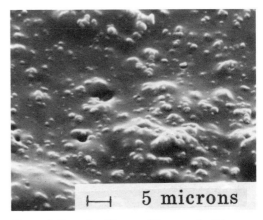

Figure 3 Scanning Electron Micrograph of the surface of an acrylic emulsion paint film, at 2,000x magnification, showing distribution of pigment aggregates in the acrylic resin matrix.

a large part in the appearance and properties of the dry film. For each pigment, the CPVC expressed as the percentage of pigment volume to total volume of the film is that point at which there is just sufficient binder to wet and fill the voids between each particle.

The second order glass transition temperature (Tg) is another critical factor determining the properties of these emulsions and their ability to form a continuous film. A hard latex with a high glass transition temperature may require coalescing agents to ensure its ability to form films. The Tg for emulsions range from -15°C (soft film) to 30°C (hard film). When the glass transition temperature of a material is too low, cold flow can take place or it can remain tacky near room temperature. The acrylic resins become glassy or brittle within a very narrow range below room temperature. These flexible surfaces can also attract particulate matter and deform readily in warm conditions. Acrylics can become glassy at temperatures as high as 5°C (40°F). Mechanical cracking can result if stress is applied at these temperatures. Thus, such high or low temperatures present problems for artworks in storage or travel, especially if they are subjected to impact or manipulation (Michalski 1991).

Relative humidity (RH), air circulation, and temperature affect the initial drying process of acrylic paints. RH is critical, as it will influence the rate of evaporation and alter the effect of the co-solvent (e.g., ethylene glycols). Suitable rheological properties of the formulation are essential to ensure the proper film formation, which can be adversely affected by excessive foaming due to surfactants and dispersants, or cracking due to excess filler material, such as cellulosics or protective colloids. In recent formulations the viscosity of the emulsions has been adjusted to facilitate film formation. Certain monomers, such as styrene and butyl esters, have been used in these formulations to improve performance. This has resulted in increased gloss, higher pigment load, and better resistance to weathering and water sensitivity (Bondy and Coleman 1970).

The acrylic emulsion paint films are readily soluble in xylene, toluene, and acetone. In certain cases, the films are soluble in hydrocarbons and even water, which can present problems for conservation treatments. This sensitivity to water and petroleum benzine is probably due to poor formulations or over-dilution, leaving the pigment vulnerable to mechanical removal. The solubility also presents a problem for artists who wish to apply a protective coating or varnish. To date there is no one simple solution for a reversible varnish on acrylic paint films.

Thus, it becomes evident that these formulations are in a constant state of flux and advancement and can vary considerably from one product to the next and even from one year to the next. Table I lists some categories of additives, with examples for each and their function within the paint film (Gachter and Muller 1985).

This brief review of the general structure, constituents, and properties of acrylic paints demonstrates the enormous range of possibilities for furthering our understanding of these materials through testing and analysis. To make informed decisions about the treatment of these paint films, we felt it was necessary to design a systematic means of identifying and distinguishing them.

The Project

The acrylic research project at The Museum of Modern Art began in 1988 as a survey funded by the Institute of Museum Services to examine approximately 150 paintings purported to be of a "synthetic polymer" medium. This generic category refers to many synthetic resins used in coatings dating from the early 20th century, including, for example, cellulose esters, vinyls, PVAs, alkyds, and synthetic lacquers (Bria 1981; Lodge 1988). During the course of the survey, it became obvious that no firm conclusions could be reached from such a general study. However, this preliminary study was essential to define the scope of the inquiry. Acrylic resins, and more specifically acrylic emulsions, were chosen as the topic for further study.

Phase 1 of the project was the completion of an extensive examination form for each painting and the collection of questionnaires sent to each artist. Photos were taken of the works and distinguishing characteristics were documented. Phase 2 consisted of an investigation into appropriate methods for precise characterization of acrylic emulsion paints.

It was difficult to actually identify these materials through visual examination alone, since their appearance was so dependent on manipulation of the material by the artist. Since the initial media attribution for each painting in the survey was based on information from The Museum of Modern Art (MoMA) curatorial files, and not scientific analysis, it was imperative that a less subjective means of characterizing these paint films be pursued. Furthermore, it was felt that information about chemical properties and variations in formulations could help facilitate treatment decisions and preventive maintenance programs.

From the 150 paintings surveyed, a small group, as representative as possible, was chosen for closer examination and testing. As a practical study, the project advanced our understanding of the artists' working methods, and elucidated potential obstacles encountered when analyzing an actual work of art, with all of the variables inherent in the creative process.

Table I

Additives: Categories and Functions

Additive	Purpose and Effect on Formulation
polyethylene glycol/glycols	plasticizer/hygroscopic/freeze-thaw stabilizer
phenyl mercury compounds/ mercury sulfide salts	fungicide/sensitive to hydrogen sulfide/can cause brown discoloration
carboxylic acids, sodium soaps of stearic and lauric acids, amine soaps, phosphates	anionic surfactants/effective for whites and extenders/hygroscopic
alkyl phenoxy polyethoxy ethanol/ alkyl aryl ethers (i.e., Triton)	ionic surfactants/hygroscopic
cellulosics, casein, polysaccharides, polyacrylic acids, gum arabic, sodium alginate	thickening agents/provide proper consistency/can affect gloss/water sensitivity/less surface smoothness
styrene	imparts gloss/increases water resistance
sulfonated oils, sulfonated esters	emulsifiers
ammonia	pH adjuster
titanium dioxide/hydrated clay/calcium carbonate/amorphous silica	extender pigments/TiO_2 may have reactive sites for water-free radical formation
soya lecithin	dispersant
primary alcohol ethoxylates	dispersant, wetting agent
tamol (chemical formula unknown)	dispersant

Methodology

We pursued the identification of acrylic resins and emulsions for three paintings using Fluorescence Microscopy, Fourier Transform Infrared (FTIR) Microspectroscopy, and Pyrolysis-Gas Chromatography (Py-GC). The works selected were *Flemish VII* (1973) by Al Held, *Dec.18,1979* (1979) by On Kawara, and *Primary Light Group: Red, Green, Blue* (1964 to 1965) by Jo Baer. These artists painted consistently with acrylic paints during the 1960s and early 1970s, and each used a unique method of application for achieving different surfaces. Their paintings will be discussed as three separate case studies.

A body of material standards was created for use as reference and for comparison to samples from actual paintings. Materials were painted out onto canvas and/or mylar, sometimes as a single layer, other times as a laminate structure to simulate a painting for cross-sectional study. Materials collected for standards included: Liquitex acrylic emulsion gessos, paints, and mediums; Golden acrylic emulsion products;

Daler Rowney Cryla acrylic emulsion products; Rohm and Haas Rhoplex acrylic emulsions; Lascaux acrylic emulsions; Magna acrylic resin solution paints and medium gels; Lefranc and Bourgeois Flashe vinyl emulsion paints; Bellini oil paints; Grumbacher oil paints; Winsor and Newton oil paints; linseed oil; and various varnishes.

These standards now serve as the basis for a library, which we are amassing for research and as a resource for other conservators.

The standards and the samples from the actual paintings were all subjected to the same scrutiny and the same tests. Each painting was examined first in visible light then in ultraviolet (UV) light, using two long-wave UV lamps. Empirical observation of these materials has proven helpful in the recognition of certain visual characteristics and autofluorescent or non-fluorescent properties of synthetic materials.

In UV light, the acrylic paints have a characteristic purple appearance, the result of a reflection as opposed to a fluorescent emission. This is distinguishable from oil paints, which emit a slight yellowish fluorescence. It is helpful to have standards prepared to compare fluorescence, as the oil paint fluorescence can be difficult to recognize without the comparison. For a discussion of fluorescence of paint and varnish see de la Rie 1982. In contrast to the behavior of oils, the purple appearance of the acrylic seems to override the primary fluorescence of the pigments.

Under stereomagnification such characteristics as pinholing or air bubbles, which form while the paint film dries, can be discerned (Figure 4). This tendency to froth is caused by the addition of surfactants to form the emulsion.

Impasto formed from acrylic paints is often rounded (Figure 5), as opposed to crisp and peaked, which is more characteristic of oils. These rounded edges of the brushwork are due to levelling, a property determined by surface tension and the addition of thickeners to decrease rapid capillary absorption into the substrate (Patton 1979). Distinctive drying cracks can occur in the surface of the acrylics if they

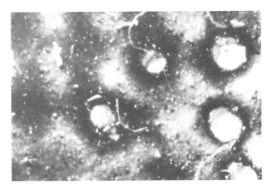

Figure 4 Detail of an acrylic emulsion paint surface illustrating pinholing and the affinity of the tacky surface for particulate matter, at 20x magnification.

Figure 5 Detail of an acrylic emulsion paint film, depicting the levelling and rounded edges of brushwork.

are applied too thickly because a dry skin will form rapidly on the surface, disallowing water evaporation from below, and forcing the formation of cracks to release underlying moisture and relieve stress.

On the whole, due to the numerous additives, thickeners, and pigment load, acrylic paints tend to dry more matte than solvent-borne paint systems.

The influence and complexity of the pigments were not thoroughly addressed in this study, although whenever possible pigment composition was determined by polarized light microscopy. In many instances, results of analysis were clearly influenced or obscured by the pigment. Black and white pigments were chosen as the focus of the study for the sake of comparison and to set some arbitrary parameters.

Microscopy/Fluorescence Staining

The fluorescent staining technique involved staining cross-sections and thin sections to determine whether any constituents or functional groups within the acrylic film could be discerned.

Experimental

Equipment: A Leitz Labor-Lux Metallographic Microscope with a xenon light source fitted with a Ploemopak A2 filter pack for viewing in normal and UV light was used. The A2 cube has an excitation range from 270 nM to 380 nM and a suppression filter from 410 nM to 580 nM. Each filter combination produces different results, due to specific excitation and emission wavelengths. Broader transmission results in a brighter, less contrasting, and generally less specific fluorescent image (Becker 1990).

The method of histological staining was chosen because of its successful adaptation to

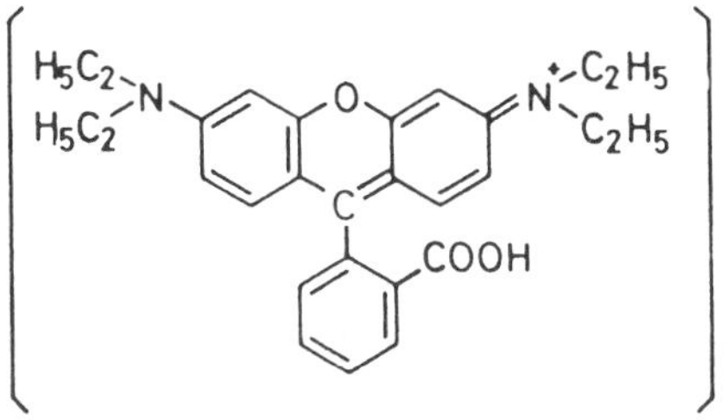

$$C_{28}H_{31}N_2O_3Cl \quad mol\ wt = 479.02$$

Rhodamine B

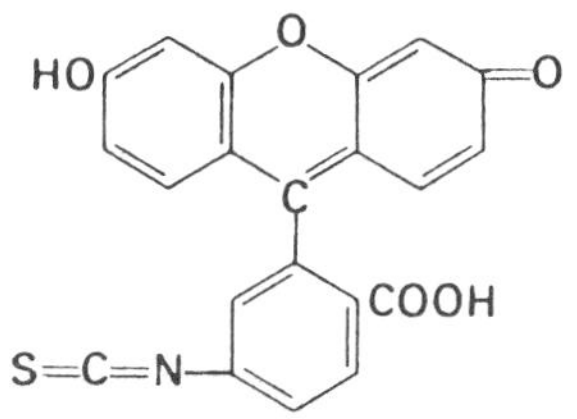

$$C_{21}H_{11}NO_5S;\ mol.\ wt.\ 389.390$$

fluorescein isothiocyanate

Figure 6 Chemical structures of Rhodamine B and FITC stains.

conservation, and its accessibility and ease of use in the laboratory (Talbot 1982; Wolbers 1987). For systematic staining of all unknowns and knowns, Rhodamine B was selected to detect lipids and fluorescein isothiocyanate (FITC) was chosen to detect proteins (Figure 6). These stains have been used on traditional painting materials to indicate the presence of functional groups contained in oil and protein binders. In an attempt to isolate a stain useful for acrylics, or to arrive at a negative attribution by elimination, samples from the body of standards and the three paintings were tested. Results of staining the acrylics proved to be quite confusing, and will be outlined in the case study discussions.

Although the stains do aid in identifying broad categories of traditional materials, such as fatty acids, amino acids, and starches, it appears that the acrylic emulsions are far too complex and the formulations too variable to be able to rely on staining techniques. Although the acrylic polymer backbone itself does not appear to have sites that would react with histological stains, there are a number of surfactants that may contain fatty acid components or amine groups that would react with lipid and protein stains. Therefore caution should be observed when making judgements about the nature of these materials through staining, and standards should always be test-stained prior to staining an unknown.

Results of this method for media identification appear to be highly dependent on technique, including pH, solvent systems, and concentrations (Clark 1983; Lillie 1990). Since acrylic polymers are readily soluble in the suggested carrier solvents for the stains, both FITC and Rhodamine B were tested in water. The FITC was buffered to a specific pH, as the literature suggested (McKinney, Spillane, and Pearce 1966). After staining, all samples were rinsed in water with pH adjusted to that of the stain. In all cases the results were more reproducible when the stain was carried in water and pH carefully controlled.

Microtomed thin sections proved to be the preferred method of sample preparation for staining. Thin sections measuring 5 μm were prepared with a Sorvall JB-4 microtome with a tungsten carbide blade. The inherent fluorescence of a material is minimized in the thin section, and the stain penetrates the entire sample. This minimizes the tendency for the stain to remain on the surface, where it can occupy vacuoles and fissures and autofluoresce.

Information gleaned from scientists at Kodak and Sigma, and literature on histological stains and their application indicated that while many of these stains do indeed have an affinity for certain materials or functional groups, they are also used as tracers, for example, to locate microfissures in metal surfaces and scratches on corneas. This suggests that there will be non-specific fluorescence, where the surface is irregular, as is often the case at the interface between two layers, not necessarily due to any affinity with the material. There is a color difference between the positive staining and the deposition in vacuoles, but this is highly subject to misinterpretation. Empirical observation indicates that rinsing the sample in the carrier solvent minimizes this problem of non-specific fluorescence. Wetting the surface with petroleum benzine after staining also quenches the non-specific fluorescence and facilitates viewing.

Ultimately, it seems problematic to use these stains to draw absolute conclusions without the use of a spectrophotometer, which would measure the wavelength versus intensity of the sample before and after staining. This would allow quantification of the reaction and reduce subjectivity. Solubility tests on the cross-sections or thin sections can also help to determine the nature of the materials present.

pH indicators applied to thin sections proved helpful in determining the properties of the films. Three solutions were used to measure the liquid acrylic emulsions and the dried films:

methyl red:	pink	pH 4.2 to 6.2	yellow
phenol red:	yellow	pH 6.8 to 8.2	red
bromothymol blue:	yellow	pH 6.0 to 7.6	blue

The acrylic paints are consistently alkaline (above pH 8.5) in their liquid state and the dried films are acidic (below pH 4.2). (This seems to disprove a widely held belief that the acrylic paints may be buffering the unprimed canvas on color-field paintings.)

As it became evident that more sophisticated means of accurately identifying these binders would be necessary, two additional methods were chosen, Fourier Transform Infrared Analysis (FTIR) and Pyrolysis-Gas Chromatography (Py-GC).

Fourier Transform Infrared Analysis
FTIR was selected as an analytical tool based on current work in the fields of Coatings and Forensics (Nielsen and Raaschou 1984; Reffner 1990) and at the Getty Conservation Institute (Derrick, Landry, and Stulik 1991). It is an expedient and accessible technique for the identification of organic binders.

FTIR has several advantages over other spectroscopic techniques, such as increased energy output and spectral resolution (Low and Baer 1977). The coupling of a light microscope with the reflecting optics for FTIR microspectroscopy allows relating the sample's morphological structure with the chemical composition, and analyzing intact layered structures.

Another advantage is the extremely small sample size necessary. Spectral libraries and computer software programs allow comparison and subtraction of spectra, and information can be readily shared and reproduced by other laboratories with different instruments. This has been demonstrated in this study by correlating samples run on two separate instruments with different operators.

Experimental
Instrument 1: Nicolet Nic-Plan FTIR spectrometer coupled to a Spectra Tech IR-Plan analytical microscope at the Philadelphia Museum of Art. One group of samples was run neat on a single diamond plate (SDP), 200 scans, with a resolution of 4 wavenumbers. An additional group of samples was run as thin sections on a

NaCl window with the same 200 scans and a resolution of 4 wavenumbers.

Instrument 2: Spectra Tech Irus plan FTIR microprobe, at the Getty Conservation Institute. These samples were all run as thin sections on a barium fluoride window, 200 scans at a resolution of 4 wavenumbers.

Samples weighing approximately 50 μg to 100 μg were taken from the paintings and mounted in Ward's bioplastic polyester embedding medium. A 5 μm thin section area measuring approximately 15 μm to 34 μm x 100 μm was analyzed. The same procedure was used for the body of standards. Dispersed samples were prepared by placing loose particles on the plates. A number of them were run for comparison to the thin sections.

One disadvantage to this method is that it is not a separation technique and therefore little information can be obtained about the additives. Complex mixtures can present problems in interpretation of the spectra, and the influence of pigments on spectral results is a field requiring extensive investigation.

Pyrolysis-Gas Chromatography

Py-GC is especially useful for the analysis of non-volatile samples, such as pigmented acrylic emulsion paint films, which cannot be completely solvent-extracted or dissolved. Pyrolyzing a sample thermally degrades it, breaking down the large polymeric molecules into small volatile molecules, which pass into the gas chromatograph. During the GC process, the sample components are separated by molecular weight and by polarity. Lower molecular weight and lower polarity components tend to pass through the column first and thus result in lower retention times.

As each component exits the column, it is detected and the response is recorded. The output, a pyrogram (pyrolysis chromatogram), is a plot of the retention time vs. degree of response.

A pyrogram of a particular material is distinctive and can be used as a fingerprint for that sample. Fingerprinting, of course, requires a reliable compound reference library. Any

changes in the analytical parameters (especially of the pyrolysis) can affect the results. For maximum reproducibility and thus the possibility for exchange of information between laboratories, experimental conditions must be identical. A recent article (Sonoda and Rioux 1990) about the use of Py-GC for identification of synthetic binders illustrates the problem of reproducibility; we found we could not directly compare our pyrograms with those published in the article.

One advantage of pyrolysis is that it requires a very small sample size and very little sample preparation. For our dried pigmented paint films, we found that a sample size of approximately 200 μg produced the best results. We weighed the samples before and after pyrolysis and found that, in general, 50% of the Magna acrylic solution paints are pyrolyzed, 40% of the acrylic emulsion paints, and 25% of the oil paints. Due to the 50:1 split injection, only 2% of the pyrolyzate enters the column, resulting in a final sample size that could be quite small.

There are paintings, though, whose smooth, unbroken surfaces or extremely thin paint layers, as in color-field paintings, may not offer a sampling site that can yield even a 50 μg or 100 μg sample without damaging the surface. Depending on instrumental parameters, it may not be possible to obtain a large enough sample size on such paintings. Because our Py-GC instrument was concurrently used for other types of sample materials, we were somewhat restricted in setting the instrumental parameters.

Experimental

Pyrolysis Unit: CDS (Chemical Data Systems, Inc., Oxford, PA) Model 120, pulse-mode system. Pyroprobe: platinum wire of 0.36 mm diameter, formed into a coil, 15 mm long by 3 mm diameter. Pyrolysis temperature can range from ambient to 1400°C. Solid samples were placed in a quartz tube, plugged at both ends with quartz wool, and inserted into the coil. Flash pyrolysis: 10 s at 650°C, although the temperature reached inside the quartz tube could be approximately 100°C to 150°C less.

Gas Chromatograph Interface: CDS GC Interface permits insertion of probe for pyrolysis, or injection needle for direct gas chromatography. The interface is connected directly to column. Interface maintenance heating temperature is 200°C to prevent condensation of the pyrolytic products on the inner walls of the chamber. The pre-heated carrier gas, helium, flow rate: 4 mL/min, sweeps the pyrolysis products from the interface chamber into the capillary column.

Gas Chromatograph Instrument: Perkin Elmer Model 8500 GC. Samples were introduced into the column in the split injection mode, ratio 50:1 (49 parts of pyrolyzed sample is vented out and 1 part enters column). Quadrex Corp. SE-54 fused silica capillary column (50 m x 0.25 mm, 0.5 μm film thickness). Column temperature (oven temperature) held at 50°C for 1 min, then increased at 8°C per min until temperature reaches 325°C where it stays for 10 min. Analysis time: 45 min.

Gas Chromatograph Detector: Flame Ionization Detector (FID).

Results and Discussion of Analytical Techniques

The body of standards analyzed with FTIR and Py-GC illustrated a number of interesting points, and allowed us to draw some conclusions about the techniques and how they can be applied to the study of acrylic paints. Monomers, polymers, copolymers, base emulsions, and pigmented emulsions were compared to determine the degree to which they can be characterized.

FTIR: The characteristic spectra of acrylic polymers show specific absorptions in the infrared region related to functional groups and molecular arrangement. For a given peak, intensity of absorption is a measure of the concentration of a functional group, which allows some quantitative estimation.

The infrared spectrum of a mixture is composed of the spectra of all components combined. The functional groups for all of the monomer units used to form the acrylic formulations are similar, and therefore it is difficult to distinguish which homopolymers form the copolymer. Additives and pigments in the paint

formulations further complicate the interpretation. Extraction and separation techniques for these formulations are worthy of further study. Nielsen and Raaschou 1984 discuss the use of a wick stick to separate the components of a paint sample for FTIR analysis.

Acrylic polymers show strong absorptions in regions of the infrared spectrum related to esters. The characteristic peaks are: a doublet around 2900 cm^{-1}, indicating C-H stretches, a sharp intense peak around 1730 cm^{-1} due to carbonyl bonds, two sharp C-H (bends) peaks at 1450 cm^{-1} and 1385 cm^{-1}. OH bends are distinguished by numerous broad peaks from 1024 cm^{-1} to 1236 cm^{-1}, which have similar configurations for all acrylic resins. The peak at 1250 cm^{-1} will be a doublet for methacrylate and a broad single band for acrylates. Comparison of pure acrylate and methacrylate polymers from spectral libraries did clearly illustrate the presence or absence of this doublet at 1250 cm^{-1}. Copolymers, however, are more difficult to recognize or determine the monomeric components present. Ethyl methacrylate and copolymers containing a methacrylate, such as Acryloid B-72 (PMA/PEMA), show a sharp peak around 1028 cm^{-1}, which is not present in spectra for acrylates (Lomax and Fisher 1990).

The paints studied here are mixtures of these polymers, and therefore are difficult to distinguish in this manner. A number of acrylic emulsion base resins were compared, such as Rhoplex AC-234, Rhoplex AC-33 and Rhoplex AC-507. The spectra are quite similar to one another and would require a more complex interpretation to elucidate specific differences in structure.

Although fingerprint comparison is very useful for broad characterization, the subtleties are difficult to ascertain without a spectral library collected with the same instrument under the same conditions and sample preparation. Comparing the emulsion Rhoplex AC-234 (PEA/PMMA) with Acryloid B-72 (PMA/PEMA) shows virtually no difference in the fingerprint region, illustrating that different copolymers of similar materials will absorb similarly.

Proprietary paints were analyzed as standards and further illustrated that complex mixtures of

Table II
FTIR Absorption Bands

Sample		C-H	C=O		C-H	C-H	C-O		O-H	
Held, top black layer PMA/dispersed		2982 2953	1728		1448	1383	1236 1178		1026	850
Held, black PMA/thin section		2982 2953	1736	1600 (d)	1448	1383	1255 1161	1073	1026	848
Held, black GCI/thin section	3518	2966 2922	1738	1609 (d)	1453	1386	1263	1162 1073	1040	856
Held, white GCI/thin section	3520 3420	2965 2941	1729	1600 (d)	1440	1376	1246	1170 1152	1064 1022	858
Held, white PMA/dispersed		2982 2953	1728		1448	1383	1236	1159	1026	850
Held, white PMA/thin section	3439 3312	2984 2951	1732	1600 (d)	1448	1383	1255	1176	1032	850
On Kawara, black PMA/dispersed		2982 2952	1732		1446	1384	1238	1175 1159 1115	1031	913 879
On Kawara, black PMA/thin section		2998 2939	1728	1600 (d)	1452	1381	1282	1161	1068	875
On Kawara, black GCI/thin section	3366	3027 2983 2940	1730	1601 (d)	1498 1452	1383	1283	1161 1124	1070 1034	840
On Kawara, brown PMA/thin section	3414	2982 2918	1743	1601 (d)	1493 1448	1381	1265	1167	1068 1033	877
On Kawara, brown GCI/thin section		3027 2985 2936	1732	1601 (d)	1493 1452	1383	1275	1163	1072 1026	877
On Kawara, gesso PMA/thin section	3696 3620	3026 2998 2932 2517	1730	1600 (d)	1452		1280	1161 1116	1068 1032	912 877
On Kawara, gesso GCI/thin section	3697 3621	3027 2983 2938 2518	1798 1730	1600 (d)	1452		1285	1175 1161 1117	1034	877
Jo Baer, white PMA/dispersed	3450	2932 2850	1730	1602 1581	1452	1400	1280	1161 1116	1032	960
Jo Baer, mock-up PMA/dispersed	3447	2928 2856	1741	1595	1481 1421	1380	1260	1172 1115	1032	938
Jo Baer, white GCI/thin section		3062 3027 2929 2857	1732	1599	1493 1452	1408	1285	1163 1123	1072	810
Liquitex acrylic gesso GCI/thin section	3698 3621	2983 2952 2936 2514	1730	1593	1447	1387	1260	1161 1117	1058 1030	877
Liquitex acrylic emulsion TiO$_2$ PMA/dispersed		2982 2950	1724		1562	1383	1242	1176 1064	1024	848
Golden acrylic emulsion TiO$_2$ PMA/dispersed		2959 2876	1736		1468 1448	1383	1240	1176 1064	1022	850
Daler Rowney acrylic emulsion TiO$_2$ GCI/thin section	3440	3027 2956 2932 2889	1732	1601 (d)	1493 1452	1383	1273	1167 1130 1072	1034	863

PMA refers to all samples run with the instrument at Philadelphia Museum of Art and and GCI refers to those samples run at Getty Conservation Institute. (d) refers to doublet, which was present at 1600 in all samples run as thin sections.

Table II (continued)
FTIR Absorption Bands

Sample		C-H	C=O		C-H	C-H	C-O		O-H	
Liquitex iron oxide black acrylic emulsion GCI/thin section	3368	2976 2933 2901 1948	1738	1600 (d)	1500 1455	1392	1278	1170 1130	1065 1034	840
Liquitex iron oxide black acrylic emulsion PMA/dispersed	no trans-mission		1732		1448	1381	1236	1161 1130	1024	850
Golden carbon black acrylic emulsion PMA/dispersed	no trans-mission	2930 2880 weak	1734		1448	1381		1160 1097	1030	840 800
Daler Rowney iron oxide black acrylic emulsion GCI/thin section	3366	2976 2942 2889 1948	1738	1600 (d)	1500 1454	1386	1278	1170 1142 1068	975	850
Magna TiO₂ acrylic resin PMA/dispersed PMA	3343	2959 2928 2874 2851	1728		1468	1383	1271 1242 1176 1155	1066 1022	966	752
Magna ivory black acrylic resin PMA/dispersed	3244	2959 2928 2874	2013 1728		1587 1468	1412	1269 1242 1147	1037	962	873 798
Grumbacher TiO₂ oil PMA/dispersed	3414	2918 2851 2264	1743		1587 1541 1464	1398 1379	1242 1167	1099	978	
Bellini iron oxide black oil PMA/dispersed		2924 2850 weak	1741		1460					
Bioplastic embedding medium	3530 3449	2918 2851	1740	1601 (d)	1493	1381	1259	1157 1120	1070 1039	744
Liquitex gel medium GCI/thin section	3366	2978 2936	1738	1600 (d)	1450	1390	1250	1170	1068 1030	850

PMA refers to all samples run with the instrument at Philadelphia Museum of Art and GCI refers to those samples run at Getty Conservation Institute. (d) refers to doublet, which was present at 1600 in all samples run as thin sections.

organic materials plus the pigments can obfuscate the interpretation of the spectra. Black and white paints from three manufacturers, Daler Rowney, Golden and Liquitex, were compared (Figure 7).

The whites appear very similar upon initial inspection with clearly resolved characteristic peaks for acrylic polymers. When a more precise comparison is made between the Liquitex and Golden whites, which are clearly the same type of material, several differences are noted. The ratios of the peaks are somewhat different. The doublet indicating the C-H peaks at 2982 cm⁻¹ has shifted to 2959 cm⁻¹ in the Golden sample, and the sharp carbonyl peak

at 1724 cm⁻¹ in the Liquitex has shifted to 1736 cm⁻¹ in the Golden sample. The C-H peaks (2850 cm⁻¹ to 2960 cm⁻¹) have a clear resolved shoulder in the Golden, corresponding to the base resin Rhoplex AC-507, while the Liquitex configuration in this area looks more like Rhoplex AC-234. Poly(methyl methacrylate) and poly(butyl methacrylate) reference spectra also have this clear shoulder peak.

Daler Rowney white has the most distinctive spectrum, which was also true with the Py-GC results. The carbonyl peak is at 1738 cm⁻¹, the highest wavenumber for this region of the three formulations, and the C-H peaks are more complex and have shifted to 2932 cm⁻¹ and

2889 cm^{-1}. (This complexity may be in part due to the bioplastic embedding medium, as this sample was only run as a thin section.) Pigment interference seems to be problematic with FTIR analysis and can influence results. Titanium dioxide has a strong absorption below 800 cm^{-1}. However, in the case of the acrylics, this has little influence on the primary peaks, which characterize the binder in the fingerprint region.

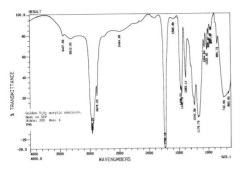

a) Golden TiO$_2$

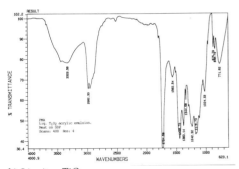

b) Liquitex TiO$_2$

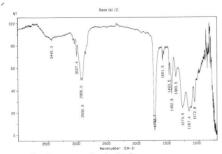

c) Daler Rowney Cryla TiO$_2$

Figure 7 Spectra for acrylic emulsions.

The black colors proved more troublesome due to the presence of pigments, such as iron oxide and carbon, which have very strong absorption patterns above 2000 cm^{-1}, and bone black, which has a strong peak between 1000 cm^{-1} and 1100 cm^{-1}. The interference from the pigment seemed to present more of a problem with the dispersed samples on the diamond plate, as it was difficult to get the sample thin enough for maximum transmission. The elasticity of the acrylics cause them to spring back when pressure is put on to smear them on the cell.

The combination of sample density and pigment obstruction resulted in inadequate transmission above 2000 cm^{-1} for these samples. A number of samples were run on different instruments using a reflectance mode, which allows analysis of a thick sample or cross-section directly from the surface with no sample preparation. Intensity of reflected radiation is dependent on the surface composition and morphology. In all cases the resolution was significantly poorer than with transmission through the sample.

Despite the pigment interference in the black formulation, several peaks were unquestionably similar in all formulations, such as the sharp carbonyl at 1734 cm^{-1}, the sharp peaks around 1446 cm^{-1} and 1380 cm^{-1} indicating C-H bends, and the broad area of peaks from 1150 cm^{-1} to 1030 cm^{-1} indicating C-O bonds.

Fewer distinctions could be made between the black formulations than was possible for the whites due to poor resolution. The Daler Rowney iron oxide black C-H peaks appear at 2942 cm^{-1} and 2889 cm^{-1} while the Liquitex and Golden seem to be a bit lower at 2930 cm^{-1}, 2926 cm^{-1}, and 2850 cm^{-1}. The Daler Rowney also has a strong peak at around 1170 cm^{-1}, while both Liquitex and Golden show a comparable peak at 1150 cm^{-1}.

The samples run as thin sections on barium fluoride windows produce clearer spectra, but it appears that the bioplastic embedding medium interferes with the results. The polyester embedding medium seems to penetrate the sample and the infrared absorption from this material adds to the spectra. The infrared absorption of polyester is quite similar to that of acrylic polymers, but it is possible to isolate the peaks of the embedding medium by comparing the same sample of acrylic run as dispersed specimen. All samples run as thin sections show absorption peaks due to the polyester embedding medium (Figure 8). Subtracting the bioplastic from the spectrum confirmed this with a drop in intensity of the corresponding peaks. By comparison with reference spectra for bioplastic and for identical samples run as dispersed films, peaks from the bioplastic can be identified: these appear as several weak but sharp peaks above 3000 cm^{-1}, a weak doublet at 1600 cm^{-1}, and a sharp peak around 1070 cm^{-1}.

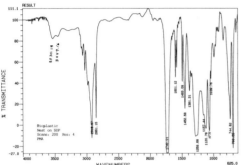

Figure 8 Spectrum for Ward's bioplastic polyester embedding medium.

Comparison of the acrylic emulsion paints with Magna, a poly(n-butyl methacrylate) solution paint, showed an identical sharp carbonyl peak at 1728 cm^{-1}, the sharp C-H peaks at 1468 cm^{-1} and 1383 cm^{-1}. The spectrum for the white Magna paint was a bit more resolved than for the black Magna, which is consistent with the results for the acrylic emulsion paints, especially in the broad area of peaks from 1170 cm^{-1} to 1030 cm^{-1}. The C-H peaks were identical in both black and white formulations (2959 cm^{-1}, 2932 cm^{-1}, 2874 cm^{-1}, 2851 cm^{-1}) and very clearly resolved. The doublet at 1242 cm^{-1} and 1269 cm^{-1} is sharply defined as expected for a poly methacrylate (Figure 9).

All of the acrylic paints can be unequivocally distinguished from pigmented oil films (Figure 10). The primary differences are: the C-H peak area is shifted to around 2920 cm^{-1} and 2850 cm^{-1}, approximately 30 cm^{-1} to 60 cm^{-1}

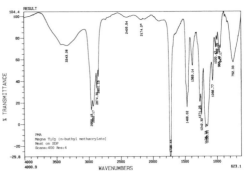

Figure 9 Spectrum for Magna TiO$_2$ white.

lower than any of the acrylic polymers. The carbonyl peak for oil is found around 1740 cm^{-1} to 1750 cm^{-1}, while for the acrylic polymers it is found around 1720 cm^{-1} to 1732 cm^{-1}. There are sharp peaks at 1464 cm^{-1} and 1379 cm^{-1}, which is the aliphatic hydrocarbon region, while the acrylic polymers show peaks at 1448 cm^{-1} and 1381 cm^{-1}. The C-O absorption bands of the oils appear at 1242 cm^{-1}, 1165 cm^{-1} and 1099 cm^{-1}. This area of the spectrum is similar in both oil and acrylics, although the ratios are different and the acrylic polymers lack the 1099 cm^{-1} peak. The most intense peak in this area for the oils appears at 1165 cm^{-1} and the major peak in the grouping for the acrylic polymers is 1159 cm^{-1}. Although the black oil shows the aforementioned pigment interference, the fingerprint region for oil has a distinctly different profile than the acrylic polymer.

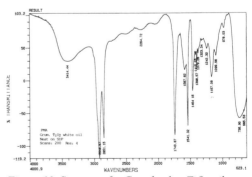

Figure 10 Spectrum for Grumbacher TiO$_2$ oil.

Py-GC: Haken and McKay 1973 have studied pyrolysis of various acrylic homopolymers, copolymers, and mixtures of homopolymers,

Table III

Py-GC Retention Times

RETENTION TIMES (MINUTES)													
MONOMERS													
MA					5.1								
EA							5.9						
MMA								6					
EMA									7.1				
nBMA											10.9		
EA-MMA mixture							5.8	6					
HOMOPOLYMERS													
MA			4.5	4.7	5.2							11.5	14.6
	16												
	24.7						30.5	30.7					
EA			4.3	4.6			6						
			17.4	18.5									
					26.9					32.8	32.9	37.8	
MMA							5.9	6.1					19.2
EMA	3.9		4.3				6		7.3				
iBMA										10.8		11.3	16.2
nBMA				4.5						10.8	11		
COPOLYMER													
MA-EMA	3.7		4.3		5.2		6.2		7.3				
	15.9	16.7	17.6		20.2								
	24.4	25.1	25.5	26.3		27.1							
BASE ACRYLIC EMULSIONS													
AC-22		4.2		4.5	5.2		6	6.1	7.2	9.2			
		16.7	17.4	18.4									
			25.7	26.1	26.8	27.1							
AC-234		4.2		4.5	5.2		5.9	6.1	7.2	9.3			
		16.8	17.4	18.5									
			25.8	26.2	26.9	27.2							
AC-507				4.4		5.7	6.2		7.6	9.3			
					20.3	20.9	23.9			24.7			
							30.3	30.7		31.9	33.5		
ACRYLIC EMULSION PAINTS													
LIQUITEX WHITE		4.2		4.5	5.2		6	6.1	7.2		10.7		
		16.8	17.5	18.5									
			25.8	26.2	26.8	27.2	28.2	28.5					
GOLDEN WHITE		4.2		4.4	5.2	5.6	6	6.1	7.2	9.3	11.2		
		16.8	17.6	18.5									
			25.9	26.2	26.9	27.3							
CRYLA WHITE				4.4		5.7	6.2		7.8	9.3			
					20.4	21	24.1			24.8			
							30.4	30.7		32	33.5		
LASCAUX WHITE				4.5		5.7	6.2		7.7	9.3	11.1		
					20.3	20.9	22.7	24	24.4	24.8			
							30.5	30.8		32	33.5		

Table III (continued)
Py-GC Retention Times

	RETENTION TIMES (MINUTES)												
ACRYLIC EMULSION PAINTS													
LIQUITEX BLACK			4.4	4.5	5.2		6	6.2	7.2		10.7		
		16.8	17.6	18.5									
			25.9	26	26.9	27.3	28.3	28.5					
GOLDEN BLACK		4.2	4.3	4.5	5.2	5.6	6	6.1	7.2	9.2	11.1		
		16.8	17.6	18.5									
			25.8	26.2	26.9	27.2							
CRYLA BLACK			4.4			5.7		6.2	7.8	9.3			
						20.5	21.2	24.2		25			
							30.4	30.7		32	33.5		
LASCAUX BLACK	3			4.5		5.8		6.3	7.5	9.4	11.2		
					19.7	21.2	22.7	24.2			26.6	26.8	
									31.5			34.6	
OIL PAINTS													
GRUMBACHER WHITE	4.4	4.6	5.2	6		7.5	9.6						
		11.7	12.3	12.9	13.7	14.7	15.7	17.6	19.3				
		21.2		22.7	24.4		25.8	26.3	26.7			28.6	
		31	31.2	32.1	33.2								
BELLINI BLACK	4.5	4.7	5	6.1		7.7	9.8						
		11.7	12.4		13.8	14.9	15.9	17.4	19.4				
		21.4		22.8	24.3							28.8	
		31.2	31.4	32.3		34							
ACRYLIC SOLUTION PAINTS													
MAGNA WHITE				4.5							11.3		
MAGNA BLACK				4.6							11.5		
PAINTINGS													
HELD WHITE			4.3	4.5	5.3		6	6.2	7.2				
		16.8	17.5	18.5									
			25.8	26.2	26.9	27.2							
HELD BLACK			4.3	4.5	5.3		6	6.2	7.2				
		16.8	17.6	18.5									
			25.8	26.2	26.9	27.2		28.4		30.8	31		
KAWARA BLACK			4.2	4.5	5.3		5.9	6.1	7.2				
		16.9	17.7	18.8									
			25.9	26.2	26.9	27.3							
BAER WHITE	4.4	4.6	5	5.8		7.4	9.5						
	11	11.4	12.1	12.9	13.3	14.8	15.5	17.4	19.1				
		21		22.7			25.6			27.4	28.4	28.8	
	30.8	31					38.6						
BAER MOCK-UP	4.3	4.5	5	5.6	6.2	7.4	9.5						
	11	11.4	12.1		13.7	14.5	15.8	17.5	19.3				
		21		22.7	24.5						28.4		
	30.9				33.1								
AGED LINSEED OIL	4.4	4.8	5.3	6.2		7.9	10						
		11.8	12.2	12.6	13.5	14.9		17	18.6				
	20.2		22.1	22.7	23.9	25	25.6					28.8	29.7
				32.2	33.2								

including the methyl, ethyl, and n-butyl esters of acrylic and methacrylic acids. They found that (regardless of the alkyl group attached to the acrylate or methacrylate) there is a constant high recovery rate of methacrylate monomer from the methacrylate polymer whether it is a homopolymer, copolymer, or mixture. For the homologous acrylate polymer, however, the recovery rate of the acrylate monomer is much lower and is dependent on whether the polymer is a homopolymer, copolymer, or mixture. The pyrolysis of an acrylate/methacrylate copolymer gives greater yield of the acrylate monomer than does the pyrolysis of either an acrylate homopolymer or a mixture of acrylate homopolymer and methacrylate homopolymer. For example, yield of the methyl acrylate monomer from the homopolymer PMA was 14%, and from a mixture of homopolymers PMA and PMMA it was 14%, but from the copolymer PMA/PMMA it was 40%.

Besides the monomer, the only pyrolysis products for methacrylates were corresponding alcohols at very low concentrations. Acrylates gave a low monomer yield with a high yield of alcohols.

It is these differences in monomer recovery that allow differentiation between copolymers and homopolymer mixtures using pyrograms. In addition to monomers, other pyrolysis products of PMMA/PMA copolymer could be methane, ethylene, hydrogen, carbon dioxide, carbon monoxide, ethyl methacrylate, and ethanol. At higher temperatures, the decomposition of the ester groups of polyacrylates results in other products, such as olefins and alcohols. Recombination reactions of degradation products during pyrolysis can also occur. In pyrolysis, PMA degrades to methyl alcohol, ethyl alcohol, MA monomer, and MMA monomer. PEA degrades to ethyl alcohol, EA monomer, and EMA monomer. PMMA, PEMA, and PnBMA degrade to mostly monomer.

The results of the Py-GC analysis of acrylate and methacrylate monomers, homopolymers, and copolymers in this study agree with the results of Haken and McKay. Chromatograms for the monomers MA, EA, MMA, EMA, nBMA, and EA-MMA mixtures were obtained. (Because monomers are in a volatile liquid form,

and cannot be pyrolyzed, about 1 μl of a solution of 6 drops of monomer in about 2 mL of methylene chloride was injected directly into the port. Consequently each monomer chromatogram has a peak at 4.5 or 4.6 min retention time representing the methylene chloride solvent.)

The pyrograms for the poly methacrylate homopolymers, PMMA, PEMA, PiBMA, and PBMA, all display a tall distinct singular peak at corresponding retention times for their parent monomers, indicating a high yield of monomer recovery. The acrylates also display corresponding monomer peaks, but with much lower relative yield, and with the presence of numerous other peaks, probably alcohols, dimers, and trimers. The PMA/PEMA copolymer pyrogram displays a high methacrylate yield and an increased acrylate monomer yield as described by Haken and McKay.

Although much information is available about methods for quantitative Py-GC, we made no attempt to determine precise quantities and ratios. Instead, where possible, we estimated the approximate relative quantities of various types of monomers recovered, or identified a material as an acrylate or methacrylate.

The Rohm and Haas base acrylic emulsions Rhoplex AC-22, Rhoplex AC-33, Rhoplex AC-234, and Rhoplex AC-507 were analyzed (Figure 11). These emulsions are based on EA-MMA copolymer (about 66:34 ratio). Although these separate emulsion products may be based on the same copolymer, they differ from each other in viscosity, for example, Rhoplex AC-22 50 Pa.s, and Rhoplex AC-33 600 Pa.s. In fact, the pyrograms for Rhoplex AC-234 and Rhoplex AC-22 are virtually identical. The pyrogram for Rhoplex AC-507 is similar, but has fewer peaks and different retention times in the early retention time area (0 to 10 min); and the dimer and trimer groups shift to longer retention times compared to Rhoplex AC-22 and Rhoplex AC-234. For Rhoplex AC-22 and Rhoplex AC-234 the dimer groups fall in the 16 to 19 min range and the trimers between 25 and 27 min. But, for Rhoplex AC-507, the dimer group is between 20 to 25 min and the trimer between 30 and 34 min.

Peaks for EA monomer (5.9/6.0 min) and for MMA monomer (6.1 min) appear in the pyrograms for Rhoplex AC-22 and Rhoplex AC-234, as would be expected. The Rhoplex AC-507 is suggested to be based on MA-nBMA copolymer (Rohm and Haas 1991). However, the peak for nBMA monomer (11.0 min) does not appear in the pyrogram — evidence that is contradictory to information given by the manufacturer. Also, note the presence of an additional distinctive peak at

9.3 min, indicating a difference in Rhoplex AC-507 from Rhoplex AC-22 and Rhoplex AC-234.

Eight proprietary acrylic emulsion paints, four black and four white, were analyzed (Figure 12). Within each brand, except for the Lascaux, the pyrogram for the white paint matches the pyrogram for the black paint, implying consistent use of the same base formulation for the two colors. For the Lascaux black and white, the peaks in the monomer area coincide, but there are variations in the dimer and trimer areas. The Lascaux white has additional peaks. Between brands, however, differences do exist in the pyrograms. In general, the Daler Rowney and the Lascaux are quite similar, except that, in the monomer area of the pyrogram, the Lascaux has an extra small peak at 11.1/11.2 min. The Liquitex and the Golden resemble each other except that, in the monomer area, the Golden has an extra peak at 9.3 min. In the dimer area, both Daler Rowney and Lascaux have peaks in the low 20s, except that Lascaux white has two extra peaks at 22.7 and 24.4 min. Lascaux black has a slightly different configuration. Liquitex and Golden both have peaks in the mid-teens in the dimer area. In the trimer area, Daler Rowney and Lascaux are both in the low 30s. Liquitex and Golden are both in the high 20s, except that Liquitex has two extra peaks at 28.2 and 28.5 min. When the Rohm and Haas base emulsions are compared to the paints, Rhoplex AC-22 and

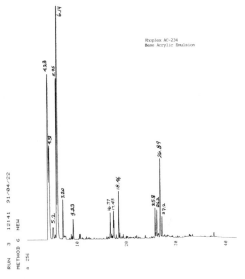

a) Rhoplex AC-234

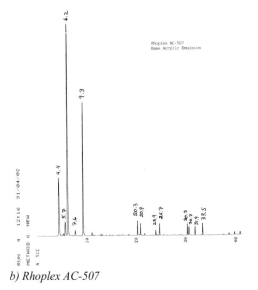

b) Rhoplex AC-507

Figure 11 Pyrograms for base acrylic emulsions.

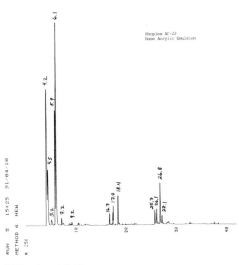

c) Rhoplex AC-22

Rhoplex AC-234 are almost identical to Golden. Liquitex is also quite close except that it lacks the peak at 9.3 min and has two extra small peaks in the trimer area. Rhoplex AC-507 matches the Daler Rowney. It is quite close to the Lascaux, except for two extra peaks in the paint at 24.0 and 24.8 min.

The medium for Magna acrylic solution paints (Figure 13) is poly(n-butyl methacrylate) resin. Magna paints produce quite simple pyrograms, that of a methacrylate homopolymer. As

expected there is a strong peak at 11.0 min, the retention time for nBMA homopolymer.

Compared to acrylic emulsions, traditional oil paints (Figure 14) produce identifiable pyrograms with a greater number of peaks, greater complexity, and a repetitive regularity in the profile.

In general, different paint media (acrylic emulsions, acrylic solutions, and drying oils) produce pyrograms with easily recognized fingerprint profiles. More specifically, different acrylic and methacrylic homopolymers and copolymers can be discerned.

As an addendum, we found that overall, the pigments do not seem to affect the Py-GC results. Weighing of the sample seemed to indicate that the pigment was still in the quartz tube after pyrolysis (40% of the sample by weight). According to the literature metal pigments can affect retention time. In our results, however, the pigment seems to have a more dramatic effect with FTIR than with the Py-GC.

Case Study I

Flemish VII (1973) (Figure 15) by Al Held was chosen as a representative example of the use of acrylic emulsion. The emulsion was applied in numerous layers to create a hard edge composition of intersecting planes, constructing an

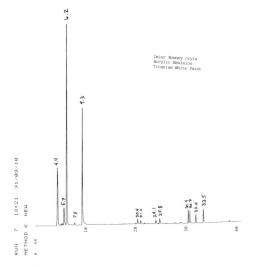

a) Daler Rowney Cryla

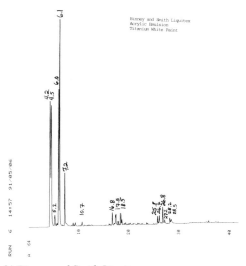

b) Binney and Smith Liquitex

Figure 12 Pyrograms for acrylic emulsion titanium white paints.

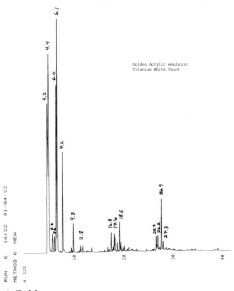

c) Golden

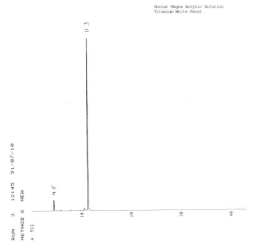

Figure 13 Pyrogram for Bocour Magna acrylic solution titanium white paint.

illusion of depth and architectural clarity (Lodge 1991). Held began using acrylic paints in the late 1950s, slowly evolving a meticulous technique of applying multiple layers, creating a masonry effect on the surface. The composition is worked out directly on the surface and pentimenti or compositional changes are visible in raking light (Figure 16). Prior to 1963 Held allowed the effects of this process to remain visible, but eventually the critics influenced his working methods by referring to traces of the process as "scar tissue," indicating numerous failures or uncertainties (Sandler 1984). At this time he began to build up the layers until he

Figure 15 Al Held, Flemish VII *(1973), acrylic emulsion paint on canvas, 60 1/8 in. x 60 1/8 in. (152.7 cm x 152.7 cm), Collection, The Museum of Modern Art, New York, Riklis Collection of McCrory Corporation (fractional gift).*

achieved the composition he desired and then used a disc sander to remove the "process" as much as possible. Marks from the sander are often evident through the surface. His very recent paintings are conceived in a full scale study and then entirely repainted on another canvas to achieve a pristine surface without unintended tape edges showing through. Held himself blocks in the composition with a base color and then numerous layers of the color are applied by his assistants (Held 1991).

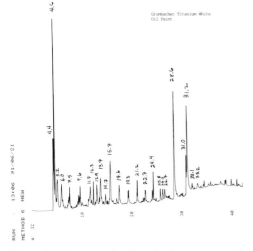

Figure 14 Pyrogram for Grumbacher titanium white oil paint.

Figure 16 Flemish VII, *detail of surface showing changes in composition.*

Flemish VII has a very high gloss, an unusual characteristic for the black acrylics, which often contain fillers and impurities causing them to dry matte (Golden 1990).

The artist recalls that in some of his earlier paintings he used a 50/50 mixture of Liquitex and Rhoplex, for example, in *The Big N* (1964, MoMA) and in his first acrylic painting, *Taxicab* (1959). He recollects that he probably mixed gel medium in the later painting *Flemish VII*, but in smaller proportions. The earlier paintings seem to hold onto more grime and particulate matter from the atmosphere. This is probably due to the large proportion of Rhoplex, which could impart a softer, tackier surface.

A test showed that black and white paints were both insoluble in water and hydrocarbons, but readily soluble in xylene, toluene, acetone, and ethanol.

Ultraviolet examination revealed the non-fluorescent nature of the medium and the characteristic purple appearance of the white. This type of fluorescence was corroborated in the cross-section that was taken from the edge of the painting where there are numerous layers and build-up.

Results of staining were as follows:

- Stained for lipids with Rhodamine B in ethanol — black uppermost layer faintly positive and the white layer strongly positive. Both layers are soluble in the carrier solvent. Same procedure with Rhodamine B in water — black uppermost layer negative, white layer faintly positive.

- Stained for protein with FITC in acetone — both layers readily soluble in the carrier solvent. Black layer spotted positive fluorescence, white layer strongly positive. Same procedure with FITC in pH 9 aqueous sodium phosphate solution — black layer is negative and the white layer faintly positive.

- Stain for pH with methyl red and bromothymol blue — indicated a pH below 4.2 in all layers.

Results of FTIR microspectroscopy for the samples from the Al Held painting confirmed the suspected acrylic binder in both the black and the white (Figure 17). The general peak pattern seems to be reproducible and consistent with the standard of Liquitex gel medium, Rhoplex AC-234, and Acryloid B-72. The Held spectra seem to be closer to the Liquitex gel medium than to the Liquitex black iron oxide, which may be due to the Held pigment, which is bone or ivory black. Liquitex gel medium was found by the Canadian Conservation Institute to be 1:1 PnBA/PMMA.

The results of the samples run neat on a single diamond plate also correspond very closely to Rhoplex AC-234 (PEA/PMMA). The Held sample is slightly more complex in the 900 cm^{-1} to 1075 cm^{-1} region of the infrared spectrum, which could be caused by pigment interference. All of the samples show a very weak peak at approximately 3441 cm^{-1}, indicating an aromatic (possibly a styrene component) or acids from unreacted monomer units.

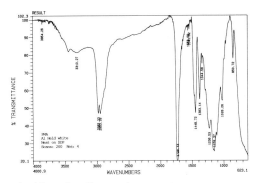

a) white paint, dispersed

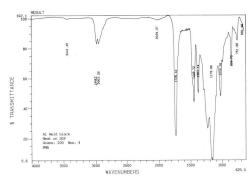

b) black paint, dispersed

Figure 17 FTIR spectra for Flemish VII.

Styrene is commonly used in more recent acrylic formulations to adjust their glass transition temperatures and to improve gloss.

The Held white sample, pigmented with titanium dioxide, closely matched both the Held black and the Liquitex gel medium. There is a very strong absorption overlay from the titanium below 700 cm^{-1}. Absorption bands match closely for the black and white samples from this painting, except the white has an intense doublet at 811/834 cm^{-1}. This peak also appears in some unpigmented emulsion formulas, such as Rhoplex AC-234, Liquitex gel medium, and Rhoplex AC-33.

When compared with white pigmented standards, the fingerprint match for the Held white sample proved to be Liquitex titanium white acrylic emulsion.

Samples of the white paint and of the black paint were each run with Py-GC. The pyrogram for the white matches that of the black and they both match the pyrograms for Liquitex (Figure 18). This again confirms information from the artist that he painted *Flemish VII* with Liquitex.

Retention times of painting and standard samples were identical, the one difference being the ratios between the monomer peaks of 4.5 and 6.2 min. This may reflect some change in ratios of the homopolymers in the formulation or in the degradation products of the naturally aged painting sample. (The standard is not aged.) The pigments do not appear to affect the results, and weighing of the sample seemed to indicate that the pigment remains in the quartz tube after pyrolysis (40% of the sample by weight).

Our effort to distinguish between the various formulations was unequivocally more successful with Py-GC than with FTIR.

Case Study II

The morning of January 4, 1966 in his East 13th Street New York studio, 39-year-old Japanese-born On Kawara began The Today Series of Date Paintings. After stamping the exact time he woke up on color postcards which he sends to his friends, On Kawara

selects a pre-stretched canvas for his daily work, a carefully painted monochrome on which is noted the day's date. If the painting is not finished by midnight, it is destroyed. By October 31, 1970 eight hundred and twenty-three of these works were completed (Denizot 1979).

The second work chosen for examination was *Dec.18,1979* (Figure 19). It is one of the three

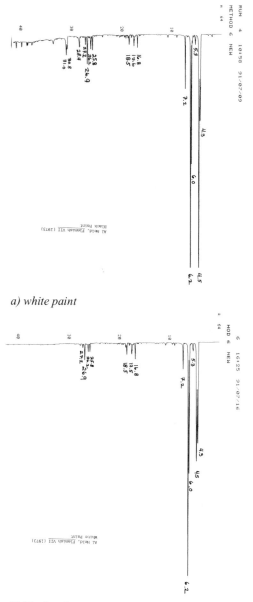

a) white paint

b) black paint

Figure 18 Pyrograms for Flemish VII.

Figure 19 On Kawara, Dec.18,1979 *(1979), acrylic emulsion paint on canvas, 18 1/4 in. x 24 3/8 in. (46.3 cm x 61.6 cm), Collection, The Museum of Modern Art, New York, Blanchette Rockefeller Fund.*

Date Paintings in the collection of MoMA belonging to the Today Series by conceptual artist On Kawara, who manipulates acrylic paints in a quite different manner from Held. He is deeply concerned with the notion of time and divisions into units such as hours and days and their relation to the earth's rotation on its axis. Each painting is housed within boxes constructed by the artist, many of which are lined with a newspaper sheet from the specific date of the painting.

The artist's meticulous painting technique consistently results in a smooth, matte, flawless surface (Figure 20). This surface could be mistaken for an oil due to its even quality and no apparent air bubbles. Air bubbles or pinholes are often an indication of the frothing of an emulsion. In fact, the artist has stated that he carefully wipes out air bubbles with a cloth, in order to eliminate this phenomenon (On Kawara 1989). However, when viewed under stereomagnification, these characteristic bubbles become more evident and the rounded edges of the brushwork appear more like acrylic, which flows and levels readily. The painting does not have a particularly plastic appearance, although the edges of the painting, which are tautly stretched and painted around the side, show no sign of stress-cracking. This would be a difficult feat if using an oil film, which is inherently much more brittle. The overall absence of cracking is also particularly interesting considering the priming layer is

rabbit skin glue, which is quite reactive and subject to embrittlement. The artist recalled that he used rabbit skin glue to prepare the cotton duck, then applied a coat of commercial acrylic gesso and then acrylic paint. He said that he purposely manipulated the paint to achieve a matte surface that should never be varnished. The paint is insoluble in water and petroleum spirits, and readily soluble in xylene, toluene, acetone, and ethanol.

Under UV light, the dark area is non-fluorescent and exhibits the aforementioned violet reflection or appearance. The white text has a purplish cast, and a slight whitish inherent fluorescence, probably due to pigment composition.

In a cross-section, the presence of three layers explained the slightly greenish color of the surface, which at first glance appeared black. Above the ground layer is a brown layer and then a black or grayish layer. Analysis of the pigments revealed a complex mixture of calcite, yellow and orange oxides, carbon black, and small amounts of an isotropic blue-green pigment.

The thin section clearly shows the porous nature of the ground and the particle distribution in the upper layers. Under UV light, the gesso layer appeared faintly fluorescent with characteristic violet overtones, the upper two layers being non-fluorescent.

Results of staining were as follows:

- Stained for lipids with Rhodamine B in ethanol — all layers stained positive. All

Figure 20 Detail of surface Dec.18,1979.

layers were readily soluble in carrier solvent, and the gesso layer was immediately broken up. Using the same procedure with Rhodamine B in water — faint positive in blacks, brightly fluorescent in gesso.

- Stained for protein with FITC in acetone — entire sample brightly positive. All layers soluble in carrier solvent. Using the same procedure in a pH 9 sodium phosphate aqueous solution — only the gesso layer is positive and brightly positive in area of sizing (rabbit skin glue).

- Stain for pH with methyl red and bromothymol blue — indicated a pH below 4.2 in all layers.

The gesso reactions in this sample from the painting corresponded to the results of staining numerous acrylic gesso standards, which consistently stain positive for both lipids and proteins. This reaction may be because of the solubility, or due to its complex mixture of fillers and bulking agents. Surfactants with hydrophilic groups (fatty acid chains) may react positively for lipids, or proteinaceous material, such as casein or gelatin, which are sometimes added as thickeners. This strong reaction is peculiar, however, since the percentages of these materials would be very small.

FTIR analysis was done on the three layers of the On Kawara sample, which was run as a thin section on a barium fluoride window. The top two layers produced nearly identical spectra (Figure 21). The priming layer appears quite different due to the interference from pigments and bulking agents in the gesso. This interference was exemplified by comparing the On Kawara gesso with a Liquitex gesso standard and reference spectra for kaolin and calcium carbonate. Both the unknown and the Liquitex gesso standard have distinct absorbency patterns for kaolin at 3676/3596 cm^{-1} and for calcium carbonate at 2502 cm^{-1}, a broad unresolved band around 1446 cm^{-1} to 1387 cm^{-1}, which is also indicative of calcium carbonate (Figure 22).

Both the black and the brown layers have absorption patterns similar to Daler Rowney and Liquitex black acrylic emulsion standards; the

Held results were similar. Reference samples that contained pure iron oxides were run as dispersed samples and often suffered from pigment interference and the thickness of the sample. There was a clear gain in energy transmission for thin section samples, but they have

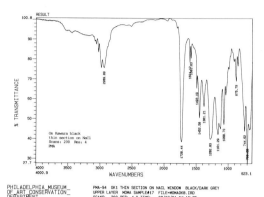

a) top black/gray paint

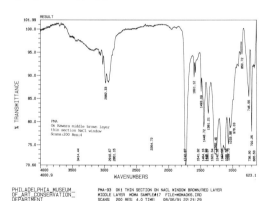

b) middle brown paint

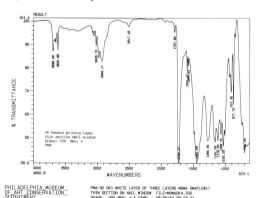

c) bottom gesso layer

Figure 21 FTIR spectra for Dec.18,1979.

434

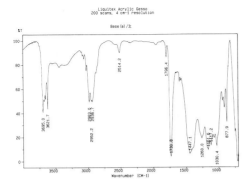

Liquitex Acrylic Gesso
200 scans, 4 cm-1 resolution

Figure 22 Liquitex acrylic white gesso.

the disadvantage of bioplastic interference. A comparison of the top layer run dispersed and as a thin section indicated that the small sharp peaks above 3000 cm^{-1}, the doublet at 1600 cm^{-1}, and the sharp peak at 1068 cm^{-1} can be attributed to the bioplastic embedding medium. Computer spectral subtraction and deconvolution of the spectrum can aid in interpretation.

Despite these obstacles, most spectra were quite well defined and could be easily matched to their corresponding standards. When the spectrum for bioplastic was subtracted from the spectra of the thin section samples taken from On Kawara paintings spectra, it was interesting to note that one of the weak but sharp peaks directly above 3000 cm^{-1} remained, which, when compared to reference spectra of coatings resins, seems only to appear when the acrylic co- or ter- polymers contain styrene.

Using Py-GC, only the top black/gray paint layer could be isolated and sampled. The pyrogram for the On Kawara black layer is identical in fingerprint and retention times to Liquitex (Figure 23). This was verified by the artist. The different pigments have little or no effect on the results.

One clear advantage of the FTIR method for this painting was the ability to analyze three discrete layers of the composite structure.

Case Study III

The triptych *Primary Light Group: Red, Green, Blue* painted in 1964 to 1965 by Jo Baer was

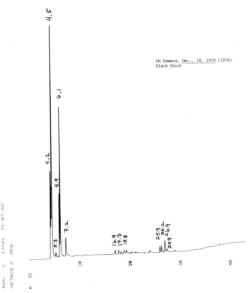

On Kawara, Dec., 18, 1979 (1979)
Black Paint

Figure 23 Pyrogram for Dec.18,1979 *top black/gray paint.*

chosen as an example of a more complex problem of identification (Figure 24). Like On Kawara, the artist is also interested in mathematical systems and sequences. She writes of this series:

> These paintings form part of a series of twelve. There are four colors in the series — blue, green, purple, yellow. There are also four sizes and shapes. ... The possibilities for combination or grouping of the paintings are the permutations of twelve (831,753,600) or whatever set factor are chosen. The paintings here are the three large squares and they use the intense color bands. All the paintings are color in a luminous mode, but this group also renders the primary colors of light: a red (magenta), a green, a blue. They are each constructed equivalent to one another as a color presence (Alloway 1966).

Figure 24 Jo Baer, Primary Light Group: Red, Green, Blue *(1964 to 1965), oil and acrylic on canvas, triptych, approximately 60 1/4 in. x 60 1/4 in. (153 cm x 153 cm) each, Collection, The Museum of Modern Art, New York, Philip Johnson Fund.*

In this work, the spatial effect of figures in a field is avoided and a unity of surface is created. To achieve this overall white field Jo Baer used a mixture of materials that she claims were chosen to avoid yellowing in the whites. These paintings use the theory of Mach band (from the physicist Ernst Mach) to create a retinal phenomenon where the viewer sees contrast enhancement, or luminous glow in certain shapes. It is easy to imagine how discoloration or cracking could adversely affect the overall impression.

According to MoMA files, the medium of the painting is oil and synthetic polymer. It was not clear upon examination if this was correct, or which areas of the painting were oil and which were acrylic. A questionnaire was sent to the artist, the painting was examined, and samples were taken to determine the nature of the materials. According to the artist, the medium used was a mixture of titanium white oil paint and Lucite 44. Lucite 44, a poly(n-butyl methacrylate) resin, was added by the artist to decrease the yellowing of the drying oil.

When the painting is viewed in a strong light, differential areas of matte and gloss are visible across the white field. The overall quality of the paint is glossy and hard, not plastic like the acrylic paints (Figure 25).

Figure 25 Detail of surface, Primary Light Group: Red, Green, Blue.

The solubility of the layer was much different than the acrylics. It was insoluble in water, hydrocarbons, xylene, and toluene. It required more polar solvents, such as acetone and ethanol, to dissolve it. The surface was quite soiled, but the particulate matter was not adhered to a tacky surface or embedded. It could be

removed easily with water, in contrast to the acrylic emulsion paints.

Under UV light the surface has a slight white fluorescence from the white pigment (found to be zinc and titanium), yet it still has the violet overtones characteristic of the synthetic resins. There seems to be an underlying layer of white that fluoresces more brightly than the surface. A cross-section was taken of the white layers to further elucidate the structure and stain for media.

Results of staining were as follows:

• Stained for lipids with Rhodamine B in ethanol — an unusual pattern of globules was outlined in the white layer. Positive stain was observed for oil in the matrix, but in the globules, negative. Paint was not readily soluble in the carrier solvent. Rhodamine B in water produced the same result. (This uneven staining of an oil matrix with non-staining globules was also noticed in a cross-section from another painting by the same artist.)

• Stained for protein with FITC in acetone and water — negative in all layers.

• Stain for pH with methyl red and bromothymol blue — indicated a pH below 4.2 in all layers.

Fortunately in this case we had the information from the artist about the materials she used. In response to the questionnaire inquiring about her technique, she wrote, "I only used an acrylic resin (Lucite 44, oil-compatible) in white paintings to insure their non-yellowing ... and only in the white parts (normal varnish [i.e., damar]/stand oil/turps in blacks and colors):
1 large tube Winsor & Newton Titanium White
3 oz. Lucite 44 (dissolved in xylene and benzine)
3 oz. benzine" (Baer 1989).

From this formula we were able to prepare a mock-up of her paint formulation to run as a standard in FTIR and Py-GC. This was composed of 4 parts Winsor & Newton Artist Oil Color Titanium White, 3 parts DuPont Elvacite 2044 resin (PnBMA) as we were unable to

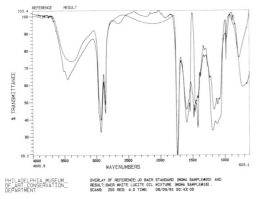

PHILADELPHIA MUSEUM OF ART CONSERVATION DEPARTMENT

OVERLAY OF REFERENCE: JO BAER STANDARD (MOMA SAMPLE#20) AND RESULT: BAER WHITE LUCITE OIL MIXTURE (MOMA SAMPLE#16). SCANS: 200 RES: 4.0 TIME: 08/09/91 00: 43: 06

Figure 26 FTIR spectra for Primary Light Group: Red, Green, Blue, *overlay of spectra from painting and from standard.*

obtain Lucite 44 (roughly about 40% concentration dissolved in xylene/hydrocarbon 50/50), and 3 parts hydrocarbon. This mock-up formulation proved extremely helpful when attempting to interpret the spectra and pyrograms generated.

In fact, the FTIR spectra generated by the unknown sample from the painting would have been difficult to interpret without the comparison (Figure 26). In the 2900 cm^{-1} region, the absorption bands had shifted down, indicating an oil, yet the carbonyl group matched quite closely to the acrylic polymer spectra. Upon initial examination it appeared to have characteristics corresponding to poly(vinyl acetate). When the spectrum of the mock-up paint

was compared to that of the painting sample, they matched quite closely.

It thus became possible to locate specific peaks that corresponded to both oil standards and standards of Magna and Elvacite, which are both PnBMA resins.

A sample of white paint from the painting and from the prepared standard were run with Py-GC (Figure 27). The overall profile of the pyrogram of the Baer white paint sample matches that of an oil paint, with one important

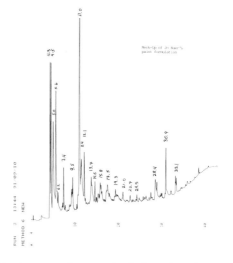

b) white paint from standard of Baer's technique

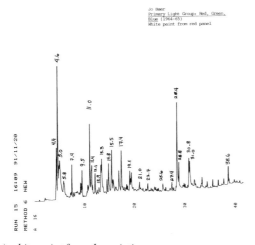

a) white paint from the painting

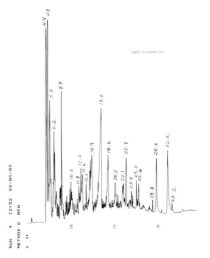

c) aged linseed oil

Figure 27 Pyrograms for Primary Light Group: Red, Green, Blue.

difference. It contains a distinct peak at 11.0 min not found in the pyrograms of oil paints. It is found, however, in the chromatograms for nBMA monomer, nBMA homopolymer, Magna white and black, and the Baer mock-up, thus demonstrating that the pyrogram of the Baer painting sample contains peaks for both the oil and the Lucite.

This case study shows the potential that exists for misinterpretation of scientific data collected from works of art, especially when materials are complex and/or have been manipulated by the artist in an unexpected or unusual way. Without such reliable precise information from Baer about the paint formulation, the pyrogram for her white paint might well have been misread.

Conclusion

Much investigation remains to be done on the identification as well as on the practical methods of conservation for acrylic emulsion paint films. The information obtained by visual examination, UV examination, and fluorescence microscopy seems to be useful, albeit limited. For more specific analysis, FTIR and Py-GC are both effective. Separation and precise identification of small components within the formulations would be a valuable area of research.

On a more general note, the results of the initial survey and examination of the body of acrylic paintings in the collection of MoMA have shown that, overall, they are in quite good condition, unless they have been mishandled or subjected to extreme environments. Of course, they have only been in existence for less than half a century, and we are unable to observe their long-term natural degradation. Future phases of the research project at MoMA will include artificial aging of paint samples (in addition to collecting naturally aging samples), and investigation of practical problems such as varnishing and cleaning these surfaces.

Acknowledgement

The authors thank the scientists who ran samples and assisted in interpreting the data.

Py-GC samples were run with the assistance of Dr. Alexander Shedrinsky at the Conservation Center, Institute of Fine Arts, New York University. IR samples were run by Beth Price, Conservation Scientist at the Philadelphia Museum of Art and Michele Derrick at the Getty Conservation Institute.

Résumé

L'identification et la caractérisation des peintures-émulsions acryliques

Un programme d'étude continu, portant sur les propriétés des peintures-émulsions acryliques, est en cours au Museum of Modern Art de New York. On a procédé jusqu'à maintenant à l'analyse du médium de quelque 150 tableaux de la collection du musée, et leur état général a été évalué. Les examens et tests usuels ont été effectués en laboratoire, et toute une série de normes a été établie à des fins de comparaison. Trois cas ont fait l'objet d'une analyse plus poussée, qui a permis d'explorer davantage un certain nombre de méthodes plus précises d'identification — des examens au microscope ou analyses par coloration locale jusqu'aux techniques de la spectrométrie infrarouge à transformée de Fourier (IRTF) ou de la pyrochromatographie en phase gazeuse, notamment.

References

Alloway, Lawrence, *Systemic Painting*, Exhibition catalogue (New York: Solomon R. Guggenheim Foundation, 1966).

Baer, Jo, personal communication, 1989.

Becher, Paul, *Encyclopedia of Emulsion Technology, Vol. 1* (New York: Marcel Dekker, 1983).

Becker, Eberhard, *Fluorescence Microscopy* (Leitz, 1990).

Bennett, H., J. Bishop and M. Wulfinghloff, *Practical Emulsions* (New York: Chemical Publishing Co., 1968).

Bondy, C., "Binder Design and Performance in Emulsion Paints," *Journal of Oil and Colour Chemists' Association*, vol. 51, 1968, p. 409.

Bondy, C. and M.M. Coleman, "Film Formation and Film Properties Obtained with Acrylic, Styrene/Acrylic and Vinyl Acetate/VeoVa Copolymer Emulsions," *Journal of Oil and Colour Chemists' Association*, vol. 53, 1970, pp. 555-577.

Brendley, W.H. Jr. and C. Karl Erhard, "Water-borne Coatings: Acrylic Polymers," *Paint and Varnish Production*, Reprint (Philadelphia: Rohm and Haas, March 1973) pp. 1-5.

Bria, Carmen, "The Development of Synthetic Polymer Resins for Artist Use," unpublished student paper, Winterthur/University of Delaware Art Conservation Program, 1981.

Clark, George, *History of Staining* (Baltimore: Williams and Wilkins, 1983).

de la Rie, Rene, "Fluorescence of Paint and Varnish Layers," *Studies in Conservation*, vol. 27, no. 3, August 1982, pp. 1-7.

Denizot, René, *Word for Word* (Paris: Yvon Lambert, 1979).

Derrick, Michele, James Landry and Dusan Stulik, *Methods in Scientific Examination of Works of Art: Infrared Microscopy* (Getty Conservation Institute Workshop, Loyola Marymount University, Jan. 1991).

Gachter, R. and H. Muller, eds., *Plastic Additives Handbook: Stabilizers, Processing Aids, Plasticizers, Fillers, Reinforcements, Colorants for Thermoplastics* (Munich: Hanser Publishers, 1985).

Golden, Mark, personal communication, Golden Paints, N.Y., 1990.

Haken, J.K. and T.R. McKay, "Quantitative Pyrolysis Gas Chromatography of Some Acrylic Copolymers and Homopolymers," *Analytical Chemistry*, vol. 45, no. 7, June 1973, pp. 1251-1257.

Held, Al, personal communication, SoHo, New York, August, 1991.

Lillie, R.D., ed., *H.J. Conn's Biological Stains* 9th edn. (St. Louis, Missouri: Sigma Chemical Co., 1990).

Lodge, Robert G., "A History of Synthetic Painting Media with Special Reference to Commercial Materials," *AIC Preprints, 16th Annual Meeting*, New Orleans, 1988, pp. 118-127.

Lodge, Robert G., "Special Report on Acrylic and Other Synthetic Media Paintings," *McKay Lodge Conservation Report*, No. 3, Spring 1991.

Lomax, Suzanne Quillen and Sarah L. Fisher, "An Investigation of the Removability of Naturally Aged Synthetic Picture Varnishes," *Journal of the American Institute for Conservation*, vol. 29, 1990, pp. 181-191.

Low, M.J.D. and N.S. Baer, "Application of Infrared Fourier Transform Spectroscopy to Problems in Conservation," *Studies in Conservation*, vol. 22, 1977, p. 116.

Martens, Charles R., *Technology of Paints, Varnishes, and Lacquers* (New York: Reinhold Publishing Co., 1968).

McKinney, Roger M., Janet T. Spillane and George W. Pearce, "A Simple Method for Determining the Labeling Efficiency of Fluorescein Isothiocyanate Products," *Journal of Analytical Biochemistry*, vol. 14, 1966, pp. 421-428.

Michalski, Stefan, "Paintings — Their Response to Temperature, Relative Humidity, Shock and Vibration," *Art in Transit: Studies in the Transport of Paintings*, International Conference on the Packing and Transportation of Paintings, London (Washington D.C.: National Gallery of Art, 1991), pp. 223-248.

Nielsen, Hans and K. Raaschou, "Forensic Analysis of Coatings," *Journal of Coatings Technology*, vol. 56, no. 718, 1984.

On Kawara, personal communication, 1989.

Patton, Temple C., "Paint Flow and Pigment Dispersion," in: *A Rheological Approach to Coating and Ink Technology* (New York: John Wiley and Sons, 1979).

Reffner, J.A. and W.T. Wihlborg, "Microanalysis by Reflectance FTIR Microscopy," *American Laboratory*, April 1990, pp. 1-6.

Rohm and Haas Co. technician, personal communication, August, 1991.

Sandler, Irving, *Al Held* (New York: Hudson Hills Press, 1984).

Schwarz, Arturo, *The Complete Works of Marcel Duchamp* (New York: Harry N. Abrams Inc., 1969).

Sonoda, Naoko and Jean Paul Rioux, "Identification of Synthetic Materials in Modern Paintings: I. Polymeric Varnishes and Binders," *Studies in Conservation*, vol. 35, no. 4, 1990, pp. 189-204.

Talbot, Robin R., "The Fluorescent Antibody Technique in the Identification of Proteinaceous Materials," *Papers Presented by Conservation Students at the 3rd Annual Conference of Art Conservation Training Programs*, Queens University, Kingston, Ontario, May 1982, pp. 140-149.

van de Wiel, H. and W. Zom, "Water Borne Acrylics and Urethanes for the Coatings Industry," *Journal of Oil and Colour Chemists' Association*, vol. 64, no. 7, July 1981, pp. 264-268.

Wolbers, Richard and Gregory Landrey, "The Use of Direct Reactive Fluorescent Dyes for the Characterization of Binding Media in Cross-Sectional Examinations," *AIC Preprints, Vancouver Conference*, Washington D.C.: AIC, 1987.